Nonfiction for High School

Nonfiction for High School

A Sentence-Composing Approach

A Student Worktext

Don and Jenny Killgallon

HEINEMANN
Portsmouth, NH

Heinemann
361 Hanover Street
Portsmouth, NH 03801–3912
www.heinemann.com

Offices and agents throughout the world

© 2015 by Don Killgallon and Jenny Killgallon

All rights reserved. No part of this book may be reproduced in any form or by any electronic or mechanical means, including information storage and retrieval systems, without permission in writing from the publisher, except by a reviewer, who may quote brief passages in a review.

"Dedicated to Teachers" is a trademark of Greenwood Publishing Group, Inc.

Cataloging-in-Publication Data is on file at the Library of Congress.
ISBN: 978-0-325-05378-3

Editor: Tobey Antao
Production: Victoria Merecki
Interior and cover designs: Monica Ann Crigler
Typesetter: Cape Cod Compositors, Inc.
Manufacturing: Steve Bernier

Printed in the United States of America on acid-free paper
19 18 17 16 15 EBM 1 2 3 4 5

In memory of John M. Crocker,
a good father, a good friend,
a good man: a model worth imitating.

CONTENTS

*If **nonfiction** is where you do your best writing, or your best teaching of writing, don't be buffaloed into the idea that it's an inferior species. The only important distinction is between good writing and bad writing.*

—William Zinsser, *On Writing Well*

NONFICTION: WORDS, SENTENCES, PARAGRAPHS

Throughout this worktext, you will learn the meanings of words in the context of nonfiction selections and study many nonfiction authors, your mentors whose writing is your apprenticeship in better reading and writing.

QUICKSHOTS: A WORD ABOUT WORDS 1

Your Turn: **Quickshot Definitions 13**

NONFICTION: A REALITY SMORGASBORD 17

Your Turn: **Informational Article 24**

A SENTENCE-COMPOSING APPROACH: A WRITER'S TOOLBOX

Throughout the rest of this worktext, you will learn valuable tools for writing. Activities are based upon sentences of skilled authors, many of whom you may recognize. Those tools are requirements for many assignments in this worktext.

SENTENCE-COMPOSING OVERVIEW 25

IDENTIFIER TOOL 31

Your Turn: **Critical Review 36**

Contents

DESCRIBER TOOL 39

Your Turn: Pro/Con Paper 44

ELABORATOR TOOL 46

Your Turn: Research Snapshot 51

TOOL VARIETY 54

Your Turn: Informational Paragraph 70

MARKING MEANING 74

Your Turn: Portrait of a Place 97

A NONFICTION SAMPLER: MINIATURE EXAMPLES

This collection of short nonfiction will strengthen your reading skills, and provide scaffolding for building your sentences and paragraphs the way authors build theirs. You'll learn to do what authors do.

QUOTATIONS: BITE-SIZE ESSAYS 102

Your Turn: Autobiographical Event 124

MIRROR IMAGES: MENTOR PARAGRAPHS 129

Your Turn: Technical Report 149

FAMOUS PEOPLE: BRIEF BIOS 153

Your Turn: Biographical Sketch 182

FAMOUS WORDS: PARALLEL STRUCTURE 186

Your Turn: Parallel Metaphor 196

OPINIONATORS: YOU SAY WHAT? 199

Your Turn: **Position Paper 214**

REPORTERS: GETTING AND TELLING IT RIGHT 218

Your Turn: **Free Choice Report 239**

NONFICTION: THE FINAL WORD 242

QUICKSHOTS: A WORD ABOUT WORDS

Nonfiction is made up of paragraphs. Paragraphs are made up of sentences. Sentences are made up of words. Sentences and the words they contain—the building blocks of meaning in nonfiction—are sometimes challenging to understand, often because of unfamiliar words.

Take this sentence by philosopher William James, from a speech he gave at Harvard University:

> *It is with no small amount of **trepidation** that I take my place behind this desk, and face this learned audience.*

A possible stumble is the word *trepidation*. The meaning of the sentence is roughly this: *I've got a lot of* [SOMETHING] *when I stand at this desk to speak to this educated group.* William's got a lot—of what? No way to guess just from context, so perhaps it's time-out for dictionary diving.

When you take the plunge, here's what you'll find, the definition from the Merriam-Webster Dictionary:

Definition of TREPIDATION (adapted)
1 *archaic*: a tremulous motion: tremor
2: a nervous or fearful feeling of uncertain agitation: apprehension <*trepidation* about starting a new job>

Examples of TREPIDATION

He had some *trepidation* about agreeing to their proposal.

Shaking with *trepidation*, I stepped into the old abandoned house.

In the first minutes, hours, or even days of fieldwork most researchers feel *trepidation* about being an outsider, a stranger on the scene.—Marie D. Price, *Geographical Review*, January–April 2001

This was an ambitious project, and a number of us felt some *trepidation* about the possible results.—Brian Phillips, *New Republic*, 13 Dec. 1999

I came aboard the 319 with *trepidation*, to join the lives of utter strangers, a man untried by the circumstances they had known.—Henry G. Bugbee Jr., "Naval History," in *Authors at Sea*, Robert Shenk, ed., 1997

Origin of TREPIDATION

Latin *trepidation-, trepidatio,* from *trepidare* to tremble, from *trepidus* agitated; probably akin to Old English *thrafian* to urge, push, Greek *trapein* to press grapes

First Known Use: 1605

Related to TREPIDATION

Synonyms

alarm (*also* alarum), anxiety, dread, fearfulness, fright, horror, panic, scare, terror, fear

Related Words

phobia; creeps, jitters, nervousness, willies; pang, qualm, twinge; agitation, apprehension, consternation, discomposure, disquiet, funk, perturbation; concern, dismay, worry; cowardice, faintheartedness, timidity, timorousness

Near Antonyms

aplomb, assurance, boldness, confidence, self-assurance, self-confidence; bravery, courage, courageousness, daring, dauntlessness, doughtiness, fearlessness, fortitude, gallantry, hardihood, intrepidity, intrepidness, stoutness, valor; audacity, guts, nerve

Whew! You took the plunge—a deep, long dive, probably finding more than you really want to know about the word *trepidation,* including its origin from the Greek *trapein*—to press grapes. (In ancient Greece, pressing grapes must have been pretty, well, trepidatious!)

This worktext presents a faster alternative to accessing the meaning of unfamiliar words. Throughout this worktext when individual words are **bold**, a fast definition—called a *quickshot*—will be *beside it* in brackets. If you already know the word, just skip ahead. If you don't know the word, the quickshot, though not a full definition of the word, will get you through the sentence without stumbling.

Though not the best seat in the theatre, a quickshot will at least allow you to see the stage. It will save you from a deep dictionary plunge, thaw brain freeze, and keep you reading, stumble-free.

It is with no small amount of **trepidation** [fear]
that I take my place behind this desk, and face
this learned audience.

With the quickshot, your trepidation about the word *trepidation* is over.

Challenges to your understanding of difficult nonfiction come often from the words themselves.

Example Sentence: *Ontogeny recapitulates phylogeny.*

This sentence has just three words—difficult words because of unfamiliarity. Unless a reader knows the meaning of each of those three words, the sentence will be incomprehensible, its meaning sent but unreceived. Even if the reader does know those words, interpreting the sentence still might be troublesome because complete understanding depends upon how those three words link to express the intended meaning.

---

ontogeny: (noun) the development of an individual from a fertilized ovum to maturity, as contrasted with the development of a group or species

recapitulates: (verb) to repeat stages from the evolution of the species during the embryonic period of an animal's life

phylogeny: (noun) the development over time of a species, genus, or group, as contrasted with the development of an individual

---

Whew! Solving that three-word sentence-puzzle is difficult. Quickshot to the rescue.

Here's the quickshot version: **Ontogeny** [*individual characteristics*] **recapitulates** [*reflect*] **phylogeny** [*species characteristics*].

It just adds up to the idea that an individual reflects the characteristics of the group to which the individual belongs: a duck has the characteristics of duckdom; a cow, cowdom; a chicken, chickendom—and a person, persondom!

Puzzle solved.

Below is an excerpt from William Styron's *The Confessions of Nat Turner*, which Styron calls a "meditation on history." The book bridges nonfiction and fiction, combining historical fact, documented events, and his own imagination.

EXCERPT—In this one ultra-long sentence, containing ten bolded words, each with a quickshot, Nat imagines what his life would have been like if he was unable to read.

> Well, under these circumstances I would doubtless have become … mildly efficient at some stupid task like wringing chickens' necks or smoking hams or polishing silver, a **malingerer** [*goof-off*] wherever possible yet **withal** [*also*] too jealous of my security to risk real **censure** [*scolding*] or trouble and thus cautious in my tiny thefts, **circumspect** [*careful*] in the secrecy of my afternoon naps, growing ever more **unctuous** [*slippery*] as I became older, always the **crafty** [*scheming*] flatterer on the lookout for some bonus of flannel or stew beef or tobacco, yet behind my stately **paunch** [*big belly*] and fancy bib and waistcoat developing, as I advanced into old age, a kind of purse-lipped dignity, known as Uncle Nat, well loved and adoring in return, a **palsied** [*shaking*] stroker of the silken **pate** [*head*] of little white grandchildren, rheumatic, illiterate, and filled with sleepiness, half yearning for that lonely death which at long last would lead me to rest in some **tumbledown** [*neglected*] graveyard. (adapted)

ACTIVITY 1: CHOOSING THE BEST QUICKSHOT

On the SAT, a test widely required for college admission, students are asked to read carefully a challenging nonfiction passage and choose from four choices the best "quickshot" (definition) for certain words in that passage. Although all four choices make some sense, the correct choice is the one that best fits the context of the passage.

Here is the official explanation from the College Board, the creators of the SAT.

RELEVANT WORDS IN CONTEXT

> The SAT focuses on relevant words, the meanings of which depend on how they're used. Students are asked to interpret the meaning of words based on the context of the passage in which they appear. This is demanding but rewarding work. These are words that students will use throughout their lives—in high school, college, and beyond.

The College Board, the creators of the SAT, gives this example:

> The coming decades will likely see more **intense** clustering of jobs, innovation, and productivity in a smaller number of bigger cities and city-regions. Some regions could end up bloated beyond the capacity of their infrastructure, while others struggle, their promise stymied by inadequate human or other resources.

The word *intense* in this passage most nearly means

A. emotional

B. concentrated

C. brilliant

D. determined.

The key point, as far as the College Board is concerned, is that *intense* is not only a word that students will regularly encounter but one that could mean A, B, C, or D, depending on the context. Here, though, choice B *concentrated* best fits the context of the passage and is the correct answer.

Directions: Do this activity twice.

- First, *without consulting a dictionary*, choose the best quickshot according to the context of the passage.

- Second, *after consulting a dictionary*, confirm or change your choice.

This passage is adapted from a speech delivered by Congresswoman Barbara Jordan of Texas on July 25, 1974, as a member of the Judiciary Committee of the United States House of Representatives. In the passage, Jordan discusses how and when a United States president may be impeached, or charged with serious offenses, while in office. Jordan's speech was delivered in the context of impeachment hearings against then-president Richard M. Nixon.

---

(1) Today, I am an **inquisitor**. (2) An **hyperbole** would not be fictional and would not overstate the solemnness that I feel right now. (3) My faith in the Constitution is whole; it is complete; it is total. (4) And I am not going to sit here and be an idle spectator to the **diminution**, the **subversion**, the destruction of the Constitution.

(5) "Who can so properly be the inquisitors for the nation as the representatives of the nation themselves?" (6) "The subjects of its **jurisdiction** are those offenses which proceed from the misconduct of public men." (7) And that's what we're talking about. (8) In other words, [the jurisdiction comes] from the abuse or violation of some public trust.

(9) It is wrong, I suggest, it is a misreading of the Constitution for any member here to **assert** that for a member to vote for an article of **impeachment** means that that member must be convinced that the President should be removed from office. (10) The Constitution doesn't say that. (11) The powers relating to impeachment are an essential check in the hands of the body of the **legislature** against and upon the **encroachments** of the **executive**. (12) The division between

the two branches of the legislature, the House and the Senate, assigning to the one the right to accuse and to the other the right to judge—the **framers** of this Constitution were very **astute**. (13) They did not make the accusers and the judges . . . the same person.

(14) We know the nature of impeachment. (15) We've been talking about it a while now. (16) It is chiefly **designed** for the President and his high ministers to somehow be called into account. (17) It is designed to "**bridle**" the executive if he [or she] engages in excesses. (18) "It is designed as a method of national **inquest** into the conduct of public men." (19) The framers confided in the Congress the power, if need be, to remove the President in order to strike a delicate balance between a President swollen with power and grown **tyrannical**, and preservation of the **independence** of the executive.

(20) The Federal Convention of 1787 limited impeachment to high crimes and misdemeanors, and discounted and opposed the term "maladministration." (21) "It is to be used only for great misdemeanors," so it was said in the North Carolina **ratification** convention. (22) And in the Virginia ratification convention: "We do not trust our liberty to a particular branch. (23) We need one branch to check the other." (24) The North Carolina ratification convention: "No one need be afraid that officers who commit oppression will pass with immunity." (25) "Prosecutions of impeachments will seldom fail to trouble the whole community," said Hamilton in the Federalist Papers, number 65. (26) "We divide into parties more or less friendly or **inimical** to the accused." (27) I do not mean political parties in that sense.

(28) The drawing of political lines goes to the motivation behind impeachment; but impeachment must proceed within the confines of the constitutional term "high crime[s] and misdemeanors." (29) Of the impeachment process, it was Woodrow Wilson who said that "Nothing short of the grossest offenses against the plain law of the land will

suffice to give them speed and effectiveness. (30) Indignation so great as to overgrow party interest may secure a conviction; but nothing else can."

(31) Common sense would be revolted if we engaged upon this process for **petty** reasons. (32) Congress has a lot to do: appropriations, tax reform, health insurance, campaign finance reform, housing, environmental protection, energy sufficiency, mass transportation. (33) Pettiness cannot be allowed to stand in the face of such overwhelming problems. (34) So today we're not being petty. (35) We're trying to be big, because the task we have before us is a big one.

(Quotations within Barbara Jordan's comments are from Federalist No. 65 by founding father Alexander Hamilton, published in 1788, which outlines actions of the United States Senate relating to the impeachment of a president.)

1. The word *inquisitor* in sentence (1) most nearly means
   a. negotiator
   b. questioner
   c. prompter
   d. traitor.

2. The word *hyperbole* in sentence (2) most nearly means
   a. fantasy
   b. lie
   c. exaggeration
   d. ridicule.

3. The word *diminution* in sentence (4) most nearly means
   a. expanding

   b. enlarging

   c. ignoring

   d. belittling.

4. The word *subversion* in sentence (4) most nearly means
   a. ruination

   b. contradiction

   c. undermining

   d. celebration.

5. The word *jurisdiction* in sentence (6) most nearly means
   a. jury

   b. area

   c. law

   d. offense.

6. The word *assert* in sentence (9) most nearly means
   a. claim

   b. deny

   c. question

   d. prove.

7. The word *impeachment* in sentence (9) most nearly means
   a. conviction

   b. denial

   c. arrest

   d. indictment.

8. The word *legislature* in sentence (11) most nearly means
   a. opinion

   b. jail

   c. government

   d. observation.

9. The word *encroachments* in sentence (11) most nearly means
   a. incentives

   b. notifications

   c. treatments

   d. trespasses.

10. The word *executive* in sentence (11) most nearly means
    a. coach

    b. counselor

    c. president

    d. principal.

11. The word *framers* in sentence (12) most nearly means
    a. creators

    b. artists

    c. planners

    d. thinkers.

12. The word *astute* in sentence (12) most nearly means
    a. hasty

    b. responsible

    c. careful

    d. smart.

13. The word *designed* in sentence (16) most nearly means
    a. invented

    b. elaborated

    c. intended

    d. comprised.

14. The word *bridle* in sentence (17) most nearly means
    a. control

    b. contradict

    c. suppress

    d. punish.

15. The word *inquest* in sentence (18) most nearly means
    a. questioning
    b. contradicting
    c. opposing
    d. strategizing.

16. The word *tyrannical* in sentence (19) most nearly means
    a. cowardly
    b. submissive
    c. dictatorial
    d. strong.

17. The word *independence* in sentence (19) most nearly means
    a. choice
    b. power
    c. control
    d. freedom.

18. The word *ratification* in sentence (21) most nearly means
    a. investigation
    b. condemnation
    c. confirmation
    d. elimination.

19. The word *inimical* in sentence (26) most nearly means

   a. stupid

   b. insane

   c. unfriendly

   d. obedient.

20. The word *petty* in sentence (31) most nearly means

   a. important

   b. significant

   c. small

   d. large.

YOUR TURN: QUICKSHOT DEFINITIONS

Using an online or offline dictionary, jot down a one-word synonym for each of the bolded words. Be sure that the synonym you choose fits the context of the sentence so readers can get meaning from that sentence.

   Here is an excerpt, with examples of a good quickshot and a bad quickshot. Both synonyms came from the same definition, but only one fits the context of the sentence. Only that definition will help the reader understand the sentence; the others will confuse the reader.

EXAMPLES

>   ***Bad Quickshot:*** Grant and Lee contrasted, representing two **diametrically** [*strangely*] opposed elements in American life.

Good Quickshot: Grant and Lee contrasted, representing two **diametrically** [*completely*] opposed elements in American life.

Explanation: The author's meaning is that the two generals were extremely different in their views of what life in America should be. Only the second quickshot *completely* matches that intended meaning by emphasizing the extreme difference in their views.

The End of the American Civil War
(adapted from Bruce Catton's "Grant and Lee: A Study in Contrasts")

(1) When Ulysses S. Grant and Robert E. Lee met at Appomattox Court House, Virginia, on April 9, 1865, to work out the terms for the surrender of Lee's army, a great chapter on American life came to a close.

(2) These men were bringing the Civil War to its **virtual** [?] finish in a scene of one of the **poignant** [?], dramatic contrasts in American History.

(3) Grant and Lee contrasted, representing two diametrically opposed elements in American life.

(4) Grant was everything Lee was not. (5) He had come up the hard way and **embodied** [?] the eternal toughness and **sinewy** [?] fiber of the men who grew up beyond the mountains. (6) He was one of a body of men who owed **reverence** [?] and **obeisance** [?] to no one.

(7) Lee, a Virginia **aristocrat** [?], **inevitably** [?] saw himself in relation to his own region. (8) He lived in a **static** [?] society which could endure almost anything except change. (9) **Instinctively** [?], his first loyalty would go to the locality in which that society existed. (10) He would fight to the limit of endurance to defend it.

(11) Different as they were, these two great soldiers had much in common. (12) Each man had the great **virtue** [?] of utter **tenacity** [?] and **fidelity** [?]. (13) In each man there was an **indomitable** [?] quality.

(14) Lastly, there was their ability, at the end, to turn quickly from war to peace once the fighting was over. (15) Out of the way these two men behaved at Appomattox came the possibility of **reconciliation** [?]. (16) No part of either man's life became him more than the part he played at Appomattox. (17) Their behavior left all **succeeding** [?] **generations** [?] of Americans in their debt. (18) Their **encounter** [?] at Appomattox was one of the great moments of American history.

QUICKSHOTS IN THIS WORKTEXT

If a word might be a stumbling block, there's a quickshot definition to get you moving again. The quickshot should be enough to unlock the word's meaning. Knowing the meaning of a key word in a sentence can often also unlock the meaning of the sentence.

*One's vocabulary needs constant **fertilizing** [enriching], or it will die.*

—Evelyn Waugh

NONFICTION: A REALITY SMORGASBORD

All of the excerpts in this worktext are *nonfiction*, the branch of literature that is not fiction, poetry, or drama. That's what nonfiction is not, but what is it?

NONFICTION DEFINED

Nonfiction is writing that's about what's real. Unlike fiction, none is made up. There are many kinds of nonfiction:

- real people (biography)
- real thoughts (essays)
- real information (articles in magazines and newspapers, print, or digital)
- real current events (news and journalism)
- real past events (history)
- real facts, processes, wikis, and blogs (information)
- real opinions about how good—or bad—things are (reviews)
- real memories (memoirs)
- real famous words (public documents, speeches)
- real memorable correspondence (letters)
- real education or instruction (textbooks, manuals, how-tos).

TRUE VS. FICTIONAL STORIES

Fiction is any story, short or long (novel), primarily from the author's imagination. Its source is the head of the author, not the history of an event (journalism) nor the facts of a real person's life (biography) nor the ideas of a person (essay) nor any other kind of nonfiction.

A fictional story never really happened except in the author's imagination. Think Harry Potter.

A nonfictional story did really happen and is based upon fact. Think Harry Truman, American two-term president from 1945 to 1953, whose biography *Truman* by David McCollough is a nonfiction account of Harry Truman's life.

Another distinction is that nonfiction is based upon factual or historical actuality; fiction, upon pretended actuality. Harry Potter, in actual truth, couldn't fly on a broomstick during Quidditch; however, in simulated truth, rendered through the skill and creativity of author J. K. Rowling (and through computer-generated images in the movie versions), Harry appears to be actually flying during Quidditch matches in the wizardly world at Hogwarts. Because of Rowling's skill in creating its realistic details, the flying seems to be actual—but isn't.

In actual truth, however, President Harry Truman did order the first and only military use of an atomic bomb to speed the end of World War II. The bombing actually happened on August 6 in the city of Hiroshima, Japan, and August 9, 1945, in Nagasaki, Japan. The true story of one of those two cities is a nonfiction book titled *Hiroshima* by John Hersey, who went to that city, interviewed six survivors, and reported their experiences and observations. Here is the opening of the book, a description of where those six survivors were at the exact moment the bomb went off.

A Noiseless Flash

At exactly fifteen minutes past eight in the morning, on August 6, 1945, Japanese time, at the moment when the atomic bomb flashed above Hiroshima, Miss Toshiko Sasaki, a clerk in the personnel department of the East Asia Tin Works, had just sat down at her place in the plant office and was turning her head to speak to the girl at the next desk. At that same moment, Dr. Masakazu Fujii was settling down cross-legged to read the Osaka *Asahi* on the porch of his private hospital, overhanging one of the seven deltaic rivers which divide Hiroshima; Mrs. Hatsuyo Nakamura, a tailor's widow, stood by the window of her kitchen, watching a neighbor tearing down his house because it lay in the path of an air-raid-defense fire lane; Father Wilhelm Kleinsorge, a German priest of the Society of Jesus, reclined in his underwear on a cot on the top floor of his order's three-story mission house, reading a Jesuit magazine, *Stimmen der Zeit*; Dr. Terufumi Sasaki, a young member of the surgical staff of the city's large, modern Red Cross Hospital, walked along one of the hospital corridors with a blood specimen for a Wassermann test in his hand; and the Reverend Mr. Kiyoshi Tanimoto, pastor of the Hiroshima Methodist Church, paused at the door of a rich man's house in Koi, the city's western suburb, and prepared to unload a handcart full of things he had evacuated from town in fear of the massive B-29 raid which everyone expected Hiroshima to suffer. A hundred thousand people were killed by the atomic bomb and these six were among the survivors.

The distinction between fiction and nonfiction is that fiction reflects scenes from an author's imagination, while nonfiction reflects events from an author's research, investigation, and discovery.

Much nonfiction, like most fiction, tells stories—but real stories of actual events (history or current events) or of real people (biography). Authors attempt to portray those nonfiction stories truthfully, factually, to reflect the actuality of the event or the life of the person.

> *Man . . . is the storytelling animal.*
> —Graham Swift, *Waterland*

Other kinds of nonfiction are not stories, but they, too, reflect the actuality of thought or procedure. A speech or a letter reveals the thoughts of the speaker or writer. An essay or an article or a review reveals the opinion of the author.

In *Nonfiction for High School: A Sentence-Composing Approach*, you'll analyze nonfiction of various types by hundreds of authors—usually excerpts of sentences or paragraphs. Some are from biographies, some from essays, some from journalism articles, some from informational texts, some from public documents or speeches, some from stories of actual events.

Among their authors are many—old and new—who are famous: Diane Ackerman, Maya Angelou, Truman Capote, Annie Dillard, Laura Hillenbrand, Langston Hughes, Erik Larson, John F. Kennedy, Tracy Kidder, Abraham Lincoln, John McFee, Barack Obama, George Orwell, Anna Quindlen, George Washington, Tom Wolfe, Richard Wright—and hundreds more established or contemporary authors.

These authors, and the others, have various ways of writing nonfiction: telling a true story about themselves or others, narrating a real event, exploring an idea or situation, reporting an incident, writing an important speech, and many other forms of nonfiction.

They all tell us something we don't know, or don't fully understand, or don't believe or accept, or don't know but would like to know. They reveal to us a world unseen, an idea unexplored, a life unimagined, a hope unrealized.

The reader finds that what might have been the author's self-absorption has been transformed into hospitality. Detail that could seem merely personal and trivial instead becomes essential and personal. . . . It is our story, too, the human story of work and rest, love and loneliness, grief and joy. We notice how the world goes on, and how often it is the simple things . . . that allow us to dwell on the issues of life and death that concern us all.

—Kathleen Norris, "Stories Around a Fire"

ACTIVITY 1: FICTION OR NONFICTION?

Listed randomly are landmark titles of fiction and nonfiction known to culturally literate readers. Write *F* for fiction, *NF* for nonfiction. If you aren't sure, research the title to find out.

1. "I Have a Dream" Martin Luther King Jr.	11. *The Old Man and the Sea* Ernest Hemingway
2. *Gone with the Wind* Margaret Mitchell	12. *The Prince* Machiavelli
3. "Theory of Relativity" Albert Einstein	13. *Hiroshima* John Hersey
4. *To Kill a Mockingbird* Harper Lee	14. *Death of a Salesman* Arthur Miller
5. "Gettysburg Address" Abraham Lincoln	15. "Self-Reliance" Ralph Waldo Emerson
6. *The Wealth of Nations* Adam Smith	16. *Frankenstein* Mary Shelley
7. *I Know Why the Caged Bird Sings* Maya Angelou	17. *Walden* Henry David Thoreau
8. *Charlotte's Web* E. B. White	18. *The Divine Comedy* Dante Alighieri
9. *The Chronicles of Narnia* J. R. R. Tolkien	19. *The Diary of a Young Girl* Anne Frank
10. "The Lottery" Shirley Jackson	20. "Of Studies" Francis Bacon

NONFICTION TOPICS

What topics are subjects of nonfiction? Count the number of grains of sand in all the deserts of the earth, and then count the number of drops of water in all the oceans on the planet, and then multiply both figures by a billion trillion. That's how many topics nonfiction has been written about—

from *A* to *Z*, from common subjects (cars, travel, sports, health, friendship, money, and a billion more) to esoteric subjects (metaphysics, astrobiology, mycology, phylogeny, ontogeny, postmodernism, and a billion more). The number is endless—with their subjects ranging tiny (an ancient history of salt) to huge (a history of the universe).

Take this example: a popular category of nonfiction about self-help or how-to books. On the Internet, amazon.com lists over 600,000 titles beginning with *How to* . . . Here are a few illustrating the range of that kind of nonfiction:

- *How to Train a Wild Elephant: And Other Adventures in Mindfulness* by Jan Chozen Bays
- *How to Babysit a Grandpa* by Jean Reagan and Lee Wildish
- *How to Cook Everything* by Mark Bittman
- *How to Be Photogenic: A Guide for Girls and Guys to Look Better in Pictures!* by F. Saeyang
- *How to Be Interesting (in 10 Simple Steps)* by Jessica Hagy
- *How to Talk So Kids Will Listen & Listen So Kids Will Talk* by Adele Faber and Elaine Mazlish
- *How to Raise the Perfect Dog: Through Puppyhood and Beyond* by Cesar Millan
- *How to Build a Fire: And Other Handy Things Your Grandfather Knew* by Erin Bried
- *How to Write a Book This Weekend, Even If You Flunked English Like I Did* by Vic Johnson

In *Nonfiction for High School: A Sentence-Composing Approach*, you'll read just a tiny bit of varied kinds of nonfiction, but through the activities, you'll increase your ability to read and write nonfiction on higher skill levels. (None will assign you to write a book over the weekend. Promise.)

IMPORTANCE OF NONFICTION

Why study methods of reading and writing nonfiction? Something done frequently should be something done well. Nonfiction is the kind of writing you'll probably read most often in college or the workplace. In college, students read textbooks, print and digital, in almost all courses and are expected to master the contents without help—scientific data, mathematical theories, psychology studies, anthropological research reports, and many others. At work, employees are often required to read database information, operational and procedural manuals, product descriptions and inventories, focus group summaries evaluating products and services, comparative market statistics, and much more. A lot of that nonfiction is rough going, requiring advanced skills of interpreting for reading and composing for writing.

The purpose of this worktext is to help you become a better reader and writer of nonfiction, including the kinds that require deep reading.

Force yourself to reflect on what you read, [sentence by sentence, and] paragraph by paragraph.

—Samuel Taylor Coleridge

UBER-LITERACY

By focusing on nonfiction sentences and paragraphs—how they are built and how they link to each other to convey meaning—this worktext *Nonfiction for High School: A Sentence-Composing Approach* promotes uber-literacy, the kind of deep reading that characterizes the most skillful readers capable of interpreting difficult nonfiction texts in college or career. The constant purpose of this worktext is to illustrate how sentences make meaning in those nonfiction texts and how understanding that process improves your ability to interpret and compose nonfiction. Carefully completing activities in this worktext, you can become uber-literate. (In case you're wondering, the prefix *uber-* means "very.")

A little knowledge is a dangerous thing.
Drink deep, or taste not the Pierian spring.
There, shallow draughts intoxicate the brain,
And drinking largely sobers us again.

—Alexander Pope, "An Essay on Criticism"

YOUR TURN: INFORMATIONAL ARTICLE

Pretend you work for a publisher of high school textbooks. Your job is to introduce the nonfiction section of a literature textbook. Your editor assigned you to write two double-spaced pages that tell high school students what nonfiction is, including the kinds of nonfiction, and to contrast nonfiction and fiction.

Directions:

1. Review the information about nonfiction in this section.

2. List important terms associated with nonfiction to explain in your introduction to the nonfiction section of the anthology.

3. Draft your introduction, including explanations or definitions of nonfiction terms or types.

4. Exchange your draft with other students in your class for suggestions to improve your introduction to nonfiction, and give them suggestions, too. Then revise several times until your review is finished.

SENTENCE-COMPOSING OVERVIEW

THE READING–WRITING CONNECTION

Reading and writing are inseparable—two sides of the same coin. Reading is the receipt of someone else's writing. Writing is the beginning of someone else's reading (unless you're writing a diary, in which case the someone else is your future self). When a sentence is composed, it is intended to be read. Sometimes, though, especially with difficult texts, what's written is not read *well*, and so the writer's intention isn't fully met. As a result, comprehension and communication are incomplete.

To understand a sentence fully, especially a difficult sentence, requires getting into the head of the writer to extract meaning from his or her writing and then importing it into your own head, without losing, distorting, or ignoring any of the original meaning in the process.

In *Nonfiction for High School: A Sentence-Composing Approach*, you'll practice ways to read and write sentences well. The sentence approach to nonfiction breaks down reading and writing to a manageable unit of meaning—the sentence—to help with interpreting and composing sentences. Sentence activities on reading and writing nonfiction in this worktext raise your skill in both to a higher level for use in and beyond high school.

> *Sentence craft equals sentence comprehension equals sentence appreciation.*
>
> —Stanley Fish, *How to Write a Sentence: And How to Read One*

SPEECH VS. WRITING

In listening and in speaking while conversing, communication through sentences, one at a time, is simple. The reason is obvious: spoken sentences are usually short, simple, with easy words. Each sentence is basic in content and style. Sentences, one after the other, are quick and easy to understand, because each is usually short and simply constructed.

In reading and in writing, compared to listening and speaking, communication is far more complex. Sentences are often long, intricate, with more demanding vocabulary. Most contain many parts in addition to a subject and a predicate. Most sentences are advanced in content and style, packed with multiple sentence parts, each with its own meaning. Together, those sentence parts require deep, slow reading for full understanding.

SPOKEN SENTENCES (OVERHEARD ON A BUS)

1. Janelle went to the mall to buy some new jeans.

2. She wanted to get some in the newest style.

3. She got a slice of pizza at the food court.

WRITTEN SENTENCES (SELECTED RANDOMLY FROM NONFICTION)

Following are the originals, then a translation of each into a series of spoken sentences showing how all the information might be conveyed in a conversation through a series of many shorter, simpler sentences, and many more words, than in the original written sentence:

1a. *In writing:* Dotted with sticker bushes, tumbleweed, and coiled rattlesnakes, the desert around our house seems to have no reason for existence, other than providing a place for people to dump things they no longer want, like tires and mattresses.

Andre Agassi, Open: An Autobiography

1b. *In conversation:* We live in a desert. It is dotted with sticker bushes. There's tumbleweeds here and there. There's even rattlesnakes coiled up. The desert seems kind of useless. The only thing people use it for is for a dumping ground. They throw stuff there they don't want, like tires and mattresses.

2a. *In writing:* One structure, rejected at first as a monstrosity, became the World Fair's **emblem** [*symbol*], a machine huge and terrifying, **eclipsing** [*overshadowing*] instantly the tower of Alexandre Eiffel that had so wounded America's pride.

Erik Larson, *The Devil in the White City*

2b. *In conversation:* One structure was rejected. It was considered at first a monstrosity. The structure was a machine, which was huge and terrifying. It outdid the French Eiffel tower that had hurt the pride of America.

3a. *In writing:* As the contest for the State Legislature that would name his successor raged in Missouri, Senator Benton stood fast by his **post** [*position*] in Washington, outspoken to the end in his condemnation of the views his **constituents** [*followers*] now embraced.

John F. Kennedy, *Profiles in Courage*

3b. *In conversation:* Senator Benton never changed his mind. He even voiced opinions that sharply disagreed with the people who had elected him. He continued to express those strong views during the battle in Missouri among the candidates who were fighting to replace him as senator.

The **juxtaposition** [*contrast*] of the written and spoken versions demonstrates that the written version is harder to understand, requiring more deep reading than the spoken version.

Throughout this worktext, you'll sample nonfiction sentences that illustrate strong writing and apply what you learn to building better sentences like those of authors.

My approach is to focus all my attention on the sentences—try to get them as good and honest and interesting as I can.

—George Saunders, author of *Tenth of December*

Reading and writing nonfiction both involve comprehending and communicating sentences that are thick not thin, long not short, packed not empty. Such sentences are the focus of activities throughout this worktext, intended to enrich and expand your ability to read and write nonfiction.

Throughout the sections of this worktext, you'll learn and apply sentence-composing skills of various kinds, with a recurring emphasis on variety in sentence structure for better reading and writing of nonfiction. Throughout the worktext, this strand focuses on three important sentence-composing tools: *identifiers*, *describers*, and *elaborators*.

To introduce you to those power tools, here are examples, with many more to follow within the activities of *Nonfiction for High School: A Sentence-Composing Approach*. Later, you'll learn exactly what they are, how they work, and why they matter for reading and writing nonfiction, or any kind of writing.

EXAMPLES

The first sentence is *before* adding the tool (underlined); the second, *after* adding the tool.

Identifiers

1a. *Before:* Sergeant Fales felt anger with the pain.

1b. *After:* <u>A big broad-faced man who had fought in Panama and during the Gulf War</u>, Sergeant Fales felt anger with the pain.
Mark Bowden, *Black Hawk Down*

2a. *Before:* One of the young men had a loose, gangly build.

2b. *After:* One of the young men, <u>a six-foot-three freshman named Roger Morris</u>, had a loose, gangly build.
Daniel James Brown, *The Boys in the Boat*

3a. *Before:* Captain Kendall had a strong jaw and a wide mouth that bent easily into a smile.

3b. *After:* Captain Kendall had a strong jaw and a wide mouth that bent easily into a smile, <u>a trait that made him popular among all passengers but especially women</u>.
      Tracy Kidder, *Among Schoolchildren*

Describers

4a. *Before:* The rest wait patiently outside.

4b. *After:* <u>Listening through loudspeakers</u>, the rest wait patiently outside.
      Susan Cain, *Quiet*

5a. *Before:* The police entered the hotel basement.

5b. *After:* The police, <u>holding their flickering lanterns high</u>, entered the hotel basement.
      Erik Larson, *The Devil in the White City*

6a. *Before:* Play is widespread among animals because it invites problem-solving.

6b. *After:* Play is widespread among animals because it invites problem-solving, <u>allowing a creature to test its limits and develop strategies</u>.
      Diane Ackerman, *Deep Play*

Elaborators

7a. *Before:* The spiders lie on their sides.

7b. *After:* The spiders lie on their sides, <u>their legs drying in knots</u>.
      Annie Dillard, "Death of a Moth"

8a. *Before:* His face was open and ordinary.

8b. *After:* His face, <u>its features unremarkable but pleasant and regular</u>, was open and ordinary.
          Daniel James Brown, *The Boys in the Boat*

9a. *Before:* The official name was the World's Columbian Exposition.

9b. *After:* The official name was the World's Columbian Exposition, <u>its official purpose to commemorate the four hundredth anniversary of Columbus's discovery of America</u>.
          Erik Larson, *The Devil in the White City*

As these examples illustrate, using those three sentence-composing tools builds better sentences—thick not thin, long not short, packed not empty—to attain variety and maturity in sentence structure in and beyond high school, for college or career.

You'll never get anywhere with all those damn little short sentences.

—Gregory Clark, *A Social Perspective on the Function of Writing*

IDENTIFIER TOOL

In the next three sections of *Nonfiction for High School: A Sentence-Composing Approach*, you'll read and write nonfiction that uses these important sentence-composing tools: *the identifier, the elaborator, the describer*. They add detail and style to writing and are indispensable tools for your writing toolbox.

Identifiers (appositives) are sentence parts that identify people, places, or things by telling who or what they are. Many begin with one of these words: *a, an, the*.

Contrast the sentences below. Notice how much identifiers (appositives) improve sentences.

1a. I came to philosophy as a last resort.

1b. A professional football player, print and television journalist, academic English teacher and world-traveler, I came to philosophy as a last resort.

John McMurty, "Kill 'Em! Crush 'Em! Eat 'Em Raw!"

2a. The study of electricity got a boost with the invention of the Leyden jar.

2b. The study of electricity got a boost with the invention of the Leyden jar, **the first device capable of storing and amplifying static electricity.**

Erik Larson, *Thunderstruck*

3a. The dictionary had a picture of an aardvark.

3b. The dictionary had a picture of an aardvark, **a long-tailed, long-eared, burrowing African mammal living off termites caught by sticking out its tongue as an anteater does for ants.**

Malcolm X and Alex Haley, *The Autobiography of Malcolm X*

ACTIVITY 1: MATCHING

Match the appositive with the sentence. Insert the appositive at the caret (^). Write out each sentence, underlining the appositive. Notice the three places appositives occur in a sentence: *opener*, *S-V split* (*between a subject and verb*), *closer*.

Sentences	Appositives
1. I started making an iceball, ^ . Annie Dillard, *An American Childhood*	a. the year that showed us we could make our own destinies
2. She had tied rags around her shoulders to keep out the spring chill and was picking through the trash while her dog, ^ , played at her feet. Jeannette Walls, *The Glass Castle*	b. a boy who could and did imitate a police siren every morning on his way to the showers
3. This was 1979, ^ . Roya Hakakian, *Journey from the Land of No*	c. a black-and-white terrier mix
4. Maria was a town character, ^ . Judith Ortiz Cofer, *Silent Dancing*	d. a perfect one from perfectly white snow
5. I looked with a mixture of admiration and awe at Peter, ^ . Robert Russell, *To Catch an Angel*	e. a fat middle-aged woman who lived with her old mother on the outskirts of town

ACTIVITY 2: COMBINING WITH THE IDENTIFIER TOOL

Combine two sentences into just one sentence. Make the underlined part an identifier (appositive) to insert at the caret (^) in the first sentence. Notice how appositives use commas for the places where they occur in a sentence: *opener*, *S-V split*, *closer*.

EXAMPLES

Opener Appositive: ^ , Sergeant Fales felt anger with the pain. He was <u>a big broad-faced man who had fought in Panama and during the Gulf War</u>.

Combined: <u>A big broad-faced man who had fought in Panama and during the Gulf War</u>, Sergeant Fales felt anger with the pain.

      Mark Bowden, *Black Hawk Down*

S-V Split Appositive: The postmistress, ^ , presides over a falling-apart post office. She is <u>a gaunt woman who wears a rawhide jacket and denims and cowboy boots</u>.

Combined: The postmistress, <u>a gaunt woman who wears a rawhide jacket and denims and cowboy boots</u>, presides over a falling-apart post office.

      Truman Capote, *In Cold Blood*

Closer Appositive: Young Masai men set off on a pilgrimage to Mount Kilimanjaro, ^ . It is <u>the sacred center of their world</u>.

Combined: Young Masai men set off on a pilgrimage to Mount Kilimanjaro, <u>the sacred center of their world</u>.

      Diane Ackerman, *Deep Play*

OPENER APPOSITIVES

1. ^ , Dodd had been a professor at the university since 1909, recognized nationally for his work on the American South and for a biography of Woodrow Wilson. Dodd is <u>the chairman of the history department</u>.

    Erik Larson, *The Devil in the White City*

2. ^ , Mother took credit for her successes, and believed setbacks couldn't stop her. She was <u>a born optimist</u>.

   Diane Ackerman, *An Alchemy of Mind*

3. ^ , Daniel Webster combined the musical charm of his deep organ-like voice, an ability to crush his opponents with a **barrage** [*bombardment*] of facts, a confident and deliberate manner of speaking, and a striking appearance to make his speeches a magnet that drew crowds. Webster was <u>a very slow speaker, averaging about a hundred words a minute</u>.

   John F. Kennedy, *Profiles in Courage*

S-V SPLIT APPOSITIVES

4. Marguerite Frolicher, ^ , accompanying her father on a business trip, woke up with a memory of her bad dream. She was <u>a young Swiss girl</u>.

   Walter Lord, *A Night to Remember*

5. The hangman, ^ , was waiting beside his machine. The hangman was <u>a gray-haired convict in the white uniform of the prison</u>.

   George Orwell, "*A Hanging*"

6. The face of Liliana Methol, ^ , was badly bruised and covered with blood. She was <u>the fifth woman in the plane</u>.

   Piers Paul Read, *Alive*

CLOSER APPOSITIVES

7. The teacher chose an escort for Clarence, ^ . He was <u>a small, wiry boy with a crew cut just growing out that resembled an untended garden</u>.

   Tracy Kidder, *Among Schoolchildren*

8. Paddy became friendly with a cow from a near-by field, ^ . The cow was <u>a big, fat, brown animal with sleepy eyes and an enormous tail that coiled about its hind legs like a rope</u>.

                   Christy Brown, *My Left Foot*

9. He lived alone, ^ . He was <u>a gaunt, stooped figure who wore a heavy black overcoat and a misshapen fedora on those rare occasions when he left his apartment</u>.

                   Barack Obama, *Dreams from My Father*

REVIEWERS

Readers want to know what you think—about that game, movie, book, restaurant, play, concert, hotel, television show, car, any product, any service. The purpose of a favorable review is to tell readers to get it; the purpose of an unfavorable review is to warn readers to forget it.

Either way, before parting with their money, readers want to know what reviewers think of it. Because of the enormous popularity of reviews of all kinds, readers frequently seek this kind of nonfiction.

ACTIVITY 3: THE BEST/THE WORST

As partners, share with each other your opinion about any one of the topics in the list below, and then open the discussion with the rest of the class. Finally, write five sentences, each about a different topic from the list, and in each use an identifier tool (appositive).

- movie or TV show you saw
- book you read
- game you attended or viewed
- music you listened to

- restaurant you visited
- concert you attended
- car you drove
- game you played
- product you bought
- tech device you used
- or anything else

YOUR TURN: CRITICAL REVIEW

For an article in your local newspaper, write a review of an event in sports or entertainment in which you include examples of the *identifier tool* (appositive) in different places: opener, S-V split, closer.

Directions:

1. Attend or recall the event.
2. List important terms associated with that event. Choose terms probably unfamiliar to your readers. For example, for the sport lacrosse, key terms are *attackman* and *midfielder*; for a movie, terms could include *computer-generated images* (*CGI*) and *docudrama*. Identify those terms by using the identifier tool (appositive) as Tim does in his review below.
3. Draft your review of the event, using appositives to identify important terms. Use appositives in different places and lengths, and sometimes use more than one appositive within the same sentence.
4. Exchange your draft with other students in your class for suggestions to improve your review, and give them suggestions, too. Then revise several times until your review is finished.

5. Create a memorable title and subtitle, with a colon between them. *Examples:* "CGI: Making Fake Real" or "Football: The Torture Sport."

Here is an example, a review of a concert by a high school student named Tim. Notice how frequently Tim identifies unfamiliar names or terms to help his readers. Study Tim's review, especially the underlined *identifiers*.

Radiohead Live: A Sonic, Techno Dazzler
by
Tim Mrozek
(***a student paper***)

(1) Radiohead is no stranger to breaking new ground, but with the release of their two new albums, <u>two highly experimental and electronic records</u>, many questions arose as to how they might perform the music live—<u>concerns that were quickly resolved at last night's concert</u>. (2) The venue was packed at the Gorge Amphitheatre, <u>a natural, outdoor music arena</u>, as many fans of Radiohead eagerly but restlessly awaited the appearance of the band. (3) Nearing dusk, Thom Yorke and the rest of his band took the stage amidst gales of applause and cheers. (4) The crowds' concern over whether or not these guys could pull off such strange and atmospheric music was quickly laid to rest as the band began with "Packed Like Sardines in a Crushed Box," <u>the first track off their newest album *Amnesiac*</u>, <u>a great kick-off for the album</u>. (5) At this point everyone realized that not only did Radiohead have the ability to perform these very experimental songs, <u>dazzlers that most bands couldn't even dream of attempting live because of the techno challenges</u>, but they were able to play them even better live than in a techno-rich recording studio. (6) As the sun began to set over the mountains in the distance, creating a very interesting mood, intensified by the very emotional moods

of Radiohead's music, Thom began to play one of the band's most recognized and adored songs, "Paranoid Android," <u>a "Bohemian Rhapsody"-like epic song consisting of three original songs put together to form what is considered by some the quintessence of Radiohead's genius</u>. (7) Thom, pumping his fist during one of the more intense parts, his voice echoing off of the mountains and into the concertgoer's hearts, brought the song together with his hauntingly beautiful vocals. (8) <u>The band's most creative and versatile member with a new show-stopper at every live concert</u>, Johnny Greenwood played one of his custom-wired guitars, giving the live version of the song the original sound for which that guitar has become known. (9) At the same time, Colin Greenwood, <u>Johnny's older brother</u>, stood between Thom and Johnny, playing the smooth yet odd bass line that really holds the song together. (10) Ed O'Brien, <u>the most "normal" of the band members</u>, was on the far left playing with his many pedals that give his guitar its unique sound. (11) All the while, Phil Selway, <u>the band's percussionist</u>, sat, sadly obscured by the others, yet heard clearly, holding the song to the proper pace and rhythm. (12) The entire concert was memorable, <u>a sonic, techno dazzler</u>.

DESCRIBER TOOL

Describers (participles) are sentence parts that picture people, places, things. There are two kinds of describers: present participles and past participles. Present participles always end in -*ing*. Past participles usually end in -*ed*.

Contrast the sentences below. Notice how much describers (participles) improve sentences.

1a. Back in London, the ship had been visited by two officers from Scotland Yard.

1b. Back in London, the ship had been visited by two officers from Scotland Yard, **patrolling the wharves in hopes of thwarting** [*preventing*] **the couple's escape**.

Erik Larson, Thunderstruck

2a. The faint light from the moon enabled me to find my way without difficulty.

2b. The faint light from the moon, **shining on the dew-laden grass**, enabled me to find my way without difficulty.

Jane Goodall, Through a Window

3a. Meanwhile, she sat stiffly in the chair.

3b. Meanwhile, she sat stiffly in the chair, **trying not to show the pain it caused her**.

Eleanor Coerr, Sadako and the Thousand Paper Cranes

4a. Phyllis was with him when her mother called her to come and see Neil Armstrong set foot on the moon.

4b. **Concerned with her father**, Phyllis was with him when her mother called her to come and see Neil Armstrong set foot on the moon.

Frank McCourt, Teacher Man

5a. One structure became the World Fair's emblem, a machine huge and terrifying.

        Erik Larson, *The Devil in the White City*

5b. One structure, **rejected at first as a monstrosity**, became the World Fair's emblem, a machine huge and terrifying, **eclipsing instantly the tower of Alexandre Eiffel that had so wounded America's pride**. (*Contains a past participle and a present participle.*)

        Erik Larson, *The Devil in the White City*

ACTIVITY 1: MATCHING

Match the participle with the sentence. Insert the participle at the caret (^). Write out each sentence, underlining the participle. Notice the three places participles occur in a sentence: *opener*, *S-V split*, *closer*.

Sentences	Participles
1. She sat in a rocking chair, her long legs curled under her, ^ . Michael Crichton, *Travels*	a. stacked in a pile of 52
2. ^ , technicians were able to gradually reduce the size of the gas bubble using a special apparatus from the atomic laboratory at Oak Ridge, Tennessee. Barry Commoner, *The Politics of Energy*	b. breaking into his Irish tenor's **rendition** [*version*] of the song "Maria" from West Side Story
3. I despised team sports, ^ . Nancy Mairs, *Plaintext*	c. looking very calm and composed

4. On a bus trip to London from Oxford University, a young man, obviously fresh from a pub, spotted me and went down on his knees in the aisle, ^ .
 	
    Judith Ortiz Cofer,
  "The Myth of the Latin Woman"
	d. spending some of the wretchedest afternoons of my life sweaty and humiliated behind a field-hockey stick and under a basketball hoop

5. ^ , the cards lay temporarily dormant. James Beltrani, "Card Trick"	e. working desperately

ACTIVITY 2: COMBINING WITH THE DESCRIBER TOOL

Combine two sentences into just one sentence. Make the underlined part a describer (participle) to insert at the caret (^) in the first sentence. Notice how participles use commas for the places where they occur in a sentence: *opener*, *S-V split*, *closer*.

EXAMPLES

Opener Participle: ^ , the desert around our house seems to have no reason for existence, other than providing a place for people to dump things they no longer want, like tires and mattresses. The desert is <u>dotted with sticker bushes, tumbleweed, and coiled rattlesnakes</u>. *(past participle)*

Combined: <u>Dotted with sticker bushes, tumbleweed, and coiled rattlesnakes</u>, the desert around our house seems to have no reason for existence, other than providing a place for people to dump things they no longer want, like tires and mattresses.

    Andre Agassi, *Open: An Autobiography*

S-V Split Participle: The hangman, ^ , produced a small cotton bag like a flour bag and drew it down over the prisoner's face. The hangman was <u>standing on the gallows</u>.

Combined: The hangman, <u>standing on the gallows</u>, produced a small cotton bag like a flour bag and drew it down over the prisoner's face. (present participle)

George Orwell, "A Hanging"

Closer Participle: Gold walked to the door and took a few deep breaths, ^ . He was <u>trying to slow down his heartbeat</u>.

Combined: Gold walked to the door and took a few deep breaths, <u>trying to slow down his heartbeat</u>. *(present participle)*

Steve Sheinkin, *Bomb*

OPENER PARTICIPLES

1. ^ , the rest wait patiently outside. They were <u>listening through loudspeakers</u>.
Susan Cain, *Quiet*

2. ^ , Spencer V. Silverthorne, a young buyer for Nuget's department store, slumbered. Spencer was <u>buried in a nearby leather armchair</u>.
Walter Lord, *A Night to Remember*

3. ^ , I stopped her constantly for details. (*Contains two past participles.*) I was <u>enchanted and</u> I was also <u>enthralled</u>.
Richard Wright, *Black Boy*

S-V SPLIT PARTICIPLES

4. The train, ^ , was forced to halt by a crowd so large that it spilled onto the tracks. The train was <u>approaching Cincinnati in mid-afternoon</u>.

   Michael Burlingame, *Abraham Lincoln: A Life*

5. His tiny feet, ^ , would have neatly fitted into a delicate lady's dancing slippers. His feet were <u>encased in short black boots with steel buckles</u>.

   Truman Capote, *In Cold Blood*

6. The police, ^ , entered the hotel basement, a cavern of brick and timber measuring 50 by 165 feet. They were <u>holding their flickering lanterns high</u>.

   Erik Larson, *The Devil in the White City*

CLOSER PARTICIPLES

7. The hanged prisoner was dangling with his toes pointed straight downward, as dead as a stone, ^ . The prisoner was <u>revolving very slowly</u>.

   George Orwell, "A Hanging"

8. Play is widespread among animals because it invites problem-solving, ^ . The problem-solving is <u>allowing a creature to test its limits and develop strategies</u>.

   Diane Ackerman, *Deep Play*

9. I passed below a troop of red monkeys, ^ and ^ . They were <u>leaping through the tree tops and</u> they were <u>uttering their strange, high-pitched calls</u>. *(Contains two present participles.)*

   Jane Goodall, *Through a Window*

YOUR TURN: PRO/CON PAPER

Pretend you are an investigative journalist for print or television. For a report, write a compilation of views pro and con about a debatable topic in which you include examples of the *describer tool* (participle) in different places: opener, S-V split, closer.

Directions:

1. Choose one of these debatable topics (or select a topic of your own), and gather information about reasons educated people have supporting, and opposing, an aspect of the topic.

   - illegal immigration
   - pay for professional athletes
   - tests and college admissions
   - English as the official language of the United States
   - single-sex versus coeducational schools
   - global climate change
   - use of animals for scientific research
   - drone strikes
   - violent video games
   - social networking
   - medical marijuana
   - death penalty
   - use of smartphones

2. Think of action phrases beginning with a present participle (an *-ing* word) or a past participle (an *-ed* word) at the beginning of the phrase.

    - For example, for the controversy about standardized test scores for college admissions, some phrases might be *ignoring the leadership positions the applicant has held in high school* (con position), or *predicting quite accurately an applicant's potential for academic success in college* (pro position).

    - For the debatable topic of use of smartphones, some phrases might be *isolated from social contact with real people through texting instead of talking* (con position), or *discovered in seconds with a few taps on the screen instead of hours spent in a library* (pro position).

3. Draft your pro/con compilation telling your readers about both sides of the debatable topic, using participles to describe significant actions associated with that topic. Use participles in different places and lengths, and sometimes use more than one participle within the same sentence.

4. Exchange your draft with other students in your class for suggestions to improve your paper, and give them suggestions, too. Then revise several times until your paper is finished.

5. Create a memorable title and subtitle, with a colon between them. *Examples:* "SAT Scores: Ticket or Torture?" or "Smartphones: Dumber Than You Think."

ELABORATOR TOOL

Elaborators (absolutes) are sentence parts that provide more information about the rest of the sentence. Many begin with one of these words: *my*, *his*, *her*, *its*, *our*, *their*.

All of them, including those that begin with other words, can be converted to sentences by adding *was* or *were*.

EXAMPLES

1. The dead man's face was coated with mud, **his eyes wide open**.
   George Orwell, "Shooting an Elephant"

2. **Her knees half-bent**, she stood in the middle of the courtyard.
   Roya Hakakian, *Journey from the Land of No*

3. In twelfth-century Florence, the elite competed by constructing a forest of towers, **each more spectacular than the next**.
   Diane Ackerman, *Deep Play*

TEST: Every elaborator (absolute) can be converted to a sentence by adding *was* or *were*.

1a. His eyes were wide open.

2a. Her knees were half-bent.

3a. Each was more spectacular than the next.

Contrast the sentences below. Notice how much elaborators (absolutes) improve sentences.

1a. I followed, walking awkwardly.

1b. I followed, walking awkwardly, **my wet clothes hindering movement**.

> Jane Goodall, *Through a Window*

2a. We walked up and down the garden rows.

2b. We walked up and down the garden rows, **the cool dirt between our toes**.

> Maya Angelou, *I Know Why the Caged Bird Sings*

3a. The houses were set out in a line under the soft green trees.

3b. The houses were set out in a line under the soft green trees, **their leaves rustling gently with the breeze**.

> Willie Morris, *My Dog Skip*

ACTIVITY 1: MATCHING

Match the absolute with the sentence. Insert the absolute at the caret (^). Write out each sentence, underlining the absolute. Notice the three places absolutes occur in a sentence: *opener*, *S-V split* (*between a subject and verb*), *closer*.

Sentences	Absolutes
1. Roger was short and bald, ^ . Frank McCourt, *Teacher Man*	**a.** my miniature binoculars and camera stuffed into my pockets along with notebook, pencil stubs, a handful of raisins for my lunch, and plastic bags in which to put everything should it rain

2. I was climbing the steep slope behind the house, ^ . Jane Goodall, *Through a Window*	**b.** his baldness offset by rich bushy black-and-grey eyebrows and a short beard
3. I came across a faded photograph of my dog Skip not long ago, ^ . Willie Morris, *My Dog Skip*	**c.** his complexion paler than usual
4. Marconi grew thin, ^ . Erik Larson *Thunderstruck*	**d.** his black face with the long snout sniffing at something in the air, his tail straight and pointing, his eyes flashing in some momentary excitement *(Contains three absolutes.)*
5. He foresaw that mankind might split into two species, ^ . Kenneth Brower, *The Starship and the Canoe*	**e.** one following the technological path which he described, the other holding on as best it could to the ancient folkways of natural living *(Contains two absolutes)*

ACTIVITY 2: COMBINING WITH THE ELABORATOR TOOL

Combine two sentences into just one sentence. Make the underlined part an elaborator (absolute) to insert at the caret (^) in the first sentence. Notice how absolutes use commas for the places where they occur in a sentence: *opener*, *S-V split*, *closer*.

EXAMPLES

Opener Absolute: ^ , the spiders lie on their sides, translucent and ragged. Their legs were drying in knots.

Combined: Their legs drying in knots, the spiders lie on their sides, translucent and ragged.
　　　　　Annie Dillard, "Death of a Moth"

S-V Split Absolute: The poor little row of forget-me-nots along the wall, ^ , came out bravely. <u>Their tiny star-like blossoms</u> were <u>all blue and white and speckled red.</u>

Combined: The poor little row of forget-me-nots along the wall, <u>their tiny star-like blossoms all blue and white and speckled red</u>, came out bravely.
Christy Brown, My Left Foot

Closer Absolute: Marconi grew thin. <u>His complexion</u> was <u>paler than usual</u>.

Combined: Marconi grew thin, <u>his complexion paler than usual</u>.
Erik Larson, Thunderstruck

OPENER ABSOLUTES

1. ^ , she stood in the middle of the courtyard. <u>Her knees</u> were <u>half-bent</u>.
Roya Hakakian, Journey from the Land of No

2. ^ , Burnham felt optimistic, despite the carpenters' strike and all the work yet to be done. <u>His mood</u> was **bolstered** [*raised*] <u>by the fine weather</u>.
Erik Larson, The Devil in the White City

3. ^ , the boat was set upon a **roiling** [*swirling*] sea. <u>Its passengers</u> were <u>left to fend for themselves</u>.
Warren St. John, Outcasts United

S-V SPLIT ABSOLUTES

4. The superintendent, ^ , was slowly poking the ground with his stick. <u>His head</u> was <u>on his chest</u>.
    George Orwell, "A Hanging"

5. Uncle Ardi, ^ , reached to kiss her. <u>One foot</u> was <u>on the tire</u>.
    Roya Hakakian, *Journey from the Land of No*

6. A windjammer, ^ , seemed to be passing along the starboard side. <u>Its sails</u> were <u>set</u>.
    Walter Lord, *A Night to Remember*

CLOSER ABSOLUTES

7. Now and then they slept ^ . <u>Their gray old heads</u> were <u>resting with painful awkwardness on the backs of the benches</u>.
    Loren Eiseley, "The Brown Wasps"

8. The official name was the World's Columbian Exposition, ^ . <u>Its official purpose</u> was <u>to **commemorate** [*remember*] the four hundredth anniversary of Columbus's discovery of America</u>.
    Erik Larson, *The Devil in the White City*

9. She burst into great sobs, ^ , ^ . <u>Her whole body</u> was <u>shaking</u>. <u>Tears</u> were <u>streaming down her face</u>.
    Michael Crichton, *Travels*

YOUR TURN: RESEARCH SNAPSHOT

You learned and practiced a sentence-composing tool for identifying (*the appositive, pages 31–35*); a tool for describing (*the participle, pages 39–43*); and a tool for elaborating (*the absolute, pages 46–50*). Now put all three tools to work for a short research report on a natural disaster or an historic tragedy. Choose one of these topics to research, or choose one of your own, and after learning about your topic, zoom in on one incident to craft an interesting report about one part of the disaster or tragedy.

NATURAL DISASTERS

- black death in Medieval Europe (1346–53)
- great Chicago fire (1871)
- Johnstown flood (1889)
- San Francisco earthquake (1906)
- Hurricane Katrina (2005)
- tsunami in Japan (2011)
- a recent natural disaster of your choice

HISTORIC TRAGEDIES

- sinking of the *Titanic* (1912)
- explosion of the *Hindenburg* (1937)
- attack on Pearl Harbor (1941)
- assassination of President John F. Kennedy (1963)
- explosion of the *Challenger* spacecraft (1986)
- attack on the World Trade Center in New York City (2001)
- a recent historic tragedy of your choice

Directions: Research a variety of sources online and offline for information about your topic. To practice synthesizing information, avoid quoting; instead, put information into your own carefully chosen words and well-crafted sentences. Somewhere in your report use these sentence-composing tools:

- identifiers (appositives), describers (participles), elaborators (absolutes) in various lengths (*short*, *medium*, *long*)
- identifiers, describers, elaborator tools in various places within the sentence (*opener*, *S-V split*, *closer*).

Note: Your teacher may ask you to visually code the three tools so they can be easily located. One possibility is to *italicize* identifiers (appositives), **bold** describers (participles), underline elaborators (absolutes).

Here is an example of an effective and interesting research snapshot, one incident from the natural disaster of the Chicago fire of 1871. The author draws the reader into the disaster by a careful selection of details, ample vivid description, and varied sentences built using the three tools you learned earlier:

- identifiers (*italicized*)
- describers (**bolded**)
- elaborators (underlined).

Incident from the Great Chicago Fire of 1871
(sample researched snapshot)

(1) Sullivan ambled down a stretch of land, crossed the street, and sat down on the wooden sidewalk. (2) **Adjusting his wooden leg to make himself comfortable**, he leaned back against the fence to enjoy the night, his mind at ease as his body relaxed. (3) The wind, **coming off the prairie**, had been strong all day, **gusting wildly sometimes**,

leaves scuttling across the street. (4) While he pushed himself up to go home, he first saw the fire, *a single tongue of flame shooting out the side of O'Leary's barn*. (5) Sullivan made his way directly to the barn to save the animals inside, *a group of cows terrified by the fire*. (6) The barn's loft held over three tons of hay, **delivered earlier that day**. (7) Flames from the burning hay pushed against the roof and beams, **struggling to break free**. (8) Sullivan entered the building, a shower of burning embers greeting him. (9) The heat was fiercely intense and blinding. (10) In his rush to flee, Sullivan slipped on the uneven floorboards, **falling with a thud**. (11) As he struggled to get up, Sullivan discovered that his wooden leg had gotten stuck between two boards and come off.

    Jim Murphy, *The Great Fire* (adapted)

TOOL VARIETY

The underlined parts illustrate the author's use of a variety of sentence-composing tools to add detail, elaboration, and style. The variety includes tools you've learned earlier plus new sentence-composing tools.

PARAGRAPH WITH A VARIETY OF TOOLS

(1) <u>In the predawn darkness, in the back bedroom of a small house in Torrance, California</u>, a twelve-year-old boy sat up in bed, <u>listening</u>. (2) There was a sound coming from outside, <u>louder and louder</u>. (3) It was a huge, heavy rush, <u>with an immense impact</u>, <u>a great parting of air</u>. (4) The boy swung his legs off the bed, <u>raced down the stairs</u>, <u>slapped open the back door</u>, and <u>loped onto the grass</u>. (5) The yard was strange, <u>otherworldly</u>, <u>smothered in unnatural darkness</u>, <u>shivering with sound</u>. (6) The boy stood on the lawn, <u>head thrown back</u>, <u>spellbound</u>.

Laura Hillenbrand, *Unbroken* (adapted)

What are the new tools? They are sentence parts added to a sentence to increase detail, variety, power, and style. Just as accessories add value to a car, tools add value to a sentence. Although they have names, here they are simply called *other tools*.

ACTIVITY 1: IDENTIFYING SENTENCE PARTS

To build a basic sentence, you need a subject and a predicate. To build a better sentence, maybe even a great one, you need sentence-composing tools. They provide information beyond the subject and predicate. In each list below, one sentence part is the subject of the sentence, one is the predicate, and the rest are various tools.

A *subject* is a topic and a <u>nonremovable</u> sentence part.

A *predicate* is a comment about the topic and a <u>nonremovable</u> sentence part.

A *tool* is a sentence part telling more information about the content of the sentence and a <u>removable</u> but desirable sentence part. Each tool is a new chunk of meaning for a sentence.

Directions: Identify each sentence part as subject, predicate, or tool. Some of the tools you will recognize; others will be new. *Notice that all the new tools are sentence parts, not sentences by themselves.*

EXAMPLE

a. Standing six foot two and 245 pounds, (***tool***)

b. my father (***subject***)

c. was an intimidating giant of a man, (***predicate***)

d. with thick, meaty hands, (***tool***)

e. every finger broken and bent. (***tool***)

AUTHOR'S SENTENCE

Standing six foot two and 245 pounds, my father was an intimidating giant of a man, with thick, meaty hands, every finger broken and bent.

Perri Knize, *Grand Obsession: A Piano Odyssey*

1a. Then,

1b. in an instant,

1c. the day's beauty

1d. was shattered.

President Barack Obama, remarks after the Boston Marathon bombings (April 18, 2013)

2a. Lost in his studies,

2b. Oppenheimer

2c. paid little attention to the outside world.

Steve Sheinkin, *Bomb*

3a. Little by little,

3b. with the sounds of the rain and the old lady's **respiration** [*breathing*],

3c. I

3d. fell asleep.

Nikos Kazantzakis, *Report to Greco*

4a. While everyone scattered,

4b. I

4c. crept into my favorite hiding place,

4d. the little closet tucked under the stairs.

Jean Fritz, *Homesick: My Own Story*

5a. He

5b. reached the fruit,

5c. dropping it to the third boy,

5d. who stood below holding out his coat as a blanket.

Christy Brown, *My Left Foot*

6a. We

6b. caught two bass,

6c. hauling them in briskly,

6d. as though they were mackerel,

6e. pulling them over the side of the boat in a businesslike manner without any landing net,

6f. and stunning them with a blow on the back of the head.

E. B. White, "Once More to the Lake"

7a. One day,

7b. when I went out to my woodpile,

7c. I

7d. observed two large ants,

7e. the one red,

7f. the other much larger,

7g. fiercely **contending** [*fighting*] with one another.

Henry David Thoreau, *Walden*

8a. At exactly fifteen minutes past eight in the morning,

8b. on August 6, 1945,

8c. Japanese time,

8d. at the moment when the atomic bomb flashed above Hiroshima,

8e. Miss Toshiko Sasaki,

8f. a clerk in the **personnel** [*employment*] department of the East Asia Tin Works,

8g. sat down at her place in the plant office to speak to the girl at the next desk.

John Hersey, *Hiroshima*

9a. Kids

9b. wanted to fight us

9c. because we had red hair,

9d. because Dad was a drunk,

9e. because we wore rags and didn't take as many baths as we should have,

9f. because we lived in a falling-down house partly painted yellow and had a pit filled with garbage in front,

9g. because they'd go by our dark house at night

9h. and see that we couldn't even afford electricity.

Jeanette Walls, *The Glass Castle*

10a. Well before dawn,

10b. in a rundown wooden building with a sawdust floor and wide gaps in the walls,

10c. Gey

10d. grabbed a screaming chicken by the legs,

10e. yanking it upside down from its cage,

10f. wrestling it to its back on a butcher block,

10g. holding its feet in one hand,

10h. and pinning its neck motionless to the wood with his elbow.

Rebecca Skloot, *The Immortal Life of Henrietta Lacks*

ACTIVITY 2: NEW TOOLS

The column on the right has only new tools. Match them with the appropriate sentence. Sentences 1–5 have one tool; sentences 6–10, two tools. Write out the sentence, studying and underlining the new tools. *Notice that all the new tools are sentence parts, not sentences by themselves.*

Sentences	New Tools
1. The explorers of the modern era are the entrepreneurs, men with vision, ^ . Ronald Regan, "Address At Moscow University"	**a.** because he was still able to move his hands
2. The teacher chose an escort for Clarence, a small, wiry boy with a crew cut just growing out, ^ . Tracy Kidder, *Among Schoolchildren*	**b.** who would jump through the open window by my bed in the middle of the night and land on my chest
3. I used to have a cat, an old fighting tom, ^ . Annie Dillard, *Pilgrim at Tinker Creek*	**c.** because then he will have sublime faith in mankind
4. Teach him always to have **sublime** [*noble*] faith in himself, ^ . Abraham Lincoln, "Letter to His Son's Teacher"	**d.** which resembled an untended garden
5. ^ , Morrie always spoke with both hands waving. Mitch Albom, *Tuesdays with Morrie*	**e.** with the courage to take risks and faith enough to brave the unknown
6. ^ , our existence would be barren and opaque, ^ . Elie Wiesel, "Hope, Despair and Memory"	**f.** long since disintegrated / whose outlines remind us how detailed, vibrant, and alive are the things of this earth that perish
7. ^ , he saw the eyes of the fifty children who had followed him, ^ . Greg Mortenson, *Three Cups of Tea*	**g.** who is an older man / who is only twenty-two

8. John, ^ , falls in love with Mary, and Mary, ^ , feels sorry for him because he's worried about his hair falling out. Margaret Atwood, "Happy Endings"	h. when Mortenson looked up toward the hole in the roof / and who were staring at the first foreigner they had ever seen
9. ^ , there is little practical distinction ^ . Margaret Chase Smith, "Declaration of Conscience"	i. without memory / like a prison cell into which no light penetrates
10. Sometimes one finds in fossil stones the imprint of a leaf, ^ , ^ . Diane Ackerman, *A Natural History of the Senses*	j. whether it be a criminal prosecution in court or a character prosecution in the Senate / when the life of a person has been ruined

ACTIVITY 3: CREATING TOOLS

Underneath each stripped-down sentence is a list of basic sentences to convert into tools to insert into the sentence. Your goal is to get all of the information *into just one sentence* by using tools.

EXAMPLE

Stripped-down Sentence: We came upon another small group of chimps.

Basic Sentences to Convert into Tools
a. This happened presently.

b. It was on an open grassy ridge.

c. One chimp was the adult male Prof.

d. Another chimp was his young brother Pax.

e. And the rest were two rather shy females with their infants.

Sentence with Underlined Tools: <u>Presently</u>, <u>on an open grassy ridge</u>, we came upon another small group of chimps, <u>the adult male Prof</u>, <u>his young brother Pax</u>, and <u>two rather shy females with their infants</u>.

Jane Goodall, *Through a Window*

1. ***Stripped-down Sentence:*** The cars traveled Reynolds Street.

BASIC SENTENCES TO CONVERT INTO TOOLS

   a. The cars traveled slowly.

   b. And they traveled evenly.

Annie Dillard, *An American Childhood*

2. ***Stripped-down Sentence:*** Fleet and Lee stood quietly on the doomed *Titanic*.

BASIC SENTENCES TO CONVERT INTO TOOLS

   a. They stood side by side.

   b. They were watching the ice draw nearer.

Walter Lord, *A Night to Remember*

3. ***Stripped-down Sentence:*** I saw the mouse vanish.

BASIC SENTENCES TO CONVERT INTO TOOLS

   a. This happened in the general direction of my apartment house.

   b. His little body was quivering with fear.

Loren Eiseley, "The Brown Wasps"

4. *Stripped-down Sentence:* He was built like an oak.

BASIC SENTENCES TO CONVERT INTO TOOLS

   a. He stood at six foot two.

   b. He was firm.

   c. He was straight-backed.

   Alex Kotlowitz, *Never a City So Real*

5. *Stripped-down Sentence:* You may not need to drink much water.

BASIC SENTENCES TO CONVERT INTO TOOLS

   a. Something will happen if you eat lots of foods naturally rich in water.

   b. These are foods such as vegetables.

   c. Those foods also include fruits, and whole grains.

   Larry Scheckel, *Ask Your Science Teacher*

6. *Stripped-down Sentence:* Phyllis was with her father.

BASIC SENTENCES TO CONVERT INTO TOOLS

   a. Phyllis was concerned with her father who lay dying in the bedroom,

   b. Phyllis was concerned but not wanting to miss the moon landing.

   c. She was with her father when her mother called her to come and see Neil Armstrong set foot on the moon.

   d. Neil Armstrong was the famous astronaut.

   Frank McCourt, *Teacher Man*

7. *Stripped-down Sentence:* The chimney sat **dormant** [*unused*].

BASIC SENTENCES TO CONVERT INTO TOOLS

a. It sat dormant for many years.

b. This lasted until the day that our father put a fish tank inside.

c. Our father was possessed of the same odd sort of inspiration that had led him for many years to decorate the lamp next to the couch

d. He decorated that lamp with rubber spiders and snakes.

Dave Eggers, *A Heartbreaking Work of Staggering Genius*

8. *Stripped-down Sentence:* Her mother was the short-order cook at the Comanche Cafe.

BASIC SENTENCES TO CONVERT INTO TOOLS

a. The Comanche Cafe was the one which was the dirtiest place in town.

b. It was also the darkest and smelliest place.

c. It was patronized by coal miners.

d. They were men who never washed their faces.

e. And they sometimes had fights after drinking cheap red wine.

f. They were such dangerous fights that the sheriff had to come.

Jean Stafford, "Bad Characters"

9. *Stripped-down Sentence:* We know that the battle against international terrorism is an armed struggle.

BASIC SENTENCES TO CONVERT INTO TOOLS

a. And we know that the battle against international terrorism is also a contest of ideas

b. Also we know that our long-term security depends on both of two things.

   c. One thing is the **judicious** [*intelligent*] projection of military power and increased cooperation with other nations

   d. The other thing is increased cooperation with other nations

   e. And we know that addressing the problems of **global** [*worldwide*] poverty and failed states is **vital** [*important*] to our nation's interest

   f. It is vital to our nation's interest rather than just a matter of **charity** [*kindness*].

   Barack Obama, *The Audacity of Hope*

10. *Stripped-down Sentence:* A baseball is made of a composition-cork **nucleus** [*center*].

BASIC SENTENCES TO CONVERT INTO TOOLS

   a. The nucleus is encased in two thin layers of rubber.

   b. One layer is black.

   c. The other layer is red.

   d. The layers are surrounded by many things.

   e. One of them is 12 yards of tightly wrapped blue-gray wool yarn.

   f. Another is 45 yards of white wool yarn.

   g. Another is 54 more yards of blue-gray wool yarn.

   h. Another is 150 yards of fine cotton yarn.

   i. Another is a coat of rubber cement.

   j. And another is a cowhide exterior.

   k. It is that exterior which is held together with 216 slightly raised red cotton stitches.

   Roger Angell, *Five Seasons*

ACTIVITY 4: EXPANDING INFORMATIONAL SENTENCES

Expand base sentences with some information from the facts provided, using whatever sentence-composing tools are effective. Include as many facts as you can. Vary the type, length, and place of your tools.

EXAMPLE

Topic: FORD MODEL T CAR

Base Sentence: The Ford Model T was ranked internationally as the most influential car of the twentieth century.

Facts:

- This pioneering car was manufactured from October 1, 1908, to May 27, 1927.
- One distinction is that it was the first car made on an assembly line.
- Once it was accepted as safe and efficient, the Model T popularized automobile travel instead of horse-drawn wagons or carriages.
- Reasonably priced for its time, this car was considered the first affordable automobile for the middle class.

Sample Result: <u>Perhaps because it was the first car affordable for the middle class</u>, the Ford Model T, <u>the first car from an assembly line</u>, was ranked internationally as the most influential car of the twentieth century.

TOPIC 1: ASPIRIN

Base Sentence: Aspirin is often prescribed in small dosages as a means to help prevent heart attacks.

Facts:

- This drug is sold in over 80 countries.
- The most successful nonprescription drug in history, it is taken by millions of people worldwide.
- It was among the first drugs available as tablets instead of a liquid.
- Perhaps the classic drug for pain and fever, aspirin is in almost all households.
- Because it thins the blood, it promotes a healthy heart by reducing the possibility of clogging.

TOPIC 2: AMERICAN CIVIL WAR

Base Sentence: The American war called the War between the States ended with the surrender of the army of the South.

Facts:

- With approximately 600,000 deaths total from both armies, this war is the bloodiest in American history.
- Because it involved Gatling guns, which resemble machine guns, the Civil War is considered the first modern war.
- It contained the bombing of Richmond, Virginia, the burning of Atlanta Georgia, and the death of President Abraham Lincoln.

TOPIC 3: CHOCOLATE

Base Sentence: Americans on average consume at least a half pound of chocolate every month.

Facts:

- Chocolate was originally a beverage, not a candy.
- In one form or another, it has been available for over 2000 years.

- All chocolate products, liquid and solid, are derived from cacao beans.
- In ancient times, the cacao bean was believed by Aztecs and Mayans to have magical properties.
- It was only in the mid-nineteenth century that chocolate became a solid candy.
- Currently in the United States chocolate is the basis of an industry worth four billion dollars annually.

TOPIC 4: AARDVARK

Base Sentence: Aardvarks are burrowing, nocturnal animals.

Facts:

- Aardvarks are found primarily in Africa.
- This mammal searches for and consumes ants and termites.
- It sticks out its tongue to catch them much like an anteater.
- Weighing between 130 and 180 pounds, it is between 3 and 4 feet tall.

TOPIC 5: VOLCANO

Base Sentence: A volcano is a rupture on the crest of a planet.

Facts:

- This rupture allows hot lava, volcanic ash, and gases to escape.
- Earth's volcanoes are the result of seventeen tectonic plates.
- These plates float on a hotter, softer layer beneath the crest.
- This means that most volcanoes are located near tectonic plates.
- The plates, either diverging or converging, create the volcano.

TOPIC 6: WART

Base Sentence: A wart is a small growth on the skin.

Facts:

- It resembles a cauliflower or a solid blister.
- It often occurs on hands or feet, or elsewhere.
- There are as many as ten varieties of warts.
- They are considered to be mostly harmless.
- They are, however, contagious.

TOPIC 7: JAVELIN

Base Sentence: A javelin is a light spear.

Facts:

- It is designed primarily to be thrown.
- The javelin can be used as a hunting weapon.
- It can also be used in sports.
- There are depictions of javelin throwers on ancient Greek vases.

TOPIC 8: FOSSIL

Base Sentence: Fossils are the preserved remains or traces of animals, plants, and other organisms.

Facts:

- They vary in size.
- They can be microscopic or gigantic.
- Fossils normally preserve only a part of the organism.
- That part was usually mineralized during life, such as bones and teeth.

- Fossils may also consist of something left behind by an animal.
- These are called *trace fossils* and are different from body fossils.

TOPIC 9: SUBMARINE

Base Sentence: A submarine is a large marine vessel capable of underwater travel.

Facts:

- It first became popular during World War I.
- Now many large navies include submarines.
- Military uses include attacking enemy ships.
- Civilian uses include marine science, salvage, and exploration.
- Most submarines contain a vertical structure that houses communications and sensing devices.
- This structure also includes a periscope.

TOPIC 10: BURJ KHALIFA

Base Sentence: The Burj Khalifa is currently the world's tallest building.

Facts:

- The skyscraper is in the city of Dubai in the United Arab Emirates.
- It is 2,716.5 feet tall.
- It has over 160 stories.
- It contains residences and offices and a hotel.
- There are 1,044 residences.
- There are 37 floors of offices.

- There is a hotel with 190 rooms.
- Underground parking holds 3,000 cars.
- Construction began January 2004.
- Grand opening was in January 2010.

YOUR TURN: INFORMATIONAL PARAGRAPH

Information about the disastrous sinking of the *Titanic* is presented below as a list of basic sentences lacking tools. Build a strong eight-sentence paragraph by converting many of those sentences into tools—*identifiers*, *describers*, *elaborators*, or *other tools*—as parts of the sentence. Vary the length, type, and place of your tools.

EXAMPLES

Here are several combinations based upon sentences 1–5. (Tools are underlined; subjects and predicates are bold.)

<u>A British passenger liner</u>, **the Titanic**, <u>built to be the largest ship ever</u>, **departed from Southampton, England for New York City April 10, 1912**, <u>sinking on its maiden voyage</u>.

The Titanic, <u>which was a British passenger liner and the largest ship of its kind</u>, **departed from Southampton, England for New York City on April 10, 1912**, <u>but sank on its maiden voyage</u>.

<u>After it departed from Southampton, England for New York City on April 10, 1912</u>, **the Titanic**, <u>a British passenger liner and the largest ship of its kind</u>, **sank on its maiden voyage**.

SENTENCE ONE

1. The *Titanic* was a British passenger liner.

2. It was the largest ship of its kind.

3. It sank on its maiden voyage.

4. It departed from Southampton, England on April 10, 1912.

5. Its destination was New York City.

SENTENCE TWO

6. It sunk in the middle of the night on April 15, 1912.

7. The ship had collided with a huge iceberg.

SENTENCE THREE

8. It carried 2,224 passengers and crew.

9. The ship carried two classes of people.

10. One class was the very wealthy.

11. The accommodations for the wealthy were luxurious.

12. They included a gymnasium and swimming pool.

13. Also included for the wealthy were high-class restaurants and fancy cabins.

SENTENCE FOUR

14. The other class was emigrants.

15. The emigrants were hoping for a better life in America.

SENTENCE FIVE

16. Over 1,500 passengers and crew died.

17. The number of lifeboats was inadequate.

18. There were only enough for half of the passengers and crew.

SENTENCE SIX

19. Many details of the sinking are available.

20. The collision with the iceberg occurred just before midnight four days into the sailing.

21. The iceberg ripped holes in the ship.

22. It opened five of the ship's sixteen watertight compartments.

23. The ship gradually filled with water.

24. Within two hours the ship sank.

SENTENCE SEVEN

25. Two hours later survivors in lifeboats were rescued.

26. A British ocean liner named *Carpathia* brought survivors onboard.

27. There were approximately 705 survivors.

SENTENCE EIGHT

28. Wreckage of the *Titanic* is on the floor of the sea.

29. That wreckage was discovered by deep-sea divers in 1985.

30. That wreckage is 12,415 feet deep.

31. The ship is split in two.

The true nature of the damage to the "Titanic" may be partly revealed as exploration of the wreck continues over the coming years, but it will often be hard to tell what was done by the iceberg and what was caused by the impact as the ship struck the ocean floor.

—Walter Lord, *A Night to Remember*

MARKING MEANING

In reading or in writing, meaning is conveyed mainly through words. If you know their meanings and understand how those words link to each other within a sentence, you're on the right track to interpret or compose meaning. Meaning comes also, however, from something else, invisible but audible in speech, visible but inaudible in writing: punctuation.

In speech, the sound of the voice—high or low, loud or soft, slow or fast—signals the end of sentences, questions, pauses, lists, interruptions, and other nonverbal cues to meaning; in writing, marks do those jobs.

Marks cue meaning, and only readers savvy enough to know what meanings those marks represent understand fully what they read. Here are the many ways commas mark meaning:

Alas, there are so many kinds of commas: those that lie like rocks in the path of a sentence, slowing its gait and requiring the reader's heed to avoid a stumble; their gentler cousins, impairing a pell-mell flow of meaning the way pebbles slow a stream; commas that indicate a pause for thinking things over; commas enclosing phrases the way the small pockets in a purse hug hairpins or collect bits of loose change; commas that return us to our last stop.

—William H. Gass, "Enter a Sentence of Elizabeth Bishop's"

Although the comma is the most common mark, several others are every bit as helpful to writers. In this section, you'll mark meaning by learning the significance of special punctuation marks used frequently in nonfiction: the dash, semicolon, colon.

After doing the activities, all with nonfiction examples of those marks, you'll gain skill and confidence to master difficult texts by fully understanding not just their words, but also their marks, and how, together, words and punctuation create and mark meaning.

> *Punctuation provides a map for one who must otherwise drive blindly past the by-ways, intersections, and detours of a writer's thought.*
>
> —Mina Shaughnessy, *Errors and Expectations*

DASH FOR INTERRUPTIONS

Sometimes a writer has an unplanned, sudden thought, so the writer interrupts a sentence to tell readers what it is.

One special punctuation mark interrupts a sentence—a dash. It indicates a spur-of-the-moment thought or an afterthought within a sentence. It's a way to mark meaning within a sentence.

A dash says to readers, "Hey! Here's something I just thought of that you should know."

> **Typing Tip:** A dash is made by hitting the hyphen key twice, not once.

Dashes indicate abruptness—a shift in thought, a change of topics, a "PS" or "BTW" within the same sentence. Sometimes the interruption is in the middle of a sentence, sometimes at the end. The interruption can be a sentence or a sentence part. In sentence 1, it is a sentence; in sentences 2 and 3, a sentence part.

EXAMPLES

1. Because he was still able to move his hands**—Morrie always spoke with both hands waving—**he showed great passion when explaining how you face the end of life.

    Mitch Albom, *Tuesdays with Morrie*

2. Cells make up all our tissues—**muscle, bone, blood**—which in turn make up our organs.

    Rebecca Skloot, *The Immortal Life of Henrietta Lacks*

3. I would stare at my father's likeness—**the dark laughing face, the prominent forehead and thick glasses that made him appear older than his years**—and listen as the events of his life tumbled into a single narrative.

    Barack Obama, *Dreams from My Father*

ACTIVITY 1: MATCHING

Match the interruption with the sentence it interrupts. Write the result.

Sentences	Interruption
1. While the preacher talked and I watched the children— ^ —my mind was busily breaking out with a rash of disconnected impressions. James Baldwin, *Notes of a Native Son*	a. the chauffeur, the other housekeeper, and her husband
2. Since it was late afternoon— ^ — we braced for one more unwelcome sales pitch. P. M. Forni, *Choosing Civility*	b. years of changing their diapers, scrubbing them, slapping them, taking them to school, and scolding them had had the perhaps **inevitable** [*certain*] result of making me love them, although I am not sure I knew this then
3. She was just what we pictured a Lab would be—^ . John Grogan, *Marley & Me*	c. two pack animals, and a half dozen head of horses

4. In a side canyon, on a late February morning, Indian Ed climbed across the rocks below the overhang where the team had spent the night with their cache of stolen goods—^ . Aron Ralston, *Between a Rock and a Hard Place*	**d.** that time is prime telemarketing time
5. That evening, her friends— ^ — would come to Aunt Tee's **commodious** [*comfortable*] live-in quarters. Maya Angelou, *Wouldn't Take Nothing for My Journey Now*	**e.** sweet-natured, affectionate, calm, and breathtakingly beautiful

ACTIVITY 2: UNSCRAMBLING

In model sentences, explain why the dashes are correct. Next, unscramble and write out the sentence parts to imitate the way the model is built.

1. *Model:* A man with murder in his heart will murder, or be murdered—it comes to the same thing—and so I knew I had to leave.

    James Baldwin, "Every Good-bye Ain't Gone"

    a. they are both so important

    b. a child with love in her life will love

    c. and so I vowed I would love

    d. or be loved

2. *Model:* Arranging a bowl of flowers in the morning can give a sense of quiet in a crowded day—like writing a poem, or saying a prayer.

    Anne Morrow Lindbergh, *Gift from the Sea*

    a. or singing a hymn
    b. a feeling of gratitude within your heart
    c. writing a note of thanks
    d. like receiving a smile
    e. during the day can provide

3. *Model:* It had taken Crocker and his team—young men, all in good condition, with some money and supplies plus horses and wagons—almost half a year to cross the plains and mountains.

    Stephen E. Ambrose, *Nothing Like It in the World*

    a. She had given Melinda and her family
    b. with no food and clothing or medicine and supplies
    c. hurricane **refugees** [*victims*]
    d. to buy some fast food and used clothing
    e. all in desperate need
    f. almost half her bonus

4. *Model:* Mrs. Hatsuyo Nakamura, the tailor's widow, got her three children—a ten-year-old boy, an eight-year-old girl, and a five-year-old boy—out of bed, dressed them, and walked with them to the military area.

    John Hersey, *Hiroshima*

    a. selected three astronauts
    b. America's space agency

c. and communicated with them during the spaceflight

   d. commander Neil Armstrong, pilot Michael Collins, and pilot Buzz Aldrin

   e. trained them

   f. NASA

   g. for the Apollo moon-landing mission

5. *Model:* Martha and Bill were lucky to have jobs—Martha's as assistant literary editor of the *Chicago Tribune*, Bill's as a teacher of history and a scholar in training—although Bill had pursued his career in a lackluster manner that dismayed and worried his father.

   Erik Larson, *In the Garden of Beasts*

   a. Elizabeth's from 1558 to 1603

   b. although Victoria's was clouded by deep mourning

   c. were destined to have long **reigns** [*monarchies*]

   d. Queen Elizabeth and Queen Victoria

   e. after the death of her husband Prince Albert

   f. Victoria's from 1837 to 1901

   g. who had loved and bolstered her

ACTIVITY 3: USING DASHES

Create an interruption for the sentence.

EXAMPLE

No Interruption: The totality of living matter on earth— ^ — makes up 0.00000001 percent of the mass of the planet.

Student Sample: The totality of living matter on earth—everything that has organs, breathes, eats—makes up 0.00000001 percent of the mass of the planet.

Original: The totality of living matter on earth—humans and animals, plants, bacteria, and pond scum—makes up 0.00000001 percent of the mass of the planet.

    Alan Lightman, "Our Place in the Universe"

---

1. A great book— ^ —demands the most active reading of which you are capable.
    Mortimer Adler, "How to Mark a Book"

2. At the time, not a soul in sleeping Holcomb village heard the gunshots— ^ .
    Truman Capote, *In Cold Blood*

3. In March, however, all the architects acknowledged that things were proceeding far too slowly —^ .
    Erik Larson, *The Devil in the White City*

4. That my father looked nothing like the people around me— ^ —barely registered in my mind.
    Barack Obama, *Dreams from My Father*

5. The arctic sun— ^ —seems not so much to shine as to strike.
    John McFee, *Coming into the Country*

SEMICOLON TO LINK TWO SENTENCES

> *I must say I have a great respect for the **semi-colon**;*
> *it's a useful little chap.*
>
> —Abraham Lincoln

Sometimes two sentences go better together because they both say something about the same person, place, object, idea, situation, or other topic.

One punctuation mark provides a way to link two consecutive sentences about a common topic; it's a semicolon. Using a semicolon is another way to mark meaning.

A semicolon says to readers, "These two sentences are linked in some way." Below are examples. Notice that the writer wants you to be alert for a link in meaning between the sentence pairs.

EXAMPLES

1. Walt Disney's father, Elias, helped build the White City**;** Walt's Magic Kingdom may well be a descendant. *(The semicolon links the Disney connection between the White City and the Magic Kingdom.)*

    Erik Larson, *The Devil in the White City*

2. The leaves were brilliant, a pale, vivid green in the soft sunlight**;** the wet trunk and branches were like **ebony** [*black*]. *(The semicolon links details about the tree's parts.)*

    Jane Goodall, *Through a Window*

3. The third week of June of 1999 was an extraordinarily happy one for my wife and for me**;** our three kids, now grown and scattered across the country, were visiting, and it was the first time in nearly six months that we'd all been under the same roof. *(The semicolon links*

reason for the extraordinary happiness concerning the adult children's visit to their parents' home.)

Stephen King, "On Impact"

ACTIVITY 4: MATCHING

By using a semicolon, join the linked sentence to the first sentence. Write the result.

First Sentence	Linked Sentence
1. That he now had two grown children seemed an impossibility; ^ . Erik Larson, *In the Garden of the Beasts*	a. it has a white (the cytoplasm) that's full of water and proteins to keep it fed, and a yolk (the nucleus) that holds all the genetic information that makes you you
2. Under the microscope, a cell looks a lot like a fried egg; ^ . Rebecca Skloot, *The Immortal Life of Henrietta Lacks*	b. leadership is doing the right things
3. My father worked hard, and my mother tended to us children and our pets; ^ . Barbara Hurd, "Refugium"	c. soon, he knew, they would be venturing off on their own and their future connection to him and his wife would grow **inevitably** [*certainly*] more **tenuous** [*weak*]
4. This Rottweiler was named Bullet; ^ . Stephen King, "On Impact"	d. the other one at home was named Pistol
5. Management is doing things right; ^ . Peter Drucker, *Management, the Individual, and Society*	e. there was always a beloved dog around, sometimes a rabbit, and, for a while, a couple of roosters

ACTIVITY 5: USING SEMICOLONS TO LINK SENTENCES

Create a second sentence to link to the given sentence. Use a semicolon to connect the two sentences.

Directions for 1–5: Write a second sentence that tells what happened next.

EXAMPLE

Incomplete: He kept a revolver in his cabin for the worst kinds of emergencies; ^ .

Student Sample: He kept a revolver in his cabin for the worst kinds of emergencies; **the sound of footsteps on the front porch steps was one of those times**.

Original: He kept a revolver in his cabin for the worst kinds of emergencies; **now he placed it in his pocket**

Erik Larson, Thunderstruck

---

1. Instead of facing problems, one runs away; ^ .
   Anne Morrow Lindbergh, Gift from the Sea

2. For a moment Augustus thought of throwing himself in the way of the horses to stop them, but before the carriage reached him, something gave way; ^ .
   Isak Dinesen, "The Roads Round Pisa"

3. I awoke to a jolting piece of news; ^ .
   Mitch Albom, Tuesdays with Morrie

4. Writers must accept the criticism of others and be suspicious of it; ^ .
   Donald M. Murray, "The Maker's Eye: Revising Your Own Manuscripts"

5. All morning I worked on the proof of one of my poems, and I took out a comma; ^ .

        Oscar Wilde

Directions for 6–10: Write a second sentence that explains the first sentence.

EXAMPLE

Incomplete: He would have to bail out of the fighter plane; ^ .

Student Sample: He would have to bail out of the fighter plane; **the engine was rapidly failing and would cause the plane to crash**.

Original: He would have to bail out of the fighter plane; **the only question was where and when**.

       Tom Wolfe, *The Right Stuff*

---

6. He kept coming back to the same conclusion; ^ .
    Erik Larson, *The Devil in the White City*

7. We had become very hungry; ^ .
    James Weldon Johnson, *Along This Way*

8. The purpose of a retreat is restorative; ^ .
    Barbara Hurd, "Refugium"

9. She said she had some luggage and her children were sick; ^ .
    John Hersey, *Hiroshima*

10. Here is exactly what reading should be; ^ .
    Mortimer Adler, "How to Mark a Book"

Directions for 11–15: Write a second sentence that contrasts with the first sentence. *Start the second sentence with the words provided.*

EXAMPLE

Incomplete: It was not an explosion; **it was the ^ .**

Student Sample: It was not an explosion; **it was the souped-up hot rod in the next block backfiring to the delight of its show-off driver.**

Original: It was not an explosion; **it was the tremendous crack of the pilot Ted Whelan, his helmet, his pressure suit, his unopened seat-parachute rig smashing into the center of the runway right in front of the horrified crowd.**

Tom Wolfe, *The Right Stuff*

---

11. In the country you are merely alone; **in the city ^ .**
    Anna Quindlen, *Lots of Candles, Plenty of Cake*

12. One brother had a weary and beaten dignity, sitting on the couch with his overcoat and a briefcase like a salesman who'd just lost a commission; **the other brother ^ .**
    Marcus Laffey, "The Midnight Tour"

13. All the joy the world contains has come through wishing happiness for others; **all the misery the world contains ^ .**
    Shantideva

14. Those who write clearly have readers; **those who write obscurely have ^ .**
    Albert Camus

15. We may call people who sacrifice their lives for another an **altruist**, but their real motives may be less selfless than we imagine; **they may be ^** .

Diane Ackerman, *Deep Play*

Directions for 16–20: Write a second sentence built like the first sentence, and join the two sentences with a semicolon. *Start the second sentence with the words provided.*

EXAMPLE

Incomplete: When I worked nights, I wrote during the day; **when I worked days, ^** .

Student Sample: When I worked nights, I wrote during the day; **when I worked days, I couldn't get any writing done**.

Original: When I worked nights, I wrote during the day; **when I worked days, I wrote during the night**.

Richard Wright, *American Hunger*

---

16. That Prendergast was a troubled young man was clear; **that Prendergast might be ^** .

Erik Larson, *The Devil in the White City*

17. If you are **idle**, be not **solitary**; if you are solitary, **^** .

Samuel Johnson

18. To play is to risk; **to risk is ^** .

Diane Ackerman, *Deep Play*

19. Ask not what your country can do for you; **ask what you ^** .

John F. Kennedy, "First Inaugural Address"

20. To err is human; **to forgive is** ^ .

                Alexander Pope, "An Essay on Criticism"

COLON FOR LISTS

Good writers sometimes include a list within a sentence—of hobbies, of groceries, of cities, of parts of a computer, of colors, and of almost anything.

    One punctuation mark provides a way to list two or more items within a sentence; it's a colon.

    A colon says to readers, "Next is the list of something just mentioned in the sentence." A writer uses a colon to alert readers to that upcoming list—another way of marking meaning.

EXAMPLES

(The underlined words are the topic of the list.)

1. She had volunteered to help these boys on the field and off, unaware of the scope and intractability of their <u>difficulties</u>: **post-traumatic stress, poverty, parental neglect in some cases**.

                Warren St. John, *Outcasts United*

2. Mary opened the Petri dishes one by one, holding them out to collect <u>samples</u> as Wilbur cut them from Henrietta's body: **bladder, bowel, uterus, kidney, vagina, ovary, appendix, liver, heart, lungs**.

                Rebecca Skloot, *The Immortal Life of Henrietta Lacks*

3. The <u>principles and practices of football and war</u> are alike: **mass hysteria, the art of intimidation, absolute command and total obedience, territorial aggression, censorship, inflated insignia and propaganda, blackboard maneuvers and strategies, drills, uniforms, formations, marching bands, and training camps**.

                John McMurty, "Kill 'Em! Crush 'Em! Eat 'Em Raw!"

INCORRECT COLONS

To the left of the colon must be a complete sentence that previews the list; to the right of the colon is that list.

The colons that follow are incorrect because no complete sentences are to the left of the colons. (*Incorrect colons below should be removed because no punctuation is necessary.*) The incorrect versions are then revised for correctness.

EXAMPLES

1a. *Incorrect:* Corey enjoyed several activities, including: playing chess until late at night, watching the late show on TV, and munching on snacks during both.

1b. *Correct:* Corey enjoyed several activities: playing chess until late at night, watching the late show on TV, and munching on snacks during both.

2a. *Incorrect:* Harry hated: robo calls on his cell, stink bugs on his wall, and starch in his shirts.

2b. *Correct:* Harry hated these things: robo calls on his cell, stink bugs on his wall, and starch in his shirts.

3a. *Incorrect:* Gavin always checked his bills for accuracy, such as: the amount of electricity used that month, the readings on his water meter, and the finance charge on his credit card.

3b. *Correct:* Gavin always checked his bills for accuracy: the amount of electricity used that month, the readings on his water meter, and the finance charge on his credit card.

4a. *Incorrect:* Miranda tweeted all her thoughts about: when she would finally get a date, how she would make up with her parents after the argument, whether she should wear the blue dress or the green one to the dance.

4b. *Correct:* Miranda tweeted all her thoughts about her life: when she would finally get a date, how she would make up with her parents after the argument, whether she should wear the blue dress or the green one to the dance.

ACTIVITY 6: MATCHING

Match the list with the sentence that previews it. Write the result, placing a colon before the list.

Sentences	List
1. Ingredients for their culture medium all sounded like witches' brews: ^ . Rebecca Skloot, *The Immortal Life of Henrietta Lacks*	**a.** my family beside me, Iranian flags soaring above, water from the canals of Tehran cascading ahead
2. Virginia Woolf wrote that in order for a woman to write fiction she must have two things: ^ . Alice Walker, *In Search of Our Mothers' Gardens*	**b.** hope that the book might succeed beyond my youthful dreams, despair that I had failed to say anything worth saying
3. The virtues that football and war celebrate are almost identical: ^ . John McMurty, "Kill 'Em! Crush 'Em! Eat 'Em Raw!"	**c.** hyper-aggressiveness, coolness under fire, suicidal bravery

4. When I beheld this view of Crown Prince Square, a parent on each arm, everything I loved was in sight: ^ . Roya Hakakian, *Journey from the Land of No*	d. a room of her own, the key and lock, and enough money to support herself
5. Like most first-time authors, I was filled with hope and despair upon the book's publication: ^ . Barack Obama, *Dreams from My Father*	e. the plasma of chickens, purée of calf fetuses, special salts, and blood from human umbilical cords

ACTIVITY 7: USING COLONS FOR LISTS

PART ONE

Create a sentence to preview the list, placing a colon between the sentence and the list.

EXAMPLE

Incomplete: a home, a family, a respectable life.

Student Sample: **In my future, after I get settled in a good job, I hope for the usual things:** a home, a family, a respectable life.

Original: **That's where the story might have stopped:** a home, a family, a respectable life.

Barack Obama, *Dreams from My Father*

1. ^ : a white cake, strawberry-marshmallow ice cream, and a bottle of champagne saved from another party.
   Joan Didion, "On Going Home"

2. ^ : biology, art, physics, history, mathematics.
   Frank McCourt, *Teacher Man*

3. ^ : hardworking, goal-oriented, driven to demanding the best of herself in any situation, refusing to settle for less.
   Ben Carson, *Gifted Hands*

4. ^ : to convert our good words into good deeds, in a new alliance for progress, to assist free men and free governments in casting off the chains of poverty.
   John F. Kennedy, *Inaugural Address*

5. ^ : wildly expensive, terribly inefficient, and poorly adapted to an economy no longer built on lifetime employment, a system that exposes hardworking Americans to **chronic** [*lasting*] insecurity and possible **destitution** [*poverty*].
   Barack Obama, *The Audacity of Hope*

PART TWO

Create a list to attach to the sentence. Use a colon before the list, and separate the items in the list with commas. For the list, add the number of items indicated.

EXAMPLE

Incomplete: I was assigned classes in English or wherever a teacher was needed: (*List five assignments for this teacher.*)

Student Sample: I was assigned classes in English or wherever a teacher was needed: **hall duty, chaperoning dances, study hall, substituting, bus duty.**

Original: I was assigned classes in English or wherever a teacher was needed: **biology, art, physics, history, mathematics**.

Frank McCourt, *Teacher Man*

---

6. This statement, which I knew almost absolutely to be false, set a number of emotions in action: ^ . (*List five unpleasant emotions.*)
James Weldon Johnson, *Along This Way*

7. On an ordinary day, the human ear is bombarded with sound: ^ . (*List brief descriptions of five irritating sounds.*)
Barbara Hurd, "Refugium"

8. They say you need three skills to be a quarterback: ^ . (*List just three words.*)
Drew Brees, *Coming Back Stronger*

9. She had made me a wonderful little writing desk there: ^ . (*List brief descriptions of six desk items.*)
Stephen King, "On Impact"

10. Mary opened the Petri dishes one by one, holding them out to collect samples as Wilbur cut them from Henrietta's corpse: ^ . (*List ten organ samples removed from Henrietta's body.*)
Rebecca Skloot, *The Immortal Life of Henrietta Lacks*

SEMICOLON FOR LISTS

Whenever any item in a list after a colon is more than ten words or already contains a comma, use semicolons, not commas, to separate the items. Separating them with semicolons makes reading easier.

ACTIVITY 8: USING SEMICOLONS FOR LISTS

After creating or researching the topic, attach a list to the sentence. The items in the list should be long, or already contain commas. Use a colon before the list, and separate the items in the list **with semicolons**. For the list, add the number of items indicated. (*The underlined words are the topic of the list.*)

EXAMPLE

Incomplete: The barn was huge, and next to it were <u>four small log buildings</u>: ^ .

Student Sample: The barn was huge, and next to it were <u>four small log buildings</u>: **a shed for storage of hand tools that my father wanted protected from the weather; a lean-to, made of rotted pieces of lumber; a chicken coop, covered with moss, now chickenless; and a playhouse he made for us to use when we were little kids**.

Original: The barn was huge, and next to it were <u>four small log buildings</u>: **the granary and the smithy; the meat house, where hides and sides of beef were cured; and the poison house, which had shelves full of bottles containing medicines, potions, spirits, and solvents, all with corks or rags stuffed in their tops**.

Jeannette Walls, *Half Broke Horses*

---

1. It's beyond my skill as a writer to capture <u>that day</u> [9-11-2001]: ^ . (*Describe in detail four images of 9-11.*)

    Barack Obama, *Dreams from My Father*

2. It seemed to me, alone on the beach and separated from my own species, that I was nearer to the birds I saw there: ^ . (*Describe in detail these birds: willet, sandpiper, pelican, seagull.*)

   Anne Morrow Lindbergh, *Gift from the Sea*

3. Abruptly there was color everywhere: ^ . (*Describe in detail four colorful objects that stood out in a big city.*)

   Erik Larson, *The Devil in the White City*

4. Nearly every famous freak of the period spent a few weeks in P. T. Barnum's circus sideshow: ^ . (*Describe in detail three acts in Barnum's sideshow.*)

   Duncan Wall, *The Ordinary Acrobat*

5. For Mary's pallbearers only her friends were chosen: ^ . (*Describe in detail one of her high school teachers, her high school principal, her doctor, her friend, her coworker, her brother.*)

   William Allen White, "Mary White"

REVIEW

DASH

Interrupts a sentence in the middle or at the end. If the interruption is in the middle of a sentence, two dashes are used, one before the interruption, one after it. If the interruption is at the end, one dash is used where the interruption occurs. (*For more information, see pages 75–80.*)

SEMICOLON

Joins two sentences linked in some way. A semicolon tells the reader that the ideas in two sentences are closely related. (*For more information, see pages 81–87.*)

COLON

Signals a list. An introductory sentence precedes the colon to preview for readers what list to expect. Separate the items in the list with commas, but if any item is more than ten words, or already contains commas, use a semicolon instead for a stronger separation. (*For more information, see pages 87–92.*)

Directions: Copy each sentence, and at the caret mark (^) punctuate it correctly with a dash, a semicolon, or a colon.

1. When the circus stayed overnight in a large town ^ Pittsburgh, Toledo, Detroit, Chicago, Milwaukee, Minneapolis ^ for extra performances, I slept on the ground under the lions' wagon.
   Edward Hoagland, "Calliope Times"

2. He made another vow that he would keep to the end of his life ^ he would never do any work that **exploited** [*abused*] someone else, and never allow himself to make money off the sweat of others.
   Mitch Albom, *Tuesdays with Morrie*

3. Since it was late afternoon ^ that time is prime telemarketing time ^ we braced for one more unwelcome sales pitch.
   P. M. Forni, *Choosing Civility*

4. We had a dispute about whether the rider had to be on his horse at the finish, and it happened so often that the horse came in alone that we made a rule ^ a horse, with or without his rider, won or lost the race.
   Lincoln Steffens, *A Boy on Horseback*

5. Looking out my study window, at the bare branches of a Japanese maple tree, I'm surprised by the different shapes snow makes atop

branches and twigs ^ pyramids, mounds, jaws, wings, candles, wedges, and animal shapes.

Diane Ackerman, *An Alchemy of the Mind*

6. Perhaps because Pete's father had been an observation balloonist in the First World War ^ an adventurous business, since the balloons were prized targets of enemy aircraft ^ Pete was fascinated by flying.

Tom Wolfe, *The Right Stuff*

7. On an open grassy ridge we came upon another small group of chimpanzees ^ the adult male Prof, his young brother Pax, and two rather shy females with their infants.

Jane Goodall, *Through a Window*

8. The parents who send their children to this modern and ably staffed school ^ the grades go from kindergarten through senior high, and a fleet of buses transport the students, of which there are usually around three hundred and sixty, from as far as sixteen miles away ^ are, in general, a prosperous people.

Truman Capote, *In Cold Blood*

9. Once in a while, sitting on the floor with my mother, the smell of dust and mothballs rising from the crumbling album, I would stare at my father's likeness ^ the dark laughing face, the prominent forehead and thick glasses that made him appear older than his years ^ and listen as the events of his life tumbled into a single narrative.

Barack Obama, *Dreams from My Father*

10. The orchard was full of extravagant smells and sights ^ low, scruffily hunchbacked things with long tails ^ squirrels that looked like gray mittens when they climbed trees ^ mump-cheeked chipmunks ^ insects that looked like tiny buttons or tanks ^ multi-colored birds in

high nests ^ chattery seedpods ^ and tall, silky flowers with long red tongues hanging out.

        Diane Ackerman, "In the Memory Mines"

YOUR TURN: **PORTRAIT OF A PLACE**

Select a city or town you are familiar with, perhaps where you live now, lived previously, or visited.

Directions:

1. Write your impression of the place using vivid images and focused details that make the place memorable.

2. Include each mark at least twice within your essay:

   - dash for interruption within a sentence (*See pages 75–80.*)
   - semicolon for linking two sentences (*See pages 81–87.*)
   - colon for a list (*See pages 87–92.*)
   - semicolon for a list. (*See pages 92–94.*)

3. Another use for a colon is between a main title and its subtitle. Create a title that names your city, followed by a colon; then create a subtitle that intrigues the reader. *Example*: BALTIMORE: BLUE CRAB BONANZA.

4. Exchange your draft with peers for suggestions for improvement.

Following are excerpts from essays about various places. Notice the kinds of details the author selected to make the description of the place uniquely memorable. Also study the author's punctuation choices (underlined) to use similar punctuation in your essay.

BIG CITY: NEW YORK, NEW YORK

(1) There are roughly three New Yorks: first, the New York of the man or woman who was born here, who takes the city for granted and accepts its size and its **turbulence** [*chaos*] as natural and **inevitable** [*certain*]; second, there is the New York of the commuter—the city that is devoured by locusts each day and spat out each night; third, there is the New York of the person who was born somewhere else and came to New York in quest of something. (2) Of these three trembling cities the greatest is the last—the city of final destination; the city is a goal. (3) It is the third city that accounts for New York's uniqueness: its high-strung **disposition** [*personality*], its poetical **deportment** [*behavior*], its dedication to the arts, and its incomparable achievements.

—E. B. White, "Here Is New York" (adapted)

TINY VILLAGE: HOLCOMB, KANSAS

(1) The village of Holcomb stands on the high wheat plains of western Kansas. (2) The land is flat, and the views are awesomely **extensive** [*vast*]: horses, herds of cattle, a white cluster of grain elevators.

(3) Holcomb can be seen from great distances. (4) Not that there is much to see—simply an aimless **congregation** [*assortment*] of buildings. (5) After rain, or when snowfalls thaw, the streets—unnamed, unshaded, unpaved—turn from the thickest dust into the **direst** [*worst*] mud. (6) The majority of Holcomb's homes are one-story frame affairs, with front porches. (7) Down by the depot, the postmistress, a **gaunt** [*thin*]

woman who wears a rawhide jacket and denims and cowboy boots, presides over a falling-apart post office. (8) The depot itself, with its peeling paint, is equally **melancholy** [*gloomy*]; the trains go by every day but never pause there.

—Truman Capote, *In Cold Blood* (adapted)

SMALL TOWN: OXFORD, MARYLAND

(1) It is comforting to know there are still small towns in America where policemen are bored: no drug busts, no high-speed chases, no assault and battery charges or alcohol-fueled domestic rages. (2) In Oxford, Maryland, the drug of choice—people drive miles to get it—is ice-cream made by a kilted Scotsman, sold and scooped by summer-job teens from an open window in the wharfside "Scottish Creamery" store. (3) It's addictive, but not criminal. (4) Instead of speeding, visitors slow their cars, admiring the charming homes in **vintage** [*old*] styles with gingerbread trim; or amble on foot, speaking to passersby; or bike, alone or in groups, through the gentle streets lined with trees and flowered lawns. (5) Couples, young and old, holding hands, **saunter** [*stroll*] down Oxford's lanes, pausing to sit on a bench at the town's centerpiece, a riverside park overlooking sailboats against blue sunny skies with vanilla clouds. (6) Noise **dissipates** [*disappears*]; the quiet assumes a texture of its own, the atmosphere velvety gentle. (7) Things slow down here, and we recall places and times less complicated: for me, a screened-in porch where I slept on a cot in the summer, a retreat from the humidity and stuffiness of a sweltering August bedroom; for my husband, a tiny pristine country cottage, on top of a hill, owned by a maiden aunt, painted and kept pure white inside and out, within a tiny sunroom a giant fern doubling as his play tent. (8) Somehow, in this lovely place of Oxford, when church bells chime twice a day, at noon and six, it feels absolutely right.

(9) With a population now of only 651—watermen, vacationers, week-enders, commuters, and a few year-rounders—this waterfront town no longer bustles as it once did. (10) Boasting a rich history, the international colonial seaport was home to a number of interesting inhabitants: Robert Morris, known as "the financier of the revolution" whose updated house still stands as an inn and now Oxford's finest place to stay; Colonel Tench Tilghman, George Washington's aide-de-camp; and sea captain Jeremiah Banning, war hero and statesman. (11) The American Revolution ended Oxford's glory days—no more British ships carrying imported goods for the colonies. (12) The town enjoyed a short rebound after the Civil War that ended when the oysters diminished.

(13) Today, commercial **enterprises** [*businesses*] are limited—no box stores or malls—and our three favorites include the country-store market specializing in sundries; the small bookstore devoted to crime novels; and the ferry crossing the Tred Avon River to St. Michaels, a popular tourist town on Maryland's Eastern Shore. (14) If you preorder at the deli counter in the Oxford market, you'll get a fabulous take-out meatloaf dinner cooked from scratch in the market's kitchen as the Friday special; its weekly availability is known only by local **cognoscenti** [*experts*]. (15) "Mystery Loves Company," the little bookstore in a former 19th century bank, sells only crime novels for those seeking mystery and excitement between two covers. (16) The Oxford-Bellevue ferry, the oldest continuous running ferry in America, crosses the river in about ten minutes, departing from the dock outside the Robert Morris Inn.

(17) *Yachting* magazine called Oxford the world's best waterfront town. (18) Yes, the world's. (19) Perhaps a stretch, but maybe not this claim—the most livable town on the Eastern Shore of Maryland. (20) Yes—at least for those who like it slow and quiet, lovely and peaceful, with fabulous Friday meatloaf and addictive ice cream.

(21) My favorite image from our week there is two girls, summer-friends, one a tweener, the other a bit younger, biking past our screened-in porch every evening, rain or shine, racing, laughing, playing—no technology required.

 Janine Wilkins, "Oxford" (complete essay)

QUOTATIONS: BITE-SIZE ESSAYS

An essay is a short piece of writing about almost any topic. Then is texting your friend an essay? Depends. Essays are usually considered expressions of authoritative or compelling opinions about a topic, carefully worded and structured. What they say is considered memorable for some reason: because it's witty, it's profound, it's insightful, it's wise, it's authoritative, or it's some other quality that makes the essay worth studying and remembering. So is texting an example of writing essays? Probably not. In most cases, definitely not.

In school, when you answer an essay question, you express your thoughts and knowledge about a particular topic, almost always the topic the teacher wants you to write about. Rarely are such essays recorded for posterity. Actually, never. So, like texting, they are not the kind of essays we're talking about.

What are the kind we're talking about? They're called *literary essays*, because they are, well, literature—writing that is expertly expressed and uniquely memorable.

The essay is a literary device for saying almost anything about almost anything.

—Aldous Huxley

Essays can be various lengths. In this section, you'll study bite-size essays—short quotations—that say "almost anything about almost anything."

Some essays are to be tasted, others swallowed, and some few chewed and digested.

—Francis Bacon

You'll decide which quotations should merely be tasted, which absolutely swallowed, and which thoroughly chewed and digested. Bite-size essays, often called *famous quotes* or *pearls of wisdom*, express an opinion about a topic, rendered memorably, often reflecting a common idea uncommonly expressed.

Throughout *Nonfiction for High School: A Sentence-Composing Approach*, you'll encounter some very complex, challenging texts to digest. Just as you need physical food for physical strength, you need intellectual food for intellectual strength. In this section, you'll feed on bite-size essays to nourish your mind.

ACTIVITY 1: CHUNKING BITE-SIZE ESSAYS

To savor these little essays, take a bite at a time by chunking them. The chunked quotations below are all about essays. A good chunk makes sense by itself; it "tastes" good. A bad chunk doesn't make sense by itself; it "tastes" bad.

Read each chunk to the slash mark (/) and you'll be able to see the difference between bad chunks (*left column*) and good chunks (*right column*).

To read well, chunk well, and then take a bite of the essay to see how it tastes. Chunking will improve your ability to read with understanding.

Bad Chunks	Good Chunks
1. The essay is a / literary / device for saying almost / anything about almost anything.	The essay / is a literary device / for saying almost anything / about almost anything. Aldous Huxley
2. The point of an / essay is to change / things.	The point / of an essay / is to change things. Edward Tufte
3. True wit is nature to / advantage dressed, what / oft was thought, but never so / well expressed.	True wit / is nature to advantage dressed, / what oft was thought, / but never so well expressed. Alexander Pope

4. The man who writes about / himself and his own time is the / only man who / writes about all / people and all / time.	The man who writes / about himself and his own time / is the only man / who writes /about all people and all time. George Bernard Shaw
5. The skill of / writing is to create a context in / which other people can / think.	The skill of writing / is to create a context / in which other people / can think. Edwin Schlossberg

ACTIVITY 2: FINDING CHUNKS

Read each pair of sentences a chunk at a time. <u>Important</u>: Read out loud, and pause where each slash mark (/) occurs. If the reading doesn't make sense, the chunks are bad. If the reading does make sense, the chunks are good. This activity helps improve reading ability.

EXAMPLE

a. I am a / writer because writing is the / thing I do best.

b. I am a writer / because writing is / the thing I do best.

Flannery O'Connor

GOOD CHUNKS: **b**

1a. Our mistakes won't / **irreparably** [*permanently*] damage our / lives unless we let them.

1b. Our mistakes / won't irreparably damage our lives / unless we let them.

James E. Sweaney

2a. Better **hazard** [*try*] / once than always be in / fear.

2b. Better hazard once / than always / be in fear.

Thomas Fuller

3a. The only person / who makes no mistakes / is the person / who never does anything.

3b. The only person who / makes no mistakes is the person who / never does anything.

Eleanor Roosevelt

4a. The important / thing is to be able at any / moment to sacrifice what we are for / what we could become.

4b. The important thing / is to be able at any moment / to sacrifice what we are / for what we could become.

Charles Du Bos

5a. All problems / become smaller / if you don't dodge them / but confront them.

5b. All / problems become / smaller if you don't dodge / them but confront them.

William F. Halsey

6a. The Wright brothers / flew right / through the smoke / screen of impossibility.

6b. The Wright brothers / flew right through / the smoke screen / of impossibility.

Charles Kettering

7a. Inspiration does not / come like a bolt, but it comes to / us slowly and quietly and all / the time.

7b. Inspiration / does not come like a bolt, / but it comes to us / slowly and quietly and all the time.

Brenda Ueland

8a. No one ever did anything worth doing / unless he or she was prepared to go on with it / long after it became / something of a bore.

8b. No one ever did / anything worth doing unless he or / she was prepared to go on with it long after it became something / of a bore.

Douglas V. Steere

9a. All the **discontented** [*unhappy*] / people I know are trying to be something / they are not, to / do something they cannot / do.

9b. All the discontented people I know / are trying to be / something they are not, / to do something they cannot do.

David Graydon

10a. In the game of life, / it's a good idea / to have a few early losses, / relieving you of the pressure / of trying to maintain an undefeated season.

10b. In the game of / life, it's a good idea to have a few / early losses, relieving you of the / pressure of trying to maintain an undefeated / season.

Diane Ackerman

ACTIVITY 3: MARKING GOOD CHUNKS

Sentence parts below are chunked meaninglessly. Copy the sentence, and then use the same number of slash marks to chunk the sentence meaningfully. This activity demonstrates your ability to create meaningful sentence parts.

EXAMPLE

Meaningless Chunks: To know what / is right and not / do it is / the worst cowardice.

Meaningful Chunks: To know / what is right / and not do it / is the worst cowardice.
                              Confucius

---

1. Failure is success if we / learn from / it.
                              Malcolm Forbes

2. We are made / kind by being / kind.
                              Eric Hoffer

3. It is never too / late to be what you might / have been.
                              George Eliot

4. **Valor** [*courage*] lies just / halfway between rashness and / cowardice.
                              Miguel de Cervantes

5. How / things look on the outside of / us depends on how / things are on the inside of us.
                              Park Cousins

6. When we accept tough / jobs as a challenge to our ability and wade into / them with joy and enthusiasm, miracles can / happen.
                              Arland Gilbert

7. We have to fight them daily, like / fleas, those many small / worries about the morrow, for they **sap** [*drain*] our / energies.
                                        Etty Hillesum

8. Everybody thinks of / changing / humanity, and nobody thinks of changing himself / or herself.
                                        Leo Tolstoy

9. It often takes more / courage to change one's / opinion than to stick to / it.
                                        Georg Christoph Lichtenberg

10. To get profit without / risk, experience without / danger, and reward / without work is as impossible as it / is to live without / being born.
                                        A. P. Gouthey

Some famous quotations are *epigrams*. An epigram is a short witty, pithy statement, pregnant with meaning. (A real tongue twister: try saying that definition three times fast.)

- It's short, usually one sentence or a few sentences.
- It's witty, so it's the thought of a clever mind.
- It's pithy, a funny word meaning full of important ideas.
- It's pregnant—not the kind that grows babies, but the kind that grows in meaning the more you think about it.

EXAMPLE

Epigram: If you think you can, or if you think you can't, you're probably right.
                                        Anonymous

Comment: This epigram suggests that both success and failure are determined mainly by your attitude. A positive attitude—the belief that you are capable of success—is desirable and a prediction of success; a negative attitude—the belief that you are incapable of success—is undesirable and a prediction of failure.

Like all epigrams, this one contains wisdom. How much wisdom depends upon your experience and belief. Any epigram is really a reflection of just one person's beliefs, delivered in a memorable and quotable style. Epigrams, in short, don't represent objective reality or universal truth, only subjective reality and individual truth.

As you do activities on interpreting epigrams in this section, decide how much truth—for you—each contains, and why.

ACTIVITY 4: MATCHING EPIGRAMS WITH MEANINGS

Interpret the quotation in the left column, and find its meaning in the right column.

Epigram	Meaning
1. Every exit is an entry somewhere else. Tom Stoppard	a. If you befriend someone, that person will become your friend.
2. It is better to light a candle than curse the darkness. Eleanor Roosevelt	b. Solving a problem is preferable to complaining.
3. The value of an idea lies in the using of it. Thomas Alva Edison	c. It is important to translate thought into action.

4. The only way to have a friend is to be one. Ralph Waldo Emerson	d. If someone is happy unaware of a problem, then it may not be a good idea for that person to learn about that problem.
5. Where ignorance is bliss, 'tis **folly** [*foolish*] to be wise. Thomas Gray	e. Leaving one thing begins another.

ACTIVITY 5: PAIRING QUOTATIONS WITH MEANINGS

Interpret the quotation in the left column, and find its meaning in the right column.

QUOTATION: Part One (1–5)	MEANING: Part One
1. **Motivation** [*desire*] is a fire from within. If someone else tries to light that fire under you, chances are it will burn very briefly. Stephen R. Covey	a. If you shield children from difficulties, you prevent them from learning how to solve problems.
2. All **misfortune** [*failure*] is but a stepping stone to fortune. Henry David Thoreau	b. If you believe in a goal, that's more important than somebody telling you what should be your goal.
3. No one can cheat you out of **ultimate** [*eventual*] success but yourself. Ralph Waldo Emerson	c. Problems can lead to success.
4. The greatest discovery of all time is that a person can change his future by **merely** [*simply*] changing his attitude. Oprah Winfrey	d. Change your attitude to gratitude to gain power and success.
5. Don't **handicap** [*disadvantage*] your children by making their lives easy. Robert A. Heinlein	e. If you fail, it's probably your own fault, and if you succeed, it's probably because of your own efforts.

QUOTATION: Part Two (6–10)	MEANING: Part Two
6. The influence of each human being on others in this life is a kind of **immortality** [*indestructibility*]. John Quincy Adams	f. Motivations are important, and if the reasons for doing something are wrong, then the behavior is wrong.
7. There is no passion so **contagious** [*catching*] as that of fear. Michel de Montaigne	g. Learning should increase knowledge and help people to understand reality.
8. The goal of education is the advancement of knowledge and the **dissemination** [*sharing*] of truth. John F. Kennedy	h. An ever-lasting aspect of a person is that person's influence on another human being.
9. The greatest **treason** [*betrayal*] is to do the right deed for the wrong reason. T. S. Eliot	i. When you express fear, people around you feel fearful.
10. The greatest weapon against **stress** [*worry*] is our ability to choose one thought over another. William James	j. If you want to reduce or eliminate worry, change your thoughts.

ACTIVITY 6: MATCHING MEANING

Choose the statement that best expresses the meaning of the quotation.

EXAMPLE

Quotation: True **affluence** [*wealth*] is not needing anything.
Gary Snyder

a. *Unacceptable*—The wealthiest are those who are poorest.

b. *Acceptable*—Those without wants are wealthy.

Explanation: Choice **b** captures the meaning of affluence, that is, having enough money to buy anything desired, and illustrates that those without wants already have everything they desire so they are truly wealthy.

TOPIC: HAPPINESS

1. Some people cause happiness wherever they go; others, whenever they go.
   Oscar Wilde

   a. Some people, near or far, bring happiness.

   b. Some people are welcome, but others are not.

2. I didn't want to get to the end of my life and find that I lived just the length of it. I want to have lived the width of it as well.
   Diane Ackerman

   a. A long life is the best life if you have few problems.

   b. A good life has important experiences as well as number of years.

3. There's no cure for birth and death, save to enjoy the interval.
   George Santayana

   a. Make the most of what happens between birth and death.

   b. Since we all live and die, make a difference.

4. Happiness leads none of us by the same route.
   Charles Caleb Colton

   a. People find happiness in different ways.

   b. Happiness is a destination, not an experience.

5. It is not the level of **prosperity** [*success*] that makes for happiness, but the **kinship** [*relationship*] of heart to heart and the way we look at the world. Both attitudes are within our power, so that a man is happy so long as he chooses to be happy and no one can stop him.

Alexsandr Solzhenitsyn

    a. Since happiness comes from our outlook and our relationships, and not from money, people can choose happiness without fail.

    b. How people look at life determines how happy they are, regardless of how much money they have or how many people they know.

Directions: The preceding five quotations are about happiness. In just one or two sentences, write your opinion about happiness, expressed, like those quotations, memorably.

TOPIC: FRIENDSHIP

6. Friendship multiplies the good of life and divides the evil. 'Tis the sole **remedy** [*cure*] for misfortune, the very **ventilation** [*oxygen*] of the soul.

Baltasar Gracian

    a. Life is better through friendship, which can bring healing to a person's life through good fortune.

    b. Friendship makes everything better, **minimizes** [*shrinks*] problems, and is like fresh air for the spirit.

7. To find a friend, one must close one eye. To keep a friend, two.
   Norman Douglas

   a. Overlooking a friend's faults promotes friendship.

   b. Keeping friends requires honesty and hard work.

8. **Adversity** [*trouble*] not only draws people together, but brings forth that beautiful inward friendship.
   Soren Kierkegaard

   a. Difficulties bring friends together to work out problems.

   b. Challenges cause friends to work together and demonstrate their good qualities.

9. The most beautiful discovery true friends make is that they can grow separately without growing apart.
   Elizabeth Foley

   a. Conflicts among genuine friends do not necessarily end friendships.

   b. Good friends find out that they don't always have to think or act alike.

10. Friendship often ends in love, but love in friendship, never.
    Charles Caleb Colson

    a. Romantic love usually fades, and sometimes disappears.

    b. Frequently love springs from deepening friendship.

Directions: The preceding five quotations are about friendship. In just one or two sentences, write your opinion about friendship, expressed, like those quotations, memorably.

TOPIC: ATTITUDE

11. Wisdom is the art of knowing what to overlook.
    William James

    a. Ignoring unimportant things is a good idea.

    b. Being able to **prioritize** [*rank*] keeps things organized.

12. The name we give to something shapes our attitude toward it.
    Katherine Patterson

    a. The label we put on something must accurately describe it.

    b. What we call something influences how we feel about it.

13. Life is raw material. We are artists. We can sculpt our existence into something beautiful, or **debase** [*corrupt*] it into ugliness. It's in our hands.
    Cathy Better

    a. Our lives are the material we craft. We can shape it into something good, or something bad. It's up to us.

    b. We cannot control our destiny. It may turn out well. It may turn out badly. We must try to influence the outcome.

14. The greatest discovery of my generation is that people can **alter** [*change*] their lives simply by altering their attitude of mind.
    William James

    a. We can succeed in improving our lives through hard work.

    b. We can change our lives by changing our thoughts.

15. Self image sets the boundaries of individual accomplishment.
    Maxwell Maltz

    a. How we see ourselves influences what we are able to achieve.

    b. We determine our future by working toward important accomplishments.

Directions: The preceding five quotations are about attitude. In just one or two sentences, write your opinion about attitude, expressed, like those quotations, memorably.

TOPIC: GOALS

16. We are conscious of touching the highest **pinnacle** [*height*] of fulfillment when we are consumed in the service of an idea, in the **conquest** [*attainment*] of the goal pursued.
    Robert Briffault

    a. When people try to accomplish something, they must stay focused.

    b. People attain satisfaction when they work passionately to achieve a goal.

17. The poor person is not someone who is without a cent, but someone who is without a dream.

Harry Kemp

    a. Wealth is measured by money, not dreams.

    b. Wealth is measured by dreams, not money.

18. Be a life long or short, its completeness depends on what it was lived for.

David Starr Jordan

    a. How complete a life is depends on its value, not its length.

    b. Longevity [*old age*] is an indication of a life well-lived.

19. A goal is a dream with a deadline.

Napoleon Hill

    a. If you can imagine a goal, you can achieve it.

    b. A worthwhile goal needs a time frame.

20. There is one thing which gives **radiance** [*shine*] to everything. It is the idea of something around the corner.

G. K. Chesterton

    a. Life looks better when something good is expected.

    b. Having a dream provides a goal for life.

Directions: The preceding five quotations are about goals. In just one or two sentences, write your opinion about goals, expressed, like those quotations, memorably.

ACTIVITY 7: PARAPHRASING MEANING

A paraphrase is an expression of equivalent meaning. For each quotation, write a paraphrase.

EXAMPLE

Quotation: Life has a value only when it has something valuable as its object.
George Hegel

Meaning: People whose lives are filled with meaningful goals lead rich lives.

Sample Good Paraphrases

1. A life is worthwhile only if the activities of that life are worthwhile.

2. Do something good with your life and your life will be good.

3. A productive life comes from a life with important purpose.

---

1. Look at everything as though you were seeing it for the first time or the last time. Then your time on earth will be filled with glory.
Betty Smith

2. Opposition **inflames** [*angers*] the enthusiast, never converts him.
J. C. F. von Schiller

3. I make the most of all that comes and the least of all that goes.
Sara Teasdale

4. **Adapt** [*change*] or **perish** [*die*], now as ever, is nature's **inexorable** [*inescapable*] **imperative** [*command*].
H. G. Wells

5. Happy he who learns to **bear** [*endure*] what he cannot change.
   J. C. F. von Schiller

6. There is no education like **adversity** [*trouble*].
   Benjamin Disraeli

7. Take the time to come home to yourself every day.
   Robin Casarjean

8. Imitation is a necessity of human nature.
   Oliver Wendell Holmes Jr.

9. New things cannot come where there is no room.
   Marlo Morgan

10. No matter where I run, I meet myself there.
    Dorothy Fields

ACTIVITY 8: TRANSLATING FIGURATIVE MEANING

Each of the following quotations conveys meaning through figurative language—the language of comparison. Translate each quotation *without using figurative language*.

EXAMPLE

Quotation: **Posterity** [*history*] weaves no garlands for imitators.
J. C. F. von Schiller

Figurative Language: A garland is a wreath of flowers in ancient times placed on the heads of champions as a crown to **signify** [*indicate*] victory. Within this quotation, a garland represents major accomplishments of **innovative** [*creative*] people, successful people who originate not imitate. Those accomplishments are recognized and appreciated by **history** [*posterity*], whereas those who only imitate their accomplishments are not.

Sample Translations:

1. Only originators of ideas are remembered with gratitude.

2. Praise for accomplishments goes to creative persons.

3. Innovators, not imitators, are the recipients of praise.

---

1. Friendship is a plant which must be often watered.
   Anonymous

2. Trouble is a **sieve** [*filter*] through which we sift our acquaintances. Those too big to pass through are our friends.
   Arlene Francis

3. Each of us makes our own weather, determines the color of the skies in the emotional universe which we inhabit.
   Fulton J. Sheen

4. Some days you tame the tiger, and some days the tiger has you for lunch.
   Tug McGraw

5. Sadness flies away on the wings of time.
   Jean de La Fontaine

6. All love that has not friendship for its base is like a mansion built upon the sand.
   Ella Wheeler Wilcox

7. The world is like a mirror. Frown at it, and it frowns at you. Smile, and it smiles, too.

Herbert Samuels

8. Hate is like acid. It can damage the **vessel** [*container*] in which it is stored as well as destroy the object on which it is poured.

Ann Landers

9. A vacant mind invites dangerous inmates, as a deserted mansion tempts wandering outcasts to enter and take up their **abode** [*house*] in its **desolate** [*empty*] apartments.

Nicholas Hilliard

10. The strongest of all warriors are these two: Time and Patience.

Leo Tolstoy

ACTIVITY 9: INTERPRETING A MEAL-SIZE ESSAY

Ready for a challenge? Written hundreds of years ago by British essayist Isaac D'Israeli (1766–1848), father of British prime minister Benjamin Israeli, this essay discusses the uses and abuses of using quotations within one's own writing. Study it **meticulously** [*carefully*].

Isaac D'Israeli, "Quotation" (adapted)

It is generally supposed that where there is no quotation, there will be found most originality. Our writers usually furnish their pages rapidly with the productions of their own soil: they run up a hedge, or plant a poplar, and get trees and hedges of this fashion much faster than the former landlords **procured** [*got*] their timber. The greater part of our writers, in consequence, have become so original, that no one cares to imitate them. However, those who never quote, in return are seldom quoted! The wisdom of the wise, and the experience of ages, may be preserved by Quotation.

It seems, however, agreed that no one would quote if he could think; and it is not imagined that the well-read may quote from the delicacy of their taste, and the fullness of their knowledge. Whatever is **felicitously** [*carefully*] expressed risks being worse expressed: it is a **wretched** [*horrible*] taste to be **gratified** [*pleased*] with **mediocrity** [*plainness*] when the excellent lies before us. We quote to save proving what has been demonstrated, referring to where the proofs may be found.

The **ancients** [*past authors*], who in these matters were not, perhaps, such **blockheads** [*idiots*] as some may conceive, considered poetical quotation as one of the **requisite** [*necessary*] ornaments of **oratory** [*speaking*]. Cicero, even in his philosophical works, is as little **sparing of** [*without*] quotations as Plutarch. Old Montaigne is so stuffed with them, that if they were taken out of him little of himself would remain. I suspect that Addison hardly ever composed a *Spectator* which was not founded on some quotation; and Addison **lasts** [*endures*], while Steele, who always wrote from first impressions and to the times, with perhaps no inferior genius, has passed away.

The Quoters who deserve the title—and it ought to be an honorary one—are those who trust to no one but themselves. In borrowing a passage, they carefully observe its connection; they collect authorities to **reconcile** [*restore*] any **disparity** [*difference*] in them before they furnish the one which they adopt; they advance no fact without a witness, and they are not loose and general in their references.

But a well-read writer, with good taste, is one who has the command of the wit of other men; he searches where knowledge is to be found; and though he may not himself excel in invention, his **ingenuity** [*creativity*] may compose one of those agreeable books that will outlast the fading meteors of his day. Epicurus is said to have borrowed from no writer in his three hundred inspired volumes, while Plutarch, Seneca, and the elder Pliny made such free use of their libraries; and it has happened that Epicurus, with his unsubstantial nothingness, has "melted into thin air," while the solid treasures have **buoyed** [*lifted*] themselves up amidst the wrecks of nations.

One word more on this long chapter of Quotation. To make a happy one is a thing not easily to be done. The happy application of a verse from Virgil is worth a talent; and there is not less invention in a just and happy application of a thought found in a book than in being the first author of that thought. The art of quotation requires more delicacy in the practice than those conceive who can see nothing more in a quotation than a mere extract. Whenever the mind of a writer is **saturated** [*filled*] with the full inspiration of a great author, a quotation gives completeness to the whole; it seals his feelings with undisputed authority. Whenever we would prepare the mind by a forcible appeal, an opening quotation is a symphony **preluding** [*starting*] on the chords whose tones we are about to harmonize.

Directions: Quote one sentence from D'Israeli's essay, and then write an explanation of D'Israeli's comment about the use of quotations by writers.

EXAMPLE

Quotation: I suspect that Addison hardly ever composed a *Spectator* which was not founded on some quotation; and Addison lasts, while Steele, who always wrote from first impressions and to the times, with perhaps no inferior genius, has passed away.

Explanation: D'Israeli claims that writers who use quotations, like Addison, tend to have an enduring readership, but writers who don't, like Steele, preferring only the expression of their own thoughts without quoting the thoughts of others, although talented writers, often are forgotten.

YOUR TURN: AUTOBIOGRAPHICAL EVENT

Choose one of the quotations from this section that you like because it illustrates something from your own life.

Directions:

1. Write a true story two to three double-spaced pages long illustrating your chosen quotation.

2. Don't include your chosen quotation directly within your narrative. Instead, illustrate it invisibly throughout your story.

3. Include varied examples of three sentence-composing tools you learned earlier: *identifiers* (*covered on pages 31–35*), *describers* (*covered on pages 39–43*), and *elaborators* (*covered on pages 46–50*). See the sample student paper by Scott below, which includes those three tools underlined.

4. Exchange your draft with peers for suggestions for improvement. Provide peers a list of five quotations from this section, one of which your story illustrates. See if peers can guess which quotation from that list your story illustrates.

Following is a sample by a student named Scott. As a young boy, Scott visited the house of an elderly couple, his great uncle and aunt. They were killed suddenly in an auto accident when a drunk driver hit their truck.

From the following quotations, choose the one Scott's narrative illustrates. Cite evidence for your choice by quoting from Scott's essay.

1. The poor person is not someone who is without a cent, but someone who is without a dream.

    Harry Kemp

2. I didn't want to get to the end of my life and find that I lived just the length of it. I want to have lived the width of it as well.

    Diane Ackerman

3. When we accept tough jobs as a challenge to our ability and wade into them with joy and enthusiasm, miracles can happen.

    Arland Gilbert

Identify the underlined sentence parts, which are Scott's use of three sentence-composing tools: *identifiers, describers, elaborators*.

EXAMPLES

Identifier: Over the mantel place there was hung a polished silvery mirror, holding a little shelf for various knickknacks: <u>memorabilia, photos, statues, buttons, postcards, nostalgic trinkets</u>.

Comment: The underlining identifies the various knickknacks.

Describer: On the long, winding street, the row house had concrete steps and an unkempt lawn, <u>littered with decaying leaves and wind-blown trash</u>.

Comment: The underlining describes the lawn.

Elaborator: Inside the living room were two chairs, <u>one of them covered up with blankets</u>, <u>the other one plain</u>. (*Contains two elaborators.*)

Comment: The underlining elaborates information about the chairs.

"No More"
by
Scott Bryant
(*a student paper*)

(1) On the long, winding street, the row house had concrete steps and an unkempt lawn, littered with decaying leaves and wind-blown trash. (2) On the door there was a small square knocker, and on the windows, long curtains with grayed white frills. (3) Inside the living room were two chairs, one of them covered up with blankets, the other one plain, displaying the wood frame of a rocker. (4) Over the mantel place there was hung a polished silvery mirror, holding a little shelf for various knickknacks: memorabilia, photos, statues, buttons, postcards, nostalgic trinkets. (5) Against one wall there was a small bulbous TV with rabbit ears on top. (6) In the middle of the kitchen sat a large wooden table, piled with unopened mail placed there every day since the accident by a neighbor, and around it were several straight-backed wooden chairs, painted white but yellowed from the years. (7) The room and the whole house smelled musty, and the furniture was makeshift and old. (8) There were no extravagances anywhere, just bare necessities—the furnishings of practicality not luxury.

(9) Looking excitedly around the room, a child not much older than 13 years of age, I stood behind my mother, trash bags and boxes in our hands. (10) My elderly great aunt and uncle had been dead for about a week now, killed instantly in their old 1970 Chevy truck by a drunk driver. (11) They had willed the house to my mother, their caretaker over the years who tended their needs when they called occasionally for her help.

(12) It was our job now to clean out their modest old house and get it ready for sale to cover their funeral costs. (13) With a look of sad determination on her face, Mom said, "Well, Scott, we aren't doing anything by just standing here. (14) We owe it to them to finish the job. Let's go."

(15) I nodded and mumbled, "Okay." (16) I tried to take a step forward, but as I put my foot down, a cat, a white mixed-breed, burst from behind the cellar door. (17) It shot up the stairs, but before reaching the top, turned around and yowled at us as if saying, "Get out! This is not your house!" (18) In a streak of white, it then vanished.

(19) Startled by the sudden encounter, I jumped back. (20) My mother, though, was unimpressed by the cat show. (21) Shaking her head and sighing, she simply said, "Now we have a cat to deal with. (22) Go and see if you can find a cage," she directed, pointing towards the kitchen.

(23) Putting the boxes and bags down, I stalked off into the kitchen. (24) The kitchen, its floors of cracked faded linoleum, a sink of peeling enamel, a fridge of ancient vintage, lacked any modern techno gadgetry. (25) As I looked around for a cage, I discovered a bag of cat food, torn open, sitting by the cellar door. (26) From another room Mother yelled, "Find a cage yet, Scott?"

(27) Yelling back to my mom, still taking in the dusty environment, I replied, "No, I don't see any sign of a cage."

(28) "Come back here then and help me. (29) There's no point of you looking for something that probably doesn't exist." (30) As I walked back, my mom sighed, "I guess we'll have to improvise." (31) Taking a high-walled box with her, she motioned for us to go up the stairs. (32) Because of the narrow width of the steep and creaking stairs, we walked up the stairway single-file.

(33) Soon we came to the top floor. (34) Looking down the hall, we saw that two doors were open—a bathroom and a bedroom. (35) Once we were inside the bedroom, Mother closed the bedroom door tight.

(36) Leaning up against the wall, my mother, a life-long cat person who knew the habits of cats, her muscles tensed for action, pointed under the bed, and then put her finger over her lips for silence. (37) As she tip-toed to the bed, she mimicked lifting the bed and motioned to me to go to the

other corner of the bed. (38) She counted slowly to three with her fingers. (39) On three, we both grabbed the bed and pushed it up against the wall. (40) Holding the makeshift-cage box, she looked under the bed, but quickly realized that the cat was not there.

(41) Glancing about for any trace of the cat, she was about to bend down when, amazed at what I saw, I tugged at her sleeve and blurted out "Look, Mom!" and pointed at the bed's metal frame. (42) There, wedged in between the mattress and the frame, was money, an assortment of 20s and 10s grouped in stacks near each side of the bed. (43) More surprising was the gaping dark hole in the wall at the head of the bed. (44) Taking a flashlight out of her back pocket, Mom bent down to peer into the hole in the plaster. (45) In it, money lay piled up in many rubber-banded stacks, a secret hoard of great Aunt May and Uncle John, their hope in an emergency, their security for the future.

(46) I stared at the discovery, small orderly money stacks, and Mother gazed disbelievingly.

(47) The cat was never found.

The wisdom of the wise, and the experience of ages, may be preserved by quotation.

—Isaac D'Israeli

MIRROR IMAGES: MENTOR PARAGRAPHS

Imitation is a necessity of human nature.
—Oliver Wendell Holmes Jr.

Within everyone is an inborn capacity to learn by imitating others—in talking or walking, in choosing clothes or grooming hair, in hitting a tennis ball or throwing a baseball, *and in composing sentences or paragraphs*. Imitating authors' sentences and paragraphs is the foundation of the sentence-composing approach to writing improvement.

WRITERS ON IMITATING

Directions: Explain what the writer means, and tell whether you agree.

1. Imitation is the sincerest form of flattery.
   Anonymous

2. Imitation is at least 50 percent of the creative process.
   Jamie Buckingham

3. In literature imitations do not imitate.
   Mark Twain

4. Imitation, if it is not forgery, is a fine thing. It stems from a generous impulse, and a realistic sense of what can and cannot be done.
   James Fenton

5. It is by imitation, far more than by precept, that we learn everything; and what we learn thus, we acquire not only more efficiently, but more pleasantly.
   Edmund Burke

6. Imitation is a perfectly honorable way to get started as a writer—and impossible to avoid, really: some sort of imitation marks each new stage of a writer's development.
Stephen King

FROM IMITATION TO CREATION

In this worktext, when you imitate sentence or paragraph nonfiction models to reflect the style of the author, you resemble an art student drawing from a Picasso painting to mirror its style, or a music student fashioning a piece to reflect Mozart. In any endeavor—artistic or otherwise, in building a skyscraper, or in building a sentence or paragraph—all imitative processes are akin to creative processes: a model is both an end-point and a starting-point. Something is borrowed from the model, and something is begun from it. Something is retained, and something is originated.

EXAMPLE

Model to Imitate: While everyone scattered, I crept into my favorite hiding place, the little closet tucked under the stairs.
Jean Fritz, *Homesick: My Own Story*

Sample Imitations
When the rain ended, Levar came out from the shelter, a makeshift tent made from a cardboard box.

After the light changed, the bus arrived at everybody's favorite restaurant, a burger joint packed with hungry students.

As a result of completing this worktext about nonfiction, you will understand the link between imitation, which is the foundation of sentence composing, and creation, which is its goal.

> *Imitation allows students to be creative, to find their own voices as they imitate certain aspects of other voices.*
>
> —Paul Butler, "Imitation as Freedom"

As you continue working through the activities in this worktext, you will learn and practice the sentence-composing and paragraph-composing tools of nonfiction authors. You'll create your own "toolbox," which you can use to develop your own style. You'll discover your own significant voice as a writer while hearing the whispers of other voices—the hundreds of nonfiction authors in this worktext, whose voices can help you discover your own.

Learning to Write

Whenever I read a book or a passage that particularly pleases me, in which a thing was said or an effect **rendered** [*expressed*] with **propriety** [*suitability*], in which there was either some **conspicuous** [*obvious*] force or some happy distinction in the style, I must sit down at once and set myself to **ape** [*imitate*] that quality. <u>Imitation, like it or not, is the way to learn to write</u>.

Perhaps I hear some one cry out: But imitation is not the way to be original! It is not; nor is there any way but to be born so. Nor yet, if you are born original, is there anything in this training that shall clip the wings of your originality.

Before he can tell what **cadences** [*styles*] he truly prefers, the student should have tried all that are possible; before he can choose and preserve a fitting key of words, he should long have practiced the literary scales; and it is only after years of such gymnastic that he can sit down at last—legions of words swarming to his call, dozens of turns of phrase simultaneously bidding for his choice—that he himself will know what he wants to do and be able to do it.

—Robert Louis Stevenson

IMITATING NONFICTION PARAGRAPHS

Nonfiction authors write about varied topics: describing a real object, place, or person; persuading readers to reach a conclusion; outlining a process telling how something happens or functions; defining a term, concept, or idea; providing information to educate readers; narrating details of an event. This section features paragraphs with those varied purposes.

Using different kinds of nonfiction paragraphs as models, you will learn how the sentences in each model paragraph are built, including their use of the three sentence-composing tools: *identifier* (*pages 31–35*), *describer* (*pages 39–43*), *elaborator* (*pages 46–50*), and then imitate that model paragraph with the same purpose, using your own nonfiction topic but building your sentences like those in the model paragraph.

I read my way as a young boy through approximately six tons of comic books, progressed to Tom Swift, then moved on to Jack London's bloodcurdling animal tales. At some point I began to write my own stories. Imitation precedes creation.

—Stephen King, *On Writing*

ACTIVITY 1: DESCRIBING AN OBJECT

The model paragraph from Anne Morrow Lindbergh's *Gift from the Sea* describes a snail shell as she inspects it in her hand.

Read the model paragraph, and the two paragraphs that follow it. Which one imitates the sentence structures in the model paragraph?

To learn how the sentences in the model paragraph and the imitation paragraph are built alike, write out two equivalent sentences as a list: sentence number (1) from the model, plus the sentence that imitates that model sentence; sentence number (2) from the model, plus the one that imitates it, and so forth.

MODEL PARAGRAPH

(1) This is a snail shell, round, full, and glossy as a horse chestnut. (2) Comfortable and compact, it sits curled up like a cat in the hollow of my hand. (3) Milky and **opaque** [*nontransparent*], it has the pinkish bloom of the sky on a summer evening, ripening to rain. (4) On its smooth, **symmetrical** [*uniform*] face is penciled with precision a perfect spiral, winding inward to the pinpoint center of the shell, the tiny dark core of the **apex** [*top*], the pupil of the eye. (5) It stares at me, this mysterious single eye, and I stare back.

Ann Morrow Lindbergh, *Gift from the Sea*

Questions to Analyze the Model

1. What sentence contains a simile (comparison)?

2. In sentence 4, what three phrases refer to the same part of the shell?

3. How do two of the sentences begin the same way?

4. How are the two main parts of sentence 5 alike?

SENTENCE-COMPOSING TOOLS

- In sentence 4, find a *describer* tool (see pages 39–43).
- In sentences 4 and 5, find *identifier* tools (see pages 31–35).

PARAGRAPH ONE

(1) Some rock stars are exciting to watch at live concerts, the fans cheering, the lights forming a kaleidoscope of color. (2) Thousands attend the concerts, which are usually held at large convention centers or outdoor theaters. (3) For weeks ahead of the concert, people get psyched, anticipating the special day when the concert hits town. (4) Despite what critics say, the behavior at concerts is loud, yes, but appropriate, with the great majority of people simply taking in the sights, the sounds, and overall atmosphere. (5) It's noisy, but nobody minds.

PARAGRAPH TWO

(1) That is a laser light, cool, ultraviolet, and invisible as air. (2) Precise and extraordinary, it gently reshapes the cornea by removing microscopic amounts of tissue from the outer surface of the cornea. (3) Innovative but expensive, it is controlled by a computer, performing to heal. (4) Under the laser is sitting with anxiety a hopeful patient, focusing on the outcome of the laser eye surgery, a medical marvel from technology, a new procedure for glass-free eyesight. (5) It beams into the patient's eye, this machine with invisible rays, and the patient sits still.

ACTIVITY 2: IMITATING THE PARAGRAPH

Investigate an object to describe, or using your own experience, describe an object you are already familiar with. Then write a five-sentence paragraph that imitates the model paragraph by Lindbergh (*page 133*).

The sentences from the model paragraph are broken down into their sentence parts to help you focus on how each part is built. Imitate each sentence part, one at a time, to write sentences for your paragraph resembling the sentences in the model paragraph.

1a. This is a snail shell,

1b. round, full, and glossy

1c. as a horse chestnut.

2a. Comfortable and compact,

2b. it sits curled up like a cat

2c. in the hollow of my hand.

3a. Milky and opaque,

3b. it has the pinkish bloom

3c. of the sky on a summer evening,

3d. ripening to rain.

4a. On its smooth, symmetrical face

4b. is penciled with precision a perfect spiral,

4c. winding inward to the pinpoint center of the shell,

4d. the tiny dark core of the apex,

4e. the pupil of the eye.

5a. It stares at me,

5b. this mysterious single eye,

5c. and I stare back.

ACTIVITY 3: DESCRIBING A PLACE

The model paragraph from Dave Eggers' memoir *A Heartbreaking Work of Staggering Genius* gives details of a quirky family room.

Read the model paragraph, and the two paragraphs that follow it. Which one imitates the sentence structures in the model paragraph?

To learn how the sentences in the model paragraph and the imitation paragraph are built alike, write out two equivalent sentences as a list: sentence number (1) from the model, plus the sentence that imitates that model sentence; sentence number (2) from the model, plus the one that imitates it, and so forth.

MODEL PARAGRAPH

> (1) The family room has always had the look of a ship's cabin, with wood paneling, with six heavy wooden beams holding the ceiling above. (2) The furniture is overwhelmingly brown and squat, like the furniture of a family of bears. (3) There is our latest couch, my father's, long and covered with something like tan-colored velour. (4) There is the chair near the couch, a sofa-chair of brownish plaid, my mother's. (5) One wall of the family room is dominated by a brick fireplace. (6) The fireplace has a small recessed area that was built to **facilitate** [*allow*] indoor barbequing, though we never put it to use, chiefly because when we moved in, we were told that raccoons lived somewhere high in the chimney. (7) For many years the chimney sat **dormant** [*inactive*], until the day, about four years ago, that our father, possessed of the same odd sort of inspiration that had led him for

many years to decorate the lamp next to the couch with rubber spiders and snakes, put a fish tank inside. (8) The fish tank, its size chosen by a wild guess, ended up fitting perfectly.

Dave Eggers, *A Heartbreaking Work of Staggering Genius*

Questions to Analyze the Model

1. Why is the room's furniture compared to "the furniture of a family of bears"?

2. How are sentences 3 and 4 alike?

3. What part of the family room is described the most?

SENTENCE-COMPOSING TOOLS

- In sentence 8, find an *elaborator* tool (see pages 46–50).
- In sentences 3 and 4, find *identifier* tools (see pages 31–35).

PARAGRAPH ONE

(1) The Claude Monet house has always had the feel of a fairy castle, flowers abounding, with twin lovely spring gardens showing the flowering hill below. (2) The flowers are breathtakingly beautiful and colorful like the splashes of an assortment of watercolors. (3) There is the lily pond, Monet's creation, still and crossed by a Japanese footbridge. (4) There is the famous Clos Normand section near the garden, archways of climbing wisteria entwined around colored shrubs, also Monet's creation. (5) One part of the Giverny garden is created by the artist's vision. (6) The property had a now famous pink brick building that was meant to accommodate family life, though Monet used elsewhere to paint, chiefly because when they

arrived, they also saw a working barn somewhere close on the property. (7) For many years the barn remained vacant until the day shortly after their arrival that Monet, inspired by the obvious utility of the space to create a studio for his various renderings of the gardens, created a light-filled studio there. (8) The artist's studio, its location chosen by a pragmatic need, ended up working nicely.

PARAGRAPH TWO

(1) The National Aquarium has been sitting on the edge of Baltimore's Inner Harbor since an urban renewal created it in 1981. (2) The building is mostly glass, a piece of modern architecture, its mission to protect aquatic life and educate for conservancy. (3) There are many award-winning exhibits, one of which is Australia's wild extremes. (4) There is a shark tank, a favorite with tourists from miles away, and especially with visiting students on field trips. (5) The upper levels of the Aquarium contain a tropical rain forest. (6) The rain forest is designed to introduce visitors to that habitat, including birds, vegetation, and animal life that might be found there, an attraction that attracts 1.5 million visitors annually. (7) The Aquarium contains a collection of 16,500 specimens representing 660 species, all within a building with architecture framed by the sky and the water of the Inner Harbor, resembling a beautiful aquatic animal itself, a stunning structure gracing the Baltimore skyline. (8) A visit to the National Aquarium, a highlight of the itinerary of virtually all tourists to Baltimore, is a must-see.

ACTIVITY 4: IMITATING THE PARAGRAPH

Investigate a place to describe, or using your own experience, describe a place you are already familiar with. Then write an eight-sentence paragraph that imitates the model paragraph by Eggers (*pages 136–137*).

The sentences from the model paragraph are broken down into their sentence parts to help you focus on how each part is built. Imitate each sentence part, one at a time, to write sentences for your paragraph resembling the sentences in the model paragraph.

1a. The family room

1b. has always had the look

1c. of a ship's cabin,

1d. wood paneled,

1e. with six heavy wooden beams

1f. holding the ceiling above.

2a. The furniture

2b. is overwhelmingly brown and squat,

2c. like the furniture

2d. of a family of bears.

3a. There is our latest couch,

3b. my father's,

3c. long and covered with something

3d. like tan-colored velour.

4a. There is the chair

4b. near the couch,

4c. a sofa-chair of brownish plaid,

4d. my mother's.

5a. One wall of the family room
5b. is dominated
5c. by a brick fireplace.

6a. The fireplace
6b. has a small recessed area
6c. that was built
6d. to facilitate indoor barbequing,
6e. though we never put it to use,
6f. chiefly because when we moved in,
6g. we were told
6h. that raccoons lived somewhere
6i. high in the chimney.

7a. For many years
7b. the chimney sat dormant,
7c. until the day,
7d. about four years ago,
7e. that our father,
7f. possessed of the same odd sort of inspiration
7g. that had led him for many years
7h. to decorate the lamp next to the couch
7i. with rubber spiders and snakes,
7j. put a fish tank inside.

8a. The fish tank,

8b. its size chosen

8c. by a wild guess,

8d. ended up fitting perfectly.

ACTIVITY 5: DESCRIBING A PERSON

The model paragraph from Rebecca Skloot's *The Immortal Life of Henrietta Lacks* describes a photo of Henrietta, a woman who died young from cancer but whose body yielded an incredible medical breakthrough.

Read the model paragraph, and the two paragraphs that follow it. Which one imitates the sentence structures in the model paragraph?

To learn how the sentences in the model paragraph and the imitation paragraph are built alike, write out two equivalent sentences as a list: sentence number (1) from the model, plus the sentence that imitates that model sentence; sentence number (2) from the model, plus the one that imitates it, and so forth.

MODEL PARAGRAPH

> (1) There's a photo on my wall of a woman I've never met, its left corner torn and patched together with tape. (2) She looks straight into the camera and smiles, hands on hips, dress suit neatly pressed, lips painted deep red. (3) It's the late 1940s, and she hasn't yet reached the age of thirty. (4) Her light brown skin is smooth, her eyes still young and playful, **oblivious** [*unaware*] to the tumor growing inside her, a tumor that would leave her five children motherless and change the future of medicine. (5) No one knows who took that picture, but it's appeared hundreds of times in magazines and science textbooks, on blogs and laboratory walls. (6) She's simply called HeLa, the code name given to the world's first immortal human cells, which are her

cells, cut from her cervix just months before she died. (7) Her real name is Henrietta Lacks.

Rebecca Skloot, *The Immortal Life of Henrietta Lacks*

Questions to Analyze the Model

1. How does each sentence begin—with its subject or something else?

2. How varied are the lengths of sentences in the paragraph?

3. How does the paragraph go from a physical description of Henrietta to her importance in science?

SENTENCE-COMPOSING TOOLS

- In sentences 1 and 2, find *elaborator* tools (see pages 46–50).

- In sentences 4 and 6, find *identifier* tools (see pages 31–35).

PARAGRAPH ONE

(1) Here's a photo in my scrapbook of a soldier I never knew, its outside edges untorn but fading with age. (2) He looks out at me and smiles, uniform shorts sagging around his waist, bare skin completely exposed, body tanned deep brown. (3) It's World War II, and he hasn't yet reached the age of twenty-one. (4) His young unblemished face is handsome, his attitude energetically ambitious and serious, unaware of the marriage that is waiting for him, a marriage that would produce three daughters and impact the world of education. (5) A buddy on the Pacific Island of Saipan took that picture, and it has lasted seventy-some years in the scrapbook where it stays, within a sepia page and a worn book. (6) He was originally named John, the unremarkable name also given to the remarkable family patriarch, who was John's

great-grandfather, born in pioneer days when courage and grit mattered. (7) People call him Johnny.

PARAGRAPH TWO

(1) On the desk is a picture, newly printed from the computer, with dazzling realistic color. (2) It shows my best friend acting silly, Waldo the Wimp, a nickname we gave him because, when we were kids, he was scared to jump off the high diving board. (3) Today, he's hardly a wimp, having been the star quarterback on Alexandria High School's team leading to district then state championships. (4) He still, though, calls himself by that nickname, even though his real name is Alfredo. (5) A good-natured guy, my best friend, he's been in my life ever since first grade, helped me through hard times, celebrated with me through good times, with the wisdom of a philosopher, the patience of a therapist, and the spirituality of a saint. (6) Now married with two kids, a boy and a girl, he honored me by making me his best man, and the godfather of his kids. (7) Friend is what I call him.

ACTIVITY 6: IMITATING THE PARAGRAPH

Place a photograph of a person you know in front of you, and write a seven-sentence paragraph that imitates the model paragraph by Skloot (*pages 141–142*).

The sentences from the model paragraph are broken down into their sentence parts to help you focus on how each part is built. Imitate each sentence part, one at a time, to write sentences for your paragraph resembling the sentences in the model paragraph.

1a. There's a photo on my wall

1b. of a woman I've never met,

1c. its left corner torn and patched together with tape.

2a. She looks straight into the camera and smiles,

2b. hands on hips,

2c. dress suit neatly pressed,

2d. lips painted deep red.

3a. It's the late 1940s,

3b. and she hasn't yet reached the age of thirty.

4a. Her light brown skin is smooth,

4b. her eyes still young and playful,

4c. oblivious to the tumor growing inside her,

4d. a tumor that would leave her five children motherless

4e. and change the future of medicine.

5a. No one knows who took that picture,

5b. but it's appeared hundreds of times

5c. in magazines and science textbooks,

5d. on blogs and laboratory walls.

6a. She's simply called HeLa,

6b. the code name given to the world's first immortal human cells,

6c. which are her cells,

6d. cut from her cervix just months before she died.

7a. Her real name

7b. is Henrietta Lacks.

ACTIVITY 7: NARRATING AN HISTORIC EVENT

Nonfiction often includes narration, in whole or part—a story that actually took place. An historic narrative chronicles details of a specific event in history.

The model paragraph from Laura Hillenbrand's *Unbroken* narrates the plight of several soldiers during World War II in a raft in shark-infested waters following their plane being shot down.

Read the model paragraph, and the two paragraphs that follow it. Which one imitates the sentence structures in the model paragraph?

To learn how the sentences in the model paragraph and the imitation paragraph are built alike, write out two equivalent sentences as a list: sentence number (1) from the model, plus the sentence that imitates that model sentence; sentence number (2) from the model, plus the one that imitates it; and so forth.

MODEL PARAGRAPH

> (1) It was June 23, 1943. (2) All he could see, in every direction, was water. (3) Somewhere on the endless expanse of the Pacific Ocean, Army Air Forces bombardier and Olympic runner Louie Zamperini lay across a small raft, drifting westward. (4) Slumped near him was a sergeant, one of his plane's gunners. (5) On a separate raft, tied to the first, was another crewman, a gash zigzagging across his forehead. (6) Their bodies, burned by the sun and stained yellow from the raft dye, had shrunk down to skeletons. (7) Sharks glided in lazy loops around them, dragging their backs along the rafts, waiting.
>
> Laura Hillenbrand, *Unbroken*

Questions to Analyze the Model

1. What words in sentences 1 and 2 describe the vastness of water surrounding the men?

2. In sentences 4, 5, 6, what details describe the physical condition of the men?

3. How does sentence 7 build suspense?

SENTENCE-COMPOSING TOOLS

- In sentences 1, find an *identifier* tool (see pages 31–35).
- In sentence 5, find an *elaborator* tool (see pages 46–50).
- In sentences 3, 5, 6, and 7, find *describer* tools (see pages 39–43).

PARAGRAPH ONE

(1) The fast mail service of 1860 to 1861 was called the Pony Express. (2) The idea was to be fast and reliable. (3) It was responsible for delivering mail from Missouri to California, with all mail and small packages transported by mounted horses. (4) Prompted by the growth of California, three industrious businessmen initiated the cross-country route. (5) Using mounted riders instead of stage coaches, their cargo heavy and slower, they intended to create a new way to deliver mail. (6) Their horses, sustained by short runs and excellent riders, carried just mail and small packages from St. Joseph, Missouri to Sacramento, California. (7) The price at that time was five dollars per half-ounce, underscoring the value of the service.

PARAGRAPH TWO

(1) The final takeoff happened July 2, 1937. (2) All she could see, in every place, was the Pacific Ocean. (3) From a tiny place called Howland Island in the mid-Pacific, world-famous aviatrix and women's rights feminist Amelia Earhart piloted a small plane named Electra, flying into unfavorable weather. (4) Seated beside her was Fred Noonan, the navigator and only other person on board the Electra. (5) On a final landing attempt, controlled by their radio, was an unclear problem, the words garbling from the plane. (6) This flight, characterized by poor planning and obstructed by a missing antennae underneath the fuselage, turned the flight to tragedy. (7) Spectators waited in nervous anticipation around the world, wanting their success in their trip around the world, fearing.

ACTIVITY 8: IMITATING THE PARAGRAPH

Investigate an historic event to narrate, or using your own knowledge, narrate an historic event you are already familiar with. Then write a seven-sentence paragraph that imitates the model paragraph by Hillenbrand (*page 145*).

The sentences from the model paragraph are broken down into their sentence parts to help you focus on how each part is built. Imitate each sentence part, one at a time, to write sentences for your paragraph resembling the sentences in the model paragraph.

1a. It was

1b. June 23, 1943.

2a. All he could see,

2b. in every direction,

2c. was water.

3a. Somewhere on the endless expanse

3b. of the Pacific Ocean

3c. Army Air Forces bombardier and Olympic runner

3d. Louie Zamperini

3e. lay across a small raft,

3f. drifting westward.

4a. Slumped near him

4b. was a sergeant,

4c. one of his plane's gunners.

5a. On a separate raft,

5b. tied to the first,

5c. was another crewman,

5d. a gash zigzagging across his forehead.

6a. Their bodies,

6b. burned by the sun

6c. and stained yellow from the raft dye,

6d. had shrunk down to skeletons.

7a. Sharks glided

7b. in lazy loops

7c. around them,

7d. dragging their backs along the rafts,

7e. waiting.

YOUR TURN: TECHNICAL REPORT

From anywhere in this section, select one of the paragraphs you imitated to include in a technical report as the first paragraph or the last paragraph or one somewhere in between—wherever it fits best.

Here are some technical topics from which to choose, or choose one of your own:

- carcinogens
- computer virus
- deforestation
- diabetes
- drones
- hydroponics
- inflation
- metastasis
- photosynthesis
- recession
- recycling
- robotics
- solar energy

Directions:

1. Study the sample below, a report about color vision by a student named Himja Shah written for her science class. Himja uses her imitation of the snail shell model on page 133 for her first paragraph.

2. Notice that the rest of her essay matches the quality of sentences she established in her imitation paragraph—but written without imitating.

3. Zoom in on Himja's abundant sentence-composing tools:

    - identifiers *italicized* (*pages 31–35*)
    - describers **bolded** (*pages 39–43*)

- elaborators <u>underlined</u> (*pages 46–50*)
- dashes ==highlighted== (*pages 75–80*).
- semicolons ==highlighted== (*pages 81–87*)
- and colons ==highlighted== (*pages 87–92*)

4. After studying how she uses those sentence-composing tools and special punctuation marks in her essay about color, after reviewing the tools and punctuation marks on the pages cited, include those tools and marks in your longer paper.

"Color Vision: A Pallet of Many Shades"
by
Himja Shah
(*a student paper*)

(1) It was an eye lens, round, bright, and transparent like a glass crystal. (2) Optic and contact, it sat wedged like filling in the hollow opening between the iris and ciliary muscles. (3) Lucid and clear, it had a whitish tone of the ground covered in snow on a cold winter morning, **unfolding to the sun**. (4) On its unbroken, contoured surface was archived with detail a perfect rainbow, **continuing inward to the distinguished interior of the eye**, *the minuscule base of the apex, the iris of the eye*. (5) It stared at me, *this radiant eye*, and I saw a masterpiece of complexion. (6) Colors make up the world we live in, <u>everyone perceiving hues of all sorts</u>, and are interpreted with optimum precision.

(7) The quest to find the perfect colors and color combinations is a common thread that ranges from great artists that have painted masterpieces to interior designers and landscapers. (8) As humans, we often judge things based on ==appearance: color==, size, and shape. (9) Color vision influences everything from art and poetry to the colors we paint our homes and the clothing we buy. (10) **Assigning colors to objects**, humans

tend to think of color as a constant, **overlooking the fact that color interpretation is a complex process that taps into our sensations and moods, as well as our eyes, neurons, and brains**.

(11) Have you ever wondered why the sky is blue, the grass is green, an apple is red? (12) Why do we see colors the way we do? (13) **Knowing what we do about color**, we can say that it is because of the spectrum of light, *the distribution of light power interacting in the eye with the spectral sensitivities of light receptors.* (14) **Centered on the light spectrum**, different colors exist for every wavelength of light, *the signal in which our eyes receive the color of an* object; our lenses use wavelengths to send signals to the brain to interpret the color. (15) The light spectrum consists of seven colors: red , orange, yellow, green, blue, indigo, and violet.

(16) Color originates in light; light , **perceived by humans**, is colorless. (17) In reality, a rainbow is testimony to the fact that all the colors of the spectrum are present in white light. (18) White light, **containing all the wavelengths of the visible spectrum at equal intensity**, can be seen broken into its color components when refracted in a prism, **revealing a rainbow**. (19) People perceive the color white due to the fact that an object reflects all the wavelengths. (20) The exact opposite happens when people perceive something as the color black; instead of all the wavelengths being reflected, they are all absorbed.

(21) So why does an apple appear red? (22) Well, light goes from the source, *the sun*, to the object, *an apple*, and finally to the detector, *the eye and the brain*. (23) All the "invisible" colors of sunlight shine on the apple; the apple absorbs all the colored rays, except for those corresponding to red, and reflects this color to the human eye. (24) The reflected red light is received by the eye, **causing a message to be sent to the brain where the color will be interpreted**. (25) <u>Lens focusing the light onto the retina</u>, the camera of the eye is where the light is absorbed by pigmented and light-sensitive cells, *cones*. (26) **Associated with wavelengths**, the color of an object is interpreted by the cones; <u>varying lengths picked up by different cones and determining the color of the</u>

object, medium cones are more sensitive to pure green wavelengths than to red wavelengths.

(27) **Looking at the world around us**, we notice that the grass appears to be green because it doesn't absorb the green wavelength. (28) Physically, objects are said to have the color of light leaving their surfaces. (29) **Arriving on an opaque surface**, light is either reflected or absorbed, usually both, **resulting in the color that we perceive**.
(30) Its composition of wavelengths unvaried, light is reduced to three color components by the eye: red , blue, and green. (31) The color white can be seen when this light stimulates all three types of color sensitive cone cells—photo *receptor cells in the retina of the eye that are responsible for color* vision—in the eye in nearly equal amounts.

(32) Complementary to vital colors in our everyday lives, colors represent the individuality of everyone through their accomplishments. (33) Without color, there would be no art and no way to express our emotions verbally. (34) Colors have many uses in society and play a big part in people's everyday lives from birth to marriage to death.
(35) **Associated by color as well**, human events take on added meaning: death is associated with the color black; white suggests purity; pink is used when a girl is born and blue for boys. (36) Colors blend into our experiences and our daily lives, **helping us to interpret, understand, and appreciate the world around us**.

FAMOUS PEOPLE: BRIEF BIOS

In this section, you will learn how the sentences in a model paragraph are built and then imitate that model paragraph by building your sentences like those.

You'll learn about interesting but little-known events from the lives of famous people and deepen your cultural literacy through learning more about the influence of those famous people.

Although this section focuses on biography, a type of nonfiction, its scope is paragraphs, not book-length biographies—just events from, not summaries of, the lives of famous people: mini-bios.

When you write paragraphs as brief bios, your content can come from your current knowledge about the person, or, more likely, new knowledge from online or offline searches.

IMITATING MINI-BIO PARAGRAPHS

When you imitate the model paragraphs, which are short excerpts from biographies of famous people, you will succeed if you focus on these goals:

BLUEPRINT FOR PARAGRAPH

Build your sentences like those in the model. The sentence structure of the model paragraph is a blueprint for your paragraph.

MATERIAL FOR PARAGRAPH

Tell something interesting your readers don't already know. Don't summarize the life of the person. You're writing mini-bios, not book-length biographies. Think tweets, not tomes. The content of the model paragraph—an up-close word picture of a little-known incident from the person's life—is the material for building your paragraph.

BUILDER OF PARAGRAPH

Write mini-bio paragraphs with two benefits for your readers: (1) new information about the person and (2) entertainment through choice of interesting details about that person's life—a humorous anecdote, an unusual experience, a startling fact, an exceptional accomplishment, a disturbing detail—or some other fascinating aspect of the person's life. In your paragraphs, pretend you are a writer for a paper or digital magazine that regularly features interesting but little-known info about famous persons—bite-size bios, appetizing tidbits that your readers will enjoy.

ACTIVITY 1: STEVE JOBS, TECHNOLOGY ENTREPRENEUR

Under his leadership, Apple produced a series of revolutionary products, including iMac, iPod, iPad, iPhone, and iTunes.

> *This is a biography about the roller-coaster life and* **searingly** [burningly] *intense personality of a creative entrepreneur whose passion for perfection and ferocious drive revolutionized six industries: personal computers, animated movies, music, phones, tablet computing, and digital publishing.*
>
> —Walter Isaacson, *Steve Jobs*

OBSERVING EQUIVALENT SENTENCE STRUCTURE

Read the model paragraph and imitation of the model paragraph with equivalent sentence structure. To see their similarity in sentence structure, read the first sentence from each paragraph, then the second, then the third, and so forth.

MODEL PARAGRAPH

(1) He was not a model boss or human being, tidily packaged for **emulation** [*imitation*]. (2) Driven by demons, he could drive those around him to fury and despair. (3) His personality and passions and products were all interrelated, just as Apple's hardware and software tended to be, as if part of an integrated system. (4) His biography is thus both instructive and cautionary, filled with lessons about innovation, character, leadership, and values.

>Walter Isaacson, *Steve Jobs*

IMITATION PARAGRAPH

(1) He was not an Ivy League graduate or privileged guy, perfectly groomed for success. (2) Fascinated by electronics, he was partnered with Steve Wozniak to revolutionize and democratize. (3) His ideas and creativity and management became iconic, just as the Apple mystique and success grew to be, as if driven by inspiration. (4) His life seemed both inspirational and unique, punctuated with moments of failure, success, disappointment, and rebirth.

IMITATING THE MODEL PARAGRAPH

Choose another famous entrepreneur or innovator, learn more about that person online or offline, and then write an imitation of the four-sentence model paragraph about Steve Jobs.

The sentences from both the model paragraph and its imitation are broken down below into their sentence parts to help you focus on how each part is built. Imitate each sentence part, one at a time, to write sentences for your paragraph like the sentences in the model paragraph. Your imitation doesn't have to be exact, just approximate, built pretty much like the model.

Model	Imitation
1a. Steve Jobs was not a model boss **1b.** or human being, **1c.** tidily packaged for emulation.	**1a.** He was not an Ivy League graduate **1b.** or privileged guy, **1c.** perfectly groomed for success.
2a. Driven by demons, **2b.** he could drive those around him **2c.** to fury and despair.	**2a.** Fascinated by electronics, **2b.** he partnered with Steve Wozniak **2c.** for ideas and products.
3a. His personality and passions and products **3b.** were all interrelated, **3c.** just as Apple's hardware and software **3d.** tended to be, **3e.** as if part of an integrated system.	**3a.** His ideas and creativity and management **3b.** became iconic, **3c.** just as the company's mystique and success **3d.** grew to be, **3e.** as if driven by inspiration.
4a. His biography is **4b.** both instructive and cautionary, **4c.** filled with lessons **4d.** about innovation, character, leadership, and values.	**4a.** His life seemed **4b.** both original and unique, **4c.** punctuated with moments **4d.** of failure, success, disappointment, and rebirth.

ACTIVITY 2: MICHAEL PHELPS, OLYMPIC SWIMMER

Holder of nineteen gold medals, Michael Phelps won the highest number of gold medals in the history of the Olympics.

Michael Phelps manipulated water like no man since Moses. Swimming had never seen anything like him.

—Paul McMullen, *Amazing Pace*

OBSERVING EQUIVALENT SENTENCE STRUCTURE

Read the model paragraph and imitation of the model paragraph with equivalent sentence structure. To see their similarity in sentence structure, read the first sentence from each paragraph, then the second, then the third, and so forth.

MODEL PARAGRAPH

(1) At first glance, the 17-year-old appeared indistinguishable from millions of American boys. (2) Raised in the suburbs, he got a **vicarious** [*secondhand*] thrill listening to rap music, had little interest in books or schoolwork, was fiercely protective of his single mother, and tried to impress the girls with a hot set of wheels, in his case a Cadillac sport-utility vehicle. (3) A baseball cap usually covered his **unruly** [*messy*] dark hair, a defense left over from adolescence, when oversized ears had made him a target of **derision** [*cruelty*]. (4) He had a pleasant, goofy grin but wore a scowl when he was introduced to a sport that wasn't his first choice. (5) That **aversion** [*dislike*] became an avocation [hobby], and was now his vocation, but it still seemed preposterous, the astonishing things the boy could do in a pool. (6) He was among a select group who had become world-class athletes before having had a chance to grow up.

Paul McMullen, *Amazing Pace*

IMITATION PARAGRAPH

(1) In record time, the boy seemed unstoppable beyond competition from other swimmers. (2) Built for the sport, he had a certain advantage expanding his young lungs, had an almost seven-foot wing span between his left shoulder and right shoulder, was singularly blessed with double-jointed elbows, and determined to maintain his one hundred and ninety pounds with

a careful regimen of dieting, in an average day a four thousand calorie breakfast. (3) An abnormally long torso characterized his young adolescent body, another advantage given him by his build, since that oversized build made Michael a competitor with an edge. (4) He had a grueling, demanding schedule and practiced a lot because he was strengthening his strokes that needed his concentrated attention. (5) That attention became an obsession, and was now his life and it no longer surprised coaches, the record-breaking results Michael could achieve in competitions. (6) He was only a sixteen-year-old who had become an Olympic candidate before having had the opportunity to begin driving.

IMITATING THE MODEL PARAGRAPH

Choose another famous athlete, learn more about that person online or offline, and then write an imitation of the six-sentence model paragraph about Michael Phelps.

The sentences from both the model paragraph and its imitation are broken down below into their sentence parts to help you focus on how each part is built. Imitate each sentence part, one at a time, to write sentences for your paragraph like the sentences in the model paragraph. Your imitation doesn't have to be exact, just approximate, built pretty much like the model.

Model	Imitation
1a. At first glance,	**1a.** In record time,
1b. the 17-year-old appeared indistinguishable	**1b.** the boy seemed unstoppable
1c. from millions of American boys.	**1c.** beyond competition from other swimmers.

2a. Raised in the suburbs, **2b.** he got a vicarious thrill listening to rap music, **2c.** had little interest in books or schoolwork, **2d.** was fiercely protective of his single mother, **2e.** and tried to impress the girls with a hot set of wheels, **2f.** in his case a Cadillac sport-utility vehicle.	**2a.** Built for the sport, **2b.** he had a certain advantage expanding his young lungs, **2c.** had an almost seven-foot wing span between his left shoulder and right shoulder, **2d.** was singularly blessed with double-jointed elbows, **2e.** and determined to maintain his one hundred and ninety pounds with a careful regimen of dieting, **2f.** in an average day a four thousand calorie breakfast.
3a. A baseball cap usually covered his unruly dark hair, **3b.** a defense left over from adolescence, **3c.** when oversized ears had made him a target of derision.	**3a.** An abnormally long torso characterized his young adolescent body, **3b.** another advantage given him by his build, **3c.** since that oversized build made Michael a competitor with an edge.
4a. He had a pleasant, goofy grin **4b.** but wore a scowl **4c.** when he was introduced to a sport **4d.** that wasn't his first choice.	**4a.** He had a grueling, demanding schedule **4b.** and practiced a lot **4c.** because he was strengthening his strokes **4d.** that needed his concentrated attention.
5a. That aversion became an avocation, **5b.** and was now his vocation, **5c.** but it still seemed preposterous, **5d.** the astonishing things the boy could do in a pool.	**5a.** That attention became an obsession, **5b.** and was now his life **5c.** and it no longer surprised coaches, **5d.** the record-breaking results Michael could achieve in competitions.
6a. He was among a select group **6b.** who had become world-class athletes **6c.** before having had a chance to grow up.	**6a.** He was only a sixteen-year-old **6b.** who had become an Olympic candidate **6c.** before having had the opportunity to begin driving.

ACTIVITY 3: J. D. SALINGER, AUTHOR

His novel *The Catcher in the Rye*, first published in 1951, has been translated into all the world's languages and has been a best-seller ever since, with over 65 million copies sold.

> *Salinger the man may be gone—and for that the world is an emptier place—but he will always live within the pages he created, and through his art remain as vital today and tomorrow as when he walked the boulevards of New York and strolled the woods of New Hampshire.*
>
> —Kenneth Slawenski, *J. D. Salinger: A Life*

OBSERVING EQUIVALENT SENTENCE STRUCTURE

Read the model paragraph and imitation of the model paragraph with equivalent sentence structure. To see their similarity in sentence structure, read the first sentence from each paragraph, then the second, then the third, and so forth.

MODEL PARAGRAPH

(1) Having enjoyed a life being spoiled by his mother, refusing to apply himself to his studies, and **flouting** [*ignoring*] the few rules ever imposed on him, entering this world of unbending discipline at Valley Forge Military Academy as a teenager came as a great shock to Salinger. (2) What made the transition even more difficult was the fact that many of the cadets at Valley Forge did not like him. (3) Salinger was a thin, lanky teen—school photographs picture him awkwardly awash in his dress uniform, always in the back row—with what some students considered a snobbish New York attitude. (4) Other cadets resented him for

entering Valley Forge two years later than most and avoiding freshman **hazing** [*punishment*]. (5) Alone, and lacking the support of his family for the first time, Salinger sought refuge in sarcasm and **feigned** [*pretended*] aloofness, attitudes that did not make him popular.

     Kenneth Slawenski, *J. D. Salinger: A Life*

IMITATION PARAGRAPH

(1) Having volunteered to become a part of World War II, enlisting to put himself into the action, but ignoring the horror always included in battle, experiencing this military world of violence on the D-Day landing in Normandy as a novice served as a lasting trauma to the young man. (2) What made the experience even more horrifying was the realization that many of his comrades at the landing did not survive. (3) Salinger was an intense, handsome soldier—the only wartime picture shows him at a table, presumably with a manuscript—with what many people thought an aloof difficult personality. (4) Some soldiers admired him for carrying six chapters of *The Catcher in the Rye* and continuing his writing. (5) Disillusioned, and wanting practice in his craft without letup, Salinger found comfort in writing and processing experience, a strategy that would make him famous.

IMITATING THE MODEL PARAGRAPH

Choose another famous author, learn more about that person online or offline, and then write an imitation of the five-sentence model paragraph about J. D. Salinger.

 The sentences from both the model paragraph and its imitation are broken down below into their sentence parts to help you focus on how each part is built. Imitate each sentence part, one at a time, to write sentences for your paragraph like the sentences in the model paragraph. Your imitation doesn't have to be exact, just approximate, built pretty much like the model.

Model	Imitation
1a. Having enjoyed a life being spoiled by his mother, **1b.** refusing to apply himself to his studies, **1c.** and flouting the few rules ever imposed on him, **1d.** entering this world of unbending discipline at Valley Forge Military Academy **1e.** as a teenager **1f.** came as a great shock to Salinger.	**1a.** Having volunteered to become a part of World War II, **1b.** enlisting to put himself into the action, **1c.** but ignoring the horror always included in battle, **1d.** experiencing this military world of violence on the D-Day landing in Normandy **1e.** as a novice **1f.** served as a lasting trauma to the young man.
2a. What made the transition even more difficult **2b.** was the fact **2c.** that many of the cadets at Valley Forge **2d.** did not like him.	**2a.** What made the experience even more horrifying **2b.** was the realization **2c.** that many of his comrades at the landing **2d.** did not survive.
3a. Salinger was a thin, lanky teen— **3b.** school photographs picture him awkwardly awash in his dress uniform, **3c.** always in the back row— **3d.** with what some students considered **3e.** a snobbish New York attitude.	**3a.** Salinger was an intense, handsome soldier— **3b.** the only wartime picture shows him at a table, **3c.** presumably with a manuscript— **3d.** with what many people thought **3e.** an aloof difficult personality.
4a. Other cadets resented him **4b.** for entering Valley Forge two years later than most **4c.** and avoiding freshman hazing.	**4a.** Some soldiers admired him **4b.** for carrying six chapters of *The Catcher in the Rye* **4c.** and continuing his writing.

5a. Alone, **5b.** and lacking the support of his family for the first time, **5c.** Salinger sought refuge **5d.** in sarcasm and feigned aloofness, **5e.** attitudes that did not make him popular.	**5a.** Disillusioned, **5b.** and wanting practice in his craft without letup, **5c.** Salinger found comfort **5d.** in writing and processing experience, **5e.** a strategy that would make him famous.

ACTIVITY 4: MARILYN MONROE, ACTRESS

One of movie's most memorable stars, the blonde actress became a pop and cultural icon, perhaps the most famous movie star ever.

She might be as modest in her voice and as soft in her flesh as the girl next door, but she was nonetheless larger than life up on the screen.

—Norman Mailer, *Marilyn: A Biography*

OBSERVING EQUIVALENT SENTENCE STRUCTURE

Read the model paragraph and imitation of the model paragraph with equivalent sentence structure. To see their similarity in sentence structure, read the first sentence from each paragraph, then the second, then the third, and so forth.

MODEL PARAGRAPH

(1) Drawn to all living things, Marilyn loved animals. (2) She would spend hundreds of dollars to try to save a storm-damaged tree and would mourn its death. (3) She welcomed birds,

providing tree houses and food for the many species that visited her lawn, worrying about them in bad weather. (4) She once had a dog that was by nature **contemplative** [*thoughtful*], but she was convinced he was depressed. (5) She did her best to make him play, and that depressed him even more. (6) On the rare occasions when he did a **pirouette** [*spin*], Marilyn would hug and kiss him, **delirious** [*thrilled*] with joy.

Norman Rosten, *Marilyn: An Untold Story*

IMITATION PARAGRAPH

(1) Raised primarily in foster homes, Marilyn married young. (2) Her husband would join the Merchant Marines to attempt to earn a steady income and would miss Marilyn's transformation. (3) Marilyn divorced her husband, focusing her energy and time on the modeling opportunities that came her way, hoping with time to create a career. (4) She eventually had an image that became in time iconic, but she was uncertain that she was talented. (5) Marilyn wanted the opportunity to play serious roles but that eluded her too often. (6) In her insecurity when she did have an important role, her lateness would upset and anger co-stars, impatient on the set.

IMITATING THE MODEL PARAGRAPH

Choose another famous actor, learn more about that person online or offline, and then write an imitation of the six-sentence model paragraph about Marilyn Monroe.

The sentences from both the model paragraph and its imitation are broken down below into their sentence parts to help you focus on how each part is built. Imitate each sentence part, one at a time, to write sentences for your paragraph like the sentences in the model paragraph. Your imitation doesn't have to be exact, just approximate, built pretty much like the model.

Model	Imitation
1a. Drawn to all living things, **1b.** Marilyn loved animals.	**1a.** Raised primarily in foster homes, **1b.** Marilyn married young.
2a. She would spend hundreds of dollars **2b.** to try to save **2c.** a storm-damaged tree **2d.** and would mourn its death.	**2a.** Her husband would join the Merchant Marines **2b.** to attempt to earn **2c.** a steady income **2d.** and would miss Marilyn's transformation.
3a. She welcomed birds, **3b.** providing tree houses and food **3c.** for the many species that visited her lawn, **3d.** worrying about them in bad weather.	**3a.** Marilyn divorced her husband, **3b.** focusing her energy and time **3c.** on the modeling opportunities that came her way, **3d.** hoping with time to create a career.
4a. She once had a dog **4b.** that was by nature contemplative, **4c.** but she was convinced **4d.** that he was depressed.	**4a.** She eventually had an image **4b.** that became in time iconic, **4c.** but she was uncertain **4d.** that she was talented.
5a. She did her best **5b.** to make him play, **5c.** and that depressed him even more.	**5a.** Marilyn wanted the opportunity **5b.** to play serious roles **5c.** but that eluded her too often.
6a. On the rare occasions **6b.** when he did a pirouette, **6c.** Marilyn would hug and kiss him, **6d.** delirious with joy.	**6a.** In her insecurity **6b.** when she did have an important role, **6c.** her lateness would upset and anger co-stars, **6d.** impatient on the set.

ACTIVITY 5: MICHAEL JACKSON, ENTERTAINER

Dubbed the "King of Pop," he excelled as a singer, dancer, and songwriter, whose unique style made him the world's most popular entertainer.

> *His brilliant contributions to music and dance, his unending humanitarian efforts, and his constant efforts to unify people and heal the world will certainly leave an everlasting impression and continue to inspire others around the world.*
>
> —Lisa Campbell, *Michael: The Complete Story of the King of Pop*

OBSERVING EQUIVALENT SENTENCE STRUCTURE

Read the model paragraph and imitation of the model paragraph with equivalent sentence structure. To see their similarity in sentence structure, read the first sentence from each paragraph, then the second, then the third, and so forth.

MODEL PARAGRAPH

(1) In front of the live and TV audiences, Michael picked up a hat and perched it on his head angled down over his eyes, and began pumping his pelvis to the opening beats of "Billie Jean" and went on to bring the house down with his moves, unveiling his moonwalk dance for the very first time. (2) He glided backward while appearing to walk forward—something most people had never seen before. (3) He seemed to defy gravity, or the laws of physics, or something. (4) TV viewers, the Pasadena Civic Auditorium audience, other artists backstage, including his brothers, were stunned. (5) Michael Jackson, who had already been enjoying uncharted success with his recent album "Thriller," and was wowing audiences with his fancy footwork in music videos, just sent his popularity soaring into the stratosphere and changed the music industry in the process.

Lisa Campbell, *Michael: The Complete Story of the King of Pop*

IMITATION PARAGRAPH

(1) With a voice like Vincent Price and its horror, Michael opened up the tombs and ghouled up his face, pointed threateningly toward the camera, and began leading the corpses to the pulsing tones of "Thriller" and went on to win an unprecedented nine Grammy awards, rewarding his most complex music video with its fabulous choreography. (2) He broke records while continuing to create music—songs his fans were always eager for. (3) Jackson appeared to revolutionize singing, the steps of choreography, and pop entertainment. (4) His costumes, gravity-defying dance steps like the Moonwalk, voice range, including his vocal hiccup, were dazzling. (5) Producer Quincy Jones, who had already shared a Grammy for "Thriller" with Michael Jackson for the best-selling album of all time, and was researching a new altruistic project with Michael plus all the most famous singers, carefully sent another tune skyrocketing with the song "We Are the World" and impacted Michael's career as a result.

IMITATING THE MODEL PARAGRAPH

Choose another famous entertainer, learn more about that person online or offline, and then write an imitation of the five-sentence model paragraph about *Michael Jackson*.

The sentences from both the model paragraph and its imitation are broken down below into their sentence parts to help you focus on how each part is built. Imitate each sentence part, one at a time, to write sentences for your paragraph like the sentences in the model paragraph. Your imitation doesn't have to be exact, just approximate, built pretty much like the model.

Model	Imitation
1a. In front of the live and TV audiences, **1b.** Michael picked up a hat **1c.** and perched it on his head **1d.** angled down over his eyes, **1e.** and began pumping his pelvis **1f.** to the opening beats of "Billie Jean" **1g.** and went on to bring the house down with his moves, **1h.** unveiling his moonwalk dance for the very first time.	**1a.** With a voice like Vincent Price and its horror **1b.** Michael opened up the tombs, **1c.** and ghouled up his face, **1d.** pointed threateningly toward the camera, **1e.** and began leading the corpses **1f.** to the pulsing tones of "Thriller" **1g.** and went on to win an unprecedented nine Grammy awards, **1h.** rewarding his most complex music video with its fabulous choreography.
2a. He glided backward **2b.** while appearing to walk forward— **2c.** something most people **2d.** had never seen before.	**2a.** He broke records **2b.** while continuing to create music— **2c.** songs his fans **2d.** were always eager for.
3a. He seemed to defy gravity, **3b.** or the laws of physics, **3c.** or something.	**3a.** Jackson appeared to revolutionize singing, **3b.** the steps of choreography, **3c.** and pop entertainment.
4a. TV viewers, **4b.** the Pasadena Civic Auditorium audience, **4c.** other artists backstage, **4d.** including his brothers, **4e.** were stunned.	**4a.** His costumes, **4b.** gravity-defying dance steps like the Moonwalk, **4c.** voice range, **4d.** including his vocal hiccup, **4e.** were dazzling.

5a. Michael Jackson, **5b.** who had already been enjoying uncharted success **5c.** with his recent album "Thriller," **5d.** and was wowing audiences **5e.** with his fancy footwork in music videos, **5f.** just sent his popularity soaring **5g.** into the stratosphere **5h.** and changed the music industry in the process.	**5a.** Producer Quincy Jones, **5b.** who had already shared a Grammy for "Thriller" with Michael Jackson **5c.** for the best-selling album of all time, **5d.** and was researching a new altruistic project **5e.** with Michael plus all the most famous singers, **5f.** carefully sent another tune skyrocketing **5g.** with the song "We Are the World" **5h.** and impacted Michael's career as a result.

SCULPTING SENTENCES

Famous Italian artist Michelangelo, who sculpted world-famous statues like "David" and "the Pieta," carved his amazing statues from blocks of stone. He believed that the stone held captive a statue but that the sculptor, using vision, creativity, and skill, could free the statue from the imprisonment of the stone. In this activity, you'll sculpt sentences about famous people out of a list of ordinary sentences, to create sentences like the ones by authors.

Directions: Each list of ordinary sentences that follows contains information about a famous person—sentences resembling a sculptor's stone waiting to be shaped into something great. Using that information, write a paragraph containing sentences built like those of an author. Sculpt superb sentences from that block of stone to create something great.

Every block of stone has a statue inside it,
and it is the task of the sculptor to discover it.

—Michelangelo

ACTIVITY 6: OPRAH WINFREY, HUMANITARIAN

Famous for widespread success as an interviewer and a philanthropist, she gained huge audiences for televised talk shows, created her own television network, and performed charitable work globally.

---

*Her **philanthropic** [humanitarian] efforts as well as her material success have made her one of the most inspiring role models not only in America, but also the world.*

—Diana Bradford, *Oprah Winfrey's Inspirational Life Story*

<u>Summary of the Paragraph</u>: Her grandmother instructed four-year-old Oprah in how to wash clothes in a bucket. Sculpt the ordinary sentences into a paragraph with FOUR sentences.

Sculpt the following information into the *first sentence* of your paragraph.

1a. It was a cold day.

1b. That day was on a lonesome farm.

1c. The farm was in Mississippi.

Sculpt the following information into the *second sentence* of your paragraph.

2a. Oprah Winfrey was a four-year-old.

2b. She sat on the back porch.

2c. She was churning up some butter for the family table.

2d. And she was watching as her grandmother poked at clothes.

2e. The clothes were floating in an old black pot.

Sculpt the following information into the *third sentence* of your paragraph.

3a. Clothespins decorated an apron.

3b. The clothespins were wooden.

3c. The apron was Grandma Hattie Mae Lee's.

Sculpt the following information into the *fourth sentence* of your paragraph.

4a. Hattie told her granddaughter several things.

4b. She told those things to her as Hattie lifted the heavy, wet laundry out of the water and hung each piece on the line.

4c. What she told her granddaughter was to pay attention.

4d. The reason she told her was because Oprah was going to have to learn to do this someday.

(Information is from a paragraph
by Ilene Cooper, *Up Close: Oprah Winfrey*.)

ACTIVITY 7: ELVIS PRESLEY, SINGER

Uniquely original in voice, gestures, and costumes, Elvis had a meteoric rise to superstardom never equaled.

> *Rhythm and blues helped make Elvis a big star. He sang R and B in his own special way. Girls screamed when he stood on stage and wiggled his hips. Boys tried to look like him. This was the start of rock and roll, and of all the rock stars to come, Elvis was the biggest.*
>
> —Geoff Edgers, *Who Was Elvis Presley?*

<u>Summary of the Paragraph</u>: The life of this legendary singer illustrates the difficulty of superstardom. Sculpt the ordinary sentences into a paragraph with four sentences.

Sculpt the following information into the *first sentence* of your paragraph.

1a. Elvis' story is heartwarming.

1b. It is also heartbreaking.

1c. It is the story of a poor boy.

1d. The boy was from the wrong side of the tracks.

1e. That boy became a king.

1f. It is the story of an outsider who pursued his dream.

1g. He pursued it despite the ridicule and derision of his peers.

Sculpt the following information into the *second sentence* of your paragraph.

2a. The story is also a cautionary tale.

2b. The tale is of dangers.

2c. One danger is the one of excess.

2d. The other is of the corruption of fame.

Sculpt the following information into the *third sentence* of your paragraph.

3a. One response to Elvis occurred.

3b. The same response to Elvis happened whether you loved him or hated him.

3c. Elvis left no one indifferent to rock and roll.

Sculpt the following information into the *fourth sentence* of your paragraph.

4a. And one thing is certain whether for good or ill.

4b. What is certain is that you loved him or hated him.

4c. He almost single-handedly changed the musical culture.

4d. He changed that musical culture not only of America.

4e. He changed the musical culture of the world.

(Information is from a paragraph
by Wilborn Hampton, *Elvis Presley Up Close*.)

ACTIVITY 8: JOHANNES GUTENBERG, INVENTOR

Inventor of the printing press, Gutenberg lay the groundwork for widespread communication through printed words.

> *What Gutenberg did to democratize books and other texts, the World Wide Web has done to democratize information.*
>
> —Peter L. Shillingsburg, *From Gutenberg to Google*

Summary of the Paragraph: Gutenberg's invention began the third of four turning points in the history of human communication. Sculpt the ordinary sentences into a paragraph with ten sentences.

Sculpt the following information into the *first sentence* of your paragraph.

1a. Human contact over the last 5,000 years has four turning points.

1b. Each of those turning points was recording moments.

1c. Those moments were when written communication flicked to a new level.

1d. The new level was of speech and outreach.

Sculpt the following information into the *second sentence* of your paragraph.

2a. The first turning point was the invention of writing.

2b. That invention allowed for the creation of big, enduring societies.

2c. Those societies were with priestly elites.

Sculpt the following information into the *third sentence* of your paragraph.

3a. The second turning point was the teaching of the alphabet.

3b. The alphabet brought writing within the reach of ordinary people.

3c. Those people were from the age of four.

Sculpt the following information into the *fourth sentence* of your paragraph.

4a. The third turning point was caused by Gutenberg's invention of printing with movable type.

4b. That invention burst on Europe.

4c. Then it burst on the world.

4d. The bursts happened in the fifteenth century.

Sculpt the following information into the *fifth sentence* of your paragraph.

5a. Printing changed things utterly.

5b. It was so utterly that it is hard to imagine a world without printing.

Sculpt the following information into the *sixth sentence* of your paragraph.

6a. The fourth turning point was the coming of the Internet.

6b. The Internet seems to be turning us into cells.

6c. The cells are in a planet-sized brain.

(Information is from a paragraph by John Man, *The Gutenberg Revolution*.)

ACTIVITY 9: JONAS SALK, SCIENTIST

His research led to the global eradication of a crippling, sometimes deadly disease affecting mainly children.

> *Jonas was intrigued by the concept of* **immunization** [protection], *a way to stimulate the body's immune system to fight disease.*
>
> —Stephanie Sammartino McPherson, *Jonas Salk: Conquering Polio*

Summary of the Paragraph: Once a widespread disease, polio was virtually eradicated by a vaccine developed by Dr. Jonas Salk. Sculpt the ordinary sentences into a paragraph with eight sentences.

Sculpt the following information into the *first sentence* of your paragraph.

1a. Polio no longer poses a threat in the United States.

1b. Also, it's not a threat in most other nations.

1c. Millions of Americans, though, still recall the terror that polio once brought into their lives.

Sculpt the following information into the *second sentence* of your paragraph.

2a. Millions of Americans also remember hearing the good news on April 12, 1955.

2b. That was when a field test showed that a new vaccine could prevent polio.

Sculpt the following information into the *third sentence* of your paragraph.

3a. Around the nation cheering began.

3b. Bells chimed.

3c. Car horns honked.

3d. Fire sirens blared.

Sculpt the following information into the *fourth sentence* of your paragraph.

4a. Reporters declared that people were rejoicing.

4b. They were rejoicing as if a war had ended.

Sculpt the following information into the *fifth sentence* of your paragraph.

5a. In a sense, the polio vaccine did end a war.

5b. The war was one that was waged against an enemy.

5c. That enemy was unseen and devastating.

Sculpt the following information into the *sixth sentence* of your paragraph.

6a. The vaccine brought down a disease.

6b. That disease held the power to steal lives.

Sculpt the following information into the *seventh sentence* of your paragraph.

7a. The leader of the research team that developed that vaccine was Jonas Salk.

7b. People regarded him as a hero.

Sculpt the following information into the *eighth sentence* of your paragraph.

8a. Salk went on to study other diseases.

8b. His study included cancer.

8c. In addition, it included AIDS.

> (Information is from a paragraph by Victoria Sherrow, *Jonas Salk: Beyond the Microscope*.)

Directions: In the next part you are not given a sentence-by-sentence breakdown. Sculpt the list of ordinary sentences into the indicated number of sentences found in the original paragraph. You may use any of the words in the sentences provided. They are from the original sentences.

ACTIVITY 10: WILLIAM SHAKESPEARE, POET AND PLAYWRIGHT

Poet and playwright most highly esteemed, William Shakespeare wrote literature timeless in beauty and ageless in relevance.

> *Shakespeare knew the human mind, and its most minute and intimate workings, and he never introduces a word, or a thought in vain or out of place.*
>
> —Samuel Taylor Coleridge, *English poet, critic, and philosopher*

<u>Summary of the Paragraph</u>: Details of William Shakespeare's birth are described. Sculpt the ordinary sentences into a paragraph with just six sentences.

1. William Shakespeare was born on April 23, 1564.

2. That was when he emerged from the womb into the world of time.

3. There was at the birth the assistance of a midwife.

4. The midwife at a birth in the sixteenth century would do several things.

5. The infant was washed and then swaddled by being wrapped tightly in a soft cloth.

6. After that, the infant was carried downstairs to be presented to his father.

7. After this ritual greeting, the infant was taken back upstairs to the birth-chamber.

8. That room was still warm and dark.

9. In the room, he was laid beside his mother.

10. Next, the mother was meant to draw all diseases from the child.

11. This process happened before the infant was put in a cradle.

12. A small portion of honey and butter was placed in the infant's mouth.

13. Also customarily placed in the suckling's mouth were rabbit's brains.

14. Those brains had been reduced to jelly.

(Information is from a paragraph by Peter Ackroyd, *Shakespeare: The Biography*.)

ACTIVITY 11: JOHN F. KENNEDY, AMERICAN PRESIDENT

Voted in periodic opinion polls the most popular American president, Kennedy brought a youthful style and vigor to his term as president, cut short by his assassination in 1963.

> *If Americans could pick a president, any president, which one would they choose to run the country today a* New York Times / CBS News *poll asked in 1996. The answer: John F. Kennedy.*
>
> —Michael O'Brien, *John F. Kennedy: A Biography*

<u>Summary of the Paragraph</u>: The PT 109 incident in World War II reveals John Kennedy's courage, persistence, and concern for others. Sculpt the ordinary sentences into a paragraph with just seven sentences.

1. The Navy rescued Lieutenant John Kennedy from a group of Pacific Islands.

2. The islands were where he had been marooned for five days.

3. This happened after a Japanese destroyer rammed his torpedo boat.

4. The boat was named PT 109.

5. He was slammed against the cockpit wall.

6. Two of his crewmen were killed.

7. After, Kennedy won a medal for courage, endurance, and excellent leadership, and extremely heroic conduct during those five days.

8. That medal became the early engine for Kennedy's political career.

9. Kennedy arranged things so that seldom a moment passed without his eyes resting on some reminder of PT 109.

10. When he looked across the Oval Office, he saw a scale model of the boat on a shelf.

11. Twice a day he swam the breaststroke in the White House pool.

12. That was the same stroke he had used while towing a badly burned crewman through shark-infested waters for five hours.

13. During that towing he was gripping the strap of the injured crewman's life preserver in his teeth.

14. Every morning he fastened his tie with a metal clasp shaped like a torpedo boat with "PT 109" stamped on its bow.

15. He saw that clasp whenever friends and aides walked into his office.

16. He saw it because he had given copies of this clasp to them.

(Information is from a paragraph by Thurston Clarke, *JFK's Last Hundred Days*.)

ACTIVITY 12: ABRAHAM LINCOLN, AMERICAN PRESIDENT

Presiding over the American Civil War, Lincoln led the country to eventual reconciliation and the abolishing of slavery.

Lincoln's moral integrity is the strong trunk from which all the branches of his life grew. His integrity has many roots—in the soil, in Shakespeare, and in the Bible.

—Ronald C. White Jr., *A. Lincoln: A Biography*

Summary of the Paragraph: Lincoln's teenage son Robert carelessly misplaced a black **carpetbag** [*briefcase*] containing the speech Lincoln was to give on the day of his inauguration as president. Sculpt the ordinary sentences into a paragraph with just nine sentences.

1. The president-elect was emphatically not amused when his son misplaced a carpetbag.
2. The carpetbag contained the only copies of his inaugural address.
3. His son Robert was not yet 18 years old.
4. Robert had accepted an invitation by fellow adolescents to see the city's sights.
5. Robert carelessly left the precious bag with a hotel desk clerk.
6. Lincoln asked his son about the location of the valise.
7. Robert replied in a tone of bored and injured virtue.
8. A look of stupefaction came over Lincoln's face.
9. Visions of that Inaugural in all the next morning's newspapers floated through his imagination.
10. The look happened as Lincoln heard what the lad had done.
11. Lincoln forced his way through the crowded corridor down to the office.
12. He swung himself across the clerk's counter.
13. He did this with a single stride of his long legs.
14. He found a small mountain of carpetbags of all colors that had accumulated behind the counter.

15. Lincoln with a little key began opening all the black bags much to the surprised amusement of onlookers.

16. He eventually discovered his own carpetbag.

17. People had never seen Mr. Lincoln so much annoyed.

18. They had never seen him so much perplexed.

19. They had never seen him for the time so angry.

20. Lincoln had seldom shown a spirit of anger toward his children.
    (Information is from a paragraph by Michael Burlingame, *Abraham Lincoln*.)

YOUR TURN: BIOGRAPHICAL SKETCH

Without imitating an author's paragraph but writing a paragraph so good it could have been by an author, write a brief bio.

Directions:

1. Select one of these famous persons below—or someone else of your own choosing.

ARTISTS
DaVinci, Matisse, Picasso, Van Gogh, Wyeth

ATHLETES
Jackie Joyner, Jesse Owens, Jackie Robinson, Babe Ruth, Johnny Unitas

AUTHORS
Jane Austen, Stephen King, J. K. Rowling, John Steinbeck, Richard Wright

CLASSICAL COMPOSERS
Beethoven, Copeland, Joplin, Stravinsky, Tchaikovsky

ENTERTAINERS
Lucille Ball, Johnny Carson, Bob Hope, Marx Brothers, Walt Disney

INNOVATORS
Alexander Bell, Jeff Beezos, Thomas Edison, Tim Berners Lee, Bill Gates

MUSICIANS
Louis Armstrong (popular), Van Cliburn (classical), Miles Davis (jazz), Benny Goodman (swing), Jimmy Hendrix (rock)

PRESIDENTS
Dwight Eisenhower, Barack Obama, Ronald Reagan, Harry Truman, George Washington

SCIENTISTS
Marie Curie, Thomas Edison, Albert Einstein, Alexander Fleming, Louis Pasteur

THINKERS
Aquinas, Aristotle, Descartes, Freud, C. S. Lewis

---

2. Learn more about the person online or offline, and then draft and revise a paragraph about that person.

3. Pretend you are a writer for a print or online magazine that regularly features compellingly interesting but little-known info about famous persons. Your job is to write an entertaining mini-bio paragraph with new information about the person—a humorous anecdote, an unusual experience, a startling fact, an exceptional accomplishment, a disturbing detail—or some other aspect of the person's life.

4. Create a paragraph that readers will believe was written by a very good writer, like the many authors you imitated in this section. Use a variety of sentence-composing tools in various positions: *identifiers*, *describers*, *elaborators*. (See the following student sample titled "Gold" for examples.)

5. Exchange your draft with other students in your class for suggestions to improve your paragraph, and give them suggestions, too. Then revise several times until your paragraph is finished.

6. Create a memorable title that your readers won't understand until after they read your paragraph. *Example:* "Taffy Ball," a title for a paragraph about basketball player Kevin Durant whose body is like "taffy" because he moves down the court in all directions.

Sentence-Composing Tools: Before drafting your paragraph, study this sample student paragraph. Notice Peter's use of sentence-composing tools in varied positions—*openers, S-V splits, closers*:

- identifiers *italicized* (*pages 31–35*)
- describers **bolded** (*pages 39–43*)
- elaborators <u>underlined</u> (*pages 46–50*).

**"Gold"
by
Peter Maleki
(a student paper)**

(1) **Once unrecognized by many people**, he used to be a nobody, *a young man so unknown that he might as well have never existed*. (2) It wasn't until the 2008 Olympics that he became one of the most widely recognized athletes in the world. (3) He won eight consecutive gold medals in one Olympic season, *an achievement unprecedented in*

the history of the Olympics. (4) His name is Michael Phelps, *a native of Baltimore, Maryland*, who began his career very early in his life. (5) *A ten-year-old boy diagnosed with attention-deficit hyperactivity disorder*, <u>his mind unable to stay focused in school</u>, Michael discovered his natural talent as a swimmer, **holding the national records for his age group**. (6) At the remarkable age of fifteen, Michael qualified for the Olympics, *the youngest age for a male qualifying as an Olympic swimmer in over sixty-eight years*. (7) *A teenager fifteen and nine months*, he had broken the world record for the 200-meter butterfly, **becoming the youngest man ever to set a swimming record**. (8) **Having won many gold medals in various events in the 2004 Olympics, including six gold medals**, he entered Beijing for the 2008 Olympics. (9) **Determined to do well**, he nevertheless had no idea that he would go on to win eight gold medals, *the most medals that can be won by an athlete in the Olympics*. (10) <u>His goal to win unwavering</u>, <u>his determination solid</u>, he competed unflinchingly, **winning one gold medal after another**—*an astonishing and unprecedented achievement*. (11) He won them all, *nineteen medals, the most gold in Olympic history*. (12) *Olympian gold-medalist unexcelled*, Michael Phelps became a worldwide Olympic superstar. (13) There may never again be another Olympic champion receiving more global and golden acclaim.

FAMOUS WORDS: PARALLEL STRUCTURE

When people wear uniforms, people look alike; wearing identical clothes shows they belong to the same group: soldiers, baseball and football players, waiters and waitresses, security guards, police, firemen, marching bands, and others.

When authors write, sometimes they list sentence parts uniformly to show they belong to the same idea. Each listed sentence part looks alike. The listed sentence parts are parallel in structure—built the same way, even sometimes beginning with exactly the same words, as in the examples that follow.

EXAMPLES

Look-Alike Sentence Parts (Same Words)

1. We have always understood **that** when times change, so must we; **that** fidelity to our founding principles requires new responses to new challenges; **that** preserving our individual freedoms ultimately requires collective action.

   Barack Obama, *Second Inaugural Address*

2. By now the bad string had reached ten in all, and almost all of the dead had been close friends of Pete and Jane, **young men who had** been in their house many times, **young men who had** sat across from Jane and chattered like the rest of them about the grand adventure of military flying.

   Tom Wolfe, *The Right Stuff*

3. Kids wanted to fight us **because** we had red hair, **because** Dad was a drunk, **because** we wore rags and didn't take as many baths as we should have, **because** we lived in a falling-down house partly painted yellow and had a pit filled with garbage in front, **because** they'd

go by our dark house at night and see that we couldn't even afford electricity.

Jeanette Walls, *The Glass Castle*

Another kind of parallel structure lists sentence parts built alike. These sentence parts don't begin with the same words, but they are constructed in the same way.

EXAMPLES

Look-Alike Sentence Parts (Same Construction)

1. We had to **pray without ceasing** and **work without tiring**.
Maya Angelou, *The Heart of a Woman*

2. All the organs of the condemned man's body were working, **bowels digesting food, skin renewing itself, nails growing, tissues forming, all toiling away in solemn foolery**.
George Orwell, "A Hanging"

3. Let every nation know, whether it wishes us well or ill, that we shall **pay any price, bear any burden, meet any hardship, support any friend, oppose any foe**, to assure the survival and the success of liberty.
John F. Kennedy, *Inaugural Address*

ACTIVITY 1: MATCHING

Match the sentence with the look-alikes (parallel structures). Write the result.

Sentence	Look-Alikes (Parallel Structure)
1. Still in pajamas, Harry Gold raced around his cluttered bedroom, ^ . *Steve Sheinkin, Bomb*	a. to increase pressure on drug criminals, and to build on anti-drug programs that have proved to work
2. After rain, or when snowfalls thaw, the streets— ^ —turn from the thickest dust into the direst mud. *Truman Capote, In Cold Blood*	b. unnamed, unshaded, unpaved
3. We need to involve more citizens in the fight against drugs ^ . *William Bennett, "Should Drugs Be Legalized?"*	c. who had never had any fresh water up his nose and who had seen lily pads only from train windows
4. On that fishing trip, I took along my son, ^ . *E. B. White, "Once More to the Lake"*	d. pulling out desk drawers, tossing boxes out of the closet, and yanking books from the shelves
5. A man in his twenties— ^ —knew we weren't going anywhere. *Annie Dillard, An American Childhood*	e. our pursuer, our captor, our hero

FAULTY PARALLELISM

If a sentence describes three favorite activities like the example sentence that follows, those activities must add up in the same way, just as one plus one plus one must equal three. In faulty parallelism, they don't add up to three. They add up to less than three.

EXAMPLE

Parallel: Pam loved (1) attending Broadway musicals, (2) shopping for bargains in second-hand clothing stores, and

(3) talking to real friends instead of texting on phones or posting on websites. *Here all three are look-alikes, expressed in the same way.*

Faulty: Pam loved (1) attending Broadway musicals, (2) shopping for bargains in second-hand clothing stores, and (3) when she talked with friends face-to-face instead of via electronics, such as on phones or websites. *Here only two of the three look alike; the third is different.*

In the example sentence, parallel structure requires three look-alikes, not just two. All three activities are equal, so they should be expressed in equal, uniform, parallel ways.

In the first sentence, the three activities are expressed uniformly—three look-alikes. In the second sentence, though, there are only two look-alikes, so they don't add up to three, and the parallelism is faulty.

Here are more examples of parallelism and faulty parallelism.

EXAMPLES

1a. *Faulty:* We felt an impulse to sing, to break into a run, and an inclination toward sniggering.

1b. *Parallel:* We felt an impulse **to sing**, **to break into a run**, **to snigger**.

George Orwell, "A Hanging"

2a. *Faulty:* Shaun was spirited but controlled, affectionate but in a calm mood.

2b. *Parallel:* Shaun was **spirited but controlled**, **affectionate but calm**.

John Grogan, *Marley & Me*

3a. *Faulty:* Tarantulas customarily live in deep cylindrical burrows, from which they emerge at dusk and to retire in them at dawn.

3b. *Parallel:* Tarantulas customarily live in deep cylindrical burrows, **from which they** emerge at dusk **and into which they** retire at dawn.

Alexander Petrunkevitch, "The Spider and the Wasp"

ACTIVITY 2: REVISING FOR PARALLEL STRUCTURE

Change the underlined sentence part to make it parallel with the other look-alike sentence parts.

1. He has got to appear resolute, to know his own mind, and <u>doing definite things</u>.

    George Orwell, "Shooting an Elephant"

2. The adversary may be a mountain, a chess-playing computer, or <u>it may be an incarnation of evil</u>.

    Diane Ackerman, *Deep Play*

3. We must therefore act together as a united people, for national reconciliation, for nation building, and <u>to give birth to a new world</u>.

    Nelson Mandela, *Inaugural Address*

4. To the people of poor nations, we pledge to work alongside you to make your farms flourish and to let clean waters flow, to nourish starved bodies and <u>feeding hungry minds</u>.

    President Barack Obama, *First Inaugural Address*

5. Here came the Rabbi, his back bent, his face shaved, <u>and on his back was his pack</u>.

    Elie Wiesel, *Night*

ACTIVITY 3: CREATING PARALLEL STRUCTURE

Expand each sentence by adding look-alike sentence parts (parallel structure). Begin those parts with the words in boldface.

Famous Words: Parallel Structure **191**

EXAMPLE

Incomplete: He taught us **to ^** , **to ^** , and **to ^** .

Student Sample Look-Alikes: He taught us **to understand programming codes, to create a mini program, and to help each other design intricate, colorful, but useful websites for various high school classes**.

Original Look-Alikes: He taught us **to aim and fire his pistol, to shoot Mom's bow and arrows, and to throw a knife by the blade so that it landed in the middle of a target with a satisfying thwock**.

Jeanette Walls, *The Glass Castle*

TWO LOOK-ALIKE SENTENCE PARTS

1. Children love to play in piles of leaves, **hurling ^** , **leaping ^** .
   Diane Ackerman, *A Natural History of the Senses*

2. Sitting beside the tree, Millie opened her packages slowly, **careful to ^** , **careful not to ^** .
   Jean Fritz, *Homesick: My Own Story*

3. A great many old people came and knelt around us and prayed, **old women with ^** , **old men with ^** .
   Langston Hughes, *The Big Sea*

THREE LOOK-ALIKE SENTENCE PARTS

4. My father taught me **to ^** , **to ^** , **to ^** .
   Perri Knize, *A Piano Odyssey*

5. I clung to the notion that politics could be different; **that voters ^** ; **that they were tired of ^** ; **that if I could ^** , then the people's instincts for fair play and common sense would bring them around.
   Barack Obama, The Audacity of Hope

FOUR LOOK-ALIKE SENTENCE PARTS

6. Our happiest childhood memories almost all included those dogs, **hiking ^** , **swimming ^** , **playing ^** , **getting ^** .
   John Grogan, Marley & Me

7. The only way to keep playing professional football was **to ^** , **to ^** , **to ^** , and **to ^** .
   John McMurty, "Kill 'Em! Crush 'Em! Eat 'Em Raw!"

8. Eating safely from dumpsters involves **using ^** , **knowing ^** , **checking ^** , and **seeking ^** .
   Lars Eighner, "On Dumpster Diving"

9. He found a door, knocked, and entered a room full of men, **some ^** , **some ^** , **some ^** , **some ^** .
   Erik Larson, The Devil in the White City

MANY LOOK-ALIKE SENTENCE PARTS

10. The nurses stayed to wipe the saliva that drooled from the dying man's mouth, **to irrigate ^** , **to suction ^** , **to clean ^** , **to pour ^** , **to put ^** , **to turn ^** , and **to change ^** .
    Barbara Huttmann, "A Crime of Compassion"

SENTENCE PARTS WITH PARALLEL WORDING

From "Declaration of Independence"
by Thomas Jefferson, July 4, 1776

We hold these truths to be self-evident:

that all men are created equal;

that they are **endowed** [*provided*] by their Creator with certain **unalienable** [*guaranteed*] rights;

that among these are life, liberty and the pursuit of happiness;

that to secure these rights, governments are instituted among men, deriving their just powers from the consent of the governed;

that whenever any form of government becomes destructive of these ends, it is the right of the people

to alter or

to abolish it, and

to institute new government,

lay**ing** its foundation on such principles and

organiz**ing** its powers in such form, as to them shall seem most likely to effect their safety and happiness.

From "Washington's Farewell Address" (1796)

I shall carry these ideas with me to my grave:

that heaven may continue to give you the choicest **tokens** [*signs*] of its **beneficence** [*goodness*];

that your union and brotherly affection may be **perpetual** [*ongoing*];

that the free Constitution, which is the work of your hands, may be sacredly maintained;

that its administration in every department may be stamped with wisdom and virtue;

that, in fine, the happiness of the people of these States, under the **auspices** [*protection*] of liberty, may be made complete by so careful a preservation and so **prudent** [*wise*] a use of this blessing as will acquire to them the glory of recommending it to the applause, the affection, and adoption of every nation which is yet a stranger to it.

From "The Gettysburg Address" by Abraham Lincoln (1863)

It is for us to be here dedicated to the great task remaining before us:

that from these honored dead we take increased devotion to that cause for which they gave the last full measure of devotion;

that we here highly resolve that these dead shall not have died in vain;

that this nation, under God, shall have a new birth of freedom; and

that government

of the people,

by the people,

for the people,

shall not perish from the earth.

SENTENCES BEGINNING WITH THE SAME WORDS

In the preceding activities, look-alikes occurred within a single sentence. Look-alikes can also occur in a series of sentences, each sentence beginning in a uniform way. Here's an example, an excerpt from a speech given by a recipient of the Nobel Prize for Literature.

EXAMPLE

Look-Alike Sentence Parts in Consecutive Sentences

I write because I have an innate need to write.

I write because I can't do normal work as other people do.

I write because I want to read books like the ones I write.

I write because I am angry at everyone.

I write because I love sitting in a room all day writing.

I write because I can partake of real life only by changing it.

I write because I want others, the whole world, to know what sort of life we lived, and continue to live, in Istanbul, in Turkey.

I write because I love the smell of paper, pen, and ink.

I write because I believe in literature, in the art of the novel, more than I believe in anything else.

I write because it is a habit, a passion.

I write because I am afraid of being forgotten.

I write because I like the glory and interest that writing brings.

I write to be alone.

Perhaps I write because I hope to understand why I am so very, very angry at everyone.

I write because I like to be read.

I write because once I have begun a novel, an essay, a page I want to finish it.

I write because everyone expects me to write.

I write because I have a childish belief in the immortality of libraries, and in the way my books sit on the shelf.

I write because it is exciting to turn all life's beauties and riches into words.

I write not to tell a story but to compose a story.

I write because I wish to escape from the foreboding that there is a place I must go but—as in a dream—can't quite get to.

I write because I have never managed to be happy.

I write to be happy.

> Orhan Pamuk, *Nobel Prize Acceptance Speech (2006)*

ACTIVITY 4: CREATING PARALLEL SENTENCES

As in the previous example, compose a series of at least ten sentences emphasizing an idea by starting each sentence in a uniform way—a series of look-alike sentences. Begin each sentence with one of the phrases below (or one of your own choosing), and repeat that phrase at the start of each of your sentences.

I read because . . .

I play (a specific sport) because . . .

I pray because . . .

I study because . . .

I text because . . .

I work because . . .

I dream because . . .

I learn because . . .

I sing because . . .

YOUR TURN: PARALLEL METAPHOR

For this last aspect of parallel structure, your writing activity combines two skills: parallel sentence parts and metaphor, the figure of speech that compares two different things, a literary equation in which *A* equals *B*.

In the following excerpt from her nonfiction book *Through a Window*, Jane Goodall, a naturalist studying the behavior of chimpanzees in their natural habitat, uses the word *windows* as a metaphor for ways to understand the world: through science, philosophy, mysticism, religion, and other glimpses into our world. Here is the excerpt:

> There are many windows through which we can look out into the world, searching for meaning. There are those opened up by science, their panes polished by a succession of brilliant, penetrating minds. Through these, we can see ever further, ever more clearly, into areas that once lay beyond human knowledge. Gazing through such a window I have, over the years, learned much about chimpanzee behavior and their place in the nature of things. This, in turn, has helped us to understand a little better some aspects of human behavior, our own place in nature.

In a latter sentence, the author uses parallel structure to describe other "windows" that help us understand "our own place in nature."

EXAMPLE

> But there are other windows:
>
> **windows like** philosophy, through which thinkers remove the shutters by their logic;
>
> **windows like** meditation, through which the mystics seek their visions of the truth;
>
> **windows like** religion, through which theologians peer as they search for purpose.
>
> Jane Goodall, *Through a Window* (adapted)

Directions:

1. Compose a similar sentence by citing three other "windows" that help you understand life and your world better—for example, beauty, friendship, love, family, nature, God, or some other aspects of human behavior important to you.

2. For parallel structure, use the frame sentence below. It uses a colon to introduce a list of long descriptive items, so separate those items with a semicolon instead of a comma for easier reading.

FRAME SENTENCE

But there are other windows:

windows like *X*, through which . . . ;

windows like *Y*, through which . . . ;

windows like *Z*, through which. . . .

OPINIONATORS: YOU SAY WHAT?

Nonfiction often tells people's opinions through blogs, essays, commentaries, reviews, letters to editors, journals, editorials, interviews, surveys, rating scales, advice. Opinionators write their own thoughts on a topic, maybe shedding new light on that topic, sometimes disagreeing with the thoughts of others, softly or loudly.

Much nonfiction conveys what people think, opinions that run the gamut—silly or serious, intuitive or scholarly, ignorant or smart.

People don't think in the same way on the same topic. Perhaps with ten people, it's possible to have ten different opinions on the same topic.

ACTIVITY 1: DIFFERENCES OF OPINION

Following are excerpts from three nonfiction sources, all on the topic of homeless dependent people, but each expressing a different opinion. Which excerpt considers the homeless inferior, which superior, and which no different from the nonhomeless? Copy illustrative sentences as evidence for your claim.

Note: In all three nonfiction excerpts below about homeless people, the authors use **describers** (*participles*), a sentence part that adds descriptive details. Describer tools are underlined. (*To review describers, see pages 39–43.*)

OPINION ONE

(1) Mom had tied rags around her shoulders to keep out the spring chill and was picking through the trash. (2) She thrust out her lower lip when studying items of potential value that she'd hoisted out of the Dumpster, and her eyes widened with childish glee when she found something she liked. (3) Her long hair was streaked with gray, tangled and matted, and her eyes had sunk deep into their sockets, but still she reminded me of the mom she'd been when I was a kid, swan-diving off cliffs and painting in the desert and reading Shakespeare aloud.

(4) Her skin was parched and ruddy from all those winters and summers exposed to the elements. (5) To the people walking by, she probably looked like any of the thousands of homeless people in New York City.

(6) I was rattled from seeing Mom, the unexpectedness of coming across her, the sight of her rooting happily through the Dumpster. (7) I worried about Mom and Dad, <u>huddled on a sidewalk grate somewhere</u>. (8) I fretted about them, but I was embarrassed by them, too, <u>ashamed of myself for wearing pearls and living on Park Avenue while my parents were busy keeping warm and finding something to eat</u>.

Jeannette Walls, *The Glass Castle* (adapted)

OPINION TWO

(1) It is worth saying something about the social position of beggars, for when one has **consorted** [*socialized*] with them, and found that they are ordinary human beings, one cannot help being struck by the curious attitude that society takes towards them. (2) People seem to feel that there is some essential difference between beggars and ordinary "working" men. (3) They are a race apart—outcasts, like criminals and prostitutes. (4) He is a mere social **excrescence** [*monstrosity*], <u>tolerated because we live in a humane age, but essentially **despicable** [*awful*]</u>.

(5) Yet if one looks closely, one sees that there is no *essential* difference between a beggar's livelihood and that of numberless respectable people. (6) Beggars do not work, it is said; but, then, what is *work*? (7) A laborer works by swinging a pick. (8) An accountant works by adding up figures. (9) A beggar works by standing out of doors in all weathers, <u>getting varicose veins, chronic bronchitis, etc</u>.

(10) As a social type a beggar compares well with scores of others. (11) He is honest compared with the sellers of most patent medicines, high-minded compared with a Sunday newspaper proprietor, **amiable** [*friendly*] compared with a hire-purchase tout—in short, a **parasite**

[*dependent*], but a fairly harmless parasite. (12) He seldom extracts more than a bare living from the community. (13) I do not think there is anything about a beggar that sets him in a different class from other people, or gives most modern men the right to despise him.

(14) A beggar, <u>looked at realistically</u>, is simply a businessman, <u>getting his living like other businessmen in the way that comes to hand</u>.

George Orwell, *Down and Out in Paris and London* (adapted)

OPINION THREE

(1) I have learned much as a **scavenger** [*hunter*]. (2) I mean to put some of what I have learned down here, <u>beginning with the practical art of Dumpster diving and proceeding to the abstract</u>.

(3) At first the new scavenger is filled with disgust and self-loathing. (4) He is ashamed of being seen and may lurk around, <u>trying to duck behind things</u>. (5) That stage passes with experience. (6) The scavenger finds a pair of running shoes that fit and look and smell brand-new. (7) He finds a pocket calculator in perfect working order. (8) He finds **pristine** [*perfect*] ice cream, still frozen. (9) People throw away perfectly good stuff, a lot of good stuff. (10) At this stage, dumpster shyness begins to **dissipate** [*disappear*]. (11) Those who **disparage** [*criticize*] his profession are the fools, not he.

(12) <u>Having survived nearly ten years of government service where everything is geared to the lowest common denominator</u>, I find it refreshing to have work that rewards initiative and effort.

(13) I find from the experience of scavenging deep lessons. (14) One is the **transience** [*impermanence*] of material being. (15) Now I hardly pick up a thing without envisioning the time I will cast it aside. (16) This I think is a healthy state of mind. (17) Almost everything I have now has already been cast out at least once, <u>proving that what I own is valueless to someone</u>.

(18) I find my desire to grab for the gaudy bauble has been largely **sated** [*satisfied*]. (19) I think this is an attitude I share with the very wealthy. (20) We both know there is plenty more where what we have came from.

(21) Between us are the rat-race millions who nightly scavenge the cable channels, *looking for they know not what*.

(22) I am sorry for them.

Lars Eighner, "On Dumpster Diving" (adapted)

ACTIVITY 2: HIGH SCHOOL SPORTS—A CON VIEW

Study the reasons the author below is against high school sports, and then focus on the list in parallel structure with each item beginning with a word ending in -*ing*.

"The Case Against High School Sports" (adapted) by Amanda Ripley

(1) Sports are **embedded** [*planted*] in American schools in a way they are not almost anywhere else. (2) Yet this difference hardly ever comes up in domestic debates about America's international **mediocrity** [*inferiority*] in education. (3) The U.S. ranks 31st on an international math test. (4) When I surveyed about 200 former exchange students last year, in cooperation with an international exchange organization called AFS, nine out of 10 foreign students who had lived in the U.S. said that kids here cared more about sports than their peers back home did. (5) A majority of Americans who'd studied abroad agreed. (6) Like most other Americans, I can rattle off the many benefits of high-school sports: exercise, lessons in sportsmanship and **perseverance** [*determination*], school spirit, and just plain fun. (7) But as I've traveled around the world visiting places that do

things differently—and get better results—I've started to wonder about the trade-offs we make. (8) From the beginning, though, some detractors questioned whether tax money should be spent on activities that could damage the brain, and occasionally leave students dead on the field. (9) Other arguments against high school sports include these:

- Allotting five times more money per student for cheerleading than for math instruction
- Having a lower student-teacher ratio for sports (coaches and other staff members) than math and reading classes
- Spending enormous amounts of money on bleachers and artificial turf, around one half million dollars each
- Funding substitute teachers when players have away games and spending huge amounts for buses, bands, cheerleaders, hotels, and meals
- Injuring around 15% of players each year with concussions and other problems
- Managing up to 10 different sports-related budgets each year
- Shifting attention during sports seasons away from academics for both athletes and non-athletes

ACTIVITY 3: HIGH SCHOOL SPORTS—A PRO VIEW

Spin the opinion in the opposite direction—now the advantages of high school sports. Draft, write, and revise a paragraph on those advantages. In addition to your own opinions, get others from the source below.

"High-School Sports Aren't Killing Academics" (adapted)
by Daniel H. Bowen and Collin Hitt

(1) If it is true that sports undermine the academic mission of American schools, we would expect to see a negative relationship between the commitment to athletics and academic achievement. (2) A research study at the University of Arkansas analyzed schools' sports winning percentages as well as student-athletic participation rates compared to graduation rates and standardized test score achievement. (3) Controlling for student poverty levels, demographics, and district financial resources, both measures of a school's commitment to athletics are significantly, positively related to lower dropout rates as well as higher test scores.

(4) Success in sports programs actually facilitates or reflects greater socialization within a school's community.

(5) The success of schools is highly dependent on social capital, defined as "the norms, the social networks, and the relationships between adults and children," with sports events providing **venues** [*places*] for parents, students, and teachers to come together, providing opportunities for increasing social capital, **bolstering** [*supporting*] rather than **deterring** [*preventing*] academic missions.

(6) Schools with well-run athletic programs benefit from superior leadership that also fosters better academic results. (7) Schools that tend to be successful in one thing are often successful in others. (8) Sports can in fact reinforce the missions of schools in ways that potentially help, not harm, academic achievement.

(9) Athletic coaches who also teach gain additional opportunities for communicating and serving as mentors that potentially help students succeed and make up for the costs of coaching commitments.

(10) If the **empirical** [*observed*] evidence points to anything, it points toward school-sponsored sports providing assets that are well worth the costs.

(11) The greater body of evidence shows that school-sponsored sports programs appear to benefit students. (12) Successes on the playing field can carry over to the classroom and vice versa. (13) More importantly, finding ways to increase school communities' social capital is **imperative** [*crucial*] to the success of the school as a whole, not just the athletes.

End your paragraph with a list of reasons high school sports are valuable. Use a colon to introduce the list, and for parallel structure begin every listed item with a word ending in *-ing*. Use bullets, as below, for your list.

EXAMPLES

- fostering a team-player spirit beneficial during and after high school
- unifying students through cheering for their own teams
- building character traits of perseverance and goal attainment

---

Honest disagreement is often a good sign of progress.

—Mahatma Ghandi

ACTIVITY 4: PRESIDENTIAL DIFFERENCES OF OPINION

In September 2013, during the conflict in Syria in which over 100,000 were killed, and millions displaced, two world leaders—President Barack Obama of the United States and President Vladimir Putin of Russia—voiced differing opinions about whether some kind of intervention was needed in retaliation for the alleged use of chemical weapons within the Syrian civil war.

President Obama, on September 10, voiced his opinion; the next day, September 11, President Putin responded. Analyze both responses below.

Directions: After each of the comments on Syria is a list of claims that are either supported or unsupported by the comments. For each claim, cite the sentence or sentences that prove or disprove the claim.

AMERICAN PRESIDENT OBAMA ON SYRIA

September 10, 2013, excerpts from his internationally televised remarks from the White House

(1) My fellow Americans, tonight I want to talk to you about Syria—why it matters, and where we go from here. (2) Over the past two years, what began as a series of peaceful protests against the repressive regime in Syria of Bashar al-Assad has turned into a brutal civil war. (3) Over 100,000 people have been killed. (4) Millions have fled the country. (5) In that time, America has worked with allies to provide humanitarian support, to help the moderate opposition, and to shape a political settlement. (6) But I have resisted calls for military action, because we cannot resolve someone else's civil war through force, particularly after a decade of war in Iraq and Afghanistan.

(7) The situation profoundly changed, though, on August 21st, when Assad's government gassed to death over a thousand people, including hundreds of children. (8) The images from this massacre are sickening: men, women, children lying in rows, killed by poison gas, others foaming at the mouth, gasping for breath, a father clutching his dead children, imploring them to get up and walk. (9) On that terrible night, the world saw in gruesome detail the terrible nature of chemical

weapons, and why the overwhelming majority of humanity has declared them off-limits—a crime against humanity, and a violation of the laws of war.

(10) This was not always the case. (11) In World War I, American GIs were among the many thousands killed by deadly gas in the trenches of Europe. (12) In World War II, the Nazis used gas to inflict the horror of the Holocaust. (13) Because these weapons can kill on a mass scale, with no distinction between soldier and infant, the civilized world has spent a century working to ban them. (14) And in 1997, the United States Senate overwhelmingly approved an international agreement prohibiting the use of chemical weapons, joined now by 189 governments that represent 98 percent of humanity.

(15) On August 21st, these basic rules were violated, along with our sense of common humanity. (16) No one disputes that chemical weapons were used in Syria. (17) The world saw thousands of videos, cell phone pictures, and social media accounts from the attack, and humanitarian organizations told stories of hospitals packed with people who had symptoms of poison gas.

(18) When dictators commit atrocities, they depend upon the world to look the other way until those horrifying pictures fade from memory. (19) But these things happened. (20) The facts cannot be denied. (21) The question now is what the United States of America, and the international community, is prepared to do about it. (22) Because what happened to those people—to those children—is not only a violation of international law, it's also a danger to our security.

(23) Even though I possess the authority to order military strikes, I believed it was right, in the absence of a direct or imminent threat to our security, to take this debate to Congress. (24) I believe our democracy is stronger when the President acts with the support of Congress. (25) And I believe that America acts more effectively abroad when we stand together.

(26) However, over the last few days, we've seen some encouraging signs. (27) In part because of the credible threat of U.S. military action, as well as constructive talks that I had with President Putin, the Russian government has indicated a willingness to join with the international community in pushing Assad to give up his chemical weapons. (28) The Assad regime has now admitted that it has these weapons, and even said they'd join the Chemical Weapons Convention, which prohibits their use.

(29) I have, therefore, asked the leaders of Congress to postpone a vote to authorize the use of force while we pursue this diplomatic path.

(30) Meanwhile, I've ordered our military to maintain their current posture to keep the pressure on Assad, and to be in a position to respond if diplomacy fails. (31) And tonight, I give thanks again to our military and their families for their incredible strength and sacrifices.

(32) My fellow Americans, for nearly seven decades, the United States has been the anchor of global security. (33) This has meant doing more than forging international agreements —it has meant enforcing them. (34) The burdens of leadership are often heavy, but the world is a better place because we have borne them.

(35) And so, to my friends on the right, I ask you to reconcile your commitment to America's military might with a failure to act when a cause is so plainly just. (36) To my friends on the left, I ask you to reconcile your belief in freedom and dignity for all people with those images of children writhing in pain, going still on a cold hospital floor. (37) For sometimes resolutions and statements of condemnation are simply not enough.

(38) Indeed, I'd ask every member of Congress, and those of you watching at home tonight, to view those videos of the attack, and then ask: What kind of world will we live in if the United States of America sees a dictator **brazenly** [*defiantly*] violate international law with poison gas, and we choose to look the other way?

(39) Our ideals and principles, as well as our national security, are at stake in Syria, along with our leadership of a world where we seek to ensure that the worst weapons will never be used.

(40) America is not the world's policeman. (41) Terrible things happen across the globe, and it is beyond our means to right every wrong. (42) But when, with modest effort and risk, we can stop children from being gassed to death, and thereby make our own children safer over the long run, I believe we should act. (43) That's what makes America different. (44) That's what makes us exceptional. (45) With humility, but with resolve, let us never lose sight of that essential truth.

Directions: Tell whether each claim is true or false. As evidence for your answer, copy any sentence or sentences that prove or disprove the claim.

1. Throughout history, the use of chemical weapons during armed conflicts has been avoided.

2. Most governments do not take a stand on the use of chemical weapons.

3. There is no question about the use of chemical weapons in Syria.

4. President Obama did not want to order military strikes against Syria without the support of Congress and the country.

5. President Putin of Russia was unwilling to ask Assad to give up his chemical weapons.

6. President Obama sees the United States as, in his words, "the anchor of global security."

7. He appeals only to the conservative right.

8. He encourages all Americans to watch the videos of the chemical attacks.

9. America cannot be held responsible for everything bad that happens worldwide.

10. The strike against Syria would, according to President Obama's words, require much more than "modest effort and risk."

RUSSIAN PRESIDENT PUTIN ON SYRIA

September 11, 2013, responding to the previous speech by President Obama in a published letter to the editor of the New York Times *newspaper*

(1) Recent events surrounding Syria have prompted me to speak directly to the American people and their political leaders.

(2) The potential strike by the United States against Syria, despite strong opposition from many countries and major political and religious leaders, including the pope, will result in more innocent victims and escalation, spreading potentially the conflict far beyond Syria's borders. (3) A strike would increase violence and unleash a new wave of terrorism. (4) It could undermine multilateral efforts to resolve the Iranian nuclear problem and the Israeli-Palestinian conflict and further destabilize the Middle East and North Africa. (5) It could throw the entire system of international law and order out of balance.

(6) From the outset, Russia has advocated peaceful dialogue, enabling Syrians to develop a compromise plan for their own future. (7) We are not protecting the Syrian government, but international law. (8) We need to use the United Nations Security Council and believe that preserving law and order in today's complex and turbulent world is one of the few ways to keep international relations from sliding into chaos. (9) The law is still the law, and we must follow it whether we like

it or not. (10) Under current international law, force is permitted only in self-defense or by the decision of the Security Council. (11) Anything else is unacceptable under the United Nations Charter and would constitute an act of aggression.

(12) No one doubts that poison gas was used in Syria. (13) But there is every reason to believe it was used not by the Syrian Army, but by opposition forces, to provoke intervention by their powerful foreign patrons, who would be siding with the fundamentalists. (14) Reports that militants are preparing another attack—this time against Israel—cannot be ignored.

(15) It is alarming that military intervention in internal conflicts in foreign countries has become commonplace for the United States. (16) Is it in America's long-term interest? (17) I doubt it. (18) Millions around the world increasingly see America not as a model of democracy but as relying solely on brute force, cobbling coalitions together under the slogan "you're either with us or against us."

(19) But force has proved ineffective and pointless. (20) Afghanistan is reeling, and no one can say what will happen after international forces withdraw. (21) Libya is divided into tribes and clans. (22) In Iraq the civil war continues, with dozens killed each day. (23) In the United States, many draw an analogy between Iraq and Syria, and ask why their government would want to repeat recent mistakes.

(24) No matter how targeted the strikes or how sophisticated the weapons, civilian casualties are **inevitable** [*certain*], including the elderly and children whom the strikes are meant to protect.

(25) The world reacts by asking: if you cannot count on international law, then you must find other ways to ensure your security. (26) Thus a growing number of countries seek to acquire weapons of mass destruction. (27) This is logical: if you have the bomb, no one will touch you. (28) We are left with talk of the need

to strengthen **nonproliferation** [*control*], when in reality this is being **eroded** [*ignored*].

(29) We must stop using the language of force and return to the path of civilized diplomatic and political settlement.

(30) A new opportunity to avoid military action has emerged in the past few days. (31) The United States, Russia, and all members of the international community must take advantage of the Syrian government's willingness to place its chemical arsenal under international control for subsequent destruction. (32) Judging by the statements of President Obama, the United States sees this as an alternative to military action.

(33) I welcome the president's interest in continuing the dialogue with Russia on Syria. (34) We must work together to keep this hope alive, and steer the discussion back toward negotiations.

(35) If we can avoid force against Syria, this will improve the atmosphere in international affairs and strengthen mutual trust. (36) It will be our shared success and open the door to cooperation on other critical issues.

(37) My working and personal relationship with President Obama is marked by growing trust. (38) I appreciate this. (39) I carefully studied his address to the nation on Tuesday [September 10, 2013]. (40) And I would rather disagree with a case he made on American exceptionalism, stating that the United States' policy is "what makes America different. It's what makes us exceptional." (41) It is extremely dangerous to encourage people to see themselves as exceptional, whatever the motivation. (42) There are big countries and small countries, rich and poor, those with long democratic traditions and those still finding their way to democracy. (43) Their policies differ, too. (44) We are all different, but when we ask for the Lord's blessings, we must not forget that God created us equal.

Directions: Tell whether each claim is true or false. As evidence for your answer, copy any sentence or sentences that prove or disprove the claim.

1. President Putin addressed his remarks to the worldwide community.

2. He is afraid that a strike by the United States might spread the conflict beyond Syria.

3. He described his fear of potential destabilization in the entire region surrounding Syria.

4. He emphasized that the bigger concern is not Syria but the preservation of international relations.

5. He acknowledges that poison gas was used by the Syrian Army.

6. He accuses the United States of interfering militarily in the internal affairs of other countries.

7. Military targeted strikes by the United States against Syria would conceivably kill persons they were designed to protect.

8. Because of the failure of international law, many countries are arming themselves with weapons of mass destruction.

9. President Putin says that President Obama sees no alternative to military action by the United States against Syria.

10. President Obama's claim that the United States is exceptional is offensive to President Putin.

Outcome: As a result of diplomacy, the Syrian crisis addressed by both presidents was lessened and United States military intervention prevented, perhaps because of the exchange of the thoughts of these two world leaders.

> *In the frank expression of conflicting opinions lies the greatest promise of wisdom in governmental actions.*
> —Louis D. Brandeis, *justice on the American Supreme Court*

YOUR TURN: POSITION PAPER

Directions:

1. Research a contemporary controversy that interests you, one of these or one of your own choice:

    - affirmative action
    - cloning
    - death penalty
    - immigration
    - minimum wage
    - standardized tests
    - stem cell research
    - tablets vs. textbooks
    - welfare

2. Decide your position (pro or con), draft a paper, and, since good writing results from rewriting, revise it several times until it resembles a paper that could appear in a publication—a magazine, a newspaper, or a book.

3. Include and underline <u>at least nine</u> sentence-composing tools—three examples of each: *identifiers, describers, elaborators*. Include some in an early draft, but add more during multiple revisions. Following is a

review of *identifiers*, *describers*, and *elaborators* with examples of those tools by Roya Hakakian from her memoir *Journey from the Land of No*.

THE IDENTIFIER TOOL (appositive phrase)

Definition—*A sentence part identifying a person, place, or thing named in a sentence.* Appositives often begin with the words *a*, *an*, or *the*. They always answer one of these questions:

> Who is he? Who is she? Who are they? (*people*)
>
> What is it? What are they? (*places or things*)

Identifiers can occur in three positions within a sentence:

> ***Opener:*** <u>A conservative Jewish woman in her late thirties</u>, she wanted us to know that it was possible to earn a degree, wear starched shirts, knee-length skirts, and bright red lipstick, and make one's own money.
>
> ***S-V Split:*** The 100,000-member Jewish community of Iran, <u>the second largest community of Jews in the Middle East</u>, after Israel, fell into disarray.
>
> ***Closer:*** This was 1979, <u>the year that showed us we could make our own destinies</u>.

THE DESCRIBER TOOL (present participle)

Definition—*A sentence part that always ends in* -ing. Many main verbs also end in *-ing*. Unlike verbs, which cannot be removed from a sentence, participles are removable with a complete grammatical sentence remaining.

> <u>Verb</u> (not removable): We were *imagining the rhythms of life at 500 Riverside Drive in New York City.*

Present Participle (removable): We spent days in reverie, *imagining the rhythms of life at 500 Riverside Drive in New York City.*

Present participle describers can occur in three positions within a sentence:

Opener: <u>Driving past the cotton fields in rural Georgia</u>, I mulled over the many details that demanded my attention.

S-V Split: Father's footsteps, <u>echoing in the alley</u>, were punctuated by the sound of Mother's heels.

Closer: We spent days in reverie, <u>imagining the rhythms of life at 500 Riverside Drive in New York City, making friends with a smart Japanese girl named Satomi, stomaching bland American meals</u>, and <u>washing dishes part-time to pay for architecture school</u>. (*Contains four consecutive present participle tools.*)

THE DESCRIBER TOOL (past participle)

Definition—*A sentence part that usually ends in* -ed. Many main verbs also end in -*ed*. Unlike verbs, which cannot be removed from a sentence, past participles are removable with a complete grammatical sentence remaining.

Verb (not removable): Father's footsteps were *punctuated by the sound of Mother's heels.*

Past Participle (removable): Father's footsteps, *punctuated by the sound of Mother's heels*, echoed in the alley.

Past participle describers can occur in three positions within a sentence:

Opener: <u>Unperturbed by the piracy</u>, Father reveled in the sensation his little verse had caused.

S-V Split: Father's footsteps, <u>punctuated by the sound of Mother's heels</u>, echoed in the alley.

Closer: She ran through the streets, unfazed by cars or pedestrians.

THE ELABORATOR TOOL (absolute phrase)

Definition—*A sentence part elaborating on the rest of the sentence in which it appears.* Absolutes are *almost* complete sentences. As a test, you can make **every** absolute a sentence by adding **was** *or* **were**.

Uncle Ardi, *one foot on the tire*, reached to kiss her.

Test: One foot **WAS** on the tire.

We walked past several rooms, *several filled to the ceiling with boxes of evidence the reverend had gathered on his own illness and that of his fellow servicemen.*

Test: Several **WERE** *filled to the ceiling with boxes of evidence the reverend had gathered on his own illness and that of his fellow servicemen.*

Elaborators can occur in three positions within a sentence:

Opener: Radio silent, in that dim light in the corner of the couch she was an old spider, stuck to her own web.

S-V Split: Uncle Ardi, one foot on the tire, reached to kiss her.

Closer: We walked past several rooms, several filled to the ceiling with boxes of evidence the reverend had gathered on his own illness and that of his fellow servicemen.

REPORTERS: GETTING AND TELLING IT RIGHT

Journalists record and then report detailed information about news stories they cover. Students research and then report detailed information about topics for different courses they take. Employees gather and then report detailed information concerning issues and topics for their work. Using sentence tools is one way to provide details.

This section covers three kinds of reports: reporting an event, reporting a process, and reporting information.

REPORTING AN EVENT

ACTIVITY 1: REPORTING A CRIME SCENE

Pretend you are a reporter who visited a crime scene of a homicide to gather detailed information and then report the story. At the scene of the crime, you wrote the following four notes, but you also took mental notes about details of the crime scene, and now are ready to write and publish the story, with lots of sentence tools for detailed information.

REPORTER'S NOTES

1. ^ The detective ^ found only one clue ^ .

2. ^ His partner ^ stood over the body ^ .

3. ^ A crime lab professional ^ worked around them ^ .

4. ^ A single bystander ^ watched everything ^ .

For each sentence, add a sentence tool in each place: *opener*, *S-V split*, *closer*. Here are various kinds of sentence tools you can add *as openers* for details about the detective.

EXAMPLES: SENTENCE TOOLS ABOUT THE DETECTIVE (OPENERS)

Identifier (appositive tool): <u>A crackerjack crime scene investigator known for his intuitive savvy</u>, the detective found only one clue.

Describer (present participle tool): <u>Combing the scene in his usual thorough manner</u>, the detective found only one clue.

Describer (past participle tool): <u>Stumped by the unique puzzle this particular crime scene presented</u>, the detective found only one clue.

Elaborator (absolute tool): <u>His face wearing a puzzled expression unusual for this master sleuth</u>, the detective found only one clue.

Directions:

1. Add sentence tools in the slots with caret marks (^). Each of the four sentences will contain tools in three positions: *an opener, an S-V split, a closer*. Use a variety of types of sentence tools: *identifiers, describers, elaborators*.

2. Immediately following each of those four expanded sentences, compose a new sentence using your choice of tools. In other words, add a second sentence about the detective, a second sentence about his partner, a second sentence about the crime lab professional, and a second sentence about the bystander. The result will be an eight-sentence, detailed paragraph: four sentences from the previous activity, alternating with four new sentences of your own.

3. Create a headline for your news story about the crime scene investigation.

ACTIVITY 2: REPORTING AN ENTERTAINMENT OR SPORTS EVENT

Your boss gives you an assignment to report a current entertainment or sports event. While attending the event (or viewing it on TV or the Internet), you take notes to report about that event. Back at your desk on your computer, you draft, revise, and submit your story for publication offline or online.

Using the format from Activity 1 as a template, write your report of the event. It should contain eight sentences, each with ample sentence-composing tools—*identifiers, describers, elaborators*—in various positions—*openers, S-V splits, closers*.

ACTIVITY 3: REPORTING ABOUT *APOLLO 11*'S SUCCESS

On July 16, 1969, Apollo 11 succeeded in placing a man on the moon, as the world cheered—an American success story. On January 28th, 1986, the spaceship *Challenger* exploded during liftoff, killing all seven crew members as the world watched, horrified.

In the next two activities, you'll learn about both events and report additional details using sentence-composing tools.

Here is information about the historic successful landing on the moon, the goal of the Apollo 11 mission.

At 9:32 A.M. on July 16, 1969, time stood still throughout the world, as thousands converged on the Kennedy Space Center and millions tuned in on live television. At that instant, the first rumbles began to shake the ground, as a small spacecraft attached to the giant Saturn V rocket several hundred feet tall started lifting off. Quickly being propelled several thousand miles per hour, it takes just a few minutes to reach a speed of 15,000 miles per hour, and just a few more minutes to enter orbit at 18,000 miles per hour. Apollo 11 was on its way to a historic first landing on the Moon. As Neil Armstrong left his first footprint on the Moon, he transmitted one of the 20th century's most famous quotations: "That's one small step for man, one giant leap for mankind."

Apollo 11: The History and Legacy of the First Moon Landing (adapted)

Directions: Each list of basic sentences contains information about the Apollo 11 mission. Using the information provided, write a report containing strong sentences built like those of the preceding paragraph—sentences so good they could appear in that same book.

Combine the following information into the *first sentence* of your paragraph, built like a sentence by an author.

1a. Apollo 11's journey had begun over a decade earlier as part of the space race.

1b. The race was between the United States and the Soviet Union.

1c. Apollo 11's journey to the Moon probably started ten years before its moon landing.

Combine the following information into the *second sentence* of your paragraph, built like a sentence by an author.

2a. Landing on the Moon was a noble goal.

2b. The goal was proposed as early as 1961.

2c. President Kennedy is the one who proposed the goal.

2d. NASA moved with urgency.

2e. The nation as a whole also moved with urgency.

2f. They moved simply to best the Soviet Union.

Combine the following information into the *third sentence* of your paragraph, built like a sentence by an author.

3a. The Soviet Union spent the 1950s beating America.

3b. They beat America to important space-related firsts.

3c. This included launching the first satellite.

3d. It also included launching the first cosmonaut in orbit.

Combine the following information into the *fourth sentence* of your paragraph, built like a sentence by an author.

4a. In 1960 the first Russian cosmonaut orbited the earth.

4b. His name was Yuri Gagarin.

4c. This happened two years before the American astronaut orbited the earth.

4d. The American's name was John Glenn.

Combine the following information into the *fifth sentence* of your paragraph, built like a sentence by an author.

5a. NASA spent $20 billion dollars on the Apollo missions.

5b. This happened over the decade from 1960–1970.

5c. This was the most expensive peacetime program in American history to date.

Combine the following information into the *sixth sentence* of your paragraph, built like a sentence by an author.

6a. Apollo 11 was only one of the missions.

6b. There were almost twenty Apollo missions.

6c. Apollo 11 was certainly the crown jewel of them all.

Combine the following information into the *seventh sentence* of your paragraph, built like a sentence by an author.

7a. Americans certainly felt the cost was worth it.

7b. They felt this way as they watched the first live shots of astronauts.

7c. The astronauts were walking on the Moon.

7d. Their names were Neil Armstrong and Buzz Aldrin.

(Information is from *Apollo 11: The History and Legacy of the First Moon Landing*.)

ACTIVITY 4: REPORTING ABOUT *CHALLENGER*'S TRAGEDY

On January 28th, 1986, the tragic accident of the *Challenger* launching was an American horror story.

>As everyone watched the liftoff on the monitors, and millions worldwide watched on live television, it looked as though the flames from the solid motors were beginning to creep upward to consume the entire *Challenger* orbiter. It took only a blink of the eye, but the moment seemed to last a lifetime. Suddenly, *Challenger* was engulfed by a huge fireball—obviously, a major malfunction. The two solid rocket motors spiraled out of the flames, creating a pitchfork-shaped white streak. Approximately three minutes later, the spacecraft plunged into the ocean, killing all seven crew members.
>
>Hugh Harris, *Challenger: An American Tragedy* (adapted)

Directions: Each list of basic sentences contains information about the *Challenger*. Using the information provided, write several paragraphs, deciding how many sentences to include in each paragraph. Build your sentences like those of an author—sentences so good they could appear in that same book

PART ONE

Combine the following information into the *first paragraph* of your report, using just two sentences.

1. A team of engineers and scientists analyzed the wreckage.

2. They also analyzed all other available evidence.

3. They attempted to determine the cause of death of the *Challenger* crew.

4. The impact of the crew compartment with the ocean was violent.

5. It was so violent that evidence of damage occurring in the seconds following the explosion was masked.

Combine the following information into the *second paragraph* of your report, using just five sentences.

6. The cause of death of the Challenger crew cannot be positively determined.

7. The forces to which they were exposed during the Orbiter breakup were probably not sufficient to cause death or serious injury.

8. The crew possibly but not certainly lost consciousness in the seconds following vehicle breakup.

9. The loss of consciousness was due to in-flight loss of crew module pressure.

10. After vehicle breakup, the crew compartment continued its upward trajectory and peaked at an altitude of 65,000 feet approximately twenty-five seconds later.

11. About two minutes and forty-five seconds after breakup the compartment then descended and struck the ocean surface at approximately 207 miles per hour.

PART TWO

Combine the following information into the *third paragraph* of your report, but you decide how many sentences.

12. It is possible, but not certain, that the crew lost consciousness.

13. This was due to an in-flight loss of crew module pressure.

14. The accident happened at 48,000 feet.

15. This was with the crew cabin at that altitude or higher for almost a minute.

16. The crew cabin was without an oxygen supply at that altitude of 48,000 feet where the accident happened.

17. Loss of cabin pressure would have caused rapid loss of consciousness.

18. Consciousness would not have been regained before water impact.

Combine the following information into the *fourth paragraph* of your report, but you decide how many sentences.

19. On March 7 the bodily remains of the crew were found.

20. This happened through the efforts of a recovery team.

21. The remains were within the shattered crew compartment.

22. The compartment was on the floor of the ocean.

23. Their remains after examination were flown to Dover Air Force Base in Delaware.

24. This was done for release of the remains to family members for burial.
(Information is from Hugh Harris, *Challenger: An American Tragedy*)

On January 28, 1986, the night of the *Challenger* accident, President Ronald Reagan was scheduled to deliver his "State of the Union Speech" but postponed it to give instead an address to the nation on the tragedy of the space shuttle *Challenger*. Here are excerpts.

> Ladies and Gentlemen,
>
> I'd planned to speak to you tonight to report on the state of the Union, but the events of earlier today have led me to change those

plans. Today is a day for mourning and remembering. This is truly a national loss.

We mourn seven heroes: Michael Smith, Dick Scobee, Judith Resnik, Ronald McNair, Ellison Onizuka, Gregory Jarvis, and Christa McAuliffe. We mourn their loss as a nation together.

For the families of the seven, we cannot bear, as you do, the full impact of this tragedy. But we feel the loss, and we're thinking about you so very much. Your loved ones were daring and brave, and they had that special grace, that special spirit that says, "Give me a challenge, and I'll meet it with joy." They had a hunger to explore the universe and discover its truths. They wished to serve, and they did. They served all of us.

I want to say something to the schoolchildren of America who were watching the live coverage of the shuttle's take-off. I know it's hard to understand, but sometimes painful things like this happen. It's all part of the process of exploration and discovery. It's all part of taking a chance and expanding man's horizons. The future doesn't belong to the fainthearted; it belongs to the brave. The *Challenger* crew was pulling us into the future, and we'll continue to follow them.

There's a coincidence today. On this day three hundred and ninety years ago, the great explorer Sir Francis Drake died aboard ship off the coast of Panama. In his lifetime the great frontiers were the oceans, and a historian later said, "He lived by the sea, died on it, and was buried in it." Well, today, we can say of the *Challenger* crew: Their dedication was, like Drake's, complete.

The crew of the space shuttle Challenger honored us by the manner in which they lived their lives. We will never forget them, nor the last time we saw them, this morning, as they prepared for their journey and waved goodbye and "slipped the surly bonds of Earth" to "touch the face of God."

REPORTING A PROCESS

ACTIVITY 5: A TECHNICAL PAPER

Writing unfolds one sentence at a time. Sentences unfold one part at a time. The most important parts of well-built sentences are the additional sentence parts built by sentence tools in various positions: *opener*, *S-V split*, *closer*. Good writing is actually a process of addition. Sentence tools create those additions.

> *Give us the tools and we will finish the job.*
>
> —Sir Winston Churchill, *British prime minister*

Directions: In a longer piece of writing (750–1,000 words), demonstrate your skill in using those sentence tools. Think about a technical process you know a lot about or have a strong interest in learning more about through research. Then draft and revise your report for educated adult readers, explaining how that process works, happens, occurs, or functions.

TOPIC SELECTION: Select a topic for your report that will benefit your readers by providing new or improved knowledge or understanding of the process.

EXAMPLES

how a human heart functions

how the confirmation process for Supreme Court nominees works

how prejudice works

how a hurricane forms

how the circulatory or respiratory system works

how inflation works

how an IRS income tax audit is conducted

how a computer's memory functions

how a child becomes an adult

how HTML language works

how the stock market operates

how society favors attractive people

how a terrorist is born

how leaves turn color in the fall

how a recession in the economy happens

how spiders use wasps as food for their young

how spyware or viruses get into your computer

how an eating disorder like anorexia or bulimia develops

how laughter promotes physical and emotional health

how DNA is replicated

how cloning occurs

how fame victimizes celebrities

how a caterpillar becomes a butterfly (*See sample essay on pages 230–233.*)

how an iPod or iPad works (*See sample essay on pages 236–238.*)

SPECIAL FEATURE: For an effective opening paragraph, imitate this model paragraph, adding your thesis sentence at the end. The purpose of a thesis sentence is to preview what your essay will be explaining.

MODEL PARAGRAPH

This is a snail shell, round, full, and glossy as a horse chestnut. Comfortable and compact, it sits curled up like a cat in the hollow of my hand. Milky and opaque, it has the pinkish bloom of the sky on a summer evening, ripening to rain. On its smooth, symmetrical face is penciled with precision a perfect spiral, winding inward to the pinpoint center of the shell, the tiny dark core of the apex, the pupil of the eye. (*Add a thesis sentence here to preview your essay for your readers.*)

Anne Morrow Lindberg, *Gift from the Sea*

SAMPLE IMITATION

He is a newborn babe, fresh, beautiful, and playful as a puppy. Comfortable and trusting, he rests peacefully with his pacifier on the bosom of his mother's chest. Smiling and gentle, he has the blue eyes of his mother, glowing with innocence. On his adorable, sweet face is reflected by genetics a facsimile, blending closely the biological composition of his parents, the genetic structure of Mom and Dad, a DNA road map. *What his parents don't realize is that already taking place is an ongoing process inside his tiny body called DNA replication.* (*thesis sentence*)

Directions for Your Technical Report:

1. Using knowledge from personal experience, reading, or the Internet, draft several paragraphs clearly explaining the process. Then begin

your report with an imitation of the previous model paragraph, ending with a thesis sentence that previews what your essay will be about.

2. Select information and details that will educate, enlighten, inform, or even entertain your readers about the process to increase their knowledge and understanding.

3. Avoid an overly technical style so that the process will be understandable by nontechnical but educated readers.

4. Expand early drafts of your report by adding numerous and varied sentence-composing tools for details of the process.

5. End your essay with a memorable paragraph as good as the first paragraph of your essay—but without imitating a model.

6. Provide an original title.

Here is an example. Notice how Evelyn meets all of the above goals, with thirty-six sentence-composing tools in various positions. Her colons and semicolons are highlighted.

"Metamorphosis"
by
Evelyn Chavez
(*a student paper*)

(1) It is a small egg, smooth, shiny, and lime green like a beautiful gemstone. (2) Secure and still, it is attached like a thumb tack on the surface of the leaf. (3) Tiny and inconspicuous, it has the color of the grass below the milkweed plant, glistening with morning dew. (4) Inside its glimmering, protective encasement is safeguarded from the dangers outside a tiny larva, waiting within the egg, the caterpillar's first home, the nutrient-rich cloak. (5) The larva awakens, a tiny creature, and the

egg starts to move. *(6) Nature is filled with many beautiful and distinctive processes, but none is like the metamorphosis of a caterpillar into a butterfly, a unique transformation that demonstrates that something beautiful can arise from humble beginnings.* (thesis sentence)

(7) There are four stages in the butterfly life cycle: the egg stage, the larvae stage, the chrysalis stage, and the adult butterfly stage. (8) An adult butterfly is very selective about the plant on which it lays its eggs. (9) For instance, the monarch butterfly only lays eggs on milkweed plants, the preferred food source of the monarch caterpillar. (10) The caterpillar has restricted mobility, so it is not able to travel very far for food. (11) The adult butterfly will deposit its eggs on a leaf, providing shelter and serving as a food source for the caterpillar. (12) After a couple of days, the egg is ready to hatch. (13) The larva, a young caterpillar that is about two millimeters long, begins to chew its way out of the egg, its mouth ripping the sheath open.

(14) Once out, the caterpillar's primary job is to eat. (15) It begins by eating the remnants of the egg; it then proceeds to eat the leaf on which it stands. (16) During this time the caterpillar starts to molt, its skin shedding up to five times during this stage. (17) The caterpillar that comes out of the egg is called the first instar; it becomes the second instar after it sheds its skin for the first time. (18) This naming system continues after each molting until it becomes the fifth instar, the final stage in the larvae stage. (19) Nearing the end of the larvae stage, the caterpillar, its need to eat reduced, starts preparing for the next stage, chrysalis. (20) The caterpillar finds a spot underneath a leaf or a branch on which it spins a silk pad. (21) Once finished, it hooks its hind legs in the silk pad and sheds its skin one last time. (22) Hanging from the silk pad, the caterpillar flexes and wiggles its way out of its old skin.

(23) Eventually the caterpillar's pale green skin becomes visible, freed from its old, restricting exoskeleton; this skin later becomes the pupa. (24) Contrary to popular belief, a caterpillar does not form a cocoon; moths come from cocoons, but butterflies emerge from pupas.

(25) For the next fourteen days, the pupa hangs from the underside of the leaf, concealed from predators. (26) The pupa's immobility might cause someone to incorrectly assume that nothing is happening on the inside, but it is quite the opposite. (27) Enzymes are quickly digesting unnecessary caterpillar tissue, providing the transforming caterpillar with much needed nutrients. (28) At this stage, the imaginal discs, embryonic cells that were stalled earlier in the life cycle, begin to grow at a fast pace. (29) Placed in various locations, the imaginal discs form different parts of the anatomy of the butterfly: the legs, the wings, the antennae, and all of the organs found in an adult butterfly. (30) Those embryonic cells divide through a process called mitosis. (31) In mitosis, the cells divide into two identical cells, and certain genes are deactivated. (32) The genes that are deactivated depend on the type of tissue being formed. (33) For example, in the area where the wings are being formed, the genes for antennae growth will be suppressed. (34) Through this process, the cells differentiate, and the body parts form.

(35) During those days, the color of the pupa also changes: starting as a pale green, turning into a brighter green, transforming into a dark teal, and ending as a dark brown. (36) The dark color signals the end of the chrysalis stage. (37) Hanging on, the butterfly slowly rips through the remains of the pupa, now a clear, plastic-like sac. (38) The butterfly emerges, its wings wet and very small. (39) Pumping liquid from its abdomen into them, the butterfly expands its wings. (40) The butterfly is ready to fly after its wings are dry enough, beginning its life as an adult. (41) Most adult butterflies only live for a couple of weeks, but some species can live longer by hibernating. (42) For instance, the monarch butterflies migrate to Mexico or southern California, and the butterflies return once the climate is favorable. (43) Once back, the butterflies mate; the female butterflies lay their eggs, and the cycle starts once more.

(44) The egg hatches first into a caterpillar like a blossoming prairie flower, the wildlife surrounding and admiring it, the new member of the

ever growing population, standing on its own for the first time. (45) The butterfly emerges last from a pupa, protecting it and transforming it into the majestic beauty that floats through the sky in perfect graceful movements. (46) The egg is the first stage, genesis, protector, and guardian, cage, and food source. (47) The butterfly is, by the end of the life cycle, the result of an incredible process, metamorphosis.

Directions: First, reread the sentence in which the tool appears, and only then identify its type: *identifier*, *describer*, or *elaborator*.

Tool	Sentence Number
1. glistening with morning dew	(3)
2. waiting within the egg	(4)
3. the caterpillar's first home	(4)
4. the nutrient-rich cloak	(4)
5. a tiny creature	(5)
6. a unique transformation that demonstrates that something beautiful can arise from humble beginnings	(6)
7. the egg stage, the larvae stage, the chrysalis stage, and the adult butterfly stage (*multiple tools*)	(7)
8. the preferred food source of the monarch caterpillar	(9)
9. providing shelter and serving as a food source for the caterpillar	(11)
10. a young caterpillar that is about two millimeters long	(13)
11. its mouth ripping the sheath open	(13)
12. its skin shedding up to five times during this stage	(16)
13. the final stage in the larvae stage	(18)
14. nearing the end of the larvae stage	(19)
15. its need to eat reduced	(19)
16. chrysalis	(19)
17. once finished	(21)
18. hanging from the silk pad	(22)
19. freed from its old, restricting exoskeleton	(23)
20. concealed from predators	(25)

21. providing the transforming caterpillar with much needed nutrients	(27)
22. embryonic cells that were stalled earlier in the life cycle	(28)
23. placed in various locations	(29)
24. the legs, the wings, the antennae, and all of the organs found in an adult butterfly (*multiple tools*)	(29)
25. starting as a pale green, turning into a brighter green, transforming into a dark teal, and ending as a dark brown (*multiple tools*)	(35)
26. hanging on	(37)
27. now a clear, plastic-like sac	(37)
28. its wings wet and very small	(38)
29. pumping liquid from its abdomen into them	(39)
30. beginning its life as an adult	(40)
31. the wildlife surrounding and admiring it	(44)
32. the new member of the ever growing population	(44)
33. standing on its own for the first time	(44)
34. protecting it and transforming it into the majestic beauty that floats through the sky in perfect graceful movements (*multiple tools*)	(46)
35. genesis, protector, and guardian, cage, and food source (*multiple tools*)	(46)
36. metamorphosis	(47)

REPORTING INFORMATION

Writing to communicate information is a popular form of nonfiction. People want facts about a topic they are interested in—with accurate details and data. People want to know what things are—everything from aardvarks to zygotes, and everything in between, including iPods, the topic of the examples below.

ACTIVITY 6: AN INFORMATIONAL PAPER

Good writing results from additions. Sentence tools like *identifiers*, *describers*, and *elaborators* build those additions. So do other tools you learned earlier (pages 54–64).

Below are two versions of an informative report: an early draft without sentence-composing tools and the final draft with those tools. *Seventy-two percent of the final version consists of sentence-composing tools in various positions.*

Notice in the revised version how the underlined sentence tools account for the high quality of the paper.

"iBaby Maybe"
(*early draft without sentence-composing tools*)

This is an iPod. It lodges easily in the case on my belt like a deck of playing cards. It stores in its small container incredible amounts of digitized music and video. On the iPod's sleek, smooth front is designed with efficiency a simple touch-control. *The iPod is an ever-evolving ubiquitous device that interfaces with your computer and the Internet to provide audio and video entertainment.* (thesis sentence)

First install the iTunes program on your computer. The iTunes software is easy to install. Click on "Download iTunes," choose your operating system (Mac or PC), and the iTunes program hurls through Cyberspace to your computer.

The software has a link to the iTunes Store. Apple provides the software for free. The route is a cinch.

The iTunes Store is the source for virtually any tune. The iTunes Store web site is easily navigated.

The fun begins. Your entire library of music and video is automatically transferred to the device. The iTunes programming will "sync" your iPod.

The iPod has become the tech gadget of the age. Walkman portables quickly became obsolete.

The name "iPod" struck gold. The iPod has gone through a number of generations.

A device like the iPod would have been unthinkable.

Babies shortly after birth may have a tiny device implanted in their brains. The tiny tech tot will be a little bundle of joy.

"iBaby Maybe"
(*final draft, with added sentence tools underlined*)

This is an iPod, digital, small, and compact as a cell phone. Lightweight and attractive, it lodges easily in the case on my belt like a deck of playing cards. Amazing and efficient, it stores in its small container incredible amounts of digitized music and video. On the iPod's sleek, smooth front is designed with efficiency a simple touch-control, providing access to its operation, the digital command center, the key to my tunes. *A technological marvel, the iPod is an ever-evolving ubiquitous device that interfaces with your computer and the Internet to provide audio and video entertainment.* (thesis sentence)

To use your new iPod, first install the iTunes program on your computer. Available as a free download, for either Macintosh or PC, the iTunes software is easy to install, taking only a few mouse-clicks, with no snags or surprises. From Apple's web site, click on "Download iTunes," choose your operating system (Mac or PC), and the iTunes program hurls through Cyberspace to your computer, an incredible digital entertainment package only seconds away.

The software has a link to the iTunes Store, the reason for the free download. To get an instant huge client base, to capture a huge market share of the home entertainment industry, including all types of music and video, to establish a virtual monopoly for easy and instant acquisition of entertainment media without having to visit a big box store, Apple provides, irresistibly and instantly, the software for free. From the iTunes

Store to your computer to your iPod, the route is a cinch, smooth, easy, and quick.

A vast music and video store in Cyberspace, owned and operated by Apple, Inc., the iTunes Store is the source for virtually any tune, in any category imaginable, from rock to opera, and any film or TV video. Attractive in design and easy to use, a virtual one-stop home entertainment center a mouse-click away, the iTunes Store web site is easily navigated, even by first-timers, for accessing information about songs or albums, films or TV shows, and reading user reviews with a five-star rating system, and, of course, purchasing and downloading tunes, videos, podcasts, and applications.

With the iTunes software on your computer, the fun begins, including making libraries of music imported from CD's or other electronic means, customizing playlists to include songs of any category imaginable, like "Jogging Tunes," "Oldies but Goodies," "Romantic Vibes," "Biggest Hits of Superstars," or any collection that can be imported from the library of tunes stored on your computer. When your iPod is connected to your computer, your entire library of music and video, including your custom playlists, is automatically transferred to the device, effortlessly and quickly. The iTunes programming, sensitive to changes, will, immediately and automatically, "sync" your iPod, to update the device's contents by adding to your iPod new music or video you've added to your computer, updating the device since the last time you connected your iPod to your computer.

The iPod has become the tech gadget of the age, consumers of all ages around the world flocking to buy the new storage device for their music, replacing almost immediately the up-until-then popular Sony product, the Walkman, a portable cassette recorder that allowed people to listen to music via headphones larger than iPod earbuds. Because the iPod, unlike the Walkman, allowed for storage of digitized music within its box—instead of having to carry cassette tapes containing the music, Walkman portables quickly became obsolete, as did the cassettes that had been the mainstream media for recorded music.

The device was introduced in 2001, a sci-fi film with that year in its title inspiring the iPod name. Based upon mention of a pod in the space film *2001: A Space Odyssey*, the name "iPod," instantly memorable, struck gold, starting a whole line of iThings like iMacs, iPads, iPhones, and others. Since its introduction, the iPod has gone through a number of generations, each adding new and remarkable features like Podcasts, which are downloadable spoken texts of every conceivable stripe, including foreign language lessons, university lectures, radio and TV broadcasts, spoken word audio books, and more.

In the non-tech past, a device like the iPod, small, reliable, affordable, storing thousands of songs and playing them through tiny speakers inserted into your ears while you jog, walk, or just sit and groove on the music, would have been unthinkable.

In a sci-fi future, as the iPod shrinks to microscopic size, although unthinkable now, babies shortly after birth may have a tiny device implanted in their brains. Unable even to crawl, the tiny tech tot will be a little bundle of joy, the joy emanating from its iBrain, where the baby's choices might be "Rock-a-Bye, Baby" for sleeping sweetly, and then, for waking rousingly, "We Will Rock You!"—plus, for in between, every tune ever recorded, playable on demand.

iBaby? Maybe.

It doesn't matter how you write the first draft or even the second draft, but it makes all the difference in the world how you write the final draft.

—Elizabeth White

YOUR TURN: FREE CHOICE REPORT

This section presented three common types of reports:

- reporting an event
- reporting a process
- reporting information.

Choose one of those three types of reports, review the activities covering that type of report, research your topic, draft the report, then revise it until it resembles a report that could appear in a publication—a magazine, a newspaper, or a book.

Directions:

1. As in the two reports in Activities 5 and 6 above—the technical report and the informational report—begin your report with an imitation of this model paragraph that ends with a thesis sentence that previews your report for your readers.

MODEL PARAGRAPH

> This is a snail shell, round, full, and glossy as a horse chestnut. Comfortable and compact, it sits curled up like a cat in the hollow of my hand. Milky and opaque, it has the pinkish bloom of the sky on a summer evening, ripening to rain. On its smooth, symmetrical face is penciled with precision a perfect spiral, winding inward to the pinpoint center of the shell, the tiny dark core of the apex, the pupil of the eye. (*Add a thesis sentence here to preview your report for your readers.*)
>
> Anne Morrow Lindberg, Gift from the Sea

2. Also like the two previous reports, include abundant sentence-composing tools—*identifiers, describers, elaborators*—in various positions: *openers, S-V splits, closers.*

3. The second report above ("iBaby Maybe") illustrates the power of revision, so rewrite your report several times because good writing is always the result of rewriting.

4. In addition to self-suggestions, get peer suggestions. Ask classmates to write their responses to your paper and begin each with whichever one of these five words fits your comment: *keep, add, delete, change, move.* Those are the five major kinds of decisions writers make when revising.

EXAMPLES
(Taken from peer reviews of reports on differing topics.)

Note: Include the reason beginning with the word *because*.

- *Keep* the focus on the elaborate lighting for the scene *because* your report emphasizes that the technical aspects of the performance were superior to the story and acting in the play.

- *Add* at least one reason why dogs prefer food made specifically for them and not cats *because* readers will believe your claim more strongly.

- *Delete* the phrase "going to the same store every day" *because* your earlier comment "never varying the store selection" already established that fact.

- *Change* the wording of your describer tool "his stomach about to relieve itself of its contents" to more blunt wording *because* the style for consistency should match the gross content.

- *Move* this describer tool "covered with the slime and mud of the soggy garden" from the opener to the closer position *because* then it would more clearly describe the dirty dog rather than Mr. Kowalski.

NONFICTION: THE FINAL WORD

Throughout this worktext, you learned the meaning of some words through a *quickshot*, a synonym approximating the word's meaning. For the final word, though, a fuller definition is needed, an answer to the question "What is nonfiction?"

Definition: **nonfiction (noun).** From the Latin, "*not*" + "*shaping, feigning*"

1. the written expression of, reflection upon, and/or interpretation of observed, perceived, or recollected experience;

2. a genre of literature made up of such writing, which includes such subgenres as the essay, the memoir, narrative, reportage, and expressive critical writing and whose borders with other reality-based genres and forms (such as journalism, criticism, history, etc.) are fluid and malleable;

3. (obsolete) not fiction.

> I often give these definitions to my students when they ask, "So, like, what *is* nonfiction?" The definitions give us a way of narrowing the field.
>
> Robert L. Root, *The Nonfictionist's Guide*

> "It's always seemed odd to me that *nonfiction* is defined, not by what it *is*, but by what it is *not*. It is *not* fiction. But then again, it is also *not* poetry. . . . It's like defining classical music as *nonjazz*."
>
> Philip Gerard, *Creative Nonfiction*

The only important distinction is between good writing and bad writing.

—William Zinsser, *On Writing Well*

****

What is *Nonfiction for High School: A Sentence-Composing Approach*?

Answer: A worktext demonstrating the difference between good writing and bad writing, helping students build better sentences in nonfiction—or almost anything else they write. Two-time winner of the Pulitzer prize for nonfiction, Barbara Tuchman says this: "Nothing is more satisfying than to write a good sentence."

ALSO AVAILABLE

The Killgallons' bestselling sentence-composing approach to building better paragraphs

Paragraphs for Elementary School

Grades 3–5 / 978-0-325-04794-2 / 2014 / 184pp

SAVE with 10-packs: 978-0-325-05749-1

Paragraphs for Middle School

Grades 5–9 / 978-0-325-04268-8 / 2013 / 224pp

SAVE with 10-packs: 978-0-325-04862-8

Paragraphs for High School

Grades 9–12 / 978-0-325-04253-4 / 2012 / 248pp

SAVE with 10-packs: 978-0-325-04632-7

For more information or to place an order, visit **Heinemann.com**.

DEDICATED TO TEACHERS

800.225.5800     @HeinemannPub

WEB **Heinemann.com** • CALL **800.225.5800** • FAX **877.231.6980**

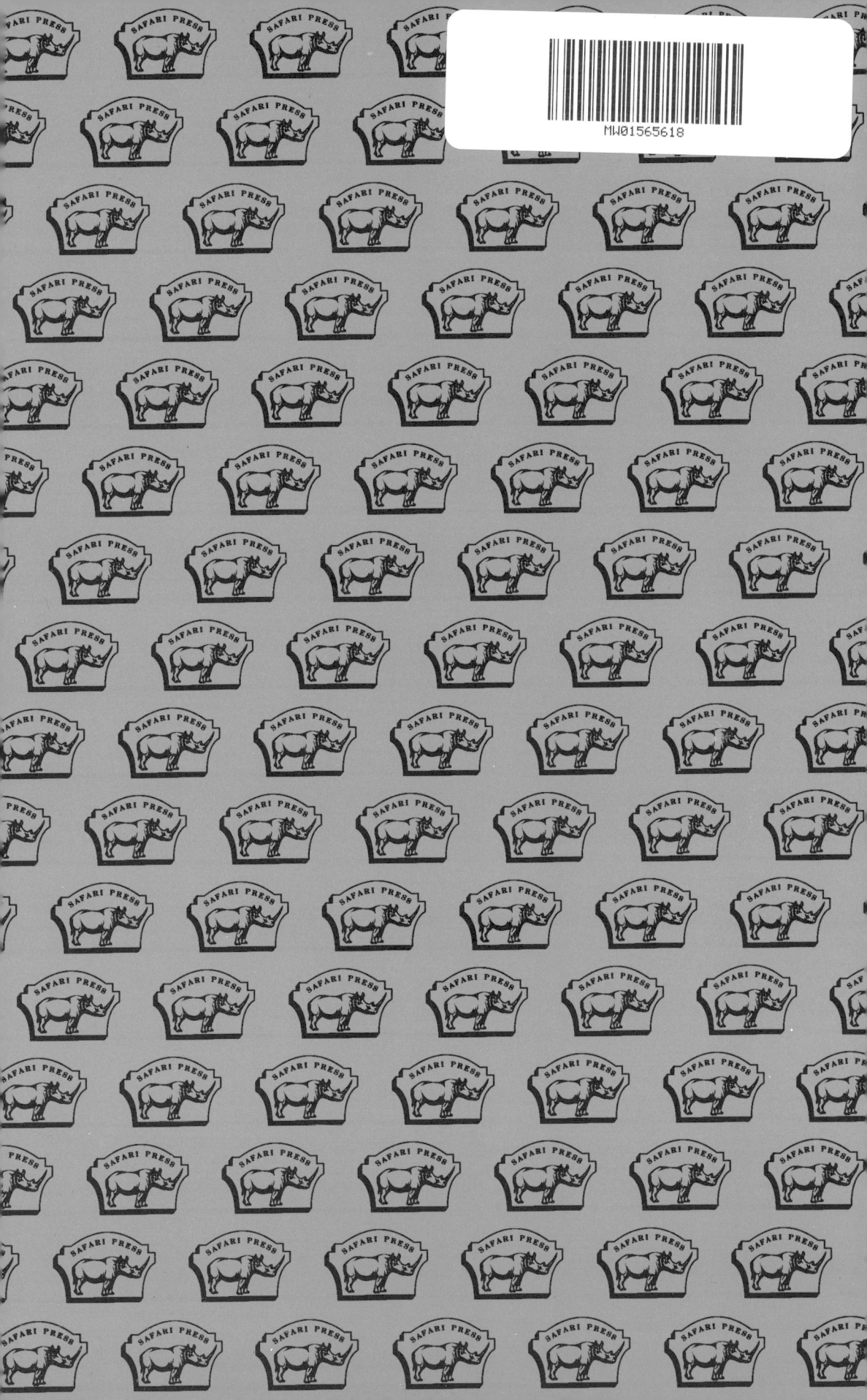

· FRANK A. PACHMAYR ·

· FRANK A. PACHMAYR ·
America's Master Gunsmith and His Guns

· BY JOHN LACHUK ·

SAFARI PRESS, Inc.

FRANK A. PACHMAYR, copyright © by John Lachuk. All rights reserved. No part of this publication may be reproduced in any form or by any means, electronic or mechanical reproduction, including photocopy, recording, or any information storage and retrieval system, without permission in writing from the publisher.

Lachuk, John

Second Edition

ISBN 1-57157-017-9

1995, Long Beach, California

10 9 8 7 6 5 4 3 2

Readers wishing to receive the Safari Press catalog featuring many fine books on big-game hunting, wingshooting, and firearms should write to: Safari Press, Inc., P. O. Box 3095, Long Beach, CA 90803. Tel: CA and worldwide (714) 894-9080; Canada and USA (except CA) (800) 451-4788.

Library of Congress # 95-69969

60th book published by Safari Press

Printed in the United States of America

CONTENTS

	INTRODUCTION	vii
I	A Modest Beginning	1
II	Frank and the .45	13
III	Custom Handguns and Rifles	27
IV	The World's Finest Shotguns	43
V	A Call to Arms: the War Years	63
VI	Gone to the Gunshop	81
VII	Pachmayr Products and Patents	117
VIII	Pachmayr Conquers the Continent	159
IX	Wonderful Wood	171
X	Frank and Friends in Field and Marsh	193
XI	Pachmayrs of the Past	225
XII	Nanitta Pachmayr	249
XIII	Pachmayr the Person	263
XIV	Man of Honors	285
XV	Pachmayr the Philanthropist	295

INTRODUCTION

When I first met Frank Pachmayr more than half a century ago, he had a modest shop. Besides himself, there were only two other technicians. Even then the arms that came out of the Pachmayr shop were top quality. In those days, the match pistol shooters fired the .38 Special revolver. Unlike today, when the .45 auto pistol is the ranking handgun, the revolver held first place. It was Pachmayr who saw that the hammer fell not only too slowly but altogether too far. He immediately set out to correct this with a determination that would not be denied.

The Pachmayr short action was a great success. Those marksmen who were keenly intent upon bettering their scores and winning more matches flocked to the Pachmayr shop for the short-action alteration to their outmoded revolvers.

This was the beginning. When the .45 auto pistol came to the fore, Pachmayr began a study of the handgun to see how it could be improved. The Model 1911 pistol as it came from Colt could just about put all its shots in the bottom of a Number 3 washtub at fifty yards. After Pachmayr altered the same pistol, it could keep all of its hits on a playing card at the same distance. I won the NRA National Championship with a Pachmayr .45 auto pistol mainly because it shot better than any of the other guns on the firing line. I've been living with and by Pachmayr pistols ever since.

(Askins amassed 117 trophies during his competitive career, winning the Texas championship five times, NRA All-Around once, and was high man on the All-American pistol teams during that period. During World War II, Colonel Askins saw combat duty in North Africa and Europe, and during his combat duty he carried and used a Pachmayr .45 ACP Colt Government Model. Editor)

Frank has an exceedingly inventive mind. He can look at any gun, whether it is a rifle, shotgun, or pistol, and immediately tell you how it can be improved. Because of this remarkable propensity for improvement and invention, he has been granted more than one-hundred, firearms-related patents.

This remarkably successful gun inventor and businessman never advertised in the shooting journals to the extent that he probably should have, but he did contribute mightily to numerous conservation organizations, such as Game Coin, Ducks Unlimited, and the Foundation for North American Wild Sheep.

Unassuming, gregarious, and good humored, Frank Pachmayr, one of my most esteemed friends, is a giant of a man as a firearms designer, inventor, and craftsman. Certainly his like will never be seen again.

–Colonel Charles Askins

ACKNOWLEDGMENTS

Many people contributed generously of their time and energy in assembling information and illustrations for this book. I must single out a number of individuals who assisted to a degree above and beyond the norm, including first and foremost the late Nanitta Gwendolyn Pachmayr, Frank's wife.

The others who helped me see this project to completion include Al Anton, Bill Artis, Bill Butler, Carl Cupp, Art Durando, Jack R. Farrar, Andrew Garner, Fred Huntington, Bill Ives, Johnny Johnson, Alex Kerr, Elizabeth Lascheid, G. G. "Gus" Michel, Elaine Nameny, Baden Powell, Dr. Robert Ingram Powell, Warren "Whitey" Shoemaker, Walter Strand, and Steve Yorba.

A special note of thanks to Richard Mellen, Frank's nephew, for helping me assemble a mass of accurate data and numerous photographs, many of which he took himself.

Quotations appearing in this book were taken from taped interviews.

DEDICATION

This book is dedicated to the memory of Frank A. Pachmayr's loving wife, the late Nanitta Gwendolyn Pachmayr. Nanitta Pachmayr was all things to her ambitious husband, Frank—business partner, advisor, confidant, understanding counselor, and loving wife.

This highly intelligent and discerning woman acted as company bookkeeper during the lean early years of Frank's gun shop and retail sporting goods store. During palmier days, she threw herself into community projects to aid the sick and less fortunate. Never critical and always supportive, Nanitta was the rock upon which Frank could always rely.

Nanitta was often Frank's hunting companion. Tough and gritty in the field, she never complained. She was often called upon to cook under primitive conditions for a gaggle of hungry hunters. She handled it all with humor and good spirits.

It was Nanitta who asked me to record her husband's life and contributions to the shooting world. It's tragic that she passed away before she could see the book that she inspired.

· Chapter I ·

A MODEST BEGINNING

In the history of American firearms, a number of men have contributed decisively to their sporting use: Browning, Colt, and Winchester ring out like bells of freedom. They made invaluable contributions to the sports of hunting and target shooting in a nation where these activities remain widely available to its citizens on a democratic basis—that is, they are not restricted to wealthy gentry or the politically privileged.

Another man who deserves recognition from shooters is Frank August Pachmayr. He has had a vast influence upon guns, long and short, rifled and smoothbore, during America's most important transitional period of firearm evolution and development. Pachmayr is one of those rare individuals who became a legend in his own time. John Browning and Samuel Colt were noted gun designers, and Oliver Winchester was a successful gun entrepreneur. Frank Pachmayr was both. He created shooting accessories that improved the effectiveness of guns. Pachmayr instinctively sensed the needs of sportsman and developed innovative products for them.

Frank remembers working in his father's gun shop for several hours a day at the tender age of seven. August Pachmayr put his sons John and Frank to work in the shop as soon as they were old enough to be useful.

Master gun craftsman and perfectionist that he was, August Pachmayr was by all accounts also a tyrant. He ran his small kingdom as a monarchy and held his entire family in servitude. His wife, Anna, ran the household, did the cleaning, shopping, and cooking. She also finished and checkered gunstocks on restocking jobs, as well as on the custom rifles and shotguns that August created with his own hands from raw wood and steel.

By nine years of age, Frank was handed the responsibility of turning the outside configurations of tapered barrels on an engine lathe. The lathe tool post moved slowly along the length of the barrel and was powered by a helical gear. It was Frank's job to control the tool bit, moving it in and out by rotating a small geared wheel. This was necessary to achieve the desired contour. In order to keep an eye on the progress of the cutting bit and watch the barrel being shaped between centers, Frank was obliged to stand on a wooden platform built for him by his father. Young boys have a notoriously short span of attention. Frank was, nonetheless, attentive to his labors and turned out some fine barrels. Then one fateful afternoon, he committed the most gross error.

Nine-year-old Frank was standing high on his box, turning a customer's barrel to a smaller diameter, when the sound of laughter from children playing marbles in the yard next door interrupted his concentration, drawing his eyes and his thoughts to the out-of-doors. His reverie was broken by the sudden and violent vibration and shaking of the lathe. There was a horrendous tearing and ripping of steel, along with a piercing shriek, as the cutting bit dug deep into the barrel. Frank instantly flipped the switch off and spun the small crank to retract the tool bit, but it was too late.

"I only looked out the window for just a minute," he relates ruefully, "but that was enough. The tool post ran into the steady rest and almost cut the barrel half. I

In the beginning, Frank Pachmayr occupied only a small corner of this store on Grand Avenue in Los Angeles, California. Eventually he owned the entire building, plus all of the others down to Pico Boulevard and around the corner.

took one look and knew the barrel was ruined beyond repair. My Old Man didn't see me for three days. I wanted to give him time to cool off!"

Gus was a wrathful taskmaster. "He could be standing just across the room from you," relates Frank, "and he would yell at you so loud the neighbors could hear him three blocks away. Hell, he could blow you right through the wall. When he wanted to get the attention of John or me from across the room, he'd throw something—anything that was handy. And we had the bruises to prove it." It was more a tribute to Frank's agility, rather than to Gus's poor aim that Frank suffered no permanent injury to his head or body.

In the heat of an argument, Gus might seize a rifle or shotgun by the barrel and use the buttstock to try to score a home run with the head of a customer or an employee. I once asked John Pachmayr if his father was perhaps only bluffing.

· A MODEST BEGINNING ·

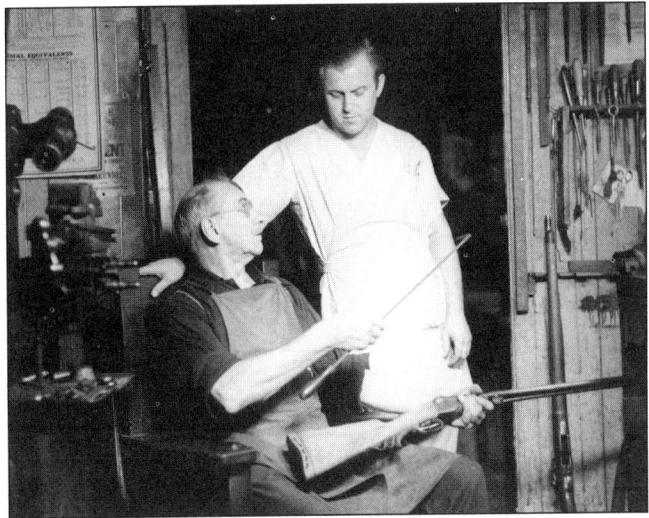

Frank continued to work for his father for paltry wages until he met and fell in love with Nanitta Laughlin. Realizing that he had to make more money before he could marry, he opened his own shop.

After all, there was no record of his ever scoring with one of his unusual "bats." John, who was openly terrified of Gus, said wide-eyed, "No one ever stuck around long enough to find out if he meant it or not."

In spite of the fact that Gus kept him pretty busy in the gun shop, Frank's entrepreneurial instincts manifested themselves early. He gathered snails in a tin bucket he borrowed from neighbors and received a dollar for ridding their yard of the pests. Quick to recognize a money-making opportunity, Frank canvassed the neighborhood and collected more snails and more dollars. Then he sold the snails to a nearby French restaurant and realized a profit at both ends of the transaction. This became an ongoing job for Frank. With the money he saved, he bought some chicks and started raising chickens.

"At one time, he had about 300 chickens in mother's back yard," Christine remarked with a chuckle. "After that, he still gathered snails, but he fed them to the chickens instead of selling them. He sold chickens and eggs and turned a handsome profit. Frank saved enough money to buy a bicycle, which he used to run a newspaper route. He was busy all the time, and Frank saved his money. Whenever his older brother John got a few pennies together, he spent them at the candy store, but not Frank. "Everything he touched turned to gold," said his older sister, Ann Christine. "We used to get ten cents a week allowance. In those days, we could buy a candy bar and go to the show on that one thin dime, but Frank stayed home and saved his money!"

Somehow, Frank found time to attend Washington Street, and later, Vermont Avenue grammar schools. Finally, he attended Los Angeles High School. Located at Olympic and Rimpau, L. A. High was a sprawling complex, covering a three-block area, with buildings three and four stories high. The main entrance was below a tall tower. Frank traveled about half an hour to and from school via streetcar. He majored in Latin because his mother wanted it. His real passion, though, was mathematics, with history ranking a close second.

Gus operated his shop for five years on the second floor of his rented home at 2000 Moneta Street in the West Adams District of Los Angeles, an area described by Christine as . . . "a very nice, wealthy parish. Theda Bera, the silent film star, used to live near us." The rococo two-story frame house boasted a broad, wide front porch where the children played and shared a series of misadventures.

"There was a big oak tree in the front yard," Christine remembered, "with limbs overhanging the front porch. One time, when I was about five years old, John and I pushed the old sofa that always sat on the porch over to the edge near the tree. I climbed onto the back of the sofa, tried to jump over to a tree limb, and missed. I was out cold for several hours and my hip was dislocated, but I had no broken bones. As soon as my hip was better, I fell downstairs and dislocated it again.

"When Frank was about four years old, a neighbor was burning some oily rags in the yard. Frank was standing nearby when some older kids came by and pushed him headlong into the fire. Frank scrambled out, but his clothes were in flames. He was pretty badly burned. In those days, you didn't go to a doctor with every little thing. Mother spread some lard over the burned areas and covered them with clean cloth. As far as I know, Frank never had any scars from it."

In his mid-teens, Frank made an abortive effort to escape his destiny. This was but the dawn of the "Big Band" era, with Paul Whiteman as the reigning "king." Gus had always loved music, especially the hofbrau bands with their noisy "um pa pa" brass section, but only as a spectator. If there was one thing that Frank was

Frank worked on .45 ACP Colt automatics for top marksmen of the Los Angeles Police Department, including top competitor Tommy Carr.

A MODEST BEGINNING

not, it was a "spectator." He was a doer from day one, and his interest in music was no different—he wanted to be a participant. He wanted to lead his own band, but he had to start someplace. In the window of a pawn shop in downtown Los Angeles, Frank spotted the glistening brass of an nearly new saxophone. Proving that he was willing to spend his hard-earned savings for something he really wanted, Frank invested in the shiny saxophone. How was he going to break the news to his father? Frank reasoned that if he could play the instrument well, he could demonstrate to Gus that his aspirations were realistic, and the old man would allow him to pursue a career as a musician.

To that end, Frank started taking music lessons on the quiet. After several months of intensive practice, Frank was able to coax several popular themes from the sax. His mother Anna was privy to his scheme and encouraged him to talk to Gus. Any outside observer could have told young Frank and his mother that the entire effort was doomed from the outset. Gus was pleasantly surprised to find that his youngest son could play a musical instrument, but when Frank talked about becoming a professional musician, his father went into a towering rage that could be heard in Santa Monica. "No son of mine is going to be a music player. You vill be a gunsmidt." With a sigh of resignation, Frank packed the saxophone away in a box in the attic never to use it again.

John Pachmayr also suffered from his father's damaging vetoes. A skilled rifleman, John qualified for the National Matches three years running. Whenever he approached Gus for time off to go to Camp Perry, Gus would rant, "You vant to go off shooding when we haf all diss vork to do? No!"

To economize on rent, Gus moved his family to 2726 Menlo Avenue to a home surrounded by open fields and tulle marshes. As a youth, Frank hunted ducks in an area now buried deep in concrete and studded with towering glass and steel structures. With his new home far removed from downtown, Gus began looking for larger, more appropriate quarters. In 1919 he settled for a loft over Lail's Garage at 812 South Grand at the hub of "Automobile Row," where new and used car dealers dominated both sides of the street. The old, yellow streetcar rumbled and rattled by on shining steel rails in the middle of Grand Street. It was powered by high-voltage electrical wires strung overhead, and it ran every quarter hour. The vehicle provided convenient low-cost transportation to everyone, including many of Gus's customers. Gus remained at that address until he had difficulty climbing the stairs in his old age.

At the Grand Street location Frank continued to work for his demanding father for $15.00 a week, a rather paltry wage even then. Gus was instilled with the "Old Country" philosophy that all members of the family worked in the business with little or no reward. This attitude was, and still is, one of the strengths of immigrant families wedging their way into the American business world. Often it leads to powerful family empires, but sometimes younger members grow restless with the long wait to enter the business and become full partners. Frequently, the young leave home and the business and the dynasty crumbles.

· FRANK PACHMAYR ·

Of course, Frank realized there were many side benefits from his apprenticeship under the unremitting tutelage of his father. He learned virtually every facet of gunsmithing from his stern father. He also made valuable contacts that would stand him in good stead when he was ready to solo.

Frank realized early that his father was not a financial wizard; in fact, Gus cared little for money. He was basically a very simple, modest person. He was secure in the knowledge that he was a more than a competent gunsmith and an excellent marksman with rifle or shotgun. He made Sunday pilgrimages to either the trap range or to nearby Schuetzen Park where he was a consistent winner of local matches. Apparently Gus cared little for handguns or pistol shooting. He aspired to no more than he had. He saw no need to strive for financial success. As long as there were enough customers to keep him busy, Gus was content.

It was apparent to Frank that if he wanted to attain financial heights, he would have to escape his father's domination. Frank's older brother, John, had already flown the nest as soon as he was twenty-one—working as a mechanic for Studebaker then later Dusenburg new car dealers. Frank planned for the day when he could start a gun shop of his own. Much of the traffic at Gus's shop actually came from Frank's steady customers. The crack marksmen of the Los Angeles Police Department beat a steady path to Gus, seeking out the skills of his talented son. Frank was already well known as one of the premier pistolsmiths in the area, long before he set out on his own.

The real catalyst finally came in the person of Nanitta Laughlin, a petite movie-star-pretty teenager, who happened along in the company of her aunt and uncle, Arline and Charles Jones. Charlie had come to Gus with an ailing shotgun. Frank admits, "It was love at first sight. I was on the phone almost before Nanitta got home. On our first date, we went ice skating up at Big Bear Lake. On weekends, I used to take her with me when I went shooting at the Elysian Park Pistol Range.

"I always test fired the pistols that I worked on, especially when I installed custom sights. Sometimes, I had to full-auto test fire an LAPD Tommy Gun (Thompson submachine gun). I maintained their entire arsenal. The Los Angeles Police Department used the Elysian range to practice and qualify. Later, Elysian Park became the Los Angeles Police Academy. Nan and I knew just about every cop in town by his first name. Chief Davis used to see us at the range, and he'd always ask, 'When are you two kids going to get married?' He invited us to many department dinners that were usually confined to uniformed personnel."

Frank knew full well that he couldn't support a wife on $15.00 a week, so he made the decision to strike out on his own. Among Gus's customers was Bud Crook, the western distributor for Caterpillar farm and garden tractors at 1220 South Grand Avenue. He had taken a liking to Frank and John. When he heard that Frank was looking for a business location, he said, "Why don't you come on over to my place? I'm moving some of the tractors out. You can have a corner of the showroom." Frank jumped at the chance.

• A MODEST BEGINNING •

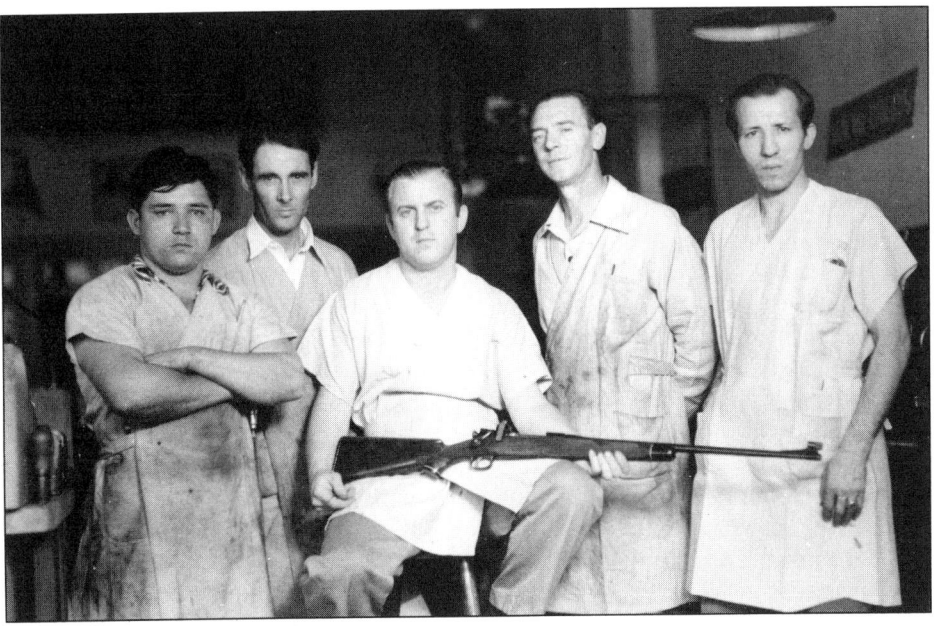

After he had established a reputation for fine craftsmanship, Frank gathered a group of skilled gunsmiths to handle the workload. This picture was taken in June 1935, nearly five years after Frank opened his shop at 1220 South Grand Avenue, in Los Angeles. From left to right are Walter Smithing, Foster Lloyd, Frank, Bert Brokeway, and Walter Strand. For most of his life Strand worked for Frank.

At the age of twenty-three in December of 1929 with America's economy poised on the brink of the biggest depression in its history, Frank set up a ten-foot work bench in a corner of Crook's showroom. He couldn't have dreamed then that someday his name would be among the most revered and honored in the field of firearms. That was way in the future.

To equip the shop, Frank borrowed $350 from Bud Crook (which he repaid out of store revenue in just six months). He bought a drill press, a grinder, a bench vice, and some basic hand tools. Included, of course, was an array of mill files that was adequate, but hardly rivaled Gus's collection. To say the least, Frank was fully schooled in the use of hand tools, but as is universally true of youth, he was aggressively seeking new and better ways to perform the customary tasks of gunsmithing. He was also looking toward new gun-oriented products to make and sell. As soon as he could afford it, Frank purchased a West Bend bench lathe to round out his machinery. If only he could have looked into the future and seen himself as the owner of hundreds of thousands of dollars worth of high tech, mass production machinery, he would certainly have been amazed.

The now world-famous Los Angeles urban sprawl was just beginning when Frank opened his modest gun shop. The city was already encroaching upon the orange groves that surrounded the civic center. Bud Crook found his market for tractors drying up. Following his customers to the outskirts of town, he moved south to Santa Fe Avenue where he shifted the emphasis of his business to making asphalt for streets and highways, and he became rich in the process.

When Crook vacated the large display room at 1220 South Grand, the recently launched Pachmayr's Gun Works took over half the frontage. Sharing the other half of the store front with Frank was an automobile insurance firm. The rear of the building was occupied by a welding shop, with "Wild Bill" Bannerman as sole proprietor and worker. Wild Bill was one of the few welders in Los Angeles at the time who could work on aluminum.

Business became brisk. Frank invited his brother John to join him. "It wasn't a formal partnership," explains Frank. "It was just a family thing. We shared the work and the income." But Frank was the businessman. He handled the money and paid the bills. Frank Pachmayr may well have been the original role model for the classic "workaholic." When he wasn't repairing or customizing guns, he was waiting on customers and selling guns across the counter. He often worked well past midnight on guns or just catching up on paperwork.

Despite an iron constitution and fierce ambition, the work load was overwhelming, so Frank hired a young gunsmith, Walter Strand. Walter worked for Frank for more than fifty years. Walter was a speed ice skater with Olympic potential. From 1929 to 1945, he was Pacific Coast Champion Speed Skater. Walter was always in training for the International Olympics and qualified for three times, but because of the expense involved and the lack of a sponsor, Walter was never able to compete. He always kept himself in shape by entering local events, though. Walter, who had the thighs and calves of a wrestler, was also an indefatigable hiker and a rugged hunter, and he and Frank often hunted together.

Walter worked for Frank on and off for most of his life. Even after he was ostensibly "retired," Walter continued to carry out assignments for Frank in his home workshop. In his eighty-seventh year, as he was making stocks for the fine custom shotguns Frank was preparing for Ducks Unlimited, Walter died of a heart attack. He was a cheerful, vital, active man up to his final day.

Walter remembered the early days with Frank. "I was working for Frank as a gunsmith," he told me before his death, "but I wanted to make gunstocks. My father was a cabinetmaker and he taught me how to work with wood. I borrowed some tools from him, and I made a stock and fore-end for an L. C. Smith double-barreled shotgun that I had. The trigger was giving me some trouble, so I took it to Frank. 'Frank, can you fix this trigger for me,' I asked him. Frank took a look at he stock and fore-end, and said, 'Did you make this stock?' I said, 'I sure did!' Frank was impressed. He said, 'Stay after work, and I'll show you how to make fine European-styled gunstocks.' Of course, I took him up on it. After Frank closed the shop, we would sit in the back with just the bench lights burning and talk about guns and hunting. We'd have a few beers, eat crackers and sliced baloney, and work on stocks.

"I learned a lot from Frank's father too, just watching him work. Gus paid me to come to his shop every week and clean up. Every week, I found his bench piled high with wood chips. He would lay his tools down and cover them up with shavings, but

A MODEST BEGINNING

somehow he always knew under which pile of chips to look for any particular tool that he wanted. The Old Man could reach into a pile of shavings and come up with the chisel, rasp, or drawknife he needed. I would sweep his bench clean with a whisk broom and carefully return each tool to the exact spot and in the same position that I found it. If I moved a tool or put it away where it belonged, he was all over me. After I cleaned up, I'd hang around and watch him work. He was a wizard with a drawknife. Sometimes he used a spokeshave. When he finished carving a stock, it didn't need any rasp work, just a little sanding. That's how close he worked. Sometimes Gus would let me help him, and that's a privilege he reserved for damn few people.

"Gus moved awful fast. I'd say to him, 'August, let's go hunting.' And he'd say, 'Ya, I vill. But I hafe to make a stock for dis rifle virst.' Then he'd bandsaw the outline on a blank according to his own pattern and have at it with that sharp drawknife. He had a lot of stamina. He'd work all night and have the stock rough finished to shoot the next morning when I picked him up to go hunting. As he got up in years, Old Gus lost a lot of weight. His face and shoulders got thinner. His old stocks didn't fit him like they did before. As a result, he missed birds that he could have easily dropped when he was younger, and it made him mad. He was always making new stocks or working on his old ones trying to get the fit back.

"And Gus was always changing the chokes on his shotguns, reaming, and re-reaming them. He thought somewhere out there was that magic choke that just couldn't miss. He used to pattern shotguns for hours on end and some of his patterns were outstanding. He was stretching the effective range of his shotguns by about ten yards, and that was using the old loads. When the sleeved shot shells came along, it changed everything. If I was hitting real good on some days, Gus would ask me, 'Vat choke do you hafe on dat gun?'

"Gus resented it when the boys struck out on their own. For a long time, Gus and the boys weren't talking to each other. I wanted to try to get them back together, so I told Gus, 'Why don't you come down to the shop and see the boys? They're anxious to see you, but they're afraid to come back here because they think that you'll kick their butts.' Gus laughed and said, 'Ya, I vould, and they know dat!' So I lured Gus down to the shop."

Whenever one of the big double doors of Pachmayr's Gun Shop swung wide, Frank and the gunsmiths were in the habit of glancing up to see if it was a customer. On this momentous day, the buzz of conversation among the boys suddenly halted as they caught sight of the tall, erect figure of Gus Pachmayr walking alongside Walter Strand. Every eye was on Gus. A lathe that was humming off in a corner of the room, whirred down and went silent. Never the timid one, Gus strode up to the gun counter, hammered the top of the bench with a fist the size of a dinner ham, and his strident voice boomed out, "Vell, vat are you poys up to now?" It was with a fervent sense of relief that Frank and John shook hands with their father after months of uneasiness and tension. After a short inspection tour—it didn't take long, because the shop was pretty small—Gus, Frank, and John repaired to the nearby hofbrau for a hearty meal and some cold beer to warm their hearts after a long, uncomfortable frost.

· FRANK PACHMAYR ·

When times were lean, Walter Strand would tour the numerous hock shops in the Los Angeles area and buy up old guns that could be repaired, re-blued, and restocked, then sold at a profit. "I'd make the stocks," Walter said, "and Frank would checker them. We could always find parts for old guns at Western Hoegee over on Main Street. If they didn't have a part, they'd get it for you. We'd rebuild guns and set them in the rack for sale. That got us through some tough times."

By 1934, Frank employed five gunsmiths, including his brother John, Walter Strand, Bert Burkow, Foster Doyle, and Walter Smith. J. B. Buchanan, who later gained fame for his work on the .45 ACP Government Model Colt, also worked for Frank.

During those early days, the welder who occupied the rear of the building moved out and was replaced by Ray Stair, who operated the Stair Rubber Molding Company. This was a happy coincidence for Frank, who was seeking a cost-effective way to produce his revolver grip adapter in quantity. Frank carved his first adapter from walnut when he was only eighteen years old, shaping a wooden block to fill the space between the grip and trigger guard of his Smith & Wesson .38 Special Military & Police revolver. It was to be many years before revolver makers offered OEM grips that considered the human hand as a design factor. The deep dip behind the trigger guard of both Smith & Wesson and Colt revolvers positioned the revolver too low in the hand, making accurate shooting difficult and causing recoil pain even when firing such a mild cartridge as the .38 Special. The New Service Colt, chambered for the .44 Special or .45-rimmed Colt, could be miserable to shoot. Military revolvers, chambered for the .45 ACP, were equally unhandy. Little wonder then that demand for the Pachmayr "Sure Grip Adapter" was brisk from the outset.

When Ray Star moved in, Frank seized upon the idea of molding the adapter from hard rubber. He designed a simple brass horseshoe clip that went on over the frame to hold it in place. The customer merely loosened the grip screw, slipped the adapter into place, and retightened the screw. The improvement in the feel of the revolver was immense. (*I had several Gold Seal Smith & Wesson .38 Special revolvers and a .44 Special "Triple Lock" Smith equipped with Pachmayr Grip Adapters. I couldn't have made it without them.*)

Frank had launched a new and profitable career. Beginning in 1931, he manufactured the Sure Grip Adapter in small, medium, and large sizes and shaped it to fit revolvers from both major makers. This item is still cataloged by Pachmayr, Ltd., and remains popular to this day. Flushed with this early success, Frank set out to design a practical recoil pad. He eagerly read every book he could find on the subject of rubber molding and directed some probing questions to local molders. In 1932, he began producing his first "Whiteline" pads with the familiar double-cross waffle pattern on the sides. Skeet and trap shooters praised the new pad.

In just five years, young Frank Pachmayr had become renowned as one of the nation's leading gunsmiths and as an inventor and manufacturer of practical and popular firearm accessories. He established a carriage-trade clientele that included industrial leaders and moneyed families in the area, as well as film stars from nearby Hollywood. By working on their guns or building custom guns for them, Frank became good friends with a number of Hollywood luminaries. Among

· A MODEST BEGINNING ·

When Frank occupied the front of the building, he installed sales counters and gun racks.

Frank's customers was Gary Cooper, a competition-level skeet shooter. Film star Robert Stack, whom Frank first met while still working for Gus over Lail's garage, became National Skeet Champion when he was only sixteen years old. Bobby Stack was only five years old and his brother Jimmy was seven when they came to Gus's shop with their father, a millionaire Chicago businessman.

An article by Jack Russell, appearing in the *Pacific Sportsman* in 1934, summarized Frank's attainments:

> Possibly nowhere else in America is there to be found a progressive gunsmith shop equal to that operated by Frank Pachmayr, 1220 South Grand Ave., Los Angeles, Calif. Its history is unique. Mr. Pachmayr is a young man, 27 years old, and has been brought up under the careful guidance of his father, Mr. August Pachmayr, who for more than fifty years has followed the gunsmith business, having learned his trade as a boy in the great Mannlicher-Schoenauer plants and other great factories of Germany. Mr. Pachmayr, Sr. has been continuously engaged in the gunsmith business in Los Angeles for more than twenty-five years.
>
> In 1929, Frank Pachmayr entered business on his own, and with his scientific and practical knowledge, the business has prospered, and today he operates the largest custom-made shop on the Pacific Slope. He has invented, developed, improved and patented many of the most practical gun appliances, among which are

the following: Pachmayr Sure Grip Adapters for Colt and Smith & Wesson revolvers, now being universally adopted by the police departments of the Western section of the nation. The White Line Recoil Absorber, purely a scientific and practical appliance for rifles and shotguns and unequaled anywhere for its effectiveness. One of the most beneficial products recently put on the market is the Sure Sight Gauger, for adjusting the adjustable sights for various ranges on Colt revolvers. Shortly the Sight Gauger will be adapted for use on Smith & Wesson guns.

For the skeet, trap, and field shooter, the new Pachmayr Pneumatic-Recoil Cushion, the only device of its type on the market, has taken the field by storm. It is said to be the one and only device that makes possible the continued long shooting over trap or skeet fields, without receiving excessive shock.

This young chap is today doing the largest portion of revolver repair, adjusting and modernizing for the Los Angeles Police Department, as well as for county and state officers.

Frank Pachmayr installed the Cutts Compensator for such notable persons as Mr. Clark Gable, the motion-picture actor, and Mr. John Barrymore, famous on both stage and screen, and for the great All Western and State champion skeet shot, Mr. Al Lucas, who broke 209 birds with the device. This attracted the attention of Mr. Henry W. Lyman, president of the great Lyman Gun Sight Corporation of Middlefield, Conn., who immediately appointed Mr. Pachmayr as southwestern representative for his company. The installation of the Cutts Compensator is now universally used by California skeet shooters. We predict that within the next ten years, Mr. Frank Pachmayr will be second to none on the American continent in gunsmith work on revolvers, rifles, and shotguns, as well as machine guns and other firearms.

Mr. Russell's prediction was more than fulfilled in the decades that followed. Pachmayr Gun Works expanded inexorably over the years. A full-service sportsmen's and outfitters' store slowly evolved, pushing the gun-repair department into the rear area of the building. Frank purchased the adjoining building to house his staff offices. He had an up-to-date machining operation turning out his Lo-Swing telescopic mount, plus tooling for a comprehensive array of recoil pad types and styles. By 1941 Frank had eight employees in the sporting-goods store, which was grossing about $75,000 annually. He was turning out hundreds of thousands of recoil pads, Grip Adapters, and Lo-Swing Mounts.

Frank was happy. He envisioned expanding markets and a broader product line all associated with firearms. He had time to hunt, fish, and operate his business at a fast, but bearable pace. These halcyon years were soon to end. It seems a diminutive Austrian paperhanger with a toothbrush mustache and a Charlie Chaplainesque look was about to make a vast impact upon Frank's life, which would change direction forever. Heartaches were waiting in the wings, but so also was a vast and lightning expansion of Frank's entrepreneurial and engineering talents. World War II was about to start.

•••

· Chapter II ·

FRANK AND THE .45

During the 1930s, the rather low scores that won pistol matches were a reflection of the crude guns of the period. Frank Pachmayr had the knack to determine a gun's shortcomings and could make alterations to correct them. He pioneered changes in the .45 ACP Government Model pistols that made it possible for this pistol to set records on NRA firing lines. Almost to a man, the ten-million soldiers fielded by Uncle Sam during World War II as well as thousands more unwilling participants in the several "police actions" since will ruefully attest that the pistol, United States caliber .45, M-1911(A1), AKA the "Government Model," or simply the ".45 Auto," is a cantankerous slab of stubborn steel that kicks brutally and is impossible to shoot accurately.

Ex-GIs might not be the best authorities on the abilities of the .45 ACP. In boot camp, they were handed thirty to fifty rounds of live ammo and given perhaps half a day of "familiarization." Rarely did anyone, except officers and MPs, handle the big pistol again during an actual tour of duty. Infantrymen had little time, and less reason, to learn to love the gun. Then again, perhaps the reputation for bad nature and poor performance on the part of the Model 1911 was honestly won. Deliberately designed with sloppy tolerances, so that a dunk in the mud served only to better lubricate it, a GI .45 ACP, and even many early commercial Colt Government Model pistols, did deliver groups roughly the size of a ten-gallon hat at fifty yards.

Despite or because of this, the .45 ACP was and is required equipment for big-bore NRA target competition. Only reluctantly did match competitors in the past take the ugly brute in hand for the big-bore leg matches. Yet today, the .45 ACP Colt or Colt-clone is the weapon of choice for most competitors, both in NRA shoots and the rapidly burgeoning IPSC and combat-styled matches.

The man who most deserves credit for this metamorphosis from beast to beauty is Frank A. Pachmayr. From the beginning, though, Frank was just another young man launching a tenuous career during a period in our nation's history when financial success was unlikely. It was in December 1929, with the nation poised on the brink of depression, when Frank rented a small corner of a showroom at 1220 South Grand Avenue, Los Angeles, California, which remained his retail store until recently. From the beginning though, Frank became known as the man to see for the finest in pistolsmithing. His father's lessons in firearm precision were still ringing in his ears.

Even before he left his father's shop, Frank was moonlighting for many officers of the Los Angeles Police Department. LAPD officers were red-hot marksmen at Regional and National Matches. They needed super-tuned equipment to remain competitive in the highly volatile target-shooting game. The wails of woe from shooters attempting to achieve winning scores with a pistol that rattled like a rusty hinge reached young Frank's ears. The .45 ACP, either in the rough-hewn military version, or the highly polished, brilliantly blued civilian Colt, had such gaping fits that the hefty pistol sounded like castanets when vigorously shaken. Frank set out to tighten the tolerances.

Beginning around 1930, Frank Pachmayr was the first commercial gunsmith to try to make this pistol shoot accurately. Charles Askins, a noted firearm authority and an important figure in pistol shooting, told me that Marine Corps armorers had tried to make some internal improvements on competition guns sometime earlier. Their work consisted of trying different inventory parts to get the best fits, as opposed to any gunsmithing operations. Frank maintains that his work on making pistols shoot accurately even predated the Marine Corps' efforts.

About 1935 United States Secretary of the Treasury Henry Morganthau decided that treasury department officers should learn to shoot. He instituted a marksmanship training program, using Coast Guard pistol experts for instructors. To encourage continued interest in marksmanship, Secretary Morganthau ordered a series of NRA elimination matches among teams representing various bureaus, such as the Secret Service, Customs, Alcohol Tax, Narcotics, Treasury Guards, White House Police, Bureau of the Mint, and Bureau of Engraving and Printing.

The Bureau of Customs gave themselves a decided edge when the entire five-man team, including the formidable Percy M. Chapman, handed their guns over to Frank Pachmayr for fine tuning. A letter from Sgt. Melton R. Rogers of the Northwest Patrol District, dated 28 May 1940, recalls a junior team member shooting ninety-four slow fire, one-hundred timed fire, and ninety-nine rapid fire over the National Match Course. He used a Pachmayr-tuned .45 ACP—not bad, even by today's standards. Frank altered .45s for such early-day NRA champions as Harry W. Reeves, Tommy Karr, Al Hemming, and Lee Echols.

As Frank describes it today, "More than forty years ago, several well-known shooters asked me if I could develop a way to improve the accuracy of the Model 1911(A1) Colt .45 auto pistol. I knew the accuracy of this fine, dependable handgun was adversely affected because the barrel moved during each firing cycle and seldom returned to exactly the same position in battery. To overcome this, I developed improvements that forced the barrel to return as nearly as possible to the same position each time. The real test came when the United States Treasury Team, Bureau of Customs Division, used our modified Colts at the Detroit 'Pre-

• FRANK AND THE .45 •

Frank Pachmayr pioneered the concept of transforming the loosely fitted Colt .45 ACP Government Model into an accurate target pistol. To test the results of his work, he constructed a machine rest in his basement target range. Here he checks twenty-five-yard target groups of ten shots in one hole.

Perry' matches that year. All five members shot with our improved .45s , and they broke the existing team record by twenty-three points."

Frank's methods were validated in competition, and today they are accepted as SOP. He must have wondered, though, when faced with that first .45, "What do I do now?" The point of initial attack was the cavernous contact between the slide and frame. Judicious wielding of a three-pound rawhide mallet along the sides of the slide and back from the area of the slide-stop disassembly slot, eliminated horizontal play. This process required patience and finesse. It was easy to close the gap too much and make it impossible to get the slide back onto the frame. It was and still is a lot harder to separate the slide rails than it was to close them. Variations in steel alloys and heat treatments among the many war surplus Model 1911s, and even among commercial Colts of different periods of manufacture, caused problems as well. A soft slide would bend too easily, and some tough ones stoutly resisted the most vigorous hammering. Frank knew how to work slowly and feel his way along.

Removing vertical play is just as tricky. Frank fabricated close-fitting adapters to support the frame in a heavy vise without damaging the weapon. Then he

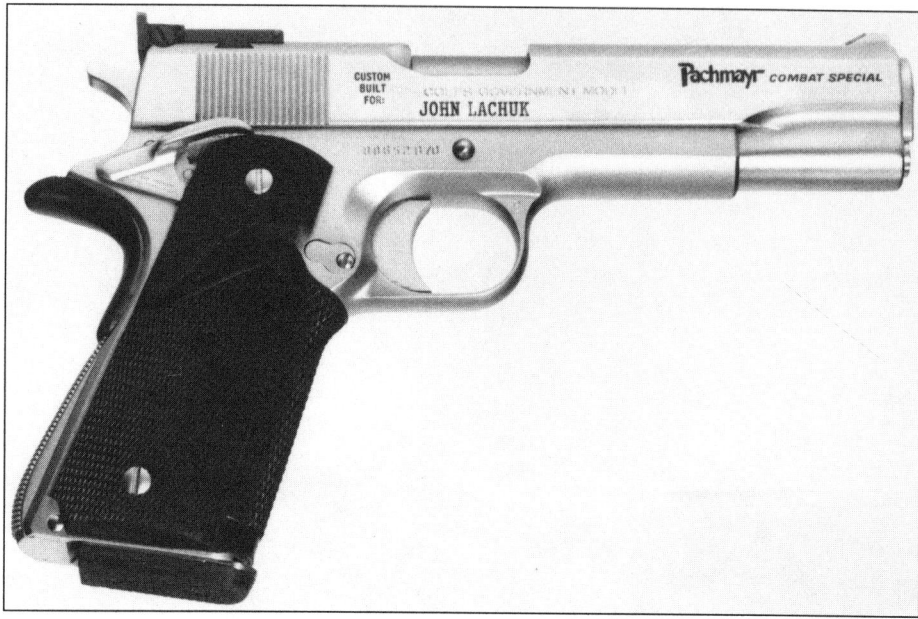

This Pachmayr Combat Special was custom-built for the author. It has all the tightening procedures Frank devised in the early 1930s. The slide-frame fit is tightened, a Bar-Sto stainless steel barrel is installed, and a Swenson ambidextrous thumb safety is added. Note Pachmayr neoprene rubber grips and grip safety.

hammered the rails with light overlapping blows, concentrating upon the areas fore and aft of the magazine well, until the slide had to be forced onto the frame. Frank refused to resort to the "easy out" used by the majority of gunsmiths—the use of an abrasive clover compound to lap the slide into place on the frame.

"No matter how much you clean the gun after using a lapping compound, abrasive particles work their way into the pores of the steel," he declares, "and that accelerates wear as the gun is used."

Despite the fact it was time-consuming, Frank preferred to use a die marker to detect tight places and carefully file and stone the contact points of the rails until the slide articulated on the frame as if it were on ball bearings. To make the fit of the barrel firm at the muzzle, Frank turned the barrel in a lathe between centers to make the outside concentric with the bore, thus relieving it one-hundredth of an inch. He began this operation ¾ of an inch back from the muzzle. He then sleeved the bushing and reamed it to a bare slip fit at the muzzle. After Colt began manufacturing their .38 Super Auto pistol with a smaller outside diameter barrel, Frank bought Colt barrel bushings with the smaller hole and reamed them to fit.

If you remove the barrel and slide from a .45 frame, then return the barrel to a locked position in the slide and survey the assembly from the bottom, you'll see as much light around the barrel hood as you would looking up through the shingles of an old barn. Frank recognized that this looseness had to be changed. To this end, he welded a bead around the barrel hood, then dressed off the excess with a file. The opening in the slide was shaped into a gentle inverted "V," and the barrel tang shaped to a wedge fit, thus eliminating rotary motion. Length was trimmed to afford proper headspace. A new longer link was fitted to raise the barrel well up into firm engagement with the locking lugs in the slide. At first, Frank tried bottoming the barrel in the locking lugs, but that tended to set the rear of the barrel at an angle that was too high, making the front sight also too high. Later he settled upon welding the barrel lug and fitting the bottom curvature where the link swiveled tightly against the slide stop pin, thus keeping the barrel parallel to the slide. After fitting, the slide locked into battery with a crisp "snap," effectively locking the slide, frame, and barrel into one solid block of steel.

Realizing that trying to measure a pistol's inherent accuracy by shooting it, even two-handed across a rest, was a poor method at best, Frank determined to

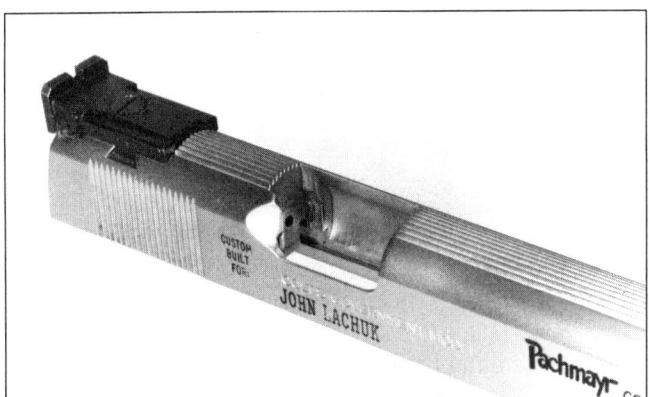

The ejection port was lowered and faired back to prevent damage to cartridge cases as they ejected, which is a boon to reloaders.

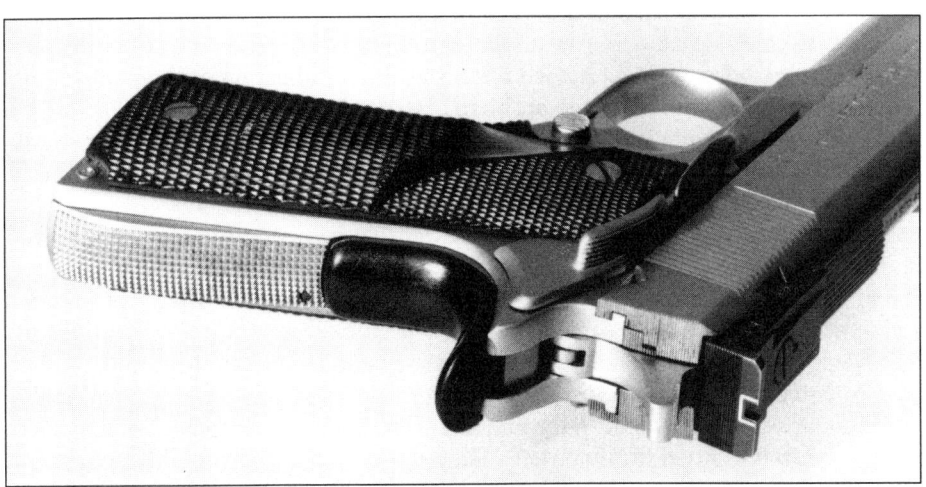

The rear of the slide was nonreflection serrated, the mainspring housing deeply checkered, and a Pachmayr neoprene grip safety installed.

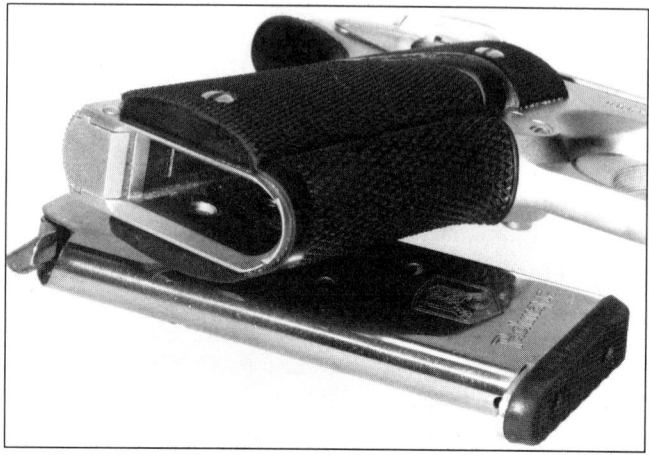

Flaring or funneling the magazine chute allows quicker speed reloading that is free of fumbling.

make a mechanical tester to remove human error from the process. He made his first machine rest large and heavy for stability. He built it on a platform that was solidly braced and bolted to the concrete-reinforced brick wall of the Pachmayr's basement indoor target range. A pair of large-diameter, heat-treated, centerless-ground steel rods, supported two "V" blocks that held the massive steel channel forming the main platform. Atop the platform, a skeleton truss held the gun (without its grips) firmly clamped between two precision-fitted, milled, steel adapter plates. A mechanical trigger fired the gun without disturbing its position. Recoil was directed straight to the rear with no effort to simulate the rotating wrist action of a shooter. Recoil momentum was quickly absorbed by friction and the weight of the platform.

Test firing in this machine gave the first true indications of the intrinsic accuracy of the famed .45 auto, before and after treatment. The mere fact of constructing such an elaborate testing device was in itself an indication of the painstaking approach Frank took to solve the problem. Before they were improved, .45 ACPs could only manage eight- to ten-inch groups at twenty-five yards. After Frank developed their accuracy, both GI and Colt Government Model autos routinely grouped well under two inches.

Frank discovered to his dismay, however, that some auto loaders simply refused to shoot well, despite his best efforts. It was then that he began to suspect that all barrels were not made equal. To test the barrel alone seemed an impossible assignment. A .45 ACP barrel couldn't be fired except in a gun—or could it? Again with the eyes of an analytical engineer, Frank Pachmayr pioneered another device, one that remains exclusive to this day. He machined a fixture that held a .45 ACP barrel rigidly outside of the gun and provided a spring-loaded firing mechanism. The fixture fitted firmly onto Pachmayr's pistol rest. He quickly confirmed his suspicions regarding inherent barrel accuracy. From a batch of new Colt barrels he had on hand, some cut a single cloverleaf at twenty-five yards. Others scattered a shotgun pattern.

· FRANK AND THE .45 ·

From that day on, Frank tested every barrel. Any barrel that couldn't deliver groups of an inch at twenty-five yards was rejected. Some barrels actually provided groups that measured an honest quarter-inch, center-to-center at twenty-five yards. When they became available, years later, Frank switched exclusively to new Colt National Match barrels, which he ordered in quantity. Testing continued with the same stringent standards, and only about half of Colt's premium barrels met Frank's standards. The balance was rejected. Even more recently, Pachmayr's adopted the exclusive use of BAR-STO Precision Machine Co. Stainless Steel Match Barrels, justly noted for their outstanding accuracy. With this adoption, the rejections ended abruptly.

Regardless of how mechanically perfect he made a Colt .45, Frank found that it was impossible to shoot accurately with the rough, creepy trigger in the design. By carefully removing tool marks from the contact surfaces of the sear and hammer notch with an aluminum oxide, Medium India stone, then burnishing the surfaces to mirror brightness with a Hard Arkansas stone, Frank removed the roughness. By making the hammer notch a little more shallow, he reduced the creep. Nevertheless, there was a limit to this. If the sear notch was too shallow, the "safety notch" above it would strike the sear as the hammer fell, damage the sear, and cushion the hammer blow, thereby causing misfires and poor accuracy.

Some shooters mistakenly regarded the safety notch, like that of the single-action Colt Frontier revolver, as a place to hang the hammer of a loaded gun. That practice is not safe even with the original Colt Peacemaker. Smart shooters leave an empty chamber under the hammer when carrying an original-styled, single-action revolver. Carrying a .45 ACP with the hammer on the half-cock notch is an invitation to disaster. The deep notch was designed by Colt to catch the sear and prevent the hammer from following the slide as it returned to battery or to prevent jarring from the sear notch and causing an accidental discharge.

With careful workmanship, Frank discovered that it was possible to achieve a crisp trigger release weighing as little as 2.5 pounds with no danger of double firing or the hammer following the slide when it was dropped on an empty chamber. Wise shooters know that it's best to lower the slide gently when not loading a cartridge to reduce wear and impact damage to action components in the gun. Dropping the slide without a loaded magazine is used as a stringent test of safety, however. If the hammer falls in response to the wrenching jar of the slide slamming into the battery, the trigger pull cannot be regarded as safe. Match rules required that the .45 ACP used in leg matches be nominally, "as issued." Tuning was not prohibited, as long as the trigger release was not less than 4 pounds. The trick for Frank was to make the trigger release crisp and at exactly the required weight, no more, no less. He devised a fixture that jigged the sear and hammer at exactly the correct angles. It held them between hardened steel inserts, allowing stoning to precise angles to get the correct pull weight.

One factor that largely escaped detection by most early .45 ACP gunsmiths was the fact that the long steel trigger itself was a problem. When the trigger release was brought within desirable limits, the inertia of the heavy, long trigger caused it to bounce back against the disconnector and drop the hammer, causing mysterious, intermittent "doubles"—two rounds released with one squeeze of the trigger. Frank's analytical mind led to an early discovery of this phenomenon, and he skeletonized the long trigger by drilling holes or by switching to the lighter-weight short trigger.

One of Frank's early techniques, which is virtually forgotten by today's gunsmiths, consisted of welding the nose of the grip safety, then carefully hand filing it to intercept the trigger bow just as the sear released, thereby eliminating objectionable overtravel. The backlash inherent in the original Colt Government Model design is anathema to target shooters because it causes the gun to move at the instant of firing, delivering those highly objectionable eight-ring hits. Today, you can buy a lightweight nylon, long trigger made by Pachmayr, with a built-in over-travel-adjusting Allen-head screw already in place at the bottom. A number of other aftermarket, lightweight target triggers are available today with the over-travel adjustment.

Despite labor, plus parts, would you believe that in the "old days" Frank's total charge for fine tuning a .45 ACP was just $25.00? As late as the early 1960s,

A long-barreled version of the Signature System became popular with pistol silhouette shooters.

· FRANK AND THE .45 ·

A key part of the Signature System was a "Slide Guide," or yoke, that attached under the frame at the rear by means of a centerless ground, long link pin and exerted upward pressure on the slide. A tension adjustment, Allen screw in a boss at the bottom impinged upon the trigger guard.

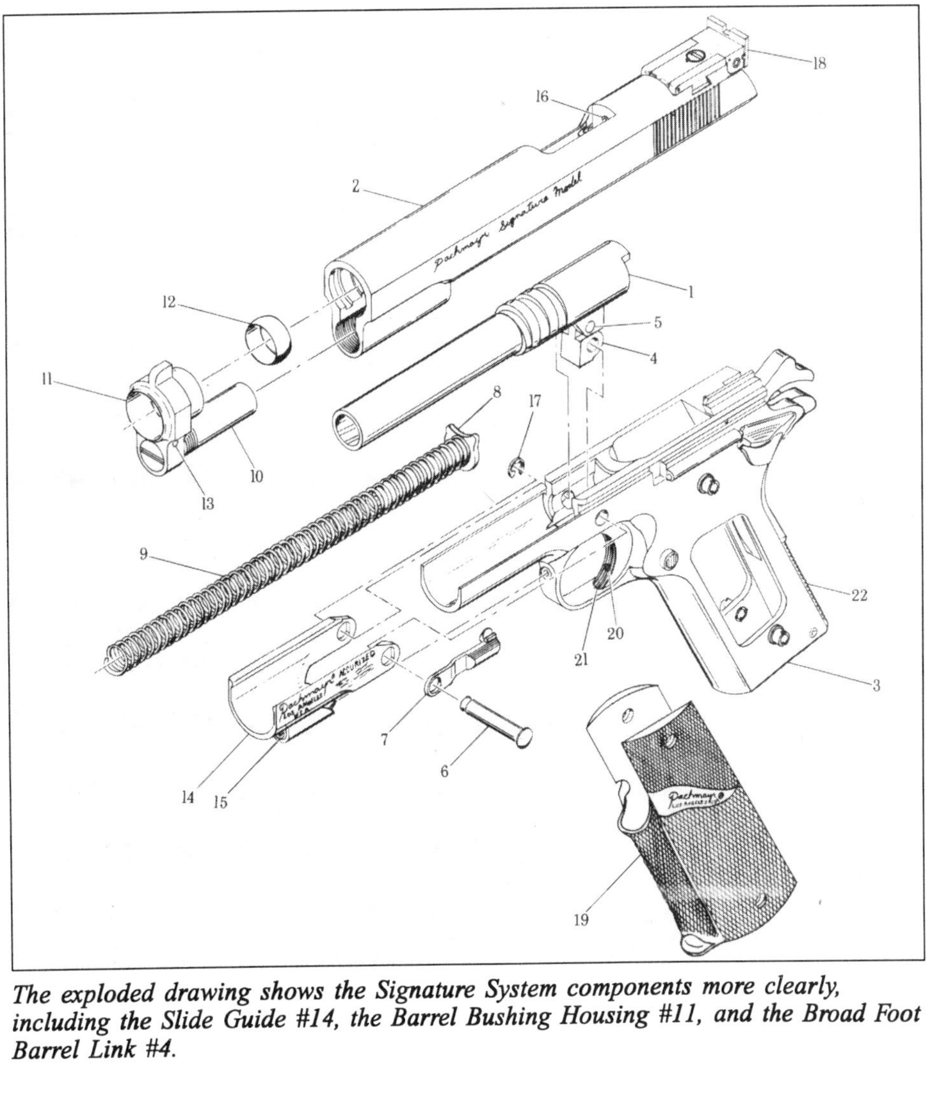

The exploded drawing shows the Signature System components more clearly, including the Slide Guide #14, the Barrel Bushing Housing #11, and the Broad Foot Barrel Link #4.

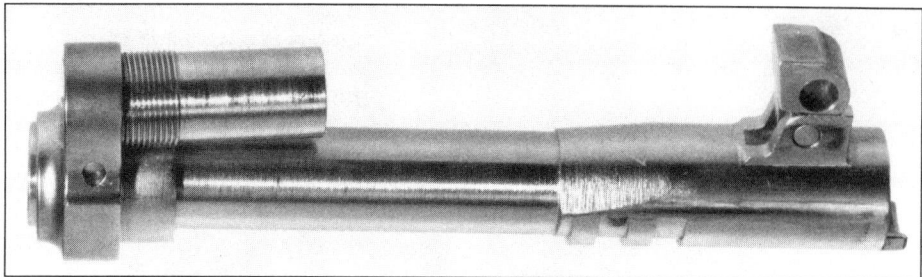

The barrel shows the Broad Foot Link and the Barrel Bushing Housing.

Here is a closeup of the Barrel Bushing Housing, showing the Messerschmidt bearing that firmly controlled the barrel, while permitting it to articulate up and down at the rear during reloading.

Pachmayr delivered a total accuracy job, complete with Micro adjustable target sights, tested and sighted for just $32.50.

Only Frank Pachmayr could raise .45 ACP accuracy to a higher state of the art with his "Pachmayr Signature Model Accuracy System," the culmination of eight years of intensive research that gained him eight separate patents. Sadly, it is no longer available. Anyone owning one of these guns has a collector's item of great value.

The kingpin of the Signature System was the Slide Guide, a yoke that wrapped around the forward portion of the frame from underneath and was secured at the rear by the slide stop pin. The two side rails were precision ground to a 120-degree included angle, forming an inverted "V" that cradled the slide, which was also ground to matching angles on both sides. An enlarged "boss" at the bottom of the yoke contained a conical-pointed Allen screw, which entered a matching tapered hole that was machined high in the front of the trigger guard. Tightening the screw increased upward pressure of the Slide Guide, allowing it to be tensioned against the bottom rails of the slide for optimum accuracy, while retaining positive function. Nylon plugs in the screw prevented loss of adjustment under fire. The practical effect was that the slide cycled in a V-block, positively eliminating deviations in any plane—up, down, or sideways. The Slide Guide was cast by precision investment from precipitation-hardening H-900 stainless steel, with a tensile strength of 200,000 psi. Bearing ways were hard chromed for greater lubricity, longer wear, and to prevent galling.

A patented, integrated, investment cast-stainless-steel bushing assembly replaced the conventional bushing. The slide was reamed out at the top of the keyhole frontal opening to barely accept the larger diameter housing and was threaded at the bottom for a hollow cap-retaining screw that took the place of the usual recoil spring plug. A coin slot at the front of the threaded plug allowed quick takedown. An absolutely tight union between the conventional Government Model bushing and barrel has always been elusive because the barrel must be free to rotate downward at the rear in order to disengage the locking lugs from the slide. The Signature barrel bushing provided absolute immobility at the front by enclosing a Messerschmidt-type, self-aligning bearing ring within the bushing housing. The hardened steel bearing was ground to a perfect sphere where it articulated in a mating spherical section within the Signature bushing. Internally, the ring was reamed to a snug slip-fit with the barrel, which was ground to a precise .575-inch outside diameter. The result was a ball-and-socket joint between the slide and barrel, leaving the latter free to pivot downward at the rear, yet with zero play in any plane at the muzzle.

To impose absolute control upon the barrel at the rear, Pachmayr devised an equally innovative redesign, completely replacing the troublesome narrow link that swivels within a milled slot in the barrel lug and disengaging the barrel from the locking lugs in the slide as it recoils rearward. In its stead, Pachmayr utilized his own "Broad-Foot Link," shaped like an inverted "T," with the full width of the barrel lug at the bottom and with the narrow leg pinned in the original slot. Nor-

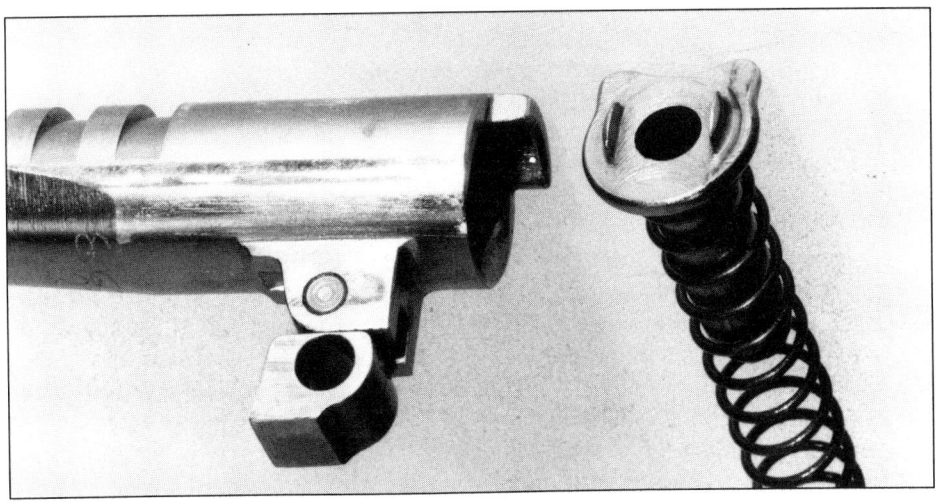

The Broad-Foot Link positively prevents barrel motion in any direction when in battery.

mally, two lugs extend down both sides of the narrow link, arresting forward motion of the barrel when they contact the slide stop pin. These were milled off to make room for the "T." A tight-fitting channel was milled into the receiver to accept the new wide link. Forward motion stopped when a square shoulder located the bottom front on the wide link and made solid contact with the bottom of the milled channel in the frame. Then the bottom of the barrel lugs were firmly seated against the top of the "T." Thus all vertical and rotary motion at the rear of the barrel came to a screeching halt. The Broad-Foot-Link was fitted to bring the barrel into battery at exactly top dead center, with no consideration given to the position of the slide in reference to the frame. If the rear of the slide didn't match with the frame, and it often did not, the gunsmith filed the frame or slide to blend the lines perfectly.

Another unique component of the Signature accuracy process was installation of the Headspace Eliminator, a spring-loaded plunger positioned in the slide above the firing pin. This places an eight-pound pressure against the head of the cartridge, assuring that it is always bottomed in the chamber. This device automatically compensated for short cartridge cases that failed to headspace correctly. Frank had determined by machine-rest tests that short rounds materially affected accuracy. They often settled at the rear of the chamber and had to be driven forward by the firing pin until the case mouths bottomed against the chamber shoulder. This had to take place before their primers could be indented sufficiently to fire, which resulted in irregular ignition and unexplained fliers on the target.

Pachmayr discovered that the slide stop pin holes placed in the frame at the Colt factory were often not square with the barrel axis, making a true precision fit between barrel and frame virtually impossible. He corrected the problem by fixturing the frame in an end mill and reaming the hole larger, exactly 90 degrees to the frame. The Signature offset slide release lever was fitted over the left leg of the Slide Guide, and an oversized pin could be slipped through both units and was retained on the right with a horseshoe spring clip.

Pachmayr's Signature system relied for its accuracy upon a number of precision machining operations instead of the skills of individual gunsmiths. It was designed to produce absolutely consistent results from one gun to another with relatively little regard for the experience of the smith. Signature .45s consistently delivered groups under one inch from the machine rest at twenty-five yards.

Signature system .45s that were chopped to sub-Commander dimensions served law enforcement officers as duty backup guns as well. With the slide left full length, barrels of Buntline dimensions were entirely practical. The unique stainless-steel bushing was machined long to accommodate the nine-inch barrel of a special order, metallic silhouette pistol that was topped by an adjustable micrometer peep rear sight and hooded front with interchangeable posts.

Looking back over the years, Pachmayr says today, "It's a lot easier to make a .45 accurate today than it was when I got started. In the old days, a standard .45 was lucky to shoot groups as big as a bowler hat. Modern .45s are a lot more accurate right from the factory. More importantly, Colt has improved its steel alloys and heat treatments, so the gun doesn't wear at such a fast rate. During the early years, an accuracy job didn't last all that long. I received a letter from a customer saying, 'I had to tighten up the slide again to make it shoot good groups.' Today, when you tighten up a slide, you can be confident that it'll last through several seasons of intensive match shooting.

"I did most of the work myself in the old days. After a while, the work load got to be too much to handle alone, and I hired Buck Buchanan to work for me. Buck took some of the burden off my shoulders, but I personally built the guns for all six of the men (five competed, the other was an alternate) that went to Camp Perry in 1935 and won team honors at the National Match."

Buck Buchanan and Frank were close friends from the time Frank worked for his father. There was a slack period, however, about three years after Buck went to work for Frank. There just weren't enough accuracy jobs to keep two men busy. Frank reluctantly let Buck go, and Buck went to work for Bill Sukale in Tucson, Arizona, making rifle barrels. Then in 1934, Frank phoned Buck and asked him to come back. Buck came a-runnin.' A few years later, Buchanan started his own shop with Frank's blessings and became noted in his own right for making the .45 ACP accurate.

"Today," says Frank, "there are a lot of ready-made, aftermarket manufactured parts to improve .45 handling, looks, and accuracy without much metal work. Most shooters can do it themselves. We had to weld up the hood of the barrel to get a tight fit with the slide. Now you can buy custom barrels cut oversized and fit them correctly from the beginning. When I had my company, I made lightweight, long nylon triggers, extended slide releases, as well as rubber grips, wide rubber grip safeties, and rubber-covered mainspring housings to make it easier to get the Colt accurate."

Of his one-hundred-plus, gun-related inventions, Frank Pachmayr's development of semisoft neoprene rubber pistol grips has been one of his most popular and enduring items, especially as applied to the slab-sided old Colt .45 ACP. Pachmayr Signature Grips offer firm control of the twisting, pitching .45 and a distinct reduction in "felt" recoil. A long-favored practice among custom gunsmiths has been to checker the .45 front strap with rasplike, sharp-edged diamonds or chisel alligator teeth down the front. The .45 auto with full-house loads could be compared to an irresistible force. Unfortunately, epidermis on a human hand is not an immovable object. After a hard day on the firing line, the front strap ends up wearing out a high percentage of the shooter's skin.

Pachmayr Signature grips offer a far less painful, yet equally effective cure. They cover the front strap with a unique wraparound cover of finger-clinging rubber and are checkered in a coarse, twenty lines-per-inch pattern. To install Signature grips, you simply attach the first grip slab on one side with two screws, then pull the second grip slab around under tension, stretching the wraparound tautly and permanently in place. Signature's sides are checkered twenty-six lines to the inch on its lower three-quarters. A thumb-rest area above bears fine thirty-line checkering. A smooth-surfaced depression on the left side allows easy access to the magazine release button. To round out the picture and finally tame the rambunctious .45 ACP once and for all, Pachmayr added neoprene-covered mainspring housings in both arched and flat configurations, plus a neoprene-armored wide-grip safety that finally provided comfort to the sensitive area between thumb and forefinger.

With minor embellishments, Frank's original .45 ACP Government Model accuracy methods remain basic among pistolsmiths to this day. After Frank retired, Pachmayr's offered the Pachmayr Combat Special system for several years, embodying many of the same steps, including slide tightening, a stainless steel Bar-Sto Match Grade Barrel, and a ramp-post front sight backed by a low-mounted radius Bo-Mar rear sight. A Pachmayr nylon National Match trigger was installed and adjusted to 3½ pounds. The Pachmayr Combat Special wasn't shipped until it delivered a 1½-inch, five-shot group from a machine rest at twenty-five yards.

•••

· Chapter III ·

CUSTOM HANDGUNS AND RIFLES

When Frank Pachmayr initiated designs that were destined to change the attitudes and tools of handgun target competition forever, he was only a young gunsmith. He had his own fledgling shop, had just recently emerged from a grueling apprenticeship with his father, and was still exploring the business world, but he distinguished himself early in his career as a pioneer in customizing handguns. Frank's work included the rattlin'-loose .45 Automatic Colt Pistol, which he helped to become the leading target pistol of modern times.

During the 1930s, the only autoloading pistols seriously considered as competition target guns were the .22 Long Rifle Colt Match Target Woodsman and the High Standard Model H-E. The Colt .45 ACP was required in NRA big-bore competition, but the loose tolerances, which were deliberately designed into the Colt Government Model 1911(A1) to assure its reliability in combat, caused it to launch its stubby .45 caliber slugs in a highly random fashion. Hitting the bull's-eye at fifty yards was generally regarded as much as a matter of luck as the result of good marksmanship. Scores with the Colt 1911(A1) were far lower than those obtained with revolvers.

But it was the wheel guns that ruled the firing lines. The Colt heavy-barreled Officer's Model was the gun of choice, chambered either for the .22 Long Rifle for small-bore matches, or the .38 Special for center-fire matches. There was also some competition from Smith & Wesson's K22 rimfire and the .38 Military and Police Target revolvers.

Double-action revolvers of the day were beautifully made of steel that was buffed flat and true, blued as deep as a tidal pool, with crisp single-action triggers, and had double actions that cycled right out of the box as if they were on roller bearings. Both Colt and Smith & Wesson shared some shortcomings, however. Both possessed long, jarring hammer falls, resulting in lengthy lock times that let the front sights wander from the bull's-eye far too long. A dedicated target buff himself, Frank was well aware of the problem.

FRANK PACHMAYR

The record indicates that Frank was probably the first pistolsmith to develop short-action modifications for double-action Colt and Smith & Wesson revolvers. He lengthened the piece that rotated the cylinder to make it engage the cylinder ratchet at the first movement of the hammer to the rear, then modified the hammer so that the sears engaged the instant the hand rotated the cylinder into battery. The hammer was also skeletonized for light weight, speeding up the long lock time and

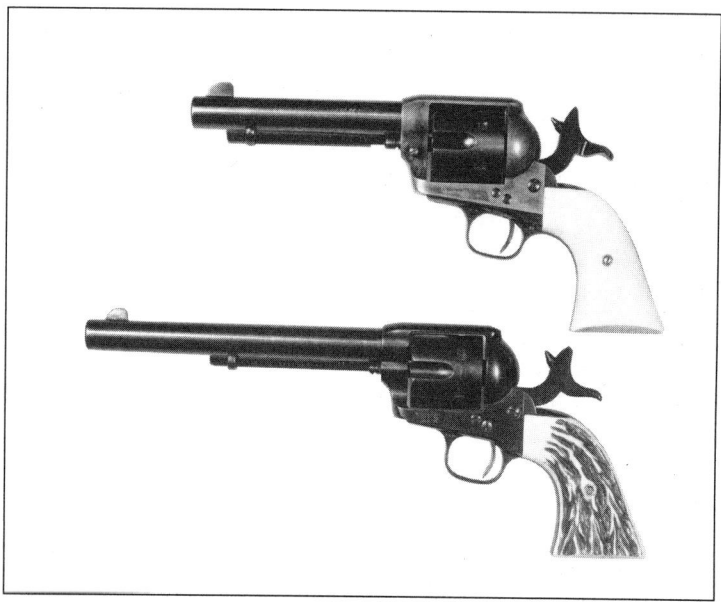

On top is a Frontier with the hammer fall shortened and the spur widened. On bottom is a standard Frontier Colt. Note the difference in hammer location at full cock.

eliminating the jarring impact from the hammer fall. Today, those short-action modifications are integrated into factory revolvers, but during Frank's time, the concept was revolutionary.

Although the revolvers were double action, nearly all competition shooters fired the entire National Match Course, including timed and rapid fire, single action. That required manual cocking of the hammer for each shot. Hammer spurs were then OEM factory offered only in a narrow width with perfunctory checkering. Frank welded steel to the sides of the hammer spurs and shaped wide beavertails with deep, sharp checkering to offer the thumb a more positive grip for more certain speedier, single-action fire. On some guns, Frank also lowered the spur slightly to allow manual cocking without having to shift the hand's grip on the gun with each shot.

These changes alone increased scores among high-level competitors, especially during the rapid-fire stage. Also among Frank's revolver modifications were milled, full-length sight ribs, with high-profile, target-adjustable Patridge sights. If a shooter wanted to arrive in the winner's circle, he had to have a Pachmayr-customized revolver just to be competitive. Frank didn't specialize in handgun modifications, so he didn't become famous for his pioneering efforts. Men like

• CUSTOM HANDGUNS AND RIFLES •

Buck Buchanan, who got his start working for Frank back in 1931, went on to acquire star reputations in handgun work by doing nothing else.

The single-action Colt Peacemaker/Frontier revolver was probably the most popular field revolver in the early days, and still cuts a pretty wide swath today. As one of the old "horse pistol's" greatest fans, I can attest to its shortcomings. Among these was a "V"-notch rear sight, barely scratched into the top of a rounded-top receiver through which the sad shooter had to hunt and seek a narrow, always-too-tall, rounded-blade front sight. I always used a sack needle file to square up the notch, making it wide enough to show light on both sides of the front sight. This was no small chore because the frames were color-case hardened. I dulled many files in this simple operation.

I'd go to the target range with a vise that I could clamp to the shooting bench and an assortment of files to sight my single-action Colt revolvers. I slowly lowered the front sight with a flat mill file, test firing as I cut, to deliver the bullets to the center of the bull's-eye. I never sighted-in at the target shooter's favored six-o'clock hold because I used the guns mostly for hunting, which required a hit at the point of aim—not three inches high. If the gun shot too far off one side, I'd have to take it home and use my barrel vise to give the frame a little tweak to the

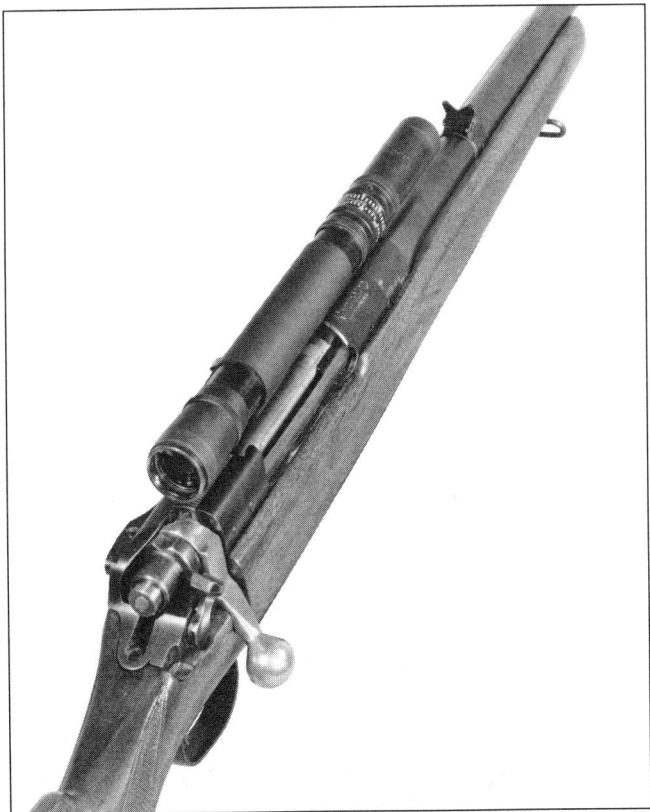

For several years following World War II, commercial rifles were in short supply. Surplus military rifles could be had for pocket change. One of the favorites for customizing was the Enfield that had huge steel "ears" protecting the rear sight. It was necessary to mill the ears from the receiver to allow use of a scope or commercial open sights. On this Enfield, Pachmayr has removed the ears to mount a scope.

opposite side. Then back to the range to try it again. If the front sight was to one side just a little, I used a big Crescent wrench to bend it slightly.

Frank was likely the first to modify the single-action Colt to update its inadequate sights and ancient action to something resembling a twentieth-century handgun. He installed a full-length sight rib, topped by adjustable target sights. He also installed a practical short action with reduced tension on the thick flat main-

This fine early controlled-feed Winchester Model 70 .357 H&H Magnum was action-honed and fully engraved for presentation as a gift from Frank Pachmayr to the late Elmer Keith. An incredibly marbled Circassian walnut stock is embellished with 32-line fleur-de-lis pattern checkering. Frank reluctantly used a Monte Carlo comb, just to please Elmer.

spring and skeletonized the heavy hammer. That modification did away with the resounding jar when the old thumb-buster landed like a sledge hammer on the frame. He installed beavertail spurs for those who wanted them. Pachmayr also offered the rare service of redoing the color case hardening. This operation is a delicate job. It is not easy to achieve color that is similar to the original Colt color and maintain the dimensional integrity of the revolver receiver without warping it.

The first article I ever wrote for publication appeared in the *American Rifleman* in 1945. It detailed the exact welding and filing steps required to change a single-action Colt to a short action. I did this without any knowledge of Frank's work in the same area, and we arrived at the same methods independently.

During World War II and for a considerable period thereafter, there were few commercial bolt-action, sporting rifles available. Model 70 Winchesters and Remington Model 720 rifles were in short supply. Only the Model 70 could be rightly regarded as a modern rifle. The Model 720 was an only slightly demilitarized version of the military 1917 Enfield rifle. It was too heavy and had a clubby feel. The end of the war was accompanied by a flood of war surplus military rifles, which were available at very low cost. I remember purchasing several Enfield rifles in new condition for only twenty-five dollars apiece. Springfields and military Mausers were available from twelve to forty dollars, depending upon their condition. The practice at the time was to turn down the bolt handles, usually by hacksawing them off and welding them back to the bolts at a turned-down angle, to allow cycling the bolts under low-mounted scope sights. The Enfield rifle had an ugly dogleg bolt, but it was already at an angle suitable for scope use. When

Pachmayr customized an Enfield rifle, he straightened the dogleg bolt to improve its appearance.

The as-issued Enfield had huge "ears" protruding upward on both sides of the rear ring of the receiver, rather like the fins on postwar-Cadillac cars, to protect the military rear sight. Pachmayr was among the first to mill these ears off, resulting in a low-contour on the rear ring of the receiver, appropriate to scope use or the mounting of a receiver peep sight. Although clumsy, the Enfield boasted a practical thumb-lever safety located at the right rear on the receiver. The original, rather bulky, spur on the safety could be readily streamlined, and it worked fine with a low-mounted scope. Conversely, Springfield and Mauser actions required removal of the military safeties, which were located on their bolt shrouds, and the substitu-

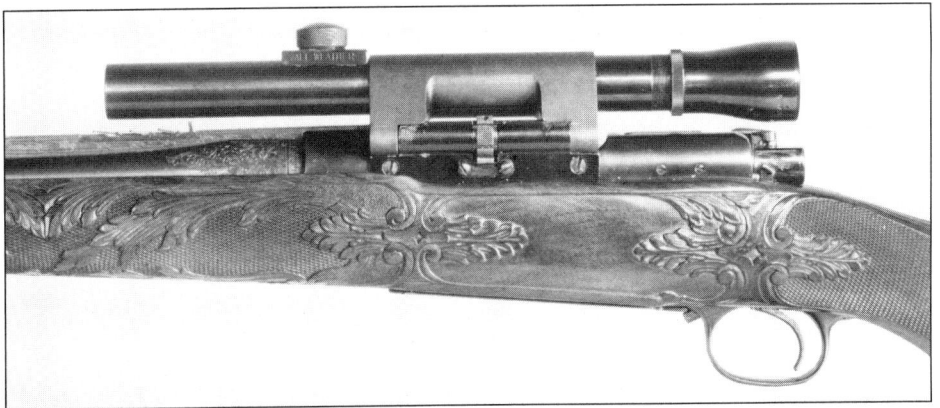

The Germanic heritage of Frank Pachmayr surfaced occasionally in high-relief, continentally styled engraving on the stock, much like the work of his father before him. This is a second-generation Lo-Swing mount with a Lyman Alaskan scope, the best available in the United States before, during, and for a time after World War II. The barrel rib has a series of foldup express sights for different ranges.

tion of a new civilian design that allowed easy access under a low-mounted scope. Several practical and attractive substitute safeties were available for these rifles in the aftermarket. One of the best was designed and made by Frank Pachmayr.

Military receivers were not predrilled and tapped at the factory to accept standardized scope-mount bases. We shooters really have it good today. It's so easy to mount a scope on a factory predrilled rifle that any reasonably talented home mechanic can perform the task. Springfield and Enfield receivers had to be drilled and tapped for a scope. Pachmayr's gunsmiths were kept busy attacking the ex-GI rifles with receivers heat-treated to a tough consistency that ruined drill bits by the case. It was also common to break off a tap in one of the holes. Pachmayr gunsmiths soon learned to use high-speed bits and carbon tetrachloride as a tap lubricant. That was only the beginning. Because heat treating on military actions was not consistent, Pachmayr sent actions destined for rebuilding to Ferro-Spec Laboratories, Inc. for a Rockwell hardness check and nondestructive testing to discover any hidden cracks that might cause sudden catastrophic failure during firing. An X-ray of the receiver clearly showed any internal flaws that might exist.

During and immediately after World War II, the best American-made scopes came from Lyman, Noske, and Unertl. The best scopes available right after the war, however, were German-made, such as Hensoldt and Ziess. Most hunters opted for good open sights or Lyman receiver sights. Few scopes were to be found in the field in early postwar America. Then there came a transition period when American scopes became coated and competent, gaining equal billing with peep sights, and finally phasing out iron sights for the most part. Frank's design of a swing-over mount was highly popular among hunters who wanted to enjoy the obvious advantages of a scope but wanted also to retain instant access to those old reliable iron sights. Early scopes were pretty rugged overall but they were frequently subject to fogging, even after internal nitrogen injection became an OEM standard feature. The sealing just wasn't totally reliable. I recall an elk hunt at Moose

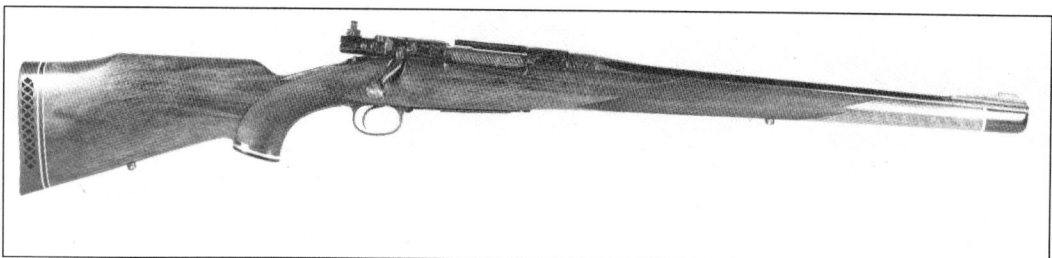

The unusual treatment given this custom Pachmayr rifle includes a slight Monte Carlo comb (seldom seen from Pachmayr), a short barrel with a full-length Mannlicher stock, and a peep sight mounted upon an extension of the cocking piece.

Creek, Idaho, when everyone's scope fogged. The six of us each had a different brand, proving that the problem was universal.

Two-stage military triggers were designed for maximum safety, rather than precision shooting. Pachmayr installed an adjustable commercial trigger, such as a Canjar, Dayton-Traister, or Timney, on each customized, military-based rifle, resulting in a crisp, single-stage trigger release. The unnecessarily long, jarring firing pin fall of the Springfield was shortened and the Enfield was altered to cock upon opening the bolt, instead of the unhandy cock-on-closing system of the original military rifle.

Military, and even commercial stocks of the day, were shaped like war clubs. They were thick and unhandy. Frank Pachmayr evolved a stock shape that was classic in contour but slender and lightweight, without being fragile. His ideas about stock design are a coalescence of his father's basic concepts of style and utility, combined with Frank's own sense of symmetry.

Frank's father, Gus, was one of the pioneers in setting early standards for American stock design, which has a more recent evolution than most shooters realize. Gus helped introduce the concepts of cheekpieces, pistol grips, and flat butt plates to the United States gun market. Until then, American gunmakers had continued the tradition of the Pennsylvania rifle—entailing excessive drop, thin combs, and sharp-pointed, half-moon butt plates—long after it was practical. Its reason for being had vanished with the long-barreled, light-recoil Kentucky rifle. During the late nineteenth and early twentieth centuries, custom rifles were unknown in America. Factory repeaters seemed to fill everyone's needs handily. Trendsetters of the day, such as Teddy Roosevelt and Zane Grey, were content to hunt anything on four legs with a big-bore, lever-action rifle, such as the Winchester Model 95 or Model 86.

The custom sporting rifle stocks designed by Frank fall into the ageless, "classic" school of stock design, but with a unique flavor that is distinctly his. Even seen from across the room, a Pachmayr rifle or shotgun is instantly recognizable as a hallmark of quality. It has symmetrical lines, superb grain, and flawless checkering. Another important asset of a Pachmayr custom stock—the tailored fit that makes it a natural pointer—has to be felt to be appreciated.

Through the years, Pachmayr has remained one of the most respected exponents of classic stock design. His rifle and shotgun stocks are always beautifully fashioned with soft flowing lines and graceful pistol grips that contrast sharply with the exaggerated lines of some modern creations. Frank detests the Monte Carlo comb because, he says, "It looks like the stock is pregnant." He prefers a straight comb, with a gently rounded, full cheekpiece, contoured to flow smoothly from the top of the pistol grip in front, curve to its lowest point about two-thirds of the way back toward the butt, then hook up and forward into a half-circle. For scope use, the comb has less drop, but remains straight. A line drawn from the toe through the pistol grip merges exactly with the intersection of the stock and trigger guard. The pistol grip is gently curved and not too low, with a steel or ebony cap at a right angle to the end of the curve. A cross section of the fore-end is round or only slightly oval, with a straight taper from the receiver to the tip. Of course, the edges must be crisp and sharp.

Though seldom used in Frank Pachmayr's sporting goods store, there was a "try gun" made by Walter Strand with a comb that could be raised or lowered from the front and rear. This provided an accurate measure of proper comb height and made it possible to adapt a custom stock to the customer's particular physical traits and shooting stance. Without the need of a try gun, Frank could study a man holding a rifle or shotgun and call out the particular dimensions that would fit him with uncanny accuracy, rather like the circus sideshow performer who always correctly guessed a person's weight.

To a shotgunner, proper stock fit means the difference between a flurry of retreating wings and meat on the table. To the rifleman, it means the difference between getting caught flatfooted or picking off that buck during the fleeting moment it becomes exposed while crossing a small clearing. For both, it means instinctive pointing that allows for concentration upon the target rather than the gun, insures positive trigger control, and avoids undue punishment from recoil. In Frank's words, "With the gun held at hip level, you should be able to choose a target, close your eyes, and shoulder the gun—then open your eyes and find that you're looking through the sights with the target under your bead or centered in your cross hairs."

Also part of the custom Pachmayr package was a deep, dark bluing of the steel components and the muted gloss of a hand-rubbed oil finish on the stock, accompanied by flawless, elegantly styled checkering. Remnants of a European influence was apparent in the occasional carving of custom gunstocks and Germanic-looking engraving. Pachmayr custom guns have always been marked with the superlative workmanship of an "old world" tradition. Guns built in keeping with these standards have proved their ability to appreciate in value with the years. Dollar for dollar, they're a better investment than stocks or bonds.

Pachmayr made complete custom rifles, usually based upon Winchester pre-64 Model 70 actions. Modifications included reshaping the blocky trigger guard and rear of action tang, plus damascening the bolt and magazine follower to improve their appearance. A new stock of fine walnut was shaped in a classic configuration with fleur-de-lis checkering, hand-bedded for guaranteed minute-of-angle accuracy, with an ebony fore-end tip, gold-insert grip cap, Pachmayr Flush Mount Sling Swivels, and Pachmayr Presentation Recoil Pad. Open sights were complemented by installation of a Lo-Swing scope mount and a scope of the purchaser's choice.

The cost of all this work, including the original rifle, as detailed in a letter from Frank to a customer, dated 2 December 1974, came to just $1,662.50. Added cost options included a new premium grade barrel, Exhibition Grade walnut blank, new one-piece trigger guard, and quarter-rib express, open rear sight. A number of steel finishes were offered by Pachmayr, including ordinary salt bluing, and rust bluing that required much more labor, but reproduced the high quality of the original finishes on many expensive guns. Usually relegated to handguns were Pachmayr's electroless nickel and hard-chrome finishes. Pachmayr Gun Works also offered original quality color case hardening for fine shotgun receivers, and single-action Colt revolver frames.

It would be an understatement to say that Frank's customers were satisfied. Quoting from a letter by Juan Brignardello of Lima, Peru:

> Dear Frank,
>
> It has been a very long time since I wrote you last, but in the meantime I have hunted a few times with the beautiful custom .270 you did for me. I must say that it is a very accurate rifle and it has performed very well. Jay Mellon [*scion of the Mellon family fortune and noted international big-game hunter*] was very impressed with it. So was Prince Abdorreza Pahlavi of Iran in our last hunt where I took him for a bear and taruca hunt. They were very impressed with your job. As you know, the prince is a .270 fan. He himself brought one made by Milliron, metal work by Burgess. For certain, I wouldn't have changed mine for his, for anything. Jay was the first to put eye on your gun, and he told me that not even O'Connor [*the late Jack O'Connor, famed gun scribe and most ardent supporter of the .270 Winchester cartridge*] would have selected a better proportion, balance, and weight for the .270. He said if the prince would order a gun, I had already everything one should ask for. So again, congratulations.

Pachmayr also made many modifications to existing rifles and shotguns. One unique service was "stock bending." It was in fact possible to bend a wood stock up or down or to the side to raise or lower the heel of the stock from half to three-quarters of an inch, and add or subtract cast-off or cast-on. The "how" of accomplishing this minor miracle was a mystery to me until I spoke to the late Walter Strand about it. He said that he performed this task at Pachmayr's by soaking the pistol grip area in boiling hot linseed oil, then exerting pressure on the butt or heel

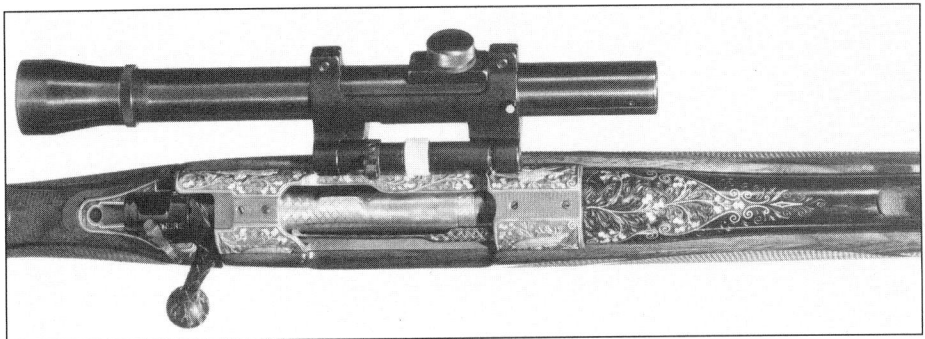

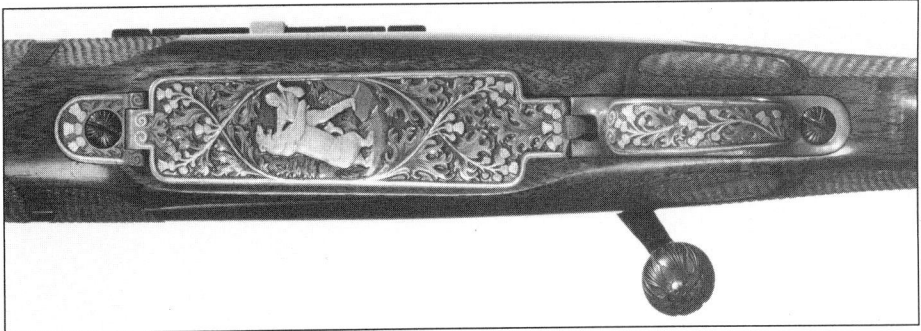

A pre-1964 Model 70 Winchester, a Pachmayr favorite for upgrading, has received a new figured walnut stock with tasteful hand checkering, plus gold-inlaid engraving and a Pachmayr Lo-Swing mount. Viewed from the top and bottom.

of the stock to get the desired movement. "I can feel just how far I can bend it," he said, "before the stock breaks." Note that this was a man who had spent most of his life making gunstocks. He knew wood as few ever do. "I let the stock stand overnight in the bent position. In the morning, I take it out of the vise and it has hardened into its new position."

When it came to building custom guns, there was one trait that Frank had in abundance, and that was patience. One particular rifle clearly demonstrates this point. One of Frank's special friends, hunting companion, and sometimes house guest was the late Elmer Keith, noted gunwriter during the two past generations and foremost proponent of big bullets at medium velocity for optimum killing power. During an Idaho elk hunt one year, Frank told Elmer, "I'm going to build you the finest custom rifle ever made."

Elmer was impressed with the idea, but he knew better than to hold his breath. Several years elapsed before Elmer saw his rifle, still in the white, during a visit to Pachmayr's in Los Angeles. Frank showed Elmer a pre-64 Winchester Model 70 barreled action. It was a .375 H & H Magnum (what else?), which had just returned from a hiatus in Germany. There it had been under the skilled hands of

Often part of the revolver improvement package at Pachmayr was a complete engraving pattern shown here on a Smith & Wesson .357 Magnum round butt, pocket pistol.

Erich Boessler, who had engraved and inlaid it with gold and silver. Centered on the floor plate was a gold grizzly bear in a menacing stance. The trigger guard, which had been slenderized and recontoured, featured the golden cameo of a bighorn sheep. On top of the receiver, the forward ring held a golden bull elk and the bridge in the rear had a gold puma, which was about to spring. Inlaid silver wire framed the deep floral engraving in the blued steel, on the receiver, and forward on the rear third of the barrel past the express-styled open rear sight and again at the muzzle, surrounding the square brass sourdough front sight. The bolt handle was deeply checkered all around. The latest model of Pachmayr's Lo-Swing scope mount was attached with a side plate, to avoid obscuring the beautiful gold inlays on top of the receiver.

Frank told Elmer, "I'm waiting for just the right piece of Circassian walnut to surface to make a stock worthy of this gun." Again the project went into the deep freeze for several more years. Then in 1975 at the National Rifle Association annual convention in San Diego, Elmer Keith saw the rifle again. (I had seen it earlier myself in Frank's office.)

As Elmer himself described it, "It [the rifle] carried the most beautiful and gorgeous stock of marbled Circassian that I have ever seen. The beautiful grain ran the full length of the stock, not just the butt end. The grain at the fore-end, just back of the ebony tip, also ran upward toward the barrel—the best possible grain structure for fine accuracy. The rifle was stocked to my old Monte Carlo cheek rest specifications and design. It was fitted with Pachmayr's finest Old English-style, solid recoil pad. The grip cap framed an engraved gold oval in the center. The sling swivels are the best I have ever seen and feature a small rounded button projecting through the butt stock and fore-end. It's barely noticeable." (Note that Frank departed from his self-imposed rule never to use a Monte Carlo stock because Elmer wanted it that way.)

The dense, hard walnut was checkered to a fine thirty-two lines per inch and in a pattern reminiscent of Gus Pachmayr's innovations. These were later expanded and enriched by Frank's nephew, Richard Mellen, who was a commercial artist before he went to work for Frank. The pattern featured two narrow, uncheckered ribs arching around the gentle curve on each side of the pistol grip and were accented by three fleur-de-lis designs on each side. The extremely fine checkering didn't obscure the wood grain as a coarse pattern often does. A solid gold grip cap was engraved simply with the name "Elmer Keith."

Typical of the refinements that Frank lavished on all custom rifles, not just Elmer's, was a wide checkered button on top of the bolt release lever, which is at the lower left on the Model 70 receiver. This was created by welding metal to the sides and the top of the OEM, stamped-steel lever and by adding material to form a wide flat on top. The result was a more attractive "button," as well as a more comfortable one to use. Even the rear tang of the Model 70 receiver was reshaped into a slender, attractive configuration.

Not only was the rifle that Frank Pachmayr built for Elmer Keith a spectacular beauty, it shot like a target rifle. Elmer reported three-shot bench rest groups measuring from $3/8$-inch to $3/4$-inch, center-to-center at one hundred yards. Elmer vowed he would hunt with his museum display rifle, but he admitted that he'd be mighty careful with it. I don't know if Elmer ever hunted with the Pachmayr rifle, but it may very well end up as a museum piece. When Elmer died of a stroke, his son Ted determined to set up a museum featuring his famous father's artifacts, including the engraved custom Winchester Model 70 built by Pachmayr. Frank made a generous contribution to the nonprofit "Elmer Keith Museum Foundation, Inc.," which is administered by the Idaho First National Bank in Salmon, Idaho.

Frank Pachmayr built many other outstanding custom rifles, each enhanced with beautiful walnut from his wood mill, hand-mated to deep, blued steel components, and with full contact end-to-end. Among these were rifles made for Pete Candy, Ike Ellis, Ed Patterson, Mike Ripley, and Arnold Shafer. The men who purchased Pachmayr custom rifles were making excellent investments that were destined to appreciate much faster than conventional items, such as gold, silver, stocks, or bonds. There is great prestige inherent in the ownership of Pachmayr guns, which are distinguished by hand craftsmanship of skilled artisans who were under Frank's personal direction.

· FRANK PACHMAYR ·

"High-grade rifles and shotguns are an excellent hedge against inflation," says Pachmayr, "ranking alongside precious stones and centuries-old artifacts. Unlike *objects d'art*, guns can be used, as well as viewed. Hunters and shooters feel a great amount of personal pride when they unlimber their favorite custom rifle or shotgun in the field or on the target range. Let their friends use the common sour grapes argument, 'I wouldn't have a gun with all that gold and engraving. I'd be afraid to use it.' My customers just smile and gloat over those covetous stares and sidelong looks of envy."

Pachmayr Gun Works was renowned for custom work. It had customers in such distant places as Africa, Belgium, England, Greece, Iran, Italy, Spain, and Sweden. Frank had wealthy and famous clients, such as Sam M. Winston, president of Winston Tires, and prominent military figures of World War II, such as General Reynear Staats, General Earl S. Hoag, and General Curtis LeMay.

Frank never forgets anything he reads or hears. He has a mind like a file cabinet, capable of indexing and retrieving information on a wide variety of subjects. As the owner of Pachmayr Gun Works, he received a prodigious amount of mail. Much of it was letters concerning guns needing repair or letters requesting information about a particular gun that the correspondent either owned or wanted to buy. He also received letters from gratified customers. Frank read every letter. He didn't reply personally to all of them, but he would pencil in a note and hand it to his assistant for an answer. Years later, Frank could remember a particular letter out of the blizzard of mail that he had received. The following is a letter from a satisfied customer James A. Suthard of Mesa, Colorado:

Dear Mr. Pachmayr:
   I received yesterday the L. C. Smith 20-gauge double that you refurbished for me. As a lover and student of wood for many years, I must say I wish the firearms industry at large shared your definition of "Field Grade." The execution of the work is, as I expected from you, soul satisfying; the wood is simply beautiful. When my ship comes in, as they say, I think I would like to rub my shoulder against what you might term "fancy" wood.

Another letter from Sam M. Winston is dated 18 July 1980:

Dear Frank:
   I picked up my .375 Winchester today and cannot begin to tell you how much I liked it and appreciate your doing it for me. It is certainly the nicest gun I possess; I can assure you I will take good care of it and think about you whenever I use it.

A letter from former *Field and Stream* shooting editor, the late Warren Page, is dated 27 March 1951:

Dear Frank:
   Last fall, I would have lost a nice black bear had not my .270 been equipped with a Pachmayr Lo-Swing mount. This is about as handsome a rifle as a man

· CUSTOM HANDGUNS AND RIFLES ·

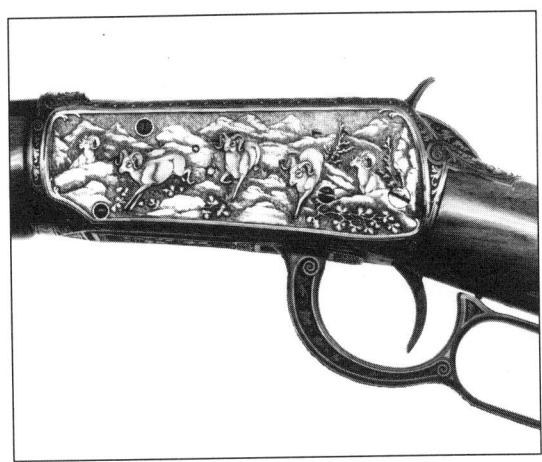

Before and after examples of Pachmayr's typical treatment of a Model 94 Winchester. He took a fine rifle and turned it into a true work of art, with high-class hand engraving and fine, highly figured walnut, finished and checkered to perfection.

Frank loved to decorate the lowly Model 94 saddle gun with extremely ornate engraving and gold inlays, depicting wildlife and realistic scenes from the Old West. He restocked them with the finest walnut to be found.

could want, there being just about enough carving around the checkering in a simple and conventional design, not too much. With the scope in place, the rifle with twenty-two-inch barrel weighs just over eight pounds. You may remember that you made this rifle for me on an FN action, with a Sudderby barrel. It has always shot beautifully for me, and I suspect that if I had to give up all of my rifles but one, this would be the one I'd hang on to.

Much of the custom work and routine repair work came to Pachmayr from outside gunsmiths, who found they could rely on the consistent high-quality workmanship—and available at a price that allowed for ample markup. Among Frank's regular customers were such well-known gunsmiths as Roy F. Dunlap, Bill McGuire, and Keith Stegall.

Typical of the specialized work performed at Pachmayr Gun Works was a special stock built for the late John T. Amber, famed editor of *Gun Digest*. Over the course of a generation, John took the annual *Gun Digest* from just another gun "catalog" to a gun journal. I wrote regularly for the journal and appeared on their masthead as a field editor for many years. John Amber was a great friend and counselor. During his declining years, he was beset by many physical debilities, but he clung fiercely to his love of shooting and was determined to remain a participant rather than a mere observer to the very end.

To John, the most troubling infirmity was the loss of sight in his right eye. It was caused from a retinal detachment from years of pounding by heavy rifles and shotguns. John phoned me one night and said that he had a shadow creeping into his right eye from the outside corner. I told him to see a doctor immediately. Time was of the essence. The symptoms were unmistakable. He called a few days later and said that he had undergone laser surgery in an attempt to reattach the optic nerve back in place. Sadly, the surgery was not successful. John tried to train himself to shoot from the left shoulder, but years of practice had worn a groove in his nerve patterns that he couldn't undo. He had to shoot from the right shoulder.

John took his problem to Frank. As John described it later, "Frank Pachmayr made a semibent stock for a Model 12 Winchester 20 gauge, which worked out very well. It was made to a pattern designed by Frank's father, August. The butt stock is not fully bent to the right; rather, one's cheek is placed over the comb to a degree and excellent alignment of the left eye with the rib is easily achieved." In this instance, Frank himself fitted the stock for his troubled friend. "I've been fitting stocks for fifty years or so," he explains. "I know what's needed to fit a stock to a particular shooter." The actual stock was made by Frank's stock maker, Walter Strand.

Over the years, Frank designed and milled speed locks from raw steel and set triggers for a variety of target rifles. He created improved single-stage triggers and practical release triggers for shotguns, installed improved ejectors, and added side plates. He designed substitute safeties to replace those found on the shrouds of Springfield and military Mauser rifles, allowing the shooter easy access under a low-mounted scope. From the outset, Frank had a philosophy to never turn down honest work. He repaired anything from a ten dollar .22 to a princely Purdey, without ever looking down his nose at a customer, however humble he might be. By the same token, he never had stars in his eyes when dealing with champions of commerce or sports, famous movie actors, or with true blue-blooded royalty.

Growing up in an age that honored the tradition of America's early Western history, Frank had a full appreciation of that colorful era. A favorite subject for his customizing was the Winchester Model 94 .30-30 carbine. In addition to hand-tuning the action, he restocked them with the finest walnut he could find, and he found some damn fine walnut. The final touch of elegance was high-relief engraving on both sides of the receivers that depicted every phase of Western life. Outstanding examples showed, in picture-perfect detail, scenes of a covered wagon train, surreptitiously observed by a palomino-mounted Indian scout peering from a distant hillside with stark, erect saguaro cactus accenting the background. Another scene showed a six-horse stagecoach pursued by a band of hostile Indians, while another presented two mounted cowboys hot after a mountain lion. Still other scenes showed deer, moose, or bighorn sheep in detailed habitat settings.

Perhaps the epitome of Pachmayr custom carbines is the Model 94 Winchester that Frank put together for President Reagan. This custom carbine is truly a one-of-a-kind combination of all that is fine and beautiful in firearms. The odyssey of the Reagan rifle began in 1981 when Frank Pachmayr decided to build a very special rifle for presentation to then-President Ronald Reagan. Frank was inspired to undertake this project because he felt a great sense of respect for the newly elected president. During the presidential campaign, Frank contributed his complete support to the conservative Republican candidate, because Reagan presented the promise of a return to fiscal and social common sense that he believed in.

Many of Reagan's roles in motion pictures were devoted to depicting early Western cowboy characters. The fact was Reagan was a real-life gentleman cowboy, able to tend the stock and horses on his Santa Barbara ranch. With this thought in mind, Frank chose to customize the consummate carbine, Winchester's lever action Model 94 .30-30. He first found a pre-64 rifle in nearly new condition and with a perfect bore. That gun was turned over to his top gunsmith for a complete internal refitting and hand honing of all the action parts to roller-bearing smoothness. Once satisfied that the action was as fine as human hands could make it, Frank turned the rifle over, with detailed instructions, to Richard Boucher (pronounced booshay), one of his most talented, precision engravers.

The idea was to depict major landmarks of Reagan's career, from playing school football to his final attainment of the presidency of the United States. In keeping with this theme, Dick inlaid a solid gold football on top of the barrel just ahead of the receiver. The right side of the receiver displays a gold microphone in honor of Reagan's days as a sports broadcaster, and also the twin masks of tragedy and mirth, depicting his days as an actor. In addition there is the seal of the Screen Actor's Guild, depicting his involvement with the labor movement and his presidency of the Guild. On the left side of the receiver, Dick placed a gold State Seal of California in honor of Reagan's two terms as Governor of California and the Presidential Seal of the United States. On the back strap of the receiver, Dick inlaid an accurate likeness of President Reagan.

For the new butt stock and fore-end, Frank chose a densely grained, luxuriously marbled English walnut blank. For this most important of all custom rifles, Frank turned to his old friend and his premier stock maker, Walter Strand. Unfortunately Walter didn't live to witness the presentation to President Reagan. After Walter shaved the stock to perfection, it went to Mike Maxwell for a precision checkering job, created in a tastefully muted design by Frank. As a final touch of elegance, the rifle was encased in a hand-crafted, velvet-lined walnut case, complete with accessories befitting the one-of-a-kind artistic work, as this certainly is.

As the Reagan rifle neared completion, Frank was informed by his personal attorney, Nicholas A. Misciagna, that any items presented to the president while he remained in office automatically became federal property and were therefore consigned to either a place in some museum, or worse, to storage in some obscure vault known only to a computer or some bespectacled clerk tending government archives. Frank wanted Reagan to carry this spectacular carbine in his saddle scabbard while riding around his ranch. Thus, it was decided to withhold presentation until after Reagan retired from office.

•••

· Chapter IV ·

THE WORLD'S FINEST SHOTGUNS

Although Frank and his staff worked on every conceivable type of firearm, clearly his first love was always premium-grade shotguns. Among his clientele were movie actors, captains of industry, and professional athletes, who appreciated and could afford high-quality smoothbores. Frank's own million-dollar collection was an impressive array of top brands, such as Parker, Perazzi, Piotti, Purdey, Holland & Holland, Boss, Westley Richards, Beretta, Winchester Model 21, and many others.

In 1964, Frank traveled to Europe and spent several months visiting major arms makers. Among them were the small Italian firms of Daniele Perazzi and F. L. Piotti, both of them virtually unknown in the United States. Frank was so impressed with the carefully handmade shotguns that he purchased several for his own use, as well as for resale. That was only the beginning. In succeeding years, Frank imported both makes of high-quality doubles in significant numbers, contributing in large part to the current popularity of both guns in the States. Frank sold thousands of recoil pads in Europe and made some lasting friendships in the process. He also ordered a prime selection of the world's finest high-grade shotguns, with features customized to his concepts. Many of these premium smoothbores found a happy home in Frank's own gun rack. Others were offered to and snapped up by Pachmayr's discriminating customers.

Nonetheless, Frank remained dissatisfied. Frank Pachmayr was beset early in life with an obsession to create the finest shotguns ever known to man. He recognized the difficulty in setting up an entire manufacturing operation such as those he had seen in Italy's famed Gardone Valley, but he could take the next best step, which was to customize well-made shotguns into masterpieces of the gunmaker's art.

Frank was always an eager buyer of fine double guns, new or used. His reputation as a collector was legendary the world over. Unsolicited offers of shotguns for him to buy arrived daily in his mail, and over the years, he built up a sizable pool of side-by-side guns that were appropriate for customizing. Many people in the trade watched for guns that Frank might want and phoned when a promising smoothbore surfaced. One day Frank received a call from his old friend Earl Taggart.

"Somehow he got wind of a real find," says Frank. "There was a little crossroads store in Pennsylvania, which was owned by a man named Howard Hewitt. The store had been built in the 1700s along the old Pony Road from Delaware to New York. Over the years that he'd operated the general store, Hewitt amassed an amazing collection of fine shotguns of every grade and gauge."

Frank and his assistant Steve Yorba jumped the first plane to Philadelphia and rented a car. Within hours they were face to face with Hewitt. Job one was to catalog the guns. It took them two days to catalog Hewitt's 136 Parker shotguns. Most of the Parkers were 12-gauge. There were also a number of relatively rare and highly desirable 20-gauge guns. There were even some old 8-gauge Parkers, with the massive Number 8 frame. Only five of these had modern, fluid steel barrels. The balance was Damascus twist barrels, too fragile for modern shotgun shells, but barrels could always be replaced. A number of the Parkers was bottom-grade Trojans, but many of them were the higher "B" and "A" grades.

"All of the guns were in great condition," says Frank. "None of them had any rust or pitting. They all closed up tight. Even the stocks were good." Apparently, Hewitt had been highly selective in his acquisitions over the years.

"He was no gun collector," explains Frank. "He was an everything collector. He had old-fashioned, hand-crank gasoline pumps, old butter churns, and ancient boxes of ammo. You name it, he had it. Along with being a combination food market, dry goods, and everything store, he was a gun dealer. He had Remington pumps and Browning shotguns, which had been discontinued for years, that were new in the boxes. After I made a deal to buy the Parkers, and he agreed to ship them, I was just walking out the door, when he said, 'Don't you want to see the European room?' Would you believe he had another big room lined with racks of prewar Merkles, Sauers, Charles Dalys, and old Purdeys?"

No need to say that all these rare and outstanding shotguns were soon residing at the Pachmayr digs. When a customer came into Pachmayr's looking for a custom shotgun, Frank took him out the rear door of the store building, across the alley to another building that he owned that fronted on Pico, and showed him a room full of almost every high-grade shotgun known to man. Here a customer could choose the gun he wanted to have completely rebuilt and customized.

Because of the great expense involved, only the finest shotguns were accepted as subjects for customizing. Two American-made shotguns, the Parker and the Winchester Model 21, both lent themselves particularly well to the upgrading procedure. The Parker has long been regarded as the premier American shotgun and has been nicknamed "Old Reliable" by hundreds of happy owners. Before the Civil War, the Parker Brothers plant at Meriden, Connecticut, manufactured coffee grinders. During the conflict, the firm accepted a contract to make breechloading carbines for the Union. Following the war, the Parker Brothers turned to making side-by-side double-barrel shotguns with Damascus twist barrels and outside hammers.

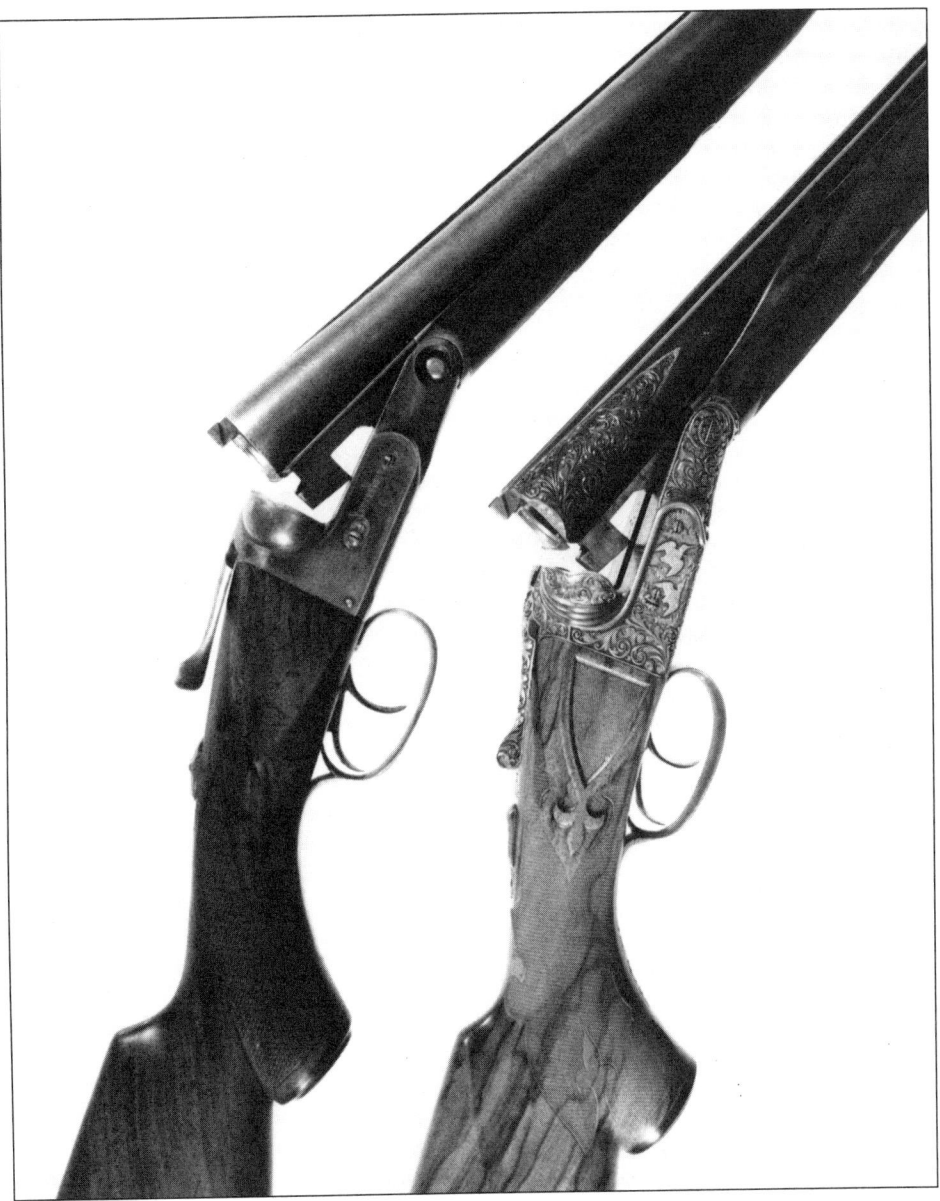

Frank Pachmayr's favorite shotgun for upgrading was the Parker. He could take a low-grade Trojan and fit it with new barrels, completely rework the action and restock it in fancy walnut. He would then have it engraved and gold-inlaid. The result exceeded the beauty and usefulness of the finest of all shotguns, the Parker Invincible Grade. Shown here is the original and an upgraded Pachmayr Parker. Note that the upgrade has side clips added for greater beauty and improved stiffness to the barrels.

Parker pioneered many important developments in the double-barreled shotgun, introducing the internal hammerless lock in 1889, automatic selective ejectors in 1902, and the first 28-gauge in 1903. In 1889 Parker adopted modern ordnance fluid steel barrels, but they continued to offer the weaker Damascus barrels on special order as late as 1926. In 1922, a Parker became available with a single selective trigger. It was designed by Herman Shura, a master gunsmith who had recently emigrated from Germany. A prior attempt at a single trigger proved unreliable and had a penchant for occasionally firing both barrels together. That problem still haunts some high-grade, European double shotguns. The year 1923 witnessed the first use of wide beavertail fore-ends, followed in 1926 by the venti-

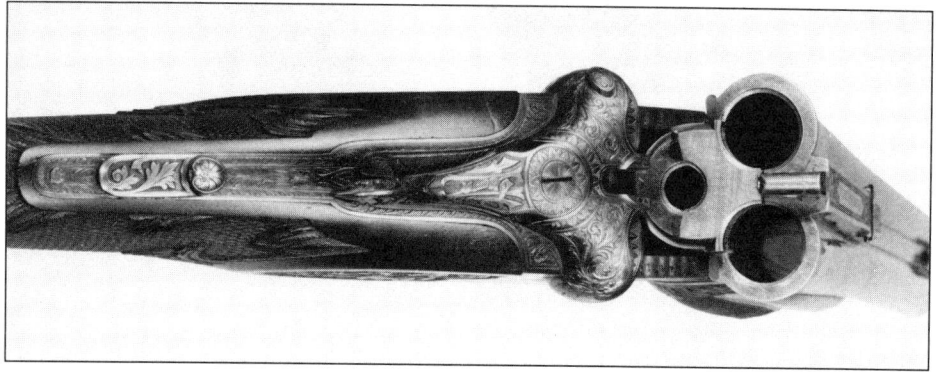

Pachmayr also reworked fine old German drillings, which have a rifle barrel under the side-by-side shotgun barrels.

lated rib, then a year later by the .410-gauge. Wide fore-ends and vented ribs were both optional features.

The depression hit the small Parker Brothers firm hard. At best it was a limited production operation, turning out barely a dozen scatter guns a week when demand was high. A sporting shotgun comes under the heading of an elective purchase. When money became short, orders dwindled to a trickle. In 1934, then company president Charles Parker sold out to Remington. Remington retained the same facilities and craftsmen at the Meriden plant, vowing, "In every respect, the Parker traditions will be continued." Parkers numbering 236,617 and up were made under Remington management.

Within a couple of years, Remington realized that the lower-priced versions of the nine different Parker grades were not cost-effective and discontinued those priced under $196. To cut costs, they moved the Parker plant to their much larger facility at Ilion, New York, in 1938. They did allow the Parker operation to retain its identity with its own separate quarters. Serial numbers 240,290 and up were made at Ilion. In 1939 Remington dropped all grades that did not have automatic ejectors. When World War II became a first priority, Remington dismantled the Parker facilities and plunged into a war production frenzy to meet the demands of the armed forces. After the war, the neglected tooling was beyond resurrection. The fine craftsmen who had assembled and fitted the guns were gone.

Parkers were handmade, in the same sense that English Purdeys are handmade. Major components were machined with excess tolerances, then hand fitted to attain the precision of a watch. From the beginning, Parker shotguns were marked by the finest workmanship. The skills required to fit the double-barreled shot-

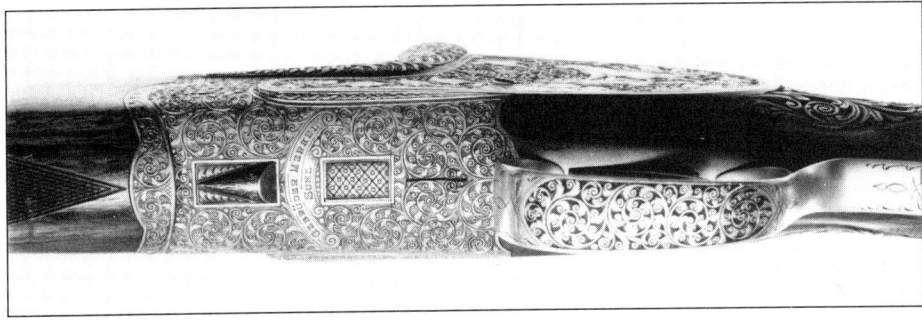

This Merkel double displays fine scroll engraving.

guns— lock, stock, and barrels—were handed down from one generation to the next. The lowest grade Parker was the Trojan, which retailed new in the early 1930s for $55. Overall, about 48,000 Trojans were manufactured. Next in grade was the Parker V. H., priced at $68, with total production placed at approximately 60,000. The top standard grade was the "A-1 Special," which had the utmost in features and materials and sold for $625. About 325 A-1s were made. Barrel steel varied according to cost and grade. The Trojan used Trojan Steel barrels and the V. H. Grade used Vulcan Steel. Both P. H. and G. H. Grades used Parker Steel. The D. H. used Titanic Steel and the C. H., B. H., and A. H. E. used Acme Steel. The A. A. H. E., a fast-swinging gun designed specifically for live pigeon shooting, and the top-grade A-1 Special used Parker Peerless Steel with barrels forged and machined entirely in the Parker plant.

The A-1 Special was lavished with infinite care in fitting. At the pinnacle of Parker production, delivery time for a special order gun ranged from six to eight months. It was also highly engraved in a variety of optional patterns and with a deep relief scroll and gold inlays. Stock dimensions were made to customer order. In an effort to top even this, Parker offered a special-order-only grade, The Parker Invincible, at $1,500 per copy, which was big money. From the Parker catalog:

> The Parker Invincible Grade places before the discriminating shooting public of the world a gun equaled by few and excelled by none. The Invincible Model is made of the very finest materials procurable. It is fabricated by artisans of superior ability, skilled in all details of high-class gunmaking, truly master gunmakers in both name and fact. No efforts will be spared in the endeavor to produce a gun of superior design, beauty and elegance of finish. The discriminating gun lover will readily acknowledge the Parker Invincible to be the finest example of the gunmakers' art ever produced by an American gunmaker.

· FRANK PACHMAYR ·

Built to order only. Parker Brothers guarantee the closest attention to our specifications and to all details of manufacture. Each item of fit and finish is most carefully accomplished by our master workmen. We conveniently offer the beautiful gun as an arm of utility and a beautiful *object d'art*.

Records indicate that only two Parker Invincibles were ever made. One Invincible was numbered 20,000. The other gun was unrecorded and to the best of my knowledge remains lost. An unrecorded Invincible, number 230,329, was discovered in 1969 and sold for $100,000. It later proved to be spurious.

I think if they were still with us, the Parker brothers would approve of Frank Pachmayr upgrading some of their fine old shotguns to the status of the Invincible. They would probably take pride in the results and they could hardly fail to be impressed. Frank's Invincible Grade Parkers are finer than anything the original firm produced and have more elaborate, more refined engraving than the originals.

This is not to say that approval is universal. Purist Parker collectors are apt to snub anything other than true originals. As one collector put it to me, "If so much as a screw has been turned, it depresses the value to some Parker perfectionists." Pachmayr's Parkers, clearly labeled "Pachmayr Invincible," don't masquerade as originals and could never be mistaken for factory issue by any knowledgeable collector. What they do offer is a practical equivalent for the original at a fraction of the cost. I anticipate, nonetheless, that someday Frank's versions of the Invincible, which can lay claim to being fine works of art in their own right, will be selling for as much as, or more than, the real thing.

One example of the Pachmayr magic touch is to be found in the Parker number 142,564, which began life in 1907 as a 12-gauge VHE Grade, with a No. 2 frame, 30-inch barrels choked, modified, and full, with automatic ejectors, double triggers, and manual safety (preferred by many shooters). Under Frank Pachmayr's watchful eye, it was stripped to its bare, white metal and completely remade. The gun was highly engraved with floral and arabesque motifs, embellished by gold inlays of ducks, pheasants, and grouse. The thumb piece of the top lever was pierced in the manner of the original Invincible. The beautiful new Circassian walnut stock and fore-end were finely checkered. The VHE sold originally for about $50.00. After customizing by Pachmayr artisans, it was valued at more than $50,000.

Frank Pachmayr's other favorite for customizing is the Winchester Model 21. It was conceived during the opulence and expansion of the 1920s in the Winchester design department headed by Thomas Crossley Johnson, designer of the monumental Model 12 Winchester pump shotgun. Assisting were George Lewis and William Roehmer. They designed the Model 21 in the light of the latest metallurgy and manufacturing methods that came out of World War I, and it became mechanically the best side-by-side double-barreled shotgun ever made. The frame and barrels were forged of the finest chrome molybdenum steel alloys. Instead of brazing and soldering the barrels together in the time-honored way, Johnson forged each barrel with half of the lump integrated with the tube, then machined each pair with interlocking dovetails. The barrel pairs were joined at the lump by the tight-fitting dovetails, then securely pinned and soldered into a single sturdy unit.

The obvious strength of this design became apparent when an off-the-shelf Model 21 was subjected to two thousand consecutive proof loads without flinching and without any dimensional changes. The bolting system of the Model 21 consists of a single underbolt engaging the barrel lump. It had to be good to make its way against the competition of such giants as the L. C. Smith, Ithaca, Fox, and

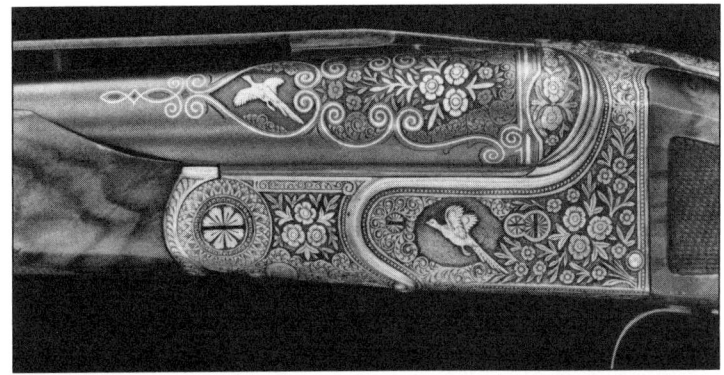

Another Parker from the side and the bottom. Various game birds are depicted.

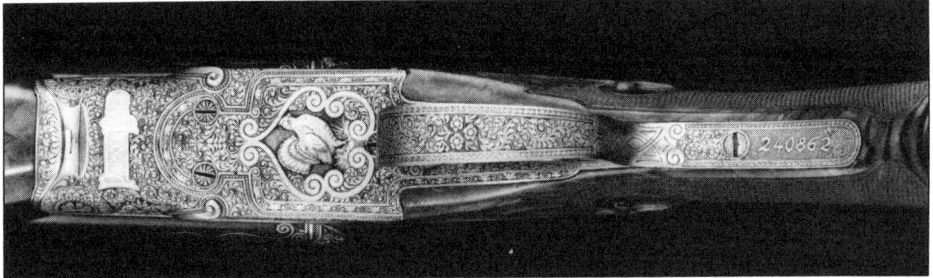

Parker. The Model 21 received little approbation at its introduction. What comment there was focused upon apparent deficiencies, such as the elimination of the familiar rib extension top lock. The only regret expressed by Frank Pachmayr was the lack of side plates.

One outstanding example of a Winchester Model 21 upgrade was the 16-gauge that Frank made for *Guns & Ammo* magazine publisher Tom Siatos. After the gun was completely benched and rebuilt, simulated side plates were added to have a broader tapestry for engraving. Both plates were graced with 18-carat yellow and white inlays of Diana, the ancient Roman goddess of the hunt. Doves and hounds attend the chaste pagan deity and golden boughs and flowers shade her. The top lever is pierced with a delicate filigree of her brother, Apollo, with drawn bow. Smoke and flames glow in the grain of the dense English walnut, full pistol-gripped stock and beavertail fore-end. Both feature precise, fine-line checkering. The butt is conservatively checkered without a plate.

After he retired from active management of Pachmayr's Inc., Frank retained the services of some of his finest craftsmen in order to continue creating nonpareil, side-by-side shotguns. He used these as a vehicle to aid the restoration of wild fowl habitats by donating the fine shotguns to various chapters of Ducks Unlimited. They were then raffled or auctioned off. The actual selling prices for these rare shotguns, usually doubled or tripled the original value of the guns. The fact that they were so rare contributed greatly to the value of Pachmayr premier shotguns. Additionally, sportsmen who support Ducks Unlimited consider purchases through the organization as a contribution to the preservation of migratory waterfowl.

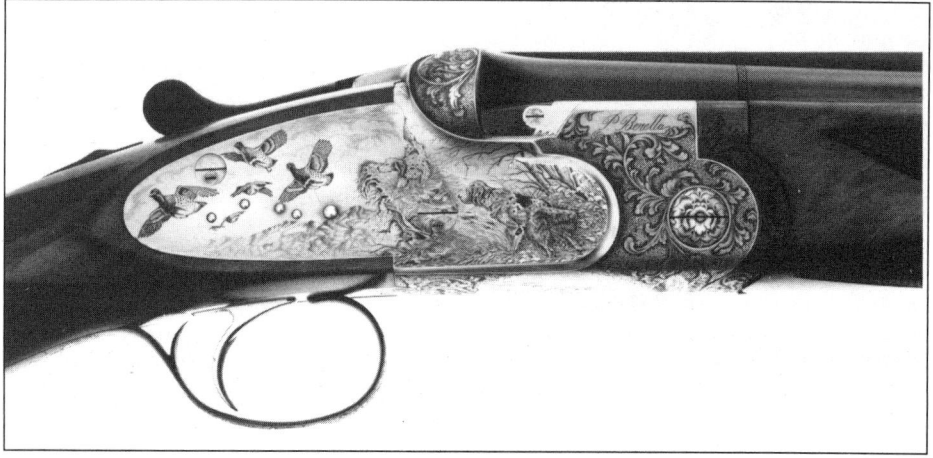

Both sides of a fine Pietro Beretta double, displaying the almost photographic quality of fine banknote engraving.

Frank Pachmayr could far more easily have simply endowed Ducks Unlimited with substantial dollars, but he wanted to contribute more of himself than that. Anyone can merely sign a check. Only the likes of Frank Pachmayr can create such superb shotguns. Furthermore, these incomparable *objects d'art* form a lasting monument to the man and demonstrate his devotion both to shotguns and to wildlife preservation.

The maestro himself didn't wield a file or graver on these shotguns any more than Henry Ford turned a wrench on the Model "T" or Model "A," but they are no less his creations. To this day, Frank chooses the various craftsmen and artisans and directs their work down to the most minute detail. It was once said of Walt Disney, "He chooses the color of the toilet paper used in the lavatories at Disney Studios." That's about the level of control exerted by Frank Pachmayr over the making of his beloved shotguns. He combines the rare qualities of taste, talent, and administrative ability that enable him to gather and direct the people who tend to the nuts and bolts. Under his watchful eye, works are created that combine perfect utility with peerless aesthetics. Products vested with pride in the making, in owning, and using may seem anachronistic in this age of space rockets and towering temples of stainless steel and one-way glass, but they serve to dramatize the contrast between increasingly rare, hand-wrought works of art and modern, consumer product clones.

The first step in recasting a quality shotgun into a genuine work of art is to totally reconstruct it mechanically. This stage of the job currently falls to a handsome, youngish, and vital master craftsman, Alain R. Laquieze of Saugus, California. Alain shapes steel with the finesse of a sculptor, adding and deleting material as required. From an engraver's point of view, boxlock, side-by-side shotguns offer a limited canvas on which to display his art. Side-plate shotguns on the other hand provide enough space to display the woodlands of Massachusetts, complete with long-haired English setters flushing gaudy pheasants. To Frank Pachmayr, the obvious solution was to simulate side plates on boxlock shotguns. Alain artfully adds side plates to any boxlock shotgun like the Parker or a Winchester Model 21 with parting lines that are all but invisible. He first mills an undercut recess into

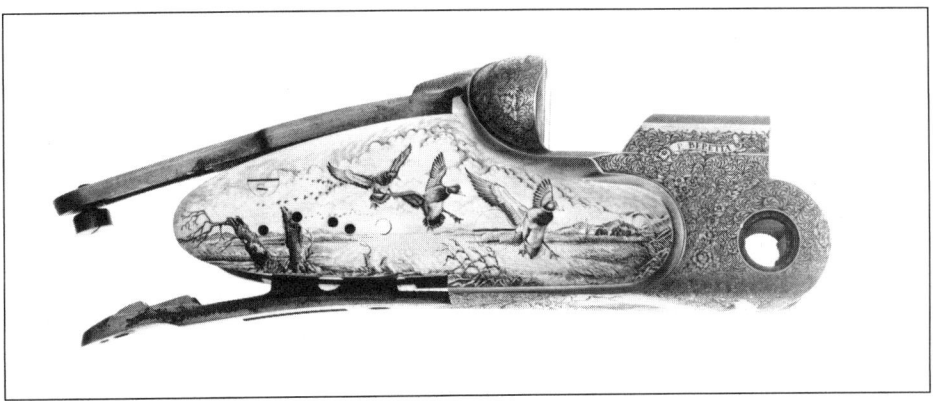

More banknote engraving on a beautiful Beretta receiver, still in white awaiting completion.

the rear of the frame, then hand fits the eighth-inch-thick steel plates. He welds side clips on both sides of the standing breech, *à la* the English Purdey. Side clips add a touch of class to a double gun and stiffen the joint between barrels and frame. Alain also welds beads of steel around the back of the outside lumps where they join the flats of the frame. Using a hammer and cold chisel, he shapes three or four delicately raised ribs and traces graceful arcs around the rear. A fine, three-cornered file removes the tool marks.

Alain transforms a common-grade Parker into the fabled Invincible by welding over the countersunk holes in the sides of the frame and replacing the original hinge pin with a new hardened steel pin. Then it is finished flush with the sides of the frame in the manner of the Invincible. The barrels are refitted to a firm contact with the standing breech and the top of the action bar (often called the water table).

He hand finishes all internal surfaces and action parts. To change the original thin splinter fore-end to a modern and practical beavertail configuration, Alain builds up the fore-end iron and adds a full support screw.

Parker parts aren't widely available these days. If replacements are not available, Alain rebuilds broken or defective action parts by welding over and reshaping worn areas and restoring the original smoothness. When necessary, he fabricates particular parts himself from high tensile bar stock and heat treats them for long wear. (When Remington decided to abandon the Parker double barrel, they sold the remaining parts inventory to a longtime employee, Larry Del Greco. Larry moved to Ithaca and went into business repairing Parkers. His son continues the work today. Del Greco is one of the few people who can color case harden a receiver after it has already been inlaid with gold.)

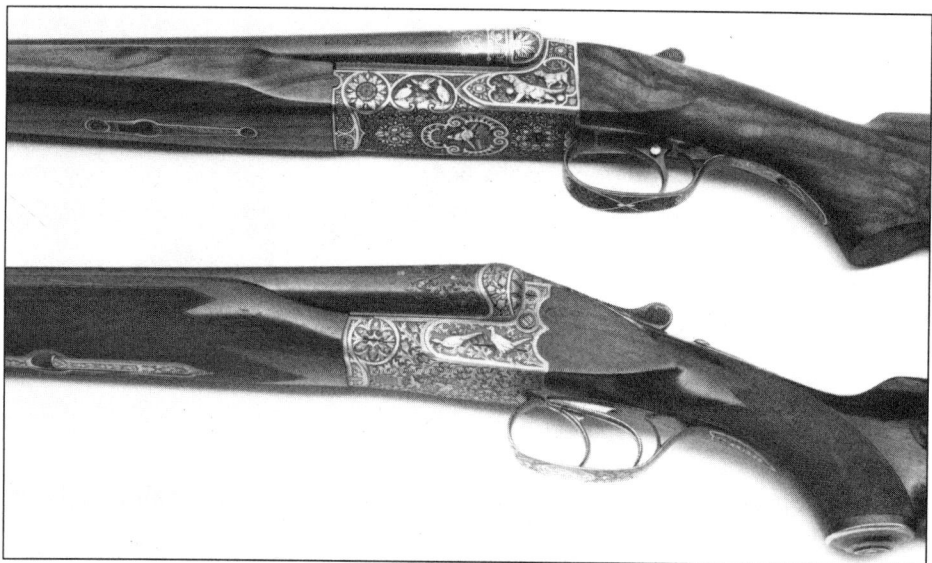

Side and bottom views of a Winchester Model 21 and a Sauer double, with contrasting styles of engraving. (Engraving by Angelo Bee.)

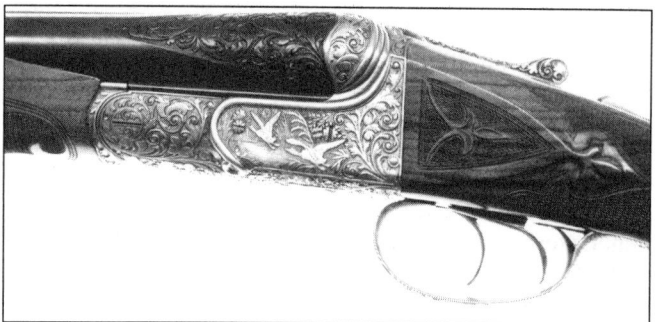

This Pachmayr displays raised beading around the back of the breech. Steel must first be welded into place, then carved into a beautiful shape. It is a difficult and time-consuming chore.

To test the tightness of the barrel-to-action fit, Alain removes the fore-end and, holding the gun upside down by the butt stock, swings the muzzle horizontally back and forth. Any play that might be present between the hook and the cross pin or any wear between the lumps and the inside of the action bar becomes immediately evident. He refits and hand hones the many internal contact surfaces until the barrels open and close with silky smoothness and with no grating or abrasive feeling. They snap shut as firmly and positively as the door of a bank vault. He checks the fit by removing the barrels and coating the lumps inside and out with the smoke from a candle. Installing the barrels, he closes and opens them. The coating must

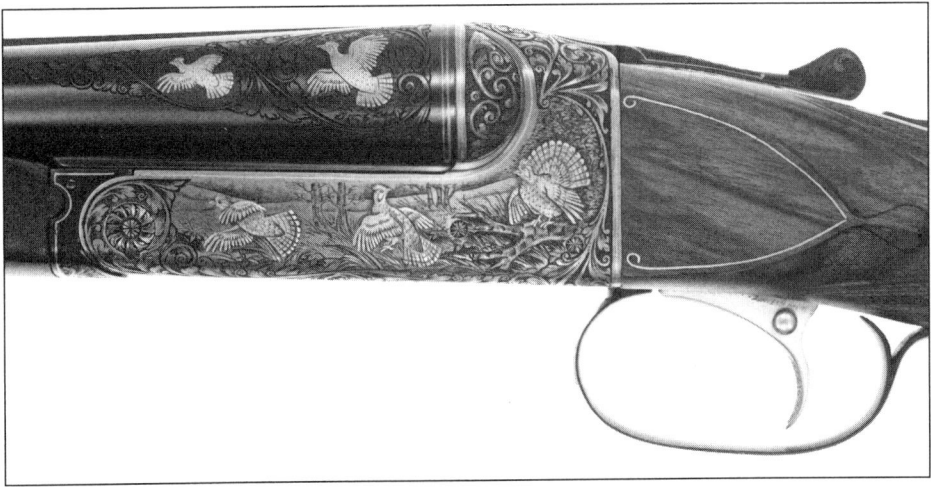

This Winchester Model 21 displays a forested home for upland game birds. Note gold wire inlaid in the stock. That's more difficult than you think!

be evenly wiped away on both sides of the lumps within the bites where the bolts engage and inside of the hook that contacts the hinge pin.

As with many dedicated gunsmiths, Alain came to his profession out of a deep love for firearms. Born in the city of Dakar, Senegal, a former French colony, in August 1949, Alain hunted the plentiful African plains game with his father, Jean-Louis, a dentist employed by the French Army. Jean-Louis and Alain's mother, Bernadette, moved back to Paris when Alain was ten years old. Removed from the distractions of African hunting, Alain devoted himself to his studies, majoring in philosophy. At maturity, Alain served in the French Army. Then a restless bent drove him to travel widely in Europe, but he finally returned to his beloved Africa where he was employed as a publicist by the French tourist agency, Havass. After a year and a half, Alain began thinking seriously about a life career. "I settled upon gunsmithing because of an enduring passion for guns," he explains. Alain entered Leon Mignon, a gunsmithing school in Liege, Belgium, and three years later earned a Superior Diploma of Gunsmithing.

· FRANK PACHMAYR ·

Part of the curriculum entailed fabricating a side-by-side shotgun receiver and lock from raw steel and fitting it to dummy barrels, using only hand files and an electric drill. I saw the results myself and I can attest to the fact that it looks as if it were machined on a mill. The flats are "flat" and every corner is square. Henri Dumoulin of Liege employed Alain, affording him an opportunity to practice every aspect of gunsmithing and fabrication. For the most part, Alain built shotguns and large-bore bolt-action rifles, typically .416 Rigby and .505 Gibbs, for African hunting, as well as double rifles. He built from scratch and installed quarter ribs and European claw-style scope mounts. In a few years, Alain became restive again and accepted employment with the premier engraver Lynton McKenzie in New Orleans. Alain left for America with his charming wife Marian and daughter Valerie. In McKenzie's shop, Alain was kept busy restoring costly antique guns and smithing high-class English shotguns.

Still beset with itching feet and seeking a balmier climate, Alain asked McKenzie about job opportunities on the West Coast, who told him to call Frank Pachmayr, a man who could appreciate a fine gunsmith. "When I got his call," says Frank, "I was so impressed with Alain's training and experience that I sent my gasoline credit card to him, so he could drive to Los Angeles." With his household possessions loaded into a rented U-Haul truck and his car in tow, Alain arrived at the South Grand address about a week later. "I put Alain to work the very next day," says Frank. "He didn't disappoint me. Alain is such a fine gunsmith that he's still working for me eleven years later." Currently, Alain operates his own fully equipped gun shop and devotes most of his efforts to customizing class shotguns for Pachmayr. His remaining time is spent on general gunsmithing, with an emphasis on customizing rifles and shotguns, including chambering and rebarreling rifles.

After performing the many functions required to restore and upgrade fine shotguns for Frank, Alain polishes and finishes the guns. He has the equipment and skill to apply hot bluing or the finest cold blue, as well as color case hardening and the gray finish so popular on the Continent.

The one thing that immediately marks a rifle or shotgun as custom, even seen from across a room, is a hand-fitted, hand-finished stock. Hallmarks of quality—elegant lines, flawless checkering, superb wood grain—are apparent even at a distance and even to the untrained eye. Much of the utility and beauty of a custom shotgun derives from the butt stock and fore-end. Only the finest wood with outstanding figure warrants use on such guns. Frank Pachmayr's fascination with fine shotguns could only be equaled by his deep affection for stock wood. Long after he retired from Pachmayr Inc., Frank maintained his own wood mill in northern California. Out of the hundreds' of tons of walnut that annually passed through his mill, Frank cherry-picked for his own use only those blanks ranking in the top one or two percent of quality wood. He based his selection on density and extravagant grain.

"In their best days," says Frank, "Purdey never saw walnut as beautiful as my exhibition and presentation grades of English, Circassian, French, Bastogne, or claro!"

Even a priceless stock blank is only as good as the man who shapes and fits it to the gun. Pachmayr's stockmaker of stature is Michael B. Maxwell of Springville, California. Mike began custom stock work over thirty years ago. Born in Long Beach, California, at the height of World War II, Mike trained to become a commercial airline pilot, but somehow his hobby of stockmaking became so intrusive that it simply pushed all other ambitions aside. Famed stockmaker, Walter Abe, introduced Mike to Frank in late 1970. That was the beginning of a long, mutually beneficial business relationship. Mike had found a patron who paid well and kept him comfortably busy.

Mike's taste in stock design parallels Frank Pachmayr's own conservative, understated lines, so he merely has to follow the classic configurations established by Frank more than two generations ago. Over the years, from fitting thousands of sportsmen, Pachmayr refined his standard shotgun stock to a size and shape that fits most upland gunners to a "T." Of course dimensions were altered to fit individual customer needs.

The day is past when custom stockmakers insist upon the masochistic drudgery of carving every stock by hand from raw wood. Woodcutting pantographs

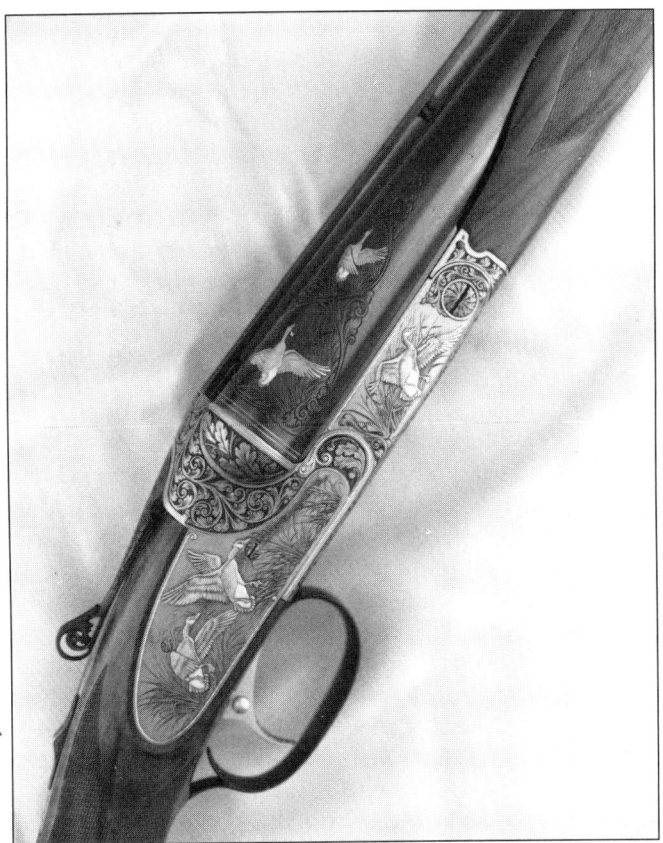

Side plates added to this Winchester Model 21 offer space for ducks descending to a reeded pond, while geese fly on the barrels. Note the perfection of the details of head, feet, and feathers!

have evolved to a high degree of precision and allow precutting of much of the stock close to final configuration. Even much of the inletting can be cut by machine, requiring a relatively small amount of hand fitting. The prestigious English firms of Holland & Holland and Purdey are now using the highly refined Precision Duplicator manufactured by Hoenig & Rodman, located at 6521 Morton Drive in Boise, Idaho. Guaranteed to cut to the incredible tolerance of plus or minus .0005 of an inch, the broadly patented, massive machine was designed by George Hoenig, a noted alumni of Frank Pachmayr's informal school of gunsmithing.

Born in Bacsalmas, Hungary, George apprenticed as a machinist in Germany. He fled Hungary to escape communism when he was only sixteen, immigrating to Los Angeles under the sponsorship of a Catholic priest. In accordance with local law, George returned to high school. While taking a metal shop class, he fabricated with relatively crude shop tools a single-shot pistol and a revolver. George received Industrial Arts Awards from Ford Motor Company in 1953 and 1954 for the guns he made in school. More importantly, the two examples of his skill and talent caused Frank Pachmayr to hire the promising youngster as a gunsmith when he was only eighteen years old. Certainly that was some kind of a record.

George Hoenig matured at Pachmayr's. He became a premier gun craftsman and stockmaker. Under Frank's direction, he developed the patented .45 ACP wide barrel link and the popular Pachmayr Dominator barrel attachment that converted a .45 ACP Government Model frame into a formidable single-shot pistol, an item once offered in a wide variety of big-bore calibers.

The epitome of good taste for custom shotguns has long been a plain wood butt free of the usual butt plate and checkered with twenty-two lines per inch or finer. This demands extremely dense, close-grained walnut. Other popular choices are sculptured, checkered steel butt plates or skeleton steel butt plates with checkered wood showing through the cutout central portion. A conventional recoil pad with exposed rubber lattice draws only frowns from shotgun epicures. Frank's Old English Presentation pad with solid sides and a finely grained leather face simulates leather-covered pads often found on high-quality shotguns.

When specified by Pachmayr, Mike Maxwell installs an Old English pad before finishing the stock with weather- and chemical-resistant polyurethane that is polished to a soft gloss. He hand checkers elaborate patterns that are subdued and in good taste. Even though the checkering sometimes is as fine as thirty-two lines per inch, a magnifying glass reveals that each diamond is perfectly formed, crisp, and sharp with no hint of runovers around the borderless perimeter.

Before the Pachmayr shotguns are stocked or finished, they are embellished with fine engraving. "Firearm engraving has always been a traditional vehicle for fine art," says Frank, "but it seems to me that modern engraving has reached a higher pinnacle of perfection than was ever attained in antiquity. The work today has become even more precise and more true-to-life in recent years. Any one of my engravers can do finer work than the best ones in the early 1900s. It's the engraving that lifts a custom-fitted shotgun from just a superb field companion to the higher plane of a true work of art."

For decades, Frank Pachmayr kept a cadre of engravers constantly hunched over their ball vises, peering intently through jewelers' loupes or magnifying glasses. With their callused palms, they pushed or lightly hammered their gravers through intricate maneuvers that magically created woodland scenes and lifelike animals or birds on a canvas of solid steel.

The beauty of fine engraving must be seen up close to be appreciated. Much of what masquerades as engraving is in fact crude and lifeless. Fine engraving, executed by a genuine craftsman is incredibly detailed and realistic. Fine-line banknote engraving achieves an almost photographic clarity. Somehow the engravers achieve that elusive third dimension. The depth is apparent to the eye. Hunting scenes are favored subjects and under skilled hands they literally come alive. An alert mule deer with head held high tests the wind with his nose, seeming ready to bolt at the crack of a twig. An eagle poised for flight with wings extended and every feather delicately defined appears ready to fly off the gun and assume a life of its own. An English setter with his hair blowing in the breeze poises on point and trembles with anticipation. A flight of mallards gracefully descends upon a reed-lined pond, and you can almost hear the swish of their wings. The result is as real and beautiful as a painting by van Gogh.

All the engravers employed by Frank are highly qualified craftsmen, all of international stature. Certainly ranked among the best is Richard R. Boucher of Torrance, California. Dick became an engraver mostly by accident. After leaving college in 1949, he answered an ad for a job in the stockroom at Hall-

This Browning over/under offers space for a remote forest sheltering a covey of fleeing bobwhite upland game birds.

mark Greeting Cards in Kansas City, Missouri. When his artistic talent came to light, he was hired instead as an engraver. Dick did copperplate and steel-line engravings of fancy greeting cards, stationery, invitations, and business cards. He engraved the presidential seals of Eisenhower, Kennedy, and Johnson. Eventually, Boucher became a supervisor and an instructor of young fledgling engravers for Hallmark.

"I discovered that aptitude plays a large part in making an engraver," he says. "I saw kids that were great at painting and sketching, but just couldn't get the knack of handling engraving tools."

One day Dick saw an engraved gun in a store and was a little startled at the cost of an otherwise ordinary shotgun. He thought, "I can do that." He experimented with some simple patterns on his own guns. "After I learned that the curved surfaces required a different technique than the flat surfaces I was accustomed to working with," says Dick, "I began to do some creditable work." Inevitably, Boucher's shooting buddies began to ask him to engrave their guns. He soon found that he was making more money at engraving guns than he was working full time for Hallmark. In 1969, he left the greeting card firm. Today, as a career engraver, Boucher earns $3,000 and up for each individual job. An average engraving job on a shotgun with a couple of gold inlays runs about $4,000.

"You have to be as much a mechanic as an artist," he remarks. "Mainly, it's a matter of cutting softer steel with harder steel. I make my own engraving tools with V-shapes from 60 to 45 degrees. Some are almost knife edged. I use a small electric grinder and stones to sharpen the tips. I can perform deep or shallow engraving, German or English style." Boucher specializes in fine-line banknote engraving.

Boucher uses only 24-carat solid gold wire and plate for his line and sculptured inlays. "Solid gold is more yellow and has a richer look," he says. "I know it's softer than 18-carat but people who buy this kind of work don't use their inlaid guns in the field all that much. If they do, and the gold wears down, they can afford to have it replaced." Boucher can inlay a design a customer wants on his gun. "One time," he chuckles, "a guy had me inlay dinosaurs and ancient ferns on a .45 Colt automatic. I prefer to make the inlays match the gun, using grouse and quail on upland game shotguns, for example. One time I put a stagecoach with wild Indians in hot pursuit on the side of a lever-action Winchester rifle."

In addition to guns, Boucher engraves custom knives. He estimates that his work averages about 70 percent shotguns, 20 percent rifles, and 10 percent knives. Richard Boucher is a professional member of both the Custom Gun Maker's Guild and the Firearms Engraver's Guild of America.

Another fine engraver on the Pachmayr team is Gino Cargnal of Simi Valley, California. It seems that much of the artistic talent available in the United States today was imported from the Continent. Gino was born in 1938 in Liege, Belgium. The precocious youngster was already turning out acceptable engraving at age fifteen. On 6 July 1954 Gino went to work at Fabrique Nationale as an apprentice engraver. The first six months were spent at design training, followed by three years of pure apprenticeship. Only then was he allowed to actually engrave simple patterns on production guns. It was almost five years before Gino was allowed to do any serious engraving upon FN rifles and shotguns. For ten years, while working full time for FN, Gino also attended the Academie Royale des Beaux Arts de Liege Belgium at night, finally graduating with a Diploma of Superior Degree for Fine and Artistic Design. He filed his school workbooks with the Belgian government to receive his professional rating, which was then required under a law dating back to 1883 and enacted under the rule of Napoleon.

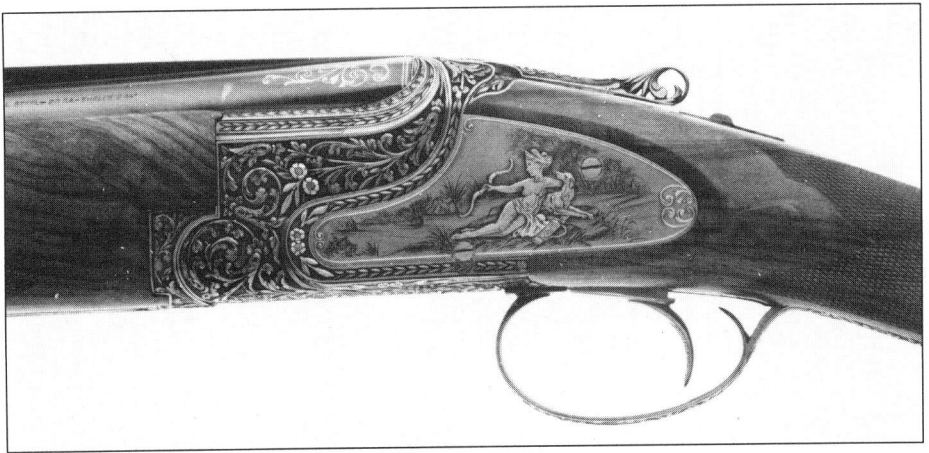

A Browning O/U with side plates added, provides a bower of rest for Diana, goddess of the hunt, and faithful hound.

Gino's work was of such excellence that it came to the attention of William Jaqua, a shotgun fancier and gun dealer in Ohio. Jaqua wrote Gino and offered him a job with his firm. In 1978 Gino sold all of his possessions, packed up his wife and two young sons, and moved to the States. He worked for Jaqua for ten years before moving to the West Coast to work for Pachmayr. Gino showed me a Model 21 Winchester with side plates added, which he had engraved in the white. The gold inlays were yet to be installed, but the work was outstanding. On page ninety-seven of the 1984 *Guns & Ammo Annual*, a completed Pachmayr Model 21 was displayed with magnificent engraving by Gino.

Another proud graduate of the Academie Royale des Beaux Arts de Liege Belgium is Angelo Bee of Chatsworth, California. Angelo was born in 1929 in Lamon, the Province of Belluno in northern Italy. At twelve years of age, Angelo migrated with his parents to Liege where he attended high school and college. He devoted two years to the study of architecture. At sixteen, he began training as a machinist at the Browning division of Fabrique Nationale. After two years, he decided to switch to the engraving department to get better pay and improved working conditions. A letter of introduction from his high school art teacher gained Angelo a place in the class of twenty young apprentice engravers.

"For the first nine months," says Angelo, "we never touched a tool. They kept us studying art and making sketches of engraving patterns." After several years of intensive training, Angelo found he was one of only four trainees who were accepted to begin engraving lower-cost Browning production guns. Angelo remained with FN for twenty-five years, studying under such masters as Felix Funken and Louis Francken. During a financial slump of the early 1970s, the Browning engraving department dropped from 140 men to just 30. About the same time, Angelo received a letter from Gene Wahrman, an executive at Paramount Pictures in Hollywood who had purchased a Browning Superposed over-under shotgun with a signed engraving by Angelo. Wahrman was so impressed with the work that he had written to Browning for Angelo's address. "We started writing back and forth," says Angelo, "with me writing in French and with him writing in English. In 1975, Mr. Wahrman suggested that I come over and visit him. During the month I was

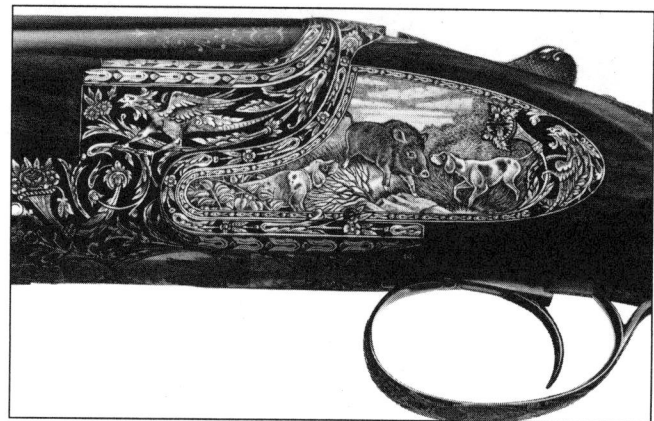

On another Browning O/U with sideplates is the scene of an encounter between a Russian boar and two hounds, flanked by winged dragons. This spectacular innovative artistic creation is set on a black background. It could easily hang in the Louvre!

here, he introduced me to Mr. Pachmayr, who sponsored me so I could move to the United States and work for him."

In addition to all styles of fine engraving—English scroll, German scroll, deep engraving, and banknote, Angelo performs specialties suggested by his customers. He has engraved such oddities as Bambi on a Perazzi trap gun and Snow White and the Seven Dwarfs on a Winchester Model 12. Although he works on pistols and rifles also, Angelo's passion is shotguns, particularly over-unders. He specializes in gold inlays with highly detailed gold wire work. His scroll patterns are cut freehanded without stencils or drawings, producing designs of free-flowing grace.

Another Pachmayr engraver, Cesario Gionvani "Rino" Greco is one of the premier artists featured in the classic book, *Modern Firearm Engravings*, by Mario Abbiatico. Born in June 1924 in Galatone, Italy, Rino soon displayed the soul of an artist. Even in grammar school, his talent at drawing was evident. As an adult, he found his paintings were saleable, but growing up deep in the heart of Italy's famed gun belt, he decided to become a firearm engraver.

He followed the well-worn path to an engraving career by going to work for Fabrique Nationale in Liege. After the usual training and apprenticeship, Rino's outstanding talent came to the attention of FN's master engraver, Louis Francken. Francken saw some of Rino's sketches of engraving patterns and found them both artistic and innovative. Soon a friendship developed between the master and his dedicated disciple. Rino took his drawings to Francken, and he taught young Rino the techniques known only to him. Soon Rino was extended the rare opportunity to work with Francken and his select team of master engravers. Of the 200 engravers employed by FN at the time, only seven belonged to that elite group. Of that chosen seven, only Francken himself and Rino specialized in engraving and inlaying the figures of animals. In 1969, Rino accomplished one of his most important works, the engraving of an FN rifle for Mr. Fessler. The gun was eventually donated to the Smithsonian Institute in Washington, D.C., where it remains.

In 1972, Rino returned to his native Italy and sought out Firmo Fracassi to learn the techniques of this noted master engraver. Then Rino was employed by Beretta, working alongside master engravers Gianfranco Petersoli, Remo Salvineli, and Mario Abbiatico, who later produced a masterwork book on engraving. In 1986, Rino immigrated to the United States and began working for Frank Pachmayr. "Mr. Pachmayr is well known in Europe as a builder of fine firearms," says Rino. "It's an honor and a privilege to work for him, even though Frank knows just what he wants, and nothing can make him change his mind. It's the best thing that has happened to me since I came to this country. I want to thank him for that."

Frank does indeed know what he wants, and he refuses to be diverted from his decisions by employees' protests. It was his supreme self-confidence that enabled him to go so far in the gun business. His well-defined sense of supervision makes impeccable Pachmayr-customized pistols, rifles, or shotguns instantly identifiable to informed shooters and collectors. Frank patrolled the line of gunsmith benches at his shop, making certain that his employees maintained his high standards of workmanship. His obsession for fine shotguns, combined with his love of duck hunting, led Frank Pachmayr to build these works of art and donate them to such wildlife preservation organizations as Ducks Unlimited and the Foundation for North American Wild Sheep for sale to discriminating sportsmen. The combination of talents that Frank Pachmayr pulled together for this effort will likely never be assembled again.

"This project gives me a reason to go on living," says Frank. "I don't want to be remembered just by a bronze plaque nailed to a tree somewhere in the wilderness. These shotguns will become my monument. Every time someone takes one of my guns to the skeet range or to the field, I'll be remembered."

Frank Pachmayr's incomparable works of art have already become collectors' items of heirloom quality, and each owner has a distinct work of art that he can display with pride and carry in the field for a lifetime of pleasure and satisfaction.

•••

• Chapter V •

A CALL TO ARMS

In the late 1930s Frank Pachmayr's gunsmithing and shooting accessories business was booming. His sporting goods store was steadily expanding, adding new product lines and hiring more salesmen. A battery of gunsmiths repaired guns and created new custom rifles and shotguns. Frank's inventive mind was overflowing with ideas for more and better shooting accessories. He had a sizable machining facility replete with lathes, mills, drills, and profiling machines in the building behind the sporting goods store that was busily turning out Pachmayr Swing Mounts, Revolver Sight Gauges, and a variety of injection molds for recoil pads.

Meanwhile, dark clouds were gathering on the international horizon. In Washington, senators and congressmen were debating whether or not the United States should again become embroiled in Europe's endless squabbling. After abjectly capitulating to nearly all Hitler's demands, Prime Minister Neville Chamberlain of England returned from the Munich Conference with the Nazi dictator, flourished his black umbrella and talking of "peace with honor" and "peace in our time." Neville's "peace" lasted one year.

President Roosevelt began preparing for what he regarded as the inevitable eventuality of war. The aircraft industry was stimulated by government contracts to get modern fighter planes and bombers off the drawing boards and into prototype stages for testing. The automotive industry was pressed to begin the manufacture of tanks.

Japan gobbled up vast areas of the Far East. Italy and Germany held sway over much of Africa. Mussolini boasted of what good fun it was to bomb and machine-gun spear-bearing natives from the air. Hitler marched into Alsace-Lorraine with no resistance from a France that was politically torn and had only antiquated defenses. After Hitler devastated Poland on 1 September 1938, France and England were obliged by treaty commitments to declare war on Germany. About six months of what became known as the "phony war" followed. Both entrenched armies faced each other across a "no-man's land" that separated the fortifications of the Maginot Line from the Siegfried Line.

· FRANK PACHMAYR ·

When Hitler elected to move, he did so with stunning suddenness and devastating effect. In May of 1940, Hitler's troops and armor overran the Low Countries and made an end run around the northern flank of the French fixed gun emplacements and concrete pill boxes. Chamberlain was ousted and Winston Churchill took his place.

The Axis were already geared for battle when the Japanese surprise attack on Pearl Harbor destroyed most of United States Pacific Fleet and killed thousands of fine, young American men. Most were trapped below deck and drowned or suffocated. Some unfortunate sailors trapped below deck in sunken warships remained alive for days, rapping out a desperate SOS on the steel bulkheads. Eventually the metallic clanking grew dim and finally ceased. Suddenly, America was united with Europe in a deadly determination to defeat the Axis.

Only the American Communist Party held out against the war. They staged street demonstrations and riots. Vociferous and volatile Harry Bridges, a leading official of the American Communist Party, and, believe it or not, president of the immensely powerful Longshoremen's Union, tied up shipping at all major ports with dock strikes and disrupted efforts to send supplies to the British. The Communists formed a group called "America First," which aimed at keeping the United States out of the war. When Hitler turned his military might against Russia, foolishly splitting his own forces, America's Communists switched sides overnight with no hint of embarrassment. Communist propaganda in the United States was then directed solely to sending arms to Russia.

Before the war intruded, American industry was busy turning out new cars, refrigerators, and other domestic products. This changed virtually overnight. Every machine that could turn a screw suddenly became committed to the war effort. Production of consumer goods stopped cold. For a half-dozen years, it was next to impossible in America to buy a pound of butter or meat, a few gallons of gas, or a new set of tires for an overage car.

Frank Pachmayr, the happy gunsmith, was reluctantly swept along in this tide and soon found himself thrust into the role of a harried industrialist. In 1942, many of the large, prime government defense contractors turned to Pachmayr as a reliable source for precision, machined components. Soon, recoil pads and Swing Mounts were as scarce as butter. Nearly all of Frank's machines were devoted to subcontracting parts for the aircraft industry. Because of the precision of his equipment and his reputation for exacting workmanship, Frank was entrusted with making parts of the finest tolerances, critical engine and airframe parts on which the Allied pilots' lives depended.

Bill Ives, a friend of Frank's, was instrumental in getting the ball rolling. Bill was an executive design and production engineer for Aircraft Accessories, a Lockheed subsidiary in Burbank, that specialized in hydraulics. Bill was in charge of the production of component parts for the hydraulic systems that were widely used in aircraft for moving control surfaces and landing gears, among others. Immediately prior to and during World War II, Aircraft Accessories was subcontracting to sixty-five firms in the Los Angeles basin. Bill Ives was well acquainted with Frank's machine shop and knew that Frank had the ability to hold critical tolerances. Also, he had the machines to profile cam sections that were required to operate valves and selectors in hydraulic systems. Bill convinced Frank Pachmayr that he should start subcontracting aircraft components.

As the war ground on, Frank grew into a major subcontractor for the aircraft industry, which was then heavily concentrated in the greater Los Angeles area. Douglas Aircraft, Hughes Aircraft, Northrop Aircraft, North American, Convair, and Lockheed were all located in or near Los Angeles. Frank bid contracts with companies outside of the Los Angeles area as well, including Rohr and Ryan Aircraft in San Diego, plus the Boeing plants in Seattle, Washington, and Wichita, Kansas, as well as Kaiser Metal Products in Trenton, New Jersey. With the passing

Pachmayr consolidated his machine shops, which were located in twenty-seven buildings and spread over an eight-block area, into this one huge three-story structure at the corner of Figueroa and 23rd Street in Los Angeles.

months, Pachmayr was awarded more and larger government subcontracts. As a high-priority manufacturer, Frank was able to purchase and lease more and larger machines to process the contracts. As his ability to produce expanded, military procurement turned to him for larger parts in greater quantities. This in turn called for more equipment. The two elements, demand and supply capability, fed on each other and caused Frank's manufacturing business to expand exponentially.

In the beginning, Pachmayr's machine shop was confined to the area in the rear of the sporting goods store on South Grand Avenue. The first expansion involved the purchase of the building next door to the south from the occupant, Ponder and Best, a prominent photographic accessories wholesaler. The purchase effectively doubled Pachmayr's floor space. Frank had offices for himself and his staff built in the front part of the new building. Behind that, four six-foot-long gunsmith benches were lined up with tool racks above and drawers below. From there to the alley was given over to the machine shop. Portions of the wall between the two buildings were removed and doors installed to allow easy access.

The rear wall of the sporting goods store was moved back to make more room up front for retail selling. The store grew in stages as new product lines, such as hunting clothes, books, and camping supplies, were added to the large selection of new and used firearms offered. Gun racks lined the new rear wall and both side walls, fronted by glass counters, and filled with handguns and gun-related accessories. Above the gun racks, Frank had rustic facades built, simulating peaked-roof log cabins. Trophy heads of deer, elk, caribou, moose, bison, and a variety of stuffed small game were displayed above that. Overhead, there hung several old wagon wheels, each with four ancient kerosene lamps suspended beneath and converted to electricity, of course. Several freestanding glass island counters were stationed out on the sporting goods floor, offering display space for a variety of fishing and hunting products, and racks of hunting clothes flanked the north wall. Several executive offices were installed on a mezzanine floor, with windows fronting into the store for observation. The shipping department was located directly under the offices. The walls of the shipping department were lined with shelves containing boxed recoil pads, grip adapters, and other products.

Building construction was virtually at a standstill during the war. As Pachmayr's role in the war effort expanded, he was obliged to spread out horizontally, building by building, along Grand Avenue, around the block along Pico Boulevard, and back up Olive Street. Before the conflict ended, Pachmayr's manufacturing operation occupied a total of twenty-seven buildings, spread over an eight-block area of downtown Los Angeles. With so many buildings, it became a major logistical problems to move spare parts to the various machining operations. Frank purchased a fleet of four GI Jeeps and outfitted each with a compact flatbed trailer. These small, maneuverable vehicles scuttled back and forth through streets and alleys among the various buildings, like so many busy beetles, each towing a trailer-load of parts in various stages of manufacture.

•••

When the atomic bomb brought the Pacific War to a sudden and largely unexpected halt, Los Angeles became a graveyard littered with the rusting "bones" of dead machine shops. Major war plants found themselves suddenly high and dry. The government yanked all their contracts without warning. Most companies were caught up in an expansion cycle and were in debt up to their ears. Many went bankrupt. For a time following the war, you could buy a fully operational machine shop in the Los Angeles area virtually for pocket change. Much of the tooling and heavy machinery involved in war production belonged to the federal government and was leased to contract companies. With the end of hostilities, these machines reverted back to government possession. Inside the huge United States Army Air Force hangers near Palmdale airport, an hour's drive north of Los Angeles, there were acres and acres of sophisticated and expensive machines gathering dust and rust. The Air Force auctioned off the machines over a period of months. Companies searching for ways to stay alive turned to proprietary products such as cigarette lighters and injection-molded plastic products. You could find about fifty different styles of plastic ashtrays manufactured around Los Angeles at the time. Obviously, the market for plastic gadgets was soon saturated.

Frank Pachmayr was one of the few prominent wartime manufacturers in the enviable position of remaining in a stable financial condition. He was able to turn some of his manufacturing facilities back to creating firearms accessories. Also, he held a number of government contracts that continued after the war since he was engaged in research and development on the next generation of weapons.

One morning Frank received a phone call from his old friend Floyd Gibbons, owner of a used-machinery business located a few blocks away. "Hey, Frank, have I got a machine for you!" Gibbons knew of Pachmayr's penchant for fine machinery, especially at bargain prices. "I know where there's a Cincinnati Hydratel for sale back East for about one-fifth of its current retail value. It cost forty-six-thousand dollars new, and this machine is in new condition."

Frank didn't own a Hydratel yet, but he well knew its capabilities. At that point in time, it was state of the art. Tape-controlled and computer-controlled milling machines hadn't been dreamed of yet. The only automatic machines made at that time were controlled mechanically by gears, cams, and levers, except for the Hydratel. This remarkable monster had a small stylus on one side that followed the contours of a full-sized wooden model of the finished part. Information from the stylus was transmitted to a battery of either three or four milling cutters via a hydraulic system called a "tracer." The Hydratel could cut three-dimensional contours of highly complex shapes, something unheard of before. The wondrous machine created either three or four duplicate parts in one operation, depending upon how many spindles it had.

Pachmayr didn't even have to think twice about it. "I'll take it," he replied. A couple of weeks later, Frank drove down to the railroad yard in East Los Angeles to view his prize with pride. The twenty-ton behemoth stood alone in all its majesty, atop a flatbed railroad car. A special heavy-load flatbed truck was required to move the massive Hydratel to the South Grand address. It was laboriously inched through the wide rear doors from the alley and eased into place on the concrete floor. The next morning when Frank came to work, he was surprised and chagrined to find that the concrete had collapsed under the load and one leg of the huge machine had actually sunk down into the floor. It became necessary to dig out a considerable section of the floor to a depth of five feet and fill it in with reinforced concrete to support the weight of the Hydratel.

Some of Frank's friends and all of his competitors saw the Hydratel as nothing more than a fine anchor for a battleship, and the war was over. Who needed battleship anchors anymore?

• FRANK PACHMAYR •

One friend asked Frank outright, "Why did you buy this turkey, anyway?"

"It's a beautiful machine," replied Frank simply. "You know how much I love fine machines. It pains me to see fine tooling still in good working order relegated to the scrap pile."

"Well," retorted the friend sarcastically, "you can't put it in the living room and pet it."

The kibitzers clucked sympathetically and looked at Frank with pity, but Frank was two jumps ahead of them. Pachmayr Corporation already had contracts that could make full use of the Hydratel's unique advantages. What's more, he kept on buying Hydratels when they became available as war surplus at a fraction of their true value. Eventually, he was to own a total of nineteen of the unique 3-D mills, more than any other company west of the Mississippi. He also bought several Rise and Fall Hydramatic mills with small wheels that followed cams to mill out two-dimensional shapes, as well as an immense production turret lathe, fifteen feet long, with a face plate that was five feet in diameter to hold oversized work pieces.

•••

In the middle of 1954, the Los Angeles City Council created a new M-1 industrial zone near the Pachmayr base of operations. Located in this new zone at 2222 South Figueroa Street, the northeast corner of the intersection with 23rd Street, was a sturdy three-story concrete and brick building that had been raised around the turn of the century to house the Pierce-Arrow automobile sales and service operations. The original tenants were long gone and the building was available. The 158,000-square-foot, steel-reinforced structure was so strong that the city building commissioner swore that it was one of a few buildings in Los Angeles that could survive an atomic attack. Frank Pachmayr saw the vacant building as an opportunity to consolidate his widely scattered machining operations. In June of 1954, the Pachmayr Corporation leased the building for five years for a total consideration of $180,000.00. Frank moved all his machines, including the huge Hydratels into his new quarters. The heavier machines were placed on the ground floor and lighter ones on the second story. Holes had to be drilled in the concrete floors to anchor the machines. A Pachmayr employee who worked on the project told me, "Nine times out of ten, the drill ran into reinforcing steel rods that crisscrossed the floors." Wide drive-up ramps, originally used to move heavy Pierce-Arrow automobiles between floors, facilitated the movement of materials and parts from one department to another.

The research and engineering department, which boasted its own machine shop and sheet metal fabricating facility for constructing prototypes, occupied the top floor. At full strength the department employed an average of fifteen engineers, fifteen research and development machinists, and a like number of sheet metal fabricators. Engineering personnel were highly qualified and experienced in all the disciplines of Aeronautical Engineering and Armament Engineering. Chief engineer for Pachmayr was Guy E. Lentz, with B.S. and M.E. engineering degrees from Oklahoma A & M. His experience included development of high-tech aircraft armament, including automatic cannons and rocketry. Lentz, staff engineer at Lockheed Aircraft Corporation, was responsible for developing the complete armament for the P2V bomber. He also developed ordnance for the Vega Model 37, the British Ventura bomber, and the B-34 bomber.

At the rail yard in East Los Angeles, Frank Pachmayr (right) views his two huge new Hydratel hydraulic milling machines with understandable pride. At the time, these machines were state-of-the-art in sophisticated mills.

On his staff at Pachmayr Corporation were such outstanding technicians as Clarence Otto, a former army paratrooper who served with army intelligence. His work experience included wing design at the American Aviation Corporation, and he was liaison engineer for the P2V prototype at Lockheed Aircraft Corporation. Another top-rated engineer was William McKinley, a graduate of UCLA and CalTech, where he studied aircraft structure and power plants, air armaments, and interior and exterior ballistics. He also worked at Lockheed designing airframes. Robert O'Brien served with the United States Air Force for 5½ years, during which time he studied all phases of aircraft design and maintenance. When mustered out, he attended Northrop Aeronautical Engineering Institute for 2½ years, graduating as a Certified Aeronautical Engineer.

FRANK PACHMAYR

These were only a few of the fine people who were employed full-time as engineers at Pachmayr Corporation. Others who served or consulted on specific projects were Walter R. Nass, a USC Mechanical Engineering graduate and former Major United States Army Ordnance at Aberdeen Proving Ground, and Cleve H. Howell, Jr., a University of New Mexico engineering graduate who served at Aberdeen and Springfield Armory on numerous ordnance projects for the army. The Experimental and Development Shop at Pachmayr's had at its disposal highly sophisticated and versatile equipment, including a battery of modern mills, drills, lathes, and profiling machines with some of the finest machinists and metal workers in the world to operate them.

The facilities and talents of Pachmayr Corporation were in great demand for intricate precision machining of key units for the aircraft program, not only from local companies but from all over the United States. Pachmayr had subcontracts with most major aircraft companies, with the Departments of the Navy and Army Ordnance Department, plus prime contracts with the United States Air Force. Pachmayr Corporation was cleared to handle classified projects up to and including those marked secret.

Among the complex items manufactured in the Pachmayr plant was a massive main wing spar for the Boeing B-52 Stratofortress, the mainstay of the United States Strategic Air Command since 29 June 1955 and still in service as of this writing. The spar began as a ponderous aluminum hammer forging that weighed 893 pounds and ended up after many machining operations as a slender, skeletonized airfoil scaling of a mere 96 pounds. Pachmayr made jet engine mounts for the original B-58 Hustler bomber prototypes, "X" (the first three experimental aircraft) and "Y" (the next ten planes), and Boeing commercial 727, also Convair's P-57 Canberra bomber, as well as the tail structure for the Boeing 707. All of these parts were extremely large.

•••

Frank's penchant for acquiring huge machines enabled him to seek out and get these lucrative contracts. After World War II, precision machines were widely regarded as worthless. Frank would visit the auctions and snap up the best of them for a song. The Korean conflict began in 1951, effectively doubling the value of Pachmayr's plant equipment overnight.

"I was at a machinery auction when the news came that the Chinese had crossed the Yalu River," says Frank. "At noon, the auctioneer, Wershow, sent out for a stack of newspapers and had them passed out to the buyers. Bid prices jumped twenty percent that day. Suddenly machinery was selling for more used than it had new." Frank's big machines brought him big contracts. He was one of the few in the Los Angeles area capable of converting a 3,000-pound rough forging into the tail structure of the Lockheed C-141, with a finished weight of just 200 pounds.

Obviously, much of the material was lost as machine cuttings. Junk dealers used to vie with each other for the contract to collect Pachmayr's untold tons of scrap metal. Sometimes, an unscrupulous dealer would slip some cash to a plant employee, inducing him to throw away good material to fatten the tonnage. On one occasion, a scrap dealer called Frank out behind the Figueroa building to see some scrap that he thought Frank could use. One look at the distinctive contours of the half-ton titanium forgings told Frank that they had been filched from his very own plant.

"I heard that you guys were using big chunks of metal like this," the junk dealer told Frank. "I bought 'em from a couple of guys with a flatbed truck. Thought I'd give you a chance to buy 'em before I scrapped 'em."

"They're stolen!" said Frank, "from us!"

"I had no way of knowing that," responded the dealer.

"Then just how did you know we could use them?" snapped Frank. "Leave them here, or I'll have the 'Junk Yard Squad' (LAPD) pinch you for receiving stolen property."

Grudgingly, the dealer responded, "Okay, take them off the truck."

When he received a new contract offer, Frank turned it over to his Product Engineering Department to develop a bid. At the same time, he would calculate costs and profit margins according to his own formula. It was uncanny how close the bids usually came to each other. If there was a wide spread, Frank sent the bid back to Engineering to be rechecked. He always read the blueprints that accompanied contract orders with the skill of a trained engineer. He read proposed production flow charts and tooling proposals, often suggesting changes that simplified and speeded the work and reduced production costs. Everyone who worked for Frank Pachmayr believed him to be a bone fide genius when it came to mathematics and mechanical design.

After receiving a contract, the Industrial Engineering Department, which was in charge of such details as materials and parts flow, production equipment, painting, ventilation, and salvage, set up tooling in the most economical and expeditious manner for handling of the part. Often improvements were made in the tooling after production began, especially if the profit margin turned out to be less than expected.

"If we were making money on a part," says Frank, "there wasn't much incentive to revise the tooling. We could be lulled into complacency, but if we were barely making a profit or maybe even losing money on the contract, we really searched for ways to alter or combine machining operations to save material and labor costs. If the number of units ordered justified the added expense, we sometimes fabricated special multiple-spindle machines just to handle a given part. We might make forging dies or patterns for casting the material to reduce waste and machining. We would experiment with different cutters and increase cutting speeds."

Sometimes, increasing the cutter speed actually resulted in improved quality. Pachmayr was a pioneer in machining such exotics as titanium and molybdenum for the aircraft industry. One contract involved machining rocket nozzles from a new heat-resistant steel.

"Theory didn't always work out in practice," remarks Frank wryly. "We phoned Metallurgical Research at North American and asked what feed speed to use on the lathe. They said to try fifty feet per minute, which was pretty slow. The surface we got was really rough. I told the machine operator to try a radically faster speed, like 600 feet per minute, to see what happened. We got a beautiful glasslike finish. The theory is to try something radically different to find clues for improvement if your current method isn't working."

•••

A view of one area of Pachmayr's huge machining facility during World War II, when he was making aircraft components.

He was in the shop as much as he was behind his desk in the office. Some of Frank's best friends were his beloved machines. He loved to work with machines. In the little spare time he had, Frank read profusely about machining, heat treating, and metallurgy. Pachmayr was largely self-trained since his formal education ended with high school. He never received a degree in metallurgy or engineering, but he employed a large cadre of engineers, and he picked their brains constantly, until the depth of his knowledge equaled or exceeded that of many of the specialists whom he employed.

Frank likes to quote the late Henry Kaiser, the titan of industry who once answered an inquisitive reporter with, "Hell no, I don't have a college degree. I don't need one. I can hire all the engineers I want." It was Henry Kaiser who furnished America with the "Liberty Ships" that carried millions of tons of war material to our allies overseas. Kaiser also built the huge aluminum plant at Ontario, California, which supplied the lightweight alloy for the first time in quantity and at a reasonable cost.

His long years of experience and inborn talent for handling mechanical things, made Frank Pachmayr an instinctively great machinist. For example, one night after attending a play with his wife Nanitta, Frank couldn't resist the urge to drop by the plant and see how the night shift was doing. As he carried out his unscheduled inspection, he stopped to watch an operator lathe-turning wheel axles for the huge Constellation.

"I thought that those axles were supposed to be heat treated before final machining," said Frank.

"They are," came the reply from the lathe operator.

"The way those chips are coming off, it doesn't look heat treated to me!" insisted Frank.

"We have the papers from Lockheed certifying that the axles were heat treated before we received them," came back the machinist.

"I went home only half convinced," relates Frank. "It troubled me all night. First thing in the morning, I called down to the plant and told the plant manager to Rockwell those axles before machining any more of them, and he was to call me right back. The axles were supposed to be heat treated to a tensile strength of 125,000 psi. The manager called back to tell me that the axles only Rockwelled to 50,000 psi. If the axles had been installed on any planes, there was every likelihood they would have failed in service. An experienced machinist should be able to tell just by watching the chips peeling ahead of his cutting bit or observing the sparks from a grinding wheel what kind of material he's working with and approximately how hard it is."

While Frank was largely preoccupied with the manufacturing and research operations, he managed to maintain an overview of the sporting goods and gunsmithing ends of the business, as well. At the end of each month, he appeared at his office and demanded, "Are the bills ready? I want to go over them and see that they're right!" Each department head from the store, repair, and mail-order sections placed his own stack of invoices, incoming and outgoing, on Frank's desk. Frank checked them one by one, carefully initialing each "F. P."

"He had an astounding memory," remarks Johnny Johnson, for many years a buyer for the sporting goods store. "He could remember the wholesale and retail prices of everything. He looked at all my invoices every month. If he saw a price that didn't look right to him, he'd tell me to call the wholesaler and check it out. If I was right, it was okay. If I made a mistake, I caught hell."

· FRANK PACHMAYR ·

Johnny Johnson, affectionately known to his friends as "Putt-Putt," continued working at Pachmayr's store for over forty years. He retired when he was eighty-three years old.

∴

Many of Pachmayr's defense contracts consisted of pure research and development, plus construction of a predetermined number of prototype units for testing. After products were brought to the production level, Pachmayr had to bid on them in competition with other government contractors with no preferential consideration. Bids were considered on the basis of cost and potential quality level. Of course, the government maintained constant oversight on product quality to be certain that specs were met. Despite this system of checks, the government sometimes favored Pachmayr over other bidders, solely because they could count on quality units without the problem of rejects.

The Pachmayr Corporation Engineering Department worked in close association with Wright-Patterson Air Force Base in Dayton, Ohio, on a number of research and development projects. One of these was a heating unit that attached to the 20mm Aircraft Gun to keep it from freezing at extremely low temperatures in high altitudes. Two of Pachmayr's electrical engineers were assigned to the project. They designed a high-temperature, 28-volt electrical resistance coil shaped to fit snugly inside the cannon receiver and impart heat where it was needed most. All components of the prototypes were fabricated in-house.

Also in conjunction with Wright-Patterson, Pachmayr developed the Airlock Ejection Chamber, a large stainless steel tube that mounted vertically in the floor of a bomber to dispense Radiosonde Beacons. Crew members wishing to mark a spot with a radio beacon, possibly to return for a rescue attempt, could simply open the lid on the dispenser and drop the radio beacon device into the tube. The lower section of the tube was depressurized by an integral automatic valve. Then the outside port was opened and cabin pressure retained in the upper part of the tube, which automatically ejected the beacon down and out of the aircraft. The tube then automatically repressurized in preparation for the next use. Pachmayr's Radiosonde Ejection Chamber was functional to a maximum altitude of 60,000 feet. The production contract for several hundred units was awarded to Pachmayr.

A major Pachmayr project involved a subcontract with Hughes Aircraft Company of Culver City, California, to develop the T101 Electric Feed Mechanism to replace the motorized AN-M2E5 feeder on the 20mm M24A1 automatic cannons that were turret mounted in America's B-36 bombers. The existing feeder was overly heavy, bulky, and subject to frequent jamming, especially in the new soft-spring mounts. Air Force specifications stipulated that the new feed mechanism be able to operate reliably in ambient temperatures from 160 degrees to minus 65 degrees Fahrenheit at a maximum altitude of 50,000 feet. The new mechanism was required to strip rounds from M10 ammunition links with either loop leading and to maintain positive control of the round until it was chambered. A firing rate of no less than 850 rounds per minute would be required.

Obviously, a number of approaches could have been taken to solve this complex problem. There were feeders in existence that used pneumatic or hydraulic power. The feeder then in use, which had proved inadequate, was powered by an electric motor. It relied in part upon the recoil of the gun for part of its chambering function. The soft-spring mounts made this system unreliable. Stubbed-round and bolt-under-round jams occurred with troubling frequency.

After the war, Pachmayr continued government contracting in research and development. Here is the T101 Electric Feed Mechanism antijamming unit that he devised for 20mm M24A1 automatic cannons, which were turret-mounted in America's B-36 bombers.

Pachmayr engineers elected to go with a constant-speed electric motor to provide torque. The motor would be constant-running with an electromagnetic clutch to provide a reservoir of torque strong enough to assure positive feeding, even when the gun was fired while aimed at an oblique angle and caused a bind in the feed chute. A pair of parallel, toothed sprockets surrounding a feed drum engaged and controlled rounds entering the gun. As the lead round lined up above the open breechblock, a spring-loaded lever positioned it positively behind the chamber. As the breechblock returned to battery, another lever detected the presence of a round in the chamber and disconnected the clutch, ending that cycle.

The electric motor was housed inside the feed drum, greatly reducing the bulk and weight of the feeder. The feeder could be adapted to draw ammo from either side to accommodate diverse space restrictions encountered in the various turret mountings in the B-36. The full-time running motor, delivering over one horsepower at 10,000 rpms, together with its magnetic clutch, provided kinetic energy storage with a flywheel effect and resulted in a high rate of torque.

Perhaps the most challenging problem was designing a clutch that could instantly tap that torque and release in only three milliseconds out of a total cycle time of seventy milliseconds without failing under severe service. Such a clutch was developed and rigorously tested before other design features were accepted. The clutch was geared to a Geneva mechanism, which rotated the sprocket one tooth at a time, providing smooth acceleration and deceleration of the feed belt. Sufficient force was available to overcome a belt pull of a hundred pounds. The feeding lever applied a force of twenty pounds to the round being chambered. The spring-loaded lever was recocked for each round by a sprocket tooth as the drum rotated. An integral brake positively stopped rotation of the drum when the clutch was released.

Initial firing tests of the new feeder mechanism were conducted at the indoor target range in the rear of the South Grand building. In spite of attempts at sound damping of the tunnel, the resulting racket caused a near panic among neighboring businessmen. The owner of a small cafe and deli on the corner of 12th Street and Grand was unfortunately baking bagels at the time. The entire batch fell flat from the concussion. Tracing down the source of the sound, he arrived at Pachmayr's front door, white apron flapping in the breeze. The white flour in patches on his cheeks couldn't mask his angry, red face. As luck would have it, Frank happened to be in his office at Pachmayr Gun Works, checking monthly bills. Once the sputtering baker calmed down enough to explain his problem coherently, Frank apologized profusely and handed him cash out of pocket, more than enough to repay him for his inconvenience and loss of income.

Pachmayr's also developed an experimental 20mm motor-powered, six-barreled rotating Gatling-gun-styled cannon, firing 250 rounds per minute and fed by two ammo boxes. This concept eventually led to the multi-barreled, fast-firing Vulcan cannon used with such devastating effect against the Vietcong. Another Pachmayr project involved driving caliber .308 steel bullets at ultrahigh velocity. An elaborate backstop was constructed, including three quarter-inch, high-density armor steel deflection plates, backed by two two-inch armor steel plates, finally ending in a sand and water trap. In spite of these elaborate precautions, some of the bullets completely penetrated all of the plates and were found in the ground behind the backstop.

Pachmayr Corporation was one of the pioneers in creating hardware to mount rockets under United States Air Force fighter wings. The AERO XIA Launcher Package consisted of a twelve-foot pod, bullet-shaped at both ends, weighing 262 pounds empty and 696.4 pounds fully loaded. It contained twenty-four 2.75-inch rockets mounted in tandem, twelve forward and twelve behind. A unique feature was that each tube was fitted with a hatch to retain full aerodynamic integrity. The hatches opened automatically when the forward rockets were fired. The design favored mass production methods without sacrificing effectiveness. Initial testing of the AERO XIA pointed up some of the weaknesses of early rocket technology. Some of the rockets made by another manufacturer failed to ignite when triggered. When this happened with the forward rocket, the rear rocket, which was automatically triggered to follow the forward one, couldn't get out of the pod. This resulted in some fireworks worthy of the 4th of July. The wrinkles were eventually ironed out in time for the Korean conflict.

Astute businessman though he was, Frank Pachmayr made one wrong guess during his years as an industrial entrepreneur. He invested heavily over a five-year period in the development of the Pachmayr Universal Fastener, a quick-release cowl fastener for the aircraft industry. He was clearly meeting a pressing need but vested interests resisted the development.

Then in wide use was the T-tipped Zeus Fastener, which required a different length of male component for every ten-thousandths of variation in the thickness of material or air gap. Airframe manufacturers were obliged to inventory thousands of Zeus fasteners to cover every contingency. With Pachmayr's design, one length handled all normal applications. The interrupted cam-lead, six-start thread on the stud, coupled with a matching receptacle, allowed engagement from the thinnest gauge sheet metal all the way up to quarter-inch thick plate with a simple quarter-turn. The stud advanced a full $1/16$-inch with that quarter-turn. The slotted head of the stud was countersunk into the outside plate. The locking nut assembly was contained in a small square housing that riveted to the bottom plate. Above the threaded nut itself were six conical spring washers, opposing each other in pairs and maintaining a constant tightening tension on the stud. This design attained far more pressure in a confined area than could ever be obtained from a coil spring. A washer with a ribbed "X" on the bottom engaged notches in the top of the nut, automatically locking the stud as it rotated closed and eliminating any possibility that the fastener might ever vibrate loose.

The Pachmayr Universal Fastener fulfilled all of the mil spec requirements of MIL-F5591 for the Number 5 fastener and exceeded strength requirements for a Number 7 fastener. Tested pull-strength for the Universal Fastener was 2,200 pounds. The Pachmayr Fastener possessed the singular facility of drawing down snug despite the uneven surfaces often encountered in aircraft.

A mere fifteen sizes of Pachmayr fasteners would have replaced one thousand Zeus units. It was a valid design, which enjoyed some sales commercially. Military procurement politics were such that it never was adopted by the Air Force, which ultimately condemned it to oblivion.

During World War II, the Korean War, and the brief peace in between, the Pachmayr work force fluctuated between 350 and 485 employees. In spite of the size of the operation, Frank personally supervised both the Pachmayr Corporation's engineering and manufacturing operations, plus the gun shop and sporting goods store. As CEO of both operations, Pachmayr was subject to a grinding work load. Of course he delegated authority. He had a director of research, Guy Lentz. He had a works manager overseeing tooling and production, and a chief inspector who was responsible for maintaining product quality and meeting military specs.

FRANK PACHMAYR

One up and coming young man, Jack Farrar, was then machine shop foreman, but was destined in time to become vice president. Jack was introduced to Frank in 1942 by a mutual friend, Bob McCullough. Jack began working for Frank part time as a machinist six months before graduating from high school. After graduating, he worked for Frank full time. Jack proved to be highly competent and trustworthy, traits that Frank always admired in any man but especially in his own employees. Jack could have had a job for life, but these were war years and many young men felt compelled to serve their country in the armed forces. In September of 1942, Jack left Pachmayr's to join the navy, even though Frank had applied for a draft deferment for Jack based on employment in a vital war industry.

For the next three years, Jack fought Japanese aggression in the Pacific theater of war. At the end of the war in 1945, Jack was mustered out to face civilian life with a wife and a son to support. The GI Bill offered the promise of a free college education. Flying in the face of advice from his mother and his wife both, Jack spurned the offer. Instead, he went back to work for Frank. Within a year, Jack Farrar was appointed foreman of the department developing and producing Pachmayr Shooting Accessories, then in their infancy. Later, he became foreman of the machine shop fabricating prototypes for the engineering department and tooling for the airframe division. Jack retained this position with Pachmayr Inc. when Frank sold his aircraft division in 1957. When the company fell upon bad times and dissolved, Jack Farrar became foreman at another machine shop in the Los Angeles area. It was late in 1964 when Frank phoned Jack one evening and asked him to come back to work for him at Pachmayr Gun Works. Remembering their happy association in the past, Jack was glad to accept.

In January of 1973 Frank appointed Jack Farrar vice president of Pachmayr Gun Works. Jack's office was contiguous with Frank's and they were in daily contact. Over the years of working together, Frank and Jack developed a very close and lasting friendship.

At the close of the Korean War, Frank became restive in his role as CEO of a large and somewhat impersonal manufacturing operation. He couldn't maintain closeness with so many employees. Frank always felt more akin to working men than executives. When a production problem arose, he often approached the men at the machines for suggestions before consulting with the engineers. As often as not, this stood him in good stead, because a solution that was obvious to the man actually making the product could be the last resort of an engineer with a slide rule in hand.

The sights and smells of guns reached out to Frank like a siren's song. He longed to return to the surroundings of his youth. He had been away from the Gun Works for too long. Ever the man of action, Frank set out to make his new dream a reality. He queried his bankers and attorney, Maynard Henry, and his accountant, Frank Thomas, for the name of a man to whom he could entrust the management of Pachmayr Corporation. He found an answer in the person of G. G. "Gus" Michele, a man with a B.S. degree in mechanical engineering from the University of Pittsburgh. Gus's job experience included thirteen years with General Electric, five years with Lockheed as manager of manufacturing planning, another five years as an independent consulting engineer, a year with Super-Cold Corporation as works manager of the mechanical division, a year with Century Metalcraft in the same supervisory capacity, and a year with Republic Engineering Corporation as general manager. At the time Frank contacted him, Gus Michele was vice president and director of manufacturing at Adel Precision Products, a division of General Metals Corporation in Los Angeles. A simple phone call set up the interview.

"When he met me," relates Gus, "I was dressed in a suit and tie, sitting behind a desk in an elaborate office. I had about fifteen employees under my direct supervision. I took Frank for a tour of our plant. We were making aircraft hydraulics systems. We performed diamond lapping, gear-cutting, light-wave measuring, and electroplating operations. The shop looked like a medical lab. We kept it so clean, you could almost literally eat off the floors. I could see that Frank was impressed, but at the same time he was suspicious. Frank always felt an affinity for the work-

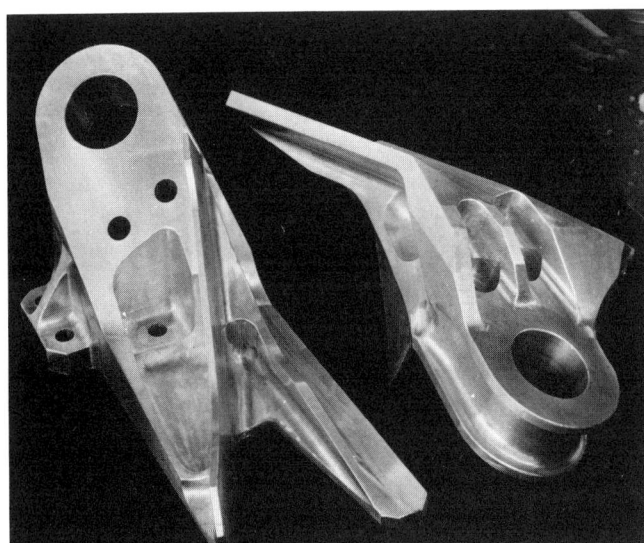

This is an example of one of Pachmayr's massive aluminum castings, after machining.

ing man, as opposed to white-collar types. He didn't find out until later that I could step up to any machine in the plant and operate it competently."

Frank was impressed enough to hire Gus, beginning in May 1956, to take his place at the helm of Pachmayr Corporation. Frank remained reluctant, however, to totally relinquish the reins of the bigger entity that had absorbed him for over a decade. He continued to oversee the plant operation for several months, in effect watching over Gus Michele's shoulder.

"Then one day," says Gus, "We received a large packet of drawings from Boeing, aimed at rebuilding the wing structure of the B52. Among them was a drawing of a replacement wing rib that was to be eight or ten feet long. It was drawn to half-scale, and it still stretched clear across my office. Frank and I both examined it, and Frank said, 'This is going to be a tricky one.' The wing rib had an aerodynamic curve, and at the same time, it made a twist. I said, 'Frank, we can set up tooling with a trunnion jig on two bearings, with a double cam in the back. One cam will follow the aerodynamic curve, and the other one will twist the rib while it's cutting.' Frank just looked at the drawing for several minutes. When he finally looked up, I think for the first time, I saw genuine respect in his eyes. He said, 'You know this is the first time in my life that someone has told me how to make something better than I could do it myself.' Then he turned and walked out of my office and left the plant. He paid me the supreme gesture of confidence. He and Nan went to Mexico for a six-week vacation. From then on, Frank trusted me to do the right thing, and he had little to do with running the plant."

Frank Pachmayr felt that he had reached a plateau at the manufacturing plant. The challenge was gone. What's more, his aircraft research contracts were winding down. He had already split his two major business into separate corporations, so when he began to think of divestiture, he could entertain the idea of selling Pachmayr Inc., which dealt with armaments. He has a good sense of timing. Alert to business trends, he anticipates major moves in the marketplace. Some of his former associates called it luck, but one of his competitors declared petulantly that, "Frank has an angel on his shoulder." It appears obvious from the record, that Frank made his own luck. Looking at the far horizon, he foresaw the imminent demise of the aircraft industry as he knew it. The military was turning increasingly from manned aircraft to guided missiles. That was the wave of the future.

"I could foresee that the aircraft industry was in its final boom stages and was due for retrenchment," recalls Frank. "The size and number of contracts began to fall off a few years after the Korean War ended. Then business took a real nose-dive in 1958. Bigger operations than mine went broke."

Over the years, Frank received a number of offers from competing corporations to buy his business, but he wasn't in a mood to sell. Suddenly, he saw the handwriting on the wall. It was time to take his winnings and bail out. On 15 July 1957, Frank and Nanitta sold all of their common and preferred stock in Pachmayr Corporation, plus machines (including the Hydratels) held in Frank's name and leased to the corporation, as well as rights to all proprietary products relating to aircraft manufacture, for approximately $750,000, to AirTech Dynamics, a corporate entity formed by Gus Michele with outside financial backing. All that Frank kept was his Cadillac.

Frank returned to Pachmayr Gun Works with new vigor, fully prepared to plow a large amount of his new capital into updating existing products and developing new gun-related accessories.

•••

· Chapter VI ·

GONE TO THE GUNSHOP

When Airtek Dynamics purchased the assets of the Pachmayr Corporation, the aircraft subcontracting operation was grossing impressive sums—$3,806,951 for the fiscal year of 1954; $3,207,040 for 1955; and $3,629,905 for 1956. Frank Pachmayr, however, recognized that the research and development work that Pachmayr Corporation was performing for the aircraft industry would soon be retrenched by the government in favor of unmanned rockets to deliver payloads half a world away.

Perhaps more important, Frank was restive with the role of CEO of a large organization that removed him from the scene of action. He longed to devote full time to his firearms business, where he could get back on a first name basis with his employees. He foresaw gross sales from his gun accessories that might someday approach those of his aircraft business. Frank was prepared to plow a sizable percentage of the capital realized from the sale of Pachmayr Corporation into new and improved firearm accessories.

Frank Pachmayr retained the South Grand address and its contiguous buildings, which contained his sporting goods store, gun accessory machine shop, and gunsmithing department. He returned to his gun business at the old address with renewed vigor. He felt that a huge weight had been lifted from his back. The responsibility for vast government contracts and the well-being of hundreds of employees were no longer his. He was exuberant and happy to be returning "home." He was in a bantering mood as he made the rounds of the store, the machine shop, and the gunsmithing benches, greeting everyone with a broad smile and a handshake.

Then he sat down behind his executive oak desk to plot a new business strategy. The words, "serve the public," have been overused by political candidates, but to Frank Pachmayr they had a deep, sincere meaning. He earnestly wanted to produce products that would improve shooting. His enlightened self-interest told him that if he made useful accessories, the public would buy them and bring profits for his firm.

· FRANK PACHMAYR ·

Using the same R and D approach that had made his aircraft manufacturing business one of the most successful in the Los Angeles area, Frank set out to revise his line of pistol grips and expand the selection of Pachmayr recoil pads, his most successful product to date. Part of the new mix would be plant improvements, including new and updated machinery. A fifty-ton punch press was added to the line for punching and forming the perforated steel backup inserts for Pachmayr neoprene grips.

The Pachmayr complex of field representatives and distributors was already the envy of the industry. Frank wanted it expanded and improved. A list of over a hundred jobbers revealed such well-known wholesalers as Alley Supply, American Wholesale Hardware Co., Olympic Wholesale (Alex Kerr's wholesale business), Western Hoegee Co., Wisler Arms, Inc., Brownell Industries, Gopher Shooter's Supply, Ken Carter Agency, Stoeger Arms, Paul Jaeger, and Williams Gun Sight Co. Pachmayr had a dozen or more field representatives constantly on the prowl for orders. He also kept his jobbers and more than three thousand direct retail customers aware of the latest in Pachmayr products. Frank knew that personal contact was the best single way to serve his customers.

Saturation advertising was not a high priority with Frank Pachmayr. He maintained a conservative but consistent pattern of modest ads that appeared in firearm publications. He ran two- and three-column ads in the *Los Angeles Examiner* from time to time, listing sale items in the sporting goods department, such as shotguns and rifles, hunting clothes, and accessories. He sent catalog sheets to such publications as the *Stoeger Shooter's Bible*. In the 1948 edition, a full-page ad displayed the Lo-Swing Scope Mount, right-angle spotting scope stand, "Clear Sight" Scope Caps, and a rubber "Muzzle Cap" to cover and protect the gun bore from rain and debris. A two-column spread in the January 1950 *American Rifleman* featured the Lo-Swing, Pachmayr recoil pads, handgun case, POWer-PAC recoil compensator, and small rubber Grip Adapter.

In a letter addressed to sporting-goods buyers, Pachmayr stated, "Our policy has always been, and will continue to be: to maintain a high level of national advertising in magazines and other media; to sell only through established factory representatives to recognized jobbers; to require rigid inspection and control of our products, insuring uniformity of highest quality and workmanship; and to maintain uniform prices and discounts."

A pricing schedule dated January 1973 shows a list price, a dealer discount of 40 percent, and a jobber discount of 50 percent, plus 10 percent on quantity orders. Policies on sharing freight costs encouraged quantity orders. Although it varied somewhat from year to year, the general policy was to prepay freight on orders of $400 or more and split that expense on orders of 200 or more. A generous dating policy encouraged orders early in the year to even out demand and make production predictions easier. A letter dated 20 May 1960 states:

> Pachmayr product orders ($200 minimum) placed now, as well as through June and July, will be billed 2% discount at October 10th, plus half of one percent

per month for early payment. Our advertising campaign will be broadened considerably in 1960, covering Pachmayr Top Mounts and other products. A stepped-up advertising campaign in all National Sporting Goods magazines will undoubtedly build a greater demand for Pachmayr products and result in increased sales by your company.

As the business grew, Frank appointed Bear Advertising Inc. to set up a structured ad budget. An invoice dated 30 April 1962 listed charges for ads placed in leading shooting magazines, including *Guns & Ammo, Guns, Gun World, American Rifleman, Trap & Field Magazine, Western Outdoors Magazine, Gunsport, Skeet Shooting Review,* and the *Jonathan Club Magazine.* The *American Rifleman* was a favorite ad vehicle with Frank. He recognized that the monthly publication reached the widest possible audience of committed gun fans, and he kept ads in

Frank as a desk-bound administrator.

almost every issue. Whenever a new product came on line, Frank sent samples to the *Rifleman* staff to test and report the results in the "Dope Bag" column. Those reports were consistently favorable not because of favoritism, but rather because the products were worthy of merit.

A principle method of Pachmayr advertising was to send catalog sheets to dealers and in response to customer queries. A purchase order to Biltmore Press Color Lithography of Los Angeles, dated 17 February 1964, listed 60,000 Pistol

• FRANK PACHMAYR •

Case catalog sheets. Each year, Frank sent a glossy color catalog illustrating the full line of Pachmayr products to dealers, along with updated price sheets and a sheet detailing dating and freight policies. Often included were dealer-assist packages consisting of counter displays, three-inch, three-color window decals and brassards, as well as picture repro-proofs for newspaper ads.

After Frank bought out the Mershon operation, separate mailings were sent for Pachmayr Gun Works and the Mershon Company, although the two companies occupied the same premises and shared identical ownership and management. The importance of the personal touch in buyer relations was thoroughly learned by Frank during his decade of dealing with military procurement people. Each year, he sent subscriptions to popular magazines such as *National Geographic* and *Human Events* to sporting-goods buyers. He also purchased four season seats to the Dodger home games at Chavez Ravine, which he made available to visiting buyers. A letter was included in each dealer mailing offering use of the tickets along with a season schedule of home games. Each year, Pachmayr's sent Christmas greeting cards to everyone on its mailing list. Frank regarded these written contacts as more useful and rewarding than hit-or-miss general advertising.

Pachmayr products were distributed mainly by major wholesalers. When dealers were unable or unwilling to go through distributors, Pachmayr would deal directly with them. To protect the jobbers markup, they received a fifty-percent discount, usually with an additional ten percent for timely payment. Dealers received only thirty percent to forty percent off the recommended retail price. Frequent special offers helped keep interest high. A letter dated 15 October 1958 detailed special onetime only sale of POWer-PACs, with price breaks at twenty-five, fifty, one hundred, two-hundred-fifty, and five-hundred units. The base price of $10.69 each applied up to fifteen units, ranging down to only $6.75 for a five-hundred-unit order.

The effects of inflation were only reluctantly passed on to customers. A letter to jobbers and dealers dated 20 December 1966 stated in part:

> A new price list will be forthcoming on all of our products. Price increases are directly related to rising costs of materials and labor. During the past twelve years, we have absorbed four raises in cost from our rubber molder, without corresponding increases in the prices of our products. We will continue improvement of engineering and design, modernization of packaging, and utilization of the most modern production tooling to reduce the unit cost of our products.

Pachmayr Gun Works had an average of a dozen field representatives covering the United States. Perhaps half that number represented Mershon products. The two groups were treated as completely separate entities with separate payrolls. Reps received 7.5 percent of the wholesale value of their sales. In 1970, Frank appointed Edward Lomax as his director of marketing. Ed was an aggressive marketing director and had a great deal of influence on the rapid rise to popularity of Pachmayr neoprene pistol grips. He secured a $100,000 contract with Colt Firearms to install neoprene grips on Colt pistols and revolvers at the factory. Colt was delighted with the product because of its high quality as well as its attraction to shooters. Colt brass also appreciated the fact that neoprene grips did not require hand fitting during assembly, as did wood or plastic grips. This represented a substantial reduction in production costs. Colt sold the Pachmayr grips as a "custom" feature, at extra cost, making the company winners in two ways. Colt's use of Pachmayr neoprene grips as OEM had a positive effect in popularizing Pachmayr grips with shooters in general.

All it really took was to acquaint shooters with Pachmayr grips, and the product took on a momentum of its own. They are simply the best. My first move after buying any revolver or pistol is to replace the OEM grips with Pachmayr's. I have a cupboard full of unused wooden and plastic OEM grips.

Ed Lomax had many contacts among firearm-marketing people and shooters. His former position as vice president of High Standard, maker of competition-quality target handguns and excellent shotguns (regrettably no longer in business), put him in an advantageous position. He made an annual pilgrimage to all the major pistol-shooting events, such as Camp Perry and the midwinter matches in Florida, where he distributed and displayed Pachmayr neoprene grips. The same grips soon became extremely popular with combat competitors as well. Today, Pachmayr, Ltd., has improved and expanded its line of neoprene grips to include more styles that fit more handguns.

Pachmayr Gun Works was represented at every important sportsman's show across the country. At the major shows, such as the annual National Sporting Goods Association extravaganza, Frank himself was in attendance. The logistics of making a sports-show appearance was a herculean effort. Early shows usually involved nothing more than renting fold-up tables and setting up a modest product display. As shows grew, both in size and importance to sellers and buyers, it became necessary to present a sophisticated facade.

It fell to Frank's nephew and employee Dick Mellen to build a proper backdrop. With a stack of two-inch by two-inch white pine, plus plywood, pegboard, and a Skillsaw, Dick created an impressive display, which had a six-foot PACHMAYR banner across the top. Huge pegboard panels over two-inch by two-inch frames allowed varied patterns of rifles, shotguns, and handguns to be hung. Dick's elaborate display made its first appearance during a celebrity interview on the television show "FYI" ("For Your Information") with talk show host Tom Frandsen, a hobby shooter, hunter, and a Pachmayr customer. The display was constructed for easy setup and easy knockdown for transport. Frank chose the guns to be displayed with an eye toward exhibiting the fine custom craftsmanship of his gunsmiths, along with a broad selection of accessories, such as recoil pads, sling swivels, scope mounts, and pistol grips. He listed the guns to be transported to the show site and helped pack them carefully to avoid shipping damage.

Since many of these guns were worth tens of thousands of dollars, security was a constant concern. In spite of the fact that show management set up round-the-clock security to restrict access during the nights, guns inevitably disappeared from some of the displays. I can remember arriving early one morning at the Ruger display during a "Shot Show" to find that it had been somehow raided during the night. Several valuable guns were stolen, and seldom are any of these guns ever recovered.

Even with stress factors like this, Frank maintained his sense of humor. At one show, he had a display that included some richly engraved and highly valuable guns. During the show, one of Frank's engravers, Richard Boucher, sat at a bench actually engraving a shotgun so that the public could watch him at work. Richard was responsible for the security of the gun on which he was working, plus several others displayed on the same table. During the second day of the show, Frank noted that Richard was facing away from the display, overly absorbed in conversation with an attractive young lady.

While Richard's attention was thus pleasantly diverted, Frank quietly slipped a highly engraved, gold-inlaid .45 Colt Government Model pistol under his coat. Frank was an inveterate practical joker; however in this case he wanted to teach Richard a lesson. After the girl drifted away into the crowd, Richard turned back to his work. A great void greeted him where there had lain an engraved Colt .45. Frank stood with his back to Richard answering questions from another spectator. Richard frantically searched the surrounding area. Finally convinced that the extremely valuable gun had indeed disappeared, he blurted out, "The .45 is gone."

Frank turned to Richard as if startled by the unwelcome news. "Where could it have gone?" he echoed.

Frank's assistant, Steve Yorba, was also in on the gag. He and Frank convinced Boucher that the girl he had been so absorbed with was a shill sent to divert his attention while her accomplice stole the gun right from under his nose. Richard was in a panic. After the full affect of the costly loss had time to sink in, Frank pulled out the gun and handed it back to Boucher.

"Here, put this back where it belongs and don't let it out of your sight again!" In telling this story on himself, Richard laughed with chagrin. He was never again careless about a gun.

At one of the early sports shows, a Pachmayr stockmaker, known to his fellow workers only as the "Mad Russian," was working in front of the booth, hand carving a rifle stock from a massive raw walnut blank. It was rather like seeing a sculptor at work. Later, he became mentally ill and was placed in an institution. When he was ready for release, Frank sent a couple of his people down to pick up the Russian and bring him home. This was just one more example of Frank's empathy for his employees.

At various trade shows, as at home, Frank was always a generous host. He usually took half a dozen or more people to dinner each night and always insisted upon picking up the check. Once, during a Weatherby Big Game Trophy Awards bash, my wife Patty and I were eating breakfast in the cafe lounge at The Stardust Hotel in Las Vegas, site of the Weatherby Awards banquet, along with Tom Siatos (then editor, now publisher of *Guns & Ammo* magazine), and Pete Brown (then firearms editor for *Sports Afield* magazine), when Frank and Nanitta strolled by.

They had just finished eating and were on their way out, but Frank and Nan sat with us and chatted for a few minutes. Then, as they rose to leave, Frank motioned to the waitress. "Put this check on my tab," he instructed her. In Chicago at one of the NSGA shows, Frank and Nan were staying at the Hyatt Regency, a posh hotel with several first-class restaurants, but Frank hosted a dinner—where else—at the local hofbrau, with an entourage of a dozen people.

Whenever he could break away from the pressures of business, Frank loved to shoot. Here he tries out the author's left-handed Savage 110-bolt-action rifle.

The last show that Frank and Nanitta attended was in Phoenix in 1981. Nan was grateful for the opportunity to get out of town and mix with people. During a lull in the show, Nan all but dragged Frank over to visit the home of the late Frank Lloyd Wright, famous architect of avant-garde buildings. Frank is no fan of museums, but he went along to please Nan. The company was already sold and Whitey Shoemaker was in charge of Pachmayr's display at the show.

"I asked Frank to come along and appear at the booth," Whitey told me later. "Frank is a legend in the industry. People come to him much as the devout visit the pope in Rome. He's the modern godfather of guns and shooting. Hordes of spectators visited the booth asking Frank questions about guns. Frank could answer almost any question right off the top of his head. He's a walking encyclopedia of gun facts dating back half a century."

Frank took some of his high-grade engraved shotguns along to display. The outstanding examples of gun craftsmanship and ornamentation drew hundreds of people to the booth. All the top names in gun writing were there to marvel over each gun. Particular friends of Pachmayr, such as Charles Askins, Jim Carmichael, the late Elmer Keith, and this author generally made the Pachmayr display their jumping off point at gun shows. It was a cozy place to visit, share a cup of coffee, the latest gun industry scuttlebutt, and a place to drop off excess heavy camera gear for awhile, knowing it was as safe as if it were in a bank.

A parade of gun journalists beat a path to Frank Pachmayr's door over the years, seeking advice from the sage of the gun world, as well as answers to technical questions. In the early days, noted gunwriters such as F. C. Ness, Phil Sharpe, Julian

The All American Trap Team of 1955 included former Greenbay Packers' football star and individual trap champion Dan Orlich of Reno, Nevada, and Pachmayr store manager Bill Harrison (second from left), as well as Pachmayr's attorney, Maynard Henry. The fourth man is not known and the fifth is Zip Eaton from Montana. This was the first trap team in which all the members broke 500 straight birds without a miss.

Hatcher, Elmer Keith, Pete Kuhlhoff, and of course Charles Askins were all frequent visitors, as were Dave Wolfe, the late Jack O'Connor, and the late Warren Page.

"If you stay in this business long enough," says Frank, "just about everything will happen to you at least once. I remember one time a customer brought an L. C. Smith double-barreled 12-gauge into the store for a trigger job. He asked how much, then wanted to know exactly how we went about it. I had an idea of what he was up to, but I told him anyway. Sure enough, he tried to fix it himself. About a week later, he was back and wanted me to repair the damage. He had taken off too much metal and ruined the sears. I told him sure I could fix it, but it was going to cost him twice as much now because I would have to replace the parts he ruined. He was sheepish about it and didn't even argue with me about the price."

Frank recognized that most shooters are not industrial magnates or movie stars, so he kept his prices in line with his customers' ability to pay. Even so, occasionally some customer would gripe about the cost of a repair job. Usually, if the counter salesman couldn't satisfy the customer's objections, he would call Frank. Frank would explain to the customer that the price was based upon the time the job required from his gunsmith. If the customer still wasn't satisfied, Frank would hand him his gun with this comment, "Okay, here take this. The job is free, but don't ever bring that gun back into this shop again because we wont work on it." As far as anyone can remember, no customer ever took his gun without paying.

"One time a guy came in and was looking at some expensive binoculars. He asked the salesman if he could take them outside and look down the street to see if he liked them. The salesman agreed. As soon as the guy got to the door, he took off running south on Grand. The salesman was the 'mad Russian,' and he had a helluva a temper. He grabbed a revolver from under the counter and took off after the thief, but he couldn't catch him and he couldn't get a clear shot, so we lost a pair of binoculars."

Once, film star Fred McMurray brought a shotgun in to have the recoil pad replaced with a new one. When he picked up the gun, he asked Frank, "Can I have the old pad back. I want to put it on another gun." Certainly the famous movie actor, one of the wealthiest in Hollywood, could have afforded a new pad, which at the time cost a nominal $3.50, but Frank obligingly found the old pad in the waste barrel out back and returned it to McMurray.

During Hollywood's heyday, Frank Pachmayr was the undisputed gunsmith to the stars. Many of the early he-men movie stars were in fact rugged outdoorsmen who loved shooting and hunting. Gary Cooper, Robert Taylor, John Wayne, Clark Gable, Bob Stack, Ward Bond, Ralph Bellamy, Dale Robertson, Wallace Beery, Don Ameche, Robert Montgomery, Rod Cameron, Rory Calhoun, Andy Devine, Chill Wills, Broderick Crawford, Frank Ferguson, Jack Holt, and John and Lionel Barrymore were Pachmayr customers. John Barrymore and Roy Rogers both had their own skeet fields in their backyards. Singing cowboy Roy Rogers was also a star on the trap fields. He broke an impressive 199 clay pigeons out of a possible 200 in the North American Clay Target Championship at the Grand American in

1979, in spite of a crowd of fans pestering him constantly for autographs. Pachmayr helped Roy's scores by customizing his shotguns.

Gary Cooper and his wife "Rocky" were both stellar shotgun competitors. "Rocky was the best woman shotgunner on the West Coast," recalls Frank. "She won the California Ladies Championship three years running and held the record as the woman with the longest run without a missed bird, and old 'Coop' was the most deadly rifleman I ever saw on running game." Among the competing leading ladies shooting against Mrs. Cooper were Joan Blondell, Jean Harlow, Janet Leigh, Claudet Colbert, Ginger Rogers, and Wendy Barrie.

As a young man, Robert Stack held a number of national skeet championships, including the World Skeet 20-gauge Championship in 1937. While still a teenager, Stack was named to the All-American Skeet Team in 1936, 1937, and 1938. Bob had the advantage of a wealthy businessman father, who sent his son to the skeet field in a chauffeured limo with a case of shells in the trunk. With all that, Bob is one of the most regular guys I ever met. Band leader, actor, and comedian Phil Harris, and his movie star wife, Alice Faye, as well as their good friend Bing Crosby, were all great shotgunners. Most of the Hollywood crowd practiced at the Santa Monica Gun Club, which belonged to Alex Kerr from 1938 to 1950. Alex, a lifelong friend of Frank and Bob Stack's and mine, also owned Olympic Wholesale, one of Pachmayr's best customers, and Kerr's, a first-class sporting-goods retail store in Beverly Hills.

A number of film executives also frequented Pachmayr Gun Works over the years. Once, Thomas Fox of Fox Film Corporation brought his thirteen-year-old son in to have a stock fitted. Gunsmith Walter Strand told me later, "The boy was small for his age and he needed a really short stock. I could only cut two inches off the stock on his Model 1100 Remington autoloader because the mainspring inside of the stock came within two inches of the butt plate. Fox was taking his son on a duck hunt in Arizona. Before leaving, he took the boy to a skeet range. The kid broke twelve targets out of twenty-five, not bad for his first try with a new gun."

Before World War II, Pachmayr salesman Art Durando worked for ten years for Metro Goldwyn Mayer as a film technician. He became close friends with MGM CEO L. K. Sidney and his son George, the noted musical director. Both were Pachmayr customers and were hunting with Art and Frank down in Mexico on the tragic day when Carol Lombard's plane crashed. Clark Gable was scheduled to join them in a float trip down the Colorado River to shoot ducks. When they heard the news on the radio that fateful morning, both L. K. and George Sidney immediately flew back to Hollywood to be at Clark's side during his time of sorrow. If some of you youngsters under forty don't recognize all these names, just ask your folks who were the greatest actors and entertainers of all time.

There was a bitter irony to this incident. Some months before, Clark had brought a 12-gauge Model 12 Winchester pump shotgun into the shop for Frank to repair. Frank returned the gun to new condition. When Gable picked it up at the gun shop, he was conveniently short of cash. Frank said it was okay to mail the money later, little knowing the aggravation that would cause him. After several months had elapsed, sprinkled with letters and phone calls that brought no response, Frank visited Clark Gable's home in Hollywood. Clark answered the door himself. He reacted angrily when he found it was Pachmayr trying to collect an overdue bill. Carol Lombard overheard the conversation and interjected, "Oh Hell, you got your damn shotgun repaired, and you said he did a good job. Pay the man." So a sheepish Clark Gable dug up the money and belatedly paid Frank.

• • •

Although glamour and adventure were a daily part of Frank Pachmayr's gun business, it was after all a business. Frank was there to make a profit, and he did. Pachmayr Gun Works exhibited steady growth throughout the years with some occasional spurts and sometimes a slight retrenchment. The calendar years of 1958 to 1960 show a steady growth pattern. Pachmayr product sales for 1958 were $353,086; $437,040 for 1959; and $412,981 for 1960. Mershon sales for 1959 were $139,323 and in 1960 they were $127,024. The slight drop in Mershon movement was offset the following year by further increases.

While Frank was preoccupied with the Aircraft Division, he allowed Pachmayr Gun Works to drift to some degree. He left several managers in charge during that period, ending with Bill Harrison. Tax schedule "C" for 1952 reveals an interesting contrast between machine shop operations, which were devoted to government subcontracting and the civilian-market, gun-oriented enterprise.

SALES 1952:				
Retail Store	Gun Repair	Wholesale Products	Machine Shop	Engineering
78,345	13,919	110,429	1,006,591	82,859

SALES SECOND HALF OF 1953:				
Retail Store	Gun Repair	Wholesale Products	Machine Shop	Engineering
136,790	19,248	244,187	NA	NA

Note that just for the ending six months of 1953, Pachmayr Gun Works almost doubled the sales of the retail store and of wholesale Pachmayr products, indicating a probable escalation in sales of four times for the year. (Incomplete records prevent a direct comparison of year for year.) Pachmayr Gun Works seemed to achieve a plateau at that point, as indicated by sales for six months ending December 31 1954:

SALES 1954

Retail Store	Gun Repair	Wholesale Products
109,792	19,942	221,539

A statistical comparison of a seven-year period extending from 30 June 1965 to 30 June 1972, exhibits flat sales in the areas of gun repair and sales of proprietary products. The retail store exhibits a steady decline in patronage, though. This area of the city went into a decline because the principal stores and businesses in Los Angeles elected to grow upward rather than outward to the metropolitan fringes. Foot traffic and even vehicular traffic in front of Pachmayr's fell to mere trickle. Many of the elite customers who supported high-end sporting goods and shooting sales were dying off or growing too old to participate anymore. The climate of discouraging shooting sports in schools, the media, and entertainment dissuaded young people from entering the shooting sports. Modern media regards any shooter as a potential mass murderer. That is, of course, total rot, but the bias is there all the same:

	Retail Store	Gun Repair	Wholesale Products
1965/66	427,429	51,158	654,957
1966/67	372,494	52,985	683,544
1967/68	378,635	50,842	724,177
1968/69	347,922	57,860	761,580
1969/70	294,007	57,131	692,212
1970/71	288,083	67,257	789,283
1971/72	286,806	58,157	809,649

Things began to look up in 1978, when sales were up by 26.9 percent and profits up by 36 percent. In 1979, sales volume was up by 36 percent, but profit increased an impressive 50.3 percent, indicating some improvement in markup. Net after taxes for the year was up 69.4 percent, even in view of generous bonuses to employees. Sales comparisons between the month of January in 1972 and 1973 show a healthy, growing business and also indicate the relative dollar volume realized from different products:

	1972	1973
Total pads	30,813	41,818
Grip adapters	430	335
Presentation grips	249	714
Sling swivels	44	372
Handgun cases	6,928	8,629
Stock blanks	7,453	517
Sports store	21,020	17,751
Custom gun service	3,474	5,107

Also enlightening is a comparison of annual sales for:

	1971	1972
Total pads	588,407	556,776
Grip adapters	10,840	10,167
Presentation grips	7,340	4,863
Sling swivels	3,225	1,249
Handgun cases	87,364	88,877
Stock blanks	36,446	14,548
Scope mounts	31,370	21,690

Note that recoil pads constituted 74.5 percent of the sales in 1971 and almost 80 percent in 1972. Neoprene grips amounted to less than one percent in both years. Pads improved. Handgun cases held steady. Stock blanks and scope mounts both slipped. Contrast this to the fiscal year of 1980/1981, the final year the company was under the ownership of Frank Pachmayr. Compare the almost seven million in wholesale Pachmayr product sales to the above sales in 1972:

SALES FISCAL 1980/81

Retail Store	Gun Shop	Wholesale Products
855,501	193,776	6,720,403

See the breakdown below. Note that the tail (rubber grips, 61 percent) is now wagging the dog (recoil pads, 23.7 percent). Cartridge packs and cartridge magazine bumpers have also become important income earners:

Total pads	1,592,737
Grip adapters	none
Neoprene grips	4,106,787
Sling swivels	41,678
Handgun cases	258,299
Stock blanks	586,295
Scope mounts	42,631
Cartridge packs	15,615
Magazine bumpers	8,956

For many years, Pachmayr enjoyed a near monopoly in the manufacture and sales of recoil pads in the United States. A large proportion of production was assigned to making original equipment manufacturer's pads, imprinted with the gunmaker's name. Among Pachmayr recoil-pad customers, were such names as Ithaca, Ruger, Weatherby, and Winchester. In 1959, Pachmayr sold almost 16,000 pads to Browning and 17,800 to Remington. The following year, the numbers were 23,000 and 10,700.

· FRANK PACHMAYR ·

Frank didn't do it all alone, and he's the first to give credit to his associates. "Certainly a share of the credit for whatever I may have contributed to the advancement of shooting sports has to go to my many friends and employees. I couldn't have done it alone. The CEO of any corporation can't do all of the actual hands-on work himself. He acts as the instigator and director of the efforts of those working for him."

•••

During the heyday of Pachmayr's store, some of the employees were Art Durando (center), store manager Bill Harrison (fifth from left), and finally store buyer Johnny Johnson, affectionately known as "Putt-Putt" (extreme right).

For years, the annual catalog and price sheets were being printed outside the company. As the business grew and demand for printed matter became greater, Frank decided that it would cost less and result in better quality if he could perform the printing in-house. One of the buildings fronting on Grand Avenue was being used for storage. It would provide ample floor space for such an undertaking. Richard Mellen was working largely with the wood mill and preshaped stock

Behind the store front, a fully equipped machine shop manufactured the Pachmayr Lo-Swing mount and other proprietary products.

blanks. Frank asked him to get a press and set up the printing operation. Dick found a good used Harris printing press, with a platen 17.5 inches by 22.5 inches.

"We could print legal-sized sheets or standard 8½ by 11-inch sheets," says Dick, "for letterheads, envelopes, brochures, price sheets, and memos to dealers, and also print the instruction sheets that were boxed along with recoil pads and pistol grips."

Richard bought a Mamya twin-lens reflex camera with standard and telephoto interchangeable lens boards to take high-definition product photos. He also acquired appropriate studio lighting. With little or no formal training, Dick evolved into a professional photographer. He took all the product photos required to illustrate advertising literature. In time, he was illustrating and printing high-quality retail product catalogs, doing all of the work, from photos and text to producing his own layouts, flats, and negatives for offset printing on a new larger press. All of this printing activity inevitably pulled Richard away from his work with Pachmayr gun blanks. Frank brought in Paul Spink to assume some of the printing chores, freeing Dick to spend more time at the wood mill to cut semifinished blanks.

•••

Surely one the most important men in advancing Frank's career was his brother Johnny. John D. Pachmayr was born 30 November 1901 in Munich, Germany. He became a naturalized citizen of the United States and attended Washington Boulevard Grammar School and Polytechnic High School, both in Los Angeles. John Pachmayr was a jolly sort of bear, called "Johnny" by his close friends and brother Frank. He looked formidable, standing just under six feet tall and weighing 180 pounds, but he was basically a happy-go-lucky, gentle person. I doubt that he ever struck a blow in anger. He was a fanatic about wrestling and never missed an important local match, and every weekly match at the nearby Legion Stadium was important to Johnny. Many of his friends were wrestlers, but he loved to shoot trap and hunt as well.

I hunted with Johnny down in Mexico several times. Art Durando handled the details of gun permits, hunting licenses, and visas. Johnny and I went down in the Pachmayr company pickup, with a camper on the back that slept two. Johnny kept a travel trailer permanently parked well below the border on the fringes of a large lake. Nearby was the adobe hut of a tenant farmer who watched over the trailer. Johnny didn't like to drive, so I ended up doing most of the driving. After a couple days of hunting, we gave all of our ducks to the tenant farmer, who was very grateful for the extra food.

I liked hunting with Johnny. He was always friendly and considerate, if something of a wag. On one trip, Johnny was shooting a fine L. C. Smith double, while I had one of the brand-new Armalite AR-16 gold-anodized, all-aluminum two-shot 12-gauge autoloading shotguns. The trigger pull on the Armalite was pretty stiff when I got it, so I filed the sears to reduce engagement somewhat and stoned the sear surfaces, resulting in an improved release. I test fired it before going to Mexico and everything functioned well, but when I was with Johnny in a boat anchored among the reeds, my Armalite "Golden Gun" played a little trick on me.

Johnny had put out a stool of decoys and was calling like a pro. We had a few good shots, but for some reason, several flights of birds had spotted us at the last moment and instead of coasting in for a landing near the decoys, they had flared up and over the boat, disappearing behind the tall stand of reeds behind us. I made up my mind the next time that happened, I was going to give it my best shot. Sure enough, the next flight came sailing in as if they were on a railroad track headed straight for the decoys. Then, without warning, they swerved as if they spotted a red light on the track and towered up and over our heads. There was no way I could get off a shot while sitting in the boat. I broke a cardinal rule by standing up.

It was like the station eight shot from the low house, and I was always lousy on that shot. Anyway, I swung hard and fast and cut loose. I was leaning backward, already off balance. To make matters worse, my trusty Armalite "Golden Gun" took that opportunity to double on me. I missed the bird and was teetering backward on the brink of disaster. Witnessing my obvious plight, Johnny thoughtfully rocked the boat and over I went.

Clark Gable and Robert Stack were Pachmayr customers for many years. They often hunted together.

Of course, Johnny knew the water was only a couple of feet deep. As I stood up on the muddy bottom, soggy and sorry, he helped me back into the boat, laughing heartily all the while. "I bet you'll remember now that you're not supposed to stand up and shoot when you're in a boat."

On the way back from one duck hunt, we stopped while still in Mexico at a small adobe bar for a couple of beers. First thing I knew, Johnny had set me up with a not unattractive hooker.

"We've got plenty of time," he assured me with a broad grin. "Go ahead." Much to Johnny's disappointment, I elected to take a "pass" on that offer.

Still a hundred miles or so south of Los Angeles, I started getting drowsy at the wheel. It's a funny thing. Even though your mind tells you that you could die if you fall asleep, that doesn't seem to do any good. I've talked to men who fell asleep at their battle stations during World War II, and even the threat of death from enemy action wasn't enough to keep them awake. Sitting beside me in the pickup cab, Johnny had been dozing off himself, with his head leaning against his closed window. He emerged from the fog long enough to look out and note how fast the telephone posts were flashing by and realize that I wasn't exactly as alert as he might want me to be. He sat up straight and shook himself awake, then reached for one of those shiny black corkscrew cheroots that he loved so. As he lit up, I coughed a couple of times and cracked the door window despite the cold bite of the wind that blasted through the narrow slit. Johnny knew what interested me the most, next to girls, and started talking about different devices and methods that were most effective in improving the .45 Colt Automatic Pistol. Suddenly, I wasn't sleepy any more. He kept up a running debate with me until we got home.

Frank Pachmayr says about his brother, "My older brother Johnny was one of the finest gunsmiths I've ever known." He declares this with obvious pride. "He was the foreman of my gunsmithing department for years. Whenever we had a tough trigger job, I had it given to Johnny, and he got most of the repair work on really top-grade shotguns. He was the best when it came to tuning up revolvers and auto pistols. Johnny was one of the best shots with a .45 I've ever seen. He shot offhand groups almost as good as a machine rest. He'd make a .45 Colt accurate, then walk over to the range and make a ragged one-hole group with it on the twenty-five-yard target."

"When we were in high school," Frank continued, "Johnny wanted to become a cartoonist, and he was good at it too. He used to draw caricatures of people that were as good as any professional ever did, but when our old man got wind of what Johnny had in mind, he wouldn't hear of it, any more than he would let me become a musician."

Johnny was a fun-loving, upbeat guy, who had an affection for beer, women, and dancing that almost surpassed his love of shooting and hunting. He broke away from his indentured service to his father Gus as soon as he could and went to work for Warren Manufacturing Company in Los Angles, where he became a carburetor specialist. When Frank struck out on his own, Johnny joined with his younger brother in the new gunsmith shop on Grand Avenue. In October 1942 Johnny made his best possible contribution to the war effort by accepting civil service employment with Army Ordnance at Camp Roberts, California, where he worked as an armorer. In November of 1946 the army was phasing out much of its operations, so Johnny became a gunsmith for Bill Beuno in San Luis Obispo. In February of 1949 he was back again as a gunsmith with Frank. Frank entrusted Johnny with the responsibilities of foreman of the gun repair department of Pachmayr Gun Works.

John represented Pachmayr's at trap and skeet shoots, which helped to exhibit Pachmayr products and to keep the company name before the public. Frank regarded this as the best kind of advertising. A large part of his sales came from competition shotgunners. How better to target his most important market share than to have his products in the winner's circle? In August 1951 Johnny sent a telegram to Frank from Dallas saying he had won the silver trophy and a third of the purse by shooting a Pachmayr-modified 28-gauge. At the 1951 Nationals held in Dallas, Johnny tied with comely Betty Ragland in the All-Gauge Handicap. After shooting 850 targets in a shoot-off for the championship, they were still tied, so the judges gave up and declared them co-champions. Pachmayr Gun Works picked up the tab for expenses on this and other trips to competitions or for hunting.

One morning in September of 1973, John Pachmayr walked out of the gun repair shop and sat down at Jack Farrar's desk. He deposited the still burning stub of a black cigar in the ash tray, picked up the phone, and dialed a number. He spoke a few words and then became silent. He didn't change position or reveal in any other way that he was in serious trouble. Whitey Shoemaker was standing nearby and he couldn't help wondering what had happened to make Johnny suddenly silent. He put a hand on Johnny's shoulder and said, "Are you okay?"

Then Johnny slumped over on the desk. He was rushed to the hospital and placed in intensive care. He recovered enough to be transferred later to Congress Convalescent Hospital in Pasadena. At the time, Johnny and his wife Grace were living at 751 Lomora Street in Pasadena, about a block north of Orange Grove. Johnny never recovered enough to return home. At 9:20 P.M. on 30 December 1973 he died from a cerebral thrombosis and was interred at Mount View Cemetery by Stump Mortuary.

From then on, Frank watched over Grace like a mother hen. He helped her collect a $10,000 insurance policy on John's life and settle her husband's affairs. At Grace's request, Frank sold most of Johnny's guns and turned the money over to her. He saw to her needs from that day on, in respect to Johnny's memory.

•••

One of Frank Pachmayr's most productive talents was his ability to recruit and instill in outstanding people his own dedicated work ethic. There's no better illustration of this fact than the person of Johnny Johnson, Frank's longest-standing employee. Johnson was born at his parent's home, located at 133 South Flower Street, in what is today the civic center of Los Angeles on 16 May 1894. Johnny's father became the foreman on the sprawling Irvine Ranch, then devoted to cattle and produce. Young Johnny became a mule skinner, driving a team and wagon with sugar beets and beans from Santa Ana to the Los Angeles produce market.

One day, Mr. Johnson sent his son Johnny by wagon to take a Model 94 Winchester lever-action rifle to Gus Pachmayr for repair. "I remember he looked forbidding as hell. He was awful gruff," recalls Johnson. "When I told him about the rifle, he said, 'Let me see that gott damn thing!' He really intimidated me, and I couldn't get out of there fast enough. Many years later, when I was working for Frank, a woman came in carrying a .22 rifle. She wanted Gus to look the gun over before she let her young son shoot it. Gus said exactly the same thing he had said to me when I was just a boy, 'Let me see that gott damn thing!'"

· FRANK PACHMAYR ·

Johnny Johnson volunteered for service in World War I and was one of the first 100,000 men shipped to France. He served in an ambulance company and witnessed the bloodiest action in the battle of Belleau Wood. About a year after he landed in France, in an ironic twist, Johnny received a command to appear before his draft board because they contended that he had failed to register for the draft.

After the war, Johnson bought a truck and started hauling produce between Los Angeles and Bakersfield. Then a field workers' strike cut off his income and caused the truck to be repossessed. He next went to work for Western Auto Supply Stores at 11th Street and Grand Avenue in Los Angeles as a retail sporting- goods salesman. He remained in this position for twenty-six years, eventually becoming supervisor of the department. On his lunch hours, Johnny would walk around automobile row and window shop for cars.

"That area was the center of new and used car sales in Los Angeles," recalls Johnny. "The old Kelley Kar Company operated Les Kelley Ford on the corner of Figueroa and Pico. Thomas Cadillac was at 1076 West 7th Street. Felix Chevrolet was located at 12th and Grand, just north of Pachmayr's. I used to drop in at Pachmayr's every now and then to visit with Warren Tucker who was store manager at the time. Warren had worked at Western Auto as a gunsmith and reel-smith before going to Pachmayr. In 1947 business was dropping off at Western Auto and Warren urged me to start working for Frank. After a short talk with Frank, I quit Western Auto and went to work for him."

Johnny Johnson became Frank's best salesman and eventually became a store buyer. "I always got along with Frank," says Johnny. "I made some bad buys sometimes, but always managed to work my way out of them without losing money. I watched the business grow and grow. We had to move the wall back to make more room to display stock. We had hunting clothes, fishing gear, and camping equipment, as well as new and used guns and ammunition. Later, we stocked some big-ticket items, like huge steel gun safes. I had good luck selling high-priced items because I only showed them to people I knew needed and could afford them."

Johnny Johnson was often Frank's hunting companion. He routinely acted as cook for Frank's camp when hunting ducks in the Navajoa area of Mexico. Johnson's life spanned the eras from buggy to space shuttle. He was twice married and twice a widower, and at last count, he had eight grandchildren.

Warren "Whitey" Shoemaker was hired by Pachmayr as an apprentice machinist in 1945, shortly after he received a medical discharge from the Naval Air Force. "I was flying the Sturman 'Yellow Peril' in training out of Oletha Naval Air Station in Kansas about thirty miles from Kansas City. One day the rudder cable on my plane broke while I was practicing low-level aerobatics. The plane went into an uncontrollable spin. I bailed out at 400 feet. The pilot chute deployed, but the main chute didn't have time to open and cushion my fall. I came down in a recently plowed field, which I guess saved my life. Luckily we were only about thirty miles from Kansas City. Two of the top surgeons in the country were there at the hospital, and they rebuilt my right knee. I was in the hospital for a year recuperating."

Whitey returned to his home in Rockford, Illinois. From then on, cold, damp weather made his leg ache, and his doctor advised him to move to a milder climate. "I chose California because I knew Roger Stokes from my hometown, and he was working out there. He got me the job at Pachmayr's. The war was still on, and we were working seven days a week to keep up with subcontracting work for Lockheed Aircraft. Eventually, I worked my way up to machine-shop foreman."

In 1946, Pachmayr resumed the manufacturing of recoil pads that had been temporarily halted by wartime rubber shortages. That first year, they sold over 100,000 units. Whitey proved such a valuable worker that Frank appointed him supervisor of the pad production. To make room for additional machine shop operations, Pachmayr had earlier purchased an entire block of buildings on the south side of Pico Boulevard. The recoil pad operation was located at Pico and Olive streets, a block east of Grand Avenue.

"We made the multiple-cavity molds and serviced them regularly" says Whitey. "The pads themselves were molded mostly by Kirkhill Rubber Company in Brea, a thousand-man plant. We kept them going three shifts a day. Frank worked closely with Bill Heney, Kirkhill's chairman of the board to come up with the best possible neoprene composition for our pads."

The neoprene composition was a tricky formula to perfect. It required balancing the need for elasticity to effectively cushion recoil against the requirement for a material that wouldn't deteriorate by either hardening or breaking down over time. The composition also needed to be able to resist compression when guns were stacked with their weight resting on the heel of the stocks. Frank had a standing guarantee that any pad that took a set from compression of the heel would be replaced free of charge.

After several years as machine shop foreman, Whitey was appointed head of the shipping department, a job that carried massive responsibility and involved the management of millions of dollars in incoming material and outgoing products. In all, he worked for Frank a total of forty years.

"He is a brilliant man." says Whitey. "He was a genius at business. It wasn't just guns. It was accounting and business in general. Each month he went through all the bills and invoices from three departments. He would check the prices and quantities and initial each one. It was amazing. He retained the price of every product from every department in his head. I only had my own department to keep track of, and occasionally I'd misquote a price. Frank would catch it every time and send it back for correction." According to Whitey,

> Frank crossed every 'T' and dotted every 'I.' He patrolled the parking lots every morning, checking to see that the cars were parked in the correct stalls and between the white lines. If any unauthorized cars were there, we called the cops. He spot checked the stock every so often by pulling boxes from the shelf. We could have 100,000 recoil pads in stock, and somehow he'd find the one that had a little 'blooming' or a tiny blemish. Then he'd make us pull every one from that lot and throw out any that were bad. Blooming was a whitish waxlike substance

that would leach out of the rubber onto the surface of the pads, indicating that they had been undercured at the factory. Usually, we could send them back to be baked a little longer, and they would be okay, but most of the time after checking every pad on the shelf, we'd find that Frank had found the only one with a flaw.

Frank could really chew us out if we screwed up, but don't let someone from outside give one of his employees a bad time. Frank really stood by you. One time Dayton Headquarters, a big jobber in Dayton, Ohio, had me on the phone and was giving me a real bad time over a delayed shipment. Frank was walking

One of Frank's great friends and long-time customer was Colonel Charles Askins, noted pistol shooting champion and gunwriter. It was Askins who wrote the introduction to this book.

by and heard part of the conversation. He took the phone from me and told one of his best accounts that they could stick their goddam order in their ear.

You've got to know Frank. He wanted everything perfect. He'd check guns before they went out. If he didn't approve a bluing job, he'd tell you to do it over. If he didn't like a trigger job, sometimes he'd stay late and do it over himself. If you did your work right, you had a job for life with Frank. He'd never fire anyone, even the poor ones. He'd say we had to try harder to motivate our people. He'd give more money to poor workers to help motivate them.

Frank was a one-man company. He would delegate authority to his three division heads and allow them to run their own departments, but he was the boss, and everybody knew it. He wouldn't put up with any backbiting or overlapping authority. If any of his employees had a personal problem, Frank would come up with a solution on the spot. He just loved to solve puzzles. I was always amazed at how intelligent and quick he was. He seemed to anticipate what we were going to say. I think he was clairvoyant. All of us consulted him often about purely personal matters.

Frank had a soft spot in his heart for folks from south of the border. He would hire them whenever possible and watch out for them like a godfather. There was one girl working for me in shipping. She had two kids but no husband and didn't make a lot of money. Frank would take me aside every now and then. 'How's she doing?' he'd ask. Then he'd hand me a hundred-dollar bill and say, 'Here, give this to her.'

Frank is a very direct man. He never had a devious bone in his body. He always says just how he really feels about something. He told the truth a lot of times when it would have been better for him to lie a little."

After Frank sold out, Whitey remained with the Pachmayr Corporation for several years before retiring. Today, he operates a Sir Speedy printing and copying franchise in Garden Grove, California.

One of Frank's most trusted employees and his perennial hunting sidekick was Art Durando, a colorful individual, to say the least. Art was born at a winery in central California, one of a chain of such establishments owned by his father. Prohibition closed them down. Thereafter, the senior Durando turned to ranching and farming, running some cattle, and raising table grapes and almonds. There was an abundance of game birds of every kind in the surrounding hills and deer hunting within walking distance of his home. Young Arthur hunted constantly. He loved the freedom of ranch life, but he had more than his share of misadventures while growing up. At about eighteen months of age, he fell into some burning brush and almost lost both hands. As a result of this accident, Art has no fingerprints, a fact that caused him no end of problems later during his naval enlistment.

Art had a three-mile walk to a country school each day. On his way home one evening when he was about seven years of age, he was run over by the teacher, who drove on as if not noticing the accident. Art staggered home battered and bloody, convinced that he had lost his right eye. Happily, he recovered completely.

There was a Chinese settlement near the ranch, and Art's father employed a Chinese cook. One day Art somehow raised the cook's anger, and the man chased Art with a meat cleaver swinging over his head. Art's father heard his son's screams and came running with a .30-30 rifle. He ran the Chinese cook off the ranch, thereby settling the dispute.

Art got into enough mischief without any help. He would hop freight trains as they slowed down for a crossing, then jump off as the trains gained speed. Each time he waited a little longer as the train gained momentum. He placed markers along the track to show where he jumped off the times before. Finally, the inevitable happened when he waited too long and jumped when the train was moving too fast. "I did about fifteen flips when I hit the ground," he chuckles. "Luckily, there were no bones broken."

Art attended junior college in Bakersfield, California. One day the supervisor of special effects at MGM Studios came up and stayed at the ranch to hunt with Art's father. He told the senior Durando that college wouldn't help Art's future.

"Send him down to Hollywood, and I'll get him into the actor's union."

Although Art had good looks and physique, as well as an outgoing friendly personality and an easy manner that should have qualified him to be an actor, he couldn't break into the union. He did land a job in the film lab and developing department. "I was getting sixty-five cents an hour in 1932," says Durando. "That was a lot of money in the depth of the depression. I was only twenty-one years old and I bought a new Cadillac convertible."

During World War II, Art Durando enlisted in the Navy and graduated from Pensacola, as a chief petty officer. Art is a fantastic shotgun marksman. It was only natural that he wound up as a gunnery instructor, teaching novice navy gunners skeet shooting with shotguns. The skill of instinctively leading their targets was later used against enemy aircraft. He accompanied his students to the gunnery range, teaching them the use of the deadly .50 caliber machine gun and 20mm automatic cannon that was swivel-mounted on moving platforms to fire at moving targets, simulating air combat. Art completed several tours of duty during the island-hopping campaign carried on by United States forces in the Pacific. He almost "bought the ranch" on several occasions.

Near the close of the war, he ended up on an island with his right arm in a cast, waiting for things to heal. In spite of the fact that he couldn't raise his arm, he spent most of his time skeet shooting. Inasmuch as he couldn't raise the shotgun to his shoulder, he simply tucked the shotgun butt into the crook of his right arm, where the cast bent at the elbow and fired from the hip.

"I began to bring down fifty straight pretty regularly," he relates, "but I kept breaking the cast from the recoil of the shotgun. The medics got pretty tired of putting new casts on me, and began demanding to know how I could keep breaking casts all the time. I told them, 'I don't know. I must be doing it in my sleep.'"

After the surrender of Japan, when Art Durando was mustered out, job opportunities were sparse, but Art returned to his job at the movie studios. He met Frank Pachmayr at a skeet shoot where both were competing. Frank was impressed with this handsome, highly personable, enthusiastic young man, who had such uncanny skill with a shotgun and a great depth of knowledge concerning all types of firearms. This was precisely the kind of person Frank wanted working in his sporting goods store, someone who could help customers choose the right gun for their individual needs.

Frank told Art, "I'd like to have you come and help me in my gun store. I think you'd make a hell of a salesman." Art didn't exactly jump at the chance, but

Another Pachmayr fan was James Arness, better known as Sheriff Matt Dillon of the TV series, Gunsmoke.

said he'd think it over, but it wasn't too many weeks before Durando was standing behind the counter at Pachmayr's. That was in 1950. Art worked for Frank over 22 years. "I used to spend eight months in the store," he says, "then spend a couple of months hunting in Mexico and a couple of months shooting in live pigeon competitions." Today, Art Durando remains one of the world's most outstanding international shotgun marksmen. He travels to major big-money shoots around the globe to compete against the world's best marksmen, and he wins.

In short order, Art became one of the most popular salesmen in the store, attracting many of his friends who knew him from the skeet and trap fields. Art also became a valued hunting partner for Frank and an unofficial liaison with Mexican authorities for south-of-the-border hunts.

General Charles "Chuck" Yeager, then only a captain, was a frequent visitor at Pachmayr's. He loved to shoot skeet and to hunt. He was stationed at Edwards Air Force Base in the arid Mojave Desert where he became the first man to break the sound barrier. He met and liked Art and invited him to come out to hunt with him.

"I know an old desert rat who lives like a hermit on a small ranch near Palmdale. He has the only pond within miles. Every evening about 6:00 the doves come from every direction to drink. Come on out and I'll show you some huntin' like you ain't never seen before. We don't hunt near the water, but we get plenty of shootin' by taking a position some distance away, along the flyway."

Frank with his long-time booster and customer, the famed gunwriter Jack O'Connor.

Chuck made the invitation in mid-afternoon, hours before quitting time. Frank was standing nearby, talking with Yeager and an air force general who had come along from Edwards. Art gave Frank a long look. Frank answered his unspoken question with, "Oh hell! You can quit early and go hunt with Chuck."

After the hunt that evening, Yeager invited Art to come up the next weekend for a skeet shoot. Art powdered a hundred straight clays, beating his host by a single bird. Then Yeager was assigned to test fly a captured MIG on Okinawa. When he returned, he phoned Art and invited him to come up to Edwards to hunt ducks.

"It got down into the twenties that day," remembers Durando. "I wore a pair of field gloves. Chuck didn't have any, so he kept his hands in his pockets most of the time. When it came time for me to drive home, I gave him my gloves. He was so grateful that he gave me his pair of Bausch & Lomb Rayban sunglasses with his name imprinted on them. Chuck was already a big celebrity, and I really treasured those glasses. Yeager was sent to Korea with his squadron, which put an end to some of the most enjoyable hunts I ever had. Chuck is one of the nicest guys I ever met."

One day Chuck Yeager brought along a friend, aviatrix Florence "Pancho" Barnes, a lusty lady famous in her own right. At the time, she was sole proprietor of the small cafe and bar near Edwards that was routinely frequented by air force test pilots. The bar was accurately depicted in the motion picture, *Right Stuff*. Although she stood less than five feet tall, Pancho made quite an imposing figure standing jauntily in the showroom at Pachmayr Gun Works. She was wearing a tan tam perched on top of a bubble of black curly hair. The tam framed her pert face, which was accented by a white silk scarf around her neck. She wore a black leather jacket over a sheer white blouse. Her tan rider's breeches puffed out at the sides and tapered into a pair of high black riding boots. She flourished a leather rider's crop in her hand. This was a costume popular with barnstorming pioneer pilots. Pancho just never stopped barnstorming. She was an early competitor in the famed "Powder Puff" air races, one of the few to give Amelia Earhart a run for her money. Pancho taught flying to army air force recruits during World War II and performed as a stunt pilot in motion pictures after the war.

Pancho was nothing if not competitive. She was always ready to prove she was as good as, nay, better than, any man. Yeager and Pancho were standing outside a counter that separated the customers from the working area of Pachmayr's gun repair department. As they talked, Pancho expressed interest in a new lathe that Frank had in the shop.

"Come around the counter, and you can take a closer look," invited Frank. Pancho backed up a couple of paces and eyed the counter speculatively. The obstacle was better than waist high to Frank, who was behind the counter, and even higher to petite Pancho.

"I'll bet I can take a shorter route than that," she declared. Frank immediately got her drift. He was something of a gambler himself, so it's no surprise that he quickly responded, "You're on for ten bucks."

Frank soon found himself poorer by one ten-spot when Pancho vaulted the bench like an Olympic high jumper and landed on her feet as well balanced as a cat.

During the middle years of Pachmayr Gun Works, the most volatile and the most rewarding ones for Frank, the guiding hand of his attorney, Maynard B. Henry, helped steady the helm and steer the enterprise through some turbulent waters. I once told Maynard, "If I ever need an attorney, I'm going to call you." He grinned at me and replied, "Johnny, I fervently hope that you never do need an attorney."

Maynard was a crackerjack trap shooter and for a time in the late 1940s, he was president of the American Amateur Trapshooting Association. Maynard was no more than medium height, but he had shoulders a yard across and he was loaded with tremendous power. He possessed the ideal build for a nonstop shotgunner, muscular and heavy, but not fat. Maynard was California State Trapshooting Champion in 1948, 1949, 1953, and 1954. He was Grand American All-Around Champion in 1953 and 1954. Whenever possible, Frank recruited his people from the field of shooting champions in the solid belief that these men had already proven their metal in combat, so to speak. His judgment proved completely justified in the case of Maynard Henry. Frank appointed Maynard as Secretary-Treasurer of Pachmayr Gun Works on 1 June 1959. He worked for Pachmayr's until his death from coronary heart failure on 11 May 1967, at Fresno Community Hospital.

Beginning 6 October 1952, William "Bill" Taft Harrison became a salesman at Pachmayr Gun Works. Bill came to California from Metropolis, Illinois. In 1947 Bill won the Grand American Open Trap shoot with a perfect 200 out of 200. His friends Maynard Henry and Alex Kerr recommended Bill to Frank Pachmayr. They knew him as a terror on the trap field and a deadly poker player. You couldn't get a better recommendation than that. Bill and Maynard were both members of the first five-man trap team on which each man broke 500 straight targets. A couple of years later, the store manager, S. Ziebert, resigned to become an importer. Frank was still deeply involved with his aircraft division, and he needed a decisive, tough supervisor to oversee the gun operations during his continued absence. Bill Harrison was only medium height, 5 feet, 10½ inches tall, and weighed a mere 165 pounds, but he nonetheless had an imposing presence, and he could speak with a granite-like voice of authority when he needed to. An announcement dated 28 May 1954 was mailed to jobbers and dealers of record, announcing the appointment of William T. Harrison as general manager of Pachmayr Gun Works.

Bill was only forty-three years old when he joined Pachmayr, but it seems as though his hair was always white. Bill and I always got along fine, and he treated me like royalty. Bill's wife, Marian, was a precision bookkeeper. She worked for Pachmayr's for a number of years and was a highly valued employee. Effective 31 July 1972, just short of twenty years after he started with Frank, Bill retired to enjoy his hobby of shooting trap full time.

Lee Greenway, a Hollywood makeup artist and personal makeup man for Andy Griffith for a number of years, was a longtime customer of Pachmayr's. Greenway, Andy, and George Nabors all grew up in the same small town in South Carolina. Lee was retiring from his job at the studios and he approached Frank with a list of ideas he had about improving the sporting goods store. Frank must have liked what he heard, because he hired Greenway as store manager. Lee remained in that position until several years later, when Alex Kerr closed his exclusive sporting goods store, Kerr's, in Beverly Hills, which set his qualified manager, Jerry Knight, at liberty. Then Jerry took over for Frank and did an excellent job.

Bill Ives exerted a huge influence upon Frank Pachmayr's life. It was Ives who first approached Frank to subcontract war material for the government, which of course led to a huge expansion of Frank's business. Later, the sale of the aircraft branch provided the capital to invest in design and tooling of many of the Pachmayr gun accessories. Before World War II, Bill Ives worked for Lockheed Aircraft and a subsidiary, Aircraft Accessories. He was largely instrumental in lining up subcontractors for manufacturing component parts of combat aircraft.

Until his death, Frank's brother, John, was in charge of the gunsmithing department. He was a skilled gunsmith and a graduate of Gus Pachmayr's stern college of home training, as well. In this 1952 picture he is working on a Parker shotgun.

"We chose them," says Ives, "on the basis of their ability to produce different parts. Frank Pachmayr had lathes, mills, and profiling machines that were capable of doing precision work. He could produce the cams and other desperately needed hydraulic components."

After the war, Bill moved to Calmec Manufacturing, where the tables turned, in effect, and Ives became a subcontractor for Pachmayr, producing major components of the POWer-PAC muzzle compensating device. In 1972 Bill retired at sixty years of age. Six months of boredom and no paychecks convinced Ives to go back to work, this time for Pachmayr, where he shared in the development and building of the Pachmayr Signature Accuracy System for the .45 ACP. When Frank sold Pachmayr Gun Works in 1983, Bill stayed on for awhile, but it wasn't the same anymore, so he retired for the second and last time to a luxurious townhouse in Brea, California, with half an acre of green in the backyard and a view of the city from the second-floor front deck.

Steve Yorba, scion of an influential family in the California area, was an important cog in Frank's well-oiled machine during the later years. The Yorba family traces its lineage back to the Spanish Dons, the original settlers of California. Steve's mother, Inez, had attended grammar school with Nanitta Pachmayr, and these two fine ladies were close friends. When Steve reached sixteen years of age, he decided he just had to have a car to maintain his standing with his peers. At the time Steve was attending high school. His father could have easily handed Steve the money, but that would have been too easy. One doesn't learn the value of money by tapping his parent's pockets, so the elder Yorba said, "If you want a car, you'll have to earn it yourself." Steve phoned Nanitta, asking about a job at Pachmayr's, and she told him to talk to Whitey. Steve recalls,

> Whitey had been used to seeing me around the store for years. I loved to hang around and look at the guns. Often Frank would take me to lunch, but this was a whole new ball game. When Whitey found out I was looking for a job, he handed me a broom and told me to be handy to chase parts for the machine shop and gun shop and to help clean recoil pads after they came back from the molding company. I used to sit in the alley behind the store along with Rosa Huber. We blew the powder out of the pads and trimmed the flash that was left from molding. I started to work for Frank in 1961, and I worked at Pachmayr's during two successive summer vacations from school. I earned enough money to buy a 1955 Mercury coupe for $600. Charley Jones was a Cadillac service manager at the time and he found the car for me.
>
> Frank was like an uncle to me for years. Frank and Nan were always coming to my folk's house for dinner. Frank took me fishing for the first time when I was only six years old. We stayed at the old Warner Springs Club located in the hills behind San Diego and fished in Lake Henshaw. Once, when I was about four years old, Frank was visiting my folks. He left the house to get something out of the car, and I remember that it was raining outside. I locked the door behind him, and I remember him standing in the rain pounding on the door to get back in.
>
> After high school, I entered the service. When I finished my stint in 1970, I went to work as a salesman for Chris-Craft boats. I made good money for awhile. Then times got a little tough and sales became spotty. I needed a steady job. I was newly married and knew that I had to settle down. I went to Pachmayr's again. Frank was out, so I was interviewed by the store manager, Lee Greenway. He said that he couldn't pay what I had been earning with Chris-Craft. I took the job anyway, figuring I could sell boats on weekends. That was on a Thursday. I was to go to work Monday. That Friday, John Pachmayr had a massive stroke.

John Pachmayr examining the "masterpiece" shotgun made by his father, Gus.

On Monday Frank saw me in the store and said, 'Let's go to lunch.'
I said, 'Okay. Did you know that I'm working for you now?'
His attitude changed immediately. He became businesslike in his attitude and his tone of voice.

The interior of the Pachmayr store was converted to a rustic atmosphere with vertical log overhangs behind the counter. Ample shelves and counterspace allowed the display of a wide range of outdoor and shooting accessories. Hundreds of rifles and shotguns were displayed in racks along the walls. Behind the counter is Frank's friend and employee, Art Durando.

I only meant to stay at Pachmayr's for just a few years, but I ended up working for Frank for eleven years. I stayed on for about eight months with the corporation after he sold out. Frank was sometimes stern with his employees, but he had to be to maintain discipline. He paid well and gave Christmas bonuses to everybody after they had been there a couple of years. For the first two years, he would hand each of the new employees a hundred dollar bill.

Frank was in the wood business because he loved fine gun stocks. He didn't care if it made money or not—he would buy 100,000 pounds of walnut just to get that dozen gorgeous stock blanks! The ordinary blanks were usually sold to factories for production rifles. We supplied most of the blanks for Browning guns, which were being made in Japan. We shipped 4,000 to 5,000 blanks at a time. Some of the fancier walnut went to Roy Weatherby.

One time, Andy (who operated the wood mill) was sick in the hospital. Frank and I went to visit him, and we met Fred Edler there. Fred was cutting walnut orchards, and he was burning the English walnut because no one wanted the light-colored wood. Frank saw it and just couldn't believe they were throwing it away. He had Edler deliver whole slabs of English to us in L.A., so he could lay out the blanks himself. Workers in the machine shop went home at 5:30. Frank had a couple of guys carry three or four slabs to the machine shop after the place was deserted. Then we would lay out patterns and cut stock blanks on the big bandsaw that was used to cut steel molds. Sometimes, Rudy would stay and help, and once in awhile, Jack Farrar would stay over. Jack just shook his head when he saw the mess we were making with sawdust all over everything. He couldn't put his men to work in the morning until we cleaned up. We were usually there until ten thirty or eleven every night for about three weeks, until we cut all of the 300 or so stock blanks. I would call my wife a couple of times each night, saying we were going to be a little longer. Finally, one night, she called Nanitta. Frank and I were somewhat surprised when they both showed up at the shop, saying it was time to quit. Frank had more stamina than any of us younger men. He wanted to work until one at night and be up again working at six in the morning.

Because of the steady attrition of the years from age, illness, or the desire to go into business for themselves, gunsmiths at Pachmayr's would leave and need to be replaced, so Frank was constantly recruiting gunsmiths. He sponsored immigration to the United States by many fine craftsmen from Germany, France, and Italy. Many of these stayed with Pachmayr Gun Works for years, but some eventually elected to strike out for themselves in new locations. A select few talented gunsmiths were discovered locally by Frank. Among these was Carl Cupp, a stalwart lad of just twenty-three years when he came to work for Frank in 1980 as a gunsmithing apprentice. Standing a solid six-feet, four inches in his stocking feet, Carl was built like a professional wrestler. Carl recalls,

> For the first three months I worked for Frank, he called me 'Harry.' He chewed me out one time because I tore some abrasive cloth cross-grain, instead of lengthwise. I tried to explain that I had to narrow the abrasive patch down some to make it fit into the .22 rimfire revolver chambers that I was polishing out. I was really depressed for a few days after that, but then the next time he came by, he showed me the proper way to hold a mill file to get a true, flat surface. Frank uses a file with such precision, you have to see it to believe it. One of his pet peeves was using clover compound to lap in a slide on a .45 Colt. He felt that the abrasive would become embedded in the pores of the steel and continue to wear as the gun was shot. He showed me just how to tighten a slide correctly, using a three-pound rawhide mallet, so it wasn't necessary to lap it in. Frank is one of the greatest gunsmiths that ever lived. More than that, he set the standards for accuracy with revolvers and pistols and showed the world how a gunstock was really supposed to look.

· FRANK PACHMAYR ·

When I first started at Pachmayr's, I only earned $5.50 an hour. It seemed to me that I had to wait a long time before I got a raise, but then, when my wife had our first baby, Frank came by to congratulate me. He handed me a hundred dollar bill, and said, 'Here, this is for the baby.' He took me to lunch many times over the years, and he never let me pick up the tab. One time, Pachmayr's got in a shipment of 1909 Argentine Mauser bolt-action rifles. I spotted one that was in perfect, as-new condition. He saw me admiring it and gave it to me. I intend to keep it original. I'll never touch a screw on that gun. A lot of Mauser rifles were carved up after the World War II to make into sporters. Today, there aren't many originals left. I think they should be preserved now.

I think the reason Pachmayr's has such a great reputation for quality products and work is because Frank trained everyone he hired in the 'Pachmayr way.' I don't know of anyone who came in the door knowing what to do. The guys that left Pachmayr's went out into the world and carried that knowledge with them. That's part of the Pachmayr heritage. To this day, I'm still overawed and star struck by the Pachmayr image. I guess you could call it hero worship. I owe a lot to the 'Old Man' and I feel privileged that I got to work for him. Someday when I retire from the gun business, I only hope that I can look back at half the accomplishments of Frank Pachmayr.

Carl is still employed by Pachmayr's, but he is now production manager. "Not bad for a guy who started out as little more than a janitor," beams Carl.

•••

At noon on 21 December 1979 Pachmayr Gun Works was the scene of a gala celebration of Frank Pachmayr's fiftieth year in business. Literally hundreds of Frank's friends were on hand to wish him well, along with film luminaries, prominent figures in sports and industry, and many local political leaders. All current and many previous employees were there to share in the celebration and sample the ten-foot long table of catered meats, cheeses, and dips. Frank and Nanitta accepted kudos and congratulations from everyone. It was a unique moment in the history of shooting and hunting sports.

In 1981 Frank suffered a debilitating stroke. He recovered, but the old zest was gone. Suddenly the business that had engrossed him his entire life began to be a burden instead of a challenge. Over the years, Frank had been repeatedly contacted by various companies with offers to buy him out. The Brown Shoe Company, which purchased Redfield Gun Sights, made an offer. The story goes that they had $720,000,000 dollars set aside for acquisitions. When word got around that Frank was seriously considering selling out, a flood of offers came in. James M. Briener, Chairman of the Board of the First Connecticut Small Business Investment Company of Bridgeport, Connecticut, expressed his serious interest in purchasing Pachmayr Gun Works, as did Thomas E. Bass of McLean, Virginia, and William P. Richards of Beverly Hills. Among the many offers made to Frank was a serious proposal by his own employees and management staff, headed by company controller Bill Tracey.

Ultimately, Frank settled upon an offer from an investment group headed by William G. "Bill" Baker, Jr., of E. F. Hutton, America's second largest securities firm. Mr. Baker holds an MBA from Harvard and served in the air force as a jet pilot and instructor. His business career included fifteen years with the prestigious Lehman Brothers investment bankers. He rose through the ranks to a position of member of the board of directors. Baker was associated with E. F. Hutton for nine years, as managing director, executive vice president, and member of the board of directors. In 1984, two years after his purchase of the Pachmayr Gun Works, Bill Baker resigned from E. F. Hutton to devote full time to his own investment company, William G. Baker, Jr., and Company, and to allow more time for pursuing his aggressive development of new Pachmayr products and sales techniques. Mr. Bruce Baker, brother to William, later became president and managing director of Pachmayr, Ltd.

Today, Pachmayr Ltd., in its new quarters at 1875 South Mountain Avenue in Monrovia, California, has a new president, Leslie H. Whitney, formerly with the famed holster company, Bianchi International. Pachmayr Ltd. currently markets an expanded line of recoil-absorbing Pachmayr neoprene rubber pistol grips, including their new American Legend Series, that combines the beauty of richly polished walnut surrounding a front insert of finger-gripped black Decelerator rubber for improved control. Over 300 different Pachmayr rifle and shotgun recoil pads are offered, including the supereffective, high-tech Decelerator pads. The Wide Barrel Link that was the keystone of Pachmayr's Signature Accuracy System is now available as a separate accessory in tough 17-4 stainless steel. The highly popular Pachmayr Handgun Cases, offered in three-, four-, and five-gun models, have been streamlined to a more modern look. A new soft-sided navy Cordura nylon Explorer case is also becoming very popular. Other new products are neoprene-handled hunting knives, dummy shotgun shells and pistol cartridges for safe testing and dry-firing, pistol sights and pistol magazines, and finally gun-care products. Pachmayr Ltd. also operates a marksmanship training school on their seventy-acre shotgun and archery range in El Monte, California.

•••

· Chapter VII ·

PACHMAYR PRODUCTS & PATENTS

After World War II, thousands of young men returned from the service who were trained to use the M1 Garand autoloading rifle, and they were interested in new styles of hunting firearms. Stodgy and old rifles were disdained in favor of gaudy and new ones. Roy Weatherby rode the crest of this wave, even pushed it along with his rococo stock styles and inlays which were accented with white spacers. Frank Pachmayr was a staunch supporter in his custom rifles of classical stock lines with muted accents, such as unadorned horn or ebony fore-end tips and pistol grip caps. He did, however, as early as 1932 produce several styles of recoil pads with eye-appealing White Line spacers.

This was actually Frank Pachmayr's second entry into mass production of firearm accessories. The first Pachmayr product manufactured in quantity was his black rubber Sure Grip Adapter, which filled the troublesome gap behind a revolver's trigger guard. Shortly after he started his own shop, Frank began molding his adapters from hard black rubber. He configured them to fit most popular double-action revolvers and made them in small, medium, and large sizes. They were held in place by a horseshoe-shaped spring clip that slipped between the grips and the front strap.

Young Frank Pachmayr was still feeling his way in the business world and lacked sophistication when his Sure Grip Adapters were beginning to sell in numbers. Therefore, he was impressed when Robert Mershon came along and promised nationwide distribution and greatly increased sales. Mershon has been described as a glib promoter with little or no knowledge of firearms, but gifted with a persuasive salesman's personality. He convinced Frank that he should form a corporation and take him in as a partner. Mershon would then be responsible for selling the adapters nationwide, and he assured Frank that sales would take a quantum leap and money would roll in.

As soon as Frank vested Mershon with a position as a corporate officer, the new partner became officious and contentious. He constantly harassed Frank to create more new products. It was at this point that Frank invented his famous recoil pad with the unique XXXX open pattern and a distinctive white line to accent its appearance. This satiated Mershon for a time because it led to further increases in sales and profits. Nonetheless, Mershon soon resumed his bickering and Frank decided to disengage himself from his partner. Frank had learned a hard lesson that made him wary of such affiliations in the future.

Mershon countered in 1935 by starting his own corporation, Mershon Company, Inc., at 511 East Broadway in Glendale, California. He introduced his own line of grip adapters and recoil pads, even including the White Line. Mershon was canny enough to apply for copyrights on all his products, a precaution that Pachmayr had yet to take. A number of years later, Mershon sued Pachmayr for use of the white line in Pachmayr pads and claimed it was his by copyright. As is often the case, justice was blind as a bat. The judge found in favor of Mershon, despite a preponderance of evidence pointing to the fact that Frank was first with the white line pad, indeed, its inventor. The judge granted Mershon an injunction, prohibiting Frank Pachmayr from using the white line in his pads or implying in any way in his advertising that he could deliver a white-line pad.

Frank appealed the decision, but the United States Court of Appeals for the Ninth Circuit upheld the earlier decision against Pachmayr. Frank then hired a new attorney, Maynard B. Henry, and carried his appeal to the State Supreme Court, which refused to entertain the petition of appeal. The case was remanded to a

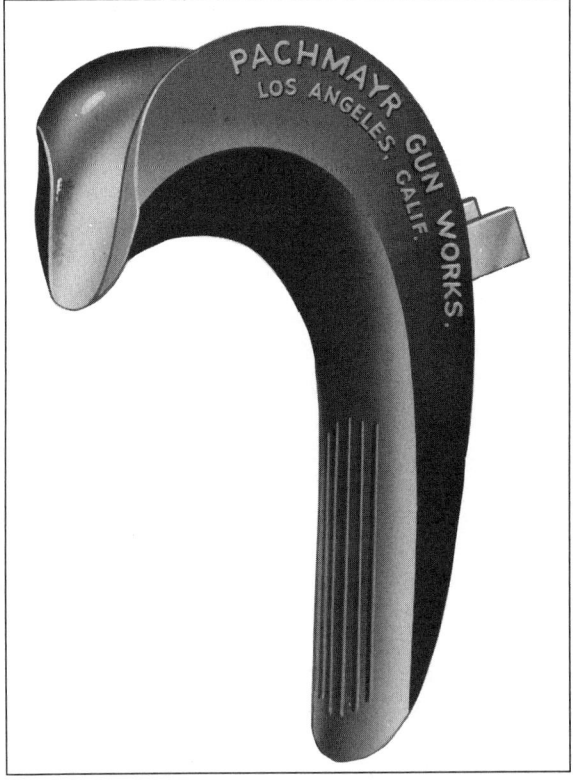

Frank Pachmayr's original proprietary product was his molded hard rubber Sure Grip Adapter, available in three sizes to fill the troublesome gap behind the trigger guard on most revolvers.

• PACHMAYR PRODUCTS & PATENTS •

Held in place by a metal horseshoe clip, the Sure Grip Adapter made revolvers much more controllable and easy to shoot.

Judge Harrison. Harrison stated that he didn't agree with the lower court decision but had no power to change it. He issued an injunction against Pachmayr from using the white line in his pads. Frank tried inserting a white plastic template in the box with each pad so the purchaser could install it under the pad. Mershon again challenged and was upheld by the court.

Judge Harrison had set up a later proceeding to determine the amount of damages to be assessed against Pachmayr. He had suggested that both parties could save money and time by arriving at an out-of-court settlement. Pachmayr's lawyers advised him to settle without more litigation. Pachmayr agreed to pay Mershon $50,000. At the same time, a stipulation dated 28 May 1956 stated that Mershon would not object to Pachmayr using a yellow accent line in his pads. A separate document licensed Pachmayr to use an aluminum spacer with a four-cent-each royalty paid to Mershon.

Frank was still preoccupied primarily with his aircraft division, so the recoil pad situation remained at a stalemate for some time. After selling out the Aircraft business, Frank bought out Mershon—lock, stock, and barrel. Mershon's tooling was poor, his designs mundane, and his corporate assets were few, but Frank turned the purchase into a business asset by setting up a new corporation using the Mershon trademark and marketing two distinct rubber product lines with Mershon at a lower price range than the premium Pachmayr pads. There was a distinct tax advantage in splitting the burgeoning sales between two corporations.

Frank continued to operate Mershon Company as an independent entity but at a new address, 1230 South Grand Avenue, adjacent to the building occupied by Pachmayr Gun Works. On 1 April 1958, under the Mershon Company letterhead, the following notice went out to all distributors and retailers on Mershon's mailing list:

· FRANK PACHMAYR ·

To All Jobbers & Buyers of Sporting Goods:
Subject: Announcement of the sale of Mershon Company, Inc., Glendale, California.

Frank Pachmayr, president and owner of the well-known Pachmayr Gun Works, Inc., has bought the Mershon Company, Inc., of Glendale, California—lock, stock and barrel. This business will be continued as a separate and competitive operation to Pachmayr Gun Works, Inc., retaining all representatives affiliated with Mershon at the time of transfer. For the past seventeen years, Frank Pachmayr has been very active as president and general manager of a large organization known as the Pachmayr Corporation, specializing in the manufacture of difficult precision structural machine parts for our latest jet aircraft. Mr. Pachmayr also maintained a very progressive and top-grade research, development, and engineering department, specializing in aircraft armament and ordnance requirements for the air force, navy, and ordnance departments of the United States government.

This company has employed up to 389 people. A few months ago, Mr. Pachmayr sold the above corporation, and will now devote most of his time to fulfilling the duties of president to both companies. White Line products will be promoted, advertised, and sold through the new company, Mershon Company, 1230 South Grand Avenue, Los Angeles 15, California, a division of Firearms Accessories, Inc., of the same address. Bill Harrison, vice president and general manager of the Gun Works, will cover the same office and duties pertaining to the new Mershon Company. Direct any questions you may have to Bill's attention. A sincere effort will be made to maintain and improve the products sold through both companies. We look forward to your continued patronage.

In addition to White-Line recoil pads, Mershon was making and marketing such accessories as Sure Grip shell packs—molded rubber belt slip-ons with loops that held ten rifle or a dozen pistol cartridges securely and quietly—Suction Grip scope caps, white-line-accented black ebonite rifle fore-end tips and grip caps, Sure Grip Adapters (unabashed copies of Pachmayr's adapter), pistol grip spacers, and 10-point rubber revolver grips.

Mershon 10-point grips were molded of black rubber. They wrapped around both front and rear straps of the revolver, making for a hefty handful, especially for those with smaller hands. The main gripping surface was stippled for increased friction. Mershon 10-point grips were not that poorly designed. They added needed length to the revolver grip, but they failed to make it to the top of the frame in the back, causing some recoil pain to the sensitive web between the thumb and forefinger. In spite of their shortcomings, 10-point grips sold, but not in great quantities. They did constitute a vast improvement over OEM grips, improving control of the gun and reducing felt recoil, especially in a .357 magnum caliber. The principle problem with shooter acceptance was the lack of eye appeal, which was a result of poor style and a clumsy feel. Even so, Frank continued to market 10-point grips under the Mershon logo.

Also under the Mershon banner, Frank sold machine-carved checkered walnut target grips for most Colt and Smith & Wesson revolvers, which were contoured to

· PACHMAYR PRODUCTS & PATENTS ·

Also marketed by Pachmayr, Mershon 10-point rubber grips never became popular because they were too bulky and poorly shaped.

match the frame in the back and had a fill in behind the trigger guard. A wide thumb shelf graced the left panel. Mershon Custom Walnut Grips were carefully cut from the best grade of finished imported walnut to a snug fit on the revolver frames, hand polished to a soft luster, and generously checkered with sharp diamonds.

Frank was ever the student and not afraid to learn from the experience and knowledge of others in his field. He was an avid reader of gun books, including those of the late Walter F. Roper, a pioneer of enlightened grip design. Before the improved .45 ACP Government Model became popular, Roper fired center-fire strings in competition with a military Model 1917 Smith & Wesson revolver at the cost of bruised and tattered skin. At the top of the grip, the narrow steel frame was then the only bearing against the tender web of the hand. Recoil of a .45 caliber revolver with original stocks was about as gentle as the business end of an ax.

Roper consulted with Smith & Wesson and was told that he could prove both his skill and manhood by learning to suffer with their original design, which was engineered to fit the mythical average hand. Instead, Roper began making his own grips and became the first popular maker of commercial custom grips. He established principles that still guide grip design to this day.

A shooter of the period was forced to clutch his revolver in a trembling death grip to prevent it from slipping down too low in the hand, or he had to hold it high and acquire the familiar black lump on the back of the second finger just above the knuckle as the rear of the guard pounded back with every shot. The Pachmayr Grip Adapter filled the gap behind the guard, then curved down the front of the frame to offer a fuller, more secure grip. Frank manufactured three sizes to accommodate every hand size. Before the advent of the .44 Magnum, the author considered the large Grip Adapter an essential adjunct to his Smith & Wesson .44 Special revolver.

In 1935 Smith & Wesson began a trend toward improved OEM grips with Magna-checkered walnut stocks that extended below the frame to lengthen the grip and also to the top of the frame above the back strap to fill the crotch of the hand and ease the bite of recoil. Magna grips, however, failed to fill the area just behind the trigger guard and left that job to Pachmayr Grip Adapters.

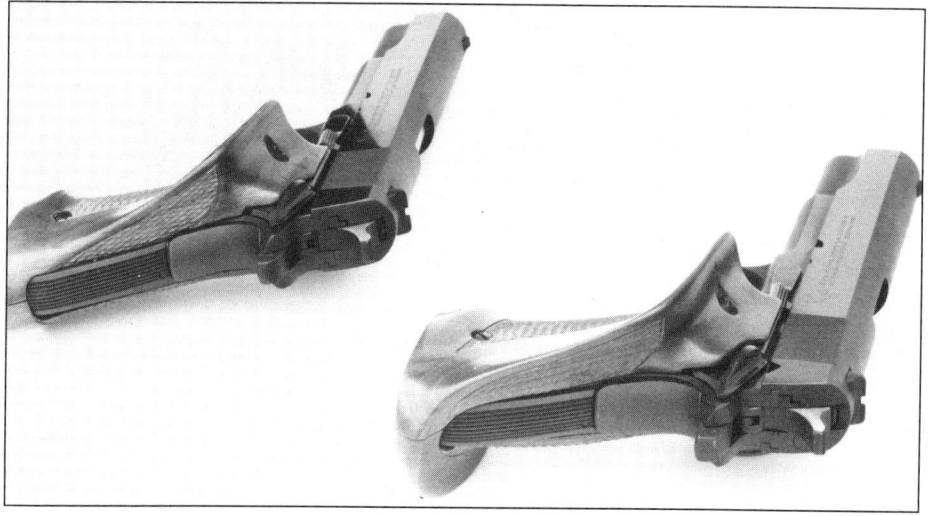

Under the Mershon corporate label, Pachmayr marketed a variety of carved walnut pistol grips, like those shown here on .45 ACP Colt Government Model pistols.

For a number of years, Pachmayr continued to produce the Mershon 10-Point rubber revolver grips with only limited acceptance by shooters. Then in late 1968, Frank decided to use rubber to absorb some of the recoil energy and take the bite out of hard-kicking handguns, but Mershon grip shapes simply weren't comfortable or appealing to the eye.

Modernizing Mershon's 10-point rubber grips was not a project to be undertaken lightly. It involved all new designs and tooling and expensive new molds, but Frank felt there was a market for black rubber grips. Eventually he proved correct, but not until he educated shooters to the benefits. Initial response to the new rubber grips was disappointing.

At the urging of his friend, Alex Kerr, Frank tried a new tack. "Frank," said Alex. "A lot of the guys out there just don't like black. Give them a choice. Offer them something that looks more like the walnut grips to which they're accustomed." Frank resisted at first but finally acquiesced. Again, it involved considerable expense. It wasn't just a matter of changing color. The lamp black used in tires and in Presentation Grips was in fact an important component of the rubber itself. Considerable experimentation followed to come up with a formula that retained the tough wearing qualities of the original and, important to shooters, the original feel. Finally, the right combination was found and Presentation Grips were offered in brown. Sales did pick up a little, but orders for brown rubber grips didn't live up to expectations, so they were eventually dropped. The essential component of shooter interest just wasn't there. As a group, shooters are a hardheaded lot and slow to accept new ideas.

Pachmayr Presentation Grips for revolvers were molded of state-of-the-art, semisoft black neoprene rubber. They were impervious to oils and common solvents, were overly contoured, had skeletonized, stamped steel-backing plates, imparted stiffness, and provided solid support for the screws that secured the grip panels to the frame. The result was a firm feel, but they were resilient enough to soak up recoil effect of hard-kicking handguns, such as the Smith & Wesson Model 29 .44 Magnum, by as much as 85 percent, according to a shooters' survey. Virtually indestructible Pachmayr Presentation Neoprene Grips retained their semisoft, warm feel even in freezing temperatures.

A checkering pattern of twenty-four lines per inch on the lower 70 percent of each grip panel augmented the tacky, nonslip feel of the rubber surface and glued the hand in position on the revolver butt in spite of recoil. Above the checkered panels were arched V-sections, lightly textured, and curving outward slightly on both sides to provide abbreviated ambidextrous thumb rests. This afforded a home for that fidgety digit without the objectionable overhang of thumb rests that interfere with holster wear and are normally found on target grips. The left panel was dished out and smooth at the top to facilitate the use of speed loaders.

Pachmayr Presentation Grips were a vast improvement over Mershon's 10-Point Grips. The new grips had style. They were "svelte" by comparison, with a slimmer silhouette, created in part by a thin wraparound over the rear strap. Because the thin web of rubber in back couldn't retain its shape if the grips were two-pieced, Presentation Grips were made like a clamshell, closed in the back. A slightly heavier, smooth-surfaced cross section wrapped over the front strap. Finger-grooved, round-butt Gripper Grips were a normal evolution of the Presentation series and were offered for medium and small-frame revolvers and the single-shot T/C Contender pistol. Compac Grips with round butt and little-finger cutout greatly improved control of small-frame revolvers, such as the Smith & Wesson Chief's .38 Special.

As a young gunsmith, Frank Pachmayr cut his teeth on the cantankerous brute of a .45 ACP Government Model Colt by developing a method of making it shoot accurately until it shot tighter groups than the revolvers that then dominated NRA competition firing lines. The one element lacking in his conquest of the stalwart .45 ACP was a set of improved grips. The only custom grips then available were either hand-carved, machined from walnut, or molded of hard, unyielding plastic. Frank determined to devise a rubber grip that would provide the best possible control of the slab-sided monster with its penchant for twisting and pitching violently in the hand with every shot. He wanted maximum support for the hand consistent with a slender profile that would allow the new grips to fit into holsters for the increasingly large contingent of law-enforcement personnel who were turning to the Colt .45 ACP.

FRANK PACHMAYR

Pachmayr Signature Grips for the Colt .45 ACP were a huge success. Initially brisk sales soon swelled to a tidal wave. Suddenly, black rubber grips were the "in" thing. Every gunwriter, including yours truly, wrote well-deserved glowing accounts of the new grips. Pachmayr Presentation Grips worked. The first time in its long and checkered history, the .45 ACP Colt and Colt-clones became controllable. It was like putting a cinch strap on a fiercely independent bronco. The recalcitrant pistol became as docile as the proverbial lamb. Instead of wrenching sideways in the hand with every shot, it remained steadfastly glued to the palm. The desperate white-knuckled clutch that marked .45 marksmen gave way to a more relaxed but firm grip that still offered complete control.

The original Signature Grip worked well for this writer. It had dual thumb rests on the sides, making it truly ambidextrous, a fact that southpaws like myself appreciated immensely. Side slabs were slightly thicker than OEM Colt grips, sharp-checkered at thirty lines per inch at the top and twenty-six lines below the thumb rests. A fabric-reinforced, twenty-line checkered rubber wraparound on the front strap negated the need for checkering or stippling the steel surface, a common custom feature. The vast majority of target and combat shooters found the new rubber grip an outstanding improvement, but some regarded it as filling the hand too much. Some combat shooters began paring down the slightly raised rib on the left slab to facilitate punching the magazine release. Others took a single-edged razor blade and cut away the lip at the bottom of the front strap to allow pulling a stuck magazine from the frame.

To accommodate both these alterations, Pachmayr offered another version of the Signature in mid-1977 with the problem areas removed. These grips proved ideal for southpaws like me. The abbreviated thumb rest was retained on the right slab where it was needed and the cutaway on the left offered easy access to the trigger. A third version did away with both thumb rests, creating an improved grip for shooters with small hands. Signature Grips were fabulous when used with the standard, steel mainspring housing, but Frank wasn't satisfied.

"I want the rear of the gun in rubber, also," he told Jack Farrar, his vice president. The result was checkered, neoprene-covered mainspring housings, both flat and arched, which provided nonslip cushioned back straps, at last removing the need for those sharply-checkered steel housings that come with most customized .45s and eat the palm of your hand like a wood rasp. The arched housings were offered in a wide configuration that completely covered the rear of the frame but required some milling at the edges alongside the housing. A later version of the arched housing afforded complete frame coverage at the rear without the need of any frame alterations.

Frank scrutinized early feedback for possible flaws in the design. He received a letter from one grateful shooter who had a real reason to laud Signature Grips. Apparently he had overloaded his .45 auto to the point of blowing up the rear of the barrel. The magazine was kicked out the bottom and the slide bulged out at the sides, but his shooting hand came through unscathed, thanks to the sturdy steel backing plates in his Signature Grips. The instant success of the Signature .45

• PACHMAYR PRODUCTS & PATENTS •

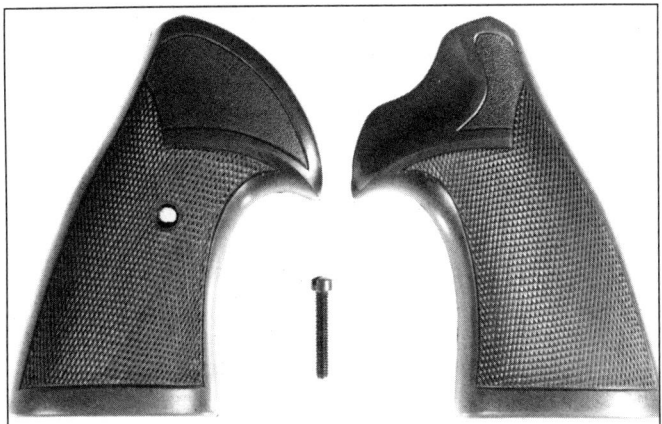

The Presentation Grips for revolvers were made of semifirm rubber. They reduced felt recoil to a marked degree and improved the overall feel of the gun.

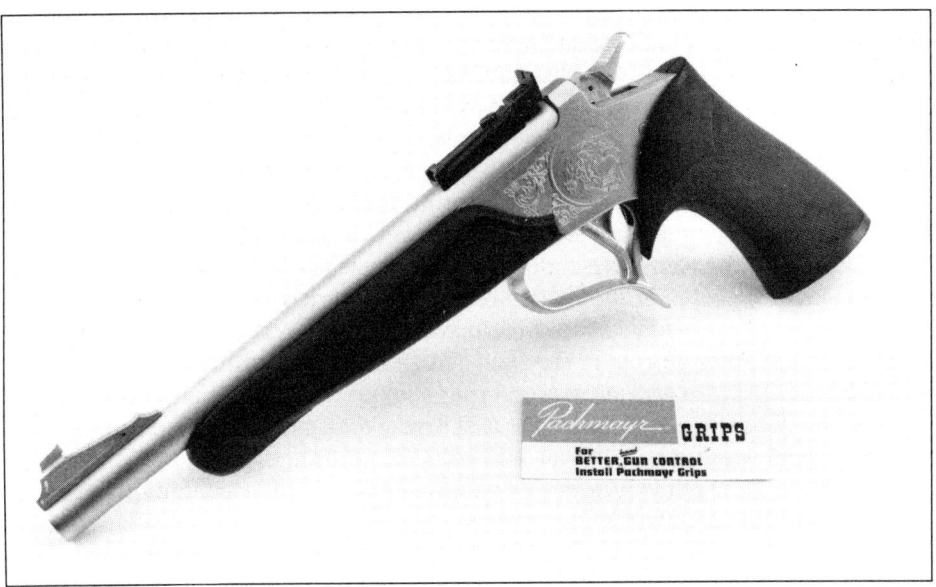

The Thompson/Center Contender single shot, top-break pistol comes in calibers up to and including the .45-70. Pachmayr Presentation Grips with hollow compression chambers at the rear helped take much of the bite out of recoil.

ACP Grip inspired release of full wraparound grips to fit the 9mm Browning Hi Power, the Smith & Wesson .39 and .59 models, plus the popular Walther PP and PPK/S 9mm pistols.

The top break, single shot Thompson/Center Contender pistol had become a favorite with handgun silhouette shooters. It was and is accurate and reliable, but in some of the big-bore calibers that were growing in popularity, it was a fearsome kicker. Pachmayr designed both Presentation and Gripper Grips for the T/C Contender with recoil-cushioning air chambers at the rear that answered a long-felt wish for a way to reduce the recoil. Even the Colt Peacemaker/Frontier single-action revolver, renowned in verse and song for the "grip that fits every hand," was improved by Presentation Grips that added depth and girth and filled in behind the trigger guard. Similar grips were offered for Ruger Blackhawk.

Proof of the continuing viability of Pachmayr Grip Adapters, invented by Frank Pachmayr well over a half-century ago, can be found in the *Guinness Book of Records* where a new shooting record was recently set. Sgt. Joe Walsh, of the Morris County Sheriffs Office, broke the fifty-one-year standing record of the incomparable Ed McGivern by firing two Smith & Wesson .38 Special revolvers simultaneously, delivering ten rounds in 9/10ths of a second, grouped into two ordinary playing cards. Rather than use custom grips to aid in setting this phenomenal record, Walsh equipped his guns with Pachmayr Grip Adapters.

For many years, the backbone of Frank Pachmayr's gun accessories was his line of recoil pads. Early recoil pads were hardly worthy of the name. For the most part, they were made of soft foam rubber that quickly wore out, sagged or collapsed with age, and accomplished little in the way of recoil reduction. About 1931, Frank introduced a new concept that used harder rubber with a latticework of XXXX openings along the side. It was sandwiched between a tough rubber outer skin, textured for a firm grip on the shooters shoulder, and had a hard rubber base to attach to the butt stock. The rubber bridge work between the base and the face of the pad crumpled under the force of recoil, cushioning the blow. Solid sections top and bottom gave the pads strength where it was most needed and made it possible to retain the pad's shape a period of years. A secondary benefit of the rubber pads was their ability to protect the butt stock from impacts with rocks and other objects in the field. In an emergency, if the rifle or shotgun had to be pressed into service as a walking stick or as an aid in climbing a rocky hillside, the neoprene pad gripped the rocks instead of skidding off, as a plastic or steel butt plate would.

In years past, classic stock design demanded checkered steel butt plates, or at the most, a solid foam pad painstakingly covered with top-grain leather. These custom pads suffered the same fate as other foam pads: They broke down with time. To offset any prejudice against rubber recoil pads on high-class custom rifles, Frank introduced his neoprene White-Line Presentation Model pad in 1965. It had solid rubber sides instead of the usual open bridge work, and it featured a tasteful basket weave face surrounded by a plain border. Because the border was sometimes cut away unevenly in fitting the pad to a gun, it was later eliminated from the Presentation Pad. The solid-sided pad was originally inspired by a request from the military to come up with a recoil-reducing pad without the open sides that collected dirt and debris. In arctic areas, open-sided pads also collected snow, making them as hard as wood.

The closed-sided Presentation Pad actually improved recoil reduction by means of an internal cavity that was supported by a waffle pattern of tapered, progressive, recoil-absorbing ribs. Another patented feature was the lightweight steel rein-

· PACHMAYR PRODUCTS & PATENTS ·

Frank Pachmayr originated the open-sided XXXX pattern of recoil pad that effectively reduced felt recoil from hardkicking shotguns and rifles.

forcement plate molded with the black hard-rubber base. Gunsmiths could appreciate that extra strength, because it was common for the brittle, black rubber base to crack during installation.

For years, recoil pad design was a hit-or-miss operation based on guesses and high hopes. It remained for Frank Pachmayr to apply engineering knowledge he gained in the aircraft industry to pad design. Using various pad thicknesses and bridge work, Frank tested and measured the rate of deceleration under controlled conditions. Frank constructed a machine rest to hold a rifle or shotgun with the butt resting against a pressure plate and backed by an electronic piezoelectric crystal pressure-measuring device. The actual recoil pressure transmitted by the gun could be measured, as could the rate of deceleration of the gun imposed by the pad that was being tested. The accumulated data was ultimately translated into a scientific approach to recoil pad design. At last it became possible to lay out a pad on paper with precise measurements for bridge structure and web thickness. Even the volume and pliability of the rubber could be factored into the equation. For the first time, pad designers had a firm knowledge of what the results would be before investing in expensive molds.

A recoil pad is no better than the mold that makes it. Pachmayr pads are the finest in the industry, not only in design but in the perfection of the finish. Frank insisted that his molds be hand polished with jeweler's rouge to a mirror brightness. Frank's molds had multiple inserts that allowed changing the faces of the pads from skeet to field configuration without altering any other factor. Even the core design that formed the waffle pattern on the sides could be switched.

Sales volume in the early days was well served with three-cavity molds. As demand increased, the number and size of the molds had to keep pace. In early 1947, Frank began making ten-cavity molds and later twelve-cavity. In 1961 Pachmayr undertook a major overhauling of his entire mold inventory, repairing and re-polishing his existing molds and adding many new ones. In a letter dated 12 February 1962, Frank wrote to his dealers and distributors: "Last year we were continually working on our molds for Pachmayr products, which, at times, did result in delayed shipments, but this rework has greatly improved our products, and we are now in a position to give you the excellent service you deserve. The pads produced by these new molds are beautifully made and will undoubtedly prove to be even more sturdy and of higher quality, if possible, than our former pads."

At the height of his operation, Pachmayr offered 216 combinations of recoil pad design from his sixty, twelve-cavity high-production molds with literally hundreds of insert variations possible. Interchangeable inserts allowed changing the name imprints on the faces of the pads from Pachmayr to Mershon or to the name of a gun manufacturer or a retail outlet. Anyone who purchased a minimum of three dozen pads could have his name and/or logo imprinted on the back. An initial fee was charged to cover the cost of machining the mold insert. Pachmayr made pads that were used as OEM on rifles and shotguns by most major United States firms and many overseas companies. Some familiar names that used Pachmayr pads were Browning, Ithaca, Remington, Ruger, Weatherby, and Winchester, as well as such overseas firms as Beretta, Fabrique Nationale, Franchi, and Perazzi.

Pachmayr directed an ongoing development program, continually upgrading his recoil pads and introducing new styles. Although Frank patented a number of different designs over the years, the original Multiple-X, open-sided ribbing originated by Frank in 1931 remained the successful standard. The Multiple-X design created a resilient bridge between the rear face of the pad and the black hard rubber base, allowing the greatest possible absorption of shock when the rifle or shotgun recoiled. Unlike many of the pads offered before by other makers, Pachmayr pads were scientifically compounded of the finest DuPont neoprene rubber. It was impervious to oil, common solvents, water, or the extremes of weather. They didn't harden with time or exposure and didn't become stiff in cold weather or become soft in hot climates. Pachmayr pads were unconditionally guaranteed for the life of the customer's gun. On those few occasions when the guarantee was invoked, Frank even paid the gunsmith's fee for installing a new pad. Small wonder that Pachmayr pads dominated the industry for decades.

Pachmayr pads are tough. They resist hardening or collapsing, even when the rifle or shotgun is stacked in a corner and forgotten for months at a time. I have one of Pachmayr's old original pads on a bolt action .30-06, and it's still perfectly serviceable after more than four decades.

Pachmayr pads are available in field, skeet, and trap styles. The last incorporates a deeply dished face that hugs the shoulder. It has coarse crosswise sawtoothed traction ribs with the sharp edges angled downward. Trap and live pigeon shooters love this pad because it slides onto the shoulder without resistance but won't slip down. Pachmayr pads are also available in smooth face, standard stippled, scalloped stippled, vertically ribbed skeet face, checkered face, screen face, basket weave, and leather face. The last was used principally on Pachmayr's white-line Old English pads, smooth-sided, and with an elegant radius that mimicked the leather-covered pads used by English gunmakers on their finest custom shotguns and rifles.

"It's the aristocrat of pads for aristocratic rifles and shotguns," says Frank. The Old English pad is hollow on the inside with a patented pattern of tapered internal ribbing that reduces felt recoil without the open-sided lattice look that some shooters find objectionable on custom rifles and shotguns. Pachmayr presentation pads are also smooth-sided and internally ribbed with a basket-weave face.

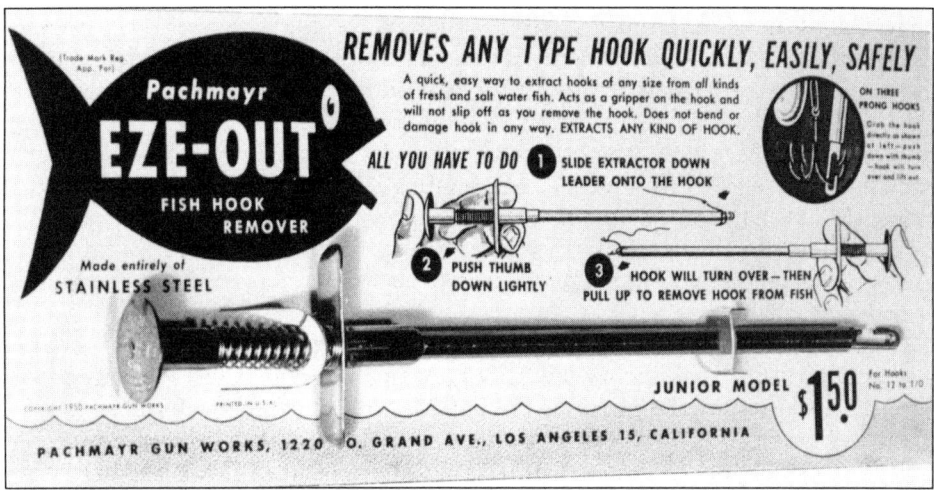

In addition to shooting, Frank enjoyed fishing. This led to his inventing the Pachmayr EZE-OUT fish hook remover, which reversed the hook for removal without harm to the fish or the fisherman.

The most effective recoil pad was Pachmayr's Triple Magnum, designed to distribute recoil energy over the entire surface of the pad. The one-inch thick, open-sided pad incorporated a four-layered lattice core of rectangular boxes in staggered rows and offered maximum damping effect. Patented sponge rubber inserts, hand-laid top and bottom, countered the normal tendency for the gun to jump forward and rebound from the shoulder after the rear shove. Triple magnum pads are still available in field, skeet, and trap versions.

The Pachmayr Pigeon Shooter was a plain-sided, hollow-core pad with the saw-toothed pattern on the face, but shaped in a normal configuration. It had only a slight rise at the heel and toe. For shooters who wanted the nonslip feel of rubber, but had no desire for recoil damping, Pachmayr offered a thin rubber, white-lined butt plate with a basket-weave or stippled face. For shooters who didn't want to deface their gun or just wanted to avoid the cost of pad installation, Frank offered a Slip-On Model Pad, which pulled on over the butt for a temporary or permanent installation. This provided protection for the gun and recoil damping for the shooter. Because considerable stretch was needed in the pad to allow slipping it over the butt of the gun, Slip-On pads were made from pure virgin rubber rather than neoprene.

Most pad models are offered in small, medium, or large sizes and come in red, brown, or black. Most models are available in three thicknesses: .60, .85, and 1.00 inch. Most are optionally available with a plain black hard rubber base or with a white-line spacer between the rubber pad and the base. A patented

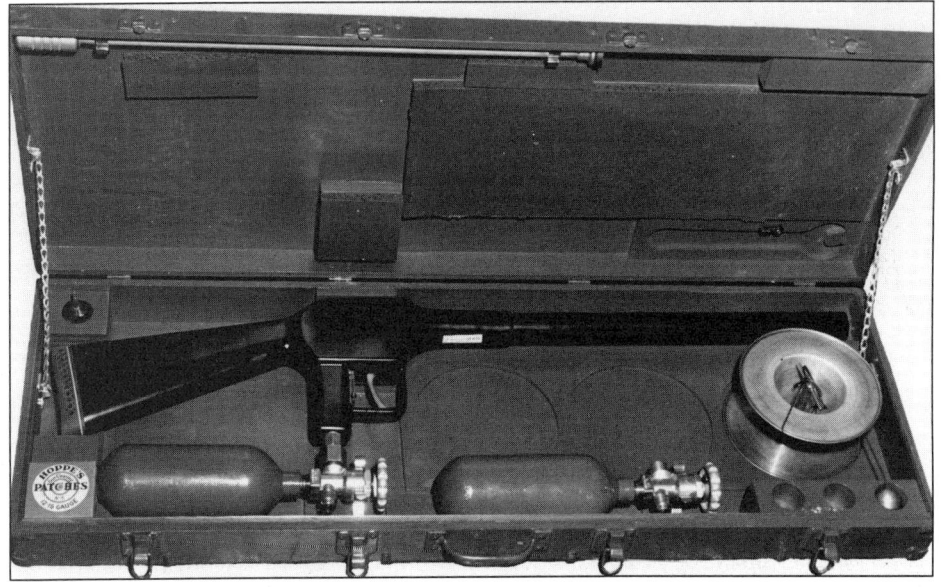

Also stemming from his interest in fishing was the Pachmayr Bos'n's Gun, a formidable compressed-air shoulder gun that launched a 1.25-pound steel harpoon at flank speed.

lightweight steel reinforcing plate was molded into the base, and the three layers were molded into a fused, inseparable unit. Most guns spend the lion's share of their time stacked in the corner or a gun cabinet with all the weight concentrated upon the heel of the butt stock. The pad needs to be pretty tough not to take a set and end up with a flat corner at the top. Pachmayr pads are guaranteed for the life of the gun, but to ease the burden on extra-thick, 1.5-inch Triple Magnum Pads, they were all packaged with a button-shank plug that slipped into the top hole in the pad and butted against the holding screw. This supported the weight of the gun and took the load off the pad.

During his forty-five years of developing firearm accessories, Frank Pachmayr was granted over 125 patents. Some patent applications were denied because the United States Patent Office believed that the innovations were not broad enough to warrant protection, or they said the principle had been previously

• PACHMAYR PRODUCTS & PATENTS •

established in another field. For example, when Frank came up with a quick detachable choke tube in conjunction with a shotgun compensator, the patent office replied that the principle of an interrupted-thread coupling had been established before in cannon breeches.

Before a patent was applied for, Frank had his law firm of Harris, Kiech, Foster & Harris of Los Angeles conduct a patent search. Sometimes they came up with a patent that was granted for an idea that was never marketed but cut across the lines of Frank's new idea. In cases such as this, Frank would contact the inventor and buy a license to use his patent or buy the patent outright. In the case of a widow, Marie E. Hawkins, Frank's sense of fairness compelled him to pay her royalties on recoil pad patents taken out by her husband Frank D. Hawkins in 1919, 1925, and 1943, even though the Pachmayr attorneys stated that the previous patents didn't conflict with those taken out by Pachmayr.

A patent that isn't protected is as good as no patent at all. Frank was called upon a number of times to defend his patents against infringement. Most of his patent suits were in connection with recoil pads. Perhaps the most exhausting suit was a civil action filed by Pachmayr Gun Works, Inc., and Firearm Accessories, Inc., (d.b.a. The Mershon Company) against Olin Mathieson Chemical Corporation, Winchester-Western Division. For years, Winchester purchased White-Line pads from Pachmayr to use as original equipment on their extensive lines of rifles and shotguns. The degree of trust involved might be judged by the fact that Olin actually sent Pachmayr a blank check, dated 11 May 1966, along with Purchase Order Number NHD 5962. The cover letter, signed by William A. Klingele, stated that the check could be filled out and cashed as soon as the order was shipped. Then, suddenly, Winchester executives decided they could save money by making their own pads, identical copies of those they had been buying from Pachmayr. In doing so, they transgressed several patents belonging to the two Pachmayr corporations.

If Frank had ignored this violation, it would have been an open invitation to the whole world to raid his designs. He had to respond. The ensuing legal battle, pitting Pachmayr's Los Angeles attorneys against Winchester's New York team of legal brains, stretched out over an agonizing eight years. This was a David and Goliath confrontation if there ever was one. In terms of monetary resources and sophisticated legal talent, Olin-Winchester far outweighed Frank Pachmayr, but it seems there is some justice after all. Frank won. After all the appeals were exhausted, Winchester was ordered to pay $150,000 in punitive damages. That sounds like a lot of money, especially in that day and age. It was just about the break-even point for Pachmayr, however. His major reward was respect for his patents throughout the world of gun accessory manufacturers.

When Frank bought out Mershon, he acquired some patent and trademark rights that belonged to the corporation. Mershon was having its recoil pads molded by an outside contractor. The pad designs were patented and trademarked by Mershon and the molds belonged to Mershon. After Frank bought the company, he moved the manufacture to a new supplier. The rubber company that was previously making Mershon pads then made its own molds and began marketing copies of Mershon pads under the trade name, Supreme Products. In 1965 Pachmayr filed suit against Supreme Products and successfully defended his patent rights.

Frank Pachmayr held a number of design patents for recoil pads. Many found their way into production models, but some were never produced. Two examples can be found in Docket Numbers 8082 and 8212, applied for in November and December of 1949. The standard specification for each of these pads reads:

> TO ALL WHOM IT MAY CONCERN:
> Be it known that I, Frank A. Pachmayr, a citizen of the United States, residing at Culver City, in the County of Los Angeles, and State of California, have invented a new, original, and ornamental Design for a RECOIL PAD FOR FIREARMS, of which the following is a specification, reference being had to the accompanying drawing forming a part thereof. The drawing shows side, rear, sectioned views, as well as an enlarged cross section of the face pattern for detail.

Number 8082 covered a pad with open sides and featured a bridgework of square boxes with cross trusses dividing them into equilateral triangles. The pad face was crosshatched with a pattern of horizontal grooves and crossed at a right angle by a fine pattern of vertical grooves. It became the Pachmayr Lightweight Field Model, a pad that really stuck to the shoulder. In spite of its mere .85-inch thickness, it did an outstanding job of reducing recoil effect. A similar lightweight pad was also offered as the Skeet Model with a vertically ribbed flat face. Docket number 8212 covered a design with open sides and had bridgework composed of a series of letter Y's successively opposing each other. The face was simply stippled. This pad was never produced.

Frank developed one feature of his pads that he didn't bother to patent. Gunsmiths were plagued with an ongoing problem when installing recoil pads on rifles or shotguns. Even if they managed to get the butt end of the stock perfectly flat after the pad was installed, there sometimes remained a slight but unsightly gap between the wood and the pad base. Some gunsmiths overcame this difficulty by dishing out the wood a little after squaring off the butt. Frank made lifelong friends of countless gunsmiths when he began molding his pads with a shallow depression in the middle of the bases so that they fit the stocks snugly all around, even if the wood wasn't exactly true and square.

•••

Although Frank Pachmayr's first love was guns, his inventive mind drifted to other fields whenever he saw a need that he thought he could fulfill. He was involved with a patent application for a drinking straw that was to be inserted into soft drink bottles at the factory. When a bottle cap was removed, the straw floated up and was ready for use. The straw was composed of two telescoping tubes. Frank received a patent for a small canister device that fitted the rear of a toilet bowl, via a snap-on bracket. The weight of an occupant on the toilet seat automatically switched on an electric squirrel-cage fan that extracted air from the toilet

• PACHMAYR PRODUCTS & PATENTS •

bowl. Three compartments filled with replaceable chemical cartridges deodorized and purified the air before venting it into the atmosphere.

It seems that inventive talent runs in the Pachmayr family. Frank's mother, Anna, was issued a patent for a unique design of a toothbrush. The bent handle and semi-circle bristles of a toothbrush successfully marketed today by a major manufacturer are shaped in a very similar pattern. Gus Pachmayr had invented a number of viable high-velocity, bottle-necked wildcat cartridges, both in Germany and in America.

Frank learned the importance of patents and trademarks after his encounter with Mershon. Pachmayr pads had carried the white-line spacer from the beginning, predating Mershon's use of it, but Mershon took the precaution of applying for a trademark on the white-line. Frank didn't have any patent protection. The lawsuit impressed Frank with the importance of filing for patents. From then on, Frank was careful to patent or trademark all of his original designs. He even had the name "Pachmayr" registered as a trademark in the United States and a dozen major foreign countries. A letter from patent attorney, William P. Green of Los Angeles and dated 9 July 1969, stated that the name Pachmayr was henceforth a "Varumarke" in Finland.

•••

One item that Frank failed to patent was a revised trigger for the Perazzi double-barreled shotgun. The expensive gun, imported by Frank from Italy, was an outstanding example of the finest hand craftsmanship, but the trigger delivered from the factory was poor. Because he loved the gun, Frank took the time to design an improved trigger mechanism with a light, crisp release. These improved triggers were installed by Pachmayr as an aftermarket option. Then Perazzi adopted the design as OEM issue. Frank never received any compensation for his design. He accepted the situation without rancor, saying only, "I'm flattered they began using my trigger."

Frank also invented a practical release trigger that was adaptable to a number of popular trap and skeet shotguns. Gunners in both competitions sooner or later begin to flinch from the constant pounding of recoil. Even the best suffer from the problem. Movie star Robert Stack, in his youth National Champion skeet shooter and still an outstanding shotgunner, told me that he resorted to a release trigger on occasion to trick his reflexes out of a flinch habit. Once the subconscious becomes acquainted with the exact instant when the gun will fire, it responds with a reflexive jerk, trying to pull the shoulder away from the gun to escape the punishment of recoil. The result is obvious—missed targets. Switching to a trigger that fires the gun when it is allowed to move forward instead of being pulled back tricks the mind into missing the moment when the gun goes off. When that routine becomes ingrained to the point where flinching resumes, the shooter merely switches back to a normal trigger and again confuses the subconscious into missing the firing time.

During the recovery period following World War II, shooters in the United States were still struggling with shortages of commercially made sporting rifles. There was, however, a surplus of military bolt-action rifles available, including United States made Springfields and Enfields, plus German made Mausers. In their military configuration, all were too long and heavy with clublike bulky stocks. A mail-order, preshaped walnut stock from Bishop or Fajen and a hacksaw improved the situation immensely. There remained the problem of a hard to access, slow to use bolt-shroud safety. Frank Pachmayr invented a replacement unit that was quick and precise. When the Winchester Model 70 again became available in numbers, Frank applied the same principles to it and created an improved safety lever that became widely used in preference to the factory original.

In addition to his pads and grips, Frank Pachmayr designed, produced, and marketed a number of lesser proprietary products. Many were patented after many years of research and development. Even as mundane an item as a cleaning rod received the full treatment from Frank Pachmayr. He engineered it with the same precision and attention to quality and detail that one might lavish on a space capsule. A dozen different versions are reflected in engineering blueprints of the original rod, dated September 1943.

A letter from Minnesota Plastics Corporation, dated 11 December 1943, traces Pachmayr's quest for the best material obtainable for the handle. In part, the letter stated, "Tenite II, technically known as cellulose acetate butyrate, is excellently suited in its physical properties for cleaning rod handles. It's tough, shock resistant to the nth degree, and very durable. We are afraid that the rather limited quantity available would not make production feasible."

Frank also invented the pistol kit, which became immensely popular with NRA pistol match competitors. Shown in its original form is his leatherette-covered, four-gun case with an Argus spotting scope mounted on the open lid.

• PACHMAYR PRODUCTS & PATENTS •

Frank was faced with the strategic materials shortages of World War II. He finally settled upon machined aluminum handles with double ball bearing sets at each end running in bronze races. He used oil-hardened spring steel rods to forestall kinks and bends and sheathed in tough plastic to protect the rifle bore from any abrasive action. Bronze burrs for the .22 and .30 caliber rods were machined with dragon's teeth arranged in neat rows all around to positively hold the patching material. To find a comparable cleaning rod today, you would have to import it from England at great expense. Picture all of the effort Pachmayr invested in this quality product, which sold for only $2.95.

Pachmayr also manufactured an official NRA precision trigger-pull weight scale, consisting of a wire bail with various weight discs suspended at the bottom that weighed from 2 to 4¼ pounds in quarter-pound increments. Handier for gunsmiths was Pachmayr's precision, spring-tension trigger scale in a solid brass body that was available in two models. One weighed a maximum of 10 pounds and the other up to 15 pounds.

A unique device from Pachmayr was his patented Sure Sight Gauge, a stamped steel device that referenced the height of the front sight on any Colt target revolver or the Colt Woodsman .22 Long Rifle against the bottom of the barrel. The Sure Sight Gauge took the guesswork out of changing the height of adjustable front sights when shifting from fifty-yard slow fire to twenty-five-yard timed and rapid fire, and back again. Elevation adjustments were set by sliding the right-angle shoulder on the bottom of the gauge against the bottom of the barrel backward from the muzzle until the angled top touched the top of the sight. The setting could then be read from a graduated scale above the sight.

Among the lesser items made and sold by Pachmayr were a set of 12-gauge red or green plastic salt and pepper shakers with screw-on brass heads and a similar set of snap caps with spring-loaded plastic buttons in place of the primers. These were designed to cushion the firing pin fall on fine break-top double and single-barreled shotguns. Snapping the hammers is the only way to relieve mainspring tension after closing the guns when they're not in use. Also produced and marketed by Pachmayr was a set of neoprene slip-on scope covers with optically flat clear-glass lenses to protect the scope's external optics.

Would you believe a mechanical fish hook remover? When Frank saw a need, he moved to answer it. In addition to being a hunter of both fur and fowl, Frank was a professional-level fly fisherman. He knew from bitter experience that frigid fingers and even colder fish combine to complicate a simple thing like recovering a fish hook from the gills. The patented Pachmayr "Eze-Out" Fish Hook Remover made it child's play. A Pachmayr catalog, dating from the early 1970s, describes the Eze-Out as, "A quick, easy way to extract hooks of any size from all kinds of fresh and saltwater fish. Acts as a gripper on the hook, and will not slip off as you remove the hook. Does not bend or damage the hook in any way. Extracts any kind of hook."

The Eze-Out consisted of a stainless steel tube with a T-handle at the top. Inside the tube was a sliding rod with a round button top over a powerful spring. At the other end, was an elongated eye with an opening on one side in the upper third. In use, the fisherman pressed the button in against spring pressure, pushing the eye out the bottom end of the tube. He slipped the eye over the leader and slid it down until he felt the crook of the hook. He then released the button, allowing spring pressure to draw the eye up against the bottom of the rod. The hook was automatically reversed inside of the fish and could be pulled free.

In the same catalog, Frank directed his attention to even larger fish when he patented his massive Bos'n's Gun, a riflelike shoulder gun utilizing CO_2 compressed gas at 800 psi, to propel a 1¼-pound steel harpoon with a bore-sealing rubber fletch some eighty yards through the air with riflelike accuracy. Enough compressed gas was provided by a 12-pound steel bottle to fire 300 shots at a cost of less than a penny each. The heavy harpoon unraveled a 750-pound test nylon line from a steel rod mounted parallel under the barrel and trailed it behind. The sharp tip of the harpoon boasted a double barb that hinged outward and resisted any effort of the fish to pull free. The 7½-pound gun loosely resembled a shotgun with a shoulder stock backed by a Pachmayr recoil pad. The pad was needed because the gun kicked like a mule. At a normal range of about forty-five feet, Pachmayr's Bos'n's Gun could shoot completely through a 500-pound fish.

One of the jobs that Frank Pachmayr always liked least was drilling the holes for sling swivels into the fore-end and butt stock of one of his fine custom rifles, not because it was a difficult chore but because he hated to deface his beautiful stocks with the protruding steel studs. He determined that one day he would find a detachable sling swivel that didn't show when the sling was removed. Frank adopted a unique concept unlike anything ever seen before. The Pachmayr Flush Sling Swivel, introduced in early 1970, utilized a case-hardened steel receptacle, a small steel drum about a quarter inch in diameter and threaded on the outside. The receptacle was fully inletted to the stock with only a slight concavity of polished and blued steel peeking above the surrounding wood. The receptacle was slotted parallel to the stock to admit a T-shaped extension of the sling loop. To attach the sling, the shooter inserted the T into the slot, pushing it in against the spring pressure and then turning the loop 90 degrees to lock it firmly in place.

When in place, the loops could swivel front to rear, but not side to side, and they couldn't twist. Loops were offered in ¾-inch, 1-inch, and 1¼-inch widths. Installing a Pachmayr Flush Sling Swivel was no do-it-yourself project. Even skilled gunsmiths were happy to have the help of a low-cost tooling jig from Pachmayr that assured a professional-looking job.

Even before he left his father's employment to set out on his own, Frank Pachmayr was a specialist in customizing and tuning handguns for the up-and-coming cadre of *pistoleros* at the Los Angeles Police Department. To test fire and sight in the pistols and revolvers after installing custom sights, Frank made a weekly pilgrimage to the Ellisian Park target range, later to become the LAPD Police Academy. For Frank, it was a sort of postman's holiday. He loved shooting, and here he had the perfect justification for burning prodigious quantities of ammunition. His least favorite task was packing half a dozen pistols, ammunition, ear muffs, cleaning gear, and other necessities into cardboard packing boxes for the trip.

• PACHMAYR PRODUCTS & PATENTS •

Ever the man of action, Frank constructed a plywood gun kit with a padded board that was notched to hold pistol barrels snugly and securely. Fellow shooters saw the pistol kit and asked Frank to make kits for them. Frank would often sell the box he was using and make a new one for himself. With each new box, Frank introduced some improvement. The top-opening lid was replaced by a side door that allowed access to shelves inside the box. He added a slide-out shelf with a vertical notched board that held the guns firmly by their barrels to facilitate re-

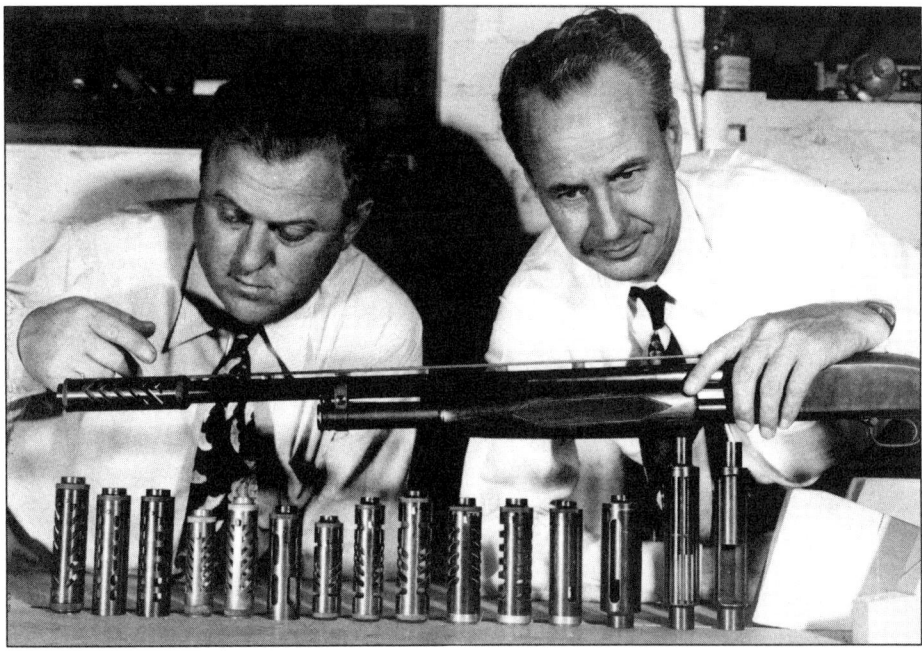

Many different shapes were tried before arriving at the chevron pattern. Frank and Powell examine a few.

trieving a pistol at the back. He braced the lid into an upright position and attached a Wollensake telescope for spotting bullet holes. The scope was collapsed and remained attached to the door when it was closed and nested into the bottom shelf.

Continued interest led Frank into offering the pistol kit as a commercial product. His original box stood a foot high and measured 8 inches deep by 16¾ inches wide. The slide-out shelf held four guns in notches or slots of varying widths and depths to allow for different barrel diameters and shapes. The opening below the pistol shelf could be used to nest a spotting scope attached to the lid or reserved for storage of ammunition and cleaning implements. The lid was attached by a full-length brass piano hinge. Frank devised a simple way to hold it open, while at the same time improving access to the pistol shelf. He simply cut the sides back in a triangle from a point about halfway up the side, back about 1½-inches at the top. The result was a winged door. The lid was held open by a spring clip that slipped over the edge and was formed by the two sections of the top, which sandwiched together when the lid was open. The shooting kit was offered in either brown or black simulated leather. All four corners were reinforced with brass hardware.

Several years later, Frank revised the kit to include another storage compartment in the rear with a key lock, and offered an expanded model to hold five guns that measured 17 by 10½ by 13 inches. A four-gun model continued to be offered. The entire plywood box was covered in a tough brown or black simulated alligator hide. The new five-gun case would accept the larger spotting scopes then becoming popular, such as the Bausch & Lomb Balscope Senior.

The pistol kits became popular among target shooters. In a testimonial to their usefulness, the Procurement Department of the Commander of the Benicia Arsenal, Benicia, California, in a memo dated 5 March 1957, placed an order for forty-one of the four-gun pistol cases and ninety-four more cases modified for use by rifle shooters.

In 1961 Frank made yet another update, introducing the new, super deluxe Pachmayr Match Shooter's Handgun Cases in three-, four-, and five-gun models. The colors offered included simulated ostrich in tan, black, or green, and simulated poncho pig in blue, green, charcoal, gold, silver, burnt umber, and maroon, plus dark brown cordovan. All of the rugged leatherette coverings were pyroxylin-coated for added resistance to abrasion and fading. The same basic, time-proven design was retained with some improvements. The top-grain cowhide leather hand grip on top was recessed to lie flat when the lid was opened or for stacking in storage and transport. All body panels were cut from first-grade California white pine plywood and all joints were marine glued and stapled with cement-coated staples by skilled cabinetmakers. All corners were rounded to reduce wear, and the hardware was all nickel-plated.

A new feature was the patented Pachmayr Lok-Grip Tray, designed by Frank, to hold guns more securely. The standard notches were at times unable to keep some pistols upright without touching during jostling in transit. Frank devised a notched tray with gaps from the crotch of each notch to the bottom. In effect, each upright wooden divider was independent of the others but retained in the tray by individual pivots at each base with a bolt all of the way through from back to front. This held them together like a stacked series of vice jaws. At the front, Frank installed a large diameter, knurled nut that could be tightened by hand to hold one gun or five rigidly in place, regardless of size or shape. Openings were configured to fit a number of different barrel shapes. The material on the jaws was chosen to have a gripping effect on the barrels without abrading or chafing the bluing. Initially offered as an option, the adjustable Lok-Grip Tray soon became a standard feature of Pachmayr pistol kits. To demonstrate to me his own confidence in the Lok-Grip Tray, Frank once took five new handguns right out of the glass display case in the sporting goods store, clamped them in a Lok-Grip Tray and without a qualm held it upside down in front of me over the concrete floor.

Another new option was the Pachmayr adjustable Tru-Vu scope bracket, which attached to the lid with four machine screws that went completely through the lid into threaded holes in the bracket mounting plate, a far stouter method than the

· PACHMAYR PRODUCTS & PATENTS ·

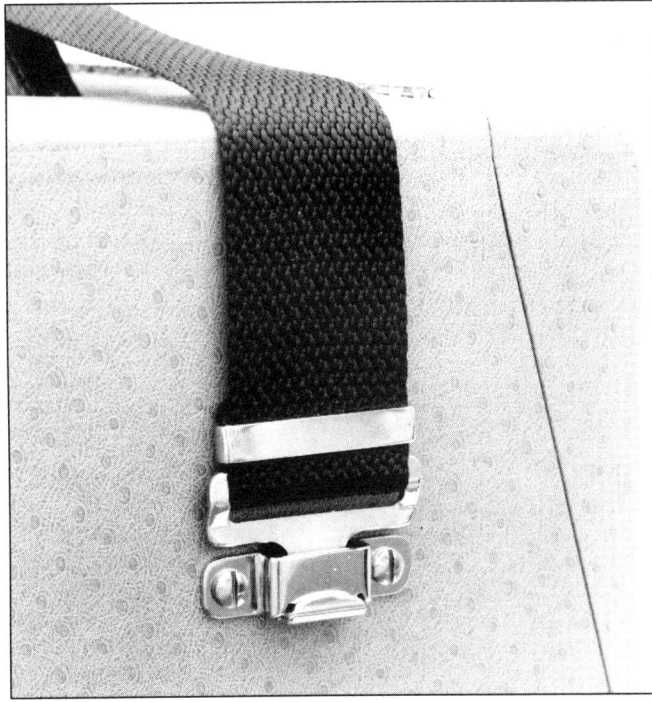

When Frank finally refined it, the leatherette-covered plywood Super Deluxe Case included a shoulder strap.

usual wood screws sunk in a thin plywood door. The bracket was strategically placed to hold a spotting scope handy when the lid was opened upright for shooting, and it nested within the bottom-front compartment when the box was closed. Pachmayr's bracket utilized a black, gold, or silver anodized aluminum cradle, mated with an aluminum base plate, via a stud through a horizontal slot in a ball-and-socket arrangement. A spring under the base plate kept the cradle friction tight in any position. A stainless steel, threaded hose clamp allowed the use of scopes of any practical diameter. A channeled rubber cushion around the clamp protected the scope finish from abrasion.

Scope brackets previously purchased by Pachmayr from other makers for use on their pistol kits had proven to be unsatisfactory because they couldn't handle many of the larger scopes that were just becoming popular at the time, such as the Bausch & Lomb Zoom 60, the Balscope Twenty, or the Swift Model 821. Some of the scopes had sharply tapered bodies. The Tru-Vu cradle could pivot horizontally on the base to permit aligning even these scopes parallel to the lid. The Tru-Vu could accommodate the smaller scopes, as well. Many contemporary mounts had a bad habit of locking the door shut if the closed case was dropped down hard, jarring the scope downward inside. The Tru-Vu was proof against this catastrophe.

It's difficult to imagine the intense effort and great expense Frank Pachmayr willingly devoted to each and every shooting accessory that he produced, regardless of how trivial or simple it might appear on the surface. A typical example can be found in his development of a shoulder strap to aid in carrying his new, larger pistol kit. When loaded to capacity with guns, ammo, and accessories, the big box scaled an impressive fifty pounds. The thought of what lugging all of this weight might do to the hand charged with the delicate job of directing pistol shots into the ten ring, prompted Frank to develop the strap. Then, too, there were a lot of ladies on the firing line. They might recoil at the thought of toting a fifty-pound box hither and yon.

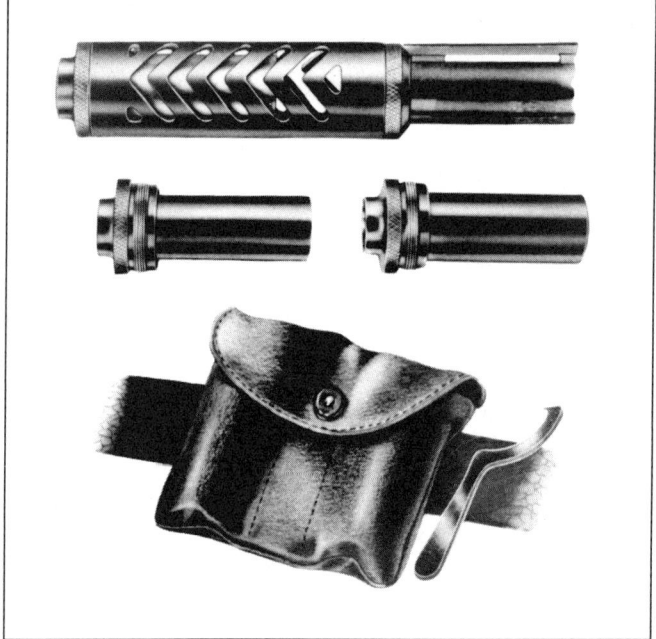

One of the most significant items in Frank's product development program was the POWer-PAC, an interchangeable choke/recoil reducing muzzle brake that delivered the best shot patterns seen at the time.

Recognizing that he couldn't do everything himself, Frank delegated the task to his project development manager, Edward B. Miller, the same Eddy Miller of Indianapolis auto racing fame. The goal was a belt that would transfer the weight from the shooter's relatively fragile hand to his sturdy shoulder on lengthy treks from parking lot to firing line. This was just another of those long overdue ideas that looked deceptively easy to attain. Merely dig up an old auto safety belt, screw it to the sides of the pistol kit, and *viola*!

It wasn't that easy, though. First, the belt had to be quickly detachable, so it could be stowed out of the way during matches to remain clean and not soil a clean shirt or jacket. Second, the belt hardware had to allow it to swivel from side to side to avoid uneven pull and possible tearing of the belt material. Third, the attachment had to have eye appeal, or else its practical value would certainly go for

• PACHMAYR PRODUCTS & PATENTS •

naught since no one would buy it. Fourth, the price had to kept within bounds without sacrificing quality. That's a big order for a small gadget.

Initially, Miller tried a pair of single post swivels attached to the pistol kit, but during several weeks of testing the posts bent under the load. Next, Eddie devised a plate and flat hook arrangement. Two belt catches or hooks were threaded onto the two ends of the belt and were attached to the pistol kit by pushing them under two catch plates, each of which was fastened to the ends of the box with two bolts into threaded backup plates. The bottoms of the catch plates were cut with a radius to allow the belt to swivel through a narrow arc. Flat leaf springs prevented accidental disengagement of the belt, while allowing a quick release.

The two-inch-wide belt was adjustable to a maximum length of fifty-five inches, long enough to go over the opposite shoulder. A number of materials were tested before selecting a high tensile strength, colorfast black nylon pebble-weave webbing, which was lightly compressed for abrasion resistance and treated to be washable.

Prototypes were distributed to a number of handgun competition shooters for field testing over a period of months. With favorable responses, production tooling was designed and built. Creating the stamping dies to punch the belt hardware out of alloy steel required four months and an investment of $25,000— more than enough to buy a comfortable three-bedroom home and lot in a good neighborhood of Los Angeles at the time. Frank dictated that parts had to have a high polish before nickel plating to achieve the quality look that spelled "Pachmayr." The load strength of the belt and hardware installed on the pistol kit was 750 pounds. Man, that's overkill! All of this effort went into the creation of a simple, unsophisticated shooting accessory that sold initially for a modest $12.50.

A spinoff of the pistol kit was Pachmayr's Black Powder Shooting Box with the same outside dimensions as the five-gun box, but with two slide-out drawers, a compartment to handle all of the myriad "necessaries" carried by muzzleloader shooters, plus black powder, round balls. Sold separately was a collapsible portable steel stand to support the box about waist level.

One of the most significant products to emerge from Pachmayr's shooting accessory development program was a combination interchangeable-choke and recoil-reducing muzzle brake, called the POWer-PAC. It took the shotgun community by storm. Trap and skeet shooters, always preoccupied with recoil and the flinching that it inevitably induces, were especially gratified with the success of the unit. The inventor of the POWer-PAC was Edward Baden Powell, a gun genius of two generations ago. Baden Powell, together with Ralph Waldo Miller, developed an impressive stable of wildcat calibers, called the Powell-Miller-Venturi-Freebore Magnums. These sharpest of sharp-shouldered wildcats were based upon standard .30-06, .308 Norma, and .300 H & H Magnum cases, necked down and up to various calibers. Powell's chronograph tests indicated that the venturi shoulder and short freebore utilized in PMVF Magnums resulted in higher velocities than the same volume of gunpowder in standard cartridges.

Baden Powell's expertise extended to many other fields as well. Baden has an impressive string of university engineering degrees. He worked in the fields of oil exploration and drilling, and water hydraulics. Baden Powell was far ahead of his time. He authored the book, *Comparative Humane Killing Power of Firearms & Ammunition on Game Birds & Animals*, and the National Rifle Association Technical Bulletin, *Killing Power*. He also contributed articles to the *American Rifleman*,

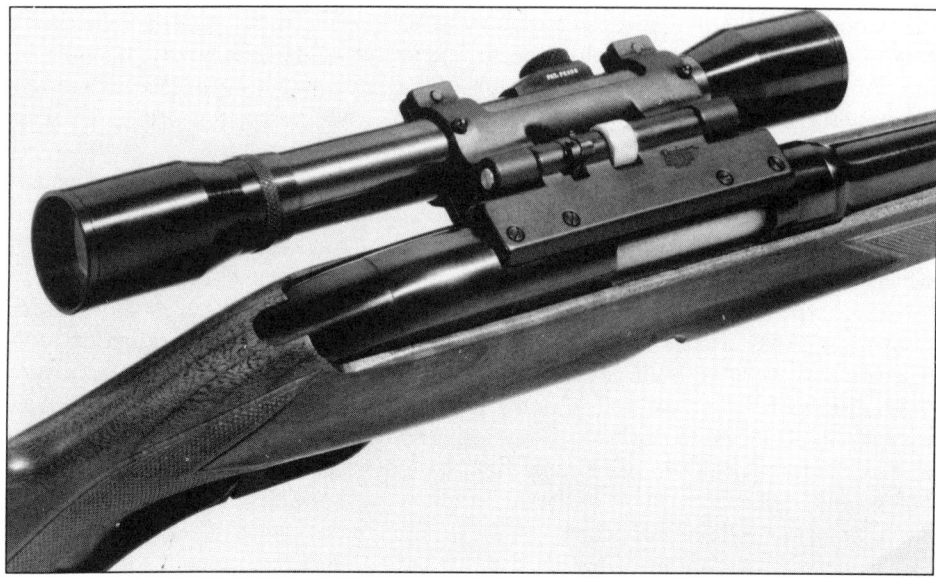

The Pachmayr Lo-Swing scope mount on a Winchester Model 88 swung to the side to allow access to the open sights.

and all his research and writing resulted in his remarkable insight into ballistics. That, coupled with his methodical approach to experimentation, provided some major breakthroughs, including the POWer-PAC. Baden began experiments with shotgun recoil and pattern control as far back as 1923. He had designed and patented more than two-dozen recoil-compensating, shot-control muzzle devices. The most promising was the one that later evolved into the POWer-PAC. Baden showed a prototype of his invention to Frank Pachmayr, who became interested in developing and manufacturing the high-tech compensator. Ultimately, Pachmayr and Powell entered into a partnership to perfect and market the device. The Patent Petition, dated 14 June 1948, applied for a POWer-PAC patent and listed both men as joint inventors. The name POWer-PAC was an obvious combination of the names POWell and PAChmayr.

Many muzzle compensators were already on the market at the time, including the Cutts Comp, popular with skeet shooters because of its ability to reduce recoil and deliver wide patterns at close range. The two main patents on the Cutts Compensator had run out by 1948, opening it up to the public domain. Some of the competitive variable-choke compensators were highly effective. The Weaver Choke and Cutts Comp both offered half a dozen interchangeable choke tubes with constrictions from open to tight. The choke tubes varied in length

• PACHMAYR PRODUCTS & PATENTS •

from less than two inches for the open choke to about five inches long for the full choke. The tubes added to barrel length and increased muzzle weight. Installation involved cutting off the barrel enough to remove the original choke constriction at the muzzle. Regardless, the result was a longer barrel overall and an unwelcome forward shift in the balance point. The standard Poly Choke, which did not attempt to reduce recoil, was varied by tightening a knurled collar at the muzzle and constricting an internal slotted collet. The Ventilated Poly Choke featured an add-on tube with a series of five right-angle slots, top and bottom, for recoil compensation.

The POWer-PAC represented a vast improvement over anything that had gone before and was unique in several ways. It was the first truly scientific approach to the problem. Baden Powell utilized his vast engineering talents coupled with an exhaustive testing program to discover what actually worked and to what degree the various design aspects were effective, both in controlling the shot pattern and reducing real and felt recoil.

In the words of Baden's son, Robert Ingram Powell, Ph.D., who participated widely in the design and prototype testing:

> What distinguished the POWer-PAC from all other devices of the time was the fact that its design was based upon scientific physical principles and extensive laboratory testing to achieve design objectives. In my capacity as Ballistics Consultant to Pachmayr Gun Works at the time, I was responsible for the mutually funded 1500 square-foot ballistics laboratory in Pasadena. That lab was a gathering place for Dad's friends, most of whom were pioneer developers of modern high-velocity cartridges. I also had charge of our field laboratory at the Pasadena Police Range, where Dad had friends. With their permission, we built a frame and clapboard shooting shack, with a steady shooting bench. We installed a state-of-the-art Remington chronograph, utilizing light screens to time the passage of the bullets. It was one of the earliest uses of this technology. We set up baffles in front of the first light screen to avoid having the shock wave precede the bullet and cause inaccurate readings. We had access to the Pasadena Cal Tech labs and Naval facilities for help on the finer points of our research.

Dr. Robert Powell had been employed for many years as a civilian research engineer by both the United States Army and Navy. During World War II, he served overseas in Army Intelligence and was instrumental in cracking the Japanese military code, which enabled a decisive victory by the United States Navy at Midway and helped to turn the tide of the war. This was a time when the Pacific Fleet was badly outgunned because of the losses it suffered during the Japanese sneak attach on Pearl Harbor. During the Korean conflict, Powell served in Naval Intelligence and trained elite troops in the field. Altogether, Dr. Robert Powell can look back upon more than twenty-eight years of government service.

At the Pasadena laboratory, Dr. Powell developed a method for taking high-speed photos of shot patterns in flight, using hand-blown strobe light bulbs filled with xenon and quenched in hydrogen to emit a microsecond flash of 50,000 volts d.c. Backed by perfect parabolic reflectors, these strobes literally froze the shot patterns in flight. The lights were triggered by a microphone, set at various distances from the gun muzzle, and allowed a running record of the shot column condition as it emerged from the muzzle and traveled through the air. This was many years before you could buy a strobe light at the corner camera store.

"Several thousand shots were taken during the period of research," relates Robert, "to observe the amount of gas dissipated and its direction and to study its effects upon the wad column and the shot charge. We could observe the angle of dispersion of gases and analyze their effect upon recoil reduction."

Part of the battery of testing devices developed by Baden and Dr. Powell was a ballistic pendulum, consisting of a vertical arm that was mounted at the top on a friction-free bearing with a shotgun fastened at the bottom end to measure free recoil. The pendulum was set up at the Eddy Cost Angeles Mesa Skeet Club range at La Brea Boulevard and Slauson Avenue in Los Angeles. Part of Robert's work was to shoot a minimum of four rounds of skeet daily at Angeles Mesa to demonstrate the POWer-PAC to the public. Robert developed a pretty good eye, racking up a total of 2,450 straights (breaking twenty-five clay birds without a miss) with many a run of 250 straight hits. Bob shot shoulder-to-shoulder with such celebrities as actors Clark Gable, Andy Devine, Robert Stack, and Rochester of Jack Benny fame. Alex Kerr, several times National Skeet Champion (as was Bob Stack), and Art Durando, International Live Pigeon Shooting Champion, were also frequent competitors at Angeles Mesa.

One day Dr. Powell was conducting recoil tests when a casually dressed man walked up and asked, "What are you up to here?"

"He was wearing a pair of faded blue jeans," relates Powell, "with tennis shoes, and a Raiders-of-the-Lost-Ark hat. Dad was a friend of the elder Hughes, so I recognized his son Howard from descriptions told to me by my father. I got to know Howard Hughes pretty well. We shot skeet together now and then. It was amusing that he was usually followed around by some starlet or other. I remember that one day he had Jane Russell in tow. Of course, she wasn't famous at the time. Howard became annoyed because she stuck to him like a pet puppy dog. Finally, he said, 'Do you have to follow me around all the time? Go over there and sit down until I call you.' Another time he came to the lab and hung around a couple of hours talking. I walked out with him when he left, and sitting in the car waiting was Ginger Rogers."

All of the Powells' testing equipment was needed during development of the POWer-PAC. The major feature that set Baden Powell's POWer-PAC apart from contemporary choke-compensator devices was the fact that Baden's unit utilized an inverted tube instead of the conventional extended tube threaded into the end of the cage. POWer-PAC variable choke tubes screwed back inside of the slotted sleeve of the recoil compensator. Thus, the length and muzzle heft of the shotgun barrel remained constant regardless of which choke constriction was used. Those two factors, however, were not among the goals of his research. He was seeking maximum recoil reduction with a minimum of noise and maximum patterning efficiency. Strobe photos of standard "control" shotgun barrels at the instant of firing revealed that the unsuspected culprits in blown shot patterns were the escaping combustion gases and the gas-sealing wads that followed the shot column up the barrel. As they exited the gun muzzle and were no longer confined and held in check by the inside of the barrel, the wads and gases drove forward into the shot column, scattering individual pellets to the side.

Existing compensators forced the shot column and the wads to traverse a long distance through a large-diameter, slotted sleeve without any side support. The rear ends of the variable choke tubes had to be funnel-shaped to gather the shot back together after they spread out in the compensator sleeve. That action inevitably deformed the outer shot in the column, scattering deformed pellets outward soon after exiting the muzzle. Perhaps more destructive to shot column cohesion was the fact that some of the powder gases went around the shot column and entered the choke tube ahead of the shot, adding further disruption of the pattern.

Because the choke tube was inside of the sleeve on the POWer-PAC, it was possible to have a gap between the barrel and choke tube shorter than the combined length of the wad and shot column, preventing gases from getting ahead of the shot. As the still expanding gases escaped the confines of the barrel, they encountered the rear of the choke tube that was effectively sealed by the wad. Seeking the avenue of least resistance, they went around the choke tube and out through the escape vents provided and countered recoil forces.

In Baden's words, "The shot column enters the choke tube before the wads behind it uncork the combustion gases in the barrel that rush forward at several times the velocity of the shot. The short distance that the shot column travels unsupported, before it enters the choke tube, doesn't allow it to spread. The choke tube has such a gentle slope on the funnel section at the rear to obviate practically all resistance that might contribute to recoil and cause deformation of shot around the outside edges of the column."

Flash photos demonstrated that a normal shotgun barrel drove the powder gases ahead of and through the shot patterns and also drove the wadding into the rear of the shot column. Fired from a POWer-PAC equipped shotgun, the shot columns were undisturbed by powder gases, and the wad fell away harmlessly immediately after leaving the bore, which allowed the shot mass to assume an aerodynamically perfect elliptical shape for greatest ballistic efficiency.

Baden Powell quoted some of the basic parameters that he and his son Robert established by actual field and laboratory testing:

> To begin with, the first vents must be not less than four inches from the muzzle to sufficiently reduce gas pressure and velocity (of the gases). Vents exhausting from the barrel must not be longer than the length of the shot column and wads in the barrel. If longer, the gases will bypass the wads and mix with the shot before and while passing through the choke ahead. Barrel vents must have an opening area at least three times the bore area of the gun. Shot must pass through at least three inches of tube after passing the vented area. At

least the last inch of the tube must be a true cylinder with parallel sides, regardless of the degree of choke taper. Vented gases must be deflected at a right angle or rearward, and the combined area of such surfaces must be at least six times the bore area of the gun.

Baden designed and patented half a dozen exhaust port configurations, including multiple rows of triangular, square, oval, cross-shaped, and chevron-shaped openings. The last was the most eye appealing and effective, with five chevrons on each side pointing forward. They were located on the upper two-thirds of the cage and vented more gases upward than down with the result that the normal upward swing of the muzzle during recoil was dampened to almost nil. This dampening effect was so pronounced that shotguns equipped with the POWer-PAC consistently delivered their shot patterns to a lower point of impact than before. At first it was necessary to bend the barrels slightly to compensate and bring the patterns back up to the normal flight path. Once the problem was clearly identified, the device was engineered to compensate and keep the sighting plane and shot plane parallel. Reduced upswing allowed the shooter to keep his target in sight during recoil and allowed quicker recovery for a follow-up shot. The chevron pattern was used in POWer-PACs that Pachmayr manufactured.

The POWer-PAC had a bronze front sight bead swaged in above a nonglare matted sighting plane. Three tubes were included and choked for short, medium, and long ranges. Pattern efficiency was phenomenal for that time. Thousands of patterns were fired to arrive at the optimum constriction for each tube. The short range tube delivered an average of 87 percent patterns into a thirty-inch circle at twenty yards. The medium range tube duplicated this performance at thirty yards and the long range tube did the same at forty yards. With larger shot sizes, Numbers 5s or larger, the long range tube delivered effective patterns for wildfowl to sixty yards or more.

The POWer-PAC was an impressive recoil reducer. According to Baden Powell: "Only part of the recoil generated in a shotgun results from the powder moving a relatively lighter mass of shot, wads, and combustion products in one direction, and at the same time pushing the heavier mass of the gun in the opposite direction. The balance of the recoil is generated by the rocketlike thrust given the gun when the gases are exhausted at high velocity from the muzzle."

The POWer-PAC reduced these recoil forces by venting the gases before the shot charge left the muzzle. Also, the impact of gases upon the rear edges of the chevrons pushed the gun forward, counteracting rearward motion and reducing free recoil by 37 percent. A 12-gauge shotgun felt like shooting a 16-gauge.

The POWer-PAC was free of the ear-piercing racket caused by most other compensators. Some trap and skeet fields disallowed compensated shotguns because of the noisy blast to the sides. The POWer-PAC was engineered to break up sound waves before they escaped from the gun and resulted in a noise level no greater or more high pitched than that experienced with a normal barrel.

• PACHMAYR PRODUCTS & PATENTS •

The POWer-PAC was installed by silver soldering a threaded adapter ring at the muzzle of a barrel after it was cut to the appropriate length. Assuring a permanent attachment, the ventilated cage threaded into place with a lock ring and Allen locking screw. The cage, which was broached from 4,130 chrome moly steel and heat treated to 60 RC, was meant to last several lifetimes. The variable choke tubes could be screwed into the cage by hand. A small wrench was included to

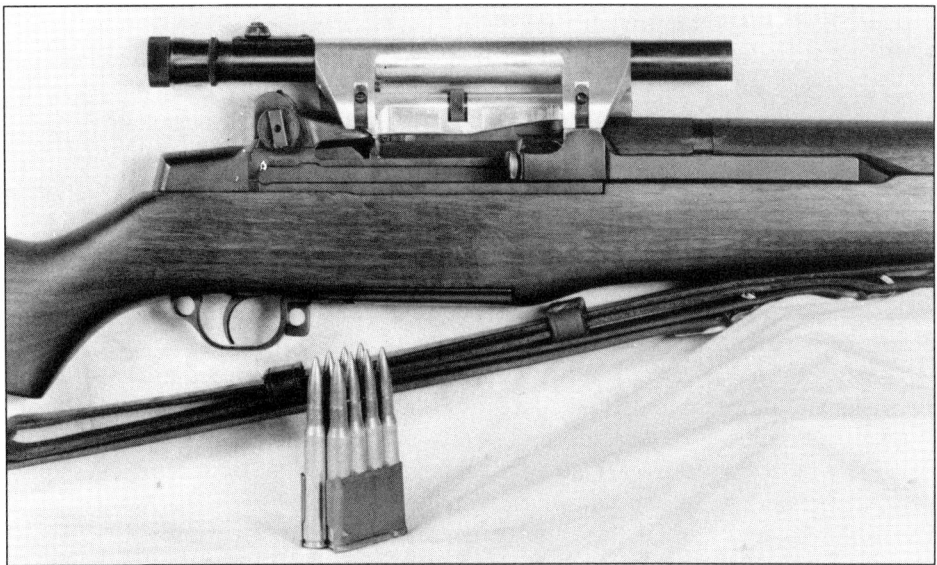

To help the marines develop a sniper version of the M1 Garand, Frank adapted the Lo-Swing to fit the GI rifle, which allowed easy top loading of the 8-shot clip.

snug up the union. A square shoulder just behind the threads sealed them away from combustion residue that often made choke tubes of competition devices freeze in place. An independent laboratory test involved firing 5000 frangible wad loads through a POWer-PAC, after which the tube could still be removed by hand without difficulty. A sturdy snap-top canvas case with belt loop was included to carry the pair of spare tubes. In addition to the chevron-shaped POWer-PACs manufactured by Pachmayr, the devices with other exit opening shapes were made under a licensing contract by High Standard and appeared as OEM on guns from Ithaca, Browning, Remington, Savage, J. C. Higgins, and Winchester.

The POWer-PAC was available to fit gauges 410, 28, 20, 16, and 12. It was launched by Pachmayr with $25,000 national advertising campaign, plus much good press, and became immensely popular, especially with trap and skeet shooters. It would still be popular today had not the ammunition makers revised their shotgun shells to incorporate plastic cups to enclose and protect the shot as it traveled up the bore. These cups began to expand the instant they were freed of the constriction of the bore and became caught inside of the exhaust cages, destroying the usefulness of the POWer-PAC.

Frank Pachmayr and his engineering staff developed yet another variable choke device. Pachmayr's patented Tru-Choke met the order that the shot should pass through a parallel section of the tube before exiting the muzzle, rather than be simply squeezed down by a taper at the end. Achieving this goal involved traveling a complicated and tortuous route. Many prototypes were tested before adoption of a cage that attached to the barrel via an adapter collar. It was similar to that used in the POWer-PAC, with a slotted recoil-reduction cage threaded onto the adapter. At the muzzle, a corrugated collar threaded onto the cage and could be rotated to vary the degree of choke. The Tru-Choke resembled already existing variable choke devices, but it was unique in that inside the cage was a two-inch long tubular collet that was slotted from both ends. The adjusting collar had two internal shoulders acting upon two shoulders on the outside of the collet, in such a way that the collet compressed uniformly along its entire length as the collar was tightened. There were twelve slots, six from each end, evenly spaced and alternating, thus allowing radial compression in response to inward wedging action of the dual-mating shoulders. The slots were so narrow that shot passing through couldn't lodge in them.

Early testing was carried out with the collets being lathe-turned of heat-treated high-tensile aluminum and slotted by saws, then hard anodized. During testing, some of the collets split through the narrow connecting webs at the ends of the slots. This problem was overcome by changing to tougher beryllium copper collets. Beryllium copper collets could be cast with the slots already in place, simplifying the machining and eliminating internal stresses that led to the original part failures. The collet tubes were easily removed for cleaning or replacement, but removal was seldom required because the design was largely self-cleaning. Inside the adjusting collar were five semicircular grooves that allowed some of the powder gases to escape through the slots and out the muzzle, which blew away any residue deposited by the wads. The outside of the collar had eight evenly spaced indices at the rear where it joined the slotted cage to define the degree of choke. An integral bronze bead front sight was centered at the front of the slotted cage.

Unfortunately, this highly efficient variable choke device was never placed in production. The Tru-Choke was set aside temporarily to make way for a push to perfect and market the Pachmayr Signature .45 ACP accuracy system. Tooling for the Tru-Choke was never resumed.

Often sudden danger inspires a flash of insight, and an idea can burst full blown upon a man. The concept of a swing-aside scope mount was born in 1934 when Frank Pachmayr, hunting on Kodiak Island, faced a ten-foot Alaskan brown bear that was headed full-bore in his direction. Frank's 4X Stith Bearcub scope was in a bridge-type mount and labeled "quick detachable" by its maker. With an angry bruin scant feet away, however, Frank had no time to reach for a screwdriver. The narrow field of the Bearcub was literally full of bear by the time Frank managed to divert the charge with a desperation shot at barely twenty-five feet.

• PACHMAYR PRODUCTS & PATENTS •

This photo of a shot in flight reveals that gases are bled off by the compensator, thus preventing disruption of the shot column, which is the real reason for improved patterns.

"There was no way I could pick my spot on that big brownie," recalls Frank. "I was lucky to turn him at all. We ended up tracking a wounded bear through a dense alder thicket—not exactly my idea of fun. I determined right then and there that I wouldn't ever find myself in that fix again."

When he returned to his manufacturing and sales complex in Los Angeles, he set out to develop a scope mount that would avoid a reoccurrence of his close encounter of the dangerous kind. Frank sketched some ideas on scratch paper. One shows a dovetailed rail on a fixed side-mounted base with a matching slot in the rings that is secured by a thumb lever to allow instant removal. His next thought was to change the dovetail to a cylindrical rail, matched by a lengthwise hole in the ring assembly with an allowance to swing the scope to the side. From there, it was a short hop to a fully hinged ring assembly and base. He still was thinking in terms of a railed union between the dual assemblies, though. It was some time before Frank's fertile mind hit upon integrating the hinge and the detachment mechanism into one compact unit.

More than one of Frank's customers questioned the need to use a scope for shooting dangerous game. "Why not just use open sights and be done with it?" a friend once asked him. "Mainly," replied Frank, "because you can't be sure of encountering your bear, Cape buffalo, tiger, or any other dangerous game at close range."

Today few hunters dispute the superiority of a scope over iron sights. A scope affords quicker target identification and positive sighting even in the poor light of dawn or dusk. Despite obvious advantages, a scope can be a liability if it becomes wet or fogged or if game is encountered at a short range. "Most shooters concede that under fifteen or twenty yards a scope is nearly useless on moving game," says Frank. In the Old Country, Frank's father, Gus, solved the problem by mounting scopes on split stilts high above the bore, which allowed the hunter to peer at his iron sights through the narrow gaps under the scope. This cure is almost worse than the malady, making the rifle top heavy and clumsy. Frank wanted to mount the scope low over the bore and hinge it to allow the hunter to flick the instrument aside when the iron sights were needed.

"The real advantage of the Lo-Swing scope mount is its ability to get out of the way in a split second," said Frank, "for emergency use of the iron sights." Even a charging grizzly should allow the split second needed to perform this brief motion. Over the years, Frank has received many testimonials for the Lo-Swing and heartfelt thanks from hunters who literally owe their lives to the hinged scope mount. Paul Strider, an Alaskan, faced that "moment of truth" with a giant Kodiak bear. He wrote, "My first encounter with a brownie was almost my last. I wounded a good-sized specimen only to have it turn and charge me. It was running through some deep sledge grass, and I lost it for a moment. When it reappeared, it was too close for me to pick up in my scope. It would have been all over except for my Lo-Swing. I just kicked the scope aside and used my open sights to drop the beast, almost at my feet."

From W. A. Heldt, a Sioux Falls, South Dakota, taxidermist, "I use the Lo-Swing on all my guns. On my two-month trip to Alaska last fall, had it not been that I was using your mount, I would never have gotten my Dall sheep. It was rain then snow, sometimes making the scope useless."

William M. Perkins of El Paso, Texas, wrote, "I recently had one of your Lo-Swing mounts installed on my Marlin. I found it extra handy in brush and heavy woods, as the scope could be made available or quickly pushed aside for fast shooting with iron sights with the flick of my left hand."

North Richland, Washington, resident Leslie P. Roache, stated, "I just want to tell you people that you have one of the sweetest mounts I have ever used on a gun in my life. Some boys were under the impression that the scope would change its line of sight by swinging it over and back. I don't know how many times mine has been swung over and back, and I never had to adjust it since I first sighted it in."

Wherever life has hung in the balance, the Lo-Swing scope mount enjoyed great popularity. In its hunting heyday, Africa consumed a high percentage of Lo-Swing scope mounts. Several years ago, Alaskan gunsmith, Arthur Skinner, reported to Frank, "I install more Lo-Swing scope mounts than all of others combined." Unfortunately, the Lo-Swing is no longer made.

The Perazzi is a Ferrari-grade shotgun from Italy and is highly regarded worldwide by shotgunners in competition. The only improvement that one can make upon this incredibly precise shotgun is to engrave it. Here is the work of acclaimed engraver Angelo Bee.

The Winchester Model 94 was Frank Pachmayr's favorite rifle for customizing and engraving. Each rifle was restocked with highly figured claro walnut, featuring a high-gloss finish and hand-checkering. The action was hand-honed to silken smoothness. Broad flats on both sides of the receiver provided ample space for dramatic tableaus of wilderness or Western life.

This Browning over/under shotgun has side plates added to provide space for four golden birds to fly, representing the major species of upland game birds. (Engraved by Angelo Bee)

This magnificent cased set of Western firearms was created by Frank Pachmayr for his life-long friend and attorney Nicholas A. Misciagna. Included are a completely customized Model 94 Winchester .30-30, a matched pair of second-generation Colt Frontier revolvers in .357 Magnum caliber, and two matched Colt Third Model Derringers. (The engraver was Richard Boucher. Photographs by Devendra Shrikhande)

A Pachmayr/Parker Invincible, upgraded to the finest shotgun imaginable, with wood and engraving that far exceed any work found on the factory originals.

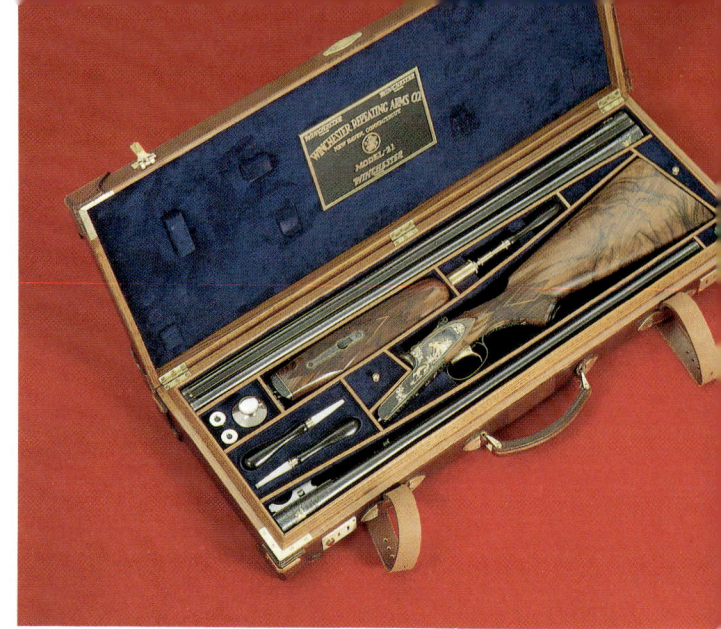

This magnificent Pachmayr-customized Winchester Model 21 was cased with two sets of barrels, for Guns & Ammo Publisher, Tom Siatos.

Side plates were added to provide a bower for Diana, goddess of the hunt, inlaid in gold, along with her hound.

The shotgun barrels were graced with gold beads, rings, and fine engraving.

(Photos by Bob D'Olivio, courtesy Petersen Publishing)

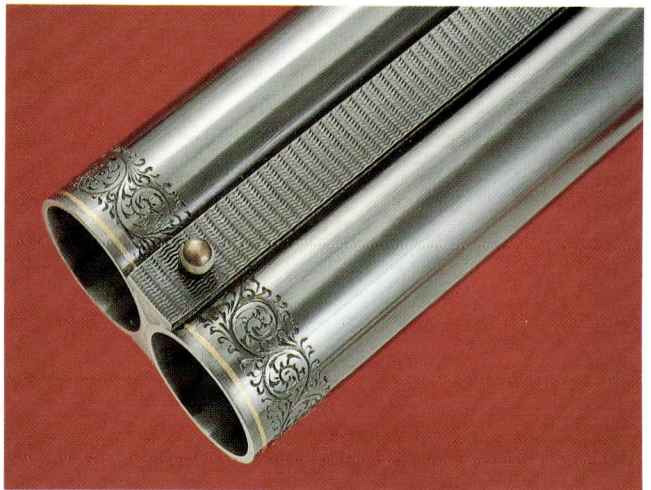

Beauty and utility go hand-in-hand with this Pachmayr/Parker double-barreled shotgun, which was upgraded to Parker Invincible level.

Both sides of a Francotte 20-gauge, with game birds on one side and fleeing rabbits on the other. This gun was meant to hunt! (Engraved by Angelo Bee)

Beautiful grain in a tastefully executed stock contributes greatly to the ultimate class of a fine custom Winchester Model 21 shotgun from Pachmayr.

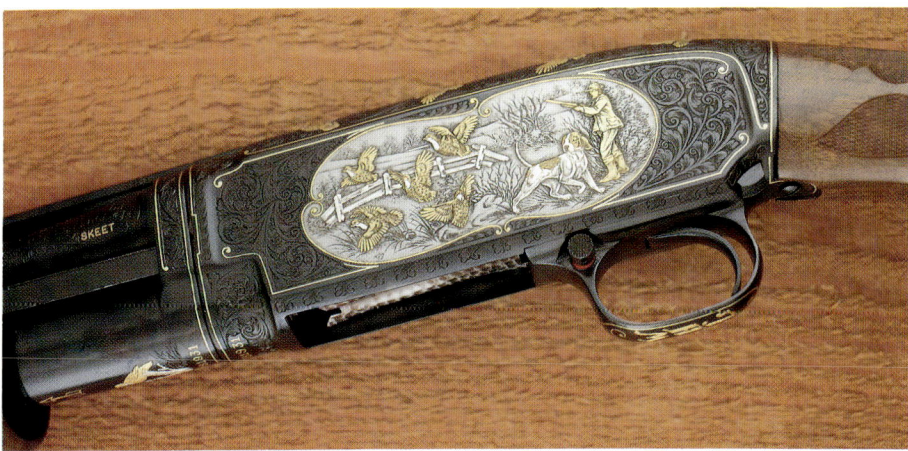

Broad flats on both sides of a Winchester Model 12 pump shotgun afford ample area for imaginative hunting scenes, including hunters, dogs, and game. (Engraved by Angelo Bee)

The Winchester Model 21 is one of the strongest shotguns ever made. However, the boxlock shotgun offers little space for decorative engraving. Frank Pachmayr added side plates to provide a wider "canvas" for the engraver, Angelo Bee.

A pair of Parker shotguns already "benched," that is completely rebuilt, and restocked. Barrels and receivers remain in the white, awaiting the engraver's skills. Note the added side clips and beading.

This Pachmayr-customized Winchester Model 94 features an ill-fated buck attacked by a leaping puma. The gold inlays are frozed forever in mid-flight, within a carved steel forest.

This ivory-handled gold-plated Colt Third Model Derringer is completely floral engraved.

This is another example of the fine engraving produced by Pachmayr. The basic gun was made by Perazzi, Italy.

On the left side of the Winchester Model 94, stocked in spectacular French walnut, a golden bison watches a fully laden golden stagecoach make its way though a cactus-studded landscape.

Frank Pachmayr loved the sturdiness and dependability of the Winchester Model 21. To offer a wider tapestry for engraving, Frank often added side plates to this boxlock shotgun. This is the work of Angelo Bee.

This Winchester Model 94 was stocked in highly figured walnut by Frank Pachmayr, then engraved and gold inlaid. Note, the stock was carved rather than engraved.

One of Frank Pachmayr's favorite double-barreled shotguns for customizing was the Winchester Model 21 shown here with side plates added. Fine engraving and gold inlays add beauty and value. This is the work of Angelo Bee.

The bottom of a shotgun provides a home for Bambi and his forest friends. (Engraved by Angelo Bee)

· PACHMAYR PRODUCTS & PATENTS ·

The original Lo-Swing mount was a pretty straightforward affair, composed of two separate side-mount bases and mated with dual rings to form a pair of hinges that pivoted on pins. Early, Frank dropped the pins in favor of two knurled screws that allowed easy scope removal. Hardened steel cones assured a return to original zero and constant alignment. The mounting procedure was exacting. If the gunsmith drilled the holes wrong, the hinges could bind or the scope could be out of alignment with the bore. Scopes of the day didn't provide constant-centered reticules and internal adjustments were rather limited. For that reason, Pachmayr performed most of the installations in-house.

Frank Pachmayr's most successful product was his rubber recoil pad, which he made available in a wide variety of patterns to fit the needs of hunters, as well as skeet and trap shooters.

One customer complained about a Lo-Swing mounted by an independent gunsmith. Pachmayr discovered that the mount was installed out of alignment with the bore. The only solution was to fill the holes and redrill the receiver. Rather than send the gun back to the customer with plugged holes, Frank shipped the customer a new rifle at no charge with his scope and Lo-Swing properly mounted and sighted in.

"We made our first mounts out of die cast," says Frank, "but some difficulty developed over air pockets in the castings. On advice of a metallurgist, we changed to a metal known as Zumac Number Five. The castings were beautiful, but after six months or so, we began getting complaints about the mounts loosening. It seems the metal had a bad habit of cold flowing away from points of pressure, in this case the screws. Continual tightening was necessary to keep the mounts in zero."

After about a year and a half, Frank abandoned the two-piece mount in favor a vastly improved design with a one-piece side-mount base and contoured on the inside surfaces to fit most of the popular rifles of the day. Installing a side mount was no easy job. The base had to be securely clamped on the rifle receiver and the scope jockeyed around until it was bore sighted. Then four holes were drilled and tapped. Pachmayr marketed a precision drill jig that accepted the rings with the scope in place to allow bore sighting. Hardened steel bushing guided the drills to assure perfect alignment.

The Lo-Swing loop assembly was shaped initially in a solid tube and slotted on the hinge side with four screws clamping the loop tight and holding the scope in place; it also provided an extra wall of protection in the vulnerable central section.

Internal diameters were offered to fit the ⅞-inch, 26mm, and 1-inch scopes then offered. At the both ends of the loop assembly, arms were hinged to the one-piece base, allowing the scope to rotate to the left well out of the way of iron sights.

Making the hinge of the Lo-Swing detachable involved inspired engineering. The rear of the base held a female 60-degree angle cone and mated to a fixed cone in the rear leg of the loop. The front of the base held a male cone that telescoped in and out in response to a knurled finger wheel in the center. The front leg of the loop held a fixed female cone to receive the movable cone in the base. A stout leaf

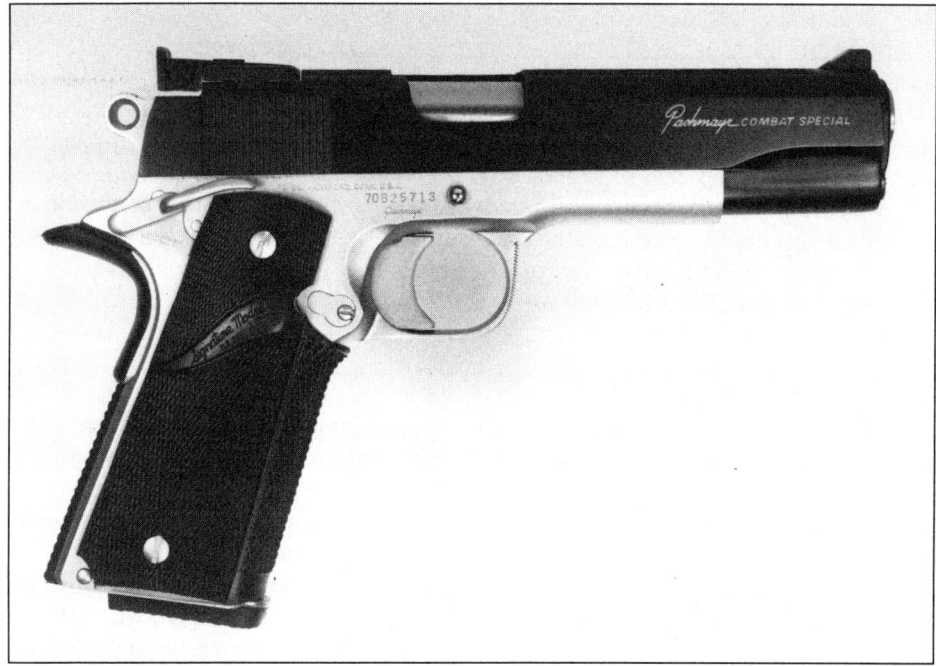

Perhaps the most popular form of Presentation Grips were those designed to rein in the cantankerous old .45 ACP pistol and keep it glued to the hand during recoil.

spring that was attached to the base hooked over a rolled pin in the loop and held the scope firmly in place over the rifle bore. Rotating the knurled wheel clockwise removed the scope from the gun in about ten seconds. Later, Frank introduced the improved "Sure Grip" latch, which replaced the pin in the loops with a spring-loaded plunger. The leaf spring on the adjusting collar on the base was replaced by a square block whose rear corner hooked over the plunger. This afforded a more positive lockup that staunchly resisted recoil of the heaviest magnum rifles, including the .458 Winchester and even massive double rifles popular for hunting dangerous African game.

• PACHMAYR PRODUCTS & PATENTS •

The solid loop style of ring used exclusively at first on the Lo-Swing was practical with scopes such as the Weaver K2.5, J2.5, J4, Lyman Alaskan, Pecar, or the early Bausch & Lomb scopes without internal adjustments. The eyepiece was removed to allow slipping the scope into the loop from the front. This procedure is contraindicated on modern scopes, but removing the eyepieces on scopes of that era caused no harm. The process of impregnating scopes internally with nitrogen gas to prevent fogging had yet to be developed. A scope opened and resealed in a dry room was no more likely to fog after than before, which wasn't saying much, because those old scopes did have a bad habit of fogging up in damp, cold weather. The original Lo-Swing mount design worked fine so long as the scopes had their internal adjustment turrets located on the tubes close to the objective lenses. When adjustment turrets shifted toward the center, it became necessary to redesign the ring assembly into split rings with two upper halves secured by two screws each to the solid swivel base. The revised design proved to be much easier to install and adaptable to a wide range of scopes.

When gunmakers began drilling and tapping holes in the tops of their rifle receivers to accept bridge mounts, such as the Buehler, ConeTrol, and Redfield, Jr., side mounts fell into disfavor. In early 1957 Pachmayr announced his new Lo-Swing Top Mount, featuring a one-piece base to fit the tops of such predrilled bolt-action rifles as the FN Mauser, the Remington Model 721/722, and Winchester Model 70. Outside tolerances on rifle receivers were pretty much at the mercy of the polishers, who were seldom devoted to precision. Internal adjustments on scopes weren't always possible to correct for discrepancies. Even if a shooter managed to sight in by cranking the adjustment screw to the limit, it was poor practice to have the reticule pulled off to the side away from the scope's optical center. Also, early scopes didn't possess the "constantly centered" reticules that we take for granted today.

Frank knew that he had to devise a means of including adjustments in his Lo-Swing top mount without adding unwanted bulk, and he came up with an ingenious idea. He made the male cone in the rear leg of the loop assembly and the female cone in the front leg eccentric instead of concentric with the centerline of the scope. The two cones were offset by precisely .0125 of an inch for a total effect of .025 of an inch. Rotating these two cones via external slotted heads provided both windage and elevation corrections up to four feet at a hundred yards. Allen screws locked the adjustments.

Theoretically, a scope that looked through the rifle bore would be the ideal sight. That's mechanically impossible, so the next best is a scope mounted as near as possible to the bore line. With this in mind, and also to allow use of factory open sights with the scope swung aside, Frank made the base of his top-mounted Lo-Swing as thin as was practical. Commonly used fillister-head screws require a counter bore almost as deep as the thickness of the Lo-Swing mount base at the front of the receiver, so Frank used special tapered-head screws. A corollary benefit was the self-centering effect of tapered-head screws. Two hemisphere-tipped pins jutted down from the rings resting against the base to precisely position the scope over the bore. Initially, these pins were short to keep the scope as near to the bore line as possible, which limited the objective lens diameter of scopes to no more than 1¾ inches. As larger objective lenses became more popular, Pachmayr offered longer pins to allow two-inch lens diameters.

Even after the popularity of side mounts had waned, Frank continued to offer side-mount bases for those who preferred them. Some flat-sided lever action, pump, and autoloading rifles were better served with a side mount. The Pachmayr

The idea for a swing-aside scope mount came to Frank when he faced a Kodiak bear so close that he couldn't get a bead with his scope-sighted rifle. This was the final model, fully adjustable for elevation and windage.

Lo-Swing was one of the few practical mounts offered to fit the highly popular Ruger Mini-14 autoloading carbine. Securely fastened to the flat left wall of the receiver, the Lo-swing offered instant access for loading, clearing jams, or use of the iron sights. Pachmayr offered custom installations in his own shop for hard-kicking guns such as the .416 Rigby double rifle, plus drillings and stack bores.

The Pachmayr Lo-Swing Top Mount was so easy to install that do-it-yourself gunsmiths could attach it on their predrilled and tapped rifle receivers, but the Lo-Swing was extremely complex to manufacture and assemble. It involved machining over two dozen parts, many with tolerance levels of .0001 of an inch. There were fifteen separate milling, drilling, and tapping operations on the base alone and over twenty-one machining operations on the loops. Pachmayr's performed most of the work in their own state-of-the-art production machine shop. The bases and loops started out as twenty-foot-long heat-treated, preshaped aluminum alloy extrusions.

• PACHMAYR PRODUCTS & PATENTS •

After machining, the parts were tumbled in a mixture of volcanic rock, soap, and cutting compound to impart the final finish before black hard anodizing.

The Lo-Swing mount incorporated a number of unique features, all worthy of protection. In mid-1946, the law offices of Harris, Kiech, Foster, and Harris, filed a patent application on behalf of Frank Pachmayr. At last, on 16 October 1951 Patent Number 2,571,935 was issued and covered the major design elements.

During World War II, Frank developed a Lo-Swing side-mount to be used on special Garand sniper rifles. None of the mounts tested by the government to that date allowed swift top loading of the Garand's eight-shot clips. The highly unsatisfactory compromise adopted by the army was to side mount scopes offset well to the left of the receiver to clear the loading clips. The Lo-Swing concept was ideal for the Garand, since it quickly turned aside, instantly flicked back into battery, and left the zero adjustment intact.

After testing a dozen Garand rifles in a vain attempt to find one with enough inherent accuracy to test the mount, Frank personally rebarreled and tuned three Garands to achieve near minute-of-angle groups. A heavy-duty, all-steel Lo-Swing was designed with precision adjustments to allow use of a scope without relatively fragile internal adjustments. Elevation was incorporated into a sturdy capstan screw at the front, while windage was adjusted by a traverse screw at the rear. The guns delivered 1¼-inch groups at a hundred yards.

The Garand mount was ready for testing by the proper military authorities but timing was inopportune. Frank dispatched Roger Stokes to Washington, D.C., to contact a number of army procurement people, including Major General Julian S. Hatcher, at the time Chief of Field Service of the Ordnance Department. Hatcher referred the matter to Colonel R. R. Studler, Research and Development Department, Office of Chief of Ordnance. The highly knowledgeable members of the *American Rifleman* staff, then composed mostly of retired military officers, also reviewed the Lo-Swing-Garand test unit. In a letter dated 18 April 1945 W. H. B. Smith of the National Rifle Association detailed discussions with the Marine Corps Development Board and stated, "Everyone here has agreed that yours is the first practical mount we have seen for the Garand."

Major General Julian C. Smith, Commanding General, Department of the Pacific, United States Marine Corps, personally ordered a test of the Pachmayr mount. In a letter addressed to Frank Pachmayr, dated 28 June 1945, he says in part, "On my return from an inspection trip to the Pacific, I found that the tests of the Pachmayr mount had been completed, as directed. Enclosed are copies of the report, and my endorsement thereon to Headquarters, Marine Corps." The report stated in part:

> The Pachmayr mount is simple, rugged, and can easily be installed by Marine Corps armorers, and can be quickly dismounted and remounted without throwing the scope sight out of line. When the scope is dismounted, the parts permanently attached do not alter the rifle in such manner as to interfere with its normal use. While as a general rule it is not considered advisable for the Marine Corps to adopt arms different from those manufactured in government arsenals, it is believed that the adoption of a different sight mount, if superior to the army type,

would be justified because the small number needed would offer no real procurement difficulties. (The army had granted a contract to Griffin & Howe for 36,000 side mounts for the Garand. The side bracket was to be attached to the Garand receivers before heat treating, with three 10-32 screws and two tapered pins. In use, the scope had to be removed each time it became necessary to reload. Bear in mind that the Garand had to be loaded from the top with eight-round expendable magazines. Even in sniper use, the delay in reloading could be dangerous. Also, the G&H mount didn't always return to zero. The scope was located so high that it became necessary to attach a 1½-inch thick lace on leather pad to the stock. The Lo-Swing was close enough to the iron sights so that it didn't require raising the comb of the stock.)

If the Marine Corps contemplates equipping M1 Rifles with telescopic sights, the Pachmayr mount is well worth both consideration and testing for this purpose. Rotating the scope to open position and reloading apparently does not throw the scope out of line. A small stud on the rear portion of the scope mount bracket has been appropriately set to keep the released empty magazine from hitting the scope after the last round in each magazine has been fired. This stud functions well, and the magazine is deflected out and to the right of the rifle. It is the opinion of shooters who fired this weapon that the sight is durable and practical, and could easily be adapted as equipment for use of sniper firing.

The actual firing tests were conducted under less than ideal conditions. The depot quartermaster noted. Personnel available were not considered the best qualified in order to obtain the desired results. The targets were not computed to size conducive to accurate sight alignment.

In spite of these handicaps and the use of standard G. I. ball ammo, hardly noted for a high degree of accuracy, the test results were encouraging. Three eight-round groups were fired at 100 yards. Mean horizontal dispersion was 1.291 inches and mean vertical dispersion was 1.598 inches, for the total of twenty-four rounds. Nine groups were fired at 200 yards. Mean horizontal dispersion was 3.185 inches and mean vertical dispersion was 2.718 inches for the seventy-two rounds. Four groups at 300 yards (maximum range available) netted mean horizontal dispersion of 3.893 inches and mean vertical dispersion of 1.5 inches. Later, as a member of the United States Wimbledon Cup team, Major General Smith fired three-inch groups at three hundred yards, using one of Pachmayr's Lo-Swing, scope-mounted Garands.

The end of the Pacific War marked the end of Frank's initial efforts to have his Lo-Swing mount adopted by the United States Armed Forces. A letter addressed to Frank Pachmayr, dated 21 August 1945, from Lieutenant Colonel Frank G. Burns, Chief, Technical Division, Research and Development Branch, said in part, "It is regretted that we were not able to test this rifle thoroughly and make a complete evaluation of it. But due to the cessation of hostilities, our testing program on all devices and weapons was immediately stopped."

Pachmayr continued refining the mount over the next few years, then tried again. Test results were again favorable. A confidential report dated 29 June 1951 from the Landing Force Equipment Board, Fleet Marine Force Pacific, Camp Joseph H. Pendleton, Oceanside, California, detailed a range test using one of Pachmayr's test Garand M1 rifles, with a prototype Lo-Swing holding a Bausch & Lomb 2.5X-10X variable scope. Paragraph two described the test:

> The Board arranged for a test-firing demonstration of the mount to ascertain, if possible, its stability under varying conditions of firing. Sixty test shots were fired, using stock ball ammunition. Sixteen shots were fired slow fire from the five-hundred-yard line. The first nine were sighting shots to get the rifle and telescope adjusted. After adjustment, the sight appeared to hold its adjustment satisfactorily, three 4s and four 5s being fired. At the 200-yard line, after preliminary adjustment (for the range) six 5s were consecutively fired, with good grouping. A string of rapid fire at the two-hundred-yard line with a different shooter resulted in a tight group slightly out of the black. In the second rapid fire string, the sights apparently moved slightly to the right.

The last sentence draws a conclusion that is hardly supported by the facts. Changing shooters is enough to change the point of impact. Two men often shoot to different points of impact with the same sight settings. The Board stated:

> EVALUATION: The sight mount is well machined and well built. Being mounted directly over the normal sights, its use is natural and easy. There is no apparent difficulty in swinging it to the left for unloading or reloading, and the catch that holds it on top of the rifle is of sufficient strength to hold it in place during firing, although it is a friction-type catch. In order to thoroughly evaluate the capabilities of this scope mount, it would be necessary to place the weapon in a rigid mount and conduct extensive firing tests. (The Board closed by recommending): a. That it be determined whether or not the need for a mount such as described in the project exists. b. If a need for such a mount exists, that the developer be contacted, and further, more conclusive, tests be made.

The "need" most certainly did exist. In 1942 the government adopted the United States Rifle M1903(A4) in .30 caliber, the common Springfield rifle, with Weaver 330C scope sight in a Redfield Jr. bridge mount in an attempt to meet that need. Weaver delivered a total of thirty-six scopes to the government during World War II. Numerous attempts were made to adapt a scope mount to the Garand M1 Rifle, but none of them met the original criteria set up by the army.

Further testing of the Lo-Swing was completed by S.O. Board #3, Office of the Chief of the Army Field Forces at Fort Bennington, Georgia, in 1953, with favorable results. A letter dated 3 May 1954 from the Ordnance Corps, Springfield Armory, Springfield, Massachusetts, signed by Lieutenant Colonel Roy E. Rayle, Assistant to the Commanding Officer, requested information regarding availability and costs.

Ruggedness is always a top priority with the military. The Pachmayr Garand Lo-Swing Mount was all-steel, secured to the Garand receiver with four stout screws. With integral windage and elevation adjustments, it weighed 1.03 pounds. A nonadjustable prototype scaled a more modest ¾ of a pound. Pachmayr was tooled to produce 5,000 units per month. To that date, Pachmayr had invested $30,000 in developing the Garand mount. Despite all of the interest expressed by United States Army Ordnance officers on the obvious utility of the Lo-Swing scope mount for the top-loading Garand M1 Rifle, a previous commitment to an inferior design apparently scuttled any hope that it would ever be adopted. Then, it's probable that the M14 Rifle was already in the planning stages, with its bottom-loading, high-capacity magazine in 7.62mm instead of .30-06, watering down the need for a swing-away mount.

Meanwhile, back at Pachmayr Gun Works, the commercial version of the Lo-Swing was rapidly gaining in popularity. Pachmayr developed a more positive cam-locking mechanism for holding the scope in battery, thus overcoming the last minuscule cause of criticism.

In 1961, Tom Siatos, then editor and now publisher of *Guns & Ammo* magazine, assigned me to test the Lo-Swing. Pachmayr installed a top mount upon my left-handed Savage Model 110 .30-06. The Lo-Swing was one of the few top mounts then offered for southpaw bolt action rifles. A couple of hundred rounds later, I had demonstrated that the Lo-Swing absolutely held its zero throughout any normal use. For one bench rest test, I swung the scope aside and then returned it to battery between each shot. Four shots clustered into $1^{1}/_{16}$ inches. One flyer stretched the overall group to $1^{11}/_{16}$ inches. I fired another five shots, completely removing the scope and reinstalling it after each shot. Extreme spread was a respectable $^{15}/_{16}$ inch, proving without a shadow of a doubt that the Lo-Swing returned to original zero after being removed and replaced. The fact that the slender sporter barrel had time to cool between shots while the scope was removed and reinstalled offers a logical explanation of the second group being tighter than the first.

I knew that the shots couldn't go too far afield because the Lo-Swing hinge pivoted upon dual hardened steel male and female cones with 60-degree included angles. The Lo-Swing loop assembly was held firmly in battery under constant spring tension. In spite of this, I had heard fears expressed that it might be jarred slightly aside during the excitement of the hunt and go unnoticed by a would-be Nimrod, who might allow his target buck to bound away unscathed. To test this fanciful scenario, I fired a five-shot "control" group. Then I blocked the scope up a half inch and fired four more, followed by another three with the scope blocked up a full inch. In the Lo-Swing mount, the hinge axis is parallel to the bore. Therefore the scope should remain parallel to the bore even when swung aside, and theoretically, the point of impact should bear a direct relation to the distance between the position of the scope in battery and the position outside of battery from which it is fired. The center of the extreme group measured two inches out from the control group. The first out-of-battery group was one inch out. The results of this test demonstrated that all of the shots would have hit the heart of a mule buck, even with the scope slightly out of battery.

My article, "Low-Down on the Lo-Swing," appeared in the February 1961 edition of *Guns & Ammo*. Frank was so pleased with my explanation and favorable assessment of his mount that he had reprints made. He sent copies to all of his field reps, with the dictum, "Read this three or four times, so that you understand it completely." Literally thousands of reprints of the Lo-Swing article were distributed by Pachmayr over the years. My own Lo-Swing mount is still in use and still holding its zero.

· Chapter VIII ·

PACHMAYR CONQUERS THE CONTINENT

"We Americans have long believed that we made the best of everything," observes Frank Pachmayr. "You have only to look at the Italian Ferrari and the German Mercedes to realize that our automotive industry is eons behind Europe in technical excellence. The European arms industry predates ours by centuries. Their craftsmen are trained almost from the cradle. They devote their lives to their work rather than to the pursuit of the biggest refrigerator or the most flashy woman. Few European craftsmen can ever afford to own the things that they make. Despite that, they appear to be content."

Frank Pachmayr had many connections with Europe, all of which could be made stronger through personal contact. His corporations, Pachmayr Gun Works and Mershon, enjoyed vigorous sales of recoil pads, pistol grips, and other gun accessories in Europe. Furthermore, Frank imported fine shotguns and rifles from Europe to serve his more affluent customers. Frank took advantage of every possible contact to locate and import high quality Circassian and French walnut stock blanks from the Continent. Also, he had close relatives in Germany.

These connections finally came together in 1964 when Frank took one of his rare departures from North America. On 12 May Frank and his entourage boarded a jet at Los Angeles International Airport for a flight to New York, where they caught a connecting flight to Madrid, Spain. Frank seldom went anywhere without Nanitta, and this trip was no exception. Along with Nan, Frank took his mother, Anna. Both women were looking forward to shopping in Spain, Italy, France, and Germany, and both were anxious to visit relatives in Germany. Anna was seventy-six at the time, but she was still in excellent health and quite able to stand up to the rigors of travel. As with all of Frank's vacations, this one was to be a mixture of business and pleasure. To Frank, business is pleasure. Nanitta once lamented to me, "We never go anywhere just for fun."

• FRANK PACHMAYR •

Included in the Pachmayr party were Art Durando, Tom McMillan, Jr., and Bill Venters. Art spoke fluent Spanish and Italian. A celebrity in his own right as a championship-level trap, skeet, and live pigeon shooter, Art was almost as expert on the subject of shotguns as Frank. Frank knew that his friend and employee would be an asset on the trip. Tom and Bill were just along for the ride to Spain.

The Pachmayr party arrived in Madrid on the thirteenth. They caught a flight to Barcelona and checked into the Mundial Hotel. The next five days were spent shopping and sightseeing, while Frank and Art set out to investigate the local gun shops and sporting goods stores. They visited S. A. Sporting Goods and spoke at length with the owner, Sr. Sebastian Coderich Sorola. Sorola told Frank that someone was selling copycat white-line recoil pads in Europe in great volume. Sorola had seen the man, a thin, dark-haired individual, standing about five feet, eleven inches tall, but he couldn't recall a name. The irony of the story was that the pads were being made somewhere in California, then shipped into a free port of entry in Algeria. From there, the pads were shipped to Spain, where the firm of AYA (*Aquirre y Aranzabal*) was distributing them throughout Europe. Located in Eibar, Spain's arms-making center, AYA is one of the largest gunmakers in Spain and purportedly the largest producer of made-to-order, double-barreled shotguns in the world. AYA box- and sidelock shotguns are marked by quality workmanship, feature fine engraving, and are styled along traditional English lines. It seemed doubtful this distinguished firm knew the pads constituted an infringement of patent or trademark rights. In any case, Frank was quite naturally vexed by the news. He sold many pads in Europe and understandably resented knockoffs usurping his market. Frank went to see J. Ponti, an attorney specializing in patents and trademarks, located at 33 Calle de Consejo in Barcelona, and arrangements were made to investigate the possibility of patent and trademark infringements. Ponti and Frank discussed appropriate moves to protect his legal rights.

Frank did a bit of shopping on his own. In Toledo, he purchased an extravagant gold cigarette case for himself. He also ordered a quantity of carved leather gun cases and some sweaters for the sporting goods store to be shipped directly to Los Angeles. On Monday 18 May the Pachmayr party flew back to Madrid and checked into the Hilton Hotel. Frank and Art Durando competed in the live pigeon-shooting championship of Madrid, one of the largest annual shotgun competitions in Europe. Some 300 shooters attended from all over Europe and Mexico. Of this number, only six managed a perfect score of fifteen birds out of fifteen. Art killed all his birds, but one fell outside the perimeter of the circle that marks the limit of flight to score. A score of fourteen out of fifteen was no reason to feel bad in this trying competition. Frank also killed all his birds, but he shoots with the same studied Teutonic precision that reinforces his canny sense of business timing. In business, deliberate haste works to his advantage. At the Madrid live pigeon shoot in 1964, it worked against him, and several of his birds dropped outside the circle. The match was won by an Italian named Sandro Asperri.

In Madrid, Art Durando was invited to a wedding party "It was held at the Ritz Hotel," recalls Art, "the most expensive place in Europe. There were about 400 people there. A friend introduced me to a beautiful woman, Maria del Carmen Gonzales, 'Marichu' for short." Art felt an immediate attraction to this educated, classy lady. "Marichu was fluent in five languages. She was a public-relations expert employed by Air France. Whenever a problem cropped up anywhere in the world, she was sent to smooth it out," he explains, with a sense of awe still apparent in his voice.

Frank brought this postcard back from Ferlach, Austria, showing a local gunsmithing school, along with examples of their students' work.

While staying in Madrid, Art saw Marichu every chance he got. During travel time through Italy and France, Art felt he was involved in a long drought. By the time the Pachmayr party reached Paris, Art couldn't stand it any longer. He returned to Madrid to be with Marichu again. As it finally evolved, after Art returned to the States, Marichu came over from Italy and they were married. They had two lovely girls, Christine and Patricia, both now young women. Art saw to it that the girls attended the finest schools in Europe, including finishing school in Switzerland. They speak and write in five languages, just like their talented mother.

On 22 May the Pachmayrs and Art Durando flew to Lisbon, Portugal. This was to be the site of the live pigeon world championships. The first day of the world title shoot was 24 May and scheduled to run through 31 May. On the first day of the three-day event, Frank missed three birds and was eliminated. Durando went straight for the first two days, along with Francis Esenlaner, a math professor at Stanford University, and Pedro Real of Spain. On the decisive third day, it was Art's bad luck to come up during a severe downpour of rain.

"When it came my turn to shoot," recalls Art, "like a fool, I left my shooting glasses on. The rain drops magnified the birds, causing me to miss my seventeenth and nineteenth targets. Esenlaner missed his twenty-third bird. Real went twenty-five for twenty-five straight to win the championship.

The Pachmayr party flew back to Madrid, then on to Rome. In Rome, Frank had a new Volkswagen bus delivered to him, to drive for the remainder of their stay in Europe. "We traveled in style," reminisces Frank, "and we took our sweet time doing it."

This time, Nanitta and Anna had their fill of sightseeing. They drove twenty-three kilometers southwest of Naples to Pompeii to examine the excavated ruins of a once proud Roman city that had been destroyed in the eruption of Mount Vesuvius in 79 A.D. Volcanic ash engulfed the entire city so quickly, the inhabitants didn't have time to flee. The ruins and the people trapped in them were frozen in time and perfectly preserved until they were unearthed centuries later to become a unique record of ancient Greco-Roman life. Next stop was the romantic city of Sorrento at a cliff side hotel with a stunning view of the deep blue Tyrrhenian Sea. Then came a leisurely drive up a twisting picturesque coastal highway back to Rome.

On 7 June, they drove north again on a sightseeing trip to Pisa. Frank and Art climbed the steep spiral staircase up to the top of the famous Leaning Tower of Pisa and peered over the side of the circular balcony, like tourists had been doing for centuries. That night the Pachmayrs were in Florence, capital of Firenze Province and the Tuscany region, in central Italy. Nanitta and Anna gloried in the exquisite gold and silver hand-wrought jewelry that could be seen in booths built across one side of the Ponte Vecchio, the "Old Bridge." A couple of days were spent looking at the vast store of art treasures on display in this historic city, including the gigantic statue of David by Michelangelo.

Then it was up and over the spine of Italy, the towering Apennines Mountains, on a tortuous macadam road and down to a verdant plain to Bologna, a city of almost half a million inhabitants, considered large in Italy. Frank had timed their arrival to coincide with the European Championship of International Trap Shooting.

"There were a lot of Russians shooting," remarked Durando. "I matched my good friend Ennio Matterelli down to the last day of shooting. There were fifty targets. Ennio was three birds behind the leader, a Frenchman, whose name escapes me right now."

The night before that last day of competition, Dr. Manfredi, the owner-operator of the internationally famed M. B. Cartridge Company threw a party for about a thousand people, including all the shooters.

• PACHMAYR CONQUERS THE CONTINENT •

"M. B. Cartridge makes the finest target shotgun shells in the world," according to Art Durando. "There was lots of good food at the party," he recalls, "and lots of wine. Best of all, there were lots of pretty women. Ennio and I both stayed late and drank and danced a lot. The next morning he told me, 'I might as well go out and have some fun. I've already lost the match.' That frame of mind took all the pressure off Ennio when he came up to shoot. He was totally relaxed. I fell behind and so did the Frenchman. The Frenchman dropped four birds. Ennio hit all fifty of his birds straight to win the shoot over me by just one bird."

In Bologna, the Pachmayrs were guests of Dr. Manfredi. After the shoot was over, Dr. Manfredi took Frank and Art on a day's tour of the M. B. Cartridge factory. Frank shipped home many cases of fine ammo for his discriminating customers. Dr. Manfredi was inordinately proud of his new Ferrari sedan. He took Frank and Art for a whirlwind tour of the town that continued late into the night.

"Over there," comments Frank, "they drive like it's just one long Le Mans. The motorists are strictly adversarial in their approach to driving in a crowd. From the back seat of Dr. Manfredi's Ferrari, I could see the speedometer on the dash clocking 127 kilometers per hour. There's no doubt that the car cornered like a racer, but we weren't wearing hard hats and we weren't even strapped in. Art and I were too busy hanging on to even enjoy the scenery."

On Thursday 11 June, Frank and Art drove northwest to Brescia, leaving Nanitta and Anna in Bologna to continue shopping and sightseeing. The first stop was the establishment of Luigi Franchi, S. P. A., Via Calatafimi 17, manufacturer of shotguns, pistols, and revolvers. After a tour of the factory, conducted by the gracious owner, Frank and Art were Luigi's guests for lunch. Before they parted, Frank had a purchase order in his pocket for 250 recoil pads.

"That was only the beginning," says Frank. "Franchi became one of our best customers in Italy." It could be said that Frank was a good customer for Franchi, as well. He ordered a 12-gauge Imperial Franchi, one of their premier shotguns, for his own use.

After lunch, Frank and Art were strolling down the main street just taking in the sights when they came upon the Tortoloni Sporting Goods Store. As they stood looking at the window display of guns and outdoor clothing, they were amazed to see about a dozen ducks placidly swimming in a plastic pond set up in the window.

Art burst out, "How do you suppose they keep those ducks from flying?"

Never one to indulge in idle speculation, Frank replied, "Let's go in and find out."

Frank learned that Tortoloni's sold an impressive 30,000 guns annually and a wide range of other sporting goods in the huge retail outlet and by mail-order catalog throughout Europe. Before Frank left, he had a large order in his pocket, along with an agreement to display Pachmayr recoil pads in the next Tortoloni catalog. For his part, Frank placed an order for fifteen dozen duck decoys like the ones he had seen swimming in the window. They were so lifelike that they even fooled two seasoned duck hunters. The action was caused by placing a fan to blow the decoys around in the water. Frank's test sample included a mixture of mallard, canvasback, redhead, and pintail hen and drake decoys for the store.

"I knew that they would sell like hot cakes in the States," says Frank. "American duck hunters had never seen anything like these decoys. They were hand-painted with low-gloss paints with colors exactly right. Individual jet-black, edged feathers stood out clearly against white or buff backgrounds. The duck bodies were molded of lightweight but rugged plastic that looked like it could last forever. They sure beat the old wooden decoys."

Frank was right in his prognostication. The decoys became popular throughout the States and dominated the market for years, and for a number of years, Pachmayr was the only importer of these fine decoys.

The following day, Frank and Art drove outside the city limits of Brescia to the Commune of Gardone Val Trompia, which was located in a small valley nestled at the foot of the Alps. Here in this tight little valley most of the firearm production of Italy takes place. There are some immense factories, and there are many more small family-owned and operated gun companies that depend in large part on farming out work to individual Valtrumplini, the 12,000 inhabitants of the area. Locks are made by one specialist and barrels by another. The parts are then assembled at yet another place, a technique not unlike that used two centuries ago.

Most of the guns imported into the United States from Italy share the small stamped letters, V.T., standing for Val Trompia. The firearm industry in Val Trompia dates back to the 1500s, when flourishing iron mines at the head of the valley supplied the metal needed to fabricate early muzzleloading guns. According to family tradition, the first gunmaking plant, the Zanotti Company, dates back to the abduction of Cassiana Zanotti by Lansquenet invaders in 1500 A.D. He was deported to Prussia where he learned the art of fabricating arquebuses. He escaped and returned to his home and established a factory making guns. Skills were handed down to the present generation with Fabio Zanotti manufacturing replicas of the guns made by his family in the 1700s.

In Val Trompia, Frank and Art headed for the largest gunmaker in Italy, the Beretta gun works, founded by Pietro Beretta in 1680. Today, Beretta accounts for more than one-third of arms production in Italy. More than half of that is exported, much of it coming to the United States. The excellence of Beretta gun design and manufacture was even recognized by the United States Armed Services when they chose the Beretta 92F 9mm autoloading pistol as their official sidearm to replace the obsolete Model 1911(A2). The Beretta factory is impressive, even by American standards. It consists of a broad complex of buildings, one of which has floor space the size of a football field under one roof. Frank met Carlo Beretta, and after a tour of the plant, received an order for 750 recoil pads.

"And that was just a starter," Frank adds. Next, the two American gun experts contacted Antonio Zoli Gun Company. There Frank purchased several high-grade engraved 12-gauge, 20-gauge, .410 side-by-side, double-barreled shotguns, and one 12-gauge over-under.

• PACHMAYR CONQUERS THE CONTINENT •

Before returning to Brescia, Frank visited the Bernardelli arms complex and several smaller firms. Among the latter was Famars, owned by partners Mario Abbiatico and Remo Salvinelli. In 1980, Mario Abbiatico authored the book, *Modern Firearms Engravings*, the definitive work on fine gun engraving in Italy. "They were making fine Anson & Deeley boxlock and Holland & Holland pattern sidelock double-barreled shotguns of very high quality," relates Frank. "Instead of just soldering the barrels and ribs, they went to the trouble of brazing them so there

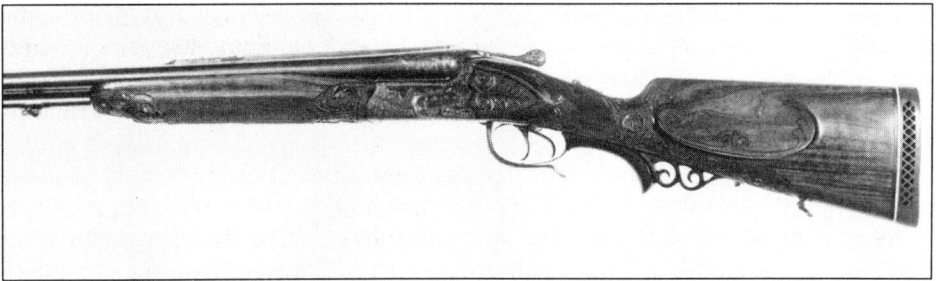

This drilling, made by Gus Pachmayr, was typical of the guns that Frank saw in Germany. Notice the elaborate engraving on the receiver and heavy carving on the stock and forearm. The small cheekpiece is also typical of traditional old Teutonic shoulder arms.

was no danger of their ever separating, even if they were immersed in a salt-bluing bath. They also did some outstanding color case hardening there."

Many of the gun firms in the Gardone Val Trompia area rely heavily on farming out various operations to accomplished artisans. They work in their own homes or small shops, each making a vital component part, such as locks or barrels. Ferlib is one such firm, specializing in hand-fitted and finished side-by-side double-barreled shotguns. Ferlib is located in the heart of the Gardone Val Trompia in a centuries-old building, which is being preserved because of its historical significance. Production is limited annually to a small quantity of guns. The firm of Perugini-Visini & Company is located in the community of Nuvolera near Brescia. Fratelli Piotti is regarded as one of Italy's top-ranking gunmakers who specializes in custom shotguns, each tailored to an individual order.

"These little companies each only make a small number of guns each year," says Frank, "but each piece is an artistic achievement. Barrels are hand fitted to the receivers with a precision that no machine can ever duplicate. Many of the guns are engraved by artisans whose names will never be known or remembered, but their work is equal to just about any I've ever seen."

Saturday night, Frank, Nanitta, and Art attended a party given by Dr. Manfredi in Bologna. There they met Sr. Daniele Perazzi and Sr. Cullio Fabri, partners in the making of some of the finest shotguns in the world. This was a fateful meeting for both the Italians and the Pachmayr organization. Frank began importing Perazzi-Fabri shotguns and talking them up to his customers. Later, the partners split up in a disagreement over manufacturing methods. Fabri continued to make guns by slow labor-intensive methods, investing from four to six hundred man-hours in each gun. The results were shotguns that Frank still regards as the finest in the world. "Equal to the best ever made by Purdey, even during their heyday between 1912 and 1958," says Frank.

Perazzi moved into more mass-produced guns, while still retaining a high degree of hand craftsmanship and quality. Pachmayr was the first to import Perazzi shotguns into the United States. Frank's vast influence on the top shooters of the day, along with Art Durando and Bill Harrison displaying the guns at major competitions, resulted in a Perazzi boom. In time, Perazzi superposed double-barreled and single-barreled shotguns came to dominate the major skeet and trap fields, including Olympic competition. Stack-barreled Perazzis are also favored by top-level live pigeon shooters.

On Sunday 14 June the Pachmayr party motored in their Volkswagen van up the tight twists of a narrow Alpine highway through massive craggy mountains, staring in wonder at the lightly-salted, but still brilliantly-green conifers that contrasted with the broad sheets of white snow covering the clearings. They topped the shivery summits and dropped down into Austria, coming to rest near the Yugoslavian border in Ferlach, another strategic European arms center.

"It's a beautiful place," says Frank. "It rains a lot there and the mountains are all a deep green." Again, Frank and Art made the rounds of gunmakers. As in Italy and Spain, Frank found that his reputation had preceded him. He was accorded a royal welcome wherever he went.

A major arms maker in Ferlach, Franz Sodia, was first on Frank's list. Not surprisingly, Frank came away with an order for 250 Mershon New Style Lightweight Field recoil pads. Frank touched base with many other gun companies, including Joseph Winkler, Joseph Just, Johann Michelitsch, Waffen Waeng, and Genossenschaft. At the firm of Lebeau-Courally, founded in 1865, Frank marveled over exquisitely precise shotguns and double rifles that had been the delight of European monarchs for over a century. Frank saw a shotgun that had been ordered by King Farouk of Egypt. Before the gun could be completed and delivered, Farouk was summarily deposed and could no longer afford such luxuries. When Frank viewed the superb side-by-side double with side locks, it was still in the white, but the lush engraving and glittering gold inlays were completed.

"They make some of the best shotguns in the world," says Frank. "I looked at that gun, with deep engraving and rich with fine gold inlays and I knew that Bob Petersen would just love to have it." Petersen is the multimillionaire publisher of such magazines as *Guns & Ammo* and *Hot Rod*. Frank bought the gun on sight and ultimately did sell it to Petersen.

For several years, Frank had been purchasing gunstock blanks from a man in Ferlach who had contracts with wood cutters in Yugoslavia and Turkey where the finest Circassian walnut is found. Some of the blanks in recent shipments had been of poor quality.

Frank told the vendor, "The only way that we can continue to do business is if you let me choose my own wood."

"But then you will pick only the best." the wood vendor protested.

"That's what I want," declared Pachmayr, "the best. I don't fool around with cheap stuff. Last time, you shipped me some inferior wood and charged me a big price for it. That's coming to a screeching halt." Eventually, the problem of getting high-quality stock blanks drove Frank into opening his own wood mill where he cut and seasoned his own blanks.

By 7:30 P.M. on Wednesday, the working tourists arrived in picturesque Vienna where they settled into the magnificent Intercontinental Hotel for a three-day stay. No time was lost contacting Franz Sarnitz, a staunch supporter and highly successful vendor of Pachmayr products in his Sport U. Waffen stores in Vienna and Salzburg. Between the two stores, Sarnitz employed a total of twenty full-time gunsmiths. A day was spent in Salzburg just sightseeing, then the party left for Traunstien.

"We were driving alongside a beautiful river at about dusk," recalls Frank. "We could see fish popping out of the water like popcorn. Art looked at me with longing in his eyes. 'I sure wish I had a fishing rod.' he said. I told him, 'Probably my Uncle Emil has a rod. More important, perhaps he has fishing rights on the river."

The Pachmayr party checked into the Park Hotel in Traunstein and Frank phoned Emil Pachmayr. About an hour later, Frank's uncle was knocking on the door. Emil was actually a half brother to Frank's father Gus, who taught Emil the art of gunsmithing. When Gus immigrated to the United States, Emil remained in Germany, content to practice his craft in his homeland. Emil had a small sporting goods store and gun shop in Traunstein and was well respected in the area. True to his family tradition, he was also a fine marksman and held a large number of shooting trophies won in the major matches periodically held in Munich. As it turned out, Emil had fishing rods to loan Frank and Art and fishing rights on a 3½-mile section of the river.

"That was the most wonderful trout fishing I've ever experienced," enthuses Frank. "The trout were still kicking when we took them back to the hotel where the hotel chef cooked and served our fish without charge. All we had to pay for was salad and beverages. The people there were polite and considerate, in marked contrast to many hostelries in the States."

There followed several days of visiting the ancestral homes of numerous relatives, cousins, nephews, and nieces, including Erik Brandhuber, his wife Gustle and two daughters, Hiltrude and Eva. Anna was thrilled to meet her many relatives in the Brandhuber clan and to see her homeland once more before she died. Reserved as he normally was, Frank couldn't suppress his own exuberance at this opportunity to see and feel his own roots.

Frank greatly admired the craftsmanship and dedication of European gunmakers, especially those in Germany, but he did have a problem with one aspect of their work habits. It seems that in Europe work started at 6:00 A.M. and proceeded straight through to 2:00 P.M. with only two fifteen-minute breaks and no time off for lunch. Frank tended to rise a little late and work a lot later. He just couldn't get used to the idea that everything was closed in the early afternoon. Reluctantly, he adapted his visits to the local business hours.

Early in 1950, a German maker of fine rifles and shotguns named Heym visited the United States and showed some of his guns to Frank. The spectacular high-relief, deep engraving on the guns greatly impressed Pachmayr. Heym told him that the guns were the work of a premier engraver in the Old Country, a German named Erich Boessler. Frank immediately sent some guns to this talented artist for engraving and was gratified to see that his work was outstanding. From then on, Frank shipped a steady stream of guns to Boessler for his incomparable deep engraving.

Frank had discussed with Erich the possibility of sponsoring his emigration to the United States. He had already sponsored a number of immigrant artisans and gunsmiths. Now that he was here in Germany, he was determined to see Boessler and discuss the idea with him. When Frank visited Boessler at 8732 Munnerstadt, Am Vogeltal, and saw the idyllic setting in which the premier Graveurmeister lived and worked, among green hills with towering conifers on every side and nothing but strikingly beautiful vistas in all directions, he exclaimed, "Jeeze, you don't want to come to horrible Los Angeles when you are in such great country. How could you ever think of leaving here to go to the United States, worst of all Los Angeles with its smog and overcrowded living conditions?"

Boessler was disheartened because he had set his mind on immigrating to the States, but Pachmayr painted such a gloomy picture of life in Los Angeles, that Boessler decided to stay where he was. The upshot of the matter was that Boessler remained in Germany and Frank continued to keep him busy with engraving jobs shipped from the States.

On 22 June Frank and his party were in Munich. From there they proceeded to Zurich where they visited with Herr Landis, of W. Glaser, Waffen AG, Lowenstrasse 42, general agents for Merkel Brothers. Merkel Brothers of Suhl are world-renowned makers of premier-grade, deep-engraved, superposed shotguns that feature Holland & Holland-type, hand-detachable sidelocks and ejectors and Bohler-Special steel barrels.

They then went to Lenzburg, Switzerland, to visit the massive, highly respected Hammerli Hunting and Sporting Arms Factory, Ltd., founded in 1863 by Johann Hammerli, a master locksmith, to produce rifle barrels for the Swiss Federal Army Administration. Since that time, Hammerli match rifles and pistols have distinguished themselves in numerous international competitions.

On 24 June the Pachmayr party was in Ulm, Germany, to see Carl Walther Sport und Jagdwaffenfabrik, 79 Ulm/Donau, maker of a wide range of rifles and pistols, including the famed P-38 of World War II. Also in Ulm, they contacted H. Krieghoff KG., Jagdwaffenfabrik, makers of some of the world's finest over-under shotguns and drillings—three-barreled guns combining side-by-side shotgun barrels with an underneath rifle barrel—which were highly popular in Europe. The final stop in Ulm was J. G. Anschutz GMBH, Daimlerstra 12, manufacturers of the finest target and sporting small-bore rifles in the world. For over three decades, Anschutz target rifles have dominated all of the international matches, including Olympic competition.

Continuing their combination vacation and business trip, Frank, Nanitta, and Anna Pachmayr, accompanied by Art Durando, motored to Wursburg, to Bad Kissinger, to Weisbaden (the favorite vacation and watering spa of Germany), and to Cologne. In Cologne, they visited the magnificent Dynamit Nobel-Genschow GMB, maker of such famed shot shells and metallic ammunition as Rottweil, Sinoxid, RWS, and the highly respected makers of fine firearms, J. P. Sauer & Sohn.

The heart of firearm manufacture in Belgium is Liege, home of the mighty Fabrique Nationale d'Arms de Guerre, the firm that launched John Browning's early career and continued to make Browning guns until recent years, as well as Henri Dumoulin & Files, s.a., maker of custom, largely handmade hunting rifles. Frank and Art made the rounds of all of the manufacturers and sporting goods sales outlets in Liege, including Auguste Francotte & Cie, Fabricants d'Armes at 61 Mont Saint Martin. This tradition-oriented gunmaker still uses the labor intensive methods of its founder Auguste Francotti. The Pachmayr Volkswagen van drove on to Paris on 3 July, and for three days, they split their time between sightseeing and visiting gun dealers.

Finally, it was time to bid farewell to the faithful Volkswagen and fly to England. Once there, Frank headed straight to the famed gunmakers, James Purdey & Sons Ltd., Audley House, London. This venerable firm was founded when King George III (best known for presiding over the British Empire during the American Revolution) perched precariously on the throne. Purdey maintains no stock of merchandise, inventorying only raw steel and stock blanks. The staid old firm counts its greatest assets as pride of reputation and the unparalleled talents of its craftsmen, apprenticeship-trained in the skills of hand-shaping steel and wood. Every Purdey double-barreled shotgun or rifle is made to order for a particular customer. They are fiercely independent, steadfastly refusing to make anything that goes beyond the bounds of their carved-in-stone traditions. Purdey is perpetually engaged in a brisk seller's market with orders far outstripping its ability to produce. Frank ordered several shotguns and well knew that it would likely be years before he would ever see them.

Located on Berkeley Square, London, is Charles Lancaster & Co., Ltd., established in 1826, armorers by Special Warrant to his late Majesty King Edward VII, by Warrant of Appointment to His Majesty King George V, and to His Royal Highness The Prince of Wales. "Lancaster is famous for its big bore double rifles that are used in Africa for dangerous game by hunters of means," says Pachmayr.

Frank visited other famous gunmakers in the London area as well: Holland & Holland, Boss & Co., Ltd., Cogswell & Harrison Ltd., Atkin Grant & Lang, Salter & Varge Ltd., and Churchill Ltd. Then it was on to Birmingham, England to visit Webly & Scott and Parker Hale Ltd. A short ride to Birmingham brought Frank to the establishment of Westley Richards & Co. Ltd., another firm dating back to the reign of King George III and also a maker of fine shotguns. From Westley Richards, Frank ordered a "Best Sidelock" 28-gauge twenty-eight-inch double barrel, choked medium and full, engraved, and with a raised vented rib.

Finally, on 11 July 1964 four weary travelers boarded a jet at Heathrow Airport for the flight back to New York. Frank lost no time getting back in touch with conditions in the States. During the first morning back on United States soil, he phoned his store manager, Bill Harrison, his attorney, Maynard Henry, Art Murtha of Kodiak Arms, a Mr. Woodcock of Ithaca Gun Co., W. T. Smith of Remington Arms Co., and Warren Page, shooting editor for *Field & Stream* magazine.

Throughout his trip to Europe, Frank took every opportunity to acquire fine walnut for resale back in the States. This activity was directly responsible for his ultimate entry into the business of cutting and selling high-grade walnut for stock blanks. Other lasting results of his European trip were closer ties with his overseas companies and contacts, leading to an expanded market share overseas for his shooting accessories; it also resulted in a marked increase in Pachmayr's importation and sale of fine imported shotguns.

•••

· Chapter IX ·

WONDERFUL WOOD

As far back as he can remember, Frank Pachmayr has carried on a passionate love affair with wood. An appreciation of wood was easy to acquire in the Pachmayr household. Chips and sawdust were flying at all hours of the day from saws, rasps, and draw knives. The gnarled hands of Frank's father, Gus, deftly carved shotgun and rifle stocks from fine walnut, and he kept ranks of walnut blanks stacked in the attic to allow time and heat to dry and cure the wood over the years.

Throughout the Pachmayr house, the scent of freshly cut wood hung in the air. Like the heavy perfume of baking bread, it penetrated every nook and cranny and was as much a part of everyday life as light and dark. Wood scraps, ranging from the size of baby blocks to those large enough to make a shotgun butt stock, were tossed into corners or pushed along with thick piles of crisp brown chips to the back of Gus's sturdy wooden work bench. The scraps provided an inexhaustible supply of subjects for young Frank to carve. With a razor-sharp Barlow folding pocketknife Frank converted shapeless scraps into effigies of animals, people, small wooden guns blackened with shoe polish, and car models, another early love of his.

Throughout his life, Frank has found the aroma of cut wood a heady incense to recall people and places from his youth. Long after he retired from sporting goods manufacturing and sales, Frank maintained an active interest in the business of cutting California walnut rifle and shotgun blanks. Rare exhibition-grade blanks were always subject to Frank's personal inspection and approval. Makers of fine guns journeyed from such as far as Italy and Japan to come to the sleepy farming community of Oroville, California, to purchase fine gunstock blanks from Frank.

Observant as a child, Frank absorbed the intricacies of stock finishing and checkering before most children his age were weaned. As early as five years of age, he was helping to finish gunstocks. Later, Gus trusted him to perform the entire procedure, and Frank learned his lessons well. He learned how to shape a stock that displayed a quiet elegance and also had a practical functionality.

Frank's concepts of stock design are a coalescence of his father's basic ideas of style and utility, combined with his own sense of symmetry. The result is the ageless, classic school of stock design, but with a unique flavor that is distinctly Pachmayr's. Even seen from across the room, a Pachmayr rifle or shotgun exhibits recognizable hallmarks of quality—symmetrical lines, superb grain, and flawless checkering. Another important asset of a Pachmayr custom stock—the tailored fit that makes it a natural pointer--has to be felt to be appreciated.

Down the years, Pachmayr has remained one of the most respected exponents of classical stock design. His rifle and shotgun stocks have always been in good taste with soft flowing lines and gracefully swept back pistol grips that contrast sharply with the exaggerated lines in some modern stocks.

Frank dislikes the Monte Carlo comb because, "It looks like the stock is pregnant." He prefers a straight comb with a gently rounded, full cheekpiece that is contoured to flow smoothly from the top of the pistol grip in front and to curve to its lowest point about two-thirds of the way back toward the butt. Then it hooks up and forward into a half circle. For scope use, the comb has less drop but remains straight. A line drawn from the toe through the pistol grip merges exactly with the intersection of the stock and trigger guard. The pistol grip is gently curved, not too low, with a steel or ebony cap at a right angle to the end of the curve. A cross section of the fore-end is round or slightly oval with a straight taper from the receiver to the tip. Of course, the edges must be crisp and sharp.

One seldom-used item in Frank Pachmayr's sporting goods store was a "try gun," in which the stock was made with a comb that could be raised or lowered in the front and rear. The pistol grip could be moved forward or back, and the butt could be raised or lowered, as well as moved in or out at the top and bottom. This allowed an accurate measure of all the critical dimensions to adapt a custom stock to a customer's particular physical traits and shooting stance. Frank, however, didn't need a try gun to size up a customer's needs. He could assess the stock requirements by merely observing the man's build and the way he handled a gun.

To a shotgunner, proper stock fit means the difference between a flurry of retreating wings or meat on the table. To the rifleman, it means the difference between getting caught flatfooted or picking off a buck during the fleeting moment it crosses a small clearing. For both, it means instinctive pointing and concentration on the target rather than the gun with positive trigger control and without undue punishment from recoil.

The rule of thumb for determining stock length consisted of holding a gun by the pistol grip with the stock lying along the arm to see if the butt touched the inside of the crook of the arm. The fact is, arm length has little to do with proper length of pull—the distance from the trigger to the center of the butt plate. True governing factors are the length of a shooter's neck and whether he tends to creep forward on the stock when he sights his gun.

"A hunter with a thin face and long neck is prone to crawling up the stock," says Pachmayr, "and needs more length to avoid poking his nose with his thumb or getting a scope in his eyebrow. The chap with broad shoulders, a bull neck, and a full face needs a relatively short stock to get his cheek to the comb. The guy who

· WONDERFUL WOOD ·

After exploring the best sources for European walnut, Frank Pachmayr began to buy California claro walnut. He pioneered new methods of drying this fine-figured wood and made it popular with custom stockmakers. Here Frank (center) is grading walnut according to degree of grain with the help of Bill Harrison and his nephew, Dick Mellen.

holds his rifle offhand almost parallel with his shoulders needs a longer stock than the one who faces his target squarely and points the gun forward."

Drop controls how high your eye will be above the bore when you shoulder your gun and is defined as the distance from the line of sight to the top of the comb. Even in straight stocks, that is with combs almost parallel to the bore, drop is usually quoted both at the point of the comb and at the heel. Pachmayr's try gun offered a positive fix on those figures.

The sliding pistol grip of the try gun measured the proper distance from the trigger to the grip. "This is more important than most shooters realize," says Frank. "If it's too long or too short, the shooter never feels comfortable with the gun.

He's always fighting it and his trigger control is adversely affected. When the reach is right, he has good control of the gun and a positive feel of the trigger."

The matter of "pitch," the angle of the butt plate in relation to the bore, is determined with Pachmayr's try gun by adjusting the position of the heel and toe of the butt plate in or out for positive shoulder contact over the widest possible area. Pitch gets the most attention from shotgunners. "Too much pitch," says Frank, "and you'll be shooting under your birds. Too little and you'll shoot over them." Pitch is measured by standing the rifle or shotgun against a wall with the butt plate touching the floor, heel and toe, and measuring out from the wall to the bore line twenty-two inches up the barrel. The sum of all of these dimensions produces a Pachmayr gun of elegance and heirloom quality. To Frank Pachmayr,

> The job of bedding a rifle really separates the men from the boys. For top accuracy, you need solid contact between the stock and the bottom of the action and the rear surface of the recoil lug. The tang and the rear of the magazine should be relieved to avoid splitting the stock from recoil. The fore-end should have upward pressure of eight to ten pounds. We never free-float barrels. We found that just about anything shoots better with some fore-end pressure.

Frank considered glass bedding to be a shortcut unworthy of his rifles. He insisted that his stockmakers painstakingly scrape and chisel away excess wood until full contact was achieved. The wood had to look like it grew onto the steel with absolutely zero gap between wood and metal.

Frank believes that fine wood is its own best decoration. He regards rococo inlays as garish rather than garnish. Pachmayr stocks confine ornamentation to artistic checkering and perhaps with a scroll or leaf pattern on the border. Checkering patterns can be rather flowery but must always be in good taste. With his background as a commercial artist, Dick Mellen was able to develop an extensive line of original checkering patterns. Often he would design a one-of-a-kind pattern at the request of a customer.

One of the most ornate examples of a Pachmayr pattern was the rifle that Frank made and presented to the late Elmer Keith, one of the foremost gun authorities of his time. The Winchester pre-1964 Model 70 chambered for the .375 Holland and Holland was stocked with a magnificently marbled Circassian walnut blank and featured stark black and tan swirls over its full length. The fore-end tip and grip cap were made of genuine ebony. On this occasion, Frank overlooked his inherent dislike of the Monte Carlo comb and shaped the stock to Keith's design, with a slightly raised comb and full cheekpiece.

The checkering pattern was one that his father Gus had originated many years before. It combined Old World artistry with New World understatement. The fore-end pattern was solid on the sides and across the bottom with simple leaf patterns fore and aft. Checkering on the pistol grip was continuous across the top. The French fleur-de-lis was inset into the checkering at three points on each side, once at the front and twice at the rear. A narrow ridge of plain wood connected the two lowest fleur-de-lis, and the checkering continued on the same lines on both sides of the ridge. The hard, close-grained walnut readily accepted a fine thirty-two lines per inch pattern. Only an extremely talented artist with the checkering files could have executed so difficult a pattern. Frank delegated the job to one of his premier engravers, Pete Thacker.

Checkering can include anything from sixteen lines per inch to thirty-two. "Fine checkering looks great," says Frank, "but when you're hunting, it isn't much help if your hands get wet and slippery. It dents and wears too easily and it fills with mud, but it does look great and it can always be touched up to make the diamonds sharp again. Coarse checkering helps you hold the gun without slipping but it looks like hell."

A checkering pattern with fewer than twenty lines per inch looks crude. More than twenty-six lines becomes too fragile. A twenty-four-line pattern is a good compromise, coarse enough to be practical but adds beauty as well. Hard, close-grained woods are the easiest to checker and give the best results in terms of sharp, crisp diamonds. Soft woods often fuzz up under the checkering file, making a crisp-looking job impossible. The work is further complicated by soft light bands of wood alternating with the harder color rings, which causes the craftsman to exert heavy pressure to cut the color and then only dig into the light bands.

All of this is academic, because, as Pachmayr says, "I would never use a soft blank. Even if it happens to have outstanding grain, it's too hard to finish and checker. It isn't strong, and it can't handle recoil. The recoil lug will set back in the wood and maybe even split the stock."

To be well proportioned, checkering diamonds should be three times as long as they are wide and cut to sharp points, using checkering files with a 90-degree angle. This results in sturdy diamonds with firm bases, twice as wide as they are high. The quality of Pachmayr checkering can be seen in the precision diamonds, all exactly the same size, marching along parallel lines of exactly the same depth. The cleanly cut diamonds don't mask the grain but allow it to show through. There are no borders and no runovers (lines that cut through the narrow outside perimeters). The checkering is treated to resist water, without taking on a shine.

For most of his gunsmithing career, Frank Pachmayr bought his gunstock wood like others in the business from many domestic and overseas sources. He traveled to Europe to explore woodcutters in France and Germany on the Continent. Once he purchased a lot of particularly fine exhibition-quality Circassian walnut blanks from a dealer in Germany. Months later, he discovered that the wood had been smuggled out of Russia. Sad to say, Russia is one of the few areas remaining with substantial stands of Circassian walnut of sufficient size to provide highly figured gunstock blanks, and they aren't selling any. Then perhaps they're smarter than our government. During the Kennedy-Johnson era, export quotas on walnut were lifted to improve unfavorable trade balance figures. America's forests were raped by Italian and Japanese furniture makers, who bought up huge tracts of standing timber, harvested the trees themselves, and shipped the logs overseas to make veneer, but they didn't concern themselves with such niceties as replanting clear-cut areas. The result is an increasingly short supply of walnut for gunstocks. Even common grades are becoming scarce. Most gun manufacturers are using walnut-stained beech or birch for factory stocks.

After exploring European sources, Frank decided that the finest walnut stock blanks for his custom rifles and shotguns were to be found in his home state from vendors such as Andy Garner in Chico, California. Frank made many trips north to inspect logs, either uncut or in the process of being cut. The author accompanied him on one such trip in 1963. It was soon apparent to me that Frank had an eye for fine figure in walnut, raw cut or uncut. Some of his skill came from many years of experience witnessing the cutting of huge old trees, but it also came from an inborn instinct for good wood.

I watched Frank supervise the cutting of a huge walnut crotch that measured eight feet across its widest section. He laid out blanks to be cut from three-inch-thick planks, or "flitches," that were cut from logs as long as twelve feet. Frank bought both dried blanks and raw, wet flitches, which he shipped home to Los Angeles and dried there himself.

An insight into Frank Pachmayr's obliging nature, as well as his pragmatic approach to machines, is offered by an incident that occurred on the trip I took with him. On the drive north, we stopped at a General Motors dealership in San Francisco where Frank had ordered a couple of new station wagons. While he completed the deal, I looked over the trade-ins on the car lot. I found a low-mileage Chevrolet and made a deal to buy it. The dealer said he would service it and have it ready to pick up on our return trip. Two of Frank's men drove the new station wagons back to Los Angeles, while Frank and I and a couple of his men proceeded to Chico.

When it was time to return, I was in a hurry to get home to my wife who had become ill. Frank offered the solution. "You can fly back from Sacramento and I'll pick up your car in San Francisco and drive it back to Los Angeles."

A few days later, Frank phoned to say he was at the store and my car was waiting there to be picked up. When my wife Patty and I drove over to get the car, Frank remarked, "I don't know why I always buy these damn Cadillacs. Your Chevrolet runs just as good, but there's something wrong with the gas gauge. I filled it up in Gorman and it still says full." Frank just wasn't aware that a little Chevy 268 c.i. V-8 didn't gobble gas like his big Cads.

Andy Garner was Frank's chief walnut supplier ever since one fateful day in 1958 when Andy visited his daughter, who was living in the San Fernando Valley, north of the Los Angeles metropolitan area. He threw some seasoned crotch-feather blanks into the rear of his pickup to sell to the late Gale Bartlett, a renowned, custom stockmaker in Lancaster, California. After choosing about a dozen blanks for himself, Gale remarked, "Instead of carrying what you have left back home, why not sell them to Frank Pachmayr. He's always on the lookout for good walnut." Gale's charming, and obliging wife, Skip, phoned Frank and told him about Andy's blanks. "Send him by in the morning," said Frank. "I'm eager to see what he has to offer."

• WONDERFUL WOOD •

About 9:00 A.M. the next day, Andy was in the spacious retail sporting goods showroom of Pachmayr Gun Works asking for Frank. Frank invited Andy into his private office. They chatted about walnut for about an hour. It was apparent to Frank from the outset that here was a man who lived and breathed wood the same way he did. Finally he could contain himself no longer. "Let's go out to your truck and take a look at the blanks you brought with you." Frank nearly flipped when he saw the outstanding grain and fine quality of the wood Andy had. He offered Andy $17.50 apiece, a good price at the time, and Andy said, "Okay."

"Do you have any more like these?" Frank asked, barely able to contain his enthusiasm. "Yeah," said Andy, "About four thousand more." Frank invited Andy back into his office and sat him down with the deference most people might accord a king. Frank

Fine old walnut trees were saved from abandoned orchards where they faced destruction by burning and were moved by trucks to the wood mill.

Heavy equipment was needed to move large logs and tree trunks.

sat on the edge of his desk and initiated a partnership that was to last a lifetime. "If you'll quit working for the city," said Frank, "and cut blanks for me, I'll take every blank you cut." At the time, Andy was working for the City of Chico, California, maintaining hundreds of huge old walnut trees growing on city property. When a tree needed to be felled because it was too old and had become a public hazard, Andy would remove the tree and cut it up for gun blanks. "I was making more from my part-time job of cutting blanks than I was working for the city," he said later.

A flitch being cut at the mill.

Frank offered to write a check for Andy on the spot as a down payment on blanks for future delivery. "I'll give you $35,000 to start," he said, "and we'll go into business." "No," drawled Andy, "You come up and see my operation first. See what I'm doing and how I'm doing it. Then we'll talk. I want you to know just what you're buying before I take any of your money." Frank said, "Okay, I'll see you in a couple weeks."

Frank couldn't wait. "I drove home," said Andy, "and late that same day, I got a phone call. Frank said, 'I'll see you in the morning.' He flew up here the next

• WONDERFUL WOOD •

Using powerful chain saws, large trees were sometimes precut in the field to reduce hauling costs.

day in his own plane, and Bill Harrison, his store manager, came with him. I showed them through the place and showed them the wood. Frank got so excited he didn't know just what to do with himself. He told me he would take everything I could cut, all grades, shotgun or rifle. We agreed on prices. The top price was to be $17.50 per blank for the best and down to $2.00 each for the plain ones. But in those days, I didn't have any plain ones."

• FRANK PACHMAYR •

Frank offered Andy the $35,000 again, but Andy declined again. "Just give me a deposit of $2.00 on each blank as I cut it and you can pay the balance when you pick them up." Andy had about 5,000 blanks on hand at the time, so Frank wrote him a check for $10,000. From then on, Andy sent Frank an accounting of blanks cut every two weeks, and Frank would forward a check for the deposit. When wood was delivered, he deducted the amount of the prior payment. On more than one occasion, Frank offered to make full payment on a wood delivery and take the deposit off a later delivery with no interest charged to help Andy's cash flow, but Andy always demurred, whose sense of honor is like a steel rod that refuses to bend. Frank had found a man with a code of conduct as rigid as his own. The kind of handshake partnership and mutual trust that both men enjoyed could only exist between two men of high principle.

Although other woods, such as beech, cherry, maple, myrtle wood, and even mesquite, have been popular with shooters and the shooting press, Frank Pachmayr has remained steadfastly loyal to one wood, and one wood only, namely walnut. Why walnut? "God gave us walnut to make fine gunstocks," declares Frank. "It has in greatest measure all the qualities we seek to make a gunstock that is light in weight, durable, holds its zero, and looks beautiful."

According to the United State Department of Agriculture, walnut has a specific gravity .55 at 12 percent moisture content, compared to .64 for beech and .62 for birch, demonstrating its comparatively light weight. In its green state, wood is composed of a high percentage of moisture, ranging from 30 to 300 percent. Internal water is a large part of the physical mass of green wood. Over time, the moisture dries out and the wood shrinks. The extent of the shrinkage gives an accurate indication of any undesirable swelling and shrinkage that is likely to occur in the finished stock under varying conditions of humidity, regardless of the waterproof finish used. Walnut demonstrates its superiority in this area, as well, with an average shrinkage of 12.2 percent in volume from the green state down to 6 percent moisture content, compared to 15.6 percent for both beech and birch. Compared to any other wood, fine walnut can hardly be challenged on any level.

California walnut has proved especially adaptable to gunstocks. General John Bidwell, an early émigré and founder of the city of Chico, planted groves of walnut trees for harvesting, as well as along every road, trail, and fence line for shade and windbreaks. These trees, planted in the mid-1880s have been the fountain of gunstock wood in California, which is now unfortunately running dry.

Because it's more colorful and lighter in weight than Eastern or European walnut, California claro became Frank's favorite stock wood. A hybrid of native, northern California black walnut (*Juglans hindsii*) with English walnut (*Juglans regia*), claro trees tend to fork nearer the ground, yielding more prime stock wood than other varieties. The first crotch provides the most color and best figure, but stocks can be cut until the trunk goes under fourteen inches in diameter. Claro, which means "clear" in Spanish, is marked by distinctive reddish-brown coloration and is streaked with dramatic greenish-black lines. Claro rivals the finest Circassian walnut for figure and displays incredible patterns of marble cake, tiger stripe, fiddleback, and the sought-after feathered crotch with its sunburst effect through the butt stock.

Frank Pachmayr gave California claro walnut something it lacked before—prestige. Most of the old-time gunmakers and stockmakers regarded claro with

Under the watchful direction of Pachmayr, Andy Garner lays out stocks on a flitch using a plexiglass form.

disdain. It was just too fancy for their tastes. Also, claro had been badly handled by some of the more flamboyant stockmakers, who went in for garish high combs, deeply flared pistol grips, and excessive inlays. Often the blanks were processed into stocks before they were completely dried, which resulted in stocks that continually changed the rifle's zero. Sometimes they were kiln-dried too rapidly and became brittle. As often as not, the grain was laid out all wrong. Frank demonstrated that claro could be handled in a way that imparted stability and strength, as well as give a look of quality to complement its spectacular beauty.

Early settlers brought English walnuts with them to California. Finding this more meaty nut less hardy than the hard-husked native black walnut, they grafted English cuttings onto black walnut root stock, resulting in fast-growing trees with a high yield. California English mimics Continental French and Circassian walnut in its hard density and golden color.

The rarest California walnut, Bastogne, is a rock-hard, dense, red, green, and gold wood that combines the brilliance of claro with the strong contrasts of English walnut. Bastogne trees are a cross between English and claro. Because they are an accident of nature and only grow in the wild, few of them exist. Andy estimates that only about seventy-five Bastogne trees remain that are large enough to make gunstocks. The owner of one such tree near Redbluff, California, was offered $35,000 for it and wouldn't sell. Estimated to be at least 150 years old, it shades a full acre with its weighty limbs that sit atop a trunk more than thirteen feet across. Andy thinks it would yield about a thousand quality stock blanks.

Increasing scarcity of good walnut caused Frank to open his own sawmill in 1975 in the community of Oroville in northern California. His nephew Dick Mellon was assigned the task of setting up the operation. Dick leased a massive ten-thousand square-foot galvanized corrugated steel agricultural storage warehouse in Oroville, in the center of the walnut orchard area, and located a sawmill in the city of Redwood on the coast.

"The warehouse was only about half finished," relates Dick. "This fellow was building it to ship to Peru where they still have more trees than houses. Before he could finish it, the deal fell through and he ran out of money. The mill was supposed to be portable, so he mounted the whole thing on a forty-five-foot, ten-wheel trailer. The rear end was extended and beefed up underneath with truss work of six-inch steel pipe. It was designed so that the engine could be picked up and placed on the trailer for transport. The drop-off table, where the cut wood came after cutting, was meant to be collapsible.

"It was really collapsible," chuckled Frank Pachmayr, as he picked up the story. "When we picked it up, the carriage wasn't even attached. There was no engine, and all the tires on the trailer were flat. The drive pulleys and shafts were all rusty. What we got was a basket of parts, but it did have potential and was the best thing around at the time."

"It took us three weeks just to do the paperwork required to move it," added Dick ruefully. "We needed a permit for every county that we crossed. We had to notify the California Highway Patrol and the local cops when we were coming. We had to have a car in front and another one behind, warning of a 'Wide Load.'

"When we finally got it to the barn," continued Dick, "We had to figure out how to assemble it without benefit of any drawings or blueprints. We set it up on the north side of the building because prevailing winds are from the south. This avoids having the sawdust blow back into the warehouse. We bought a Caterpillar D-8 bulldozer just to push the sawdust away from the mill."

"We needed plenty of horsepower to run all of this equipment," continued Dick, "so we bought a big standing-diesel engine. We set up hydraulic rams to power the carriage that moved the logs and the dogs or teeth that held the logs in place. Two huge, four-foot diameter, circle saw blades were mounted one above the other, offset just enough so that they couldn't touch when they were spinning. We extended the carriage to a length of sixty feet. We could cut lengthwise on logs up to four feet in diameter and up to twenty-four feet long. The cut log dumped onto a track with cogs attached to endless chains that would push the log over, slide it forward, and feed it into a secondary set of blades. This resawing unit was ten feet wide. The log was clamped with dogs at one end of the carriage, which was riding on 'O'-gauge railroad tracks. It could be moved laterally to align the log with the blades. Then the carriage fed the log through. We could cut just a couple of inches deep, just under the bark and sap wood, to look for color and grain in the log."

"Sometimes you had to turn the log," Frank interjected, "maybe 30 degrees, maybe 180—maybe two or three times to find the best color and figure, or you had to twist it or raise it a little. Fiddleback adds a lot to the value of a stock blank, whether it's for a rifle or shotgun. If you cut a log wrong, you might only see the ends of the fiddleback grain, losing the whole effect. What should be $500 blanks could turn into $2 blanks. You could waste the whole log. You want the fiddleback patterns to run across the width of the blank."

"We'd cut the slab three inches thick," resumed Dick. "It ran down a chute where a chain shunted it aside to make room for the next one. We'd get the slabs out of the sun right away and into the barn, especially if it was hot. The hotter it was, the more likely the slabs were to start checking on the ends. Once started, the cracks would go two or three inches deep. If we couldn't cut slabs into blanks right away, we sealed the ends with a nondrying petroleum and wax solution called Mobile-CER-M. "Inside, we laid out the gun blanks, using transparent acrylic patterns of rifle and shotgun blanks. We'd move the patterns around to get the best grain. Sometimes the grain looked good on one side, but when you turned the slab over, the grain wasn't good on the other side and we'd have to lay it out all over again. We used chalk to outline the patterns, so we could wash it off if we goofed. Some of the slabs weighed 300 to 400 pounds each. Whenever we could, without ruining the grain, we'd cut them down the middle on a big band saw to about eight-foot lengths. After cutting the blanks on the bandsaw, we sealed the ends and any knots. Then we segregated the blanks into three rough grades and stacked them as high as six feet on four by four-foot pallets, with one-inch-square stickers between layers to allow for air circulation.

"The tall stacks of blanks were covered by clear plastic tarps. The plastic stopped just short of the concrete floor, to allow air to circulate through the blanks. Moisture from the wood collected inside of the plastic and ran down its sides. Literally gallons of water drained off the wood. After about eight months, the runoff stopped and we pulled off the tarps. The blanks were air dried for another eight to twelve months before they were ready to market."

Why did Pachmayr tie up so much capital in a product that took months to prepare for market? Simply, because he loves wood, and Frank would never compromise quality. He tried drying California claro in a kiln, but the results weren't up to his quality standards. Because of its cell structure, claro can't be forced to dry in a hurry. The microscopic parallel cells are staggered like bricks in a wall, instead of one directly above another, and water molecules are obliged to travel around corners to escape. Any form of forced drying causes the external cells of claro to close up and trap the moisture inside like an eggshell. Once this happens to a claro blank, it never will dry enough to make a good stock. Frank and I chose an outstanding, highly figured, semidried blank for one of my big-bore rifles. Unfortunately, it was one of the early blanks that Frank sent early for an experimental kiln dry, and it was ruined in the process. The kiln operators tried to force the drying and all the blanks collapsed.

Old-time gunsmiths knew that you couldn't hurry the drying of walnut. Frank remembers that his father stored gun blanks in a dank corner of the basement for years in the Old Country tradition before transferring them to a dry loft for more years of stabilizing and drying.

A moisture content of seven percent is generally acceptable in a blank. The fact is that it's pointless to dry wood lower than the normal atmospheric conditions to which it will be exposed. Most of the United States has an average humidity of about eight percent. A relatively dry six percent average is found in an area encompassing Nevada and parts of its contiguous states. A thin strip of the lower Pacific Coast, a wide band of the Gulf states, and the lower Atlantic seaboard are a damp eleven percent. Inevitably, any stock will normalize at the average humidity of the area where it's kept, regardless of how well it's sealed by the finish.

So-called impermeable finishes can at best protect against abrupt atmospheric changes, but cannot entirely prevent moisture absorption. For years, the basis for impermeable plastic finishes was pure phenolic resins that were used in fine marine finishes because of their high resistance to water and chemicals. They were unsatisfactory in gun finishes because the resins crazed and yellowed. Pachmayr used only the newer, tough, non-yellowing polyurethane resins with an ultraviolet ray shield added. Polyurethane forms an almost watertight seal with a rugged surface that turns aside minor blows and scrapes that might otherwise dig into the stock. It shows wood grain to the best advantage with great apparent depth and without darkening the wood. It can be finished with a high gloss, if desired, or given the muted glow that is the hallmark of fine Pachmayr rifle and shotgun stocks.

How do you recognize good grain in a gunstock? "Picking a blank for a custom gunstock is something you have to do for yourself," says Frank. "You might as well try to pick a man's wife for him as his gunstock blank. It doesn't take a genius to know good wood. The basics of laying out a blank are simple. Yet I see a lot of gunsmiths doing it wrong, because they cling to the old idea that a crotch feather should fan out from the comb toward the toe. That puts the grain structure across the pistol grip, and that's just asking for a broken stock, especially on a rifle. The old-timers got away with this kind of layout on shotgun stocks, partly because they aren't given all that much abuse, and partly because the wrist is reinforced either by the side plates or by a through-bolt. For greatest strength, the grain in a blank should curve around the pistol grip. That makes the crotch feather fan out from the grip cap toward the heel of the stock. With the exception of fiddleback, fancy grain should be kept out of the pistol grip of a rifle or shotgun and out of the fore-end of a rifle. The best rifle blank has the grain tracing the curve of the pistol grip and parallel to the barrel through the fore-end. The straight grain is less likely to warp hither and yon with changes in humidity.

Andy Garner, Frank, and Bill Harrison examine cut walnut.

"Most rifles shoot better with some fore-end pressure," adds Frank. "Fancy grain or cross grain in the fore-end causes the pressure to change or shift sideways with every switch in the weather and changes a rifle's point of impact. The hunter doesn't know anything's wrong until he misses his game. A lot of times, the hunter blames his marksmanship when it's really the fault of his rifle.

"When someone asks me how to choose a good stock blank," says Frank, "I tell them to look at the ends and edges. Look for fine texture and small pores in the wood. Look for narrow annual rings. Both of these indicate that the wood wasn't over-watered. If a tree has it too good, it grows fat and pithy. The tree that has to struggle for existence produces harder, more dense wood. It's stronger and less prone to warp. It takes checkering better and finishes better. Look at the way the grain runs at the butt end. If the grain runs more or less straight across the thickness of the blank, that means it was quartersawed. Only two or three center-cut planks or flitches from a large log provide quartersawed blanks. The grain is generally similar on both sides of the blank. These are the truly select blanks that yield crotch feathers. Quartersawed blanks from farther down the trunk, away from the limbs, are liable to look sort of drab, but they are strong and stable. They make good shooters. The rest of the flitches cut up into what we call plain-sawed blanks. From the butt, you can see the grain running more or less across the width of the blank, usually at an angle. From the sides, plain-sawed blanks show edge grain and annual rings. Properly dried, they make stable stocks. When the curve of the stock is shaped, the sides have a leaflike pattern that's very attractive."

In 1975 Dick Mellen received a business offer from a Texas entrepreneur that he just couldn't resist. He was commissioned to set up and operate an extensive printing plant in Dallas. Although Frank felt keenly the loss of his nephew's guiding hand at the wood operation, he wished him well in his new job.

Frank remembered his pleasant and productive association with Andy Garner. He called Andy and asked him to take over the woodcutting operation. "If you'll take it," promised Frank, "I'll buy the warehouse and you can have a permanent home there. I have also had my eye on another property that has been on the market about fifteen years now. I think I can get it at a good price."

Andy said later, "After all that man had done for me, how could I turn him down when he needed me?"

The property that Frank offered to buy was a long-abandoned twenty-four-thousand-square-foot citrus storage warehouse located just a few miles from the sawmill in Palermo. Also made of galvanized corrugated steel, it dwarfed the original ten-thousand-square-foot building. With the added storage space of the new building, Pachmayr was able to stockpile vast quantities of walnut that might otherwise have been lost.

In spite of the fact that walnuts were California's seventeenth-ranked agricultural crop in the late 1970s and grossed $168,000,000 in 1979, a number of factors were coming to a head that made the walnut-growing industry uneconomical. Orchards planted a century or more earlier were past their peak production years and made many operations marginal at best. Younger walnut orchards were still producing robustly and were holding their own, but many small walnut farmers could barely keep their heads above water. The pressure of urban development was pushing real estate values sky high, and with it, property taxes in the area were rising, sometimes faster than the real estate. Even farmers who loved the walnut business were forced to sell to developers or to substitute more profitable crops. Entire ancient orchards were being torn out to make way for rice, kiwi fruit, and other more profitable crops.

Frank Pachmayr recognized the enormous loss the world at large, and shooters in particular, would suffer if this wood was thrown away for lack of a market. He knew that some orchards had actually been burned and buried by their owners because there were no buyers at hand when the trees were pulled up. Frank determined to absorb as much of this precious walnut as possible. He bought three entire orchards, totaling hundreds of trees, on one trip north. In one year, Andy Garner took out nine orchards. He bought up one orchard in Butt Meadows that he had had his eye on for fourteen years. Andy flew to southern California with Frank to check out an orchard in Ramona. "There were hundreds of trees," Andy observed later, "but not a one of them was wider than a car's steering wheel, and we don't cut any tree that's under a yard across."

At one point in 1981 Pachmayr Wood Products had 700 tons of walnut stumps waiting to be processed. They were mainly from orchards given up in the Clear Lake, Porterville, and Visalia areas. Already cut were 12,000 gunstock blanks, stored in the Oroville and Palermo warehouses. At his Los Angeles headquarters,

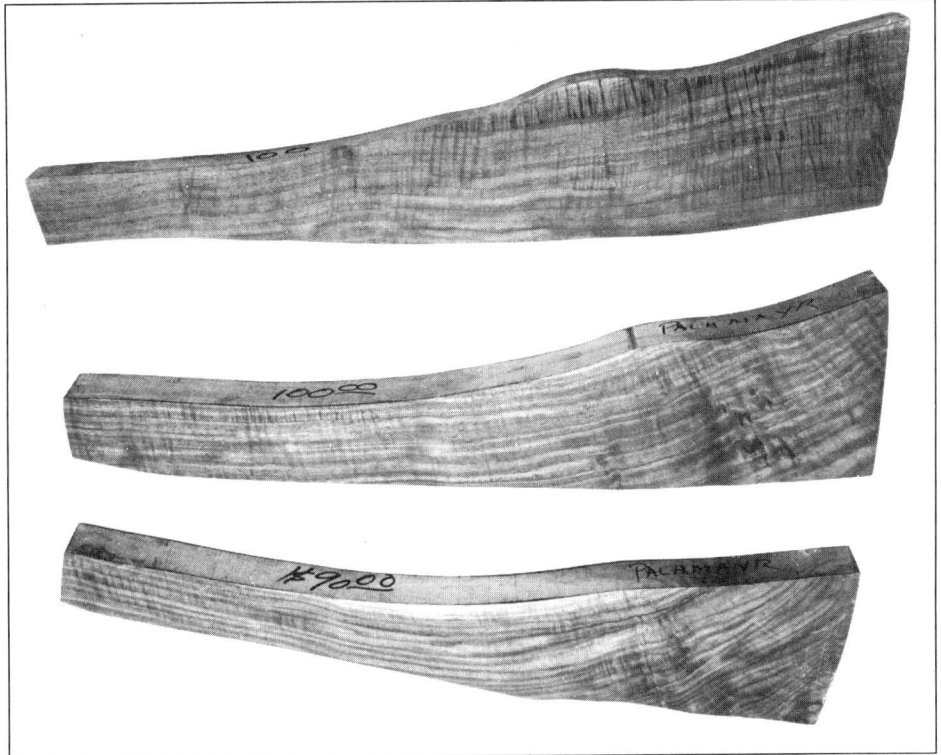

Three of the standard-grade Pachmayr claro walnut blanks.

Frank had another 12,000 cut blanks. The market for raw shotgun and rifle blanks had an early saturation point. The sale of raw blanks to gunsmiths for custom rifles was limited by the small number of artisans in the United States, as well as the fact that custom stocks usually required weeks to complete and slowed sales. Although Pachmayr kept a number of skilled stockmakers constantly busy, he could use only a limited number of blanks in-house. Even large-batch sales to various gun manufacturers in the United States and abroad couldn't soak up the large inventory.

To Frank, the obvious answer was to open new markets. He set out to sell machine-shaped and inletted rifle blanks to gunsmiths and general consumers. Dick

Mellen was still with Frank at the time, and it was his responsibility to purchase a modern woodcarving machine. He selected a North Star thirteen-spindle precision pantograph, which could deliver up to a dozen stocks with identical outside dimensions and precisely inletted closely to final dimensions. Normally, only some touch-up inletting and final external finishing remained to be done. Frank determined that Pachmayr partly inletted stocks were going to be among the finest available. To that end, he assembled a collection of master patterns valued at approximately $25,000. Dick said later, "It seems that half of my time was spent creating new patterns. Just when I thought that we must have a pattern for every bolt-action rifle known to man, something new would show up. Mauser-styled rifles were particularly bad, because each manufacturer made them a little differently."

Machine-shaped and inletted blanks have been offered for years by large-volume wood firms in the East. They were most popular with do-it-yourself shooters, bent on changing military surplus rifles into sporting rifles after World War II. Precut blanks were generally regarded with scorn by custom stockmakers. Frank wanted to produce something that even premier stockmakers wouldn't be ashamed to use. With precision equipment and punctilious workmen, he was able to machine closely to final dimensions. This degree of accuracy was attainable only with careful attention to detail. Tooling was changed a total of seven times during a single run. Wood was shaved in thin layers, rather than hogged off in a hurry. The inletting looked as if it was cut on a milling machine, rather than a pantograph.

The stocks all featured classic configurations and were styled in the manner of Pachmayr custom stocks. A muted Monte Carlo comb was offered for those who preferred that design. The quality of Pachmayr's wood was also something seldom seen before in the industry. A total of eight grades were offered, ranging from plain to exhibition. Grading was done with an eye to giving the customer the most for his dollar. If there was any doubt about a particular blank, it was graded lower and sold for the lower price, instead of the other way around.

When Frank Pachmayr sold his business in 1982, all corporate entities, including Pachmayr Wood Products, were sold together as a complete package. Recognizing the great implications that the change in ownership could have on his vice president, Andy Garner, Frank flew up to Oroville to tell him in person, instead of merely phoning the news to him. "Your job is guaranteed," Frank told Andy, "under the terms of the sales agreement." As it worked out, the head of the syndicate that purchased Pachmayrs, James Baker, was only too happy to leave the wood operation entirely in Andy's capable hands. "You'll have to handle the wood," he told Andy. "I don't know a damn thing about it."

After a couple of years in retirement, Frank grew restless with inactivity and longed to be in business again. He turned back to his first love, gunstocks. His offer of something over a quarter of a million dollars fell on receptive ears. Overnight, Andy was again working for Frank, a happy fate for both of them.

During Frank's absence, the corporation had sold the smaller of the two warehouses, and Andy had set up a new facility at the larger warehouse. Andy installed

• WONDERFUL WOOD •

a new $19,000 Alaskan Portable Sawmill with a sixty-inch wide chain that was driven by a hydraulic pump and powered by a massive fifteen-horse, 220-volt, three-phase electric motor. The eight-foot tall mill was capable of cutting logs up to fifty-four inches wide and twelve feet long. The hydraulic system had a bypass valve that stopped the chain whenever it encountered excessive resistance, for instance when it hit a flat iron or a railroad spike. Andy mounted the sawmill on a concrete pad next to the loading dock, which was happily downwind of the building and had a wide shed roof for protection from the elements.

"This huge building was erected by the late William Randolph Hearst, the newspaper and magazine magnate," announced Frank, with an expansive wave of his arm to encompass the entire 24,000 square feet of floor space, "somewhere around the turn of the century. He used it to warehouse and process oranges that were grown in his orchards hereabouts. He even set up his own sawmill to make lumber from trees cut on his property in the hills around here. There was a railroad spur set up right next to the building just to load his produce.

"The building has nine full-width gables with windows for light. There was no electric power in here when I bought it, but it had a strong floor and a solid roof and was sound as a brick outhouse. Best of all, it had twelve large, independently sealed rooms, which took up about a one-third of the north end. You know the building is longer than a football field—320 feet long to be exact and 110 feet wide. Hearst used the rooms to store and ripen oranges with steam registers producing heat. We found them ideal to dry blanks.

"Andy handles the whole Oroville operation for me. He buys the trees and pulls them out, then stacks the logs and stumps in the three-acre yard behind the loading platform until he's ready to cut them up for blanks."

At the time, Andy wasn't buying orchards anymore. "These days, about 90 percent of the trees are too small for gunstocks," he said. "Most of the big trees still around are Eastern black walnut. They don't have any figure. They're just plain, straight-grained wood. Now I have to look for individual trees, usually in people's yards, that have gotten so old they're dangerous and have to be cut. I know every tree man from Yreka to San Diego. If one of them finds a good tree, he'll call me. I drive over and take a look. I can tell a good tree by just looking at it, even from a distance. Sometimes, I just drive by. I can tell if it's no good for gunstocks. We used to cut nothing but the big trees. Now it's rare to see one that's five foot in diameter."

One time, Frank and Andy bought a walnut tree 9½ feet in diameter in Chapman Town, "where Diamond Match had their office when I worked for them right after World War II," says Andy. "The crotch of the tree was so high, I drove my flatbed truck up to it and stood on the truck while I sawed it in half with a six-foot chain saw. We got fifty-six crotch blanks from that one crotch. That tree had 34½ tons of fine gunstock wood in it."

Andy treated each and every walnut tree with tender, loving care. First, he topped the tree, cutting away all small branches and brush. Then he dug out around the tree, exposing the roots. He notched the roots on one side to provide hinges and cut the roots on the sides and back a few at a time, allowing the tree to fall over gently. "I could get a fifteen-ton log within four feet of the ground," he proclaimed proudly, "before it finally broke loose and toppled over."

All the while, Andy controlled the speed and direction of the tree's fall with cables from a large boom truck attached well up the trunk. "I took half an hour to lay a tree down gently," he says. "Some guys just pulled it down, or came up and pushed it over with a bulldozer. They think they're saving time. The fact is, they may ruin the tree. If a tree just crashes to the ground, there's a good chance it'll splinter internally and just shatter like a glass bottle. It doesn't show on the outside. It might not show up when they cut the slabs or rough out the blanks. It might not show until the blanks dry, then they split all through the grain. I've seen blanks that other people cut split from end to end. After putting in all that time and labor, they get nothing for their efforts but firewood. You can get into trouble even when you do everything right. Some big old trees with tremendous tops get twisted by the wind, causing wind shakes. The internal cracks don't show up until the blanks are dried.

"I had my own system for drying blanks," Andy continues. "First, I stacked them on edge with one end on a two-by-four. The slight slant helped drain off excess water. After four to six weeks, I would treat the ends of the blanks to prevent cracking and transfer them into one of the sixteen-by-twenty-foot drying rooms. Using a controlled dry heat source, I increased the room temperature slowly over a period of four to six weeks until it reached 85 degrees. Room temperature and humidity were monitored four times a day, and the rooms were vented to allow the moisture to escape. It took about three months of steady heat before the blanks became the same temperature all the way to the center of the wood. Each batch of blanks remained in the drying room for about a year. There is no forced air circulation. One large walnut company back East tried using fans from various directions to hurry up the drying, and they lost one-third of the blanks. I never lost more than 2 percent, sometimes none. I could tell when they were getting dry by just striking two blanks together. When they were wet, they gave off a dull, sodden sound. After they dried out, they rang like a bell."

Andy used a West German electronic moisture register that cost $600. It went under the unlikely name of Fauchtigkeitsnessgerat Testor. "This was the first tester I ever found that could tell you if the center of the blank is actually dry. A lot of registers indicated dry. Then when you cut into the wood, you found a thin sliver of wet wood left in the middle." Andy pronounced a blank dry when it registered between five to seven percent moisture content.

Andy cut flitches 2½-inches thick on the Alaskan Sawmill. "I could keep an eye on the grain," he says, "and jack up the log on one end or the other or roll it over a little to get the best grain." Frank and Dick Mellen made similar comments about this part of the process. "I kept a sharp watch for steel chunks that could ruin a $140.00 chain saw in a few seconds," says Andy. "If there was a black spot in the wood, you could bet there was a nail or something under it, and I usually chopped it out with an axe to save the chain. Sometimes I had to scrap a log because it was full of steel. Once I found a row of railroad spikes in a tree. Someone had driven them in the trunk to make a ladder, probably for a tree house. Over the years, the tree grew around them, encasing the spikes inside where they couldn't be seen. When I saw the bark worn in the center of the Y, I knew that kids had been playing in the tree. Anything was liable to show up hidden inside, from roller skates to a monkey wrench."

Andy used a hydraulic hoist to pick up the slabs from the end of the mill and stack them on a pallet, then used a forklift to move them to the big band saw near the mill. "I laid out the stocks, using transparent plastic patterns to get the best lay of the grain," he explained. "If you want top quality, you can't be greedy when you're laying out blanks. Most times, you have a choice of getting a half dozen blanks with outstanding grain or ten with mediocre grain. You might make more money with the ten, but you won't have the quality. I know a lot of people who lay out their patterns for maximum yield. They use skimpy patterns and cut right on the line to get the most blanks they can. I always used to cut long and wide around the pattern to allow the gunsmith plenty of leeway in laying out his stock."

Andy Garner continued to operate Frank Pachmayr's wood mill, cutting premium stock blanks for domestic and international trade until 1993 when a high-tension power line dropped, sparked, and set the huge building ablaze. The century-old wooden structure was tinder-dry. In minutes, it was reduced to a massive pile of glowing embers, taking hundreds of irreplaceable walnut stock blanks with it. Frank and Andy mourned the loss of the blanks more than the sizable financial loss that both suffered in the fire.

On Christmas of 1993 Andy received a check from Frank in the amount of $100,000, a "thank you" for all the years of honesty and faithful hard work. Andy handed it over to his wife Sharon, with carte blanche on its disposition. Sharon opened an intimate little gift shop in Oroville. Andy plans to resume cutting walnut stock blanks, albeit on a smaller scale because of the loss of the heavy equipment and storage space.

•••

· Chapter X ·

FRANK & FRIENDS IN FIELD & MARSH

If you analyze Frank A. Pachmayr to choose one trait that was the engine of motivation propelling his career, it would have to be his passion for hunting. His love of guns sprang from this fountainhead. Frank grew up hunting birds and rabbits around his Los Angeles home. Perhaps that's why he prefers shotgun shooting at airborne feathered targets to toting a rifle or handgun in quest of furred and horned creatures. Withal, Frank is an outstanding marksman with all types of rifled arms, as well as with smoothbores.

In his love for any kind of bird hunting, Frank willingly travels to get into the thick of wing shooting. The dense jungles of Africa, teeming with game animals of every kind and size, and the plains and towering peaks of Asia dotted with exotic trophies like Marco Polo sheep—both destinations of choice for many modern-day hunters—did not hold the intense allure for Frank that a rustic, reedy duck blind in northern California or Baja California could exert. After his business came of age and certainly after he sold out the aircraft division, Frank could have easily afforded to journey to Africa or Asia, in fact the four corners of the earth, and hunt big game that was so plentiful then. Somehow, that didn't appeal to him. Frank has always had a great respect for wildlife, and he was never comfortable with the killing of large game animals.

About twenty years ago, after I returned from an elk hunt in Moose Creek, Idaho, I took pictures of my trip over to show Frank. He had hunted Moose Creek himself, so I was pretty sure he would be interested in the elk that I had taken in the High Sierras during a raging blizzard. Frank sat behind his desk as I fanned the photos out in front of him, and he solemnly examined each one in turn. "These are great pictures," he commented, "but there's one here I don't like." Then he reached over and picked up one of the photos and gave it a wry look, saying, "You ought to throw this away. The elk is a noble animal. It shouldn't be shown like this." I looked at the picture that Frank objected to. It was a flash photo taken in the dim dusk by my guide. It showed me standing beside the huge bull after we had finished caping the carcass with its head severed at the neck and lying on the ground. I looked at the photo and saw it through Frank's eyes. "You're right." I conceded, as I pitched the print into the round file beside his desk.

On another occasion, one of Frank's friends was proudly displaying photos of his African safari. Frank groaned at the sight of an elephant lying dead on its side. "How can you bear to kill a huge animal like this?" he demanded. Frank does love a good deer hunt, though, which for him is as much a social event as it is a hunting trip. He savors the camaraderie, the hours spent with old friends gathered around a campfire by the tent, or in front of a potbellied stove in a mountain cabin.

These days, Frank has wound down, as all of us do with the passing of years. He fought his way back from a stroke in 1981, but failing health didn't prevent him from going duck hunting in the grasslands near Oroville. As always, Frank combined business with pleasure. He visited his wood mill and helped his foreman, Andy Garner, select fine shotgun blanks for a large shipment to Japan.

For several years in the late 1950s and early 1960s, Frank operated the Indian Creek Guest Ranch located on the middle fork of the Salmon River in Idaho. Frank and Bill Jay were partners in running a booking service for hunters, called Sportsmen Holidays, with headquarters at Pachmayr's sporting goods store at 1225 South Grand Avenue. During September, October, and November, for a nominal $350.00, sportsmen could enjoy ten days of hunting elk, deer, and bear in the primitive area of Idaho. The ranch held packer rights on approximately nineteen hundred square miles in the Salmon, Bitterroot, and Payette National Forest of Idaho. Some of the largest elk herds in the country were to be found there. Hunters also had the opportunity to fish the famed "River of No Return," the Salmon and Middle Fork.

No hunt, even in a primitive area, is any better than the guide who helps find the game, helps the hunter get a good shot, and then finds the way back to camp. Professional guides at Frank's Indian Creek Ranch were members of Idaho's Outfitters and Guide Association, assuring that they would be competent guides. For a $500.00 fee, Sportsmen Holidays included a direct flight from Los Angeles to Salmon, Idaho, aboard one of Frank's corporate planes—a 310 Twin Cessna, a C-18 Twin Beechcraft, or a Beech Bonanza. The alternative was land travel to Boise, then a half-hour flight by private plane to the ranch.

"There were only two directions there," remarks Frank wryly, "up and down. When you weren't struggling for breath climbing up some mountain or other, you were slipping and sliding down, trying not to get killed. Sometimes we would walk the ridges, which was relatively easy going. Then we'd sit and scan the opposite ridges with binoculars. That was about the best way to spot game in that rugged, heavily timbered range.

"The only way in and out of the ranch was by plane. We had a backwoods landing strip that got a little icy in the winter. It wasn't long enough to land my Twin Beech, but planes as big as a Twin Cessna could make it if you didn't come in too fast. Of course, if a guy had no spirit of adventure, he could get there by backpacking for a week or so," added Frank with a twinkle in his eye and a grin on

· Frank & Friends in Field & Marsh ·

Frank Pachmayr's father, Gus, was an inveterate hunter his entire life. He began hunting as a boy with Frank's grandfather in the forests of Bavaria. Even in his declining years, Gus could walk the legs off men half his age. Gus hunted until the infirmities of old age finally kept him at home.

his face. "It was a great place to get away from it all, and elk and deer certainly did thrive there. I remember one guy from Los Angeles who was the first to take elk and deer during the 1960 season. He got a 150-pound buck his first day out. Later, he shot a 400-pound bull elk no more than a mile and a half from camp.

"The rest of us didn't have such good luck that year. The weather was lousy. It was below zero much of the time and the wind cut right through you. We saw elk tracks every day but never seemed to catch up with the herd. I remember one day we followed elk tracks in the snow right up to the lip of a precipitous ridge. It looked like the elk had just walked off the edge, but I knew elk weren't that stupid. I think they just sprouted wings. Then we did something I never would have allowed if the weather hadn't been so rough. We sprouted some wings of our own. We had Jack Curnow along, and I wanted him to have a good hunt. At the time, Jack was outdoor editor for the *Los Angeles Times*, so although I don't like to take unfair advantage of wild game, I okayed the use of my plane. We flew over the area and spotted several elk herds. Then we flew directly back to the air strip at the ranch and headed out on foot right to the spot where we had seen elk only hours before. In spite of our recon flights, all we saw were tracks. I swear you had to be in good shape to hunt that country. We started out before light and came back after dark, totally wasted almost every day."

In his *Los Angeles Times* column dated 20 November 1959, Jack Curnow recounted a hunt with Frank. The column was datelined Sulfur Creek Ranch, Boise, Idaho:

> So this is elk hunting—one party goes out from Sulfur Creek before the season ended up there last Sunday and shoots elk at the end of the airplane runway. Another party goes out from this ranch (Pistol Creek Ranch) where the season runs until 30 November and stumbles onto a herd and gets meat on the table. A gang from southern California spends a week here without getting an elk.
>
> Our party of Frank Pachmayr, Los Angeles gun-works specialist, Corliss Pipher, Capistrano Beach contractor, and yours truly hunted hard for three days and we get but one elk, and that was shot by Pachmayr at long range. Some of us have seen elk on other ridges a mile or two away. We tracked elk in the snow by the herd. We smelled elk—no kidding, you can if you're to the lee of them, and you better be. Never have we caught up with them.
>
> These ranches are located on the middle fork of the Salmon Rivers, five minutes apart by light plane. You get full information about them from Bill Jay at Pachmayr's Gun Works in Los Angeles. There are plenty of elk in this country. All you have to do is fly around and you can see them easily, but finding them on horseback and afoot is another story. Let me tell you about a typical day of elk hunting.
>
> Floyd Posing, our guide, wakes us at 4:00 A.M., usually with these words, 'Today's the day they give elk away, time for elk hunters to be up and about.' You

crawl out of the sack and find that it's a nice day—ten degrees above zero this morning. You put on your arctic underwear—you've really been sleeping in them—slip on socks, pants, and shirt. You brush your teeth. Breakfast is ready.

Sourdough hotcakes, two or three eggs, bacon, coffee. You gorge. Now you put on a second pair of pants, another pair of heavy socks, wool shirt, heavy jacket and boots, a muffler, gloves, a heavy cap with earmuffs.

You struggle onto a horse warm as toast—you, not the horse. Your rifle is in the scabbard with shells in the magazine. Now you start on a six or eight-mile ride. You're warm for maybe fifteen minutes before you turn up a can-

Frank owned several corporate planes, including this twin Beech that took him and his guests on many hunting trips. He had his own personal pilot on constant call.

yon. The temperature here is zero or below and you slowly get numb. You get real numb, especially a thin-blooded southern Californian. You get off and walk, you ride, you walk. But you can't possibly keep warm despite all the ads about that underwear.

Finally you get off the horse and start uphill. In this primitive area of Idaho there are but two directions, up and down. You start climbing the 300 feet or more to the ridge of the mountain. That's where the elk are. This takes two hours or more of what becomes sheer agony for an office worker. Keep going or you'll freeze. You've already quit wondering when the fun stopped and the work began. You can't even enjoy the beauty around you. You just want to quit, but you can't let the others know.

They're feeling the same way, but won't admit it for the same reason. You stop often to look over the area for elk. That's what you say, anyhow. Now you're on top and the sun is hot. You've eaten your lunch long since to stoke up energy. Sit around half an hour, and you're a new man.

Where are the elk? That's a good question. Five hours later you've covered seven miles of ridge, waded through snow, slipped on slushy rocks, stumbled over fallen trees. You've become excited six-dozen times over all the fresh tracks, but haven't seen an elk. Sure positive, they're around, but where? Only the elk knows, and he's not telling.

Now it's a couple of hours straight down the hill. Then a walk to the horses. That's easy, that's easy, only a couple of miles because the guide has plotted your ridge course and descent all the way. Now you're on your horse and that chill starts working again, the sun having gone down. It's a long way back. It's cold again. Ride, walk, ride, walk.

Now you're back in front of the roaring fire at the lodge. You're telling big whoppers, including what fun you had. Now a tremendous dinner. Now more lies around the fire. Only you're too tired to take part. There's a four-o'clock call in the morning. It's starting to snow again. You hope it turns into a full-blown blizzard. You can sleep in then. We've got to hurry to bed. Sure, going elk hunting in the morning. Maybe.

In another column, Jack Curnow wrote:

Instead of being out elk hunting yesterday as planned, we spent the day loafing around the lodge, warming our tootsies and watching the snow come boiling down. Sometimes you could see the peaks briefly, but mostly the high ridges were out of sight. Some of us were a little perturbed because the guides decided before daylight that it didn't make much sense to go out in a semiblizzard. The elk, being cagier than the hunters, would be huddled down warmly in the high country out of the wind. It behooved hunters to take a cue and stay indoors. If you really felt bad about the situation, you could always look up at the sign over the mantle. It says, 'I had no shoes and complained, until I met a man with no feet.'

Our group is made up of Frank Pachmayr of the famed gun works, Corliss Pipher, Capistrano Beach contractor, pilot Chuck Fischer of Santa Ana, and yours truly. We flew to Boise in Pachmayr's Twin Beech, then were flown in here by Marvin Hornback, operator of Pistol and Sulfur Creek ranches, in his Cessna.

We barely got in ahead of a snowstorm Saturday morning. It quit snowing long enough for Hornback to fly out. Since then it's all been radio conversation. It's anyone's guess when he gets back here. A veteran bush pilot, he doesn't fly until conditions are perfect.

Frank saved the yellowed newspaper clippings because, he said, "Jack really laid it on the line. Elk hunting's a hell of a thrill, but it's just as tough as he said. That trip still stands out in my mind after all these years because the weather was so foul. After elk hunting hard for four days in bad weather around our main camp at Pistol Creek, we decided to try for some of the huge mule deer down around the Flying 'B' Ranch located several miles south. It only took about a quarter-hour flying time getting there. Then we set out on horseback with Shorty Jessup as our guide. To look at him, you wouldn't know that Shorty was all of seventy years old. He was rawhide tough and about as fat as a yank of venison jerky, and he couldn't find anything good to say about us city fellers."

After a few hours on the trail, it began to warm up some, but Frank and his companions were still on the shady side of the mountain, so they had no desire to remove their thickly padded goose-down jackets. Jack Curnow was leading the way with Corliss Pipher close behind. Shorty and Frank brought up the rear. The party had to ride single file as the horses picked their way along a narrow mountainside trail. "A single missed step by one of our horses could have sent any one of us on an early trip to the Happy Huntin' Grounds," observed Frank.

Suddenly Jack jumped off his horse—no mean trick on that narrow trail—and waved Pipher to bring his gun. "I could see the buck about 150 yards away on the opposite hill," recalls Frank. "Pipher swung off his horse on the right side, which was uphill. There was no downhill side. Almost in the same movement, he plucked his saddle carbine from its leather boot." Most range ponies would come unglued if a rider dismounted on the off side, but these were mountain horses, and they had been trained to stand firm when a rider boarded or got off on either side.

"Corliss scrambled around to the front of his horse and ducked under its head to get a clear view of the running buck," continues Frank. "Then standing in an awkward position with all of his weight on the downhill leg and with the reins hooked over his left arm, he made a great offhand shot on the running buck, bringing it down with one round."

The sound of Pipher's gun startled Jack's horse, and it reared, almost bumping Jack off the mountain. Shorty wasn't at all upset. "Never seen old Susie do that before," he mused. Shorty grinned widely and chuckled as he watched Jack, who was white-faced and clinging to his horse's bridle with both hands. At the same time, Jack was peering over the side of the sheer drop and mentally calculating his chances of survival had he been nudged off the trail.

"After we gutted out Pipher's buck, we decided we might just as well stay put and have lunch," Frank continues. "While we were eating, Shorty wandered off to scout the neighboring ridges with his binoculars. I had about finished my ham and Swiss on rye, when he strolled back and asked, 'Any of you slickers able to shoot 600 yards?' Jack and I both got up and grabbed our rifles. Pipher's rifle had only factory open sights, so he settled for spotting for us with his 7X binoculars. I was shooting a .270 Winchester Model 70 Super Grade with a 4X Stith Bear Cub in my own Pachmayr swing mount. I held the tapered post just above the deer's back in line with its shoulder and squeezed the trigger, and I saw the buck drop. I let out an exultant yelp, but so did Jack. We both shot about the same time, and we both saw the buck drop. Each one of us thought we had hit it; in fact, I knew I had hit it.

"Now I might have deferred to Jack on a lot of things, because after all, he was my guest on this hunt," says Frank. "But when it comes to giving up my deer, especially one that I bagged at 600 yards, I don't back down to anyone. We were just getting into a hot discussion over possession, when Shorty came up behind us laughing fit to bust. 'Neither one of you dudes hit anything,' he said. Then Corliss, who was still searching the hillside with his Bausch and Lomb, said, 'There goes the buck limping over the top of the ridge.' Well, I headed up the ridge to the right at a run, and Jack hot-footed it up the other side of the wide 'V' formed by another ridge to the left. We hoped to keep the deer between us. As I topped the crest and looked over the other side, I spotted my buck trotting along about a hundred yards downhill. There was no mistaking that spectacular rack. When I took my first shot at long range, it had looked like an elk through my rifle scope, despite the distance. Now at nearly point-blank range, I brought it down with one standing shot. End of story. Or so I thought.

"Then I was startled to hear a whole barrage of shooting from the direction of the other ridge. I looked over to see Jack shoot right over the back of another buck," Franks continues. "So there were two. This buck was somewhat smaller than the one I had just bagged, but it was still a respectable trophy, and it also ran with a peculiar halting gait, like it was wounded. Jack fired his first shots at the wounded buck at about 100 yards. The deer was still making full steam till it got out about 250 yards, then it paused and turned broadside to look back. Jack fired one shot from a sitting position and the buck fell like a stone. 'Gol Dang,' exclaimed Shorty, 'you finally got it. Guess I owe you both an apology. Appears there was two deer, and each of you got one.'

"Jack explained with some embarrassment, 'I got so conditioned to shooting high when the buck was way out there, that I just kept shooting over it at close range.'

Shorty snorted, 'Well I can't say as I've seen better long shots, but I'll be danged if I ever saw worse short shots.'

"After our successful deer hunt, we returned to Pistol Creek for several more days of elk hunting," Frank adds. "I managed to connect with a bull—the only one taken on this trip—again at extreme range. I think we were all pretty worn out and anxious to get home by then, but we got snowed in there for over a week. We tried to fly out five times without success. Each time, the storm closed in and sent us scuttling back to the ranch. Once, we got about halfway to Boise before we were forced to turn around. We landed in almost zero visibility, barely ahead of a blizzard. By the time we got the plane lashed down to D-rings implanted in the ground, the storm broke. We finally got out by flying low under the cloud cover. We couldn't get high enough to clear the mountain ridges, so we threaded our way through the canyons by way of Sun Valley and Hailey. Trips like that one can be frustrating and trying. When you're there, you wish you were back home toasting your feet next to the fireplace, but I wouldn't trade the experience for a million dollars!"

In November of 1961, Frank organized a Colorado deer hunt. Frank's party included his brother John, his nephew Richard Mellen, and Vince Martin, all from Los Angeles, as well as Roy Coykendall of El Monte and Les Walters of Covina. They flew in Frank's Twin Beech to Meeker, Colorado, then drove in a Jeep into the high country around Yellow Creek to Violet Ranch, a spot marked clearly by an old dilapidated windmill. When the Jeep trails ran out around 7,000 feet, they made camp in a grassy, green swale that was surrounded by jagged snowcapped peaks. Every morning, they were up before light to labor on foot to top out at more than 8,000 feet above sea level.

The mule deer in this remote area were huge, with thick, massive antlers. Because the deer were present in such abundance, the Colorado Fish and Game Commission had authorized two-deer permits. Using his Winchester Model 70 .300 H&H Magnum, loaded with Remington 180-grain Core-Lokt bullets, Frank bagged two immense bucks. Both had antler spreads in excess of thirty inches.

Frank and his brother John often hunted doves and ducks together in the area of Navajoa, Mexico.

Frank's first buck dressed out at 215 pounds. The deer was in a full gallop about 400 yards away when Frank spotted it. It was quartering away on an opposite slope and stretching the range with every hoofbeat. By the time Frank found the antlers in his scope, he was holding high for 500 yards. With his horizontal cross hair level with the animal's back, Frank swung ahead and lead his target just as if it were a highflying Canada goose. He brought it down with two deliberate shots.

A couple of days later, Frank spotted what he described later as, "The largest buck I ever saw in my life." It was a crisp morning when Frank hunkered down on the shady side of the mountain with his back pushed into a bush to conceal his

Nanitta Pachmayr was one of the quickest to drop any bird on the wing. Frank said no one hunting with her ever got a shot until Nan limited out.

outline. He trained his binoculars on the opposite slope, which was now highlighted by the first rays of a tepid sun that was just topping the hill behind him. At first, the hillside appeared deserted, but as he watched, he began to pick out a doe here, a buck there, but nothing worthy of his metal.

Suddenly a set of craggy antlers popped up behind a tall patch of bitterbrush, only to vanish for a few seconds, then reappear. An alert old buck was warily grabbing a tuft of grass, then raising his head to scan for enemies, as he munched resolutely. Frank watched for perhaps a quarter hour, as the wary old buck browsed along behind the brush. Then the buck tentatively came into a clearing, knee-deep in green grass. With the buck now completely exposed, Frank could see the broad thickness and wide breadth of his rack towering above a massive old head. The buck was graying at the snout, and Frank realized that this was a prize worth having. He plotted his stalk.

Should he attempt to cross the grassy meadow that separated the two mountain slopes, Frank was certain the sage old buck would spot him. He would have to go sideways at least a couple of ridges, then cross, and cut back to find the buck. The wind was from his left, so Frank traveled to the right in order to return upwind on the opposite slope. Over an hour of hard going over deadfalls and occasional patches of impenetrable brambles brought Frank near the spot where the biggest deer he ever saw had been grazing. Frank was approaching cautiously, rifle ready, when he heard a great commotion in the brush ahead and caught a glimpse of towering antlers and a gray-brown body hightailing it through the forest. With his scope, he tracked the buck fleeing to the right through a fence of trees until it crossed an opening wide enough to offer a shot. The Winchester roared and reared back, and the buck disappeared.

Frank hurried to the spot where he last saw it and discovered the big deer crumpled up against the base of a towering spruce twenty yards away. Frank was exultant, but as he examined the great buck more closely, he began to doubt that it was the one he had spotted earlier through his binoculars. With a sinking feeling in his stomach, he worked his way through the patch of mixed fir and pine toward the clearing where he had first seen his big buck. There it was, still browsing near the large bitterbrush patch within easy rifle range, totally unaware of a human presence. With an inward groan, Frank realized that both of his deer tags were filled.

Lesser men have been known to yield to the temptation to shoot the larger trophy and just leave the smaller one to the coyotes, but Frank Pachmayr was ever a man of unbending principle. He refused to shoot. "I just stood there," says Frank, "watching that magnificent muley for ten, maybe fifteen minutes. I was wishing that I hadn't left my camera back in camp. I knew the guys would never believe me when he told them just how big this buck really was."

Knowing that there was no need for concealment, Frank stepped out of the shielding shadows into the open. The grizzled buck was so startled, it just stood staring at Frank for several seconds. Then in the gesture so common to mule deer, it attempted to tiptoe away, his head bobbing with each high, reaching step. Then he broke into a dead run, predictably uphill and out of sight. Frank was happy with his two Colorado trophies, but he has never ceased to mourn "the one that got away."

Hunting above Yellow Creek, there were other long shots made by members of Frank's party. Dick Mellen, shouldering a Model 721 .280 Remington, fired one 125-grain spire point at 350 yards to bag his buck. Vince Martin made a one-shot kill at 400 yards. All in the party bagged their limit, except Mellen, who contented himself with one deer, although he had ample opportunity to take two. Among them, the six-man party bagged eleven deer, all of trophy dimensions, with an expenditure of less than two boxes of ammo.

In relating the experience later, Dick said, "It was snowing the entire time we were there. We nearly froze on those ridges, with the wind blowing right through us. We counted nearly a hundred deer each day, even with the naked eye and under poor visibility. We also saw plenty of sage hens and a mountain lion. To make it even more perfect, there was a herd of almost a hundred mustangs running free over the range. It was a thrill to see those big devils kick up their heels and take off over a mountain every time we spooked them."

· FRANK PACHMAYR ·

After a heady taste of Colorado deer hunting, Frank Pachmayr was anxious to make it a habit and share it with his many hunting buddies. Along with his friends, Charles F. Shield, Sr., and guide-outfitter Vern Caldwell, Frank set out to find some secured hunting rights in the area. In 1953, he asked Vern to scout around for some promising property that could be used to form a hunting club. Frank was sure that he could line up a number of hunters who would be eager to join him in the project. Vern found a Mrs. Reagle willing to sell 160 acres of clear-title homestead property for $2,000. Approximately 125,000 acres surrounding the property were open to public hunting. Frank Pachmayr assigned his attorney, Maynard Henry, to form a California corporation to operate the club. The Shield-Caldwell Hunting Club, Inc. was registered, effective June 1953. Enough memberships were sold to cover costs, and the funds were deposited in a Meeker bank. In August 1953 Shield flew back to record the title deed in Meeker, Colorado, Rio Blanco County, in the name of the Shield-Caldwell Hunting Club. It was owned by fifteen members who each paid $3000. Initial annual dues were $25 per member. Guests were assessed $30 for each hunt.

During the first season, the hunting club suffered a number of start-up woes. Charles went up in September to build a cook's cabin that was mandated by the first board meeting held in Westmoreland, California, earlier that same month. The bulldozer broke down and caused building delays. Opening day, 24 October, was greeted by a blizzard. Luckily, the cook shack was standing and a small shed, housing a used Kohler power generator, adequately powered the refrigerator and provided lights. By the second year, the thirty-year old machine gave out. Parts were no longer available for the aging and ailing unit, so it was replaced with a 1,000-watt, 115-volt AC manual-start generator. The first year income of the club was $5,245.00. Costs, including the land purchase, totaled $5,053.18, leaving a bank balance of $191.82. Most years the club just about broke even, but Frank never intended it as a profit-making venture. By close of the deer season on 9 November, nine members had hunted, including Frank Pachmayr. His private pilot, Earle Shade, was a guest of Frank's during this christening season.

The Shield-Caldwell Hunting Club was located at a 7,000-foot elevation, with surrounding mountains topping 8,000 feet, in the northwest corner of Colorado in Deer Management District Number 22, Tamarack Area, Piceance Creek drainage. The club property and large surrounding area were federally mandated wilderness areas. District Number 22, encompassing the territory along both sides of Piceance Creek Road up to Cathedral Bluffs, was designated as a multiple-deer area, allowing the purchase of any number of tags the hunter wanted. The surrounding districts were only allotted two deer tags. Hunting success was virtually 100 percent. Any hunter worthy of the name could be assured of bagging one or two sizable bucks. It was common to have twenty deer hanging from the trees around the camp. Occasionally the number could be double that. The average four-point buck dressed out about 190 pounds. "We never shot anything with less than four points," says Frank. Charles Shield's son, Bill, shot one 14-point cactus buck with a 33½-inch spread that dressed out at 204 pounds.

• FRANK & FRIENDS IN FIELD & MARSH •

Nested in the Cathedral Bluffs area, approximately fifty-two miles west of Meeker, fifty miles north of Rifle, and twenty miles east of Rangely, the club was accessed from Highway 64. Driving south on a dirt road that roughly paralleled Piceance Creek to a fork that headed west through Ryan Gulch, to Cross "V" Cattle Co., then hard north through a locked gate at Yellow Creek Road to the 84 Ranch, then west again over eight miles of wagon ruts and horse trails, you would reach the hunting camp. After several years of bouncing over ruts and washouts, the club members voted to bring in a small bulldozer to even up the rough spots.

Duck hunting in California or down in Mexico held more appeal for Frank than hunting exotic game in far-off lands.

• FRANK PACHMAYR •

Hunters caused a modest boom in Meeker. Frank always booked an individual bungalow at Arthur Amick's Stagecoach Park Hotel in Meeker as a stopover for his guests and to provide a place for hunters to take a shower on the way home. The local landing strip was taxed by the hunting season influx of private planes. Bad weather brought muddy landing strips at the Meeker Airport. Frank remembers the day his Twin Beech was mired to the axles on a soggy strip, and a bulldozer was needed to dig it out. Meeker Airport was privately owned and operated by K. E. Cowdery. It and he were entirely adequate to the needs of a lazy cattle community, but Meeker was suddenly receiving a rocket boost into the twentieth century. In addition to the increased activity generated by a great many out-of-state hunters, Meeker was becoming heavily involved in uranium mining and oil exploration. The nearest major airport was Denver, over 200 miles away. Businessmen relied almost wholly on air transportation to expedite travel in and out of Meeker. Recognizing the immense importance of an all-weather airport to the future economic development of the area, Rio Blanco County Commissioners voted to purchase the airport and surface the takeoff and landing strips.

The largest migrating deer herd in the world, with an estimated population of 50,000, was the White River deer of Colorado. In January 1956, in a move to restore and preserve the winter feeding grounds for the White River elk and deer herds, the Colorado Game and Fish Division purchased the entire ranch holdings of the Square "S" Land and Cattle Company, including 14,000 acres of patented land on Piceance Creek and control of thousands of acres of public domain in the Piceance and Yellow Creek drainage area from owner Alphonso E. Bell, Jr., of Bell Petroleum Company. The $375,000 purchase price was derived 75 percent from Pittman-Robinson funds, a tax upon arms and ammunition that American sportsmen had voted on themselves to support wildlife conservation. The move also assured a huge area of public access for hunters.

This sudden development caused consternation among the members of the Shield-Caldwell Hunting Club. Government acquisition could have had a devastating affect upon the hunting club because of contiguous borders and rather informal access easements, but it proved to be a tempest in a teapot. The club continued to operate pretty much as it had without interruption, but the foreboding wasn't entirely unjustified. The hunting club was indeed doomed but not by the government. It was the inexorable hand of progress that finally brought them down. Ominously, in Grand Valley just ten miles north of Meeker, Union Oil Company was ready to throw the switch on their new five million dollar oil shale plant.

Frank's twin Beech and big DC-3 shuttled back and forth between Los Angeles and Meeker three or four times during the two-week deer hunting season with a full complement of hunters. Frank took pleasure in inviting his friends to hunt with him, and also invited business acquaintances and executives of companies and subcontractors he did business with as goodwill gestures.

Charles Shield managed the deer camp, but the official greeter for Frank Pachmayr was his nephew, Richard "Dick" Mellen. Each year, Dick drove a station wagon from Los Angeles to Meeker with a sturdy Jeep CJ-5 in tow, accompanied by another man driving a ¾-ton stake body pickup truck that was towing another Jeep. Both vehicles were usually crammed with equipment and supplies for the deer camp. After a couple seasons in damp, drafty tents, several members, including Frank, built their own hunting cabins. Dick would set up the cabins for guests and be waiting at the Meeker airport to transport them to their final destination.

In 1955, John Amber, then editor of the *Gun Digest* came to hunt with Frank. Along with John, came famed gunwriter Warren Page, then shooting editor for *Field and Stream* magazine. That was a memorable hunt for everyone. In a letter dated 21 November 1955, John Amber wrote to Frank, "I had a hell of a good time, and I never saw so many deer in my life, aside from the Kaibab many years ago. A damn nice bunch of guys too, and I'm grateful to all of them for the kindness and help they extended to Warren and me."

Frank's nephew, Dick Mellen, was the constant companion of John and Warren during their hunt. He piloted their Jeep for them and helped with such details as gutting and hauling back game. When the trio set out in the Jeep at 6:00 A.M. the first morning, they began counting deer, just for fun. "They were all over the hillsides," says Dick. "From a distance it looked like a convention of jackrabbits." By 1:00 P.M., they had counted upwards of 600 adult deer. Between sightings, Amber and Page debated ballistics.

"When those two got together and talked guns," says Dick, "it was like hearing it from the mouths of the Gods." Warren Page was famous for his long shots. He would chuckle over gun pundits who said it couldn't be done consistently or humanely. Warren was a championship bench rest shooter and worldwide hunter, who fathered the modern 6mm Remington and .243 Winchester cartridges that we know today.

Quoting the fact that big bore, ten-shot, three-quarter-minute groups had been achieved at a thousand yards, it followed logically, according to Warren, that a good marksman with good equipment could routinely bag elk at 400 to 500 yards. Warren often spoke of holding dead on at ranges to 300 yards, "shooting through a six-inch pipe," meaning no more than three inches high at mid-range with no more than three inches of drop at the longest dead-on range. At longer ranges, he advised holding a foot high. Of course, his own field reckoning was much finer.

"That morning," says Dick, "we passed up a lot of ordinary bucks and some were damn good, but those two were looking for only one-in-a-thousand racks—the kind of old loners who hang out high on the ridges, even after the herds have begun feeding the valley floor. Sometime during the morning of the second day, we were tooling along a side hill, when I felt Warren come to attention. He motioned for me to stop and trained his binoculars on a hill across the canyon from us."

Warren jumped out of the Jeep with John Amber hard on his heels. He held his 7X50 binoculars steady for several tense moments. "Well?" John Amber finally burst out impatiently. "It's a beauty." exclaimed Page, as he handed the binoculars over to Amber, who echoed his own assessment. Page grabbed his rifle from the rear of the Jeep and almost ran downhill for about sixty yards toward the edge of a bluff overlooking the canyon. He was instinctively crouching, although the deer in the distance was oblivious to his presence. Page pulled up short at a fallen fir tree. By sitting on a stout bare limb that jutted out parallel to the ground and twisting his body toward the target, Warren was able to improvise a bench rest across the huge tree trunk. His familiar peaked cap padded the forearm of "Old Betsy Number One," Warren's custom 7mm Mashburn Magnum Mauser, scoped with a fixed-power 4X Redfield.

John and Warren had a brief debate over the distance and required holdover. Under a sodden sky, they looked across a wide valley. Mist filled the broad expanse like soup in a bowl, which made the estimation of distance more uncertain. Trees were as quiet and still as cardboard cutouts. Across the canyon the buck, standing broadside, was quietly feeding. The morning air was all but motionless. It was agreed that no wind compensation was required. The range consensus was 600 yards, prompting Warren to hold his cross hairs about one-fourth of the way up the towering antlers to compensate for the two-plus feet of drop he anticipated. Warren squeezed the trigger as deliberately as if he were in a bench rest match. The rifle coughed and jerked upward. Warren had time to lower his rifle from recoil and watch through the scope as the bullet landed. John Amber, hunkered down by the roots of the fallen tree and eyes glued to the binoculars, jumped up and let out a yelp, almost dropping the glasses. "I saw dust from his shoulder." he exulted. Then a dull "Whop," sounded across the canyon. The buck seemed suddenly tired, as he lay down and rolled over on his side.

Even with the adventurous Dick Mellen at the wheel of the Jeep, it required about two hours to get down one mountain, across the narrow valley, and up the other one. The buck was indeed stone dead. Dick said later, "It dressed out well over 200 pounds, and the spread was damn near a yard wide. A couple of days later, they did the same damn thing," he added. "It was a huge buck at about 600 yards. Only this time John Amber was doing the shooting."

John Amber and Warren Page had one final adventure waiting for them on their flight home. Pachmayr's Twin Beech was used as a shuttle to bring in guest hunters from Los Angeles, Cody, Dayton, and Las Vegas. Pilot for the season was Loren L. Reibe, Hollywood stunt flyer who had a hand in filming such movies as *The High and the Mighty*. Loren was taking John and Warren to Denver to catch a commercial flight back to Chicago. Apparently in a throwback to his Hollywood stunt-flying days, Loren just couldn't resist the temptation to circle back and buzz Meeker airport. Frank and Dick Mellen, who were seeing John and Warren off, watched as the Twin Beech zoomed over the hard-packed dirt runway no more than five feet off the ground when it passed them. Clearly visible through one of the portholes was John Amber with a look of stark terror on his ashen face.

To Frank Pachmayr, deer hunting was always more a social event than a pure hunt. To be sure, he hunted, but he spent far more time attending to the comfort and enjoyment of his guests. He was also attentive to the proprieties of sportsmanship and game management. Those who do not hunt find it hard to understand that Nimrods feel great respect and affection for wild animals. Most of the present-day "eco-freaks" who march around protesting hunting have never experienced the out-of-doors beyond a National Geographic documentary, and they can't appreciate the kinship that man and game develop. Frank loves animals, wild and domestic. His greatest dread especially with inexperienced hunters brought to the deer camp as guests was that they might wound and lose game. The thought of a wounded animal suffering was too much for him to bear. He would go to any lengths to track down a wounded animal and put it out of its misery. It was not uncommon for Frank to set out from camp in the Jeep to a spot where an animal had been hit, but not recovered. He would then track it on foot all day, if necessary, to bring it to bag.

Dick Mellen recalls, "One night, after Frank went out to track a deer some guy had shot and lost that morning, he didn't come back to camp. We began to get really worried by 10:00 P.M. It was pitch black outside and cold as the South Pole. Finally, I couldn't stand it any longer. I jumped in the Jeep and went looking for him. I knew about where the deer had been hit. I headed for there and hoped I might run into Frank along the way. I found him about midnight where he was bedded down for the night. He told me there was nothing to worry about. 'Next time wait till daylight before coming to find me.' He had the deer, too, all gutted and hung in a tree to cool. The next time he went off chasing some other guy's wounded deer, I decided to wait him out. He came waltzing in about noon the next day with the deer in the back of his Jeep."

Frank's wife, Nanitta, hunted elk for the first time at the Shield-Caldwell Hunting Club. She brought down a mature bull with her pre-64 Winchester Model 70, .270 rifle that was topped by a 4X Bearcub scope in a Pachmayr Swing Mount. In all, Nan hunted at the club four seasons and took a trophy buck every time. "Once I was hunting with John and Frank in a Jeep without a top," she related to me before her death. "Richard was driving, and we were making our own roads over rough terrain. Those boys do the dangdest things. We were driving over hills and into canyons and across gullies. Then we drove into this curtain of fog and you couldn't see the front of the hood. I told Richard, 'You'd better stop and take a look before you drive over a cliff.' Against his will, he stopped and walked ahead to see what was there, and sure enough, we were headed for a sheer drop."

Camping conditions were pretty primitive on the first trip. "They promised me a tent the second time we went because we couldn't get anyone up there to build a cabin for us yet. They did have a tent for me that was set up on a raised sixteen-foot square wooden platform." The second year, they didn't get a cook up to the camp, so Nan doubled as camp cook. "My mother-in-law gave me a recipe for sauerbraten, using wild game. I made it with venison and everyone just loved it," she commented in happy recollection. "Eventually, we had a regular bunkhouse built, with thirty-six bunks for members and guests. Several of the members built their own personal cabins, beginning with Dick Anderson in 1955."

The average success ratio in Colorado at the time was about 60 percent, pretty good by any measure. During the halcyon days, the Shields-Caldwell Hunting Club enjoyed nearly a 100 percent success ratio. No one ever had to go home without his venison. On 15 October 1955 eight hunters bagged eight bucks on that first day of the season. When the surrounding mountains were exploited by oil companies for shale, the deer population dropped abruptly. Hunting became hit-or-miss. Eventually in 1976, the club sold its strategic 160 acres to Standard Oil and ARCO, the very demons that had devoured the land and rendered it barren.

Nanitta Laughlin knew when she married Frank Pachmayr that he was an inveterate hunter. With Frank it was always, "What you see is what you get." He was never one to indulge in pretense, and you always knew where you stood with him. During their courtship, Nanitta accompanied Frank on many forays to rifle-pistol target ranges, skeet-shooting ranges, turkey shoots, and even on some local hunts after pheasants, quail, and doves. Nan admitted, however, that even she was a little taken aback when her honeymoon turned out to be a deer-hunting trip.

•••

Frank Pachmayr came by his love of hunting honestly. His father, Gus, was a dedicated hunter from the first day he walked at his father's side in the Bavarian forests of Germany. Gus in turn took Frank and John hunting many times. In his declining years, Gus often went hunting with Frank. Nanitta graphically recalled one of these hunts.

"It was the early part of October when Frank and I and Gus drove to Utah for a combination deer and pheasant hunt as guests of Bob Ramsey on his ranch near Richfield, southeast of Salt Lake City. The countryside was something to behold with green fields of alfalfa for miles around. Some of the fields were already harvested, which made the pheasants concentrate in hedgerows and brush along roadside ditches. It was a beautiful time of year with the trees turning a golden copper shade, and the air was fresh and crisp. We arrived at Ramsey's home just in time for supper. Later, we brought our gear in and retired early, because Bob said we would be setting out early the next morning after pheasants.

"We were awakened before dawn. After breakfast, we began driving along the side roads around Bob's ranch and looking for cock pheasants with their brilliant colorful plumage. If one flew up, usually not too alarmed, it would land within a hundred yards or so. Then we'd start out on foot to find it. Of course, we flushed a lot of mud-colored hens along the way, but they were illegal to shoot. Gus soon became impatient with this style of hunting. He wanted to set out by himself on foot. Bob protested that Gus might not be able to find his way back to the ranch because he wasn't familiar with the territory. In his broken English with a heavy guttural accent, Gus assured Bob that he could find his way back. My father-in-law was nearing sixty years of age, but he was a powerful man, standing over six feet tall. His long legs covered a lot of ground. He could outwalk any of the younger people.

"We hunted until about 11:00 o'clock, then returned to the house for lunch. Gus wasn't back yet. After we ate, we started talking about going to look for Gus. About that time, we heard a loud knock on the door, and a familiar booming voice demanded entry. Bob opened the door, and there stood Gus, little the worse for wear,

With the use of the company camper, the author and John hunt in Mexico.

grinning from ear to ear. He was proud and beaming. He had his limit, five fat pheasants hanging from his belt—all hens. Gus was hard of hearing, so everyone in the room shouted at once, 'Where did you get all of those hens?' 'Vat hens?' came his reply. 'Dese are just young cocks.' No one said another word about it. Although he wasn't actually anticipating a visit by the game warden, Bob had the cook clean the birds immediately, and the next night, we had 'young cocks' for dinner.

"Both the deer and pheasant hunts were unqualified success stories," Nan summed up, "Everyone returned to Los Angeles with their limits of deer and birds."

•••

• FRANK PACHMAYR •

Apparently, Gus had more than his share of hunting misadventures. In the early days, Los Angeles was a center for gambling, bootlegging, and prostitution, and a pretty tough crowd used to visit with Gus. He found they were people he could understand and enjoy. After all, Gus was a pretty hard case himself. To balance out the seamy clientele, Gus also worked for such men as auto-magnate Walter Chrysler, Fairbanks Morse, of scale fame, James Langford Stack—father of actor Bob Stack and a successful money magnate.

Among Gus's particular friends was wrestling promoter Hugh Nickols. Nickols held the title of light-heavyweight wrestling champion of the world for fifteen years. He was still as tough as a two-dollar steak with bulging muscles that knotted up as hard as steel when tensed. Even wrestling fans didn't realize how hard these men really were. Even if you believe that wrestling matches are staged and largely pretense, you have to admit these men absorb a terrible amount of punishment in an ordinary match.

After his wrestling career was over, Hugh Nickols became a wrestling promoter at the Hollywood Legion Stadium. He had enough money to have Gus create a custom drilling—a combination gun with two shotgun barrels on top and a rifle barrel nested in the crotch below that shared a common breech and single trigger. These handmade guns were a specialty with Gus, and his idea of heaven was to be allowed to go on making them forever. During the year that it took for Gus to painstakingly carve the gun out of raw steel and wood—lock, stock and barrel—he and Hugh had many an argument over gauge and caliber, stock shape, and carving design. To an outsider, it might appear that the giants would come to blows at any moment, but they were evenly matched in strength and temperament. It was rather like two grizzly bears sparring. Neither one wanted to throw the first punch. Gus always prevailed in these spats. Finally the drilling was finished—and a work of art it was—and Hugh was delighted. The two men became good friends and hunting companions.

Of course, Hugh's wrestling cronies became Gus's friends also. They sported such colorful names as Yukon Jake and Gorgeous George. One horrendous hulk was whimsically called The Angel because he was so incredibly ugly. Once, when Gus was hunting with a group of wrestlers, one of the party shot an illegal doe and hung it out in the trees for camp meat. Everyone knew that Gus never knowingly broke the law, so they just neglected to mention it to him. The next morning when Gus asked what they were cooking over the camp fire, they told him it was lamb stew. When it came time to go hunting, no one wanted to stay behind to feed the fire and stir the stew, so Gus volunteered. As luck would have it, while Gus was tending the stew, a game warden came by checking hunting licenses. Gus told him there was lamb stew on the fire, and he was welcome to sample it. The warden only had to taste the stew to know that it wasn't lamb. A cursory search revealed the doe carcass. He immediately arrested poor innocent Gus and hauled him off to jail. When the wrestlers returned to camp that evening, they found Gus gone. Hugh made an astute guess about what happened and went to the local sheriff's office. Sure enough, the sheriff told Hugh that Gus

Pachmayr was at that very moment occupying a cell. Nickols in truth feared no man, yet he had a healthy respect for Gus, especially when the old man's dander was up. Hugh told the sheriff, "Look, I'll pay the old man's fine, but don't let him out until tomorrow morning, and if you don't mind, I'll take his gun back for him. I'll leave enough money with you for his bus fare home. As for the rest of us, we're leaving right now." After a few days, Hugh phoned Gus to make sure he was all right. Gus let loose a stream of invectives that scorched Hugh's ears, and he waited another month before venturing back to the gun shop of Gus Pachmayr.

•••

Gus hunted often with Frank at the deer club in Colorado. During one hunt there, Gus came down with a cold, so he stayed in camp one day by himself. When everyone came back that evening empty-handed, they found Gus contentedly puffing his stubby cigar, while a fine buck hung in the shade of a tree, cooling out. Gus shot his deer within fifty yards of the cabin.

During another season, Gus was riding in a Jeep with his son, John, while his grandson, Dick Mellen drove. As Dick tells the story, "We were driving along and spotted a pretty good buck. Gus didn't want it. He was waiting for something bigger, so John got out of the Jeep and shot the deer. I walked down the hill with John where the deer had fallen. When we got there, I could see that my uncle was getting a little green around the gills. He told me he couldn't gut out a deer without losing his lunch. He wanted me to gut it for him.

I said, 'What about Grandpa?' My uncle was more scared of his father than anything else. 'If he finds out you can't gut a deer, he'll give you holy hell.'

John said, 'Tell him that I went down the hill after another deer.' I said, 'I hope it works.' Grandpa was already halfway down the hill toward us. My uncle all but ran to the bottom and hid in the trees.

"I started gutting out the deer. Lord knows I had plenty of practice since we started up the deer club. Grandpa came up to me and watched for a minute. 'Vere's Chonny?' he demanded. 'He went down the hill after another deer,' I said without looking up. I was afraid the old man would guess that I was lying if he saw my face."

For several minutes, Gus stood rooted like a scraggly old oak, his head rotating slowly as his eyes methodically scanned the area like a radar beacon. Dick deliberately pretended not to notice and busied himself with gutting the dead deer. Finally, Gus raised his rifle and peered through the scope, scrutinizing every shadowy nook and cranny of the canyon. Finally the old man spoke again, "Iss dere a deer down dere?" he said in a tone that obviously implied considerable doubt. Dick decided to hedge his bets. "Johnny said he saw one down there," he replied. Gus was poised like an eagle prepared to launch. Dick knew that once Gus decided to search for John, he would pursue the hunt relentlessly, until he discovered his eldest son down the hill where he had taken refuge behind a tall fir tree.

Dick moved to intercept Gus. "Grandpa, can you help me get this buck back up to the Jeep?" Dick knew that Gus couldn't resist a challenge. "I can carry that jackrabbit up on my shoulders," Gus declared contemptuously. "No gramps, you'll get all bloody. Just grab a horn, and we can drag it back." By the time they arrived at the Jeep, about eighty yards up the hill, John was at their side. He had been watching their progress through binoculars and decided that it was safe to return. The old man glowered as John made lame excuses for not gutting his own deer. Dick deliberately picked a path for the Jeep that made it necessary for everyone to just hang on and effectively diverted Gus's attention from John. By the time they reached camp, Gus had all but forgotten the incident.

Dick and his grandfather remained fast friends for all of Gus's life. When Dick was a boy, Gus often took him hunting in Frazier Park and the Angeles Crest areas near Los Angeles. "The Old Man always knew just where to find the birds," says Dick, "be they pigeons, doves, quail, chukar, or pheasants. He could tell where they would be at any given time of day. He knew what they would be doing and where they were doing it. He taught me how to use the 12-gauge, double-barreled shotgun, which he loaned to me."

● ● ●

John and Frank Pachmayr naturally adopted many of their father's friends. Both were avid sports fans, and Johnny was a regular at the local wrestling matches. He often went hunting with his wrestling buddies. On one occasion, he and Hugh Nichols and four other wrestlers were returning from a pheasant hunt near Bishop, California. As they entered Tejon Pass, just north of Los Angeles, they were trapped behind a busload of college football players, who were returning victorious from a game. The narrow, curving road through the mountains was appropriately nicknamed the "grapevine," by hapless truck drivers who had to traverse it on a regular basis. More than one eighteen-wheeler went over the side of that tortuous highway. Hugh was driving his new Chrysler Airflow, an aerodynamically designed car ahead of its time, and it led the way in reducing air resistance in cars, as well as having power and maneuverability. Hugh impatiently honked his horn at the bus as it was laboring up a steep grade. The driver refused to pull over. At the first opportunity, Hugh passed. As the car pulled alongside the bus, the college ball players leaned out the open windows, jeering at the occupants of the car and motioning for Hugh to pull over, little knowing that they were courting disaster.

Hugh was not one to let a challenge go unanswered. He pulled over in front of the bus. The bus stopped and the ball players, flushed with their recent victory came boiling out, spoiling for a fight. They certainly got what they came for. Hugh and his four rugged companions proceeded to thrash the entire complement of ball players, estimated to number more than fifty. After the wrestlers finished with them, many of these stalwart youths required medical attention. John didn't like ten-to-one odds, so he remained firmly rooted in the rear seat of the Chrysler throughout the free-for-all.

These wrestlers were always full of mischief, and they had a tendency to play rough. Just receiving a friendly pat from one of these bruisers was rather like getting cuffed by a grizzly bear. One time, Hugh Nickols and another wrestler named Larue went pheasant hunting with Frank, John, Gus, and a friend named Howard Vermilion. Howard was an excellent shot, and he never let anyone forget it. He was forever engaged in a game of one-upmanship. On this trip, he made it a point to always shoot more birds than Hugh Nickols and then gloat loud and long about it. He should have chosen his victim with a little more discretion. By the end of the second day, Hugh had it. He pulled Frank aside, and growled, "I'm going to fix that S.O.B."

Knowing full well that once his mind was made up and knowing that Hugh Nickols was about as easy to stop as a freight train, Frank just stepped back to watch the entertainment. That evening, everyone had a few drinks to wind down from a long day in the field. When he could see that Vermilion was getting pretty mellow, Nickols grabbed him by the seat of the pants and the scruff of the neck and chucked him head-first into a sleeping bag. Then zipping up the bag, he grabbed it at the head and spun it around the room like a centrifuge until he was satisfied that the occupant was thoroughly dizzy. Then he dropped him with a thud. Vermilion couldn't walk a straight line the rest of the evening, and the next day, according to Frank, "He couldn't hit a barn with a baseball bat." Vermilion was refreshingly quiet that night.

On another hunt, Nickols hid Gus's rifle in the woods. Gus turned the cabin upside down searching for it to no avail. Finally, when everyone was ready to go hunting, Hugh gave the gun back to Gus. The old man was so mad that he stomped out declaring, "I'm going home." Frank used some gentle persuasion to talk his dad out of walking the 500 miles back to Los Angeles.

Sometimes it seemed as if John Pachmayr had only bad luck. Why else would a guy almost drown in his own bed? In early January 1960 Art Durando and Bill Jay, Frank Pachmayr's partner in the guided tour company, Sportsman Holidays, organized a bird shoot down in Navajoa, Mexico. Frank and Nanitta were along, and also John Pachmayr. The party of hunters enjoyed outstanding hunting of such large ducks as canvasbacks and redheads.

On the night of 11 January, John, Art and some of the other hunters, "tied one on," in one of the Navajoa cantinas. Fun-loving John might have sampled a little more tequila than the others. Perhaps that's why he didn't respond when the flood alarm was sounded at about 4:00 A.M. The area was hit by torrential rains early that morning. Engineers at the Mayo River Dam above Navajoa were elated. They wanted a full reservoir for the upcoming dry spell, but they overplayed their hand. About 3:00 A.M., water began spilling over the top of the dam. The engineers were forced to open the sluice gates to relieve pressure on the dam and reduce erosion that could undermine the huge concrete structure, but first, they had to alert all the people downriver that they were about to be flooded out.

The manager of the El Rancho Motel received a phone call that sent him pounding on doors to rouse the *Norte Americanos* who monopolized his motel during the four-month bird-hunting season from October through February. Art Durando woke up members of the Pachmayr party. When he got to John, he opened the door and yelled, "John we have to clear out of here in 15 minutes. There's going to be a flood." John gave a halfhearted grunt, that Art accepted as acknowledging his warning. Art ran to Frank's room, where all of the shotgun shells were kept. If they got wet, it could ruin everybody's trip. He herded most of the group of hunters to the Del Rio Motel in Navajoa, that he knew was on higher ground. Frank was concerned for Nanitta. He opted for a move even higher, up to Alamosa, a quaint foothill village.

In the confusion that ensued, no one noticed that John wasn't among them. Art thought he had gone with Frank, and Frank assumed that his brother was with Art. Both were wrong. John was still fast asleep on his bed at the motel. John was dreaming about sailing, when the fact that his bed was actually afloat finally forced itself upon him. He awoke with a start and leaped out of bed—into water up to his waist. After the initial panic, he gathered his sodden gear and flagged down a passing boat that was ferrying hapless inhabitants to higher ground.

Several small villages had been washed away, and the people escaped with little more than the clothes on their backs. The American hunters took up a collection to aid the displaced persons and donated all the game they shot for food. Art Durando's group, which now included John, found excellent hunting about twenty miles south of Navajoa, and Frank was equally happy in the area he had chosen.

Ducks are thought to be creatures of the water. When it's raining "cats and dogs," as we like to say, "it's good weather for ducks." The ducks of Navajoa, however, thought it was too much of a good thing. They migrated to dryer climates farther south, and the quail moved up into the foothills, which is where Frank Pachmayr was waiting. There were swarms of white wing and mourning doves and towering flocks of wild blue pigeons remaining near Navajoa, nonetheless. Just a couple of hours south by car was Los Mochis, a traditional hangout for squadrons of huge, sweet-eating black brant geese and a haven for refugee ducks from the Navajoa flood.

Ed Seagram, heir to the Seagram whisky empire in Canada, was scheduled to join Frank Pachmayr and Art Durando in Navajoa. Seagram flew into Obregon just north of Navajoa, but the one road into Navajoa from the north was rendered impassable by two severe washouts. The railroad trestle that could have offered an alternate route around the blocked road was still standing, but it was weakened by the flood waters to the point where no trains were running. Demonstrating extraordinary resourcefulness, Seagram rented an ambulance, loaded his guns and dogs into it, and drove across the railroad trestle to join up with the hunting party.

Navajoa was a favorite bird-hunting area for Frank Pachmayr. He was always taking friends and business associates down in his Twin Beech to hunt the largely unexploited area. Navajoa is located about 900 miles south of Los Angeles, halfway between Sonora and Los Mochis in the narrow valley between the Gulf of California across from the Baja peninsula and the narrow spine of the Sierra Madre mountains. This is the southern end of the migratory birds' Pacific Flyway. The area is replete with brackish coastal ponds and swampy lagoons, backed inland by rich fields of rice, sugar cane, milo, and wheat, plus a generous sprinkling of fresh water ponds. In the winter, these attract bluebills, spoonbills, sprigs, teal, red-

A photo of John Pachmayr when he bagged the limit in Navajoa. Note his young face. The Pachmayrs hunted in Mexico for many years.

heads, and widgeon in prodigious numbers. The abundance of feed also attracts massive flights of whitewing doves and wild blue pigeons, known as *palomas zuelas* to the natives.

The one fly in the ointment was a Mexican government restriction dictating that only four guns and 100 rounds of ammunition for each were allowed to cross the border from the United States. With the abundance of game available in the area, 400 rounds constituted a grossly inadequate supply. The result was a constant struggle to sneak extra ammo into Mexico. On one occasion, John Pachmayr was ferrying shells into Mexico by car. Crossing the border at Nogales, he proceeded sixty miles south to the checking station. The Mexican officers found the hidden shells and turned John around. Another member of the hunting party was also caught and sent back to the United States to off-load some ammo. They were obliged to leave the excess ammo with a Pachmayr dealer in Nogales.

One season Frank became ill and had to fly back to Los Angeles to recuperate. In a about a week he flew back to Mexico, landing in Hermosio. The Mexican authorities inspected the Twin Beech and found no ammunition. "Where is your ammunition? We must count it," said the Mexican customs agent. Frank explained that he had been down before and had left his ammunition behind when he returned to the States, but they weren't buying it. "Show me some shells by tomorrow morning," said the customs officer, "or I'll tear this plane apart." This was a troublesome threat to Frank. He had hidden eight cases of 12-gauge shells in the nose cone of the plane, and the Mexican authorities were empowered to seize the plane if contraband were found aboard.

Art Durando was waiting in Navajoa for Frank to arrive. He began to worry when the plane didn't show up by dark. Finally, he received a long distance call from Frank, who laid out the problem, then added, "Call Al Hoffer or John Hoffer at the San Oberto Hotel and see if they can't exert a little influence here." Art was able to reach John Hoffer and explain Frank's dilemma. Hoffer interceded, and the next morning, Frank was waved on his way.

The noted shooting and hunting author, the late Jimmy Robinson, was a close friend of Frank Pachmayr, and a frequent guest of his in Navajoa. Beginning in 1926 as trap and skeet editor, Robinson wrote about shotgun hunting and competition for *Sports Afield* magazine for half a century, until he died on 18 June 1986. Accepted at the time as "dean" of sports writers, Robinson reported in the 25 February 1972 issue of *Outdoor News*, "Clara and I are back from ten days in Mexico, where we hunted out of Navajoa with sporting-goods dealer Frank Pachmayr, his wife Nanitta, and Jim Brazina, outdoor editor of the *Los Angeles Times*. There is excellent whitewing dove and duck hunting from Navajoa to Mazatlan (950 miles on good road south of Los Angeles). I am not exaggerating when I say we saw a hundred thousand or more whitewings in one field, and some farmers beg you to shoot them. The limit is twenty-five a day, fifteen whitewings and ten doves. You can take ten ducks a day, except on Saturday and Sunday when the limit is twenty ducks." Jimmy hunted quail with Frank and John just sixty-five miles south of the border. He later swore that they flushed more than sixty large coveys each day. He commented, "It was the best wing shooting I have ever experienced."

Frank Pachmayr and Nanitta were often guests of Jimmy Robinson at the Sports Afield Lodge, St. Ambroise on the Delta Marsh, in Manitoba, Canada, where Jimmy entertained the royalty of Europe and Hollywood. Among his guest duck hunters were Clark Gable, Robert Taylor, Gary Cooper, and Ernest Hemingway. A number of Hollywood celebrities were customers of Pachmayr's Gun Works and often hunted in Mexico with Frank.

•••

An almost constant hunting companion to Frank, especially in Mexico, was Art Durando. Art became the unofficial organizer of south-of-the-border trips, setting up the required permits for guns and ammo and hunting licenses. Art still performs that service to dozens of American hunters who visit Mexico each year. He is one of the finest shotgunners in the world today. In his youth, he was all but unbeatable, but he was still able to learn from an old master, like Frank Pachmayr.

During the first few trips to Mexico, Frank couldn't help noticing that Art would jump the gun, taking targets well before they were in range of less skilled shooters. Often hunters in neighboring blinds couldn't get a shot because the birds were too distant. Frank decided to correct this. He took Art with him into a duck blind one morning, and said, "I want to teach you how to hunt ducks." Art thought he already knew, but Frank was the boss. Frank set out three dozen decoys on the water and settled back for some fancy calling. When a flock flew by, Frank started to call. Sure enough, part of the flock peeled off and circled his decoys. Then Frank coaxed them in with a gabbling sound that said, "come on in, the water's fine and the chow's good." Art was too impatient for this studied routine, he stood up to shoot as soon as the ducks circled into range, but Frank pulled him forcefully back down by the coattail. "Wait until they settle into the decoys." he whispered. So Art waited as the birds circled several times, then set a glide path for the decoys. As the drakes lowered their landing gear, they seemed to hang in the air almost motionless. "Now." hissed Frank. They stood up together and both scored doubles, with the dead birds almost landing in the blind. Durando began to appreciate the skill and artistry of this style of hunting. Besides, he didn't have to wade across a swamp to pick up the dead birds. Frank and Art were hunting companions many times after that, and Art always remembered this lesson he learned from Frank.

•••

Frank preferred to hunt with a retriever at his side whenever possible. Early in 1960, wealthy oil magnate Ed Crowley, a close friend of Frank's, gave him a long-eared puppy. It was part of an experimental litter resulting from the cross of a black Labrador retriever and a golden retriever. The lab's genes were dominant, resulting in an all-black dog. Frank named his new pup "Davey," and trained him himself. As Davey grew to maturity, he proved to be the smartest dog Frank ever had. He seeming to know instinctively what Frank wanted him to do. Davey adored his master, and Frank returned that affection in kind. It tickled Frank to watch Davey show up his friend's expensive purebred dogs.

"While one of their dogs was out retrieving one duck," beams Frank with pride, "Davey would retrieve two or three. He kind of stacked them in his mouth.

He was a hell of a quail dog, too. Once I wounded a quail, and Davey took off after it. He was gone about fifteen minutes, and I was beginning to worry. He'd never been gone that long before. Then he came trotting up proud as could be with the live bird in his mouth. Once he brought in a wounded duck. When he dropped the bird at my feet, it took off half flying, half running into the bulrushes. Davey was off like a shot and caught it. This time I tried to catch the bird as he let go, but somehow it got away again. Davey caught it in about three hops this time, and he brought it back and slammed it against the ground, as if to say, 'Stay there.'"

Frank doted on Davey. In his executive Twin Beech plane, the rear or lounge section was equipped with plush leather upholstered seats. Just behind them, in a space that was too small for a full-sized seat, there was a jump seat. Frank threw a pillow on this and assigned it to Davey. The dog would sit upright on the seat and look with great interest out the window during the flight.

Dick Mellen made many of those flights with Frank and Davey, and bears witness to the fact that Frank held Davey's interests paramount. "Frank was always feeding Davey snacks," recalls Dick. "I'd buy beef jerky to eat on the hunt and Frank would feed it Davey. The first time we took Davey down to Navajoa, he wasn't used to cactus. He ran pell-mell through cactus patches, and ended up with his chest, nose, lips, and ears full of cholla. We spent hours pulling cactus quills out of him. Cholla has barbed tips, and some of the ends stayed under his skin. We rubbed him with a soothing lotion, and that was the end of Davey for that trip." It was two years before Frank decided to take Davey back to Mexico. Remembering the hours spent pulling cholla from the dog, Dick objected to the idea, but Frank insisted. "Hell, he'll be all right," said Frank to Dick's protests. "He learned his lesson the last time." It was true. Davey never again picked up any cactus quills. He had learned to skirt cholla patches while retrieving ducks.

"I've seen Davey bring in a hundred or more ducks in a single day all by himself." declares Frank.

"Yeah," adds Dick, "he'd retrieve everyone's ducks, all right, but he'd take them all to Frank. I could be in a blind right next to Frank, and Davey would go out to get one of my ducks. Coming back, he'd run right by me and drop the duck at Frank's feet. I have to admit, though, that Davey was pretty selective. If I shot a small duck, like a teal, say, he'd bring it to me, but if I shot a big fat prime sprig, Davey took it straight to Frank. If somebody missed a bird, Davey would look up at the sky, then turn to the shooter with a look of sheer disgust on his face."

"Many times, Davey would bring back two ducks at once." recounts Frank. "If one bird was dead in the water, and the other was still paddling away, Davey would take out after the live one first. Then he'd come back and push the dead duck into his mouth on top of the first bird."

Once Frank shot a double on mallards, and the first bird dropped right in front of the blind. The other one fell in the tules behind him. "We had a box of rocks inside the blind," he recalls, "to throw out in the water to show the dogs which direction the bird was. I threw one toward the tules to give Davey the direction. He headed out, but stopped at the edge of tules and looked back at me, as if to say, 'What now?' I motioned for him to keep going. He disappeared into the reeds, and was gone about ten minutes. I was beginning to get a little concerned, when he came trotting back, proud as a peacock with the duck in his mouth."

Davey lived a dozen years and was Frank's hunting companion for every one of them. Frank deeply mourned the passing of his beloved four-legged friend. He

Although Frank enjoyed hunting ducks, geese, and doves more than he did hunting deer or other big game, he was nonetheless an excellent marksman with a rifle.

felt there was something missing for a long time after that. Denied the services of his retriever, Frank was obliged to gather in his own dead ducks. Art Durando described one of Frank's subsequent hunts. "Frank and I were shooting over this small pond. It was getting kind of late and both of us had about shot our limits, so I was gathering in my decoys when I see half a dozen dead ducks swimming across the pond. I was thinking maybe I should change my brand of whisky when I see this baseball cap floating along in front of the ducks. Then I see Frank's head under the cap, barely above water."

Hearing this tale, Frank hastened to explain. "I thought the water was shallow enough to wade across. I started out to gather up my kills. Pretty soon the water was over the top of my hip boots. My boots were already filled with water, so I thought I might as well go all the way and be done with it."

•••

Frank Pachmayr could never have hunted so often or so widely after he sold his planes. He could and did on occasion drive to Navajoa, staying on the road for almost twenty hours without stopping. The same trip by plane required less than four hours. In late October 1958 Frank, his father Gus, Joe Chastek, Bill Jay, and newspaper columnist Jack Curnow set out from Los Angeles in Frank's Twin Beech with Chuck Fisher as pilot. The destination was Idaho Falls. They were to meet another trio of hunters, Earl Sheib, Jim Hamm, and Earl Shade. It was not to be. They cleared the Rocky Mountains and were just passing over Las Vegas when the Twin Beech suddenly became a single engine aircraft. The right engine blew up like a bomb. Frank was nonplused. He just had the plane completely overhauled. Obviously somebody goofed.

Fisher made an emergency landing on one engine at McCarran Airport in Las Vegas without any casualties. Frank was unruffled by the harrowing experience, and he wasn't about to let a little thing like a broken airplane deter him from his hunting plans. He rented a car at the airport and resumed his trip at ground level. Frank, Gus, Joe Chastek, and Jack Curnow continued on. Chuck Fisher and Bill Jay stayed behind to arrange repairs on the crippled plane. Then they returned to Los Angeles to pick up Frank's other Twin Beech, which they flew to Idaho to rejoin the hunting party.

Frank maintains a fatalistic view of flying. "I know a lot of guys who were killed flying to or from a hunting trip. No one really knows when his number's coming up, but you can't worry about it all of the time. In the summer of 1957, Red Higgins, a friend of mine, invited me to come up to his ranch for some fishing. Red's Horse Ranch is located northeast of Baker, Oregon in the Wallowa Mountains, near the Minam River. Earl Shade was flying me back from a business trip to Portland. I told him to fly over Red's Horse Ranch, to get a look at his landing strip, and Earl made a practice pass over the strip without actually landing.

"He told me, 'It's damn short for a heavy plane like this Twin Beech, but I guess we could make it all right.' So I called Red and told him we'd come on up. Since we only figured to stay a few days, Earl decided he'd just hang out with us at the ranch. He wanted to bring his wife, Shirlee, and I said okay. We met Earl at the Santa Monica Airport about 10:00 A.M., and flew to Bishop to pick up some friends, Al and Eleanor Morris. From there, we flew to Baker, Oregon, to refuel. Since Earl was a little antsy about Red's landing strip, we decided to leave the girls in Baker and make that first landing at Red's place without them.

"Earl had to make a steep approach, but he set the plane down smooth and light. Earl hit the wheel brakes immediately, but we still rolled all the way to the end of the strip by the time he got the plane stopped. He was more worried about the takeoff than he was about landing, because the strip was rimmed with tall pines, and he had a pretty steep climb just to clear a ridge. It didn't make us feel any better to see three wrecked planes plastered against the hillside. Red had to admit that they crashed trying to take off from his strip. He had neglected to mention that to me over the phone. Red was full of explanations. The pilots were not skilled enough. Their engines weren't in good shape. Wind conditions were wrong when they took off, and so forth. It also came out that only one twin-engine plane had ever landed there before, and it took a week before the pilot could get up enough nerve to take off again. Before he left, he pumped out as much gas as he dared, in order to lighten the plane for takeoff. Anyway, we off-loaded all our gear, making the Twin Beech a lot lighter for the trip back to Baker to get the girls."

Nanitta picked up the story from there. "Earl looked a little drawn when he landed at Baker, but we force fed him a Coke and a hot dog, and he was ready to take off again. Since Earl was alone, I got to sit in the copilot's seat with my 16mm motion picture camera. I wanted to get a shot of the ranch from the air before we landed, but I wasn't quick enough. It all happened too fast. Suddenly I caught sight of an opening in the seemingly endless carpet of green trees, then a river, and then we were coming in for a perfect landing. The landing strip was surrounded by fields of wild yellow buttercups in full bloom. I was kicking myself because I didn't record the beautiful sight on film. The men were all standing at the end of the runway by the time the plane stopped rolling. They had heard us coming."

After several days of marvelous fishing and eating succulent trout, the Pachmayrs and their guests faced the prospect of taking off with a fully loaded plane from a minuscule landing strip. Happily there was a smart breeze blowing down the valley to give them some added lift. Anyway, Earl decided to chance it. "It was a tight fit," recalls Frank, "but we made it okay. The real kicker came some weeks later when Earl was talking to some other pilots in San Francisco. They knew about Red's Horse Ranch, all right. It was famous. Or perhaps I should say infamous among pilots who flew the Northwest area. One pilot told Earl, 'Sure, lots of guys land at Red's place, but most of them can't take off again.' We didn't go back there again."

Nanitta told me of one more flying adventure that she recalled quite vividly. "We were flying south in the Twin Beech and had just passed over San Francisco. I remember it was a beautiful night with a full moon shining on the water of the bay. We were about 3,000 feet up, and I could see the crisscross pattern of the city lights as we passed over. It was clear and crisp with no sign of fog. All of a sudden, I saw the running lights of a plane right next to us, flying almost wing tip to wing tip. I could see that it was a swept-wing military jet. I could even make out the pilot and navigator looking over at us. I yelled at Earl Shade, the pilot, 'Don't move. Don't change your flight path. There's a big jet right by us.' About that time, Earl got a radio contact from Edwards Air Force Base. We were over restricted airspace. Earl tried to cut the corner and he cut it a little too close. They told him to veer off by so many degrees, and he just said, 'Yes sir.' As soon as he answered, the military jet disappeared, just like that."

Certainly Frank Pachmayr has had more hunting experience than ten average sportsmen. Advancing years now limit his visits to the uplands, but he continues his efforts to support and maintain the game birds he loves to hunt.

•••

· Chapter XI ·

PACHMAYRS OF THE PAST

Every man is a product of his heredity and environment. Frank Pachmayr's legacy can be traced from his father, August M. Pachmayr, to generations of Germans from the fractured principalities of the mid-sixteenth century through the domination and unification of Frederick William I. The individual and collective power of this inheritance was all embodied in the towering stature and physical prowess of August Pachmayr.

The Teutonic roots of the Pachmayr family can be easily traced back over three centuries, and then the trail becomes spotty. Court documents found in the main state archives in Munich disclose scattered mentions of the Pachmayr family dating back to 20 January 1381, when a Wernher Pachmayr was a notary. In 1420 Ulrich Pachmayr appeared as a witness in a contract dispute. In 1553 Hans Bachmayr, of Pornbach, made a barter deal with the Convent of Scheureni. (Early writings interchange the letters B and P, often resulting in different family spellings.)

In 1665 Wolfen Pachmayr is shown to own a farm in Heissmanning. Wolfen's mother Margaretha died on 24 October 1661, at a hundred years of age. Beginning on 26 November 1663, there is a clear genealogical trail of the Pachmayr family in Germany with the marriage of Johann Pachmayr, son of Vitus and Margarethe Pachmayr, innkeepers in Reichertshausen, to Maria Magdalena Winther, daughter of innkeeper Philipp Winther of Hohenkammer.

In the early seventeenth century, the Pachmayr family established themselves as postmasters in the Hohenkammer-Pfaffenhoffen area and handed that distinction down through one generation after another until 1 March 1808, when the Kingdom of Bavaria usurped all postal services for itself. From then on the office was assigned only to members of the nobility. Denied the postmaster's position, the Pachmayrs became gamekeepers and forest supervisors, again in virtual perpetuity.

Many Pachmayrs entered government service, including H. Josef Bachmayr, mentioned in the 1912 *Court-State Handbook of the Kingdom of Bavaria* (p. 87) as the Royal Road and Bridge Inspector. He was given direct supervision of bridge and road construction for the nine districts of the Kingdom of the Upper-Danube District.

In the middle of the nineteenth century, the Pachmayrs once again began receiving commissions in the postal department. Many members also distinguished themselves in the military service and attained the rank of officer. The family name of Pachmayr was also known in the popular vernacular of the seventeenth century as "Tafelmayer." The family name of Anton was also intermingled with the Pachmayrs. Members of these families distinguished themselves as doctors, entrepreneurs, and beer brewers.

Johann Ludwig Bachmayr, son of the Prince-Electoral Finance Office Surveyor, Josef Bachmayr, entered the priesthood on 15 August 1827, and later edited a book, *The Seven Holy Sacraments of the Catholic Church*. Portraits painted in 1847 of First Lieutenant Wilhelm Pachmayr and his daughter Marie hang in the Regensburg Museum. The *Bavarian Courier* of 1848 mentioned that a Doctor John Pachmayr was practicing in Geltendorf, County Court Bruck. In 1843 Max Pachmayr became Postmaster of Pornbach, contracting to keep a minimum of eighteen fit horses and two stage coaches with lanterns. A photograph still exists, showing Max with a group of other members of the Marksmen's Association, demonstrating that an interest in firearms existed early in the family history.

Karl Pachmayr, born 6 April 1890, became a Vice-Corporal of the 4th Company, 16th Bavarian Infantry Regiment. On 14 October 1916 he led a small command in an assault up a steep hill at Ormului Heights, driving firmly entrenched Russian troops from the hill and capturing about thirty prisoners. With his small command, he held the hill against counterattack until reinforcements arrived. Karl Pachmayr was promoted to lieutenant and saw numerous battles until he was mortally wounded in the battle of Flanders and died 4 October 1917.

Ferdinand Pachmayr, Frank's grandfather, was born about 1820. He was at various times a stage line operator, an innkeeper, a hops grower for the flourishing beer industry of Germany, and finally a gamekeeper and supervisor of forest use for the community of Pfaffenhofen in Bavaria. Ferdinand married three times, leaving many children. Among the children of his third and last marriage was August Martin, born in Pfaffenhofen on 29 December 1870. August proved to be a bright youngster and loved to accompany his father on hunting trips in the neighboring woods. As older fathers are often wont to do, Ferdinand doted on his young son and taught him the ways of the woods at the early age of five years. In the field, young August kept the hunting dogs from getting lost, but his abiding interest centered around the guns used by hunters. So intense was this fascination that his father presented August with his first gun at the age of seven when the boy could barely raise it.

By the time he was nine, August was certain that he wanted to become a gunsmith. Pursuing the system of craftsmanship handed down over centuries of ancient Europe, Ferdinand apprenticed his son, then only thirteen, to an old master named Fisch. Apprentices in the Old World spent their early years as little more than servants and were delegated the most menial chores. Young August worked

· PACHMAYRS OF THE PAST ·

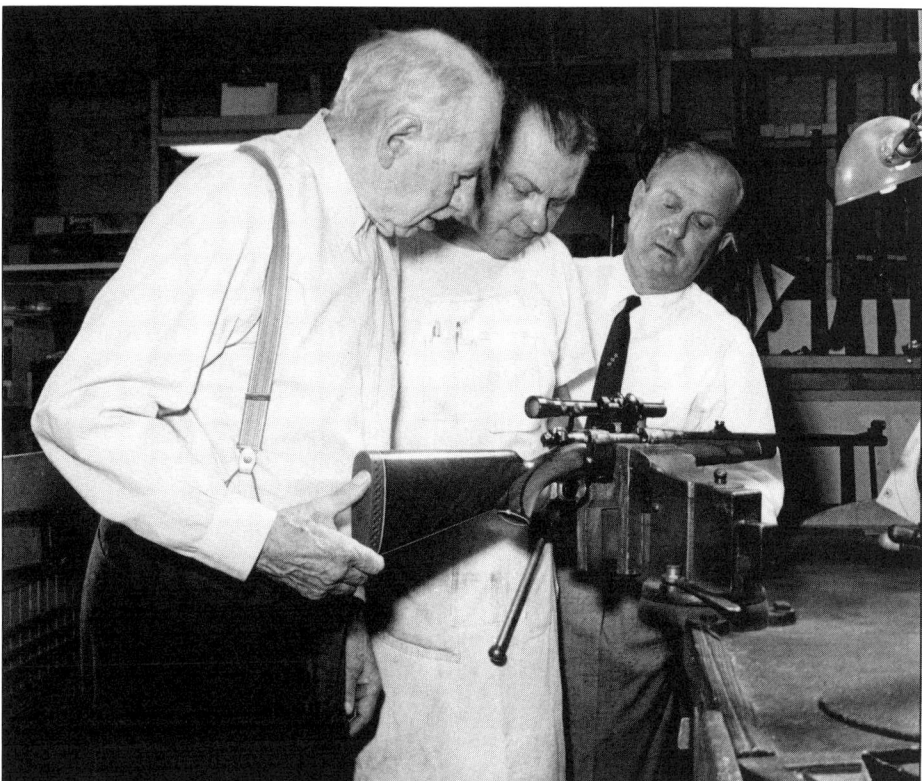

August, "Gus" Pachmayr, taught his sons, John and Frank, the intricacies of gunsmithing from an early age. After Frank and John struck out for themselves, Gus continued to advise and consult with his two brilliant students.

twelve to fourteen hours a day, seven days a week at the whim of his master. He soon tired of the unending job of cleaning up after the old gun builder, but he kept his eyes and ears open and learned. The experience left its mark. When August finally opened his own gun shop, he delegated cleanup chores to others. If no one was around to clean up after him, the shop simply remained dirty.

For four years, August's father paid the equivalent of a hundred dollars a month for his son's servitude. At the time and in that place, this amounted to a small fortune. During his fifth and sixth apprentice years, August worked full time without any pay except his room and board. It was then considered he had learned enough to be worth as much as he cost.

Hard work seemed to agree with August. He grew taller than his father and taller than most of those around him. He grew as tall and thick in the trunk and limbs as one of the few primeval oaks that still stand in the mountain forests of Bavaria. August shared as well the self-assurance and confidence of the oaks. They grew slowly, unlike the Johnny-come-lately conifers that sprang to sudden maturity, looked outwardly strong, but were pithy inside. August could have been a direct descendant of Thor, the god of war. Had he been born a century and a half earlier, he could have become one of the elite Grenadier Guards of Frederich William I, second king of Prussia, all of whom were six feet or taller. August had large, heavy hands with long, thick fingers that were strong enough to carve game scenes in wood or steel, but with fine, intricate lines and detailed filigree. August also possessed a Germanic aptitude for mechanical design and fabrication.

Following his apprenticeship, August worked for Carl Stiegle and later for Ludwig Oberhammer in Munich. Both were well-known makers of drillings, three-barreled combination guns, usually fashioned with two side-by-side shotgun barrels on top, plus a rifle barrel nested on the bottom. August learned to cut by hand receivers and lock parts, such as hammers, triggers, sears, and springs from raw steel, using only saws and files. Milling machines, power lathes, and profilers were yet to be invented. He learned the ancient methods of heat treating to give strength and hardness to gun parts and long life to springs.

Almost five years more were spent in the employ of the famed firm of John Jacob Reeb of Bonn on the Rhine. It was here that the fledgling gunmaker built his first complete gun, his masterpiece—a double-barreled, outside hammer, 16-gauge shotgun—lock, stock, and barrel. This gun marked his becoming a master gunsmith. According to his own recollection, the year was about 1893. This selfsame gun came back to haunt August after more than five decades. While with Reeb, young August learned about the new Anson and Deeley hammerless actions, which he was to refine and utilize in later guns of his own. Even at this early point in his career, August displayed the precision and attention to detail that was to mark the guns he created for the rest of his life.

Shaping massive blocks of steel into receivers for drillings and shotguns by using little more than a battery of huge files allowed a gunmaker a lot of time for woolgathering. As all young men do, August had his daydreams. Most of them had to do with someday hunting buffalo in America, which he imagined as one huge prairie inhabited by cowboys and Indians and overrun with great hairy bison.

At the age of twenty-eight, with his apprenticeship and his internship finally at an end, gun craftsman August M. Pachmayr returned to the town of his birth and opened his own shop. For centuries, the families of Pachmayrs had been content to live and die within the borders of Bavaria. Surely young August would do the same.

A couple of years later, though, in search of a wider clientele, August moved his business to Munich. At last, he felt that he had found a permanent home. He had no idea that there was another destiny in store for him, one that would transport him halfway around the world from his beloved *heimat* (homeland). Over the next ten years, August achieved a considerable reputation as a superior gun craftsman. He built several outstanding guns for Germany's Kaiser Wilhelm himself, all by hand from butt plate to muzzle.

Business was brisk by the standards of the time and place. Guns were still laboriously crafted by hand and were expensive. Most of August's customers were far from wealthy, though. Usually, they could afford one or maybe two guns at best. This fact alone explains the popularity of drillings in Germany. Added to that was the nature of hunting in the forests, where feathered or furred game could be encountered at any given moment. Drillings, though, were intricate and costly to make. The average hunter and gun enthusiast was far more likely to have one shotgun and one rifle his whole lifetime. As August was to say later with a sly grin, "A man chose his gun as carefully as his vife. Ya, maybe more carefully."

Among his unique products were custom takedown rifles that were capable of accepting any number of different barrels. They came in various calibers for hunting everything from mice to moose.

Machine mass-produced firearms were still years away. A man wanting a gun had to contract with a local gunsmith for his lifelong weapon. Endless conferences were involved that dealt with gauge or caliber, barrel length and diameter, stock style and length of pull, type of sights, and other elements of design. Often, a year or more of waiting passed before the gun was finally completed.

Young gunsmith August was witness to, rather a participant in, the vast transition from black to smokeless powder. Many a customer came to him with a fine Damascus steel shotgun that had burst from the new ammunition. Early efforts at improved steels to withstand the higher pressures of smokeless powder in shotguns proved futile until the 1890s when the great German arms firm of Krupp finally introduced their revolutionary "Fluid Steel." August saw rifle velocities leap suddenly to levels that caused severe barrel leading with the lubricated lead bullets that had sufficed earlier. Gradually, jacketed bullets evolved.

The adoption of the 8mm Lebel bolt-action rifle by the French army introduced smokeless powder and jacketed small caliber bullets to the military. The Rifle Testing Commission in Spandau, Germany, developed the rimless 7.9mm Infantry Rifle 88, sometimes referred to as the Mauser Model 88, which was adopted by the German army. With the emergence of bolt-action rifles, a sonorous death knell began to ring for Old World gun craftsmen. Machines made relatively crude, but workable shoulder arms at a fraction of the cost. August recognized the inevitable. When an army officer obtained a Model 88 for his own use and brought it in for alterations to adapt for hunting, August shortened, lightened, and smoothed the relatively crude rifle, creating what may well have the been the first military rifle converted to sporting use.

Store manager Bill Harrison aids Gus in choosing a stock blank for his next rifle.

• PACHMAYRS OF THE PAST •

Always the leaders in optics, the Germans had sporting and military telescopic sights decades before they became popular in the States. August was fitting scope mounts to rifles as early as 1890. The Germans were also pioneers in the development of high-velocity varmint cartridges. The .22 Hornet burst like fireworks on the American scene and took woodchuck and squirrel hunters by storm about 1931. Based upon a souped up version of the old .22 Winchester Center Fire that used jacketed bullets, it was already common on the Continent decades earlier as the 5.6x52R. It was widely used in drillings and remains highly popular in Europe today. It was also a favorite for barrel inserts used in shotguns, a type of device that reached a high state of sophistication in Germany. They had elaborate mechanisms for zeroing the devices to coincide with existing sights and offered sportsmen there an alternative to the expensive three-barreled drilling.

August Pachmayr was no stick-in-the-mud. He was trained in the dogma of the old school of gunsmithing, but he recognized that survival depended upon adapting to modern ways. He saw that bottle-necked, high-velocity cartridges were the wave of the future. He began experimenting with a number of wildcat rounds, some of them years before the more widely publicized experiments of Charles Newton. One of August's developments was the .257, a rimmed round that became a favorite among German gunmakers for the third barrel on their drillings.

August loved his homeland. His roots were centuries deep there. The hofbrau beer gardens were there and were frequented by his friends. An expert marksman with shotgun or rifle, he could hunt in his beloved woods, participate in the weekly Schuetzen Matches, and go ice skating. August cut quite a figure in those days. At the frozen pond, he met his bride-to-be, Anna Brandhuber, who worked as a bookkeeper for her father Franz in Munich. Anna had been born on 29 June 1880 in Partenkirchen. Early in 1899 August and Anna were wed. First a son, John, was born in November 1900. Then a daughter, Anne, was born to the happy couple in September 1904, and Frank August Pachmayr was born in Munich in 1906.

By the turn of the century, it became apparent that the days of old-time German gunmakers were numbered. Many gave up the struggle to remain viable in a world suddenly flooded with machine-made sporting firearms. August felt that there was no room to expand in Munich. He became increasingly restless and searched for new worlds to conquer. He must have recalled his childhood dreams of hunting bison on the American plains with Indians on both flanks. Years later, when asked why he decided to emigrate to the United States, he replied with a mischievous grin, "I tink it vas dos buffalo."

Two half-brothers, Xavier and Otto Pachmayr, preceded August to the United States and settled in the sunny, sprawling, but still sparsely settled metropolis of Los Angeles, California. Otto owned a huge water storage tower and water works at 130th Street and Moneta, now Broadway, that serviced much of the metropolitan area. August hadn't seen either of his brothers since 1886, but they wrote about the wonderful financial opportunities in the New World. They also wrote about the sporting delights of duck shooting in nearby sloughs and reedy marshes, which were located where the downtown intersection of 9th Street and Figueroa bustles today.

With such inducements, it was only a matter of time. Finally, on 9 October 1907, the August Pachmayr family, complete with cherubic one-year-old baby Frank, boarded the transatlantic steamer, *Chemnitz*, and set sail for America. Arriving in Galveston, Texas, on 28 October, they boarded a train for California.

Otto helped August and his family locate a new home at 80th Street and Moneta, not too far from his own residence. For a time, August worked for Joe Singer, a veteran gunsmith of the Los Angeles area and one of the finest Schuetzen rifle shots on the West Coast. August was delighted to find that his favorite Sunday afternoon sport had preceded him and had an avid following in the New World. There was even a fine hofbrau nearby with beer by the stein and plenty of cooked red cabbage and *hausenpfeffer*. There was even a polka night with dancing to a spirited German brass band.

August was actually only one of a wave of German gunmakers of the old school that invaded the United States in the early 1900s. They brought with them a wealth of knowledge and expertise that was to shape our sporting arms industry in an entirely new direction. Such sterling smiths as Fred Adolph of Genoa, New York, and Adolph O. Neidner of Dowegiac, Michigan, made invaluable contributions. Neidner developed a number of wildcat cartridges and made many of the barrels used by Townsend Whelen, the noted rifleman and arms authority of the past. Hans Wundhammer of Los Angeles became famous for the "Wundhammer swell," a hump in the pistol grip of a rifle that fills the palm of the hand. He also developed the first sporters based upon GI Springfield rifle actions for Captain Edward C. Crossman, a famous rifle authority, and Stewart Edward White, noted novelist and African hunter. Both of these two were famous during the first half of the twentieth century. These Teutonic titans of gunmaking redefined shoulder arms for American sportsmen and instilled an appreciation for precision and beauty in rifles and shotguns. They influenced the swing to accurate falling block and bolt-action rifles, and they refined shotguns from clubby and clumsy to slender and responsive.

Gus Pachmayr was one of the Germanic pioneers who set new standards for American stock design, which has a more recent evolution than most shooters realize. Gus helped introduce the concepts of practical cheekpieces, pistol grips, and flat-butt plates to American shooters. United States gun manufacturers continued the tradition of the Pennsylvania rifle. This included excessive drop, thin combs, and sharply pointed half-moon butt plates long after the practical reasons for their existence had vanished with the long-barreled, light-recoiling Kentucky rifle. During the late 1800s and early 1900s, custom rifles were unknown in America. Factory repeaters seemed to fill our needs completely. Trendsetters of the day, such as Teddy Roosevelt and Zane Grey, were content to hunt anything on four legs with big-bore lever actions, such as the Winchester Model 86 or Model 95.

Even in the company of the leaders among established German gunmakers, August stood out from the crowd. In a photograph that appeared in a publication entitled *Western Field*, (date unknown) August, or Gus, as he became known in

America, was pictured with eight other California gunsmiths. Most were casually dressed, but not Gus. He was wearing a three-piece suit with a dark coat and pants and a contrasting vest, starched collar, black tie, and a Tyrolean hat, set at a rakish angle. He lacked only a pair of lederhosen to proclaim his Old Country origins. Gus learned English, of course, well enough to communicate intelligibly, but he never dropped his heavy German accent, which added emphasis to everything he said.

After two years, during which he became familiar with his new country, Gus opened his own gun shop on the second floor of his home on Moneta. Later, he set up shop in a loft over Lail's Auto Livery Ltd., an automobile rental agency, at 815 South Grand Avenue. Gus had already established his reputation as a maker of fine firearms and as a dedicated perfectionist in gun repair or alteration. He purchased a power lathe and constructed his own rifling machine, which was an intricate assembly of gears, pulleys, and levers that could cut any desired rate of twist. Gus could now bore, ream, rifle, and turn his own rifle or shotgun barrels. The

Gus making the presentation of a trophy to a match winner (unknown). Gus often contributed the winning trophy. Once he almost won his own trophy.

Gus Pachmayr deer hunting in the High Sierras in 1947.

walls of his new shop were lined with row-on-row of files of every imaginable size and cut. One huge milling file measured four inches wide by three feet long.

To Gus, this was the height of modern utility. He could still remember when he had to shape and taper his rifle barrels with only a set of over forty files. As much as ninety percent of the work on his early guns was accomplished with nothing but files. His huge, gnarled, and work-hardened hands filed with such deftness that he could true a piece of steel as square and flat as a milling machine. He fitted the break-top receivers and sidelock actions of his shotguns and drillings with such precision that years of use resulted only in a slight burnishing effect between moving parts. Hammers, triggers, sears, and springs were literally carved from raw bar stock. Gus became famous as a maker of parts to fit older guns or one-of-a-kind guns for which factory parts were not available. He could even make a nonstandard screw by using Swiss needle files to cut the threads.

Fine wood held as much fascination for Gus as did steel. He was disdainful at the idea of using a blank precut on a pantograph. He could size up a roughly hewn stock blank for the proper flow of grain, then attack it with a drawknife with such gusto that chips literally flew as if from an explosion. A raw walnut plank would emerge as a gunstock in a few hours. After chiseling the receiver and barrel channel tightly so that wood and metal were welded together, Gus would finish the outside with a spokeshave, making it so smooth that it hardly needed to be sandpapered. He finished the gun with engraving, checkering, and carving that was equal to any man who was dedicated to engraving and carving alone. It was the miracle of August Pachmayr that he combined all of the skills normally associated with a half dozen dedicated specialists and did every job as well as the very best.

Stocks were shaped by Gus in the conservative classical tradition, often with a continental flavor. He regarded as abominations the rococo stocks with deeply curved pistol grips and gaudy inlays that became popular. The sight of one was likely to elicit a Teutonic tirade of such vehemence that every living being within hearing would cringe. "Vat da hell kind of gun is dot?" he would shout indignantly. "Anyvune who vould own it, his taste iss all in der taste buds, right on der tongue."

Gus was a precise workman in wood as well as metal. When he finally laid aside his planes and files and pronounced a stock finished, it was already so smooth that it scarcely needed further attention. Nevertheless, his wife Anna took the stock from her husband and carefully sanded it with progressively finer grades of abrasive paper, beginning with 2-O and ending with 4-O. She wrapped the paper around sanding blocks to prevent the abrasive from digging deeper into soft strata in the wood grain, which imparted a "bounding main" effect to areas that should remain level. Between sanding sessions, Anna sponged the surface with hot water and held the stock above an open gas flame on her kitchen range to raise the grain. She resumed the sanding, going against the grain to remove the fine whiskers. This routine was repeated many times until wetting no longer had any effect. Then Anna applied boiled linseed oil and rubbed the surface with the palm of her hand until it refused to absorb any more oil. After an hour or so of rubbing in the finish, the stock took its place in a long drying rack to remain there sometimes for weeks until the oil hardened. Then the hand rubbing process was repeated. This ritual continued until the pores of the stock were filled and appeared smooth under bright light. The velvety surface of the wood glowed with a soft luster and the grain looked as deep as a tidal pool.

Now the stock was ready for checkering and/or carving. In the Teutonic tradition, Gus often combined the two on the same gun, usually with carved borders surrounding a field of checkering. Much of the job of carving and checkering requires tedious repetition. Gus was always impatient with anything that he felt was wasting his time. Eventually, he enlisted his wife to complete some of this chore. He began by laying out checkering patterns and having Anna finish up by deepening the grooves until the diamonds became sharply pointed. Anna displayed an innate aptitude for checkering that came as a happy surprise to Gus. Realizing that his wife had hidden talent, Gus gradually turned more and more of the checkering and carving over to her. Anna learned her husband's style so well that no one could ever tell their work apart. She could even pick up in the middle of a carving or checkering job that Gus had begun and complete it to perfection without any coaching.

They combined forces on one notable job. Gus laid out a checkering pattern, cut it part of the way, and left the tops of the diamonds flat. He then drilled tiny holes in the centers of each of the diamonds. Anna cut short lengths from a roll of silver wire and lightly hammered a small silver insert in the center of each diamond. Gus then finished cutting the checkering until each silver-centered diamond was tack sharp.

Gus continued to make guns—lock, stock, and barrel—for clients who were well-to-do and not impatient. He built a traditional German drilling for Hugh Nickols, a promoter of wrestling and boxing events at the Hollywood Legion Stadium during the forties and fifties. Other customers were Walter Chrysler (cars), Eddie Maier (Maier beer and auto racing), Fairbanks Morse (scales), and James Langford Stack, noted financier and father of movie actor, Bob Stack.

Gus was an avid experimenter. While still in Germany, he invented the .256x46.5mm, a rimmed cartridge that became a favorite chambering for the rifle barrel in drillings. He continued his experiments in America and made his own barrels and reloading dies for a wide array of calibers that were based for the most part on either the rimmed .30-40 case or the rimless .30-06. Gus necked the .30-06 up to as much as .40 caliber, and down as small as .22 caliber. The small-bore version proved unrewarding ballistically, because canister powders of the time burned too fast and caused a severe overbore problem. Gus designed his .22-06 case with considerable taper, duplicating the pattern of bottle-necked black powder cartridges that had been adapted to smokeless powder use and reducing to some degree the unwanted overabundance of powder capacity. The wildcat cartridge chambered and extracted well, but it offered little ballistic advantage over the popular .22 Savage Hi-Power, which had been designed by Charles Newton and was based upon the black powder .25-35 case. Gus used the old, jacketed 70-grain Savage bullet in his experiments. He was convinced that

· PACHMAYRS OF THE PAST ·

During World War I, Gus (front row, far right) became a member of the National Guard. He is seen here in Calexico in 1914. His skills as an outstanding marksmen won him a job training recruits.

his cartridge would have been successful if only .22 caliber jacketed bullets could have been obtained weighing 95 grains. It was his contention that a bullet with such superior sectional density could literally have ignored the wind, which was the major enemy of long-range varmint hunters. Better performance rewarded Gus in his experiments with the .30-06 that he necked down to .25 caliber and 6.5mm, as well as a dead ringer for the .35 Newton and a 7mm that could have been a model for the .270 Winchester.

The carefully documented tests by August Pachmayr were carried out principally between 1910 and the early 1920s, about the same time as Charles Newton's most rewarding experiments. The two were friends and shared data. In fact, Gus made barrels for Newton. Gus had his own theories about rifling depth, pitch, and number of lands. He felt that small caliber rifles delivered superior accuracy with four lands and grooves, while .30 caliber or larger did better with six.

Gus continued to make complete guns, including his own personal trap shotgun, with which he scored in the high 90s. He also reshaped countless military Springfield and Mauser rifles, before, during, and after World War II. His sporters were marked by smooth-working actions, crisp triggers, and simple classic stocks. His fine-line, borderless checkering was always impeccable.

· FRANK PACHMAYR ·

This informal portrait of August M. Pachmayr reveals some of the innate power of this grand old man, both his physical and moral strength.

A notable innovation by Gus was his takedown system for sporting rifles. He created a number of Springfield and Mauser sporters with barrel-forearm assemblies that separated from the receiver and butt-stock section with a simple twist of the wrist. The original barrel-receiver threads were utilized with the barrel cinching up and properly headspaced just as the forearm and stock reached perfect alignment. Both front and rear wood sections were capped with steel plates and a spring-loaded latch kept them securely aligned. Most of the rifles were made in short-barreled Mannlicher configurations and were equipped with either micrometer receiver sights or simple open sights.

Disassembled, they required little storage space. Another advantage Gus offered was alternate barrels that he made in different calibers to fit the same action. One Mauser rifle was equipped with a .270 Winchester barrel and a .35 Whelen barrel assembly. One customer had eight barrels in calibers ranging from .250-3000 to a .400 Whelen. He was capable of taking game from ground squirrels to elephants with the same rifle by merely changing barrels. Gus was either first or among the first to convert a Springfield service rifle to fire .22 Long Rifle ammunition. He contrived a new magazine box that fed the tiny rimfire cartridges and shortened the bolt throw. Some say that his rifle inspired the United States Army to introduce a GI version for training and target shooting.

Gus was no stranger to the army himself. He served with distinction in the national guard for several years during World War I, and he soon proved to be the best marksman in his platoon. It was natural for him to train army recruits in the fine art of rifle shooting. When Gus became a naturalized citizen, he

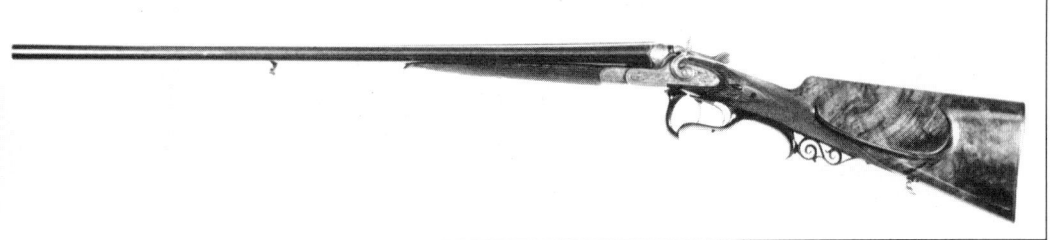

This 16-gauge, double-barreled shotgun was young August Pachmayr's "masterpiece," made while he was still in the employ of John Jacob Reebe, in Bonn, Germany. The intricately shaped trigger guard was hand carved of American buffalo horn. It was this gun that finally qualified Gus as a master gunsmith.

forbade anyone in the family to speak German, even at home. As a result, his children never learned to speak German.

Gus was no stranger to shotgunning. He was a championship-caliber trap shooter and was a member of the Amateur Trapshooting Association of America, the Northern California Skeet Shooting Association, and the California Golden State Trapshooters Association. He competed on a regular basis at the Rancho Angeles Trap & Skeet Club in Gardena and at the Long Beach-Dominguez Gun Club. He traveled to Fresno, Las Vegas, Reno, Phoenix, and many other places for major shoots. His interest in trap competition extended to contributing winning trophies to some regional matches. On at least one occasion, he almost won his own trophy. Gus was also deadly on game birds in the field, and he never passed up a chance to hunt. In the *Pacific Fish & Game News*, dated 31 July 1953, the cover story related:

> In an American Trapshooting Association Registered shoot held at the Long Beach-Dominguez Gun Club last weekend, August Pachmayr, 84 years young on his next birthday and businessman-resident of Los Angeles for about 50 of them, proved that he still has what it takes to make younger shooters look to their laurels. Firing under a difficult crosswind that made right-angle birds take off like homing pigeons, all squads found certain angles very hard to take, and scores suffered accordingly. Pachmayr shot a sparkling 23-25-24 for his first three rounds

of the 100 target handicap feature event, for which he had donated the trophy, and was well up in the final standings until three fast right cross birds dumped his final score down in the listings. The elder Pachmayr was still shooting from the twenty-yard line.

Making complete shotguns or customizing and repairing them was a major part of Gus's work. During his testing of a large number of shotguns over a period of years, Gus decided that factory-made shotguns from both European and American makers were underbored. The only exceptions he found were the better British double-barreled guns. In most instances, he maintained that the chokes were all wrong. His own theories of proper shotgun chokes were backed with calculations enough to stump an Einstein. More to the point, Gus could show test patterns to prove his contentions. He could point to patterns from guns that he had choked, which followed his theories and remained effective out to the hundred-yard line. He didn't advocate, however, shooting at ducks and geese beyond sixty yards, because the lead shot lost most of its energy and penetration at extreme ranges.

It might have been mere coincidence, Gus admitted, but he always obtained the best patterns with odd-numbered shot, such as 7s, 7.5s, and 9s. He also discovered that a choke that performed well with large shot was less effective with small shot, and vice versa. In the process of choking hundreds of shotgun barrels, Gus always determined what manner of game his customer was after and choked his gun accordingly.

When Gus made his own 12-gauge, single-barreled trap gun, he worked his witches brew over the muzzle and the result was a gun that powdered clay birds even from the twenty-seven-yard line. When Gus stood up in a cold, damp blind and drew a bead on a highflying honker, sprig, or canvasback, it was dead certain the bird would splash close by. Gus delighted in making those tough shots on pheasants or the tricky, fast-flying mourning doves.

Making complete guns was not cost-effective in the New World, and Gus came to pursue it only as a part-time hobby. He specialized instead in barrel making, as well as reboring and re-rifling barrels. At a time in our history when money was scarce, this was an attractive alternative to buying a new barrel, then having it threaded, fitted, and chambered. All of these steps were already accomplished on the original barrel. Gus had only to ream the bored barrel to the next largest appropriate caliber, perhaps .30-30 to .32 Winchester, then re-rifle the tube and screw it back in. Invariably, he obtained accuracy that was as good or better than the original. Often he rebored and rechambered .30-06 Springfield or Enfield rifles for his own .35 A. M. Pachmayr cartridge or for the .35 Whelen for hunters who wanted greater killing power. This was of course the heyday of Elmer Keith, who excited a lot of interest in large-bore hunting cartridges.

For all the work of reboring and re-rifling, Gus charged only $20. A price sheet without a date shows the cost of a new custom-fitted rifle stock to be $65, with $10 to $25 extra for fancy wood. In a typewritten paragraph of explanation, Gus wrote, "When restocking an Enfield, I use the complete Springfield trigger guard and floor plate for better appearance and to lighten the gun." Gus charged

· PACHMAYRS OF THE PAST ·

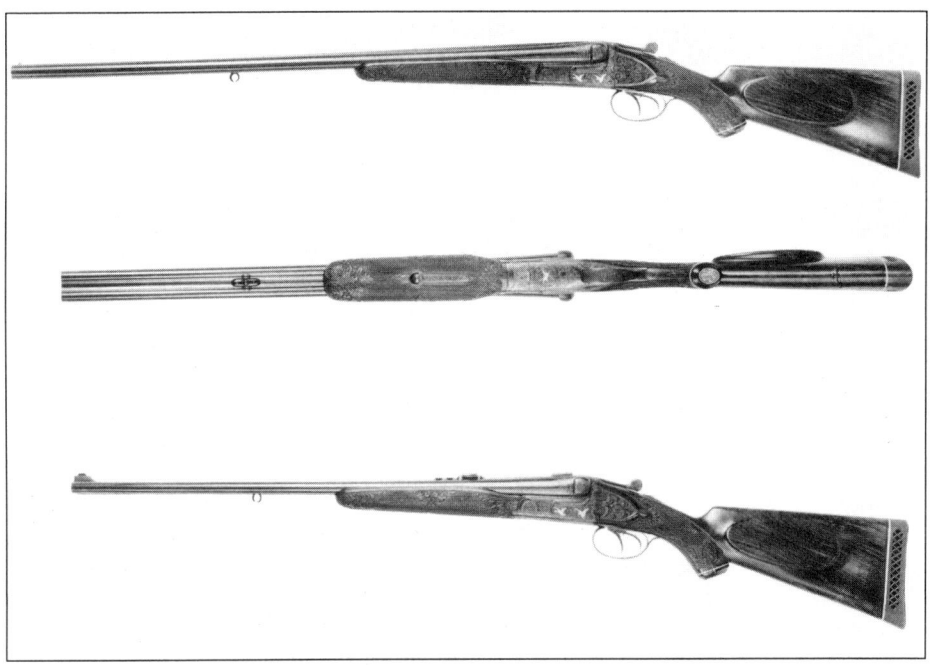

This late double rifle reveals how the design ideas of Gus Pachmayr slowly became more "Americanized" and less in the style of the "old country."

Closeup of Gus's steel engraving. Gus could perform all of the various aspects of gunmaking as well as anyone who specialized in one part of the operation.

just $5 to mill the ears from a GI Enfield and refinish it. Installing a Pacific Receiver sight cost $9.50, plus $6.75 for a bead and ramp front.

Gus didn't work just for work's sake. If it was more cost-effective to order something from another gunsmith, he would do it. A letter from W. A. Sukalle, famed barrel maker of Tucson, Arizona, dated 25 July 1934, went:

> Dear Friend Gus,
>
> Your welcome letter received and will say that I will get those two 20-gauge barrels drilled for you first of this coming week. I have been awfully busy this year. In regards to that barrel you say is .2845-inch grooved diameter, I must of got a hold of the wrong blank as I make the .270 with a .269-inch bore and groove diameter of .278 inch. So please return the barrel and I will turn up another one. Also send the action so I can fit it. I will close with regards.

Gus worked on everything from Purdeys to original matchlock rifles. To him, it was all in a day's work. "Der basic vorking principles iss all der same," he would say in a matter-of-fact tone. Amidst the chaos of his cluttered workshop was a kind of order. Gus could put his hands on the appropriate file, screwdriver, or drawknife, even if it was buried under a foot of wood chips and shavings. A mountain of cigar boxes contained untold treasures. He could reach into a dust-covered unlabeled box and come up with an appropriate sear, hammer, trigger, or spring for guns of every age and breed. On one occasion, a customer came to pick up an eighteenth-century flintlock pistol, which Gus had rebuilt. Delighted with the rehabilitated smoothbore, the owner needed only some spare flints to shoot it. Gus rummaged through his collection of spare parts and came up with a handful of flints. "I brought dem over from der Old Country," he beamed. "You never know ven somet'ing like dis vill come in handy."

On those very rare occasions when Gus allowed a customer to actually stay and wait for his gun, the onlooker would stand in awe as the old master reduced the piece to an array of screws and action parts, apparently strewn carelessly on top of his already cluttered work bench. When one anxious customer complained, an amused Gus reassured him, "You shtand more chance of vorgetting vat your vife looks like, den I do of getting der gun parts mixed up." Guns were put back together magically, as Gus's calloused fingers flew unerringly to the correct screws and lock parts, following a blueprint indelibly imprinted on his mind by years of experience.

In his later years, Gus came to be regarded by some as something of an eccentric. If public opinion was of any concern to him during his younger years, it certainly did not trouble him at all later on. Few men dared contradict him on matters of gun function or design. His sulphurous wrath was well known to intimates and to ostentatiously rich clients who locked horns with the old man about some gun they wanted made or repaired their way. Money was never an inducement to Gus. He worked on guns out of love for the art, and it was an art form with him. Never once did Gus prostitute his ideas of good design and mechanical effectiveness for financial gain. He routinely turned down work that failed to conform to his basic ideas of good gun design.

In November of 1926, Gus and Anna were divorced, and he devoted himself even more to his passion for firearms. He was happiest when working quietly in his shop, which was still located over Lail's automotive garage. If you had an

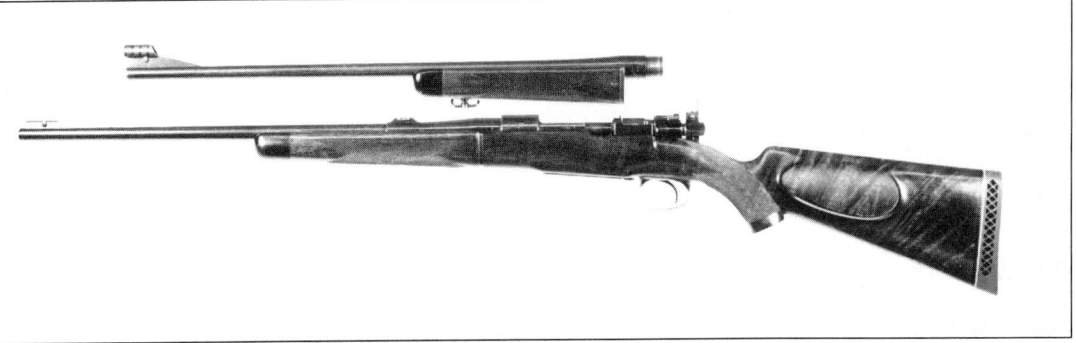

Gus had one exclusive device--interchangeable rifle barrels on Mauser or Springfield actions. Shown here is a military Mauser with two barrels.

ailing firearm that you wanted Gus to work his magic on, you had to pass through the wide garage entrance, which was open all day, thread your way between cars in various states of disrepair, and ascend a flight of rickety, wooden stairs. At the top, a modest sign declared simply "Gunsmith." Hung next to it was another sign, marked "Open" on one side and "Out to Lunch" on the other. A nearby hofbrau supplied Gus with most of his food. He slept in the shop and worked odd hours, impelled sometimes by financial necessity, but more often merely because the project was of absorbing interest to him.

Noted gunwriter Jack O'Connor once described the shop of Gus Pachmayr as, "small, with a minimum of power machinery in an era of power. It had a small lathe, a long workbench, and hundreds of specialized tools hung on the wall. Adjoining it was a smaller room containing a cot. California fails to penetrate it, as the windows look as though they haven't been washed since 1919, when the proprietor moved in."

At the close of World War II, the Allied occupation forces confiscated all firearms from the German military and civilians alike. Happily, many fine guns were "liberated" and returned to the States hidden in duffle bags, rather than burned or otherwise destroyed. Late in March 1946 one of these found its way into the gun shop of Frank Pachmayr, youngest son of August. It was in the hands of an ex-GI named D. W. McDonald, who happened upon the old side-by-side, 16-gauge double-barreled shotgun in Bonn, Germany. Frank examined the uniquely shaped trigger guard of American buffalo horn and gently traced the pattern of fine old Germanic engraving on the receiver with his fingertips, cocked the smooth-working, graceful outside hammers, and listened to the lock, which ticked like a gentle grandfather's

Gus always said that he came to the United States to hunt buffaloes, but it seems likely that his two half-brothers, Xavier and Otto Pachmayr tempted him more than a little. Otto owned a huge water tower that serviced much of the Los Angeles metropolitan area.

clock. He marveled at the fact that a gun apparently dating back before the turn of the century had clearly been used a lot yet could still close with the certainty of a bank vault, leaving no gaps between the barrels and the standing breech. Frank gladly paid the $300 asking price, thinking as he did that the gun was in fact priceless. Little did he know. Several weeks later when his father Gus came to visit, Frank was startled as the old gentleman exclaimed, "Gott in Himmel! Frank, vere did you get dis gun?"

• PACHMAYRS OF THE PAST •

"A soldier picked it up in Germany," replied Frank, "and brought it home with him. He offered to sell it to me and I bought it. Why do you ask?"

"Vhy?" said Gus excitedly. "Because I made it, dots vhy. Could you ever vorget a gun dot you sveated over for veeks—even if it vas fifty years ago? Especially if you vere getting paid only three marks a day." Gus took the gun in hand, and confirmed that it was indeed his "masterpiece." The barrel was marked J. J. Reebe. The gun remains a valued addition to the personal collection of Frank Pachmayr.

Many of August Pachmayr's guns have survived him. One of these, a Schuetzen rifle brought to the States after World War II, clearly exhibits his superb craftsmanship. Constructed with a Martini-type action, it boasts a 29.5-inch full octagon barrel, fluted nineteen inches back from the muzzle for decoration and reduced weight. On the top flat near the receiver, the maker's name is inlaid in

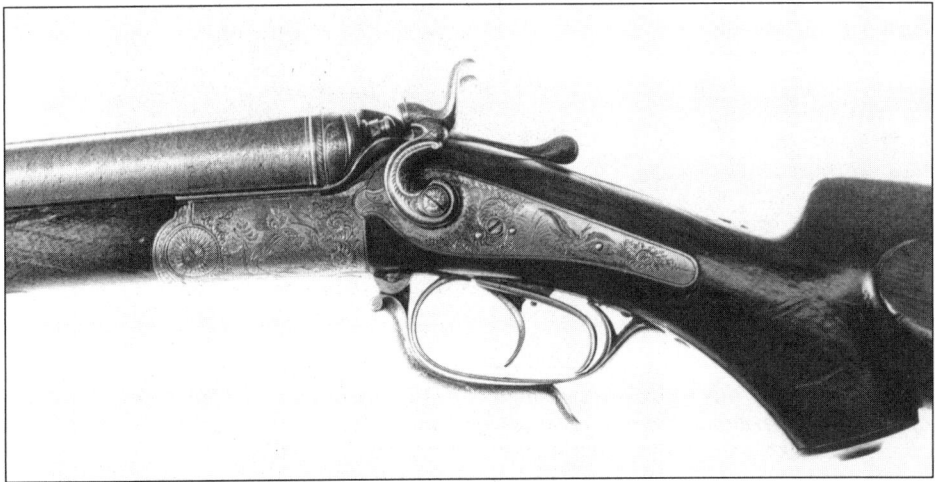

Early in his career, Gus made his guns lock, stock, and barrel. Here is an early double-barreled shotgun that he made with Damascus barrels.

silver: A. M. Pachmayr Pfaffenhoffen A/Um. The bottom flat is grooved to accept a cleaning rod that slides through two steel ferrules and back into the forearm. It was originally chambered for the 8.15x46R, the target shooter's Normal Patrone. The bore diameter is .3027 inch with a groove diameter of .3127. The fine old gun was unfortunately rechambered to accept .32-40 cartridges, probably after its arrival in America. The 12.5-inch length of pull (distance from trigger to center of butt plate) is shorter than average, indicating that the rifle was made for a man of about five feet, ten inches tall. A full cheekpiece indicates that he was probably of slender build. As befits a gun built exclusively for offhand shooting, the stock has a deep drop to a deeply arched, slightly hooked butt plate. The Martini-style action features a firmly fitted breechblock that hinges downward from the rear and is actuated by a smooth-working, gracefully sculptured trigger guard. The double-set trigger is a refined five-lever type, sharp-edged and crisply executed in every detail. The lock time is notably quick, which is an important asset to a gun that is fired only from offhand. The weight of pull is adjustable down to a few ounces by means of a slotted screw accessible from the outside. The gun exhibits an inherent distinction and grace that is roughly analogous to a fine old Kentucky rifle or a French dueling pistol. In the Old World manner, it is embellished with ornate

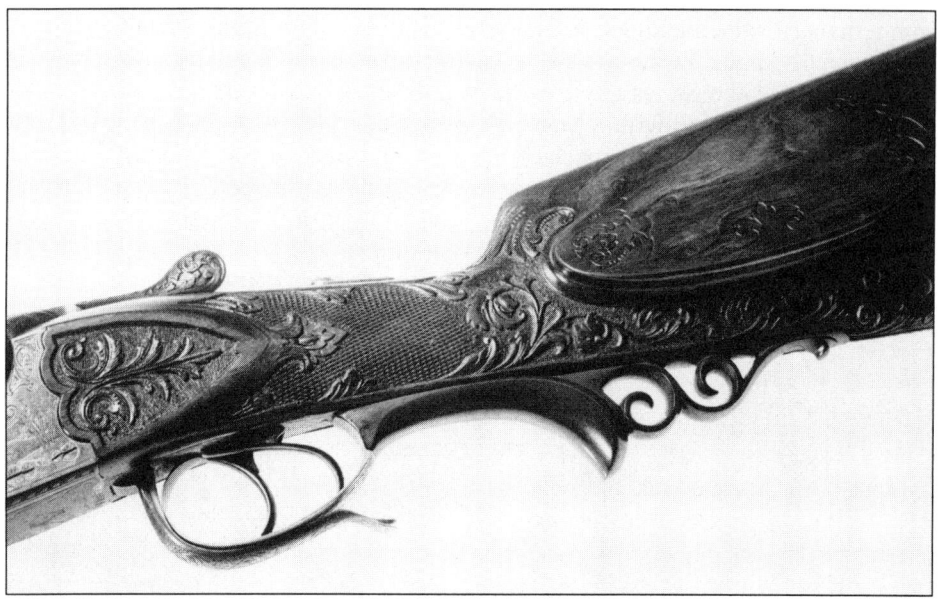

The butt stock of this early drilling made completely by Gus Pachmayr exhibits some of his heavy Germanic carving style, which can be seen in this European-styled eliptical cheekpiece. The ornate grip is carved American buffalo horn.

carving from muzzle to butt. Hardly a single surface was ignored. In an oval on the right side of the receiver and framed in finely detailed floral patterns is a huge lifelike wild boar beset by two hounds. Fine-line etching provides a dark background that makes the figures stand out in three dimensions. In another oval on the left side are a regal stag and doe lying in the shade of a spreading walnut tree. Fine scrollwork graces the top and bottom of the receiver, which is beautifully color-case hardened. The blued barrel is highlighted with simple scroll engraving around the open rear sight with a knurled ring next to the receiver. A fragile pinhead front sight is guarded on both sides by flanges. The forearm and receiver sport matching bosses. For added accent, the forearm is carved with leaf patterns front and rear. The stock is also carved in graceful sweeps with leaves that frame sections of fine-line checkering. A shallow thumb rest on the right is matted on top and carved beneath. Behind the smooth-surfaced cheekpiece is what one expects was probably a head-and-shoulders likeness of the gun's owner.

Gus worked on a regular basis until he was ninety-one years of age. He came to be regarded affectionately as "Old Gus" by his many friends, and his reputation as a curmudgeon faded as he mellowed in his declining years. He may well have been the last of a vanished breed of gunmakers who could construct a fine firearm from butt to muzzle without resorting to another man's hand. His basic tools, as he said many times, "are mine hands, mine eyes, and mine heart. Vidout proper of use of dese, no vun can turn out a goot gun."

Gus believed that hidden in every piece of fine steel and quality walnut there was a gun. If one could but cut, scrape, file, and smooth away the excess material, a masterpiece would be created. The masterpieces of this venerable craftsman, lovingly and laboriously whittled from steel and wood over three-quarters of a century, are now regarded as highly prized collector's items, and they will never again be duplicated.

August Martin Pachmayr died one hot July day in 1966 at the age of ninety-five. He left a legacy unlike any other. In addition to the many priceless guns he left behind, his skills and knowledge lived on in his son Frank, who continued the Pachmayr tradition of fine gun products and unswerving dedication to quality.

•••

• Chapter XII •

NANITTA PACHMAYR

*Nanitta Gwendolyn (Laughlin) Pachmayr was born on
10 June 1912 in Long Beach, California.*

Frank Pachmayr's mother, Anna, was as sweet and understanding as his father, Gus, was stern and unforgiving. That Frank could find another woman to share his life who was the image of his mother beggars the imagination. Yet he did. One of Frank's business associates once remarked, "Frank has an angel on his shoulder." He was trying to explain Frank's uncanny sense of timing in the business world, but the same could have been said of Frank regarding his choice of a bride. Nanitta Pachmayr was all things to Frank—business partner, advisor, confidant, understanding counselor, and loving wife.

His own personal "angel" must surely have been looking out for him on the day when young Frank Pachmayr first met the glowing, laughing, effervescent teenage Nanitta Laughlin—a beautiful girl to look at and a joy to hear. She had a warm sensuous voice and the sound of her laughter was like the tinkling of silver bells. Frank was impressive himself in those days. He had a muscular, square-shouldered, athletic body, and a shock of unruly yellow hair over piercing blue eyes and sharply etched, classic Germanic features. Frank had the square-jawed, determined look of a young man who knew his own mind. Although he never quite reached the six-foot-plus height of his father, Frank had an imposing, commanding presence. Nanitta was favorably impressed, to say the least. As for Frank, he gave his heart the first moment he saw Nan.

As so often happens, this momentous event took place by pure chance. In Nanitta's own words, "The first time I met Frank, he was working for his father above Lail's Garage at 8th and Grand Avenue in Los Angeles. My cousins, Arline and Charlie Jones introduced me to Frank and his father Gus. Charlie had work to be done on his shotgun, so he took it to Gus, who he knew was a fine gunsmith. I just went along for the ride. "I was attending Los Angeles Junior High School at the time, and it wasn't long after our meeting that Frank started courting me. Our first trip together was to Big Bear Lake for some ice skating. Then we went to all of the school baseball and football games. I enjoyed sports as much as Frank, and he was almost a fanatic on the subject. Frank invited me to go with him to the 1932 Olympic Games at the Coliseum located on the campus of the University of Southern California in Los Angeles. We watched as Dutchie Smith and Georgie Coleman won honors for diving and Frankie Wycoff won the relays. From then on, we spent weekends at the Elysian Park Pistol Range, where Frank taught me how to shoot a pistol. We went to turkey shoots, trap shoots, and skeet shooting. We went hunting for doves, quail, and pheasants. Our 'engagement' lasted over a year, because my mother wanted me to finish school before getting married.

"My first real safari with Frank came a week after we were married in 1935," Nanitta recalled. "We went deer hunting up at Checker Meadow near Bass Lake with John Wayne and Lloyd Foster. That was an experience I'll never forget. It was the big thrill of my life, because it was my first deer hunt and I was meeting the 'Duke' for the first time. This was the beginning of a wonderful marriage that lasted over half a century."

If you remember that everyone was still young and John Wayne was something of a cutup, it is not hard to believe that he would pick up his wife and toss her bodily across the campfire to Lloyd, who caught her and tossed her back to John. She managed to wriggle free and stomped off in a huff. Duke eyed petite Nanitta and sized her up as the next victim. He took a long step toward her. Nan backed up a step and put her right hand on the butt of the .38 Special Smith & Wesson she carried conspicuously in a hip holster. "You touch me," she said evenly, "and I'll shoot you." As she told the story, Frank chuckled and added, "She sounded like she meant it, too. You can bet that Duke kept his distance from Nan the rest of the night."

Nanitta Pachmayr hunted with Frank many times during their life together, and she was a spunky little hunter. She kept up with the men and never asked for special consideration. She accepted the inevitable hardships of the field—getting up before dawn in freezing cold, sometimes rain or snow, long hard hikes, wet feet, and aching muscles—all without complaint.

From the time they first started keeping company, Frank was coaching Nanitta in the use of handguns, rifles, and shotguns. She quickly caught on and became an outstanding shot with pistol or rifle, but she just couldn't seem to get the hang of using the smoothbore. Frank watched young Nan as she shot skeet and trap and noted that she had trouble positioning her face on the comb of the stock. She was always trying to overreach. He had a sudden inspiration. "Nan," he said, "try holding your forefinger up at arm's length in front of you. Focus on something in the distance and note the position of the finger in relation to the distant object." Nanitta followed Frank's directions. "Now close your right eye," instructed Frank. "Does the finger move?" "No," replied Nan. "Now close your left eye. Does the finger move?" "Yes," said Nan. "There's your problem," exclaimed Frank. "Your left eye is your master eye. You've been shooting from the right shoulder. You'll have to become a left-handed shooter, at least with a shotgun."

· NANITTA PACHMAYR ·

Frank and Nanitta were indeed a handsome young couple, as shown in this portrait taken shortly after their marriage.

As Nanitta told me later, "It was awfully awkward at first because I've always been naturally right-handed. But after I finally got the hang of it, I began hitting with the shotgun, for the first time." Nanitta soon became an ardent fan of trap and skeet shooting, competing in local shoots, usually winning or placing in her class. She even became a serious competitor in live-pigeon shooting in Mexico and Spain, a much more difficult game. Nan placed second among women contestants in a match held in Tijuana, Mexico, in mid-June of 1960.

Nanitta shot a 12-gauge Winchester Model 12 pump for a time, but the recoil was too punishing. She turned to various 20-gauge shotguns for most shooting, sometimes changing to a 28-gauge or even a .410 for dove and quail hunting. Frank told me once, "If you go bird hunting alongside Nan, you won't get many shots until she limits out. She's so quick on the bird, she has it dead in the air before anyone else can get his gun to his shoulder. Nan hunted right along with the men, shot for shot, and she usually skunked us. One time, I saw her shoot twelve pheasants with twelve shots. She didn't wing them. She nailed them dead center.

Nanitta (center) was a devoted skeet shooter and a formidable competitor. She is seen here at Eddie Kost's Skeet and Trap Club in Angeles Mesa, California.

They dropped like stones. If you try to match Nan, shell for shell, she's going to beat you every time. If a covey of quail or doves flushes in front of Nan, she can pick out the biggest bird and drop it. She calls her shots. Deer hunting, she would pick a particular buck out of a herd because he had good rack or was the biggest. Then she waited for the right moment to get a clear shot, and she never missed."

Nanitta Pachmayr had her share of misadventures in the field. "Once," she told me, "we went hunting on this fella's ranch, with permission, of course. We were crossing this pasture when I saw a huge old bull staring me right in the face. He sort of pawed the ground like he meant to charge, then he started trotting toward us. I told Frank, 'You'd better shoo that bull away, because he's heading for us.' Frank says, 'I'll fix him,' and fired his shotgun into the air. The bull stopped, but it still looked like it wanted to charge. I fired a shot from my 20-gauge into the ground just ahead of him and the bull took off running. There was a barbed wire fence around the pasture, and the bull just sailed over it like it wasn't even there.

"One time Frank, Gus, and I were hunting down in the Imperial Valley," Nan related further. "It was 115 degrees in the shade. I was walking along when I felt something pepper my behind. I looked back and saw that Gus was shooting in my direction. My clothes were a brown duck color that just matched the dried grass we were in. He didn't see me there when he shot at a bird. I'd just about had it anyway with that insufferable heat. There wasn't a cool spot around. In those days, we didn't have air conditioning in cars. There was an old tractor parked there. I got under the tractor in the shade. Frank tried to coax me out, but I wouldn't come out until they were ready to drive back to the air-conditioned hotel."

Most of the time, Nanitta stood up to the hardships of hunting as well as any man. There was a time, though, in the early days when she reacted in typical feminine fashion. Nanitta was on a hunt with Frank on the western slope of the High Sierras. They were backpacking in with an outfitter named Herman Cambaugh, who had a string of packhorses to carry the tents and duffel. The small party of hunters was strung out single file on a narrow trail that threaded its way across a fairly steep side hill. One of the party spied a black bear browsing in apparent unconcern in a berry bramble on the opposite hillside. Without stopping to think, he shouldered his new Model 71 .348 Winchester lever-action rifle, fired at the bear, and missed. The startled bear responded by barreling pell-mell down the hill toward the nearest cover it could see, which happened to be in the direction of the hunting party. The would-be bear killer shouted a frenzied, "He's charging." With wildly flailing arms and legs, he tried to scramble up the hill in the opposite direction. It would have been comical had the rest of the party understood the situation, but everyone was self-absorbed climbing the steep trail and they were caught flatfooted. With the shot suddenly ringing out, followed by the warning shout, and the sight of a large black bear headed in their direction, they were unnerved to say the least. Startled out of her reverie, Nan looked up and saw the bear running toward her. She gave a little squeal of alarm and grabbed at Frank with both arms like a drowning child. Frank said, "Here, get up on this rock." Clasping his two hands together, he made a stirrup for her foot to boost her on top of a large boulder. Then he unslung his rifle and took up a guard position at the base of the rock.

By that time, the bear had reached the thicket at the bottom of the ravine and galloped into it like a runaway war tank, amidst much crashing and crackling of broken branches. Suddenly everything was silent. The party of hunters waited expectantly for the bear to clear the brush and charge up the hill at them, but he never came. Apparently, the bear was fully content to remain hidden in the brush, safe from all the rifles.

In 1950, Frank, Nanitta, and her brother, Homer Laughlin, had a near brush with death, and it had nothing to do with hunting. I would give odds that more hunters are killed every year in flying or automobile crashes than ever perished from accidental gunshot wounds. Frank, Nanitta, and Homer were en route to a two-week fishing and hunting vacation in Colorado. Nan was at the wheel of Frank's new four-door Cadillac Seville. It was late at night and both Homer and

Frank were fast asleep. Nanitta was getting drowsy, but she pressed on, thinking they might make their destination by early the next morning. As they neared Del Norte, Colorado, Nan dozed off. The expensive automobile swerved off the road, across a wide ditch, through a stout barbed wire fence, and into a pasture. The front end dug into the soft turf, and the long sedan flipped end-for-end three times. Luckily, the pasture was cushioned knee-deep in thick prairie grass.

The farm owner, awakened by the noise, hurriedly pulled on his trousers, grabbed a jacket, and hightailed it to the pasture, which was eerily quiet now. He could be excused for expecting the worst as the beam of his flashlight picked out three figures scattered at random on the ground and the mangled Cadillac lying upside down with the wheels still spinning. Then one of the figures stirred. At least they weren't all dead. In a few minutes all three had regained consciousness and were up and walking around. Miraculously, although the car was beyond repair, the three occupants, who were tossed like rag dolls out through open doors, escaped with no more than bruises and sore muscles. The farmer invited the trio to stay the night at his house.

Early the next morning Frank, Nan, and Homer went out to inspect the Cadillac. Frank wrote the car off with a glance. Nanitta was distraught over wrecking the car. "Forget it, honey," said Frank. "I'm just glad that no one was hurt." Determined that the accident wasn't going to ruin their trip, Frank phoned the Cadillac agency in Los Angeles, where he had purchased the car only a few months before. Then he phoned Art Durando at the Pachmayr retail store. Frank said, "Art, we had an accident and totaled our car. I want you to pick up a new Cadillac for me and drive it to Del Norte, Colorado. We're staying with the owner of the farm where we ran off of the road. A wide river runs right through his property. I'm going to do some fishing today. I already called the agency. The car will be serviced and ready to go by noon. Remember that this is Saturday and they close early."

Art asked two questions, "Was anyone hurt?" and, "How do I find Del Norte?" Then he added, "Catch some fresh trout for me. I'll be there in time for lunch tomorrow."

"I drove all night," says Art, "and I did get there about one o'clock the next day, just as they were sitting down to a lunch of fresh trout. I traveled with them for the next two weeks. We had a ball fishing, mostly in the Gunnison River."

Frank routinely hunted ducks and geese once or twice a year at the North Butte Duck Club, one of three gun clubs located at the north end of the Butte Mountains near Marysville, California. Nanitta told about their first trip to the Butte Club. "It was mid-January when 'Kip' Brown, a friend of Frank's, called to ask if we would like to hunt up at Butte. I needed wool socks and longies, so I went shopping at Kerr's Sporting Goods in Beverly Hills. Although Alex Kerr was my husband's competitor, he and Frank have always been the best of friends. Alex saw me come into his huge sporting goods store and insisted upon waiting on me himself.

"The next morning, Frank and I piled all of our gear in the trunk and back seat of the big four-door Cadillac and found there wasn't any room left over to stow the icebox to bring back our birds. By then, it was almost noon, and we were supposed to meet Mr. Brown in the Marysville Hotel, which was over 400 miles north, then drive together the twenty miles or so to the gun club. When we reached the end of the ridge route north of Los Angeles and started dropping down into the desert, Frank groaned. There was a white blanket of tulle fog covering the desert floor like a huge cloud as far as the eye could see. That area was the scene of several disastrous auto pileups, one time involving almost a hundred cars and big

During the early years, Nanitta functioned as bookkeeper for her young husband's fledgling gun company. As business improved, Frank hired a bookkeeper so that Nanitta could be a housewife. She was still a frequent visitor to the gun store.

eighteen-wheel trucks. There was one accident. Then the others just kept piling into the back of the wrecked cars because no one could see far enough to stop in time. If we hadn't known that Kip was waiting, we might have turned back, then and there. As it was, we drove in the fog almost all the way to Marysville.

"It was long after dark when we finally arrived. It seemed like everyone must already be in bed. The street lights were dimmed and there wasn't a soul around. This was our first time there, and we had some trouble locating the Marysville Hotel. When we finally made it to the lobby, we found Mr. Brown sound asleep on a couch. Frank introduced us, and I saw a small boy sitting beside him. I spoke up and said, 'Oh, that must be your grandson.' Kip was graying and well past middle age. He laughed, and said, 'No, he's my son. I just got started a little late.'

"It was late that night when we arrived at the North Butte Duck Club. A few people were staying up, playing pinochle. They greeted us. Someone explained the club rules and said that we would be awakened at 4:30 in the morning by the chef, Elmo, so we hurried off to bed.

"It seemed like our heads just hit the pillows, when an alarm went off. It was as loud as a school bell and startled us out of our wits. Frank and I dressed in a hurry and hustled down to breakfast. Elmo served a real gourmet breakfast, just like a big hotel with eggs, ham, bacon, and biscuits, along with orange juice and coffee. Kip Brown and his five-year old son, 'Kippy,' sat across from us. Kippy was bundled up inside a hooded parka, so you could hardly see his little face, but he was as anxious to get started as any of the hunters.

"Kip and his tiny son went down the stairs outside of the clubhouse and picked up their golden retriever from the kennel underneath. All of the hunters were throwing their gear into boats, starting their motors, and heading out to the blinds. It was like a race to see who could get there first. This was my first time hunting from a permanent blind. Each blind was a platform set on stilts in the water and camouflaged with reeds and tulles so the birds couldn't see them. There were two hunters to a blind. Frank and I set out our decoys, got into our assigned blind, and loaded our guns. The sky was turning light, and we could see the buttes in silhouette. In a little while, the first rays of the sun were filtering through the willow trees. It was a beautiful sight.

"The Duck Club is located right on a flyway, and there is a game refuge next to it. We had no trouble getting our daily limit of mallards and teal by the time the sun was high enough to warm the frigid air. Frank and I went back to North Butte Duck Club many more times over the years, but I never lost my sense of wonder at the beauty of the place."

•••

Frank purchased his present residence on a hill in Cheviot Hills in 1963 for $80,000. The house was modest by today's standards, but located in a conservative middle-to-high income neighborhood. Nanitta set out to bring the home up to her standards, ultimately spending more on remodeling than the original cost. Frank gave Nan a free hand with renovating the home to her own tastes, and Nanitta designed some ambitious house additions herself. She began with a fifty-foot-deep family room with a high, beamed ceiling that was added to the rear of the original structure. In the rear left corner, she had a massive fireplace built from floor to ceiling from gray flagstone, which had been taken from some property that Frank owned in Arizona. Pecky wood panels flanked the fireplace. The opposite wall featured a built-in pit barbecue that Nan really used to cook for guests. The barbecue and the wall around it were constructed of the same gray flagstone as the fireplace. The entire floor of the family room was flagstone. The flat rock then extends out past the all-glass wall with its wide French doors surrounds a kidney-shaped, tiled, concrete swimming pool, around which is a generous flagstone deck for entertaining guests. Nan built a large bath house behind the pool.

· NANITTA PACHMAYR ·

The house faces east. The kitchen dinette and formal dining room are at the front of the house to catch the warm rays of the morning sun. The pool in back is bathed in the afternoon and evening sun to allow basking in the sun until late in the day. Sitting in two of the battery of deck chairs by the pool on balmy California evenings, Nan and Frank could see the azure expanse of the Pacific Ocean in the distance merging with the blue horizon. At night, they often sat enjoying the sight of Culver City lights stretched out before them like stars in a black sky that was somehow misplaced on the floor instead of the ceiling. They also saw an unending parade of planes taking off and landing at Los Angeles International Airport (LAX).

In the family room, two king-sized couches were each arranged at a right angle, one facing the fireplace and the other facing a large-screen television set on the

Frank and Nanitta frequently attended local social functions, including this Weatherby Big Game Trophy Award Banquet at the Beverly Hilton Hotel in December of 1967. (Left to right) Bert Klineburger, Frank and Nanitta, Ray Watson, and two identified only as "the couple from Las Vegas."

south wall, a gift from Frank's employees several Christmases back. Four marble-topped coffee tables front the long couches. In the contiguous living room, located in the center of the house, there is another large sofa, flanked by round, marble-topped tables that support a pair of tall Grecian urn lamps. A pair of overstuffed chairs, a narrow-waisted walnut grandfather clock, a grand piano, and a large glass-fronted china cabinet round out the furniture. Inside the china cabinet are mementos of years of traveling on several continents.

A large painting of a Spanish flamenco dancer in full costume was painted by Nan's brother, Homer Laughlin, a contractor in the Los Angeles area for many years. Nan's interest in art is further reflected in several other original paintings and art pieces, such as a five-foot brass figure supporting a floor lamp.

Several years after purchasing his present home, Frank bought a choice piece of property in the Rolling Hills Estates, located among the lofty Pacific Palisades that overlooked the Pacific Ocean south of Venice. He planned to build a new home there for Nan, but the project was postponed for various reasons until it was too late.

A major interest in Nanitta's life was her work with the Bel Air Chapter of The Flower Guild Charities For Children, founded by Mrs.Paul William (Gladys) Lawrence during World War II to help the wives of servicemen. The Flower Guild is affiliated with the National Plant, Flower, and Fruit Guild that was organized in 1893 in Montclair, New Jersey. In 1914 the National Guild was the first organization to help France feed Belgian refugees. In 1917 they shipped 4.5 tons of food to overseas hospitals and aided reforestation in war-torn England, France, and Italy.

The Los Angeles area Flower Guild Charities For Children is a philanthropic organization dedicated to improving medical facilities for children, mainly at the Los Angeles County University of Southern California Medical Center, formerly called the Los Angeles County General Hospital, widely known as the "Gray Lady." For many years, Nanitta worked hard at raising funds for therapeutic equipment, such as a respirator incubator for babies unable to breathe for themselves, an infant heart-lung machine, wheel chairs, walkers, feeding tables, television sets, and even playpens. Donations were made to the Heart Clinic, Cardiac, Communicable Disease, and Occupational Therapy Departments, as well as the Premature and Newborn Service at Southern California Medical Center. "Sometimes, I just took care of children at the hospital," explained Nanitta. "They were such dear things. My heart went out to them."

The Flower Guild also supports the Child Care Center at the Nora Sterry School in West Los Angeles. In addition, the philanthropic group built and maintains ninety-two child care centers strategically dotted up and down the Pacific Coast. Collectively, the ladies of the Guild have donated thousands of hours to the hospital. In 1958, the Flower Guild established a Memorial Children's Heart Fund to maintain the Flower Guild Children's Heart Clinic, which enabled hundreds of children to undergo open-heart surgery. As a society leader possessing wide-ranging contacts with many Los Angeles business leaders, Nanitta was in a position to bring major money into the organization and obtain contributions of furs, jewelry, and cosmetics for benefit raffles. She also arranged such special events as a benefit harness race at the Hollywood Turf Club. Nan was Press Chairman for the Guild for two years.

"I was up until 1:00 A.M. on many mornings before and after various events, typing newspaper releases. I had to vary each release a little for different papers, because they wouldn't print the material if they thought that they were duplicating some other paper."

Nan was Guild Vice President in 1964 and President during 1966. She often acted as hostess for informal teas or Guild business meetings at her home. The major fund raiser for the Guild was their annual ball held at such prestigious locations as the Ambassador Hotel, the Beverly Hills Hotel, and the Biltmore

Here we see Nanitta and Frank (right) with the late Jimmy Robinson, famed field editor of Sports Afield *magazine, and his wife Clara, during a hunting trip to Navajoa, Mexico. They were after white-wing doves.*

Hotel. Local businesses bought ads in the annual ball program and Frank was always first in line with a full page ad. Guests were charged by the plate with all proceeds going to charity, and all labor was contributed. Nan served on the Guild Board of Trustees and was appointed Assistant Ball Chairperson for the 1965 affair. She was also chairperson of the Flower Guild's Twentieth Annual ball in 1966. Nanitta chose a Hawaiian theme for the affair and everyone wore appropriate costumes. She also arranged the 1970 ball held in the Beverly Wilshire Hotel's Sans Souci Suite.

Nanitta was also involved with other civic groups, such as the Cheviot Hills Garden Club and Cheviot Hills Republican Women Federated. It wasn't all work and civic duty for Nanitta. The Los Angeles area has long been a vacation land of almost inexhaustible attractions. Frank and Nan made good use of these. They attended the opera. They even went to Earl Carrol's nightly "Vanities," a girl review displaying scantily-clad beauties to rival anything that Florenz Ziegfeld could have dreamed up. Just across Wilshire Boulevard, Nan and Frank went dancing at the famed Palladium, where the greatest of the "big bands," including Artie Shaw,

As they grew older, Frank and Nanitta acquired a quiet dignity.

Glenn Miller, and Benny Goodman performed regularly. The Biltmore Theater, downtown at Fifth and Olive Streets, staged many of the latest Broadway hits, featuring such names as Maurice Evans and Lunt and Fontaine. The El Capitan Theatre featured Ken Murray's Blackouts, where Marie Wilson, the empty-headed, saucer-eyed, buxom blonde bombshell, displayed her endowments nightly. Incidentally, I knew Marie and she was no dummy.

Nan and Frank attended the Drunkard Theatre Mart, a dinner theater on Clinton Street many times. Nan and Frank also dined frequently at the celebrated Brown Derby and Lawry's Prime Rib Restaurant. The Turnabout Theater on La Cienega Boulevard, Los Angeles' "restaurant row," ran Elsa Lanchester and a mixed review for years. The Shrine Auditorium played Metropolitan Opera with major performances every year, featuring ranking artists, such as Rise Stevens, Lilly Pons, and Lauritz Melchior. The Stage Theatre featured current plays and stage musicals. The Theatre Mart, a dinner theater, played a period drama, "The Drunkard," for over sixteen years. The Pasadena Playhouse featured current dramas. The Philharmonic Auditorium offered top symphonic performances by eminent artists. The Wilshire Ebell Theatre offered a wide range of events from The Icecapades to symphonies. The Hollywood Bowl still stages everything from heavy opera to ear-splitting rock artists. Many of these attractions are closed today, but all of them beckoned to Frank and Nanitta in their prime, offering a year-round smorgasbord of entertainment, which they liberally sampled.

Frank considered Nanitta a full partner in everything that he did. In the early days, she worked as a bookkeeper at Pachmayr Gun Works. Frank invariably included his wife's name on ownership papers of corporate stock and other assets. She usually accompanied him on hunting and business trips. In the fall of 1947 Nanitta traveled with Frank and Baden Powell to visit High Standard, in a successful effort to sell them on using the POWer-PAC on their shotguns. Some trips were more for vacations than for business, but Frank made it a point to visit his dealers in every city he could.

On 14 August 1957 Frank and Nan left for an extensive trip through Canada and Alaska. They drove north on old Highway 99 with a stop at Bakersfield that enabled Frank to see several of his dealers, then on through Redding and Red Bluff to Yreka, where they attended a friend's wedding. Then they traveled north through Grants Pass to Portland and Seattle. Again Frank made a tour of dealers in the large northwest cities. The next stop was Vancouver, where they set sail on a commercial liner for a trip through the famed Inland Passage. Nanitta recorded these trips in detail in her daily diary. It was evident from her remarks that she reveled in the beautiful scenery on all sides and the closeness that she and Frank enjoyed during these trips.

Nanitta Pachmayr was always an elegant lady, who never acted haughty or talked down to anyone. She was gracious to everyone she met and especially considerate of other people's feelings. I recall once that my late wife Patty and I were attending a reception at Robert Petersen's home, publisher of *Guns & Ammo* magazine, *Motor Trend, Teen*, and many others. Patty and Nan were chatting, when Elmer Keith's wife, Lorraine, grabbed Nan by the arm and said, "Come on let's go upstairs to the nursery to see Marjorie's new baby." Lorraine ignored Patty, possibly because they weren't well acquainted, but Nan took Patty's hand and said, "Of course. We'll all go."

At the time of her death, Nanitta Pachmayr was engaged in writing a definitive history of the Culver City area, dating back to early times. The pity is, it will never be finished. Throughout her life, Nanitta maintained an optimistic, serene, and generous attitude, and so it remained till the end. She was a valiant fighter, and she resisted the ravages of abdominal cancer for three long years after the doctors had written her off, holding the disease at bay despite severe physical suffering. I never heard a moan or complaint, and somehow she always had a smile for those around her.

The last time that I saw Nan alive, she was sitting up in bed, going over the monthly household bills with her personal secretary. Toward the end, she had difficulty speaking. The pain she endured was reflected only in her husky voice and labored breathing. Yet she struggled to tell me all that she could to help this book become a reality. I believe that one of her greatest regrets in leaving this world was that she could never see Frank's biography in print. Nanitta Pachmayr died quietly in bed on 5 November 1986. Her death was deeply mourned by all who knew her.

●●●

· Chapter XIII ·

PACHMAYR THE PERSON

Frank Pachmayr is widely regarded by his contemporaries as the "dean of gunsmiths." One well-respected gunsmith dubbed Frank Pachmayr, the "master gunsmith emeritus." Although now retired, Frank is one of the few men remaining in the New World who possesses the skill to create a complete gun—lock, stock, and barrel—from raw steel and wood, with no outside help.

"My older brother John and I both learned gunsmithing from our father. There was a popular misconception about my dad," explains Frank. "There was an article in *Outdoor Life* written by Jack O'Connor that depicted my father as a primitive workman who didn't have any machine tools and couldn't use them if he did. It was hogwash. My father could use any of the machines that were available. He made his own milling cutters and even ground his own reamers for the dozens of wildcat cartridges that he designed. He did use files a lot, so well that he could shape a shotgun receiver about as fast and with as much precision as another man could work with a mill."

Frank learned another object lesson from Gus. "You can't make any real money just repairing guns," he says with vehemence. Many of his father's best customers were well-heeled industrialists and businessmen, but none of that wealth ever rubbed off on Gus. "I guess my father was happy in his own way. He didn't ask much of life, but I could see that there was more to it than just work, so I decided to go into business for myself."

Young Frank A. Pachmayr could hardly have dreamed just how successful he would one day become. He was an entrepreneur in the Horatio Alger tradition. If he hadn't entered the gun business, no doubt he would have made it at least as big in some other endeavor, but he took as great a pleasure in his work as his father did in his. Until his retirement, Frank's greatest pleasure in life was to run his business from behind his executive oak desk, which was surrounded by one of the finest collections of custom rifles and shotguns ever assembled in one location. Gun racks, fronted by sliding glass doors, lined three walls of Pachmayr's comfortable office and contained more than a hundred long guns. A world-renowned connoisseur of fine firearms, Frank chose for his personal collection only those guns that were either rare or lavishly embellished with high engraving, or both. Among his favorite smoothbores are original Merkels, Parkers, Purdeys, Wesley Richards, and highly engraved Winchester Model 21s. The one thing I don't remember ever seeing in Frank's office was a .45 Colt Government Model, in spite of the fact that he is probably most famous for his work with the .45 ACP. Among the rifled arms in Frank's collection are several guns made and engraved by his father, alongside modern custom rifles built and engraved in Frank's shop.

Fine engraving improves the appearance and investment value of any gun. "Sportsmen have more respect for a gun, or any other tool for that matter," offers Frank, "if it's beautiful, as well as mechanically and functionally perfect. Of course, the engraving also increases the gun's value and makes it more desirable as an heirloom. Having a beautiful gun with gold and silver inlays dates back to the days of royalty and the antebellum period when hunters were highly respected. In the past, hunters were esteemed by the public for their skill, daring, and knowledge of the woods and wildlife. An engraved gun was the mark of a gentleman or a community leader. The same is true today, in spite of efforts to discredit hunters and hunting."

Frank still adds to his collection of fine shotguns, such as Piotti and Francoti. He has presented some of his finest guns to Duck Unlimited and the Foundation for North American Sheep, of which Frank is a founding member, as well as other wildlife conservation organizations. These guns are auctioned off to raise funds for wildlife preservation. Presently, his collection is estimated to be worth upward of five million dollars.

Frank's office at Pachmayr Gun Works was like a working museum. He was never too busy to show his fine firearms to interested visitors. He took special delight in showing his collection to children, to whom he patiently explained every facet of each gun's manufacture and function. On the walls above the glass-fronted gun racks were many mounted trophies of mule deer and elk with impressive racks.

•••

Often, after a particularly harrowing morning, or perhaps in celebration of closing an important deal, or just because it was noon time, Frank would invite some friends or employees to join him for lunch. Frank loves good food. He's a confirmed gourmet, with a deep appreciation for all kinds of cuisine, but he has always kept his waistline in check, except when he traveled to Italy, where he was exposed to the best pasta in Rome. By the time Frank left Italy, he had gained fifteen pounds.

He learned to love German food at his mother's table. His all-time favorite eating place was the Turner Inn Munich Hofbrau, which was situated near the Los Angeles Convention Center at 645 West 15th Street, before it was razed to make room for new development. Frank was such a familiar figure at the Hofbrau that they named a sandwich after him. The Frank Pachmayr Reuben Sandwich was made with hot corned beef piled high on rye bread, spread with thousand island dressing, topped with sauerkraut and chopped apples, and served with kosher pickles and potato salad. The Hofbrau was noted for its dark German beer and wines, authentic German sauerbraten, wienerschnitzel, *kassler rippchen*, bratwurst, Hungarian goulash, and *kalbshaxen*. At night, a full German brass band rocked the oak dance floor.

Exotic menus were always favored by Frank. He acquired a taste for Chinese food at the Blue Moon Cafe near the wholesale vegetable market in Los Angeles. Whenever Frank and his work crew went up to Oroville to pick up a load of walnut stock blanks or to help with a particularly large export order, he would take the entire group to Chico for a Chinese dinner. In the beginning, everyone loved it, but by the fourth trip north, they all grew bored and cooked up a plot to avoid Chinese food. Everyone was in on the scheme. At the end of a long day of packing pallets with fine walnut blanks, when Frank proposed, that they all go to dinner at the Chinese cafe in Chico, Steve Yorba stepped forward. "Frank," he started out rather tentatively. "That place burned down a few weeks ago. It's out of business now." Frank was openly disturbed, but never one to be daunted by a minor mishap, he chose another cafe in Marysville.

One day, I was visiting Frank's old stockmaker, Walter Strand. As noon approached, Walter suggested that we eat at El Pollo Loco. "It's one of Frank's favorite eating places," he explained. As we finished eating, I pondered aloud, "I wonder if I could take a cooked chicken back to Frank's house." I knew that Frank was on a restricted diet, but Walter responded with his customary enthusiasm, "Sure. Take Frank some chicken. He'll love it."

"What if Nanitta catches me trying to slip him some *verboten* food?" I asked.

"If Nan catches you," replied Walter with a grin, "just tell her it was my idea."

When I arrived a Frank's house, I found the front door locked, so I was obliged to enter by the side door, which meant I had to walk right through the kitchen. The minute I reached the kitchen, I knew I was undone. Nan saw the box of chicken, piping hot, and smelling like manna from heaven. She gave me a stern look and reproached me with, "Frank can't have this." She was implying that I should know better, which of course I did. "I just thought maybe he could use a break from that bland food," I replied lamely. Nan took the chicken box and shoved it into the refrigerator, well to the rear of the shelf. "The doctor says he can't have it," she said with a tone of finality that told me the discussion was ended. After Nan's death, Frank fired his cook and went back to eating what he liked, including lunches at the German Hofbrau.

•••

Frank loves animals even more than good food. This obvious affection for wild and domestic creatures manifests itself in many ways. One year, Frank was hunting in his customary migratory bird haunts near Navajoa, Mexico. As usual, Art Durando was hunting alongside him. Art borrowed several dozen Canadian goose decoys from a friend and deployed them the night before so that he and Frank could move into the blind before daybreak with as little fuss as possible. As the first light of day began to creep in, along with the honking of live geese, Art peered anxiously into the dim dawn for his decoys. His first hint of trouble came when he saw that the decoys weren't in the same position as the night before. As the light increased, he realized that the decoys were askew on their wire stands with some completely knocked on their sides. Incredibly, the geese didn't seem to mind. They came into the pool anyway. By mid-morning, Frank and Art both

Next to being in the field hunting, Frank most loved to be in his famous gun and sporting goods store, with his guns and gunmakers.

limited out. With hunting over, Art checked his decoys. They had been torn and ravaged by coyotes, apparently in the belief that they were flesh and blood instead of plastic.

Decoys that effective interested Frank. He found out that they were made in the small family-owned plant of G. and H. Goose Decoys in Henriette, Oklahoma. The idea of producing the decoys himself interested Frank. He sent a representative, Carl Brown, to the plant to investigate the possibility of purchasing the business. The owner declined, but allowed Pachmayr to produce the decoys under a license from them. Frank considered the offer at some length, but ultimately decided to pass it up. "The idea was tempting," he said later. "I knew I could make a lot of money by mass-producing those decoys, but they were just too damn good. I was afraid if I put them into the hands of thousands of hunters, before long all of the geese would soon be shot down."

Frank's love of nature and wild creatures was often shown in simple ways. For years he had a daily ritual of feeding a flock of pigeons in the alley behind Pachmayr Gun Works by broadcasting corn as the birds clustered around him. Apparently birds can communicate. Somehow the word got out and the flying freeloader flock grew. In time, the flock became so huge that it nearly covered the whole alley in all directions. Frank just bought more corn to feed his rapidly expanding bird population.

Once Frank was invited to a barbecue at a friend's house and found a pair of friendly Labrador retrievers penned in the back yard. He wanted to let them out, but the host objected that the dogs might annoy his guests. Frank did the next best thing by putting together a barbecue plate for each of the dogs, and he fed the dogs before he ate himself.

Dogs have always been an integral part of Frank's life, and he doted on his retriever, Davey. Davey could sit upright on the seat and look with great interest out of the window during flights in the plane. Dick Mellen made many of those flights with Frank and Davey and bears witness to the fact that Frank put Davey's interests first. Frank has owned a succession of dogs and he loved them all. Nanitta also liked dogs around the house, but not big hunting dogs. The perfect house dog is of course the poodle, who is a smart dog with a distinct personality. Poodles don't shed fur, are small enough to remain inconspicuous, and ever ready to sound an alarm when strangers approach. Today, Frank still has two of Nan's white poodles and they adore him. I remember once reaching over to shake hands with Frank, who remained seated as I was leaving his house. One of the poodles sitting in his lap leaped at me with a warning growl and a nip on the hand, obviously fearing that I intended to harm his master.

●●●

Frank always did things in style. If he were in business today, he would be flying a Lear Jet. As it was, he operated two Twin-Beech, low-wing monoplanes with cabin space for twenty people. Frank had his own 3,700-foot-long landing strip in Mexicali to facilitate hunting in Mexico. He had two large tents set up permanently in the camping area during the wildfowl hunting season. When upland birds and migratory waterfowl were in season south of the border, Frank flew down every weekend with parties of hunters. Art Durando would leave the store at noon on Friday and drive down to set up the hunt. Johnny Johnson, another store salesman, was permanent chef. Among Frank's guests were many prominent political and military men, as well as such celebrities as cinema actors Lionel Barrymore, Rod Cameron, Gary Cooper, Clark Gable, and Robert Stack. Indus-

• FRANK PACHMAYR •

trial magnates, such as oil billionaire Bill Doheny, Hubert Eaton, owner of Forest Lawn Cemetery, and Hupp Haldeman, millionaire Chrysler auto dealer, were frequent guests.

Frank owned and used dozens of different hunting rifles, but his favorite was a .300 Holland & Holland Magnum, custom-built on a pre-64 Winchester barreled action with a Leupold 4X scope in a Pachmayr Swing Mount. He preferred Parker shotguns, electing to carry and use engraved, gold-inlay guns that are usually relegated to display only. Of course, Frank had the luxury of having any dings or dents repaired in his shop. Once, when I marveled at his carrying a $100,000-gold-inlaid Parker shotgun in the field, he replied, "Oh, the gold doesn't wear much."

Frank is intrinsically such a generous man that he often loaned out guns that were worth thousands of dollars as if they were common rifles and shotguns. One such occasion was recalled by Pachmayr gunsmith Carl Cupp. "Frank would always lend you a gun if you needed it," says Carl. "He heard I was going deer hunting in northern California with Steve Yorba, and he insisted that I use one of his personal rifles, a highly engraved, gold-inlaid, pre-64 .270 Winchester Model 70 with a fabulous claro walnut stock. I took it along because Frank insisted, but I didn't hunt with it. Frank would always hand you a gun that was so valuable you were afraid to actually use it."

Frank always maintained a discerning eye for detail in his business. He spot checked his products and his employees constantly. Often, he would stroll through the shipping area, randomly snatching boxes from the long lines of shelves lining the walls. He pulled the product and examined it minutely. Head of the shipping department for decades, Warren "Whitey" Shoemaker recalled a time he said to Frank, "You never say anything when everything is all right. You only speak up when you find something wrong." Frank replied, "I don't worry about things that are right. I only worry about things that are wrong. Then I fix them."

Frank is always a cool head in a crisis. Art Durando tells of one incident that illustrated that personality trait pretty well. "Frank and I were fly fishing some distance apart along the banks of a lake when I heard three shots behind me. It seemed as if someone was shooting in our direction. I yelled at Frank to watch out, but he was too concerned with the fact that one of his favorite bamboo fly rods had just broken. Then I saw a black bear headed right for Frank with three guys running after it shooting as they came—all of them missing. Finally, Frank turned his attention to the ruckus behind him. I was ready to jump off the point into the lake as the bear got closer, but Frank held his ground. Finally, one of the hunters connected, bringing the bear down. Frank just calmly accepted the whole thing as if it was a normal everyday occurrence. We had roasted bear for dinner that night."

Durando continued with another story, "Once Frank and I checked into a motel owned by a guy who said he used to work for Remington as an exhibition shooter. We had a few drinks together that evening, and he told us that he had once broken 700 trap targets in a row without a miss. I guess he noticed our raised eyebrows. 'Just to prove I'm not a liar,' he told Frank, 'I'll show you some trick

· PACHMAYR THE PERSON ·

A particular friend of Frank's is the famed championship pistol shooter, distinguished soldier, and noted gunwriter, Colonel Charles Askins. Frank customized many guns for his friend, including this fine Pachmayr Combat Special .45 ACP.

shooting in the morning.' The next morning, this guy turns up with a Remington Nylon 66, one of those little plastic automatic .22 rifles. I'd throw bottle caps, coins, and steel washers into the air, and this guy hit every one. Finally he asked Frank to hold a cigarette in his hand, and Frank stood there while the guy cut the cigarette in two with his .22 rifle. Then he shot cigarettes out of Frank's ears. I would never have done it. Frank is just too damn brave."

Frank has a sense of humor that can pop up at any moment. Once he and Art Durando were fishing a little stream in a wilderness area. The fish weren't biting, and Frank could see that Art was getting restless and impatient with the lack of action. Frank thought he'd wake up his fishing companion. In a hoarse stage whisper Frank called out to Art, "There's a grizzly sow with a cub in the brush behind you, and she doesn't look very good to me." Art dropped his fishing pole and whipped around to look behind. "Where is it?" he hissed. Frank laughed. "I'm only kidding," he said.

Frank routinely stopped by the several work benches located behind the store area to see how work was progressing and to impress his gunsmiths with his desire for high-quality workmanship. This helped to keep his employees on their toes. If he thought a man was getting careless in the way he handled parts from a gun he was working on, Frank might pocket a small part, then look on in amusement as the gunsmith panicked searching for the missing component.

Frank Pachmayr feels quite comfortable about flying. Minor misadventures don't phase him, and his impish streak sometimes surfaces at unexpected times and places. During one flight in a Twin-Beech, Dick Mellen was acting as copilot. "We were about thirteen thousand feet somewhere over the Rockies and headed home from a hunting trip when we began to smell smoke. The pilot, Earl Shade, responded instinctively by cutting the ignitions to both engines. A fire in that place and time would have meant certain death." As the twin three-bladed props slowed and finally stopped, Dick and Earl searched desperately for the source of the smoke. Dick glanced back anxiously over his shoulder to see if Frank was reacting to the sudden silence of the engines. "Frank had his head down between two of the seats. Then he came up for air, and I could see he was laughing. He held up a piece of string for me to see with the end on fire. Earl had some trouble getting one of the engines restarted. After he finally had things under control again, he handed the helm over to me and went back and chewed Frank out for scaring the hell out of him."

Frank has always believed that in business, saving pennies results in dollars of profit. He hates waste. Often, a gunsmith would leave for lunch without turning off the neon light fixture positioned over his workbench. Frank would walk over and turn it off. Frank's nephew, Dick Mellen told me, "I once read a magazine article that said it was cheaper to let a neon fixture remain lighted than it was to turn it off when you were going to be gone for just an hour or two, because the power required to restart it was more than that used by the tubes that remained burning. I explained all of this to Frank one day just before we went to lunch. He listened patiently to me. Then he headed for the office door. "Okay," he said, "turn out the lights, and let's go eat."

An instinctive abhorrence of wasted motion is an integral part of Frank's character. Whenever possible, he combines tasks. Before making his rounds of the machine shop and gun repair area each morning, he would try to accumulate several errands and perform them in one trip. This was not laziness, but rather a useful habit that enabled him to do more work than many other people could do in a restrictive time slot. He also believed in focusing his attention completely on a given task by pushing all distractions aside. His mind had a habit of racing past what he was doing to anticipate and even plan the next move. He constantly had to rein in his thoughts and direct them back to the job at hand. His mind was constantly problem-solving, mulling over dilemmas, and working out effective solutions.

When Frank and Nanitta purchased a home in exclusive Cheviot Hills, they had a large swimming pool built in the back. Offset to the downhill side at a lower level, they had a large concrete storage room built. Concrete is not impermeable, even when it is supposedly sealed. Inevitably, there was some water seepage through the cement walls into the storage room. Frank phoned Nan's brother, Homer

• PACHMAYR THE PERSON •

Laughlin, a contractor, to see if he could offer a solution to the problem. Homer said they would need to dig a trench sixteen feet deep and three feet wide around the perimeter of pool on the side facing the storage room and fill it with coarse rocks to interrupt the seepage and drain it off downhill.

Homer provided a written bid, which Frank thought was too high. Never at a loss for a quick course of action, Frank told Jack Farrar, "I want a dozen of the beefiest guys from your machine shop and grinding room over at the house Monday morning." When this improvised crew arrived, Frank set them to digging the trench. When lunch time came, he sent Steve Yorba out for several barrels of Kentucky Fried Chicken. "The guys were glad to get it," recalls Steve, "but the second day, Frank had me get more of the same chicken and the guys grumbled a little. The third day, he had me bring chicken again and the whole crew went into an open rebellion. Frank couldn't understand it. He can eat the same thing every day and be perfectly content."

Frank always treated his wife Nanitta with courtesy and respect. He witnessed the verbal abuse heaped upon his mother by his father Gus Pachmayr and was determined never to resort to such tactics himself. He was unfailingly polite and considerate with Nan. He included her in his business dealings, as well, placing business assets, including stock, half in her name, as if she were a full partner in the business. As a result, Nanitta had her own personal fortune.

A great sense of patriotism and intense civic pride makes Frank an avid participant, rather than a mere onlooker in local and national governmental affairs. Frank is always at the forefront of citizens in favor of law and order. Years ago, when Los Angeles became embroiled in race riots, the Los Angeles Police Department was suddenly faced with a massive emergency for which they were completely unprepared. Large sections of southwest Los Angeles were ablaze with arson fires, and firefighters found themselves shot at by unseen snipers in the windows of adjoining buildings. Calls of, "Shooting, with officer down," went unanswered for a lack of sufficient armed personnel. Pachmayr saw the need. He offered the Los Angeles Police Department unlimited access to arms and ammunition from his massive stock. He handed out over a hundred 12-gauge Browning autoloading shotguns to uniformed officers, along with a hundred rounds of ammunition for each man. Additional ammo was dispensed as it was needed. After the emergency, most of the guns were returned, but of course, they could only be sold as used for less than wholesale cost. Pachmayr never received any compensation from the city for the use of the guns or his contribution of ammunition, but he never lodged any complaints or filed any claims for his volunteering them.

• • •

Next to shooting and hunting, Frank's greatest passion, especially as a young man, was powerful cars. Pachmayr's was a popular hangout for race drivers in the Los Angeles area at a time when racing was big business and big money around the city. Frank's racing buddies used to hold informal drag races up and down Grand

Avenue. Famous Indianapolis race drivers, like Riley Brett, Lou Meyer, and Roy Richter, were close friends of Frank's.

Frank often employed race drivers and race-car designers in his business. Riley Brett worked for Pachmayr and designed one of the first rocket-launching pods for fighter planes. "He was an outstanding machinist," recalls Frank. "When I was working on a new type of detachable aircraft panel fastener for the government, I showed the design to Riley. The male section of the fastener had to be machined with an interrupted helical fast thread and mated with a matching thread inside of the nut. These fasteners weren't very big. I knew they'd be tough to make. I went to Riley's office and unrolled the blueprints on his desk. He studied the drawing for a few minutes and then looked up at me. I said, 'I bet you can't make this.' He glanced back at the blueprints, then back at me. 'The hell I can't,' he declared, and he went ahead and made them."

Frank sponsored and financed a large commemorative bronze plaque of Riley that stands in the Indianapolis Speedway Museum in Indiana. In a letter to Bob Laycock, Executive Secretary of the Indianapolis 500 Old-Timers Club, Inc., Frank stated:

> "I think all of the racing world, and especially the Indianapolis Motor Speedway, and all of the people who knew and did business with Riley throughout the years should give him this honor of record. When I worked for my father back in 1922, my brother John, my father, and I knew Riley Brett as a customer, a shooter, and a hunter. About that time, Riley worked for Harry Miller, who built the Miller racing cars. My brother also worked there under Riley for a couple of years in the carburetor department."
>
> "During the early years, Riley was the chief mechanic for Jimmy Murphy, next for Harry Hartz, and then for Frank Lockhart, who got killed in an accident at Daytona Beach, Florida, in 1928 when he blew a tire in the run back of his test, setting a record of 232 mph in a car built entirely by Riley Brett. It had two eight-cylinder Miller engines sitting side by side with a special gear train and dollar-sized pistons to obtain this speed. Riley built this car personally. I saw it in his small upstairs shop in a building located at 11th Street and Figueroa in Los Angeles."

The bronze plaque was etched by artist Ron Burton, under the supervision of Speedway Museum Director Jack Martin. It has a bigger-than-life-sized face of Brett in helmet and goggles, depicted at the height of his quarter-century-long racing career and next to his famous V-16 Sampson Motors Incorporated Special, Number 32, that he owned and drove in the 1939 Indianapolis 500. Presentation of the plaque was made 23 May 1983, at the annual barbecue of the Indianapolis 500 Old-Timers by Vice President Lou Meyer. Frank was unable to attend because of illness. The Sampson Special car itself was on display along with the plaque.

Frank also employed famed racing personality Eddie Miller as a designer. Eddie was involved in designing prototype rocket pods for United States fighter planes while working for the Pachmayr Corporation. Later, he performed the lion's

• PACHMAYR THE PERSON •

share of design work and tooling on the Pachmayr Signature Accuracy System for the .45 ACP, as well as the shoulder strap and hardware for Pachmayr's pistol case.

Frank is loyal both to his friends and to his favorite brand of car. Over the years, he has owned a number of Cadillac automobiles. He traded for a new one every year or two. His good friend Charlie Jones was service manager at Martin Cadillac, first in Los Angeles, then at the Santa Monica outlet, and he gave Frank

Among Frank's distinguished customers was popular television personality Tom Frandsen (left), host of the daily TV show, "Tom Frandsen F.Y.I." that aired for over fourteen years from KNBC, Los Angeles.

an inside track to the best car and price. Frank's loyalty to Cadillacs has remained unflagging throughout his life. "I like the comfort of a big car," he once told me, "and if you're ever involved in an accident, you're a lot safer in a big car."

• • •

There's a strong fatherly interest in Frank for his employees. When he sold the Pachmayr Gun Works corporation to a group of investors, he presented each of his employees with a block of shares in the new corporation, both to give them a stake in their jobs as continued motivation and to provide them with bargaining chips when dealing with the new management. Frank also extracted a promise from the new owners that there would not be a wave of firings that so often marks the entrance of new corporate management. Frank's own secretary, Elaine, stayed on with the corporation for a couple of years before being terminated. Frank was still coming into the plant three days a week in his role of corporate advisor and consultant, and to take care of personal correspondence. It happened that one Wednesday, he came into the office just as Elaine's son, Craig, was picking her up. She was in tears over losing her job.

"Frank walked over to me," Elaine told me later, "and put his arms around me. He told my son, 'Don't worry about your mother, I'll take care of her. From now on, she's working for me.' Then he told me to take two weeks vacation. When I came back, he'd have an office set up for me." For a number of years, Elaine continued acting as Frank's personal secretary.

•••

The clothing Frank wore during his working hours was virtually always the same. He usually wore tailored, tan dress slacks, a starched checkered dress shirt, and a dark brown wool cardigan sweater. When going out to lunch, he put on a tailored tan blazer. He wore a braided leather string tie that had been given to him by Los Angeles Police Department Chief Davis. It had a gold bolo the size and shape of an arrowhead that pointed down. On the face was a miniature police department badge. He always wore polished black Florsheim oxfords. "Good shoes are cheaper in the long run," he says. "They fit good, and you don't have trouble with your feet." In years past, Frank was a man who enjoyed fine whiskey, in quantity. He was a hard-drinking man for most of his life, but only after hours when it didn't interfere with his work.

Despite the fact that Frank can afford the best of everything, he chooses to live a simple life in modest surroundings, but like all of us, he does occasionally have the impulse to splurge. One day, I was in Frank's office, when his then secretary, Vivian Tew, announced a visitor. Frank told her, "Send him in." An average-looking man, probably in his early thirties and dressed in a conservative dark business suit, entered the office. The visitor reached across the desk and greeted Frank with a handshake. "Need any watches today?" he asked. "I'd like to see what you have," responded Frank. The visitor pulled off his jacket and draped it over a chair back. Then he rolled up both shirt sleeves, revealing dazzling rows of solid-gold wrist watches, stacked from his wrists to his elbows. Included were such luxury watches as Patek Philippe and Rolex. Frank examined each watch in turn, as the unorthodox salesman handed them to him. "I'll take this one and this one," he said almost casually. I saw the check when Frank made it out. It was in four figures.

•••

• PACHMAYR THE PERSON •

Frank and Nanitta knew intimately many famous people. General Curtis LeMay, Commander of the Strategic Air Command, given the mission of deterring a Russian attack for many years, was a regular customer at Pachmayr's. Many greats of the entertainment industry and sporting world, baseball, tennis, and football, were Pachmayr customers, as well as astronauts and World War II flying aces, such as Joe Foss and Pappy Boyington.

Frank Pachmayr is a political conservative. He threw his full support behind his friend Ronald Reagan when he decided to "pay his dues" and enter politics. Frank exerted his immense personal influence with friends and business associates, as well as contributing generously to Reagan's gubernatorial campaign. When Reagan ran for the presidential nomination against Gerald Ford, Frank was at the forefront of his supporters and was disappointed when that attempt failed.

After Ronald Reagan was elected to the presidency in 1980, Frank joined the Republican Presidential Task Force, a blue-ribbon advisory group with a direct "hotline" to the president. Frank supported efforts to stem the tide of antigun legislation in 1968. He was one of the founders of FAIR (Firearms and Individual Rights), an organization formed in the Los Angeles area to combat antigun legislation by presenting the views of gun owners to the public. He felt, as gun owners do, that the liberal press in Los Angeles told, and still tells, only the antigun viewpoint.

Frank has always been a fair and reasonable man. At a meeting that resulted in the founding of FAIR, Frank proposed that the group take a stand that some carefully considered legislation would be acceptable. I told him, "Frank, if we take a reasonable view, we have no bargaining chips, no room to maneuver. We're certain to be pushed back by the politicians, so we have to take a stand to the right of what we actually expect to achieve." As FAIR got underway, Frank provided financial support, full access to his printing facilities for issuing newsletters, banners, and other printed material.

Frank is also a generous supporter of the National Rifle Association Institute for Legislative Action, the so-called "gun lobby" that liberal politicians oppose. A long list of political organizations count upon Pachmayr for support. He is a sustaining member of the Republican National Committee, a member of the President's Committee, Citizens for the Republic, the United States Senatorial Business Advisory Board, and the United States Senatorial Club. Frank often bought entire tables at costly fund-raising dinners for conservative political candidates, some local, some not so local, and some as far away as New York City? Frank is a supporter of such groups as the American Federation of Police, the American Security Council, and the National Tax Limitation Committee.

A number of nonpolitical groups also have Frank Pachmayr as a valued member. He belongs to the California State Chamber of Commerce and the Smithsonian Associates and is an honorary member of the Municipal Motorcycle Officers of California. Perhaps Frank most enjoys his membership in the Jonathan Club. It occupies a large building in the heart of downtown Los Angeles and has a complete gym where Frank can work off daily stress and maintain his waistline. The club also has a fine restaurant where he occasionally takes me to lunch. In years past, the Jonathan Club held summertime beach parties with several hundred members in attendance and served gourmet fresh fish dishes of every description. Nanitta and Frank were nearly always at these parties.

Frank always carries an American Express Card. At Pachmayr Gun Works, he often handed it over to employees to buy gasoline for company cars or purchase supplies. Once, he even mailed it to an aspiring young gunsmith who worked for Jaqua's Fine Guns back in Findlay, Ohio, so the young man could drive to Los Angeles and go to work for Pachmayr's. Such was the great respect that Frank Pachmayr commanded that he was never once ripped off by anyone carrying his card.

Frank Pachmayr may well be the last of a vanishing breed—an honest all-round gunsmith who can literally do everything. During his days as a full-time gunsmith, Frank could take any job offered him on any gun ever made in full confidence that he could handle it right and expeditiously. He knew virtually every brand of gun that could be found in America, regardless of where it had been made. He knew each gun intimately, down to the last tiny spring and screw. He always admonished his gunsmiths, "Don't throw any usable parts away. If you run across a part you don't recognize, save it anyway. You never know when it might

Frank also enjoyed his days at the skeet range.

come in handy. Some day you might be glad to have it." For years Frank saved boxes of old miscellaneous small parts and screws in closed cupboards in his office. When one of his gunsmiths needed a trigger, a firing pin, or a screw for some old gun that was long since out of production and no parts were available, nine times out of ten, Frank could rummage through his boxes of old parts and find the exact item needed. The true miracle of this performance was the fact that he could remember what the part looked like and knew exactly where to find it.

There were times, however, when even Frank Pachmayr could become vexed with a gun. In the old days, when Frank worked at his gunsmithing counter in the front of the store, he was trying to get an old Colt Lightning revolver correctly timed. The Colt Lightning is said to be the gun carried by Billy the Kid. The Kid thought it gave him an edge because it was double action, which could be fired faster than the single-action (manual cocking) Colt Peacemaker/Frontier or Remington revolvers. The Lightning was a notorious prima donna, however, and liable to become cantankerous at the drop of a hat. Once it went awry, the old revolver stubbornly resisted all efforts to get it back in time. Always impatient with anything that was unreasonable or slow to respond, Frank was having some problems with this gun. Suddenly his patience just gave out, and he heaved the recalcitrant revolver right through the open double doors in front of the store and into the middle of Grand Avenue

As a teenager, I used to hang around to watch Frank work. He would be standing behind his well-ordered bench and be dressed in a blue bibbed apron. I remember once a customer brought back a .45 Colt auto that Frank had made accurate. The man complained that the hammer followed the slide down. It's not a good idea to just drop the slide of a Government Model on an empty chamber because there is risk of damage to the delicate sears. A good practice is to hold the hammer back with the thumb under the slide, then ease the slide down on an empty chamber. If there are rounds in the magazine, just drop the slide. Easing it down might prevent the slide from going fully into battery, but the hammer should still be held back to protect the sears and make it impossible for the gun to go full auto.

Faced with a complaining customer, Frank restrained himself from any inclination he might have had to lecture the man on proper .45 ACP use. Instead, he tapped out the pin holding the mainspring housing, slipped the housing out, and lifted out the sear spring. He bent one of the three prongs on the spring forward slightly to increase pressure on the trigger sear, then he reassembled the gun and dropped the slide. The hammer followed the slide down. He disassembled the .45 and bent the spring some more and again reassembled it and dropped the slide. The hammer followed the slide. All the while, the customer stood there watching. Frank concealed his embarrassment, but I could see the red rising up his neck to his ears. Finally, he turned to the customer and said abruptly, "You'll just have to leave the gun a day or so. I have to adjust the sear angles a little." Years later, Frank devised fixtures that held the sear and hammer precisely to stone the sear engagement surfaces to the exact angles needed to get a completely safe, but crisp and light pull.

· FRANK PACHMAYR ·

Later, when Frank became an executive with many gunsmiths under his command, he would require that they show him their finished jobs. If he wasn't satisfied with the results, he would have it done over. Many times he would send a gun back to be reblued again because of a small blemish that had escaped the eyes of his employee. Sometimes he would stay late just to personally rework a trigger job that one of his gunsmiths couldn't seem to get right. It could be said that Frank's real hobby was conducting his business. After he retired as CEO of Pachmayr Gun Works, Frank continued for years to operate his wood mill and to cut and sell fine walnut for gunstocks.

•••

Shotguns have always been Frank's first love. He loved to make them, work on them, and shoot them. Whenever the pressures of business allowed, Frank headed for a hunting jaunt or a trap field. Frank's father Gus was an outstanding trap competitor and even sponsored a number of trap events in the southern California area. An aptitude for trap shooting was one of the greatest gifts that Gus handed down to his two sons.

Frank qualified as an expert on trap technique and was capable of offering cogent advice to neophyte competitors. "The first thing that you need to shoot trap," Frank advises, "is a 12-gauge, single-barrel or over-under, double-barrel shotgun with a full choke bore. You need a full-length ventilated rib for a long, flat sighting plane and to reduce mirage (wavering lines of heated air rising from the barrel that distort your view of the target). The rib should have two bright brass bead sights, a large one at the muzzle and a smaller one halfway back. When you're holding the gun correctly, both beads should appear as one. Some shooters use a pump action, like the Remington 870 or the Winchester Model 12, for shooting both singles and doubles. An autoloader is okay if you put a shell catcher on it, so you don't pepper the shooter on your right with empty shells.

"Whatever gun you choose, it should have as straight a stock as possible, so that you can hold your head erect. Some guys lace a leather cheekpiece on a field stock and shoot it at trap, but they get knocked silly after a few rounds because the gun recoils upward every time and belts them in the face. That straight stock also reduces recoil effect. A trap stock should have a full pistol grip because the right hand exerts the most control over the gun." Frank Pachmayr is an expert at properly fitting individuals with custom stocks.

"Weight of the gun should be well forward," says Frank, "with the balance point at the hinge of a break-top shotgun and at the front of the action on a pump or autoloader. Barrels are generally longer, from thirty to thirty-two inches. A muzzle-heavy feel helps steady your swing and follow through."

Trap shooting is the oldest organized shotgun sport known. It was first mentioned in the English publication *Sporting Magazine* about 1793. Originally, wild pigeons were released from traps to provide shooting for English gentry, who used cylinder-bored flintlock, then later, cap-lock, muzzleloading shotguns. In 1831 the

• PACHMAYR THE PERSON •

first trap competition was held in America at the Sportsmen's Club in Cincinnati. The first national championship was held in New Orleans in 1885 and was won by the famed marksman, Dr. W. F. Carver. The Amateur Trapshooting Association be-

John Pachmayr (left) was in charge of Pachmayr Gun Works gunsmithing department until his death. Frank then looked after John's widow on a continuous basis.

came America's governing body of the sport. It conducted the Grand American Tournament competition annually on their extensive trap grounds at Vandalia.

A trap field consists of a low-slung trap house with a single mechanical trap that throws clay birds away from the shooting positions at random angles, which are unknown to the shooters. Five shooting positions are arranged three feet apart in an arc sixteen yards behind the trap house. A squad of five shooters is assigned to each trap and each shooter fires five shells from each position at single targets. Then the team of shooters rotates to the right for another five targets, until each shooter has fired a total of twenty-five shots, five at each position. This event is known as sixteen-yard singles. A second event in registered shoots involves handicaps that place higher-ranked shooters farther from the trap house, somewhere between eighteen and twenty-seven yards. The third event is doubles, in which two birds are launched at once at diverging angles and fired at from sixteen yards.

"Proper stance is just as important in achieving good trap scores as it is in playing good golf," declares Frank. "Stand quartering to the trap house with your left foot forward and your right foot angled outward behind. Flex your left knee and lean into the recoil. Stay relaxed and not tense. Bring your gun up to your cheek, then back, and raise the shoulder to meet it. Don't shoulder the gun so low that you have to lean down to the comb. That one fault accounts for about 90 percent of missed birds. Hold your gun muzzle just at the top edge of the trap house. Any higher, and it will cover up the bird. Focus your eyes out ahead of the house where the bird will appear and call, 'Pull.'

"Beginners always want to know exactly how many feet to lead a given target. Trap is a game of instinct shooting, not an exact science. I never have any conscious recollection of lead. I just swing smoothly past the bird and fire. The lead seems to take care of itself. Learn to shoot quickly. After the bird gets out there about thirty-five yards, it sinks like a rock, or in a high wind, it may veer up or off to one side. It gets real tricky trying to hit those long shots. Remember you aim a rifle, but you point a shotgun."

Although the game of trap began as a sport confined to the English gentry, today it's the most democratic of sports. In registered shoots, top guns are handicapped severely by adding distance from the trap house to the point where amateurs often bring home the bacon, and handsome bacon it is. Prizes often include new automobiles and large cash awards.

Although trap is fiercely competitive, shooters enjoy a great feeling of camaraderie. That is the part that Frank Pachmayr likes best. Many of the shooting accessories developed by Pachmayr were directed toward improving convenience and easing pain for trap shooters. Frank invented a "release trigger," a kind of set trigger that cocks when the trigger is pulled back and fires the gun when it is released. This device tricks the shooter's reflexes and prevents flinching—the bane of every seasoned trap shooter. Almost every serious competitor is afflicted with "flinchitis" at some point in his career.

Pachmayr recoil pads were largely inspired by the trap shooter's need for recoil relief. At one point, Frank developed a two-piece stock with a butt and comb section that telescoped over the grip section and had a pair of hydraulic cylinders in between to cushion the blow. Springs returned the stock to battery after each shot. The device was highly successful but expensive to make and market, and only a limited number of units were produced. Frank also marketed a number of less significant trap accessories, including a leather shell pouch and shooting jackets.

Although trap was his first love, Frank shot his share of skeet. Skeet was designed to simulate field shooting of live birds under controlled conditions, but the game soon became an end unto itself and was pursued by experts, who used specialized equipment. A skeet field is laid out like a clock face cut in half. The semicircle is marked off one through seven for shooting positions. Station eight is located at the hub of the clock. At station one, there is the high trap house that launches clay pigeons from ten feet above ground level. At station seven, the low house launches birds from three and a half feet. Unlike trap, where birds are launched at various angles, skeet birds are all launched in the same direction each time. Different angles are achieved by moving the shooter from station to station. Two clay pigeons are fired singly from each position in turn, first from the high house, then from the low house, followed by doubles with both birds launched simultaneously.

Explaining the basics, Frank says, "You can't very well use the same gun for trap and skeet, because stock specs are entirely different. For skeet, you need about the same drop on your stock as for a field gun, usually about an inch and a half at the comb, and about two and a half inches at the heel. Barrels are generally short, twenty-six to twenty-eight inches, and skeet bored, which is about the same as an ordinary improved cylinder choke. You want your gun to deliver about a thirty-inch pattern with Number 9 shot at twenty-five yards. Auto loaders and pump guns are the most popular for skeet, and a few guys use over-under doubles.

"Stance for skeet is about the same as trap. Point your body toward the center of the clock, then rotate at the waist until your muzzle is pointing about ten to twelve feet in front of the trap house. Pick up the bird as it leaves the trap. Swing into your lead, fire, and follow through."

Undoubtedly the postgraduate shotgun competition is live pigeon shooting, a game that Frank Pachmayr loved as much as life. Over the years, Frank, Nanitta, and his friend and employee, Art Durando traveled to Tijuana and Nuevo Laredo, Mexico, as well as to Italy and Spain, to compete in matches. There are two styles of live pigeon shoots. In one, the birds are simply released from traps at ground level. In the other, the Valencia matches originated in Old Spain, live pigeons are thrown into the air by a "Columbaire," a thrower. The Columbaire regards it as his mandate to outsmart the shooter by throwing the birds in as wild and unpredictable a fashion as possible. The thrower watches for any shooting weakness of a contestant and skillfully plays upon it to make the gunner miss. Just before launching the bird, the Columbaire deftly plucks a few tail feathers to make the pigeon's flight erratic and difficult to track. The gunner is allowed two shots to drop the bird inside a hundred-meter circle. Any birds that fall outside of this limit are scored as misses. "I wouldn't try to advise anyone on how to shoot live pigeons," remarks Frank. "By the time they're good enough to try it, they'll have their own ideas about their gun and how to use it."

In spite of the fact that trap and skeet are both shotgun competitions that fire at flying targets, the two are entirely different disciplines. Seldom does an expert at one take the time and effort to become adept at the other, but Frank Pachmayr was an exception to that rule. He was a formidable competitor at both, as well as live pigeon shooting. Notwithstanding the fact that he was a crackerjack trap and skeet shot, Frank never made the circuit of competition events that culminated in the annual Grand American and the Vandalia. It required too much time to compete on a regular basis. On the other hand, Frank's store manager, Bill Harrison, and his attorney, Maynard Henry, were both inveterate trap competitors and perennial champions of the sport. Both were members of the first five-man team to break five hundred birds straight. Of course, Bill and Maynard wore shooting jackets emblazoned with the name "Pachmayr," which helped spread the word about Pachmayr products.

The favorite game bird for Frank was without a doubt the duck, but he is first to admit that the most challenging winged target is the chukar. "If there was ever a game bird that can make a man think he's got rocks in his head," says Frank, "it's the chukar partridge. It's the ghost of the uplands, first you see it, then you don't. I've worn out a couple pair of good Redwing boots just trying to catch up with those devils. You can hear them on a hillside a couple hundred yards away, so you tiptoe over there, pick your way between the cactus and sagebrush, and find nothing. Just to add to your frustration, you now hear them cackling away in the exact same spot where you were standing before."

The ground-nesting chukar, which has managed to thrive in California's steep, barren, rocky highlands, in spite of predation by fox, coyote, and bobcat, earned its name by calling out a throaty chuck . . . chuck . . . chucka-a-a-ar, whenever it becomes alarmed. It can sneak away from a dog on point, then run on its spurred red legs like an Olympic sprinter under the brush without leaving a clue as to its direction. When it leaves the ground and resorts to air transportation, it launches like a carrier jet with rocket assist and all engines redlined. It can travel like a bullet for 200 yards without deviating from its path, then vanish into the scrub, pinyon, and sagebrush. The pastel gray to tan plumage with black-banded wings, throat, and head blends perfectly with its surroundings, as if it were native to the area. Actually, the chukar was transplanted from its native Himalayan foothills to the United States before the turn of the century and prospered in the rough regions of the High Sierras.

Both Nan and Frank have hot-footed it uphill and down dale many times in the exasperating chukar chase. "It's rather like hitting your head on a stone wall," suggested Nan. "When you finally stop, it feels so-o-o go-o-od. When you finally limit out on chukar, the feeling of triumph can't be matched by any other bird." Nan needed no cannon to connect. She did quite nicely with her richly engraved, gold-inlaid, 20-gauge Parker double. In spite of advancing years, Frank's father Gus was able to keep pace with the younger chukar hunters. In fact, he could outdistance and outguess them more often than not. He had an instinct for knowing what the birds were going to do.

There is no doubt that Frank loved his crusty, irascible father, in spite of his harsh discipline. Gus was only acting out the traditional treatment of his forebears. Regardless, Frank felt a great respect and affection for his father, which is reflected in his comments regarding Gus today. "During his declining years, my father was one of the few fully qualified gunsmiths left in the country. He knew the business from the ground up. He was one of the finest hand workmen left in the world. The internal inletting that he did just couldn't be duplicated in quality by anyone in the country. When he inletted a side plate, it snapped into place. There may have been a few workmen of his caliber left in Germany or England, but not in this country. I don't think that he ever received the credit he deserved."

• PACHMAYR THE PERSON •

For a number of years after Frank had established himself both as a premier gunsmith in the Los Angeles area and as a highly successful entrepreneur, Gus continued to operate his one-man gun-repair and gun-building business in a loft above Lail's Garage at 815 South Grand Avenue. The business card of A. M. Pachmayr read, "Expert gunmaker, repairing and duplicating any gun parts, stocking, bluing, boring, rifling, etc."

Gus had his own well-established clientele, and Frank often referred repair jobs to his father when he thought the old man might benefit by the added revenue or because a particular repair job was especially suited to his father's extensive ability. Occasionally, a customer might enter Pachmayr Gun Works and think he was at Gus's business location. Then he might request that a certain repair job be performed by Gus, either because he knew from Gus's reputation or was aware by previous contact that the old man was a reliable and exacting workman. Frank was always happy to send the gun to his father.

Gus was perfectly happy amid the grime and clutter of his cold and drafty workplace of many years, and Frank was content to have him remain there until one day in the early 1950s Gus slipped on the grease-soaked wooden steps of the loft and came tumbling down to the concrete floor. Gus suffered no broken bones in the fall, but Frank realized the danger. Frank owned twenty-six units that stretched south on Grand from Pachmayr's to Pico Boulevard and around the corner. Frank had all of Gus's work benches, machines, and tools moved to a new location into a building fronting on Pico, just a half block south of Pachmayr's. Frank had a nice apartment created in adjacent rooms, complete with a new radio and a television set, which was still a novelty at the time. Gus loved the television, but frequently threatened to kick out the screen when he couldn't find a western movie playing. That was before the days of VCRs.

Richard Mellen, Frank's nephew, wanted to become a gunsmith for Frank. Frank suggested that Dick work in the engineering and machine shop for a time to learn the basics of metal working, so Dick went to work just across the street from Gus's new quarters. "In the evening after work," Dick recalls, "I used to go over to the Gus's and help him out any way I could. Sometimes, I'd clean up for him or help him with something on a gun. He showed me how to work on various guns and always took the time to explain the reasons why he did things a certain way. I learned a lot from him. Of course, Gus and I were already great friends. When I was a kid, he often took me bird hunting in Frazier Park. It was Gus who taught me how to shoot and hunt."

Occasionally Gus would come up with a project that could be done more quickly, perhaps even better, on a mill, which he never felt palmy enough to purchase. Note, he was no fool. He well knew the limitations of files, in spite of the fact that he handled them with the deftness of a magician. "Gus asked me to mill a ventilated full-length rib for a shotgun he was working on," recalls Dick. "I checked with Frank, and he said it was okay to use shop machinery. The old man was really grateful to me. You know, he softened up a lot in his later years. He was actually polite with me most of the time. He still cussed a blue streak when he got ticked about something, but it seems he was more even tempered as he grew older."

Somehow, Frank managed to inherit his father's strong character and self-assurance without assuming his irascible nature.

•••

· Chapter XIV ·

MAN OF HONORS

Frank A. Pachmayr is one of the few men who have lived to see his name become a byword. From Los Angeles to Munich, from Johannesburg to London, the name "Pachmayr" is synonymous with fine guns and shooting accessories. Frank is repeatedly referred to as "a living legend." In addition to his financial rewards, Frank Pachmayr has received many formal honors.

On 20 April 1980 Frank was awarded the Certificate of Appreciation by the Utah Wildlife and Outdoor Recreation Federation for "Dedicated service to the conservation of our natural resources." In 1983 Frank A. Pachmayr received the Award of Distinction–Craftsman from the Hunting Hall of Fame, California Division. Founder, Kenneth W. Vaughn, says, "We honored Mr. Pachmayr not only for his practical contributions toward improving the hunter's field equipment by means of his inventions of a unique swing-away scope mount, effective recoil pads, rubber pistol grips, and the creation of fine custom rifles and shotguns, but also because he created firearms that were in effect elaborate, one-of-a-kind works of art. Mr. Pachmayr has also been one of the major monetary supporters of wildlife and wildfowl preservation efforts."

At the thirteenth annual O.A.H.A. conference in 1985, Frank Pachmayr was honored as the "Outstanding American Handgunner" of the year. That was only one of many formal honors accorded the famous gun magnate. The highest award that can be given by the Southern California Safari Club is the Don Warren Award, named in honor of the late Donald R. Warren, a dedicated and fiercely ethical big-game hunter. The Don Warren Award was presented to Frank A. Pachmayr by club President Thomas J. Radoumis on 16 May 1987 at the annual banquet held at the Los Angeles County Museum. "This award is given to a member only once in his lifetime," explained Mr. Radoumis, "for exemplary conduct in the field of hunting, sportsmanship, and conservation. The nominee is judged on his honesty and integrity, hunting qualifications, and contributions to the club." Mr. Radoumis presented Pachmayr with a statue of an African bongo, an elusive trophy and symbolic of the Don Warren Award.

• FRANK PACHMAYR •

In his acceptance speech, Frank said, "I am in the twilight of my years and I figure I can be a little nostalgic . . . about organizations and members thereof. I have been fortunate in the groups I have belonged to and the friends I have made. . . and it's difficult to find the words that express my appreciation for the most prestigious award the Southern California Safari Club gives, the Don Warren

Famed gun inventor and manufacturer, the late Roy Weatherby, was on hand to congratulate Frank Pachmayr when he received his Hunting Hall of Fame Award.

Award. The friends I have made in the Southern California Safari Club have made my life richer, and I assure you that the compliment of this award is one of my life's treasures. Thank you for your warmth and comradeship. I wish you good hunting throughout life." Frank received a standing ovation from the members after his remarks.

In 1982, the Mzuri Safari Foundation, an organization dedicated to big-game conservation in Africa and America, recognized Frank Pachmayr with a Special Award of Appreciation. At the MGM Hotel in Reno, Nevada, on 16 February 1984, Frank received the distinctive and coveted David D. Bohannon Award from the Mzuri Safari Foundation as Conservationist of the Year.

Frank was one of the founders, along with C. J. McElroy, of Safari Club International, a nonprofit corporation dedicated to conserving wildlife. This group

• MAN OF HONORS •

started with a small nucleus of hunters and expanded to one of the largest such organizations in the world. They relocated endangered African game animals to protected plains areas in the States where they have thrived. So successful was the program that Safari Club International was later able to repopulate some areas in Africa with their own native game.

The American Custom Gun Makers Guild, Inc. granted Frank Pachmayr an honorary membership in 1983 for his outstanding contributions to modern rifles and shotguns, as well as his unswerving dedication to quality craftsmanship.

On 19 May 1982, in Reno, Nevada, at the forty-fifth annual meeting of the Board of Trustees of Ducks Unlimited, Inc., Frank Pachmayr was unanimously elected to the position of Honorary Trustee. This alliance dedicated to the preservation of waterfowl honored Frank again in May of 1987 at the Ducks Unlimited Annual Convention held in Vancouver, British Columbia. Frank received the Platinum Teal Award, the highest honor offered by Ducks Unlimited.

Frank A. Pachmayr achieved the distinction of having his name and that of his wife, Nanitta, placed together upon the Ducks Unlimited Benefactor's Roll of Honor. The bronze plaque, mounted upon a walnut base, was presented at a luncheon ceremony held at Scandia Restaurant in Hollywood California on 20 January 1988. Several score of Pachmayr's friends and as-

Frank Pachmayr sits at his desk, flanked by some of the many awards he received over the years, including the Outstanding American Handgunner Award on the right.

· FRANK PACHMAYR ·

Here we see Frank Pachmayr and President Reagan in the latter's Century City office during the presentation of four fine firearms to the former chief executive.

sociates were in attendance, including publisher Robert Petersen and famed gunmaker, the late Roy Weatherby. Few people have done as much as Frank Pachmayr to provide funds to Ducks Unlimited conservation projects. Seventeen major wetlands projects in Saskatchewan and three others in Alberta, Canada, are named for Frank and Nanitta, as well as one in northwestern Iowa and another in Sonora, Mexico.

In 1990, the Alaska Outdoor Council presented an engraved plaque to Frank in gratitude for his donations.

In spite of this deluge of accolades, Frank still values, more than any other tribute, the ones paid him by his customers when they said, "Good job," or, "These grips fit my hand better than any I ever used," or, "This is the best recoil pad I ever had." Certainly formal honors are an important gauge of Frank Pachmayr's great influence on hunting and shooting sports. Perhaps even more significant are the many heartfelt tributes from friends and associates. Their comments cast some light on the character of the man.

· MAN OF HONORS ·

From C. John Olson, a gunwriter and magazine editor of note, in a letter dated 20 June 1984:

Dear Frank,
I was stunned to learn that you've sold out and have gone into semiretirement. I couldn't help but be saddened by this because there are so few truly knowledgeable firearms "gentlemen" left in the marketplace . . . the type of people to whom a handshake was a binding agreement that was never violated. I feel that our long business relationship was on this level. In fact, I can't think of a single marring incident in the thirty-some odd years that we dealt with each other.

From James Carmichael, shooting editor for *Outdoor Life* in a letter dated 30 May 1983:

Dear Frank,
Let me thank you again most sincerely and wholeheartedly for the breathtaking customizing you did on my Model 21 Winchester. It is of course my most treasured gun, and I will never be able to thank you enough. I will of course use it well in spreading word of the incomparable service offered by Frank Pachmayr.

Since it arrived, I have shown it to dozens of gun lovers here in East Tennessee, and all are completely dazzled. Invariably, they say it is the most beautiful gun they have ever seen. As always, some insist that I could never bring myself to shoot such a beautiful gun, but I told them I have every intention of shooting it—and often.

Last weekend I took it to the local skeet club to try it out on the skeet field, but found that a tournament was in progress and therefore the fields were closed to casual shooting. So, finding that there was an opening on an upcoming squad, I simply signed up for the tournament, figuring this to be as good a way as any to get in a few shots with the new gun. So it came to pass that the first shot fired in your beautiful gun was in actual skeet competition. And I simply could not miss. The upshot of it was that I won the tournament without missing a bird, and right now the High Gun Trophy is on my desk. I can't wait to use the gun on dove this fall.

In a letter from Carmichael addressed to me and dated 19 November 1987:

Dear John:
There are a lot of good things I would like to say about Frank Pachmayr, but it would take a lot longer than a letter. Though the name Pachmayr is very well known in shooting circles, I do not think that most sportsmen understand the depth or the variety of Frank's involvement in the shooting game, nor do they fully realize the enormous impact he has had on many areas of sports

shooting. The Pachmayr recoil pad is a family name in the shooting industry, but how many folks are aware that Pachmayr was one of the first and best accurizers of .45 ACP tournament-grade pistols? This involvement goes back before World War II, when a Pachmayr accurized auto loader was the only way to go. And the legions of handgun shooters, who tote their Pachmayr pistol shooter's kit to the firing line, probably cannot imagine the fantastic Pachmayr custom guns that originate at the famed Pachmayr shop in Los Angeles.

Every time I have visited the Pachmayr building in Los Angeles, I go prepared to spend the day. Frank loves guns more than anyone I know and loves to show them to anyone who is interested. Invariably, the gun rack behind his desk is filled with the most luscious rifles and shotguns that one can imagine. He is a perfectionist, and even when he is proudly displaying one of his company's artful creations, he will invariably point out how this or that could have been done better.

And my God, how Frank loves stock wood. His warehouse is a treasure trove of some of the most beautiful stocks to be seen anywhere. I've spent hours in his warehouse as he pulled one blank after another, discussing the merits of each blank in detail.

If Frank Pachmayr had not been born, it would have been necessary for him to have been invented. No individual that I know encompasses such an enormous amount of skills, talents, and knowledge. I certainly consider myself privileged to be his friend.

This a letter from Roy E. Weatherby to me, dated 11 March 1987:

Dear Johnny,

Frank and I have known each other since 1945. I used to spend a lot of my time in his store on Grand Avenue. In fact, when I came to California in the fall of 1937, I imagine that I probably started visiting his store shortly afterward. In those days, Frank was very active in his retail store. Frank and I used to visit a great deal when I would go to his place.

When I started in business in 1945, I remember in our retail store we were selling Pachmayr's Lo-Swing scope mounts. I had one salesman in the retail store, and apparently he tried to unsell a customer that asked for a Pachmayr mount and sell him another brand. The customer left our place and drove downtown to Frank's store and told Frank about the incident. Frank called to tell me about it. So believe me, Johnny, I certainly got all over the salesman in our store.

As far back as I can remember, when I started making guns, I was using Pachmayr recoil pads. We've never used anything but Pachmayr pads; we also sold them in our retail store. When he began to sell stock wood, I remember I would go down there and Frank and I would select the wood I was going to buy. And Frank, being like myself, a person who really appreciated beautiful wood, naturally hated to let any of the unusual wood get out of his hands. I can remember him saying, "No, Roy, not that blank. That's a much more expensive piece of wood."

• MAN OF HONORS •

Frank was a very well-liked person. Later in life, I got to know his wife, Nanitta, also, and, as you remember, for many, many years, I've invited both of them to the Big Game Trophy Dinner. Frank has been a real gun enthusiast for as long as I have known him. I remember as far back as the late thirties when anyone was talking about guns, it seemed as though Pachmayr's was the place to go.

I guess, Johnny, I've known Frank just about as long as I've known you. I'm sure that Frank's name will no doubt be remembered for many, many generations as one of the very respected names in the gun and hunting world and also as a very fine person.

In a letter from Fred T. Huntington, founder of RCBS reloading tools, dated 9 March 1987:

Dear John,

I was in and out of Frank's shop and plant from the late 1950s on. I never had the pleasure of hunting with him. In 1982, he and Nanitta came to Oroville for a weekend. I immediately suggested that my wife Barbara and I could take them to our summer home at Lake Almanor, because it was quite hot here in Oroville. It was a Friday afternoon, and we started out in my Cadillac. Before very long, the car began to overheat. I pulled into a service station and refilled the radiator. Pretty soon, it got hot again. This time, I discovered a leak in the lower radiator hose. So I phoned my son Buzz and had him drive up with our station wagon. Buzz stayed behind to get the Cadillac fixed.

Because of the car trouble, we arrived at our lakeside cottage rather late. Through all of this, I never heard a word of complaint from Frank or Nanitta. They loved our small place, enjoyed the front porch and breezes, and good sleeping nights. I found they did not drink much and seemed to enjoy good California wines rather than any hard liquor. Barbara cooked some fine lunches and dinners, and they ate heartily. When leaving, they both said they'd like to return next year, but illness kept them from coming back.

Frank is a very fine man, much devoted to his wife. They seem to love each other very much, and get along fine together. In the three days they were with us, I never heard a cross or unkind word from either of them. Frank treats everyone with respect and his usual friendliness.

In a letter to me dated 26 March 1987, Pachmayr's former secretary, Vivien Tew, said of her boss:

Dear Mr. Lachuk,

I have a great deal of respect for Frank Pachmayr. One thing, besides Frank's excellent knowledge of guns and wood, was his "calculator" type mind. When I first went to work for Pachmayr Gun Works, about 1951, there was just a small number of office personnel. The mail would be opened at the switchboard and the switchboard operator would run an adding machine tape on all of the payments received for the day. When Frank would come in, before he would start work, he would stop at the PBX and pick up all the checks, adding the totals in his head. Sometimes there would be twenty or thirty checks. The total amount he would come up with was always within a penny or two of the adding machine tape total and many times right on the button. He delighted in doing this, and we all got a kick out of it because his accuracy was amazing.

I worked for Frank until 1980, and up until the time I left, he retained a phenomenal memory. If someone was looking for a gun part which did not seem available, he had only to ask Frank if such a part existed in his personal inventory, even just a small screw of a particular kind. He knew just exactly where to look for it. This would be true even if the item had been put aside ten or fifteen years prior. This was unique inasmuch as this inventory of parts was kept in boxes on his desk, in his cupboards, in fact, places you wouldn't believe. His desk was always cluttered with boxes filled with parts, magazines, newspapers with articles he wanted to retain, and letters to be answered. No one had better touch anything because as cluttered as it was, he always knew where some letter or article was if he wanted to see it.

Frank always had a number of wood blanks stacked in his office, and we would occasionally have some cockroaches trying to make a home in them. One day I was in Frank's office taking dictation, when one of these monsters wandered across the carpet. It was truly Godzilla. I was engrossed in the dictation, and when I happened to glance over and see the bug, I screamed like a banshee. This didn't startle Frank. He just went into hysterical laughter, and said, "Oh well, it couldn't eat much."

Frank always appreciated mechanical skill and ability in his gunsmiths and machinists. Inasmuch as he himself was an excellent craftsman, he recognized ability in others. He was quite hard headed, and it was difficult to change his mind once it was made up. But he always seemed to bend when it came to a difference of opinion with one of the machinists or gunsmiths whose work he admired.

Probably due to working around machinery most of his life, Frank was hard of hearing. In later years, he was pressured into wearing a hearing aid, but it stayed more in its original box than near his ear. This partial deafness caused him to speak quite loud at times. Naturally, his employees never commented on it, but one time Mr. Pachmayr was showing a distinguished visitor through the store and shop areas, and speaking very loud—to the point where the man asked him not to yell. Frank said he was sorry but that he spoke loudly because he was a little deaf. The visitor smiled, and said, "Well, I'm not."

Nanitta Pachmayr was a very fine and wonderful lady. When I first went to work for Pachmayr, she used to help with the office work. She had a delightful personality.

• MAN OF HONORS •

In a letter I received from Bruce Baker, former president of Pachmayr, Ltd.:

Dear John,

I have always been impressed by the reputation of the Pachmayr name in the shooting sports world. Throughout this country, of course, and especially in Europe, the Pachmayr name is almost revered. Reflecting on that, I've reached some of my own conclusions. Frank had a knack for discerning a need for a shooting accessory, and then building a quality product to meet that need. Utility and quality were always his watchwords.

Frank also insisted upon quality gunsmithing. In my brief tenure as manager of the custom gun shop while we were looking for a qualified manager, I was always impressed by his obsession with perfection and quality. Frank never allowed himself to be pushed into delivering a gun that wasn't ready. No detail of a project escaped his attention. He demanded the very best from his employees. And no one could put something over on him. He would accept no excuses for shoddiness or laziness. He would not tolerate a dirty and disorganized workbench.

Frank is also a very generous human being in his own unique way. At times I felt he was taken advantage of by some people. Frank is frugal, yet generous, and would go the extra mile and expense to make a job right.

When my brother Bill bought the company, he wanted Frank to always feel welcome down at the shop. He did that because we recognized that Frank still had a lot to offer. It's been a good association. We've learned a great deal from Frank, and I think he appreciates what we've been able to do for the company, maintaining its image and reputation.

Today, Pachmayr Ltd. has a new president, Leslie H. Whitney, formerly with the famed holster company, Bianchi International. Pachmayr Ltd. currently markets an expanded line of recoil-absorbing Pachmayr neoprene rubber pistol grips, including their new "American Legend Series," that combines the beauty of richly polished walnut that surrounds a front insert of finger-gripped, black decelerator rubber for improved control. A full line of over 300 different Pachmayr rifle and shotgun recoil pads are offered, plus pistol sights and pistol magazines, handgun cases, and gun care products. The company also operates a marksmanship training school on their seventy-acre shotgun and archery range in El Monte, California.

•••

• Chapter XV •
PACHMAYR THE PHILANTHROPIST

Any man who acquires a reputation for generosity can expect to be deluged with requests for contributions to a variety of "just causes." Frank Pachmayr is no exception. He was always besieged by a parade of petitioners at his Pachmayr Gun Works business office. Some even became pushy and obnoxious, but Frank always treated them with courtesy and consideration, regardless of the sincerity of their appeal. He gave each petitioner a patient hearing and often helped with contributions even when the request might appear to be of dubious merit.

Frank always included Nanitta's name when sending contributions, because he felt that she had as great a stake as he did in supporting humanitarian causes. Among the groups to which Frank and Nanitta contributed are youth-oriented organizations, such as the Boy Scouts of America and the Young Americans for Freedom, as well as such regional groups as the Los Angeles YWCA and Southern California Salvation Army, plus national groups such as the American Cancer Society and National Audubon Society. Educational facilities also benefited from Frank's largess, including the University of California, Heritage Hall, and the ARCS Foundation (Achievement Rewards for College Scientists). Frank was always a staunch supporter of law enforcement and veteran's groups, such as the Municipal Motorcycle Officers of California and the Los Angeles Area Vietnam Veterans Leadership Program.

Frank Pachmayr has always fought fiercely for the rights of gun owners. To this end, he contributes regularly to such organizations as the Firearms Coalition in Silver Springs, Maryland; the Gun Owners of California in Sacramento; Gun Owners of America in Springfield, Virginia; and the Second Amendment Foundation in Bellevue, Washington. Always at the top of Frank's list of good gun groups was the National Rifle Association. Frank also supported the Southwest Pistol League and the Elmer Keith Museum Foundation, Inc.

When the Outstanding American Handgunner Awards (O.A.H.A.) found itself in financial difficulties, Pachmayr leaped into the gap with a substantial monetary contribution that enabled this organization to survive. The O.A.H.A. Foundation, Inc. was formed in 1973 by Lee Jurras and incorporated in New Mexico in 1975.

"It was my sincere belief," said Jurras, "in establishing this award that the handgunners of this country needed to have their own 'All-Americans' and 'Hall of Fame.' I further felt this program needed to be a self-supporting entity, unencumbered by industrial politics or lobbying interests. The membership should be made up of handgun enthusiasts, whether they be plinkers, collectors, competitive shooters, hunters, or those who just believed in this American heritage."

In describing Lee Jurras, Frank says, "He has received far less recognition by today's pistol shooters than he deserves. Almost everybody has forgotten that it was Jurras who pioneered factory-produced pistol ammo with lightweight bullets at high velocity. Lee founded Super Vel Cartridge Corporation and forced the big name companies to follow his lead. The result was more effective pistol ammunition, which we take for granted today. Lee was also one of the pioneers of handgun hunting and did a lot toward publicizing and popularizing the sport." In 1977 Lee Jurras handed the helm of O.A.H.A. over to Larry Kelly, who is best known for his Mag-Na-Port Arms barrel venting system that reduces recoil in pistols and revolvers. In a ceremony held in San Antonio, Texas, on 18 May 1979, Jurras received the award that he originated from the hands of Steve Vogel of Sturm, Ruger & Co.

Of course, high on Frank's list is wildlife conservation. He has offered monetary support to many wildlife preservation programs, to groups like the Wetlands for Iowa Program, National Fish & Wildlife, California Wildlife Federation, Foundation for North American Wild Sheep, Game Conservation International (Game Coin), Sacramento Safari Club, the Los Angeles Audubon Society, and the Utah Wildlife and Outdoor Recreation Federation.

In January of 1984 Frank donated two Pachmayr Custom Rifles to the Wyoming Game Wardens Association. Valued at $10,000 each, both guns were pre-64 Winchester Model 70 bolt action rifles, custom stocked, and richly engraved and gold inlaid by Pachmayr engravers. One was a .270 Winchester caliber and the other a .264 Winchester. Both were equipped with scopes on Pachmayr Lo-Swing Mounts. The following year, Frank donated a Pachmayr Custom Deluxe Rifle in .300 H&H Magnum and a Custom Deluxe 12-gauge Browning shotgun. These guns were auctioned off to raise money for animal and habitat preservation and to fund university and high school scholarships in game management.

Later the same year, Frank donated two rifles to the Hunting Hall of Fame. One was built along the lines of the Winchester pre-64 Model 70 bolt action, the other was based upon an FN Mauser bolt action. Both were .270 Winchester caliber and richly engraved and inlaid. Even after Frank sold Pachmayr Gun Works, his company's tradition of charitable giving continued under the stewardship of Bruce Baker. In 1985 the corporation donated the first gun in its Americana Series to benefit the Metropolitan Museum of Art in New York.

Frank A. Pachmayr loves all kinds of hunting, but if he had it his way, he would have spent most of his life in a boat or blind that was rimmed by reeds and rustling sawgrass. The decoys would be riding the wavelets in ranks and tempting the mallards and pintails within range of his favorite 12-gauge Parker double. This passion for duck hunting drove Frank's obsession for the preservation of migratory

Frank and Nanitta were close companions in the field, as in all other pursuits, including their extensive philanthropic efforts.

wildfowl. It is a cause that he backs with the same skills he used to create rifles and shotguns of regal quality.

Frank has presented over $8,000,000 worth of classic long guns to wildfowl preservation organizations. They were created by skilled artisans appointed and supervised by Frank. To the sometimes incredulous query, "Why do you do it?" Frank simply replies, "Because we did a very good business with our hunting products. I believe in putting something back into the sport that, to put it candidly, made me rich. Besides, I believe in what Ducks Unlimited and other regional organizations are doing to preserve our wildlife and game habitat. Somebody's got to do it. Without an effort to save what we have left and build for the future, our sons and daughters won't be able to enjoy the sport that we love. Another thing, I've noticed that a lot of my rich friends are starting to follow my example, getting involved, and contributing to wildlife preservation. One thing, though, you have to watch out what group you're giving money to. A lot of them that make the most noise about helping animals, marching around demonstrating against hunting and medical research involving animals, manage to funnel nearly all of

Nanitta and Frank Pachmayr standing beside the marker that commemorates their $100,000 contribution to the Ducks Unlimited Lake George wetlands conservation project in Canada. This was a small portion of the many contributions made by Pachmayr to wildlife conservation over the years.

the money into 'administrative expenses.' Little money ever goes to help the poor animals."

On occasion, Frank has funded specific projects, such as the marsh preservation program carried out by Ducks Unlimited at George Lake in Canada. Some 70 percent of the continental migratory waterfowl population breeds in Canada, and 200,000 or more pairs have been counted annually at George Lake, which is located 276 miles northwest of Edmonton, Alberta, near the town of Hines Creek. About half of the surrounding, mostly flat, land is privately owned, with the balance in the hands of the Crown. As far back as records were kept, George Lake has been a productive breeding ground for migratory wildfowl, including mallards, pintail, widgeon, and shoveler, all feeding upon underwater growth of clasping leaf, sago, duckweed, and smart weed that are rooted in the murky bottoms.

Sharing the ponds and marshes are beavers, who industriously build dams that raise the water level enough to threaten the grades of a nearby railroad and highway. This annual hazard led to government proposals to drain the entire area. On the other hand, developers wanted to raise the water level by six feet and convert the clear, fresh water lake into a vacation retreat. Either idea would have ruined the area as a wildfowl nesting ground. Others that would have suffered from development were muskrats, deer, moose, and various predators. The Canadian arm of Ducks Unlimited in cooperation with Canadian Fish and Wildlife managed to place a hold on development of the land until a practical plan for game preservation could be worked out and funded.

In 1973 Ducks Unlimited worked out a cooperative program with the Alberta Department of Environment to constantly maintain the water level one and a half feet lower than the average annual level. This was achieved through an inlet diversion on the east side of the lake, which would be built by the Crown. A 9,000-foot outlet ditch on the west end, which was controlled by a concrete structure containing three escape valves, was to be built by Ducks Unlimited, which would also build five farm crossings and a temporary earthen dam to prevent drainage of the lake during construction. The result was projected to be a constantly flooded area of 1,350 acres, surrounded by fifteen miles of irregular shoreline. This project, one of many sponsored by Ducks Unlimited, was designed to maintain adequate waterfowl breeding grounds even through severe drought periods, such as those experienced in 1981 and again in 1988.

Ambitious plans are well and good, but without money, they are like a toothless lion—all roar and no bite. Frank Pachmayr provided the bite in the form of funding to the tune of $100,000. The effort was appropriately titled by Ducks Unlimited as "The Pachmayr Project." On 9 October 1981 the project was formally dedicated by Frank and Nanitta Pachmayr. They unveiled a bronze plaque embedded in the front of a five-foot-tall concrete cairn. The plaque reads:

GEORGE LAKE PROJECT
A CONSERVATION PROJECT UNDERTAKEN FOR THE PERPETUATION
OF NORTH AMERICA'S WATERFOWL RESOURCES.
COMPLETED IN 1980 BY DUCKS UNLIMITED (CANADA) AND THE
PROVINCE OF ALBERTA DEPARTMENT OF THE ENVIRONMENT
WITH THE COOPERATION OF LOCAL LANDOWNERS FUNDS PROVIDED BY
THE PROVINCE OF ALBERTA
AND
NANITTA AND FRANK PACHMAYR

· Frank Pachmayr ·

Frank Pachmayr's sponsorship of Ducks Unlimited began some twenty-five years ago. His commitment is outstanding even in this organization that celebrated its fiftieth anniversary in 1987. It has had phenomenal success in fulfilling its original purpose of wetlands restoration. Ducks Unlimited's parent was a group called More Game Birds that originated in 1937. It grew from concerns of sportsmen who had witnessed an alarming decrease in fall wildfowl migration from four hundred million at the turn of the century to a mere

Frank and Nanitta were partners in everything. They shared in owning the business, even though Nanitta wasn't involved on a daily basis in later years, and they also shared in the donations to worthy charities and game habitat preservation.

thirty million by 1937. Many species were on the brink of extinction. The concern spread across Canada, the United States, and Mexico, all strategic habitat areas.

These sportsmen banded together to form Ducks Unlimited, the first international wildlife conservation organization. By its fiftieth year, Ducks Unlimited had managed wetlands restoration projects that resulted in the annual bird migration increasing to a hundred million, more than triple its all-time low. Other threatened fowl have benefited from the Ducks Unlimited projects, including the whooping crane and bald eagle, plus forty species of mammals and three hundred species of fish.

• PACHMAYR THE PHILANTHROPIST •

Frank was largely responsible for the formation of more than one conservation group, and he breathed new life into many others. The Iowa Natural Heritage Foundation wanted to form a Wetlands for Iowa wing of their organization but lacked the funds. They estimated that to start out with five wetlands projects they would need $100,00. Bill Artis, National Trustee of Ducks Unlimited, contacted Frank Pachmayr with a request for assistance. Frank responded by contributing two shotguns each valued at $35,000. A matching contribution from publisher Ted Meridith put the fledgling group over the top. To date, Pachmayr has contributed well over a half million dollars to the Iowa's Natural Heritage Foundation, enabling them to launch eighty more ambitious wetland projects.

Bill Artis, who acted as a conduit for many of Frank's gun contributions to various groups, estimates the total dollar amount that he personally handled exceeds seven million dollars. On one occasion, Bill transported sixty shotguns and rifles valued from $25,000 to $35,000 each to the Canadian Ducks Unlimited in Winnipeg, Canada.

To demonstrate how casually Frank committed himself to monumental contributions, Bill Artis relates that he and Matt Connolly, Executive Vice President of Ducks Unlimited, were Frank's guests for lunch at the Jonathan Club in Los Angeles. During the course of conversation, Frank said, "I'll contribute a gun for every state in the union, and we'll call it the 'fifty-gun salute.'" Then reconsidering, he said, "No let's make that two guns for each state, and we'll call it the 'hundred-gun salute.'" You can appreciate the enormity of this commitment when you realize that these guns were valued from fifteen to fifty thousand dollars each.

The final benefit from the Pachmayr gun donations far exceeded the value of the guns, because they were usually auctioned off or sold at raffles for far more than the basic cost. On one occasion, a fine engraved shotgun was raffled off and netted a total of $300,000. The winning ticket was held by a multimillionaire in Canada. He immediately donated the gun again, and it sold at auction the next year for a quarter of a million dollars.

Other beneficiaries of Pachmayr's charitable giving include the North American Waterfall Plan, the Izaak Walton League, and the National Fish and Wildlife Foundation. Frank's contributions of more than six hundred thousand dollars to the latter have a double impact, because donated funds are matched dollar for dollar by the federal government.

Frank Pachmayr continues his donations of fine engraved and inlaid shotguns and custom rifles to various habitat preservation organizations in a continuing effort to offer them assistance. It takes time for Frank to create these matchless examples of gun craftsmanship. In addition to fine custom rifles, Frank's contributions include shotguns, mostly side-by-side doubles, such as Browning, Winchester, L. C. Smith, Parker, Perazzi, Purdey, Webley, and W&C Scott, along with a smattering of high-grade auto loaders and pump action shotguns. The guns feature different original engravings and overlays of precious metals, making every gun one-of-a-kind.

Certainly, Frank Pachmayr has more than "paid his dues." He has richly endowed the sports of hunting and shooting far beyond anyone's wildest dreams—including his own.

•••

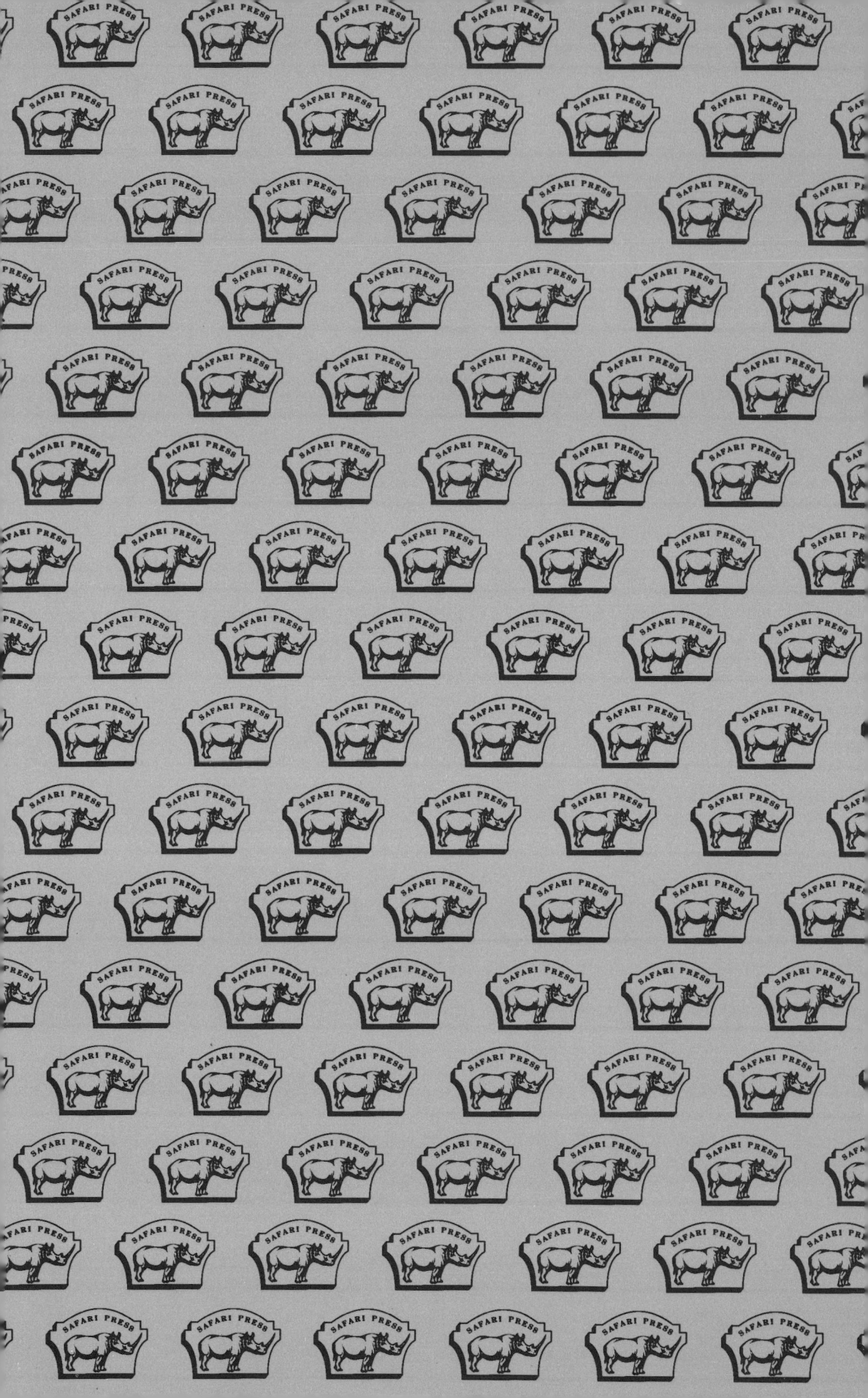